PRICE THEORY AND APPLICATIONS
SEVENTH EDITION

This new seventh edition of *Price Theory and Applications* adds extensive discussion of information, uncertainty, and game theory. It contains more than 100 real-world examples illustrating the applicability of economic analysis not only to mainline economic topics but also to issues in politics, history, biology, the family, and many other areas. These discussions generally describe recent research published in scholarly books and articles, giving students a good idea of the scientific work done by professional economists. In addition, at appropriate places the text provides "Applications" representing more extended discussions of selected topics including rationing in wartime (Chapter 5), import quotas (Chapter 7), alleged monopolistic suppression of inventions (Chapter 9), minimum wage laws (Chapter 12), the effects of Social Security on saving (Chapter 15), fair division of disputed property (Chapter 16), and whether one should pay ransom to a kidnapper (Chapter 17).

Jack Hirshleifer is Distinguished Professor of Economics, Emeritus, at the University of California, Los Angeles (UCLA). He is the author or coauthor of the six previous editions of *Price Theory and Applications* and the author or coauthor of six other books, including *The Analytics of Uncertainty and Information* (1992, with John G. Riley) and *The Dark Side of the Force* (2001), both published by Cambridge University Press. Professor Hirshleifer is a Fellow of the American Academy of Arts and Sciences and the Econometric Society, a former president of the Western Economic Association, and a former vice president of the American Economic Association, which named him a Distinguished Fellow in 2000. He has served on the editorial boards of the *American Economic Review*, the *Journal of Economic Behavior and Organization*, and the *Journal of Bioeconomics*.

Amihai Glazer is Professor of Economics at the University of California, Irvine. He has taught at the Hebrew University, Carnegie Mellon University, and the University of Tampere, Finland. The author of more than 80 articles in professional journals, Professor Glazer is coauthor with Jack Hirshleifer of the fifth edition of *Price Theory and Applications*, coauthor with Laurence Rothenberg of *Why Government Succeeds and Why It Fails* (2001), and coeditor with Kai Konrad of *Conflict and Governance* (2003). He is a coeditor of the journal *Economics of Governance*.

David Hirshleifer is the Ralph M. Kurtz Professor of Finance at the Ohio State University. He previously taught at the Anderson School of UCLA and the University of Michigan Business School. The coauthor with Jack Hirshleifer of the sixth edition of *Price Theory and Applications*, David Hirshleifer has served as a director of the American Finance Association, as editor of the *Review of Financial Studies*, and as associate editor or coeditor of several other journals in finance, economics, and corporate strategy. His papers have received a number of research awards, including the 1999 Smith–Breeden Award for the outstanding paper in the *Journal of Finance*.

PRICE THEORY AND APPLICATIONS

Decisions, Markets, and Information

SEVENTH EDITION

JACK HIRSHLEIFER
University of California, Los Angeles

AMIHAI GLAZER
University of California, Irvine

DAVID HIRSHLEIFER
Ohio State University

CAMBRIDGE
UNIVERSITY PRESS

CAMBRIDGE UNIVERSITY PRESS
Cambridge, New York, Melbourne, Madrid, Cape Town, Singapore, São Paulo

Cambridge University Press
40 West 20th Street, New York, NY 10011-4211, USA

www.cambridge.org
Information on this title: www.cambridge.org/9780521818643

First published 2005

Printed in the United States of America

A catalog record for this publication is available from the British Library.

Library of Congress Cataloging in Publication Data

Hirshleifer, Jack.
Price theory and applications / Jack Hirshleifer, Amihai Glazer,
David Hirshleifer. – 7th ed.
   p.   cm.
Includes bibliographical references and index.
ISBN-13: 978-0-521-81864-3 (hardback)
ISBN-10: 0-521-81864-8 (hardback)
ISBN-13: 978-0-521-52342-4 (pbk.)
ISBN-10: 0-521-52342-7 (pbk.)
1. Prices.   I. Glazer, Amihai.   II. Hirshleifer, David Adam, 1958–   III. Title.
HB221.H62   2005
338.5 – dc22   2005011729

ISBN-13   978-0-521-81864-3 hardback
ISBN-10   0-521-81864-8 hardback

ISBN-13   978-0-521-52342-4 paperback
ISBN-10   0-521-52342-7 paperback

Contents

Preface

Theory is useless unless it leads to applications. But real-world problems remain a buzzing, blooming confusion absent a systematic theory to put them in intellectual order. Earlier editions of this book pioneered an approach, not totally new but given unusual emphasis by us, that weaves together economic theory and real-world applications. Most current intermediate microtheory texts have come to follow our lead and also now try to enrich the theoretical exposition with selected applications. Our enthusiasm for and experience in discovering, describing, and analyzing how microtheory works out in the real world nevertheless lend a special strength to *Price Theory and Applications*.

To this end the many brief "Examples" that direct attention to specific applications remain, as in previous editions, a hallmark of *Price Theory and Applications*. This edition contains more than a hundred such examples. These discussions generally describe recent research published in scholarly books and articles and so also give students a better idea of the scientific work that professional economists actually do. (The media typically picture economists as a band of squabbling soothsayers – some saying business will be good, others always predicting doom. Students may be surprised to find that there are any scientifically validated results in economics.) In addition, at appropriate places the text provides "Applications" representing a wide range of topics, among them rationing in wartime (Chapter 5), import quotas (Chapter 7), alleged monopolistic suppression of inventions (Chapter 9), minimum wage laws (Chapter 12), the effects of Social Security on saving (Chapter 15), fair division of disputed property (Chapter 16), and whether you should pay ransom to a kidnapper (Chapter 17).

Two other key themes guide this text. First, that economics is not a body of facts or propositions to be memorized. It is instead a way of thinking about the world. There are diligent students who say, "Prof, just tell me what pages you want me to learn and I guarantee I'll know every word." But memorization is not enough. Even the ability to derive and prove logical or mathematical propositions does not suffice. Insight and intuition must also be cultivated. Insight and intuition tell us what theories or propositions apply in any given context. Yet not everything can be left to inspiration. Insight and intuition have to be earned by hard intellectual labor.

Second, traditional economic theory has been guilty of tunnel vision in focusing so strictly on rationalistic individual behavior and market interactions. Humans are not always entirely rational, and market interactions are only one of the many domains of social life. Economics as a universal science applies outside these boundaries, whenever humans (or even animals!) have to cope with resource scarcity. Market decisions are of course amenable to economic analysis. But so are personal choices (how many children to have, whether to live in the city or the suburbs, whom to seek as friends) and political ones (balancing between affluence and defense, between regulation of improper behavior and individual freedom, between relief for persons unable or unwilling to work versus providing incentives to those who are productive). Accordingly, the text employs a range of materials from scientific work in anthropology, psychology, political science, social biology, and other fields that all serve to illustrate economic principles.

Critics of economics sometimes object that, under the pressures of everyday life, people have to make decisions without using esoteric economic concepts such as marginal analysis. But biologists have discovered that marginal analysis explains many aspects of the behavior of animals (see the "Smart Ants!" example in Chapter 4), and humans are surely cleverer than ants. Yet people, individually or collectively, do sometimes make irrational choices. During the high-tech stock market boom in the late 1990s, investors seem to have displayed "irrational exuberance" (see Example 1.5 in Chapter 1).

Critics have also accused economics of being unscientific in failing to test theories by experiments. This is an uninformed criticism. Experiments are playing an increasingly important role in economic research. The examples in the text report on many experimental studies. Among them are ingenious methods devised to test whether economics students are more selfish than noneconomics students (Chapter 1), whether children make choices that are logically consistent with one another (Chapter 3), whether markets work well even when there are only a few traders on each side (Chapter 14), and whether residents of different countries vary in how much they are inclined to cooperate (Chapter 16).

As to coverage and level of difficulty, this is not a minimal "thin gruel" book. Apart from meeting immediate classroom needs, we aimed to achieve growth potential. The material is ample enough in scope and rich enough in content to serve as reference and guide for additional self-study or coursework beyond the intermediate level. But perhaps the main reason for the wide coverage is to illustrate the wealth of fascinating implications and applications of economic theory. In consequence, this text contains more than can usually be handled in a one-term microeconomics course. Instructors and students in more compact courses will find that Chapters 1 through 8 can serve as core readings covering the essentials of individual optimization and supply–demand equilibrium in product markets. Some teachers, in accordance with student interests and time constraints, may want to add selections from the remaining chapters. A two-term undergraduate price theory course can cover the entire text.

A number of expository aids are provided to facilitate readability and comprehension. First, detailed descriptive legends accompany the diagrams. The analytical high points of a chapter can often be efficiently reviewed by studying the diagrams, with their legends, in sequence. Second, almost every chapter contains worked numerical exercises. Third, each chapter ends with a summary and two groups of questions – one group to test recollection and recall, the other to provide challenges for further thought and discussion. (Answers to about half of the questions, those marked by a dagger, appear at the back of the book.)

This seventh edition of *Price Theory and Applications* bears the subtitle *Decisions, Markets, and Information*. Reflecting recent exciting advances in economic analysis, the subtitle highlights the increased emphasis in this edition on the economics of information. Especially but not exclusively in Chapter 11, there is new coverage of risk and its distribution in the economy, of information acquisition as a way of overcoming risk, and of rights in intellectual property – especially patents and copyright. Specific new topics include option value, the problem of "lemons," herd behavior, and the informative content of advertising.

The text employs game theory from time to time, with emphasis on practical relevance rather than on abstract theorems. Game theory is notably helpful in addressing topics such as oligopoly (Chapter 10), public goods (Chapter 16), and cooperation versus conflict (Chapter 17).

Several additional features of this book improve on conventional textbook coverage:

- Traditional intermediate texts slight the topic of transaction costs. In Part Five the analysis of exchange subject to transaction costs shows, among other things, why and how a monetary commodity comes into being. Even earlier, Part Three indicates that the costliness of exchange explains why business firms exist. And Part Seven emphasizes how transaction costs affect the real-world relevance of the Coase theorem.
- Textbooks rarely discuss product quality and product variety. Chapter 9 examines how markets, under both competitive and monopolistic conditions, determine the quality levels and the product assortments that suppliers offer to consumers.
- Saving and investment, often treated as topics entirely separate from mainline microeconomics, are explained in Chapter 15 in terms of the economic theory of choice and equilibrium over time. The analysis here provides a bridge to macroeconomics and to the business finance literature.
- In addition to the traditional normative issues of welfare economics, Chapter 16 provides a unified treatment of public goods.
- The final Chapter 17 presents a positive analysis of government. The same chapter puts forward a unique game-theoretic approach to the broad social problem of conflict versus cooperation.

As in previous editions, calculus is used only in marked mathematical footnotes. However, students who know calculus can interpret the delta (Δ) notation used for marginal concepts as signifying a derivative or differential.

Whether we have struck a proper balance between coverage and simplicity, between theory and application, between technical accuracy and intuitive suggestion, only the reader can judge. We will be grateful for guidance on this point from instructors and students, and also for specific corrections where errors appear.

Over the years the authors have been dismayed to observe so many intermediate texts putting out repeated editions, in machine-gun style, every 4 or even every 3 years! That might possibly be smart business practice, creating forced obsolescence in order to discourage students from buying used copies of the current edition. But it is not warranted on educational or intellectual grounds. The subject simply does not change that fast. Nor can authors on a 3-year cycle devote enough time to really think through needed improvements in style and content. The 6 years since the previous (sixth) edition of this textbook have given us the chance to add many new examples, applications, and questions and to include new topics such as the economics of information and networks.

Finally, we have been delighted to work with Cambridge University Press as publisher of this seventh edition.

As in past editions, the *Instructor's Manual for Price Theory and Applications, Seventh Edition*, contains teaching tips and expanded answers to a number of questions in the textbook, plus an assortment of additional numerical, essay, and multiple choice questions for each chapter. It was prepared by Ray Bromley, building on work done for earlier editions by Michael Sproul.

Resources for instructors and students using *Price Theory and Applications* are available online at http://www.pricetheoryapplications.com. These include additional applications and examples, studying tips, text corrections, and downloadable teaching aids.

Previous editions of this text have benefited from helpful reviews by many colleagues, too numerous to be individually named here. For this seventh edition we are particularly grateful for a detailed and insightful analysis and commentary by Eric Rasmusen. We also thank the teachers, students, and other readers who have independently taken the trouble to send valuable corrections and comments. For the current edition we have benefited especially from input by Robert Murphy of Hillsdale College.

Over the years a number of research assistants have worked mainly on the examples and on the questions and answers for the various chapters. Once again the number has grown too large for a complete listing, but we would especially like to name Charles Knoeber for his outstanding assistance on the initial edition of the book and Kyoo-Il Kim for his help on this edition. Thanks are due to Enpei Lan, who prepared the indexes. We also thank Scott Parris of Cambridge University Press for shepherding this new edition through the publication process.

Finally, the senior author is happy to report that his coauthors on several earlier editions, Amihai Glazer and David A. Hirshleifer, both participated as coauthors for this edition.

I INTRODUCTION

1 The Nature and Scope of Economics

Economics concerns decisions – choices among actions. Every action has its pros and cons, pluses and minuses, benefits and costs. Are you thinking about taking up tennis? The game may trim your figure and improve your disposition, but will take time from your studies and could damage your joints. How about dropping out of college to take a job? You would likely earn more money now, but earn less later in life. Similarly in business and government. Whether it's a small action, as when your neighborhood market sets its price for potatoes, or a big one, as when Congress decides on declaring war, almost always there are valid arguments for and against. Faced with such opposed considerations, how should individuals, firms, or governments make decisions? Economics shows how to determine the *best* action, through a systematic assessment of the costs and benefits.

Few decisions are made in a vacuum. Other people are likely to react. Thinking like an economist means taking these reactions into account. A law firm that raises its billing rates may find customers switching to another provider of legal services – so the higher price might not increase profit after all. Or imagine that Congress, aiming to widen use of the Internet, were to require Internet service providers (ISPs) to charge very low prices. Before concluding that this is a good idea we would need to know how the ISPs would react. They might provide access at those low prices. Or they might reduce the quality of service, so that consumers find busy signals when trying to connect. (Although this might seem a rather wild example, something similar occurs when rent-control legislation freezes apartment rents during a period of general price inflation. Such a price freeze makes landlords less willing to supply and to maintain rental housing.)

Economics has been called the "dismal science."[1] That's probably because economists are often messengers bringing bad news; for example, that a superficially appealing project or scheme may not be such a great idea once all the consequences are taken into account.

Table 1.1 lists a number of individual and social problems, together with some purported "solutions." Also shown are possible bad consequences that an economist might point out. Can you add other possible objections? And on the other side, can you think of counterarguments that might rebut these objections?

Proponents of plans and projects tend to overlook possible flaws, while opponents tend to ignore the evidence in favor. Because people committed to one side of a question generally do not want to listen to contrary arguments, thinking like an economist – trying to impartially weigh the pros and cons – may not make you popular. But it is likely to improve your private decisions, enhance your prospects of business success, and make your views on social issues more balanced.

1.1   ECONOMICS AS A SOCIAL SCIENCE

Economics is a science. Like other sciences it consists of explanations (theories) that help us understand and make valid predictions about the real world, together with the empirical evidence for and against them. More specifically, economics is a *social* science. Its subject matter is the interplay of choices made by living beings. Economics addresses

---

[1]   Not a gay science . . . no, a dreary, desolate, and indeed quite abject and distressing one: what we might call, by way of eminence, the *dismal* science.

– Thomas Carlyle (1795–1881)

Table 1.1 Finding solutions to social problems

Problem	Solution	Possible adverse consequences
1. Our country's steel producers are threatened by competition from imports.	Impose a tariff on imported steel.	a. The price of steel will rise, so steel-using industries will have higher costs and will have to raise prices to consumers. b. Foreigners, because they will be selling less steel to us, will buy fewer of our country's exports.
2. Apartment rents are rising, putting decent housing out of reach for the poor.	Freeze apartment rents.	a. Landlords will skimp on upkeep and repair of apartments. b. In the longer run, fewer rental units will be constructed.
3. Women's wages are lower than men's.	Adopt "comparable worth" laws requiring equal pay for men and women doing comparable jobs.	a. Employers will become less willing to hire women. b. Costly bureaucratic and judicial proceedings will be involved in setting wages.
4. Commercial fishing for tuna kills large numbers of dolphins.	Require domestic fisheries to use special nets that let dolphins escape.	a. Consumers will have to pay more for tuna. b. Foreign fisheries, not subject to our laws, will take over more of the tuna trade.
5. Medical costs are very high.	Require government to pay a share of medical bills, especially for the poor.	a. Doctors' bills and hospital charges will rise even more than they have previously. b. Taxes will have to go up.
6. Many people are addicted to drugs.	Toughen enforcement of narcotics laws.	a. Street prices of narcotics will rise, forcing addicts to steal to feed the habit. b. Huge financial stakes in the narcotics trade will lead to more corruption of the police and judiciary.
7. Many people are addicted to drugs.	Abandon enforcement of narcotics laws.	Increased availability and lower prices of narcotics will increase usage and addiction.

questions such as: Will a reduction in the capital gains tax make the stock market rise? Will higher tariffs make consumers better off? Will increased prison terms reduce crime? Will easier divorce improve the status of women? Will a high-price (meaning low volume of sales) strategy lead to more profit for a firm than a low-price strategy?

A cynic might deny that economics is a science. Here is a possible complaint: "Economists always disagree with one another. That doesn't give me much confidence that economics has arrived at scientific truth. Furthermore, if economists can scientifically predict financial and commercial events, why aren't they all rich?"

It's easy to exaggerate the disagreement among economists. Controversy makes news; consensus rarely does. The great majority of economists agree that price controls lead to shortages, that free trade improves the international division of labor, and that uncontrolled printing of money will bring about inflation.[2] What is more important, disagreement is essential if a science is to advance. In astronomy the heliocentric hypothesis of Copernicus challenged Ptolemy's 1,000-year-old geocentric model. In chemistry the phlogiston theory of combustion was superseded by Lavoisier's oxidation theory. And in biology creationism was countered by Darwin's theory of evolution. It is not universal agreement that characterizes science, but rather *willingness to examine the evidence*. All important issues of economics – for example, how taxes affect incentives to work, whether trade unions raise workers' wages, whether stronger copyright laws promote creativity – are under continuous re-evaluation in the light of the evidence. Economists may continue to disagree, perhaps because the problems are complex or the investigators insufficiently skilled, but unresolved issues persist in any living science.

Engineers, despite having well-validated theories and a vast amount of evidence as to strength of materials, commonly add a huge safety factor (50 or even 100%) before building a bridge or a dam. And even so, bridges still collapse and dams wash away. In Los Angeles during the 1994 earthquake, reinforced freeways designed to withstand an even more severe jolt than actually occurred nevertheless collapsed. As another example, meteorology is certainly a natural science, yet meteorologists hardly even claim to predict the weather for more than a week or so ahead. If economists predicting the extent of unemployment or forecasting the rate of inflation were permitted as wide a safety factor as engineers or meteorologists, they would rarely be seen as going very far astray.

EXAMPLE 1.1 THE ECOLOGIST, THE ECONOMIST, AND THE STATISTICIAN

In 1990 the ecologist and popular author Paul Ehrlich sent a check for $576.07 to the economist Julian L. Simon. It was a payoff on a bet made 10 years previously. Ehrlich, though not an economist, had made startling economic predictions in his 1968 bestseller *The Population Bomb*. Take, for example, his opening sentences: "The battle to feed all of humanity is over. In the 1970s hundreds of millions of people are going to starve to death."

Ehrlich's predictions utterly failed. Despite an "oil crisis" in mid-decade and again toward the end, overall the 1970s were a decade of remarkable economic growth. Yet the author continued to be highly acclaimed. In books, speeches, and articles that received worldwide attention he prophesied that accessible supplies of many key minerals would be nearly depleted by 1985.

Meanwhile the economist Julian L. Simon had been predicting just the reverse for the 1970s and 1980s: continuing improvements in human well-being, and lower prices for raw materials. Simon challenged Ehrlich to back his contrary forecast with hard cash, and Ehrlich accepted the challenge. The result was a 1980 bet about whether the prices of five important metals – chrome, copper, nickel, tin, and tungsten – would, after allowing for inflation, rise or fall by 1990. The economist let the ecologist choose the specific commodities. Once again, the economist Simon was proved right and

---

[2] *Scientific* consensus need not imply general agreement about *policy*, however. See the section on "Positive versus Normative Analysis" below.

Ehrlich wrong. The 1980s were also a decade of prosperity, and raw materials prices generally fell. The ecologist had to pay off on the bet.

Ehrlich's analytic error was to look only at the demand side, and specifically at growing world population (more mouths to feed). Julian Simon, with his better economic understanding, also considered the supply side. More people mean more mouths, but also more hands and brains. Simon also took account of other favorable economic trends such as greater liberalization of national economies and increased international trade.

So the predictions of economic analysis were vindicated. Nevertheless, Paul Ehrlich continued to publish highly popular books forecasting, as mistakenly as before, environmental doom in the near future. Just as regularly, up to his death in 1998 Julian Simon was providing sound analysis and well-validated economic forecasts, culminating in his volume *The Ultimate Resource* (2nd ed., Princeton University Press, 1998). But none of his books were best-sellers.

What was going on here? An economic interpretation might be that these two authors were supplying different commodities. Julian Simon was supplying correct economic analysis. Paul Ehrlich was and is in a different business, rather comparable to horror-story writers such as Stephen King. Evidently, at least when it comes to selling books, the demand for horror stories far exceeds the demand for sound economic analysis.[a]

A later exhaustive and careful study by the Danish statistician Bjorn Lomborg (*The Skeptical Environmentalist*, Cambridge University Press, 2001) has updated Simon's results. Initially intending to refute Simon's analysis, Lomborg found his research instead confirming it. Despite rising world population, per capita incomes have maintained their upward trend and real prices of important resources have continued to fall.

As a rather strange sidelight, upon publishing these results Lomborg became the target of personal attacks that reached an extraordinary level of intensity. At one of his public presentations a cream pie was dumped on his face and clothing. He was even accused of "intellectual dishonesty" by a scientific body with official standing in Denmark. Ultimately, all the charges were conclusively refuted, and the improperly motivated proceeding against Lomborg was dismissed. (Which does not necessarily mean, of course, that all of Lomborg's estimates and forecasts will ultimately prove to be correct.)

One possible lesson: sound economic analysis can sometimes be riskier than you might think![b]

---

[a] For a detailed history of the Ehrlich-Simon wager see John Tierney, "Betting the Planet," *New York Times Magazine*, December 2, 1990.

[b] A summary of the Lomborg controversy is provided in Jim Giles, "The Man They Love to Hate," *Nature*, v. 423, May 15, 2003.

The cynic's second challenge to economists – "Why aren't you all rich?" – sounds crass. But economists, of all people, cannot dismiss it. First of all, as the preceding Example showed, correct economic analysis need not have greater market appeal than incorrect but psychologically appealing assertions. More generally, scientific knowledge in any field does not guarantee riches. If Michael Jordan had studied the aerodynamic equations governing the motion of spheroidal missiles, would that have improved his basketball point scores? This argument shouldn't be pressed too far, though. After all, what's the use of economics (or of aerodynamics, for that matter) if not the practical results obtained? So it's reasonable to expect that better understanding of economics and markets would lead to more wealth. Although most people can hardly match the life achievements of geniuses like Tiger Woods in sports or Bill Gates in business, training in economics ought to increase income. And, as the next Example shows, apparently to some extent it does.

EXAMPLE 1.2 EARNINGS OF MALE COLLEGE GRADUATES, BY FIELD

The table shows median annual earnings for men with bachelor's degrees, by selected fields, for the year 1993 – the latest year for which such data have been published. Only selected fields are shown here, and the ranking is among those selected fields. (The source also tabulates earnings for women graduates, but the female tabulation unfortunately omits economics.)

Median annual earnings for men, by selected fields, 1993

Field	1993 earnings	Rank
Engineering	$51,600	1
Mathematics	50,500	2
Pharmacy	50,500	3
Physics	50,400	4
Economics	48,100	5
Accounting	47,800	6
Nursing	43,500	7
Business, other	43,000	8
Political science and government	41,600	9
Psychology	40,700	10
Biological/life sciences	39,600	11
Sociology	38,800	12
History	38,300	13
English language and literature	37,600	14
Education	34,500	15
Visual and performing arts	32,100	16
Social work	30,600	17
Philosophy, religion, and theology	29,700	18

Source: Table 5 in Daniel E. Hecker, "Earnings of College Graduates, 1993," *Monthly Labor Review*, December 1995.

In this tabulation, economics is the best-paying social science degree, ranking just below a high-earnings group that includes engineering, physics, mathematics, and (surprisingly perhaps) pharmacy. (Though not shown in this tabulation, pharmacy is actually the top-ranking field for women.)

One cannot be sure that these high incomes are due specifically to educational preparation. To earn a degree in engineering, math/stat, or physics you have to be pretty smart to begin with, and perhaps that applies also to economics. Also, the life styles associated with different occupations may be attractive or repellent. Higher pay may be needed to induce people to become bill collectors or hangmen, and conceivably economics suffers from a mild version of such distaste. Perhaps the category of philosophy, religion, and theology ranks at the very bottom of the tabulated wage distribution because many people find such employment to be a noble activity, a "higher calling." (How such nonpecuniary considerations influence occupational wage patterns will be studied in Chapter 12.) Overall, it seems reasonable to conclude that studying economics does pay off, to some extent, in terms of higher income.

What about the other social sciences? Sociology, anthropology, political science, social psychology, and sociobiology also attempt to explain behavior. The boundaries between economics and these other sciences are indistinct, in part because economic reasoning has shown itself to be of value in those fields as well. Anthropologists use economic techniques to analyze the foraging choices and birth-spacing decisions of primitive peoples. Political scientists use cost-benefit analysis to predict how many citizens will cast ballots and which way they will vote. And sociobiologists, on the hypothesis that economically sound strategies are more likely to survive the test of evolutionary selection, employ economic analysis to explain, for example, why some animals choose to defend territories while others do not. (This book will be illustrating economic principles with instances drawn from these and other related social sciences.)

Although the boundaries may be indistinct, economics has a central core. First, on the individual level of choice economists generally postulate "economic man,"[3] a hypothetical being whose decisions are based upon the rational pursuit of self-interest. Second, economics concentrates upon one type of human interaction: *market exchange*. In this book we necessarily emphasize the "narrow economics" associated with these core ideas. But there is a "broad economics" that goes beyond them. Economists can and do attempt to take account of irrational and nonselfish behavior. And economists certainly devote effort to studying *nonmarket interactions*, ranging from family relations to violent conflict.

However, first steps first. We must begin with the central core of economic reasoning.

1.2 "ECONOMIC MAN"

The term "economic man" is frequently used in a derogatory sense, as an implicit criticism of economic reasoning. Since people are not always *rational* and not always *self-interested*, economics is, critics allege, built on bad foundations. But the economist does not contend that rational and self-interested behavior are universal and absolute facts. Rather, they constitute a working hypothesis, whose validity in any context can only be assessed only by its usefulness. Does that assumption help us understand what actually happens in markets and elsewhere?

Rationality

Rational behavior has at least two meanings in common use. The first meaning refers to method, the second to result. When speaking of *method*, rational behavior is action selected on the basis of reasoned thought rather than habit, prejudice, or emotion. When speaking of *result*, rational behavior is action that is effective in achieving desired goals. The two meanings differ. Good methods can sometimes lead to bad results. ("The best

---

[3] *Note:* "economic man" includes "economic woman"!

laid schemes o' mice and men/Gang aft a-gley" – Robert Burns.) And the seemingly inferior methods available to animals, even some with tiny brains, often work very well. A human being chasing a fly with a swatter often loses the contest. But in general, we expect that considered thought leads to better action.

Everyone behaves irrationally to some extent – out of passion, thoughtlessness, mental defect, or just plain perverseness. So how can rationality be assumed in economics? Assuming rationality is justified only if doing so helps predict how people will behave. Economists find that for the most part, though not literally always, the assumption of rationality does work.

Operating a motor vehicle involves many decisions, among them how aggressively to drive. It might seem that driving aggressively is always irrational, but that depends upon one's ends. A rational person values safety, but also values other goals such as saving time and avoiding inconvenience.

EXAMPLE 1.3 RATIONAL DRIVERS?

Airbags reduce, on average, the severity of auto injuries and the risk of death from motor accidents. But given that additional safety margin, it might well be rational for motorists to drive more aggressively!

Is such an adaptation observed? Steven Peterson, George Hoffer, and Edward Millner examined statistics collected by the state of Virginia about fatal two-car accidents in 1993.[a] In 30 such accidents, one car was equipped with an air bag and the other was not. The accident reports identified in each case the supposed "initiator," the party driving more aggressively. The table indicates that in 22 of the 30 accidents (73%) the initiators drove cars with airbags, although only 50% of the cars involved in accidents were equipped with airbags. So, the indications are, having an airbag increased the likelihood of a driver initiating an accident.

Two-car accidents with/without airbags (Virginia, 1993)

	With airbags	Without airbags
Number of cars	30 (50%)	30 (50%)
Number of "initiators"	22 (73%)	8 (27%)

Source: Adapted from Peterson et al., p. 262.

Any single bit of evidence such as this can only be indicative, not conclusive. And even if entirely valid, these results do not necessarily imply that regulations requiring airbags are inadvisable. Although drivers of airbag-equipped vehicles may indeed be more inclined to take risks, the increased aggressiveness may not entirely cancel out the overall beneficial safety effect of airbags.

---

[a] Steven Peterson, George Hoffer, and Edward Millner, "Are Drivers of Air-Bag-Equipped Cars More Aggressive? A Test of the Offsetting Behavior Hypothesis," *Journal of Law and Economics*, v. 38 (October 1995).

For a person receiving disability pay, the rational choice of when to return to work depends upon the costs and the benefits. What would you expect to happen if disability benefits were increased?

EXAMPLE 1.4 RATIONAL MALINGERING?

Under U.S. federal regulations, each state's workmen's compensation program re-imburses injured workers at a certain "replacement ratio" (usually around 2/3 of pre-injury wages) up to a specified maximum. For a rational decision-maker, the higher the compensation for remaining on disability status, the less the incentive to return to work. Bruce D. Meyer, W. Kip Viscusi, and David L. Durbin examined a "natural experiment" testing whether changes in incentives had any visible effect upon the return-to-work decision.[a]

In 1980 the state of Kentucky raised its maximum weekly benefit from $131 to $217 – by about 66%. In 1982 the state of Michigan raised its maximum from $181 to $307 – by about 70%. (Other provisions of the states' compensation arrangements were largely unchanged.) Crucially, these adjustments impacted only upon relatively high-wage workers, those with incomes big enough to benefit from the higher compensation caps.

If remaining on disability status were purely a medical matter, higher payoffs would not have affected returning to work. But taking monetary incentives into account, a rationally calculating high-wage worker would be more likely than before to remain on disability status. In contrast, low-wage workers, unaffected by the higher cap on disability payments, had no financial incentive to defer returning to work.

After the change in regulations in Kentucky, the median duration of temporary total disabilities for high-wage workers rose from 4 to 5 weeks, while remaining at 3 weeks for low-wage workers. Similarly in Michigan, the median duration for high-wage workers rose from 5 to 7 weeks, while the low-wage median remained constant at 4 weeks. So both high-wage and low-wage workers responded in ways consistent with the rationality assumption.

COMMENT

We ought not jump to the conclusion that workers who chose to remain longer on disability status were malingering. It may well be that family responsibilities and other financial needs had previously induced some workers to return to work too early, before their injuries were fully healed.

[a] Bruce D. Meyer, W. Kip Viscusi, and David L. Durbin, "Workers' Compensation and Injury Duration: Evidence from a Natural Experiment," *American Economic Review*, v. 85 (June 1995).

Despite these and many other examples of rational choices being made even in some-what unexpected contexts such as automobile driving, one often hears about "irrational" behavior – even from so eminent an economist as the Chairman of the Federal Reserve Board.

EXAMPLE 1.5 "IRRATIONAL EXUBERANCE"

On December 5, 1996 Alan Greenspan, the chairman of the Federal Reserve Board, expressed concern that the high level of stock prices represented "irrational exu-berance." And indeed, by historical standards, the stockmarket was extraordinarily high. At the beginning of 1980 the Dow Jones Industrial Index had stood at about 800. A decade later it had risen to about 1,800 and by December 1996 to around 6,900. Although the market dipped a bit after Greenspan's remark, by the beginning of the year 2000 it reached almost 11,000.

Stock prices can be said to be "too high" or "too low" only in relation to actual and anticipated corporate earnings. In his book *Irrational Exuberance* (Princeton University Press, 2000), the economist Robert Shiller contended that not only were stock prices historically high, but the price-earnings ratio (P/E) also far exceeded all historical levels. According to his data, the inflation-adjusted P/E, whose previous high had been around 32 (just before the 1930s Depression), had reached an unprecedented 44 in the year 2000 (as estimated visually from Figure 1.2 in the Shiller book).

But other analysts maintained that the unusually high stock prices reflected ongoing favorable economic developments such as the computer revolution, which promised continued gains in productivity. Also important, though less often mentioned, were the reduced risks of cataclysmic war after the collapse of the Soviet Union. Along with that, there was an improved climate of opinion for private business, owing to the declining appeal of communist and socialist ideologies.

So at the time it was not so clear whether the stockmarket levels were "irrational." The table here indicates that the Dow Jones Industrial Index did indeed move downward for some years after the publication of Shiller's book in 2000, but it recovered almost all the lost ground by early 2004. Whether stockmarket levels of 8,000 or 10,000 or whatever are truly "irrational" is something all investors (including the authors of this book!) would really like to know.

Date (January)	Dow Jones industrial index
2000	10,940
2001	10,887
2002	9,920
2003	8,053
2004	10,544

Human Goals – The Self-Interest Assumption

"Economic man" is supposed to be not just rational but also self-interested. Who can doubt that self-interest, though certainly not the only human goal, is an important aspect of what humans seek in life? Adam Smith said: "It is not from the benevolence of the butcher, the brewer, or the baker, that we expect our dinner, but from their regard to their own interest."[4]

Traditional "narrow economics" does not inquire into the origins of our goals in life, our *tastes* or *preferences*. In one society individuals may protect children but eat cattle; another society may protect cattle but permit infanticide. Often, however, people's goals and preferences do have analyzable sources. Psychologists explain them in terms of primitive instincts, as reinforced or suppressed by socialization. Anthropologists analyze how culture helps determine individual purposes; sociologists examine the role of class or of other group identifications. Sociobiologists explain human tastes and preferences as the product of evolution through natural selection. Partly stimulated by this line

---

[4] *The Wealth of Nations* (1776), Book I, Chapter 2.

of scientific work, "broad economics" has begun to study the cultural and biological sources of preferences. As one example, teenage boys take more risks than do teenage girls, as evidenced by the higher auto accident rates (and correspondingly higher auto insurance premiums) for young males. Male risk-taking may make biological sense, since males must compete harder with one another to gain the attention of the opposite sex.[5] (Biological and other possible sources of preferences will be discussed in more detail in Chapter 3.)

Another question is whether tastes and preferences are *stable*. In analyzing taxes on alcohol, economists usually assume that the craving for alcohol, a taste, will be constant. If so, taxing alcohol makes drinking more costly but will not affect the underlying desire to drink. As a matter of historical fact, however, the taste for liquor has been known to change dramatically. Around 1850 the remarkable temperance campaign of Father Matthew in Ireland cut the consumption of spirits in that country from 12,000,000 to 5,000,000 gallons per annum. (But only temporarily!) And think of the fashion industries – their very existence is based upon ever-changing tastes. What is far more important, many of the crucial social changes in human history have been due to shifts in people's goals for living. Economic analysis may trivialize fundamental values and goals by suggesting that they are mere arbitrary "tastes." From the prophets of ancient Israel to the ministries of Jesus and Mohammed to the recent decline in religious belief in the West, the changes in the kinds of rewards that people seek from life have enormously affected human societies. Economists have mostly not attempted to explain these important determinants of human behavior.

Self-interest is the human goal attributed to "economic man." But benevolence ("wishing well" to others) certainly exists,[6] and malevolence ("wishing ill") as well. For biologically evident reasons, people are mainly benevolent toward their own children, or at any rate to close kin. Yet people also extend very large sums, in the form of charity, to strangers. Economists for the most part do not attempt to explore the underlying sources of such behavior. Nevertheless, economists would assert that, if it were cheaper to be benevolent (for example, if tax deductions for charitable giving were to become more generous), more benevolence would be elicited. And even though there is a biological explanation of parental aid to children, economists would still predict that greater financial inducements would induce even more assistance to one's offspring.

It has been alleged that this emphasis upon self-interest makes *economists* more selfish than they would otherwise be. Perhaps economics students are being "taught to be selfish"![7]

---

[5] See Paul H. Rubin and Chris W. Paul II, "An Evolutionary Model of the Taste for Risk," *Economic Inquiry*, v. 17 (October 1979).

[6] Indeed, Adam Smith also said:

> How selfish soever man may be supposed, there are evidently some principles in his nature, which interest him in the fortune of others, and render their happiness necessary to him, though he derives nothing from it, except the pleasure of seeing it.

This is the opening sentence of *The Theory of Moral Sentiments* (1759).

[7] This allegation has been made even by economists: Robert H. Frank, Thomas Gilovich, and Dennis T. Regan, "Does Studying Economics Inhibit Cooperation?" *Journal of Economic Perspectives*, v. 7, 1993.

EXAMPLE 1.6 SELFISH ECONOMICS STUDENTS?

In a study at George Washington University the economists Anthony M. Yezer, Robert S. Goldfarb, and Paul J. Poppen[a] examined two questions: (1) When asked about *hypothetical* situations, do students in economics courses report they would be more selfish than before they took the course, as compared with students taking non-economics courses? (2) When the *actual* behavior of students is observed, are economics students in fact more selfish?

Table A compares the *self-reported* unselfishness of students in economics versus noneconomics classes. Each student was asked to state the percent chance that, after receiving a bill containing a substantial error in his/her favor, he/she would voluntarily ask to be charged the correct amount due. The same question was asked at the beginning of the course ("Before") and at the end ("After").

Table A Results of survey question (self-reported hypothetical "unselfish" actions)

	Before	After
Two economics classes	53.4%	50.0%
Two noneconomics classes	52.5%	53.8%

Source: Calculated from Yezer, Goldfarb, and Poppen, "Question 2," in Table 1, p. 181.

Though the difference is small, these data do provide some slight support for the contention that economics instruction led to an increase in student selfishness – as self-estimated for such a hypothetical situation.

The investigators then went on to conduct a much more significant experiment, this time with real money. Envelopes containing $10 in cash were "lost" in economics and noneconomics classrooms. Each envelope was addressed and stamped, and also contained a message to the effect that the money was in repayment of a loan. Since the envelopes were already addressed and stamped, an unselfish person had only to seal the envelope and drop it in a mailbox. A selfish person could just keep the money.

The investigators left 32 envelopes in economics classes and 32 in noneconomics classes. See Table B for the results.

Table B Results of "lost letter" experiment

	Returned	Not returned
32 letters in economics classes	18 (56%)	14 (44%)
32 letters in noneconomics classes	10 (31%)	22 (69%)

Source: From description in Yezer, Goldfarb, and Poppen, p. 181.

Table B shows that, when it came to real decisions with real financial stakes involved, *fewer* economics students acted selfishly. The self-estimated hypothetical survey reported in Table A, which appeared to indicate the contrary, may have shown

only that economics students are more frank in admitting they might sometimes behave selfishly.

***

[a] Anthony M. Yezer, Robert S. Goldfarb, and Paul J. Poppen, "Does Studying Economics Discourage Cooperation: Watch What We Do, Not What We Say or How We Play," *Journal of Economic
Perspectives*, v. 10 (Winter 1996).

So, it appears, studying economics does not make a person more selfish. However,
economics instruction may make the student more willing to admit that he or she will,
in certain circumstances, act selfishly. What about economics professors?

EXAMPLE 1.7 SELFISH ECONOMICS PROFS?

In a number of academic professional associations the dues schedules rise with
income. But members are permitted to fit themselves voluntarily into the appropriate
income category (the "honor system"). David N. Laband and Richard O. Beil studied
a number of professional associations using this procedure.[a]

A member of the American Economic Association (AEA) in 1994 who placed himself
or herself in the lowest dues category (declared income less than $37,000) would pay
dues of $50, whereas self-placement in the highest category (declared income greater
than $50,000) required dues of $70. For the American Sociological Association (ASA),
the dues structure ran from $34 at the bottom end (for income less than $15,000) to
$180 at the top (for income greater than $50,000). For the American Political Science
Association (APSA) the comparable numbers were $65 (for income less than $30,000)
and $125 (for income greater than $70,000).

Were the self-placements into dues categories truthful? The authors tested this
by sending a separate questionnaire asking members of each association about
their incomes during the year. The questionnaires had no obvious connection with
professional dues, but replicated the income categories in members' annual billing
statements.

It was found, for example, that in responding to the questionnaire only 3% of
American Economic Association members indicated that they fell into the lowest
income category. But when it came to paying dues, 25% placed themselves in that
category. So evidently, many members "cheated." Somewhat similar results were
found for the other associations.

One way of comparing the different professional associations is to calculate
what the "true" average dues payment would have been, if members of each
association had placed themselves in the correct categories as indicated by the
independent questionnaire. Some of the relevant averages are indicated in the table.

Average dues liabilities and payments in 1994/95

	"True" dues liability	Actual dues payments	Actual/true
AEA	$67.74	$62.83	93%
ASA	$147.60	$112.52	78%
APSA	$105.15	$96.05	91%

Source: Laband and Beil, pp. 96–97.

Although in percentage terms the economists appear to be relatively truthful (and, to that extent, unselfish), the comparison in the table is perhaps biased. Since the AEA is considerably cheaper than the ASA and APSA, the temptation to cheat is less. Still, it is at least doubtful whether economists are any more selfish than other academics.

[a] David N. Laband and Richard O. Beil, "Are Economists More Selfish than Other 'Social' Scientists?" *Public Choice*, v. 100 (1999), pp. 85–101.

Ignorance and Uncertainty

To say that people are rational is not to say that they are all-knowing. Almost all decisions are subject to uncertainty. A consumer may not be aware of the quality of the goods offered for sale, a job-seeker may not know which employer would be willing to pay the highest salary, a computer manufacturer may be unsure about what products its competitor may bring to market, a politician may be doubtful whether the public will approve of a proposed policy.

Much of this book deals with decision-making under uncertainty. How much should one be willing to pay as an annual premium for fire insurance? Should a person choose a safe but lower-paying job over a risky one offering higher rewards? Which stocks should an investor buy?

As a subtler point, individual decision-makers should take into account the behavior of others. A person who thinks a stock is underpriced ought to ask why other investors let that stock's price get so low. Moreover, any one person should recognize that others may attempt to take advantage of his or her own ignorance. Later chapters will analyze how these considerations affect the terms of insurance contracts, the prices of assets, and the employment contracts that firms offer.

1.3   MARKET AND NONMARKET INTERACTIONS

We all need food. But there are many ways to go about getting it. Someone who wants bread from the baker can work at a job and earn the price of a loaf. An alternative would be to steal the bread. As still another option, consumers might try to persuade bakers that it is their charitable duty to give away bread. Or consumers might organize a political movement aimed at forcing bakers to do so. "Narrow economics" concentrates upon the first of these interactions, that is, upon *voluntary exchange through the market*. For the most part, crime has been left to sociology, the techniques of persuasion to psychology, and the uses of state power to political science, and. But "broad economics" goes beyond these boundaries.

EXAMPLE 1.8 CRIME AS AN ECONOMIC CHOICE – "THREE STRIKES"

Crime sometimes does pay. It may be entirely rational, though certainly not ethical, for a criminal to steal rather than work if he feels the gains are worth the risks. Conventional criminology, a field historically dominated by sociologists, has regarded criminals as "deviant" individuals who do not make rational choices. According to this traditional view, the solution to crime lies on the psychological level – for example, improving the mental health of potential lawbreakers, or providing them with better role models. Economic analysis, without necessarily denying that criminals are psychologically "deviant" in some ways, suggests that even criminal activity will respond to incentives.

Imprisonment can reduce the crime rate in two main ways: incapacitation or deterrence. *Incapacitation* does not involve rationality: a person in jail is simply not in a position to commit crimes against the public. *Deterrence*, in contrast, operates through the potential lawbreaker's calculation of the costs versus the benefits of criminal activity. So a deterrence policy implies at least some degree of rationality on the part of potential law-breakers.

This distinction became crucial in the debate over "three strikes" laws – proposals to sentence habitual criminals to life imprisonment. If *incapacitation* is the important consideration, "three strikes" laws are seriously flawed. The propensity to commit crimes is known to decrease with age, so such laws would fill the prisons with relatively aged inmates who would not be committing offenses anyway. But if *deterrence* matters most, the threat of being put away for life might discourage even young criminals.

A study by Steven Levitt attempted to separate the two effects.[a] Using data for the period 1970–1992, he examined how the number of crimes in one statistical category such as assault responded to arrest rates in another category such as burglary. Given that a large number of lawbreakers commit both types of crimes then, if *incapacitation* is the main force at work, a higher arrest rate for assault would reduce both assaults and burglaries. But if *deterrence* is the predominant influence, a higher arrest rate for assault should lead criminals to commit fewer assaults – but just as many (or maybe even more!) burglaries and other crimes.

The evidence suggested that deterrence was more important than incapacitation in reducing the crime rate. In fact, deterrence alone explained about 75% of the overall impact of higher arrest rates on crime. The study therefore provides some support for "three strikes" laws, though of course the effect on crime rates is not the only consideration in evaluating such legislation. (Another element that needs to be weighed are the costs of building more prisons and dealing with a larger inmate population.) Recent evidence from the states of Washington and California tends to confirm that, in those states as well, the higher incarceration rates associated with "three strikes" have reduced the number of offenses.

In another study, the same author asked why juvenile crime rates rose much more than nonjuvenile rates in the period 1978–1993.[b] (In that period the adult arrest rate for murder fell by 7%, but the juvenile arrest rate rose by an extraordinary 177%!) The main explanation, he concluded, was that in the period of study the average juvenile punishment rate per crime – already lower than the adult rate – fell by around 20%, whereas the adult punishment rate rose by about 60%. He also noted that the crime rate falls sharply in the year that an age cohort moves out of the (more lenient) juvenile justice system and into the (more severe) adult system.

---

[a] Steven D. Levitt, "Why Do Increased Arrest Rates Appear to Reduce Crime: Deterrence, Incapacitation, or Measurement Error?" *Economic Inquiry* (July 1998).

[b] Steven D. Levitt, "Juvenile Crime and Punishment," *Journal of Political Economy* (December 1998).

So it appears that economic analysis can be usefully applied to crime as one form of nonmarket behavior. Charity is another. A third form of nonmarket interaction, sometimes not too far removed from crime, is politics. The economic approach to politics will be covered in Part Seven of this book.

Market interactions have two crucial characteristics: they are *mutual* and they are *voluntary*. Among the possible nonmarket interactions, charitable giving is voluntary but is a unilateral rather than a mutual transaction. Theft, of course, is involuntary on the part of the victim.

But is the market interaction really voluntary? Can a poor person refuse a job that pays low wages but will at least put food on the table? Isn't he just a "wage slave"? Or suppose a highwayman threatens his victim, "Your money or your life!" Isn't he offering a voluntary deal? Then how can criminal extortion be distinguished from market exchange?

The explanation of these puzzles rests upon the concept of *property*. The highwayman is proposing a market deal: he will refrain from murder, in exchange for money. But under our legal system each person has property in his or her own life. The seemingly voluntary transaction proposed by the highwayman is based on his seizing power over something to which he has no legal title – the victim's life. As for the wage slave contention, it is true that a rich person can buy more of what he or she wants than can a poor person. This may or may not be inequitable, but poor people are not enslaved. Their working capacity is their own property, and they can bargain with alternative employers for the best available terms. Slaves cannot market or trade their labor, for it is not legally theirs to sell.

1.4   ALLOCATION BY PRICES – THE MARKET SYSTEM

Consider the allocation of seats in your economics classroom. Some seats are more desirable than others. One possible rule is first come first served. Or the professor could make the assignments on any basis he or she preferred. Or the students might elect a committee to work out the assignment. In less friendly situations such as rock concerts, good seating might depend on your ability to jostle and trample others. All of the above represent *nonmarket* ways of apportioning a scarce resource. On the other hand, rights to seats might be assigned by a market technique, for example, by an auction.

EXAMPLE 1.9 BIDDING FOR FACULTY OFFICES

William J. Boyes and Stephen K. Happel reported on how the College of Business at Arizona State University, upon moving to a new building, dealt with the problem of assigning faculty offices.[a] The Management Department gave first choice to the most senior professors. The Finance Department followed a first come first served rule: a sign-up sheet was posted outside the Chairman's office, and choices were awarded in order of signing up. The Statistics Department used a randomizing device – rolling dice.

The Economics Department chose to hold an auction. (The financial proceeds, which turned out to be around $3,200, went to a fund supporting graduate student scholarships and dissertation research.) The single highest bidder paid $500 for the right to have the first choice of offices available.

COMMENT

The auction led to some adverse publicity. A number of citizens felt that the professors were auctioning off public property for their own benefit. The complaint was unwarranted, since the offices were not being sold to the detriment of the taxpayers. What was being sold was only the right to choose ahead of other professors. Also, the proceeds were not used for the benefit of the bidders but for the benefit of graduate students. Once this was made clear, opposition dissipated.

[a] William J. Boyes and Stephen K. Happel, "Auctions as an Allocation Mechanism in Academia: The Case of Faculty Offices," *Journal of Economic Perspectives*, v. 3 (Summer 1989).

The key feature of markets is *price* – the terms on which goods are exchanged. To acquire a commodity buyers must be willing to pay the market price, while successful sellers are the ones willing to give up control of the good in exchange for the same market price.

Market prices ration goods and resources to consumers. As the preceding discussion has shown, there are other ways of rationing: first come first served, dictatorship, violence, lottery, and so on. But price has one feature these other methods lack: the commodities go to those individuals with the highest willingness to pay. Economists do not claim that this principle is necessarily ethically attractive. Among other things, wealthier people are able to pay more. So anyone who has acquired wealth, even unethically, has the power to buy lots of desired goods. On the other hand, all other conceivable methods for rationing goods and resources might also be subject to objection on ethical grounds, perhaps more so. Setting ethics aside, it is "efficient" (in a sense to be made more explicit in the chapters that follow) for goods and resources to end up in the hands of those most willing to pay.

From the point of view of sellers or providers, *prices guide production*. Whenever the current market price of a commodity exceeds its cost of production, producing more of the good becomes profitable. Not only are current producers likely to increase output, but new providers will have an incentive to enter the industry. In consequence, more goods will be provided precisely where consumers' willingness to pay is highest. This is the principle that Adam Smith called "the invisible hand."[8] Even if a person seeks only private advantage, he or she is led to serve the public by producing those goods or services that others most desire.

Perhaps this idea, that self-interested motivations can lead to actions that end up helping other people, seems obvious. Yet many people, in Adam Smith's day and in ours, believe that the only way to help others is by intentionally "doing good." More sophisticated individuals appreciate, as did Adam Smith, that in helping others *trade* can be more effective than charitable *aid*.

Still, it is not immediately evident just how self-interested behavior manages to avoid mutual harm or even total chaos. Los Angeles is fed by converging food shipments from all corners of the earth – without any benevolent dictator to make sure that the Kansas farmer, the New England fisherman, and the Florida orange grower deliver food to the city. Though no one is ordered to do so, and none of these suppliers need be motivated by any particular love and concern for Angelenos, the city is fed. Why? Because Kansas farmers simply find it more profitable to ship their wheat to Los Angeles than to eat their crops themselves, and similarly for all the others.

Adam Smith put it this way: "in civilized society [man] stands at all times in need of the cooperation and assistance of great multitudes, while his whole life is scarce sufficient to gain the friendship of a few persons."[9] How can a person who has only a few friends

[8] Adam Smith, *The Wealth of Nations*, Book IV, Chapter 2.
[9] Adam Smith, *The Wealth of Nations*, Book I, Chapter 2.

nevertheless get the assistance of multitudes? The answer lies with the invisible hand of self-interest, which leads an individual to work for the good of persons practically unknown to him. The market system leads us all to work for the good of one another. The result is an orderly economy that meets people's needs and desires without anyone having planned for it to do so. (Ironically, it was the "planned economies" of Communist China and Soviet Russia that had difficulty keeping the grocery shelves stocked.)

1.5   BEHAVIOR WITHIN ORGANIZATIONS

Though traditional "narrow economics" has concentrated on the study of markets, one of the directions in which "broad economics" has moved has been to examine behavior within organizations. Within organizations, to some extent at least, resources are allocated not by exchange but by command. Government is the most prominent example. American congressmen enact legislation without buying one another's votes. (But, as will be seen in Chapter 17, "log-rolling" represents a kind of exchange of votes among members of a legislature.) In the executive branch, the President is empowered by law to direct the activities of the subordinate officers of government. Similarly within business firms, managers exercise authority over the actions of subordinates.

Yet "economic man" is also at work within organizations. In democratic political systems, voters are likely to support the candidate regarded as most likely to improve their well-being. Politicians are likely to adopt positions that maximize their career prospects. Within firms, managers are notoriously interested in their compensation packages. And when a Board of Directors fires a CEO, the usual reason is inadequate performance in terms of maximizing shareholder income.

1.6   POSITIVE AND NORMATIVE ANALYSIS: "IS" VERSUS "OUGHT"

In its scientific aspect economics is strictly *positive*. It answers questions such as "Is this theory (explanation) really true of the actual world?" But economics also has a *normative* aspect, dealing with questions such as "Should this policy be adopted?" Given an objective, economists can use their knowledge of "what is true" to analyze the problem and suggest ways of achieving "what ought to be done."

Adam Smith had in part a normative purpose in writing *The Wealth of Nations*. He opposed the then politically dominant mercantilists,[10] favoring instead the policy he called "natural liberty" – free trade among nations, and laissez faire within. This book is less concerned with normative issues (policy recommendations) than with positive matters (scientific understanding). Looking at the positive aspect, Adam Smith's even more fundamental thesis was that the economy follows objectively determinable laws. In early times, some people thought the planets were pushed in their courses by angels. Newton showed how the principle of gravity explains planetary motions. Similarly, to explain the universe of economic behavior, Smith put forward the idea of the market system as a mechanism, driven by the self-interest of participants, yet integrated so that each is led to serve the desires of others.

The distinction between positive and normative analysis sheds new light upon the question raised earlier about disagreement among economists. Economists may disagree

---

[10] The mercantilists believed that national well-being required the accumulation of gold and silver. To achieve this end, they recommended regulations to encourage exports and discourage imports.

on policy issues because they seek different normative goals. One might be more concerned with social equality, another with individual freedom. Even complete scientific understanding will not resolve such philosophical conflicts. But often disagreement among economists is over *means* rather than *goals*: not over what to do, but how to do it. Scientific progress in positive economics will, over time, tend to eliminate this source of disagreement.

EXAMPLE 1.10 WHEN DO ECONOMISTS DISAGREE?

In the early 1990s several surveys of economists collected opinions on a variety of important positive and normative issues. The table here summarizes results for six questions, which we have classified as either positive or normative.

	Agreement among economists			
Proposition	Generally agree	Agree with provisions	Generally disagree	Index of consensus
POSITIVE ISSUES				
A minimum wage increases unemployment among young and unskilled workers.	56.5%	22.4%	20.5%	36.0
A ceiling on rents reduces the quantity and quality of housing available.	76.3%	16.6%	6.5%	69.8
The cause of the rise in gasoline prices that occurred in the wake of the Iraqi invasion of Kuwait is the monopoly power of the large oil companies.	11.4%	20.3%	67.5%	56.1
NORMATIVE ISSUES				
The distribution of income in the United States should be more equal.	48.5	24.4	26.7	21.8
Antitrust laws should be enforced vigorously to reduce monopoly power from its current level.	34.9	36.9	27.6	7.3
The level of government spending relative to GNP should be reduced.	35.6	19.03	44.6	−9.0

Note: The column labeled "Index of consensus" was constructed by comparing "Generally agree" with "Generally disagree," subtracting the smaller of these from the larger. ("Agree with provisions," the middle position, was omitted.)

Source: Adapted from Richard M. Alston, J. R. Kearl, and Michael B. Vaughan, "Is There a Consensus among Economists," *American Economic Review*, v. 82 (May 1992), pp. 204–5.

COMMENT

Notice that the "Index of Consensus" among economists is quite high for the *positive* issues, but considerably less so when it comes to *normative* issues of public policy.

1.7   ELEMENTS OF THE ECONOMIC SYSTEM

Decision-Making Agents in the Economy

There are three main types of economic decision-makers: individuals, firms, and governments.

Individuals are the basic units of a society. The consumption decisions of individuals are discussed in Part Two of the text, and their resource-supply decisions in Part Four. Actually, recognizing the mutual support and cohesiveness of the family, economists sometimes consider the household to be the effective consumption unit. Except where otherwise specified, the individual here will be understood as making decisions for his or her family or household.

Business firms are artificial units. Every firm is ultimately owned by or operated for the benefit of one or more individuals. Surprisingly, this fact is often overlooked. One hears it said, for example, that "we should tax corporations, not the people." But taxes levied upon a corporation must ultimately come from the pockets of human beings. The company's owners will likely earn lower profits, its workers may have to forego wage increases, its customers may pay higher prices. At the same time, of course, the tax revenues might be used in ways that benefit other people. (As usual, every choice of policy involves both costs and benefits.) The firm is best regarded as an aggregation of individuals gathered together for the purpose of production, for converting resource inputs into desired outputs. The market supply decisions of firms will be discussed in Part Three, and their resource demand decisions in Part Four.

Governments are also economic decision-makers. The most important activity of a government is to set the legal framework within which the entire economy works. Like firms, governments are artificial groupings. Unlike firms and individuals, governments have the legal right to take property without consent (as by taxation). Furthermore, government decision-making is determined by political rather than market processes, a topic that will be examined in Part Seven.

Modern economies have still other decision-making units. Trade unions and cartels are organizations of sellers in markets. And there are also voluntary associations such as clubs, foundations, and religious institutions, through which individuals combine for collective consumption choices.

Scarcity, Objects of Choice, and Economic Activities

The source of all economic problems is *scarcity*. People's desires can never all be satisfied. Even if all material commodities were present in unlimited quantities, we would have insufficient time to enjoy them all. And, in addition, we all desire intangibles such as power, love, and prestige. There can never be enough of these. Scarcity is what forces people to make economic decisions – where to work, what to produce, how much to sell – with a view to obtaining what we most desire.

The objects of economic choice are called *commodities* or *goods*. These terms are usually understood to include not only merchandise but also services. Services represent a flow of benefits over a period of time, which might be derived either from physical goods (e.g., the shelter provided by a house) or else from human activities (e.g., the entertainment provided by concert performers).

Consumption is the ultimate economic activity, and in a sense the explanation for all the others. In their consumption decisions, individuals choose the goods they like best, given their incomes and the prices they face.

Production by individuals and firms is a second economic activity. Production transforms resources into consumable goods. The process of production can modify physical form, as in the conversion of leather and human labor into shoes, but not necessarily so. Moving goods over space (shipment of oranges from Florida to Maine) and over time (storing potatoes after harvest to distribute consumption over the year) are also forms of production.

Of course, to be economically rational, production should represent conversion from a less desired to a more desired configuration. Burning an antique Chippendale chair for heat is production, but would normally be ill-advised. (Yet a person in danger of freezing to death might find the conversion from chair to warmth highly advantageous.)

The third main economic activity is *exchange* (to be discussed in Part Five). For the individual, exchange, like production, is also a kind of conversion – a sacrifice of some objects for others. But from the social point of view, exchange is distinguished from production by the fact that the totals of commodities are unaffected. Trade neither creates nor destroys goods and services, but only reshuffles them among the different decision-making agents in the economy.

1.8 MICROECONOMICS AND MACROECONOMICS

A distinguished professor of logic, deploring the division of his subject between deductive reasoning and inductive reasoning, once declared: "In our textbooks on deduction we explain all about logical fallacies; in our textbooks on induction, we then commit them." Economic theory has a similar split. In much of microeconomics we explain how and why the Invisible Hand operates so well, how and why self-interest leads people to serve one another in a spontaneous system of productive cooperation. But macroeconomics examines why the system of coordination of economic activity through markets may sometimes break down.

Microeconomics concentrates on equilibrium in particular markets, presuming an equilibrium of the market system as a whole. But, it seems, the overall equilibrium of the market system is not always robust. Economic activity may become disrupted, with consequences such as inflation or large-scale unemployment. Macroeconomics investigates how and why such disruptions occur.

For some time starting with the "Keynesian" ideas of the 1930s, macroeconomists attempted to develop modes of reasoning largely independent of any microeconomic foundation. Some theorists even dismissed classical microeconomics as obsolete or irrelevant. It is now generally recognized that the study of microeconomics is necessary even for a proper understanding of macroeconomics. However, it may be that such an understanding will require employing "broad economics," and in particular taking account of imperfect rationality.

SUMMARY   The core of economic analysis deals with the *rational and self-interested behavior* of individuals and firms, as they interact with one another through *market exchange*. Rational behavior is the appropriate choice of means for achieving given ends, which requires comparing the benefits and costs (advantages and disadvantages) of all the available courses of action. Economists do not ordinarily ask why people are self-interested or why they have specific desires, but instead treat these as facts to be studied by the other social sciences.

Individuals can try to satisfy their desires in a number of ways, for example by persuasion, by force, by theft, or by calling upon government assistance. But economics mainly studies market relations, in which people seek to achieve their aims through voluntary exchange.

Economic thinking has, however, moved outward from this central core. In an attempt to achieve more complete understanding of reality, "broad economics" applies economic methods of analysis to nonmarket interactions such as crime and politics. It also attempts to allow for non-self-interested actions (such as benevolence in the family) and for the fact that humans sometimes deal with one another in ways that seem irrational.

Adam Smith's principle of the Invisible Hand shows how persons who are interested only in their own welfare are nevertheless led to cooperate with one another through market exchange. The market economy is an unplanned yet integrated arrangement, whose functioning follows scientifically determinable laws.

The main decision-making agents in the economic system are individuals (possibly acting on behalf of their families or households), firms, and governments. Individuals are the only agents who consume. Though individuals may also produce goods and services, in modern economies production mainly takes place through business firms – artificial agents created by individuals for that purpose. *Production* transforms the physical shape, location, or availability of commodities. *Exchange* reshuffles the existing goods and services among the economic agents to better accord with individual desires.

Economics has both a *positive* and a *normative* aspect. From the positive or scientific point of view, economics attempts to explain what the real world is like. In its normative aspect economics studies questions of policy, for example, how large a fraction of the tax burden should be borne by the rich. Although scientific progress in economics tends to eliminate disagreements among economists on positive matters, when it comes to normative issues unanimity can never be expected. The reason is that economists, like other citizens, diverge in the policy goals they seek to achieve. This book concentrates upon the positive aspect of economic analysis.

QUESTIONS
†The answers to daggered questions appear at the end of the book.

For Review

†1. a. In what respects can economics be considered a science?
   b. Give an example of a prediction that modern economic science can confidently make.
   c. What predictions has economics not yet been able to make?

†2. a. What is rational behavior?
   b. Give examples of rational and irrational behavior.
   c. Can the economist's postulate of rationality be useful even when irrational elements strongly influence behavior?

3. Does the economist assume stable preferences? Give an example of a change in preferences that has had important economic effects.

†4. Does the economist assume that everyone is selfish? Give an example of unselfish behavior that has important economic consequences.

5. Market transactions are said to be both *mutual* and *voluntary*. Give an example of a nonmarket interpersonal transaction that is not voluntary and an example of one that is voluntary but not mutual.

6. What are positive issues in economics? What are normative issues? Give an example of each.

†7. a. How does the Invisible Hand lead self-interested individuals in a market economy to cooperate?
   b. Would self-interested behavior lead to voluntary cooperation in a monastic economy where all income was equally divided?
   c. In a dictatorship where the political authorities confiscated the lion's share?
   d. In an economy with no property, so that any person could try to seize whatever he or she needed from other people?

8. "The principle of the Invisible Hand asserts that self-interested behavior on the part of resource-owners leads inevitably to chaos." True or false, and why?

9. What is the difference between production and exchange?

For Further Thought and Discussion

1. Jack Vance, in his novel *Wyst: Alastor 1617*, described a planet whose economy was based upon egalism, a system in which all resources are shared and accumulation of private property is considered a crime. In this self-styled utopia, theft is considered a virtue, as it prevents anyone from accumulating private property. Would you like to live in such a society? What would be the advantages and disadvantages?

†2. a. Other things being equal, would you expect the murder rate to be lower in jurisdictions applying capital punishment?
   b. If the income-tax exemption granted for each child were increased, would you expect the birth rate to rise?

†3. The psychiatrist T. S. Szasz argues that mental illness is the result of rewarding people for disability. Not only is the patient motivated to become "ill," but there is a financial advantage to the healing professions in declaring personal problems to be "illnesses." How could mental illness be made less "rewarding"? Would doing this reduce mental illness?

4. If government were to increase relief payments to the unemployed, would you expect unemployment to rise?

5. Explain why some individuals are wealthy (in a position to consume a great deal in the product market) and others are poor.

†6. If the Invisible Hand leads individuals to serve their own interests by serving others, why are some people led to a life of crime? Why do some corrupt politicians find it advantageous to serve themselves at the expense of their constituents? Why are dictators motivated to seize power? [*Hint:* Does the principle of the Invisible Hand apply to all kinds of social interactions, or does it hold only when individuals interact in a particular way?]

†7. Would an effectively enforced law requiring drivers to wear seat belts tend to reduce driver deaths? Pedestrian deaths?

†8. Dr. Samuel Johnson said, "There are few ways in which a man can be more innocently employed than in getting money." But the French writer Charles Baudelaire declared "Commerce is satanic, because it is the basest and vilest form of egoism." What do you think each had in mind?

9. Classify each of the following statements or propositions as either *positive* or *normative*. (Does the classification "positive versus normative" have any bearing upon truth or falsity?)
   a. Smoking in enclosed public spaces should be banned.
   b. Prohibiting smoking in public places would reduce the demand for cigarettes.

    c. Legislation to limit the places where smoking is permitted would be opposed by the tobacco industry.

    d. Nonsmokers' rights to breathe clean air are more important than smokers' rights to pollute the air.

    e. Antismoking laws will have no effect on sales of cigarettes because smokers will light up just as much as before but confine their puffing to legal areas.

10. It may become possible to predict the place and time of earthquakes, weeks or even months before their occurrence. Some influential writers have argued that such predictions should be kept secret, or even that investigations leading to such predictions should be banned. Allegedly, the panic caused by predicting an earthquake would be more damaging than the earthquake itself. What does this view imply about individual rationality? Would you favor or oppose a ban on earthquake prediction?

11. According to traditional economic analysis in which all economic agents have perfect information about market opportunities, a worker who is unemployed can get a job promptly simply by agreeing to accept a lower wage. In a sense, any unemployment would be voluntary.

    a. Suppose that employers do not know whether a particular worker will be a good match for the firm without interviewing the worker. How do you think this would affect the unemployment rate?

    b. Suppose that some workers prefer to be temporarily unemployed rather than receive a pay cut. Consider a company that faces a drop in demand, and needs to pay its employees less. Do you think it matters whether price levels are stable, or whether the economy is in a period of rapidly rising prices (so that each dollar is worth less each year in terms of the real goods and services it can command)?

2 Working Tools

Table 2.1 Optimization problems versus equilibrium problems

Optimization problems	Equilibrium problems
1. Should I buy a new car or keep my old one a while longer?	1. Are new car prices likely to be lower next year?
2. Will I be happier working, or should I drop out of the rat race and live on handouts?	2. Would generous "welfare" benefits for the unemployed raise the unemployment rate?
3. Should I buy a condo or live in a rental apartment?	3. What determines the ratio between the annual rental of an apartment and its purchase price as a condominium?
4. Should narcotics laws be made stricter or more lenient?	4. If use of narcotics were decriminalized, would drug usage increase?
5. Should our union go on strike, or had we better accept management's offer?	5. Do strikes raise the wage of workers?

Let's start with some good news. Remarkably, the microeconomics we study in this book deals with only two classes of problems: (1) *finding an optimum* and (2) *finding an equilibrium.* Facing any economic question, your first step should be to ask: "Is this an optimization problem, or is it an equilibrium problem?"

Look at Table 2.1. Notice that *optimization problems* always take the form: "Would it be better for me (or possibly, depending upon the point of view, for my business or for my nation or even for humanity as a whole) to choose this action or that action?" In short, what's the best thing to do? *Equilibrium problems* ask instead: "How can we explain what we observe in the real world?" For instance, why are diamonds so expensive when a more essential commodity, water, is cheap?

The questions listed in Table 2.1 all concern market dealings. But as argued in Chapter 1, optimization problems and equilibrium problems arise not just in markets but in all areas of life. *Some optimization examples*: an airplane designer is considering titanium versus stainless steel for an aircraft wing; a physician is choosing whether to prescribe an antibiotic or a placebo; an army commander is deciding whether to attack or retreat; a manager is considering whether to buy or lease new office space. *Some equilibrium examples*: in biology, why is the male/female sex ratio at birth almost always close to 1:1; in anthropology, what makes some cultures egalitarian and others highly hierarchical; in international relations, why are some nations large and others small; in finance, what determines the prices of different shares traded on the New York Stock Exchange? In each group of questions, all but the last lie outside the range of "narrow economics," yet the methods of economic reasoning remain entirely applicable.

For each of the two classes of problems, economics uses a characteristic technique. (1) To deal with equilibrium problems economists look for a *balance between supply and demand.* (2) To solve optimization problems economists *find a minimum or maximum by comparing marginal magnitudes.* This chapter reviews the two techniques.

2.1   EQUILIBRIUM: SUPPLY-DEMAND ANALYSIS

Balancing Supply and Demand

The supply-demand diagram of Figure 2.1 should be familiar from earlier courses, but let's review some of the details. The horizontal axis shows the *quantity Q* of some

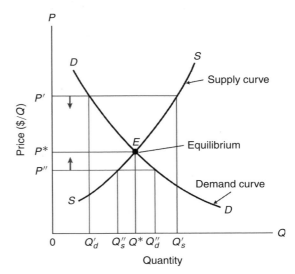

Figure 2.1. Demand and Supply

At the equilibrium point E, the quantity that consumers wish to purchase equals the quantity that sellers want to sell. The equilibrium price is P^* and the equilibrium quantity is Q^*.

good, for example, memory chips.[1] The vertical axis represents *price P*, in dollars per megabyte. [*Note:* Prices are usually quoted in money terms, but more fundamentally a price is the *ratio of exchange* between two goods. If a megabyte of memory costs $1.00 while an inkjet cartridge costs $15, then the price of memory, in terms of a cartridge, is 1/15.]

The demand curve DD shows the quantity that consumers would want to buy at each price P. The negative slope of DD reflects *The Law of Demand*: the fact that, as the price of memory chips or telephone calls or shoes decreases, buyers generally want to buy more. Though there are exceptions, surely the Law of Demand broadly describes behavior. Here's a bit of evidence: Stores often place ads claiming they offer low prices. Have you ever seen a retail store advertise that its prices are exceptionally *high*? Since that never or almost never occurs, retailers must generally believe that lower prices increase sales. (And if they are to remain in business, they had better be correct about such beliefs.)

Similarly, the supply curve shows how much sellers would offer at each possible price. The positive slope of the supply curve indicates that the higher the price, the greater the quantity offered.

In Figure 2.1 market equilibrium occurs at point E where the supply curve and demand curve intersect. The coordinates of E are the equilibrium quantity Q^* and equilibrium price P^*. To see why this is an equilibrium, consider a market price higher than P^* – for example, P' in the diagram. At price P' suppliers want to sell the quantity Q'_s, while consumers want to buy only Q'_d. Since suppliers in aggregate are unable to sell all they want to at price P', at least some of them are likely to offer buyers better terms. So, as indicated by the downward-pointing arrow, at P' there would be downward pressure on price. Consider next a market price initially lower than P^*, say P'' in Figure 2.1. At such a low price, the quantity Q''_d that consumers want to buy exceeds the quantity

---

[1] Sometimes it is convenient to interpret quantity on the horizontal axis as a *rate per unit time*, for instance, thousands of chips per month or per week.

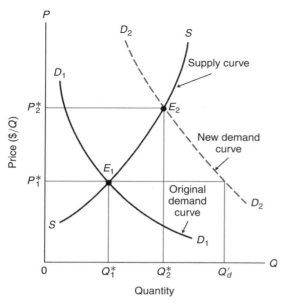

Figure 2.2. Increase in Demand

When consumers' preferences change, so that they desire to purchase more at each price, the demand curve shifts to the right from $D_1 D_1$ to $D_2 D_2$. Equilibrium price and equilibrium quantity both increase.

Q_s'' that suppliers want to sell. As indicated by the upward-pointing arrow at price P'', there would be upward pressure on price.

Whenever price differs from P^*, one or the other process will always be at work. Only at P^*, where the supply curve and demand curve intersect, does the quantity that consumers want to buy exactly match the amount suppliers are willing to sell. This equality defines the market equilibrium quantity Q^*.

CONCLUSION

The point where the demand curve intersects the supply curve determines the equilibrium price P^* and quantity Q^*.

There is no implication that being in equilibrium is either good or bad. Recalling the distinction made in Chapter 1, that would be a *normative* question – whereas here we are engaged in strictly *positive* analysis. There are an equilibrium price and quantity of good things like housing, but also an equilibrium price and quantity of bad things like heroin.

How valid is this analysis? Economics, like all sciences, employs *models* that only imperfectly depict reality. A model of reality is like a map of a city. A good street map is a highly incomplete picture of the real city, but it tells you enough to get you where you want to go. So one ought to ask not that models be literally true, but rather that they be useful. Supply-demand analysis is useful in explaining why prices – for disk drives or for potatoes or for politicians – are sometimes high, sometimes low.

How Changes in Supply and Demand Affect Equilibrium

What happens if circumstances change, for example, if costs of production fall or if consumers' incomes rise? Such changes affect the equilibrium pictured in Figure 2.1 by altering the supply curve, by altering the demand curve, or by altering both.

Suppose that, perhaps as a result of increased income or changed preferences, people now want to buy more paper goods than before at each possible price P. This is called an *increase in demand*. As shown in Figure 2.2, the demand curve shifts *to the right* (from

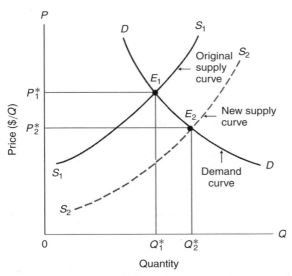

Figure 2.3. Increase in Supply

When a change in conditions induces sellers to offer more at each price, the supply curve shifts to the right from $S_1 S_1$ to $S_2 S_2$. Equilibrium quantity increases, but equilibrium price falls.

$D_1 D_1$ to $D_2 D_2$). The old equilibrium price and quantity were P_1^* and Q_1^*, and the new equilibrium price and quantity are P_2^* and Q_2^*.

How does the change come about? Suppose that after the demand curve shifted to $D_2 D_2$ the price had initially remained unchanged at P_1^* Then consumers would want to buy the amount Q_d'. But at price P_1^* suppliers still want to sell only the quantity Q_s^*. Since the quantity demanded exceeds the quantity offered, price tends to rise until it reaches its new equilibrium level P_2^*.

This description is oversimplified in several ways. In the model all transactions are assumed to take place at the equilibrium price. But in actual markets some sales may occur at "wrong" (nonequilibrium) prices. Furthermore, these "wrong" transactions may affect the terms at which later sales take place. An apple seller at a local farmers' market might be lucky enough to dispose of half his barrels early in the day, at a high (disequilibrium) price. He might choose to go home and celebrate rather than bother selling his remaining stock. But once the remaining barrels are taken off the market, prices for the remainder of the day could be affected. Economists analyze such issues under the heading of "economic dynamics," a topic that requires more advanced techniques than used in this text. Instead, we will use what is called the *method of comparative statics*. This means that, as shown in Figure 2.2, two supply-demand equilibria are compared, one under the initial conditions, the other under the changed conditions. So, in analyzing some change in economic circumstances, the basic technique is simply to ask: Does the change shift the supply curve, or does it shift the demand curve, or both?

Consider next an increase in supply. This means that at each price sellers want to sell more than before, so the supply curve shifts to the right (from $S_1 S_1$ to $S_2 S_2$), as shown in Figure 2.3. Here the new equilibrium quantity Q_2^* is larger than the old Q_1^*, but the new equilibrium price P_2^* is less than P_1^*. [*Caution:* Resist thinking of an increase in supply or demand as an *upward shift* of the corresponding curve. That would be correct for shifts of the demand curve, but wrong for shifts of the supply curve. To avoid error, always interpret an increase in supply or in demand as a *right-ward shift*, as a larger quantity offered or desired at each possible price.] Last, you can verify that a simultaneous increase in both supply and demand will make the new equilibrium quantity greater than before, but the equilibrium price might move either way.

PROPOSITION: An *increase in demand* causes the equilibrium price P^* and quantity Q^* to both rise. An *increase in supply* causes equilibrium Q^* to rise but equilibrium P^* to fall. A simultaneous *increase in both supply and demand* makes the equilibrium quantity Q^* greater than before, but the new equilibrium price P^* could be higher, be lower, or remain unchanged.

EXAMPLE 2.1 SCARCITY AND PRICES IN MEDIEVAL WINCHESTER

That unusually scarce supply leads to high prices is sometimes denied. In 1973 and again in 1979, the Organization of Petroleum Exporting Countries (OPEC) sharply reduced their petroleum exports. Oil prices rose sharply. Nevertheless, some commentators attributed the price increases not to the reduced oil supply but instead to corporate greed or to consumer irrationality.

Yet the connection between low supply and high prices has been observed since earliest times. The table here is derived from records of wheat production in the period 1211–1448 on estates owned by the Bishopric of Winchester, as reported in a study by H. Flohn.[a] As can be seen, in periods with low yield/seed ratios (bad weather), wheat prices were high. The top row, for example, indicates that when the yield/seed ratio was the least favorable (in the range 2.0 to 2.5), the wheat price was the highest (12.0 shillings per quarter of wheat).

Wheat yields and prices, Winchester 1211–1448

Average yield/seed ratio	Average price (shillings per quarter)
2.0–2.5	12.0
2.5–3.0	8.8
3.0–3.5	7.1
3.5–4.0	6.2
4.0–4.5	5.5
4.4–5.0	4.8
>5.0	5.1

Source: Estimated visually from Figure 12.1 in Flohn.

---

[a] H. Flohn, "Short-Term Climatic Fluctuations and Their Economic Role," in T. M. L. Wrigley, M. J. Ingram, and G. Farmer, *Climate and History* (Cambridge University Press, 1981).

What brings about shifts in demand curves or supply curves? It is sometimes useful to distinguish between changes that originate outside and inside the economic system. Possible "outside" sources of variation include:

(1) *changes in tastes* (a news report about the dangers of cholesterol may make some people avoid butter)

(2) *changes in technology* (the integrated circuit greatly increased the supply of electronic devices)

(3) *changes in resources* (an important oil discovery would enlarge the world's supply of petroleum)

(4) *changes in legal rules* (decriminalizing marijuana would increase both its market supply and its market demand).

"Inside" sources, influences upon supply and demand for a particular good that originate elsewhere within the economy, might include:

(1) *changes in prices or quantities of other goods that are related in demand* (a decrease in the price of printers increases the demand for paper)

(2) *changes in prices or quantities of other goods related in supply* (increased beef production boosts the supply of hides)

(3) *changes in income* (the higher incomes received by stock brokers in the 1990s increased their demand for luxury cars).

EXAMPLE 2.2 POTATOES/DRY BEANS VERSUS STRAWBERRIES

Vegetables and fruits are cheapest at harvest time. The reason is not hard to explain. The demand for food is fairly uniform over the year, but the supply can vary drastically over the seasons.

The table here compares seasonal price variations for potatoes and dry beans versus strawberries. Potatoes, which dominate the potatoes/dry beans totals, are usually most expensive in July, just before the main potato harvest in August and September. As the new crop arrives, prices fall for several months before beginning to rise again in November. The strawberry price pattern is strikingly different. The price is usually much higher in the winter months (December and January) before strawberries begin to arrive in early spring.

Although the potato harvest is highly concentrated in the fall, notice how small the price variation is over the year: the highest monthly price (July) exceeds the lowest monthly price (October) by less than 50%. The main reason is that potatoes are easily storable. Although few potatoes are produced in winter, prices remain low owing to carryover from the fall harvest. As the stored potatoes are gradually consumed, prices rise toward their peak in July.

The main strawberry crop comes in earlier, and prices are lowest in late spring and early summer. Also, since strawberries are less storable, their price varies considerably more over the year. Indeed, strawberries are so perishable that it may seem surprising the seasonal price variation is not greater. The reason is that the strawberry harvest is more evenly distributed over the months of the year.

Monthly prices (2000–2002)

	Potatoes/dry beans (1990–1992 = 100)	Strawberries ($/CWT)
Jan	99.3	129.4
Feb	105.0	96.1
Mar	110.3	76.6

Apr	112.7	68.2
May	114.3	53.7
Jun	118.3	59.7
Jul	128.0	59.7
Aug	117.3	73.2
Sep	95.3	66.2
Oct	86.7	81.5
Nov	95.7	102.2
Dec	100.0	122.5

Source: U.S. Dept. of Agriculture, National Agricultural Statistics Service, Agricultural Prices (April 2003).

The original source of agricultural supply variation over the year is the "outside" element of God-given seasonal climate. But, as the Example shows, human decisions in the form of storage activities modify the force of the external factors. Other "inside" responses – improved transportation, changed agricultural practices, development of new seed varieties, and so on – also tend to stabilize prices over the year.

Examples 2.1 and 2.2 dealt with the supply and demand of ordinary commodities like wheat and strawberries. But supply and demand are also relevant in many other contexts, among them the "marriage market."

EXAMPLE 2.3 BABY BOOMS, MARRIAGE SQUEEZES, AND WOMEN IN THE LABOR FORCE

Shoshana Grossbard-Shechtman and Clive W. J. Granger[a] studied how the relative numbers of marriageable men and women affect female labor force participation. An important feature of the "marriage market" is that women tend to marry men a few years older than themselves. Therefore, when women born in a baby-boom year mature, they find suitable (slightly older) male partners relatively scarce. The marriage rate necessarily being lower, women are then more likely to enter the labor force.

Baby booms and female labor force participation

Dates (bb = baby boom)	Sex ratio*	Increases in women's labor force participation (in comparison with preceding cohort)		
		At age 20–24	At age 25–29	At age 30–34
1965 (pre-bb)	0.96	3.6%	6.3%	7.2%
1970 (1st bb)	0.94	7.8	12.1	12.1
1975 (2nd bb)	0.92	6.4	9.4	6.2
1980 (3rd bb)	1.0	4.8	4.7	3.1

* Ratio of unmarried men 20–29 to unmarried women 18–29.
Source: Adapted from Table 1 and Figure 2 in Grossbard-Shechtman and Granger.

Moving downward in each of the last three columns, we see that all the entries are positive: every female age group had a higher percentage in the labor force than did the preceding cohort. That of course is mainly the consequence of the strong long-term trend toward increasing women's labor force participation. But notice that the percentage increases in the second row are all markedly greater than those in the row above. This reflects the fact that women in 1970 found marriageable men relatively scarce compared to 1965, and hence were more likely to enter the labor force. The remaining rows show that the increases tapered off for the later (and smaller) baby booms. By 1980 the sex ratio had recovered to the 1.0 level (relatively favorable to women). And so the increases in female labor force participation were lowest in this time period.

---

[a] Shoshana Grossbard-Shechtman and Clive W. J. Granger, "Women's Jobs and Marriage, Baby-Boom versus Baby-Bust," *Population*, v. 53 (September 1998). [In French.]

Supply and demand affect not only the frequency of marriage but the terms on which brides and grooms get together.

EXAMPLE 2.4 DOWRIES

In some societies the family of the bride pays a dowry to the groom (or to his family). Actually, the reverse pattern – "brideprice," a payment from the groom or his family to purchase a wife – has been far more common over the range of human societies. Most societies have permitted polygyny (when a man can have several wives). In communities where powerful or wealthy men can bid for multiple wives, it is not surprising that marriageable women become relatively scarce and command a high brideprice.

Building upon these supply-demand considerations, Steven J. C. Gaulin and James S. Boster[a] hypothesized that dowry rather than brideprice would be observed mainly in *non*polygynous societies, where a man is limited to one wife. Such societies are either monogamous or, rarely, polyandrous (when a woman can have multiple husbands). And since dowries are payments to obtain a more highly desired husband, they argued, dowries should also be more common in highly stratified societies – where power and wealth disparities among potential grooms are large.

The table here compares the prevalence of dowries among societies classified as (1) polygynous versus nonpolygynous and (2) stratified versus nonstratified. Each cell indicates the number of societies in each category, as described in the *Ethnographic Atlas*, and the number of societies where dowry payments were observed. The table shows that dowries are indeed paid almost exclusively in societies that are both nonpolygynous (usually monogamous) and stratified.

Prevalence of dowries as determined by polygyny and stratification

	Polygynous societies	Nonpolygynous societies
Stratified	5 of 268	27 of 72
Nonstratified	1 of 625	2 of 101
Number of societies	893	173

Source: Adapted from Gaulin and Boster, Table 1.

---

[a] Steven J. C. Gaulin and James S. Boster, "Dowry as Female Competition," *American Anthropologist*, v. 92 (December 1990).

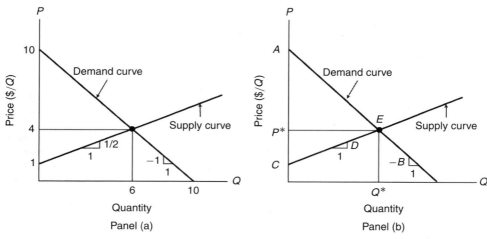

Figure 2.4. Linear Supply and Demand Curves

Panel (a) pictures the specific linear demand curve $P = 10 - Q$ and linear supply curve $P = 1 + Q/2$. The equilibrium is the point of intersection where $Q = 6$ and $P = 4$. Panel (b) pictures the more general straight-line demand equation $P = A - BQ_d$ and supply equation $P = C + DQ_s$. At the equilibrium point E, the quantities demanded and supplied are equal.

Algebra of Supply-Demand Analysis

The preceding analysis showed how equilibrium price and quantity are determined diagrammatically, by the intersection of the supply curve with the demand curve. To find the equilibrium algebraically, *supply* can be expressed as an equation relating price to the quantities offered. And *demand* can be expressed as an equation relating price to the quantities that buyers are willing to buy. The solution to these simultaneous equations determines the two unknowns: price P and quantity Q.

The algebra is especially easy when the demand and supply curves are straight lines, as pictured in Figure 2.4. Panel (a) shows a hypothetical demand curve with the equation $P = 10 - Q$. The supply curve corresponds to the equation $P = 1 + Q/2$. To find the equilibrium, either the prices or the quantities in the two equations can be set equal to one another. Let us equate the prices on the left-hand sides of the two equations. Then, since the right-hand sides must also be equal, $10 - Q = 1 + Q/2$. Solving, $Q^* = 6$ is the equilibrium quantity. Now insert $Q = 6$ into the demand equation to find the equilibrium price: $P^* = 10 - 6 = 4$. (Or we can obtain the same price by substituting $Q = 6$ into the supply equation: $P^* = 1 + 6/2 = 4$.)

EXERCISE 2.1

As in the preceding paragraph, suppose the demand curve has the equation $P = 10 - Q$ and the supply curve is $P = 1 + Q/2$. Find the equilibrium by equating quantities rather than prices.

ANSWER: Rewrite both equations to put Q on the left-hand side. The demand curve becomes $Q = 10 - P$ and the supply curve becomes $Q = 2(P - 1)$. Setting the two right-hand sides equal leads to the condition $10 - P = 2(P - 1)$. Solving, $P^* = 4$ is the equilibrium price. To find the equilibrium quantity, substitute $P = 4$

in the supply or the demand equation to obtain $Q^* = 6$. The answer is of course the same as before.

Panel (b) of Figure 2.4 pictures the general linear demand equation, which can be written $P = A - BQ_d$. Here Q_d is the quantity demanded, and A and B are positive constants. Geometrically, A is the intercept of the demand curve on the vertical price axis. Think of A as the "choke price for demand," meaning that for any price P greater than or equal to A, purchases will be zero. In this linear equation, $-B$ is the slope of the demand curve.

The general linear supply curve has the equation $P = C + DQ_s$, where Q_s is the quantity supplied. The positive constant C, the intercept of the supply curve on the vertical axis, is the "choke price for supply." At any price P less than or equal to C, none of the good will be supplied. The positive constant D represents the slope of the supply curve.

At equilibrium, the quantity demanded equals the quantity supplied:

$$Q_d = Q_s \tag{2.1}$$

Since $Q_d = Q_s$ at the equilibrium, we can drop the subscripts and just write Q in the equations for demand and supply:

$$\begin{cases} P = A - BQ & \text{(Demand)} \\ P = C + DQ & \text{(Supply)} \end{cases} \tag{2.2}$$

Solving equations (2.2) algebraically, the solution is:

$$Q^* = \frac{A - C}{B + D} \quad \text{and} \quad P^* = \frac{AD + BC}{B + D} \tag{2.3}$$

EXERCISE 2.2

What if the demand and supply curves are not straight lines? Suppose the demand curve is described by the equation $Q_d = 12 - P^3$ and the supply curve is $Q_s = P^2$. Find the equilibrium price and quantity.

ANSWER: Since at equilibrium $Q_d = Q_s$, the right-hand sides of the equations must be equal: $12 - P^3 = P^2$. By inspection, $P = 2$ satisfies the equation. Checking the quantities demanded and supplied, $Q_d = 12 - 2^3 = 4$ and $Q_s = 2^2 = 4$. So the solution is $P^* = 2$, $Q^* = 4$.

Let us now turn to the algebra of *comparative statics*. Shifts in either the demand curve or the supply curve can take many forms. One possibility is that the demand curve might shift parallel to itself: the intercept changes but the slope does not. Another possibility is that the slope changes in such a way that the curve rotates about an unchanged intercept on the vertical axis.

EXERCISE 2.3

Start with the demand and supply equations of Exercise 2.1 in the form $Q = 10 - P$ and $Q = 2(P - 1)$. Now suppose the quantity demanded becomes twice as great at

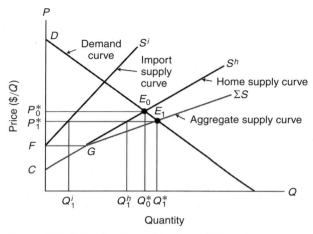

Figure 2.5. Introduction of an Import Supply

In the absence of imports, the equilibrium E_0 is at the intersection of the demand curve D and the home supply curve S^h. The aggregate supply curve, labeled ΣS, is the horizontal sum of S^h and S^i. The new equilibrium is E_1.

each price. Then the new demand equation is $Q = 2(10 - P)$. (a) Does this change in demand represent a shift of the *intercept*, a change of the *slope*, or is it a more complicated type of change? (b) Find the new equilibrium price and quantity.

ANSWER: (a) The "choke price for demand" remains $P = 10$, so we have here a change in the *slope* only. (b) To determine the equilibrium, first equate the right-hand sides of the unchanged supply equation and the new demand equation, $2(P - 1) = 20 - 2P$. Then solve this equation, obtaining $P^* = 5.5$, $Q^* = 9$. Compared with the previous solution ($P^* = 4$ and $Q^* = 6$), here the equilibrium price and quantity have both increased. Notice that even though the new demand curve indicates that consumers will buy double the quantity at each given price, the new *equilibrium* quantity does not quite double. The explanation, of course, is that the equilibrium price has risen.

An Application: Introducing a New Supply Source

A more challenging problem is illustrated in Figure 2.5. Suppose a country that had previously barred imports of steel now permits them. The demand curve for steel is D. The "home supply curve" S^h shows the amount of steel that domestic firms want to sell at each price. The "import supply curve," which shows the quantities foreign firms want to sell, is S^i. With no imports, the equilibrium E_0 is at the intersection of the D and S^h curves. When imports are allowed, the new equilibrium E_1 is determined by the point where the demand curve intersects the "aggregate supply curve" that allows for both home supply and imports. This is the curve labelled ΣS in Figure 2.5: it is the horizontal sum[2] of the S^h and S^i curves.

In the diagram, imports reduce the equilibrium price from P_0^* to P_1^*; they raise the equilibrium quantity from Q_0^* to Q_1^*. There is one slightly tricky feature. At any price

[2] The Greek letter Σ, capital sigma, signifies summation.

below F, the choke price for import supply, no foreign steel enters the market. Therefore at prices below F the aggregate supply curve ΣS is identical to the home supply curve S^h. At prices above F, however, ΣS diverges to the right of S^h by the amount of imports. So the aggregate supply curve that allows for *both* home and import sources has a kink at point G (which is at the same height as point F).

EXERCISE 2.4

Let demand be $P = 300 - Q_d$, and suppose the home supply curve is $P = 60 + 2Q_s^h$. To find the initial equilibrium with no imports (E_0 in the diagram), set the domestic demand equal to the domestic supply, $300 - Q_d = 60 + 2Q_s^h$, and let $Q_d = Q_s^h$. Numerically the E_0 solution is $P_0^* = 220$, $Q_0^* = 80$. Let the import supply curve be $P = 80 + 4Q_s^i$. If imports are permitted, find (i) the new equilibrium price, (ii) the amount sold by domestic firms, and (iii) the amount imported.

ANSWER: Note first that the import choke price, 80, is lower than the original equilibrium price, $P_0^* = 220$. So foreign firms will want to sell in this market. The aggregate supply sums the amounts that foreign firms want to sell and the amounts that domestic firms want to sell. To determine this sum, put Q on the left-hand sides of both the foreign and the home supply equations. [*Caution:* Do not put P on the left side of the equations and then sum; that would be adding the prices, where what we want to do is to sum the quantities!] The home supply curve can be rewritten as $Q^h = (P - 60)/2$. For imports, $Q^i = (P - 80)/4$. The sum of the two is $Q \equiv Q^h + Q^i = 3P/4 - 50$. Equating the right-hand side of this sum to the right-hand side of the unchanged demand curve we have $3P/4 - 50 = 300 - P$. Solving, at the new equilibrium the price is $P_1^* = 200$ (compared with the previous $P_0^* = 220$) and the quantity is $Q_1^* = 100$ (compared with the previous $Q_0^* = 80$). So the import quantity has risen from zero to $Q_1^i = 30$. The quantity supplied from home sources falls from $Q_0^* = 80$ to $Q_1^h = 70$.

Taxes on Transactions

Transaction taxes can take several forms. The two simplest are a *unit tax* (a fixed dollar amount for each unit of the good sold) and a *proportionate tax* (a fixed percent of the price).

EFFECTS OF A PER-UNIT TAX　A tax in the amount of T per unit sold creates a gap of T between the price paid by the buyers (the *gross price* P^+) and the price received by the sellers (the *net price* P^-):

$$P^+ \equiv P^- + T \tag{2.4}$$

[*Note:* The symbol $\equiv$ is used to emphasize that the equation is a definitional *identity*.]

One result that can be derived from the algebra is that, regardless of whether the seller or instead the buyer is the one legally obligated to pay the tax, the results are the same. (If the seller has to pay the tax, he will charge enough extra to cover the tax; if it is the buyer, she will reduce the amount she is willing to pay by the same amount.) For convenience, let's assume it is the seller who has the legal obligation to pay the tax.

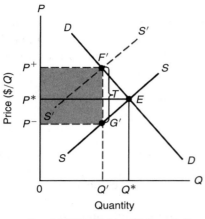
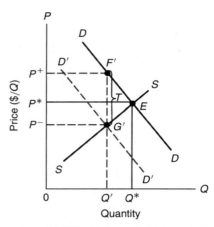

Panel (a) The "Add-on" Interpretation   Panel (b) The "Take-away" Interpretation

Figure 2.6. Effects of a Unit Tax

Panel (a) depicts an "add-on" analysis, where the tax is regarded as shifting the supply curve SS upward by $\$T$ per unit. The intersection with the unchanged demand curve DD determines the equilibrium quantity Q and the *gross price* P^+. Panel (b) depicts a "take-away" analysis, where the tax is regarded as shifting the demand curve DD downward by $\$T$ per unit. Here the intersection with the unchanged supply curve SS determines the same equilibrium quantity and the *net price* P^-. Regardless of which type of analysis is used, the equilibrium quantity falls from Q^* to Q'. In comparison with the old equilibrium price P^*, the gross price P^+ is higher and the net price P^- is lower than before.

Both panels of Figure 2.6 show an initial demand curve DD and supply curve SS. The equilibrium price is p^* and the equilibrium quantity is Q^*. Let government now impose a tax $T = \$2$ on each unit sold. Sellers may think of this in either of two ways. First, a seller may regard the tax as raising unit cost by $T = \$2$. This "add on to cost" interpretation is illustrated in Panel (a). Here the *supply curve shifts up* by the amount T; the new curve represents the quantity offered on the market at each *gross price* P^+. Alternatively, a seller may think of the tax as reducing receipts by $T = \$2$ per unit sold. This "take away from receipts" interpretation is illustrated in Panel (b). Here the *demand curve shifts down* by the same amount T; the new curve represents the *net price* (the after-tax price) P^- received for each possible quantity sold.

In the "add on" picture of Panel (a), the intersection of DD with the new (upward-shifted) supply curve $S'S'$ at point F' generates the new solution values for quantity Q' and for the gross price P^+. The net price P^- is found in Panel (a) by simply moving downward from F' to G' along the original supply curve SS.

In the "take away" picture of Panel (b), the intersection of the new (downward-shifted) demand curve $D'D'$ generates the solution values for quantity Q' and the net price P^- at point G'. To find the gross price P^+ we simply move upward from G' to F'. The locations of the points F' and G' are the same in both diagrams, and the solutions for Q', P^+, and P^- are identical.

When these solutions are compared with the original equilibrium at E, the unit tax reduces the quantity exchanged from Q^* to Q'. However, care is required in describing the effect upon price. In Panel (a) the intersection point F' occurs at a higher price than at E, but in Panel (b) the intersection point G' occurs at a lower price. So does a unit tax raise price or does it reduce price? The answer: it does both! The *gross price* P^+ is higher than the original P^*, but the *net price* P^- is lower than P^*. In short, consumers pay more but sellers receive less.

> **PROPOSITION:** A unit tax on transactions reduces the equilibrium quantity sold. It raises the gross price P^+ (inclusive of tax) paid by consumers, but lowers the net price P^- (the net-of-tax amount) received by sellers.

Algebraically, the demand and supply equations (2.2) and the tax identity (2.4) can be combined into a new system of three simultaneous equations:

$$\begin{cases} P^+ = A - BQ & \text{(demand equation)} \\ P^- = C + DQ & \text{(supply equation)} \\ P^+ \equiv P^- + T & \text{(tax identity)} \end{cases} \tag{2.5}$$

Skipping over the details, the algebraic solution is:

$$Q' = \frac{A - (C + T)}{B + D} \qquad P^+ = \frac{AD + B(C + T)}{B + D} \qquad P^- = \frac{(A - T)D + BC}{B + D} \tag{2.6}$$

When equations (2.6) are compared with to equations (2.3), where there was no tax, the algebra shows that (as in the diagram) Q' must be less than Q^*. A tax on transactions reduces the quantity bought and sold. And it is also algebraically evident that the new gross price P^+ must be greater than the original price P^*, whereas the new net price P^- must be lower than P^*. This too confirms the geometrical result. Also, the new gross price that buyers pay rises by less than the full T, and the new net price that sellers receive falls by less than the full T. So buyers and sellers share the "incidence" of the tax.

EXERCISE 2.5

Suppose that as before the original demand function is $P = 300 - Q_d$ and the supply function is $P = 60 + 2Q_s$. A unit tax $T = 15$ is imposed. What is the effect of the tax in comparison with the previous no-tax equilibrium $P^* = 220$, $Q^* = 80$?

ANSWER: An easy way of solving the three-equation system (2.5) is to substitute the right-hand sides of the first two equations into the third. This yields the single equation $300 - Q = 60 + 2Q + 15$. The solution for quantity is then $Q' = 75$. Substituting into the other equations gives $P^+ = 225$ and $P' = 210$. So consumers pay $5 more per unit, while sellers receive $10 less.

EXAMPLE 2.5 BEER TAXES AND DRINKING BY HIGH SCHOOL STUDENTS

Although taxes on beer have risen in recent years, these increases have not kept up with inflation. So the real (inflation-adjusted) tax on beer has declined. Michael Grossman et al[a]. estimated how beer drinking by high school seniors would have responded in 1989 to a Federal excise tax increase of about 76 cents per six-pack (an amount calculated to adjust the Federal tax to the inflation that had occurred since 1951).

In the table, the "Actual distribution" figures were based upon a survey of high school students conducted at the University of Michigan. The "Distribution after tax adjustment" figures were calculated from an economic model of how prices would affect the drinking decisions of individuals in the various groups.

Beer taxes and drinking by high school students, 1989

Category (# of drinking occasions in past year)	Actual distribution	Estimate after tax adjustment
Abstainers (none)	15.3%	18.6%
Infrequent (1–9)	44.4	46.1
Fairly frequent (10–30)	27.1	24.7
Frequent (more than 30)	13.2	10.6
	100.0	100.0

Source: Adapted from Table 2 in Grossman et al.

If the economic model is correct, higher beer taxes would have reduced drinking – increasing the proportions of students in the abstaining and infrequent-use groups and decreasing the proportions in the heavier-drinking groups. The authors of the study claimed that these hypothesized tax increases would have been more effective than increasing the minimum drinking age to 21, a reform that by 1989 was adopted in all the states of the United States.

[a] Michael Grossman, Frank J. Chaloupka, Henry Saffer, and Adit Laixuthai, "Effects of Alcohol Price Policy on Youth," National Bureau of Economic Research, Working Paper #4385 (June 1993).

EFFECTS OF A PROPORTIONATE TAX   Since the same general principles apply as for a unit tax, the proportionate tax can be analyzed in more condensed fashion. The main difference is the way in which the demand or supply curves shift.

If the proportionate tax is calculated as a percentage *t added on* to the seller's net price P^- (ordinary retail sales taxes are quoted this way), the tax identity (2.4) becomes:

$$P^+ \equiv P^-(1 + t) \qquad (2.7a)$$

Alternatively, sometimes a tax is quoted as a percentage that the government *takes away* from the gross price P^+. Denoting the percentage taken away by such a tax as τ (the Greek letter tau), the equation becomes:

$$P^+(1 - \tau) \equiv P^- \qquad (2.7b)$$

Any percentage of tax can be expressed either way. Simple algebra shows that t and τ are related by:

$$\tau = t/(1 + t) \quad \text{or} \quad t = \tau/(1 - \tau) \qquad (2.8)$$

So a tax of 25% quoted as a percentage "added on" to P^- is equivalent to a tax of 20% "taken away" from P^+.

Figure 2.7 resembles the preceding Figure 2.6. Once again Panel (a) represents the "add on" picture and Panel (b) the "take away" picture. (The graphs are constructed to represent an add on tax rate $t = 100\%$, which implies a take away tax rate $\tau = 50\%$.) But whereas in Panel (a) of Figure 2.6 the supply curve SS was displaced upward parallel to itself, here it is displaced *proportionately* upward by the percentage t. Thus the vertical intercept shifts upward from C to C', where $C' = C(1 + t)$. Moving to the right, the

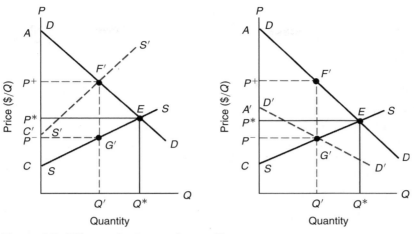

Figure 2.7. Effects of a Proportionate Tax

As in Figure 2.6, panel (a) depicts an add-on analysis and panel (b) a take-away analysis. In panel (a) the supply curve SS is shifted upward by $t = 100\%$ to become $S'S'$. In panel (b) the demand curve DD is shifted downward by $\tau = 50\%$ to become $D'D'$. In either case, the new equilibrium quantity Q' is less than the no-tax equilibrium Q^*. As before, in comparison with the old equilibrium price P^*, the gross price P^+ is now higher and the net price P^- lower than before.

new supply curve $S'S'$ diverges increasingly from SS as the price rises. A similar pattern holds for the take away picture in Panel (b). Whereas in Figure 2.6 the demand curve was displaced downward parallel to itself, here the vertical intercept decreases from A to A', where $A' = A(1 - \tau)$. And, moving to the right, $D'D'$ converges upon the old DD – the two necessarily intersect at the horizontal axis where price is zero.

Algebraically, equations (2.5) remain valid except that the tax identity must be written in the form (2.7a) or (2.7b), depending upon whether the tax is quoted as an add on percentage t or a take away percentage τ.

EXERCISE 2.6

Using the same supply and demand curves as in the previous exercise, suppose that an add on tax $t = 100\%$ is imposed. (This is equivalent to a take away tax rate of $\tau = 50\%$.) What is the effect of this tax in comparison with the no-tax equilibrium $P^* = 220$, $Q^* = 80$?

ANSWER: Start with equations (2.5), but replace the third equation with $P^+ = P^*(1 + t) = 2P^-$. So the gross price will be twice the net price. The quantity solution is $Q = 36$. The gross price is $P^+ = 264$, and the net price is $P^- = 132$. The quantity exchanged declines sharply in comparison with the no-tax equilibrium, as would be expected given such a steep tax. The gross price paid by buyers rises only moderately; the net price received by sellers falls drastically. So the "incidence" here is more heavily upon the sellers.

An Application: Interdicting Supply

In 1920 the Prohibition amendment to the United States Constitution made it illegal to produce or import alcoholic liquor. Soon thereafter a vast bootlegging industry developed. Despite costly police efforts, the interception of supplies from foreign or illegal domestic sources eventually became so ineffective that Prohibition was repealed in 1933. Instead, with the continuing aim of discouraging liquor consumption, the government imposed high liquor taxes.

On the whole, these taxes have been effective. Although bootlegging continues, police efforts hold it to tolerable levels. And the liquor taxes raise large revenues for Federal and state governments.

Currently, the United States is attempting to use the interdiction technique for narcotic drugs, leading to smuggling and bootlegging problems resembling those of the 1920–1933 Prohibition era. Some commentators have suggested that, following the precedent of alcoholic beverages, buying and selling narcotics should be legalized, but subject to heavy taxation.

This *normative* policy question, which involves philosophical and moral issues as well as narrowly economic ones, is not addressed here. But from a *positive* point of view, one can ask about the relative effectiveness of interdiction versus taxes for discouraging usage.

From the take away point of view of the preceding section, taxes intercept part of the *price* paid by buyers before the money reaches sellers, whereas interdiction intercepts part of the *quantity* produced by sellers before it reaches buyers. So, one might at first think, perhaps a 50% take away tax would be as effective in reducing consumption as a 50% interdiction of supply. But this analogy is imperfect. In fact, a 50% interdiction rate – if it could be achieved – would more effectively reduce consumption than would a 50% tax.

In dealing with transaction taxes, recall that it is essential to distinguish the *gross price* P^+ paid by buyers from the *net price* P^- received by sellers. With interdiction there is only one price, but the *gross quantity* Q^+ (the total manufactured) must be distinguished from the *net quantity* Q^- (the amount actually delivered to buyers).[3] Call i the interdiction (interception) rate. Then the relation between the two is:

$$Q^- \equiv Q^+(1-i) \tag{2.9}$$

Panel (b) of Figure 2.7 pictured a *take away tax* $\tau = 50\%$. Figure 2.8 shows a *take away interception rate* $i = 50\%$. Without any attempt at interception, the equilibrium price and quantity are P^* and Q^*, where the supply curve SS intersects the demand curve DD at point E. Now consider interception from the point of view of the producers. First, since half their output will be intercepted and thus never reach any buyer, suppliers will be willing to supply any specified quantity Q^+ only at double the price. So, as shown in the diagram, the adjusted supply curve $S'S'$ for manufactured quantities Q^+ will be twice as high as SS throughout.

But the story does not end there. Recall that the amount Q^- delivered to buyers is only half the Q^+ produced. So, from the buyers' point of view, the supply curve is $S''S''$ (a horizontal displacement of $S'S'$ half-way to the vertical axis). Thus,

---

[3] This analysis does not attempt to deal with the complicated delivery chain from grower to smuggler to wholesaler to retailer.

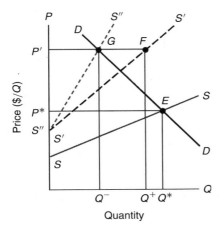

Figure 2.8. Interdiction of Supply

Here the government intercepts the fraction $i = 50\%$ of the amounts supplied before they are delivered to buyers. As suppliers require a price $1/i = 2$ times as high to produce any given quantity, the new supply curve $S'S'$ is twice as high as the original SS. This $S'S'$ curve pictures the *produced* quantity Q^+ at each price. Since the *delivered* quantity $Q^- = (1-i)Q^+$ is just half the produced quantity, the effective supply curve $S''S''$ to buyers is found by shifting $S'S'$ inward by 50% toward the vertical axis. In comparison with the original equilibrium price P^*, the new equilibrium price P' is higher. The quantity produced, Q^+, is smaller than the original equilibrium quantity, Q^*, and the amount actually delivered, Q^-, is much smaller.

interception has a kind of "double whammy" effect upon sellers' incentives. First, interception increases the price suppliers must receive (if they are to stay in business) for any unit manufactured, and second, it reduces the amount delivered below the amount manufactured. Geometrically, first SS shifts to $S'S'$ and then $S'S'$ shifts to $S''S''$.

The interdiction equation system can be written:

$$\begin{cases} P = A - BQ^- & \text{(demand equation)} \\ P = (C + DQ^+)/(1-i) & \text{(supply equation)} \\ Q^- \equiv Q^+(1-i) & \text{(interdiction identity)} \end{cases} \qquad (2.10)$$

The only possibly unexpected element here is on the right-hand side of the middle equation. The $1 - i$ in the denominator corresponds to the upward displacement from SS to $S'S'$ in the diagram. For example, if $i = 50\%$, at each Q^+ the price P received by suppliers would have to be twice as high.

EXERCISE 2.7

Use the same underlying supply and demand curves as in the previous exercise, but now assume an interception take away percentage $i = 50\%$. What are the effects upon (i) the price P, (ii) the quantity manufactured Q^+, and (iii) the quantity delivered Q^-?

ANSWER: Using the equation system (2.10), the demand equation remains as in the previous exercise, but now write it as $P = 300 - Q^-$. The supply equation is modified by the expression $1 - i$ in the denominator on the right-hand side, becoming $P = (60 + 2Q^+)/(1 - i)$. Assuming $i = 50\%$, and skipping the algebraic details, the solutions $Q^+ = 40$, $Q^- = 20$, and $P = 280$. Whereas a 50% take-away tax reduces consumption from 80 to 36, an interdiction rate of 50% would bring it farther down to $Q^- = 20$.

Why does interdiction have this double whammy effect upon consumption? A tax that reduces the profitability of output induces sellers to cut back, and in doing so they reduce their production costs. But with interdiction, suppliers suffer the costs of producing units that will be intercepted and will not reach consumers.

The fact that interception has such a powerful discouraging effect may appear to favor the current interdiction policy as opposed to the tax alternative. Several important considerations, however, may cut the other way. Among them are:

1. A take away tax of 50% was compared with a take away interdiction rate of 50%. But it is far easier to enforce a tax rate of 50% than to achieve an interdiction rate of 50%. In fact, current liquor taxes are far above 50% on a take-away basis (that is, more than half of what the consumer pays for a bottle goes to the government rather than to producers),[4] whereas current narcotic interdiction rates are believed to be only in the neighborhood of 20%. An interception rate of 50% is probably not feasible.
2. In contrast with interdiction, taxes generate revenues that might be used for antidrug education or other useful purposes.

Recall, last, that even a fully satisfactory *positive* analysis would only partially resolve the *normative* issue of which policy to adopt. Among other things, social values are involved. Although some people regard drug use as a merely regrettable activity, for which a tax constitutes a sufficient penalty, others think that drugs are a moral evil to be fought without compromise.

Price Ceilings and Price Floors

Governments sometimes attempt to repress inflation by price ceilings or "freezes." In contrast, during the great depression of the 1930s in the United States, through what was called the National Recovery Administration, the U.S. government attempted to impose *minimum* wage-price controls (floors). Whether price ceilings or price floors can cure a general inflation or cure a general depression are macroeconomic questions not considered here. Instead, the analysis will examine the effects of price controls on the markets for particular goods.

In Figure 2.9, Panel (a) depicts an *effective* ceiling price at the level P'. (To be effective, the ceiling must be lower than the equilibrium price P^*.) At price P' the quantity demanded Q'_d exceeds the quantity supplied Q'_s so there is upward pressure on price. (Note the upward-pointing arrow.) The arrow, however, is blocked by the fixed ceiling.

If we can assume there are no dealings in illegal black markets, what quantity will be exchanged? A fundamental maxim of exchange is: "It takes two to tango." That is, trade requires willing buyers *and* willing sellers. At the ceiling price the buyers want to buy Q'_d but the sellers want to sell only the smaller quantity Q'_s – so Q'_s is the amount that will be traded. (Notice that the amount traded is not a compromise between what consumers want to buy and what sellers want to sell; it is always the *smaller* of the two.) The final outcome is at point C in the diagram. The distance CH represents the "shortage," the excess of the demand quantity over the supply quantity at the legal ceiling price.

---

[4] According to the organization Americans for Tax Reform, in 2002 on average 60% of what was paid for a bottle of distilled spirits went to the government in taxes.

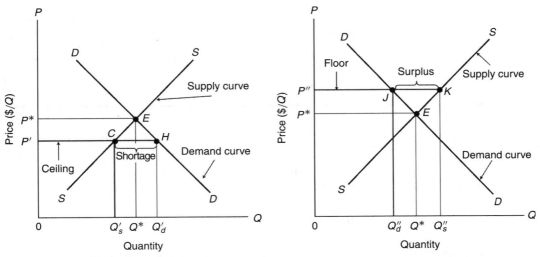

Figure 2.9. Ceilings and Floors

In comparison with the unregulated equilibrium price P^* and quantity Q^*, panel (a) pictures an effective price ceiling $P' < P^*$. The quantity exchanged falls to Q'_s, the supply quantity at price P'. Because consumers seek to buy a larger quantity Q'_d at this price, there is a perceived "shortage" CH. Panel (b) pictures an effective price floor $P'' > P^*$. Here the quantity exchanged falls to Q''_d, again smaller than Q^*. An effective price floor thus creates a perceived "surplus" JK. *Exception*: If the price floor is supported, the amount Q''_s will actually be produced and the surplus will be absorbed by government purchases.

EXAMPLE 2.6 POSTWAR SHORTAGES AND TREKKING

During World War II, Germany and Japan had covered their huge fiscal deficits largely by printing money. The inflationary pressures generated were repressed by keeping prices frozen at low ceiling levels, enforced by severe penalties. After the war ended, Allied occupation authorities in both Germany and Japan continued the previous system of controls. But, given the huge accumulations of money stocks in the hands of the public, after a few years the control system broke down. The price ceilings had become so unrealistic as to paralyze legitimate trade. The shelves in retail stores were bare.

In both Germany and Japan a pattern called *trekking* was observed. City-dwellers would leave town for the day and scour the nearby countryside for food – sometimes making private black-market deals with farmers, sometimes bartering household goods, sometimes simply stealing. On one single day, it is reported, over 900,000 persons trekked from Tokyo to the countryside.[a]

In 1948, with the approval of the Occupation authorities, Germany introduced the Erhard economic reforms, which reduced money stocks by a currency conversion from old marks to new marks. Shortly afterward, the price ceilings were abolished. Almost immediately, goods reappeared in the stores. Trekking abruptly ended. There was one unexpected consequence. The German state railroads suddenly faced a financial crisis, owing to an immediate 40% decrease in short-haul passenger traffic.

The sharp drop reflected the huge amount of trekking to the countryside that had previously been taking place.[b]

---

[a] Jerome B. Cohen, *Japan's Economy in War and Reconstruction* (University of Minnesota Press, 1949), p. 378.

[b] Lucius D. Clay, *Decision in Germany* (Doubleday, 1950), p. 191.

Panel (b) of Figure 2.9 pictures an effective price *floor* P''. At P'' the quantity Q''_s offered by sellers exceeds the quantity Q''_d desired by buyers, so there is downward pressure on price. But, as the blocked downward-pointing arrow in the diagram indicates, the legal floor prevents price from falling to its equilibrium level P^*. Once again, because "it takes two to tango," the quantity traded is the *lesser* of Q''_d and Q''_s – in this case, Q''_d. Note that although effective price ceilings and price floors have opposite effects upon price, they have parallel effects upon the quantity traded: in either case, the quantity exchanged is less than the equilibrium Q^*. With price ceilings, black-market dealings take place at illegally high prices; with price floors, black-market transactions involve illegally low prices.

This picture changes when price floors are *supported*. Support takes the form of a "buyer of last resort." In the United States, the Federal government has been such a buyer for several farm products. In Panel (b) of Figure 2.9, private buyers are only willing to buy the amount Q''_d at the high floor price P''. Now suppose the government will buy any amounts left unsold. In the diagram this is the "surplus" amount *FG*. So with a supported floor no black market appears. Instead a problem of surplus disposal arises – the buyer of last resort accumulates larger and larger unwanted holdings.

CONCLUSION

Effective ceilings hold down prices; effective floors keep them up. In either case, the quantity exchanged is *less* than in unregulated equilibrium. If, however, the floor is *supported* by a "buyer of last resort" willing to accumulate inventories, the quantity supplied will be greater than under the unregulated equilibrium.

EXAMPLE 2.7 AGRICULTURAL PRICE SUPPORTS

Since the 1930s the U.S. government has attempted to maintain "parity" prices for agricultural products. Parity means the relationship between agricultural and nonagricultural prices that obtained during the years 1910 and 1914, a period of farm prosperity. Throughout the 1950s and 1960s, high parity price floors were maintained by government purchases. A federal agency, the Commodity Credit Corporation (CCC), would buy any otherwise unsold quantities of supported crops at the support level – usually at 90% of the parity price.

The "surpluses" purchased by the CCC were mostly stored; the federal government hoped to sell them in years of small harvests. But the amount produced almost every year was greater than the amount consumers would purchase at the artificially high supported prices. By 1960 the CCC held in storage as much wheat as that year's entire crop.

To reduce the cost of holding such huge stores, Congress passed food stamp and school lunch programs subsidizing food prices for some consumers. A variety of "supply management" programs were introduced to reduce quantities produced. In addition, the price support levels were reduced. The table shows that, accordingly, in the 1960s government purchases were much smaller than in the previous decade.

Yearly acquisitions of three supported crops by the commodity credit corporation, selected years

Grain	Sorghum	Corn	Wheat
1953	40.9	422.3	486.1
54	110.1	250.6	391.6
55	92.6	408.9	276.7
56	32.5	477.4	148.4
57	279.5	268.1	193.5
58	258.0	266.6	511.0
1963	125.1	17.9	85.1
64	66.8	29.1	86.9
65	85.0	11.2	17.4
66	0.3	12.4	12.4
67	9.1	191.0	90.0
68	13.7	34.4	182.9

Source: Commodity Credit Corporation charts, November 1972, pp. 49, 75, 115.

Over the years, political support for the policy of buying surpluses has declined. Instead, a variety of other techniques for maintaining farm prices have been increasingly used, the details varying from commodity to commodity. Generally speaking, these restrict either the number of acres that can be planted or the amount of product that can be sold. Such methods of "supply management" have been supplemented by other programs aimed at maintaining farm incomes, among them direct payments to farmers for acres not planted or for crops not sold.[a]

---

[a] These programs are described in Chapter 2 of M. C. Hallberg, *Policy for American Agriculture: Choices and Consequences*, Iowa State University Press, 1992. See also Chapter 12 of M. C. Hallberg, *Economic Trends in U.S. Agriculture and Food Systems since World War II*, Iowa State University Press, 2001.

2.2 FINDING AN OPTIMUM

Optimizing, finding the action that leads to the best outcome, is the second of the two major problem-solving methods used in microeconomics. Economists typically solve optimization problems by means of *marginal analysis*, a technique that does the work of the mathematical calculus without requiring any formal knowledge of calculus techniques. To find the profit-maximizing level of output, for example, a firm should rationally balance its Marginal Revenue (the increment to receipts when it increases output) against its Marginal Cost (the added charges incurred in producing an extra unit). Optimization problems arise for all types of economic agents. Consumers choose how best to spend their incomes, resource-owners try to maximize income by choosing among different ways of employing their assets, and governments seek a preferred

Table 2.2 Total, average, and marginal revenues

Quantity (Q)	Price or average revenue (P = AR)	Total revenue (R = PQ)	Marginal revenue (MR)
0	10	0	
			9
1	9	9	
			7
2	8	16	
			5
3	7	21	
			3
4	6	24	
			1
5	5	25	
			−1
6	4	24	
			−3
7	3	21	
			−5
8	2	16	
			−7
9	1	9	
			−9
10	0	0	

balance between taxation and expenditure. This chapter mainly reviews the analytical tools for optimization decisions.

The Logic of Total, Average, and Marginal Concepts

Consider a firm's revenue from sales. In Table 2.2 the first column shows possible output quantities ranging from $Q = 0$ to $Q = 10$. (We will usually be treating variables as *continuous*, so that intermediate quantities like $Q = 2.7$ are also permitted.) The second column lists hypothetical prices at which these quantities can be sold. These two columns are the tabular equivalent of a standard demand curve. The third column is Total Revenue (or Revenue, for short), defined as price P times quantity Q:

$$R \equiv P \times Q \qquad (2.11)$$

The data corresponding to the third column are plotted in the upper diagram of Figure 2.10. Note that as quantity Q increases, Revenue R first increases but eventually begins to decline as buyers become saturated with the firm's product.

Revenue is a *total* magnitude, whereas price P is an *average* magnitude. Specifically, price P is definitionally identical to Average Revenue (AR), as follows obviously from the equation preceding:

$$AR \equiv R/Q \equiv P \qquad (2.12)$$

When Revenue is measured in dollars ($\$$), Average Revenue or price is measured in dollars per unit quantity ($\$/Q$). In Table 2.2, at quantity $Q = 2$ the Total Revenue is 16.

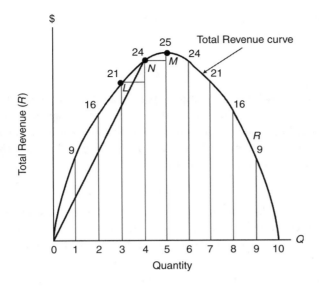

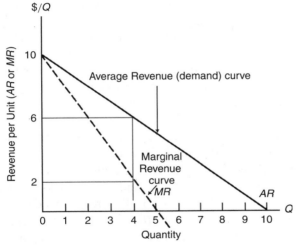

Figure 2.10. Geometrical Derivation of Average and Marginal Magnitudes

The upper diagram pictures a Total Revenue R function, and the lower diagram the associated Average Revenue AR and Marginal Revenue MR functions. For the specific quantity $Q = 4$, Total Revenue is $R = 24$. The height of the AR curve in the lower diagram corresponds to the slope of the bold line ON in the upper diagram, so that $AR = R/Q = \frac{24}{4} = 6$ at $Q = 4$. The height of the MR curve at $Q = 4$ corresponds to the slope along the Total Revenue curve. It is approximated by averaging the slopes of LN and NM. The slope of LN is $(24 - 21)/1 = 3$ and that of NM is $(25 - 24)/1 = 1$, the average being 2. Therefore, in the lower diagram, 2 is the height of the MR curve.

Average Revenue at $Q = 2$ is $16/2 = 8$, which corresponds to the price along the demand curve for that quantity.

Marginal Revenue MR is shown in the fourth column of Table 2.2. Its definition is:

$$MR \equiv \Delta R / \Delta Q \qquad (2.13)$$

where ΔR and ΔQ signify *small changes* in Revenue and in quantity.[5] Like price, MR is measured in dollars per unit quantity ($\$/Q$).

> **WARNING**
>
> A total magnitude (such as Revenue in the upper panel) should *never* be plotted on the same diagram as average and marginal magnitudes (such as Average Revenue and Marginal Revenue in the lower panel). The units of measurement are not the same. The vertical axis of the upper diagram of Figure 2.10 is scaled in dollars ($\$$), whereas the lower diagram is scaled in dollars per unit quantity ($\$/Q$).

In Table 2.2, if the supplier sells two units instead of one, Revenue rises from 9 to 16. Over this quantity interval of size $\Delta Q = 1$, Marginal Revenue is $MR \equiv \Delta R/\Delta Q = (16 - 9)/1 = 7$. If output were increased further to $Q = 3$, over the next unit quantity interval MR would be 5, and so on.

In numerically calculating Marginal Revenue, there is one tricky point. For an increase in output from say $Q = 1$ to $Q = 2$, the MR of 7 applies *between* $Q = 1$ and $Q = 2$ (rather than *at* $Q = 1$ or *at* $Q = 2$). (The jagged "staircase" in Table 2.2 suggests this.) At least as an approximation, then, $MR = 7$ applies best halfway between, at $Q = 1.5$. To find the MR specifically *at* $Q = 2$, the best estimate is to take the average of the MR of 7 over the "lower interval" (from $Q = 1$ to $Q = 2$) and the MR of 5 over the "upper interval" (from $Q = 2$ and $Q = 3$). Thus, as a good approximation, at $Q = 2$ the MR is about 6 (the average of 7 and 5). By similar reasoning, at $Q = 3$ the MR is about 4 (the average of 5 and 3).

It is sometimes said that Marginal Revenue is the increment to revenue due to "the last unit produced" or "the next unit that might be produced." The first statement looks at the downward interval (so that, in terms of the numbers in the preceding paragraph, at $Q = 2$ the MR would be 7). The second statement looks at the upward interval (so that at $Q = 2$ the MR would be 5). Our recommended procedure is to average these two figures, yielding the result $MR = 6$ at $Q = 2$. When the increments R and Q are quite small relative to R and Q, the more precise approximation may make little difference, yet sometimes the disparity can be large. Since it is only trivially more difficult to do so, it is good practice always to use the better approximation. And in fact, for a straight-line demand curve like the one tabulated in Table 2.2, the recommended method always coincides with the calculus answer and so will be exactly correct.[6] When the demand curve is not a straight line the recommended procedure will not be quite perfect, but it will almost always be more accurate than the alternatives.

---

[5] *Mathematical Footnote*: For infinitesimally small changes, Marginal Revenue becomes the calculus derivative:

$$MR \equiv dR/dQ \equiv \lim_{\Delta Q \to 0} \Delta R/\Delta Q$$

[6] *Mathematical Footnote*: The demand-curve equation underlying Table 2.2 is $P = 10 - Q$. Then Total Revenue is $R = PQ = 10Q - Q^2$. Taking the derivative, Marginal Revenue is $MR = R/dQ = 10 - 2Q$. At $Q = 2$, therefore, $MR = 6$. This exact answer is the same as shown by our recommended method of approximation.

EXERCISE 2.8

For the nonlinear demand curve $P = 100 - Q^2$, compare the recommended method with the less precise methods for approximating MR at $Q = 4$.

ANSWER: Since Revenue = Price × Quantity, the Total Revenue equation becomes $R = (100 - Q^2) \times Q = 100Q - Q^3$. Total Revenue R is 273 at $Q = 3$ and 336 at $Q = 4$. So *between* $Q = 3$ and $Q = 4$, the recommended method associates the revenue increment $336 - 273 = 63$ with output $Q = 3.5$. Symbolically, the estimated Marginal Revenue at $Q = 3.5$ is $\Delta R/\Delta Q = 63/1 = 63$. Similarly, *between* $Q = 4$ and $Q = 5$, MR is $(375 - 336)/1 = 39$, which approximates the MR at $Q = 4.5$. The estimated MR at $Q = 4$ is found by averaging: $(39 + 63)/2 = 51$. (The exact calculus result at $Q = 4$ is $MR = 52$, close to the recommended approximation $MR = 51$.) In contrast, the less precise method of identifying Marginal Revenue at $Q = 4$ as the revenue increment from the "last" or fourth unit produced would lead to the poor estimate $MR = 63$ at $Q = 4$. Or saying that the MR at $Q = 4$ is the revenue increment from the "next" or fifth unit would imply an even worse estimate: $MR = 31$. The recommended method is a *much* better approximation than either of the other two.

What if the units of output are *discrete* rather than continuous, so that it is meaningless to calculate Marginal Revenue for fractions of units? In that case one cannot avoid having two different estimates for MR: one over the "upward interval" and the other over the "downward interval." Which estimate should be used depends upon whether the decision to be made involves an upward or a downward choice.

EXERCISE 2.9

Suppose that only exact integer amounts of output are possible. Imagine that the cost of producing remains constant at 6 per unit (so 6 is both the Marginal Cost and Average Cost at all levels of output). Using the data of Table 2.2, verify that $Q = 2$ is the best output to produce.

ANSWER: Starting from output $Q = 2$, the table indicates that over the "upward interval" (from $Q = 2$ to $Q = 3$) the Marginal Revenue is $MR = 5$. Since the cost of producing one more unit is 6, it is evidently unprofitable to increase output. Over the "downward interval" Marginal Revenue is $MR = 7$. Then reducing output to $Q = 1$ would also be unprofitable: it would reduce Revenue by 7 while reducing costs by only 6. So $Q = 2$ is the best amount to produce.

The preceding exercise suggests the following general rule:

RULE: When only discrete choices are possible, output is at an optimum when Marginal Revenue is *less* than Marginal Cost over the smallest allowable "upward interval" and Marginal Revenue is *greater* than Marginal Cost over the smallest allowable "downward interval."

EXAMPLE 2.8 PROFESSORS AND PUBLICATIONS

Professors' research results are usually reported in scholarly articles. Professors with many publications gain professional recognition and tend to receive higher salaries.

Howard P. Tuckman and Jack Leahey[a] estimated the effect of article publication upon professors' salaries in the 1970s. The table here compares the *average* and *marginal* salaries associated with varying numbers of published articles, in comparison with baseline salaries for professors with no publications. (Multiple authorship was disregarded, so that each coauthor received full credit for any published article.)

The general relations between the tabulated average and marginal salary figures resemble those shown in the lower panel of Figure 2.10, taking number of publications as the quantity variable. In the data shown here, averaging over all professors the first article was associated with a marginal salary gain of $543, whereas the marginal salary gain from the 35th article was only $49. (This declining pattern reflects the Law of Diminishing Returns, to be discussed in Chapter 6.)

Published articles and salary gains

Number of articles	Average salary gain	Marginal salary gain
1	$543	$543
5	295	191
10	227	153
15	194	120
20	174	109
25	160	100
30	149	93
35	150	49

Source: Adapted from Tuckman and Leahey, Table 2.

COMMENT

The number of publications is necessarily discrete. The authors' marginal estimates represent the "upward interval" interpretation of the marginal concept for discrete variables. The first figure, $543, is the salary increment looking upward from zero to 1. This would be the relevant figure for a professor deciding whether or not to make the effort of producing a first article.

[a] Howard P. Tuckman and Jack Leahey, "What Is an Article Worth?" *Journal of Political Economy*, v. 83 (October 1975).

How Total, Average, and Marginal Magnitudes Are Related

When the variables are continuous rather than discrete, the relations among total, average, and marginal magnitudes are most easily interpreted in terms of geometry. The two main principles are:

1. The *marginal* magnitude is the slope of the total function.
2. The *average* magnitude is the slope of a ray from the origin to the total function.

The first principle is demonstrated in Figure 2.10. Corresponding to the data of Table 2.2, the parabola in the upper diagram shows Total Revenue R for each level of output Q. As Q rises from 4 to 5, R rises from 24 to 25, so the revenue increment is $\Delta R = 25 - 24 = 1$ between $Q = 4$ and $Q = 5$. Slope is defined as "rise over run." Here the rise is $25 - 24 = 1$ and the run is $5 - 4 = 1$, so the slope is

$\Delta R/\Delta Q = 1/1 = 1$ in this range. Corresponding to the recommended approximation method described above, this slope of 1 is best associated with the in-between quantity $Q = 4.5$. (It would be wrong to say that the slope is 1 *at* point M, where $Q = 5$. Since M is the maximum of the parabola, the slope of the curve has to be zero there.) To approximate the slope specifically at $Q = 4$, the recommended method averages the slopes at $Q = 3.5$ and at 4.5. From the Marginal Revenue column of Table 2.2, these two slopes are 3 and 1, respectively, so the recommended estimate of the MR at $Q = 4$ is 2.

The second rule states that Average Revenue at any given output is, geometrically, the slope of a line that connects the origin to the point on the Revenue curve corresponding to the output level chosen. Look again at the upper diagram in Figure 2.10. At $Q = 4$, Total Revenue is $R = 24$. From the definition of Average Revenue, divide R by Q to obtain $AR = 24/4 = 6$. Now compare the ray ON. The slope of segment ON is the vertical distance or rise (24) divided by horizontal distance or run (4), yielding 6 once again. So the geometrical result is the same, as follows numerically from the definition Average Revenue $\equiv R/Q$.

The lower panel of Figure 2.10 depicts the Average Revenue and Marginal Revenue curves that correspond to the Revenue function shown in the upper panel. Both AR and MR in this panel are falling throughout. MR is declining throughout because, in the upper panel, the R curve that relates revenue to quantity is always becoming (algebraically) less steep moving to the right. Thus the slope of the Total Revenue curve is initially positive, becomes zero at $Q = 5$ (where R reaches its maximum), and is negative for larger levels of Q. Similarly, Average Revenue AR also falls throughout, because the slope of the ray from the origin to a point along the Revenue curve declines steadily in moving to the right. (For example, OM is less steep than ON.) Note that at $Q = 10$ the line from the origin to the Revenue curve is flat. Its slope is zero. This means that AR is zero at the output where the demand curve intersects the horizontal axis, which obviously must be true since Total Revenue is also zero there.

However, as long as Total Revenue rises with increasing quantity, Marginal Revenue remains positive. But past the peak of the Total Revenue curve, the slope along the R curve becomes negative and so MR turns negative. Extending these ideas to general relations between total and marginal functions leads to the Propositions:

PROPOSITION 2.1a: When a total magnitude is rising, the corresponding marginal magnitude is positive.

PROPOSITION 2.1b: When a total magnitude is falling, the corresponding marginal magnitude is negative.

Last, when Revenue reaches a maximum (or a minimum) the Revenue function is neither increasing nor decreasing; it is level. Drawing the obvious inference:

PROPOSITION 2.1c: When a total magnitude reaches a maximum or a minimum, the corresponding marginal magnitude is zero.[7,8]

---

[7] *Mathematical Footnote:* When $dR/dQ < 0$, the Total Revenue function R is increasing; when $dR/dQ < 0$, it is decreasing; when $dR/dQ = 0$, the function is stationary.

[8] *Mathematical Footnote:* As a technical qualification, Proposition 2.1c is valid only when the associated minimum or maximum is "flat." In the upper diagram of Figure 2.10, R has a flat maximum at $Q = 5$: the Revenue curve is horizontal, and Marginal Revenue is $MR = 0$. But the Revenue curve also has minima at $Q = 0$ and $Q = 10$,

When a *total* magnitude is at a maximum, it does not follow that either the corresponding *average* magnitude or the corresponding *marginal* magnitude is at a maximum. Indeed, as was just seen, when a total magnitude is at a maximum the associated marginal magnitude equals zero. And although the associated average magnitude will normally be positive, it will not be at its maximum.

Since optimization consists of finding a maximum of some desired variable such as profit or utility, or a minimum of an undesired variable such as cost, Proposition 2.1c suggests how economists solve optimization problems. Suppose you were packing for a voyage for which you would be charged a unit fee proportional to weight carried (a continuous variable). The optimum number of pounds to pack would balance the marginal benefit of another pound (or fraction thereof) against the additional fee you must pay. Similarly, a firm's profits are maximized at the level of output where an additional unit neither increases nor decreases profit.

The lower diagram in Figure 2.10 illustrates still another principle:

PROPOSITION 2.2a: **When the average magnitude is falling, the marginal magnitude must lie below it.**

Think of the average weight of people in a room. If someone walks in and the average weight falls, the *marginal* weight (the weight of the person who just walked in) must have been less than the average weight.[9] In Figure 2.10 each new unit lowers Average Revenue (*AR* is always falling); hence the Marginal Revenue curve *MR* lies always below it.

Using similar reasoning:

PROPOSITION 2.2b: **When the average magnitude is rising, the marginal magnitude lies above it.**

PROPOSITION 2.2c: **When an average magnitude is neither rising nor falling (at a minimum or maximum), the marginal magnitude equals the average magnitude.**[10]

In Figure 2.11, the upper diagram shows a firm's Total Cost curve *C*.[11] To derive Marginal Cost *MC* from the Total Cost function shown, remember that *MC* is the slope of *C*. The slope along the cost curve in the upper diagram falls, moving to the right, up to point *K*. After that the cost curve becomes steeper. Correspondingly, in the lower diagram *MC* falls, reaches a minimum at point *K'*, and then starts rising.

The Average Cost *AC* at any output is given by the slope of a ray from the origin to the point on the Total Cost curve corresponding to that output: the vertical distance

---

yet the curve is not flat at those points; that is, $MR \neq 0$. In this book we will deal almost always with flat minima or maxima, for which Proposition 2.1c holds.

[9] A careful reader will note that number of people is a *discrete* rather than a continuous variable. Nevertheless, the proposition certainly continues to hold true. A question at the end of the chapter asks how to reinterpret Propositions 2.1a,b and Propositions 2.1a,b,c when the underlying variable is discrete.

[10] *Mathematical Footnote*: Let us verify Proposition 2.2a of the text, and specifically that *MR* is below *AR* when *AR* is falling. For *AR* to be falling it must be the case that:

$$0 > \frac{d(AR)}{dQ} = \frac{d(R/Q)}{dQ} = \frac{Q(dR/dQ) - R}{Q^2}$$

The inequality dictates that the last numerator must be negative. It follows that $dR/dQ < R/Q$, or $MR < AR$: Marginal Revenue is always less than Average Revenue. Similar proofs apply for Propositions 2.2b and 2.2c.

[11] In Figure 2.11 Total Cost is shown as positive even at an output of zero. The explanation is that fixed costs (such as the rent on a factory building) must be paid even if nothing is produced.

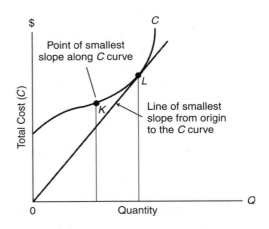

Figure 2.11. Derivation of Average and Marginal Magnitudes from Total Function: Cost

The lower diagram derives Average Cost *AC* and Marginal Cost *MC* from the Total Cost function *C* in the upper diagram. At the quantity where the slope along the Total Cost function is least, *MC* is at a minimum. Where the slope of the line drawn from the origin to the curve is least (point *L* in the upper diagram), *AC* is at a minimum. When *AC* is falling, *MC* lies below it; when *AC* is rising, *MC* lies above it.

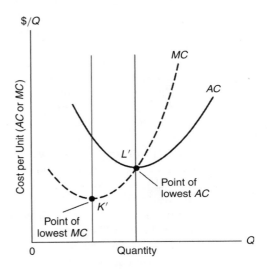

(cost *C*) at that point divided by the horizontal distance (output *Q*). Moving to the right along the Total Cost curve, the slope of the ray out of the origin falls until point *L* – after which the slope begins to rise. So, in the lower diagram, *AC* falls until point *L'* and rises after that. This means that *AC* is at its lowest value when output is *L'*. (Note that if fixed costs are positive, Average Cost $AC \equiv C/Q$ is infinite at the vertical axis where $Q = 0$.)

In the upper diagram, anywhere to the left of *L* a ray from the origin to the cost curve is steeper than the slope of the cost curve itself. Since the slope of the ray is greater than the slope of the cost curve, *AC* is greater than *MC* for any output level in this range. This again confirms Proposition 2.2a: when *AC* is falling, *MC* lies below it.

To the right of *L*, a ray from the origin to a point on the cost curve is flatter than the cost curve itself at that point, so *AC* is less than *MC*. This confirms Proposition 2.2b: at those values of *Q* for which Average Cost is rising, Average Cost is less than Marginal Cost.

Lastly, the ray from the origin to point L along the cost curve has the same slope as the cost curve itself at point L. This means that here Marginal Cost = Average Cost, confirming Proposition 2.2c.

The following Example describes a policy error seemingly due to ignorance of marginal concepts.

EXAMPLE 2.9 THE OIL ENTITLEMENT PROGRAM

In 1973 and 1974 the Organization of Petroleum Exporting Countries (OPEC) drastically reduced petroleum production, causing the world price of crude oil to soar from about $2 to almost $12 per barrel (see the OPEC Example in Chapter 8). The U.S. government, concerned about its balance of payments, tried to reduce oil imports. However, American policy-makers also wanted to eliminate "inequitable" gains to those domestic producers of crude oil who were profiting from the higher world prices. Unfortunately, the method chosen to achieve the second objective tended to defeat the first.[a]

To prevent domestic producers from reaping windfall gains, the price of *domestic* crude oil was frozen. (It was impossible, of course, to freeze the price of imported oil.) But some refineries, owing for example to vertical integration or to pre-existing contracts, had access to domestic crude while others did not. In the interests of "equity" the Entitlement Program was undertaken. The basic idea was that every refiner was entitled to buy, at the low ceiling price, the nationwide *average* fraction of the (artificially) cheap domestic oil. Refiners having access to domestic crude had to compensate refiners making more than average use of expensive imported crude.

The unanticipated effect was to encourage imports of the high-priced foreign oil. From the point of view of the nation as a whole, the Marginal Cost of crude oil was the high-cost imported crude at $12 per barrel. Had all refiners been required to pay this world price for imported crude oil, they would have wanted to import less oil. But under the Entitlement Program, each barrel imported entitled the importer to a great bargain: the right to obtain an equivalent amount of domestic crude at an artificially cheap frozen price! So in effect, refineries were subsidized to make heavy use of high-cost imported crude.[b]

---

[a] This is necessarily a very simplified discussion of the enormously complicated details of U.S. oil policy. In particular, the legal distinction between so-called "new domestic oil" and "old domestic oil" has been omitted here.

[b] Many discussions of the oil entitlement program are available. See, for example, C. E. Phelps and R. T. Smith, *Petroleum Regulation: The False Dilemma of Decontrol* (Santa Monica, CA: RAND Corporation, 1977).

Straight thinking about average and marginal concepts is also helpful in considering the tax implications of earning higher income.

EXAMPLE 2.10 TAXES

The table here shows the personal income tax schedule for single taxpayers, calculated from the Internal Revenue Service's Form 1040 Instructions for the tax year 2003. For any "Taxable Income"[a] in the first column, the next columns show the tax at the lower end of the bracket and the marginal tax rate for additional dollars of income within the bracket. At an income of $28,400, for example, the tax is $3,910. This is the sum of a tax rate of 10% paid on the first $7000 of income and a rate of 15% paid on the remaining $21,400. The marginal tax on the next dollar earned would be 25%.

The following fallacy is sometimes encountered. Suppose an employee's taxable income is indeed $28,400 at the top of the 15% Marginal Tax bracket, so that her tax is $3,910. Her employer offers a raise of $100, but the worker refuses the raise because it would put her in a higher tax bracket! The worker may think that in moving up to a higher *marginal* tax rate (25% instead of 15%) she would be taxed the extra 10% on *all* her income, ending up worse off than before. This is false. The worker's additional tax would be only 25% of $100, or $25. Accepting the raise would increase her after-tax income by $100 − $25 = $75. The loss due to refusing the raise is one of the costs that arise from inability to use correct marginal reasoning.

Personal income tax schedule for single taxpayers

Taxable income	Tax at lower end of bracket	Marginal tax rate
$0 to $7000	$0	10%
$7000 to $28,400	$700 (= $7000 × 10%)	15%
$28,400 to $68,800	$3910 (= $700 + 0.15 × $21,400)	25%
$68,800 to $143,500	$14,010 (= $3910 + 0.25 × $40,400)	28%
$143,500 to $311,950	$34,926 (= $14,010 + 0.28 × $74,700)	33%
> $311,950	$90,514 (= $34,926 + 0.33 × $168,450)	35%

a "Taxable income" is earned income minus the exemptions, deductions, etc., provided in the tax law.

An Application: Foraging – When Is It Time to Pack Up and Leave?[12]

In the early history of humankind, foraging was a major economic activity. Human bands and tribes collected resources from the environment by hunting or fishing or gathering fruits and vegetables. Some modern activities are logically analogous to foraging. Travelling salesmen, for example, might be said to be foraging for customers.

A crucial choice for all foragers is how to distribute the available time over different sources of food and other usable resources. Imagine a human band roaming a desert, empty except for occasional resource patches in the form of oases. At any given oasis, living needs will gradually exhaust the available resources. So the band must eventually move on. The economic problem is just when to do so.

Suppose all oases are equivalent and equally distant from one another. Figure 2.12 shows the total food yield y collectable from a given oasis, as a function of the "stay time" s that the band spends at that location. However, when the band moves on, a certain amount of "dead time" d occurs in travelling from one oasis to another.

The Total Yield curve $y(s)$ in Figure 2.12 is analogous to the Total Revenue curve of Figure 2.10. The main difference is that the curve emerges not from the origin but from a point $(d,0)$ along the horizontal axis. This is in order to allow for the foragers' dead time.

[12] The analysis here is an adaptation of a result in Eric Charnov, "Optimal Foraging, the Marginal Value Theorem," *Theoretical Population Biology*, 9 (1976), pp. 129–36.

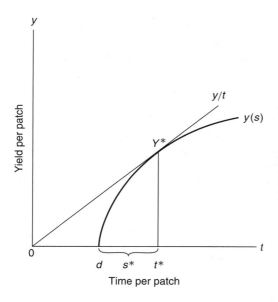

Figure 2.12. Foraging – Optimal Stay Time

The optimal stay time s^*, at any single resource patch with yield $y(s)$, occurs when the Marginal Yield in that patch equals the Average Yield (y/t) taken over the entire period – dividing the yield per patch y by the overall time per patch t, where $t = d + s$. That is, the average time per patch includes not only the stay time s but the dead time d spent traveling from one patch to the next.

If the group has a fixed amount of time per season that can be devoted to foraging, it will want to maximize y/t, the Average Yield over all resource patches, where t is the sum of the dead time and stay time per patch. As with all average magnitudes, the Average Yield is shown geometrically as the slope of a line drawn from the origin to the curve. The maximum Average Yield is the slope of a line from the origin that is just tangent to the curve (at point Y^*).

As is consistent with Proposition 2.2c, when the average magnitude is maximized here the marginal magnitude equals the average magnitude. That is, at Y^* the Marginal Yield, the slope along the Total Yield curve, is equal to the Average Yield represented by the slope of the line OY^* from the origin to the curve. So the optimum stay time is characterized by the property that the Marginal Yield from remaining one more day in a particular resource patch equals the Average Yield over all patches, allowing for both stay time and dead time. The interpretation is that, having maximized average daily food intake over the entire season, it does not pay to stay at any particular oasis once its marginal yield has fallen below the average yield that the band is able to achieve overall.

EXAMPLE 2.11 FORAGING CHOICES

The Aché people of Paraguay obtain their food mainly by foraging. When encountered on a foraging expedition, food items typically require additional effort before actual capture. Animals must be pursued, fruits and berries have to be picked, tubers must be dug up, and so forth. So for each encounter a decision must be made: whether to devote the extra time and effort needed to actually acquire the item, or else pass it up in the hope of finding something more profitable later on.

For Aché foragers, calories can be taken as the value or yield associated with different food sources, to be measured against the cost in terms of time required for acquisition and preparation. If the Aché are choosing rationally, they should invest the time needed to acquire any food item whose marginal payoff (ratio of calories/hour) exceeds a certain cutoff level, passing up those with lower ratios. The cutoff level should be the average payoff achieved over all food types actually harvested or collected.

Observing the Aché, the anthropologists Hillary Kaplan and Kim Hill[a] were able to classify 28 frequently taken food items in terms of the calories/hour ratio. As the table indicates, Aché foragers almost always invested the effort to take very high-ranking food items (high marginal yield per unit time) – a group including honey, deer, and armadillo. The average rank of these foods was 11.6 (rank 1 being best). Relatively lower-ranking items such as palm nuts might or might not be acquired, depended upon circumstances. And finally, many possible food sources with very low calorie/hour ratios (not shown in the table) were never taken at all.

Aché food choices

	No. of items	Average rank (calories/hour)
Items almost always taken	14	11.6
Items sometimes taken	14	15.2

Source: Interpreted visually from p. 175 of Kaplan and Hill.

[a] Hillary Kaplan and Kim Hill, "The Evolutionary Ecology of Food Acquisition," in Eric Alden Smith and Bruce Winterhalder, eds., *Evolutionary Ecology and Human Behavior* (1992).

SUMMARY   On the intermediate level there are two main techniques of economic analysis: finding an equilibrium, and finding an optimum.

Equilibrium price and quantity are geometrically determined by the intersection of a supply curve and a demand curve. Changes in demand or supply are shown by shifts in these curves. An increase in demand (more of the product is desired at each price) raises both the equilibrium price and quantity. An increase in supply (more of the product is offered at each price) raises price but lowers the quantity sold.

A tax on transactions reduces the quantity bought and sold. The tax raises the *gross price* (the price a buyer pays) but reduces the *net price* (the price a seller receives). The volume of transactions always decreases.

If a price ceiling or a price floor is effective, the quantity bought and sold is the *smaller* of the quantities demanded and supplied at that price. The market is not in equilibrium. An effective price ceiling necessarily leads to upward pressure on price, and an effective price floor to downward pressure on price. The typical consequence will be black markets or other attempts to evade the price controls.

The solutions to *optimization* problems depend upon the relations among total, average, and marginal magnitudes. Comparing marginal and total magnitudes:

1. When the total magnitude is rising, the marginal magnitude is positive.
2. When the total magnitude is level, the marginal magnitude is zero.
3. When the total magnitude is falling, the marginal magnitude is negative.

Comparing marginal and average magnitudes:

1. When the average magnitude is falling, the marginal magnitude is below the average magnitude.
2. When the average magnitude is level, the marginal magnitude equals the average magnitude.

3. When the average magnitude is rising, the marginal magnitude is above the average magnitude.

QUESTIONS

†The answers to daggered questions appear at the end of the book.

For Review

†1. Which of the following are optimization problems? Which are equilibrium problems? [*Note:* You need not give the actual answers to the questions, but you might think about them.]
  a. Is it more profitable for a business to offer occasional special sales at reduced prices, or to stick with moderate prices year-round?
  b. Would a gold discovery in Hawaii raise apartment rents on the island?
  c. If the punishment for murder were made more severe, would there be fewer murders?
  d. As a military commander, should I attack now when the enemy doesn't expect it or wait for my reinforcements, even though the enemy will then be alerted?
  e. Over the year, why is the price of strawberries more variable than the price of potatoes?
  f. If my wife and I have had three girl babies in a row, should we give up or try again for a boy?

2. Is supply-demand analysis the key tool for equilibrium or for optimization problems? For what class of problem is the relation among total, average, and marginal quantities the key tool?

†3. In what sense is price a "ratio of quantities"?

4. Explain why market equilibrium is determined by the *intersection* of the supply curve and the demand curve.

5. How does an "increase in demand" shift the demand curve? How does an "increase in supply" shift the supply curve? Does an increase in demand affect the equilibrium price and quantity in the same direction? What about an increase in supply?

†6. In the analysis of a $T per unit tax, we shifted the demand curve downward by $T to find the new equilibrium. Would the same result have been achieved if instead the supply curve were shifted upward by $T? Explain.

7. Draw supply and demand diagrams, with upward sloping supply curves and downward sloping demand curves, to illustrate the following possibilities:
  a. A large demand increase may have little effect on equilibrium price.
  b. A demand increase may raise price substantially, while an equal supply decrease would hardly affect price.
  c. A small demand decrease may produce a large drop in equilibrium quantity.
  d. Supply changes may have no effect on the monetary values of total sales.

†8. In each of the following cases, state whether an excise tax will raise the (gross) price *paid* by consumers, or reduce the (net) price *received* by sellers, or both.
  a. Supply curve slopes upward and demand curve slopes downward.
  b. Supply curve horizontal, demand curve slopes downward.
  c. Supply curve vertical, demand curve slopes downward.
  d. Supply curve vertical, demand curve horizontal.

9. Suppose the government pays a $5 per unit *subsidy* on sales of flags. What would be the effect on the quantity exchanged? On the gross and the net price?

†10. a.   What is an "effective" price ceiling or price floor?

  b.   Why do effective floors and ceilings both *decrease* the quantity traded?

  c.   What happens, however, if a price floor is "supported" by government purchases of any amounts unsold in the market?

11. Starting from the Total Revenue function, show how the Average Revenue function is derived. Show how the Marginal Revenue function is derived.

12. Starting from the Total Cost function, show how the Average Cost function and the Marginal Cost function are derived.

†13. The Lackawanna Social Club, which has 20 resident members, keeps a refrigerator stocked with soda. Soda cans are obtained from a local distributor for 30 cents per can. Each member has free access to the refrigerator and can consume as many cans as he likes. At the end of each month, the total cost of the soda is divided equally among the members. What is the marginal cost per can to the club? To a member?

†14. In terms of the general relations among total, average, and marginal quantities, which of the following statements are *necessarily* true, and which are not?

  a.   When the total function is rising, the marginal function is rising.

  b.   When the total function is rising, the marginal function is positive.

  c.   When the total function is rising, the marginal function lies above it.

  d.   When the marginal function is rising, the average function is also rising.

  e.   When the average function is falling, the marginal function lies below it.

  f.   When the marginal function is neither rising nor falling, the average function is constant.

†15. In the application on interdicting supply, suppose a tax rate of 50% and an interdiction rate of 20% are about equally easy to enforce. Which would have a bigger effect upon consumption?

For Further Thought and Discussion

†1. In the year 302, the Roman emperor Diocletian "commanded that there should be cheapness." His edict declared:

> Unprincipled greed appears wherever our armies, following the command of the public weal, march, not only in villages and cities but also upon all highways, with the result that prices of foodstuffs mount not only fourfold and eightfold, but transcend all measure. Our law shall fix a measure and a limit to this greed.

  a.   Why do you think Diocletian found food prices higher wherever he marched with his armies?

  b.   What result would you anticipate from the command that "there should be cheapness"?

†2. Suppose that the supply curve for gold is very steep (positively sloped, but almost vertical).

  a.   Would a T tax tend to have a relatively large or a relatively small effect upon the quantity exchanged in the market? Would there tend to be a relatively large or a relatively small effect upon the gross price paid by buyers? Upon the net price received by sellers?

  b.   Explain in terms of the underlying economic meaning.

3. Analyze correspondingly the case where the demand curve is very steep (negatively sloped, but almost vertical).

†4. a.   If the price of gasoline rises as a result of a reduction in petroleum supplies, what effect would you anticipate on the price of automobiles?

b.   Upon the relative price of small, light cars versus large, heavy cars?

†5. a.   What assumptions underlie the "method of comparative statics"?

b.   Will these assumptions ever be met in the real world?

6. During World War II, the British government imposed a ceiling price on bread. Explain why there was upward pressure upon the price of bread. What consequences would you anticipate, given continuing enforcement of the ceiling? To alleviate the upward pressure on the bread price, the British government took fresh bread off the market; all bread sold had to be at least one day old. Would you expect this regulation to achieve the desired effect?

†7. Owing to congestion, Gregory Peck International Airport wishes to limit the number of daily airplane departures to one hundred. (The airlines are eager and willing to provide two hundred flights a day.) It is proposed to auction off the rights to use the terminal, thus in effect imposing departure fees on the airlines. What are the likely consequences?

†8. The table below gives a partial tabulation of a demand function. Estimate Marginal Revenue at $Q = 3$.

Quantity	Price
0	30
3	20
6	12

9. The following is part of a price schedule, showing the quantity discounts offered by a printing shop. Does something peculiar happen as the size of your order approaches the upper limit in a given price range? Explain in terms of Marginal Revenue to the printing shop. Can you think of a more sensible way for the printing shop to offer quantity discounts?

Size of your order	Your price ($)
1–10 units	.50 each
11–20 units	.40 each
21–50 units	.35 each
Over 50 units	.30 each

†10. In Example 2.8 (PROFESSORS AND PUBLICATIONS), why are the average and marginal figures inconsistent in the last two rows of the table?

11. In a recent book, the philosopher John Searle stated:

During the Vietnam War . . . a high official of the Defense Department . . . went to the blackboard and drew the curves of traditional microeconomic analysis; and then said, "Where the two curves intersect, the marginal utility of resisting is equal to the marginal disutility of being bombed. At that point they have to give up . . . " I knew then that we were in serious trouble, not only in our theory of rationality, but in its application in practice.

Searle here questions the applicability of rational analysis to warfare. Leaving aside that larger issue, show that the "high official" is applying marginal reasoning incorrectly. (Or perhaps the philosopher misunderstood what he said.) [*Hint*: Does the intersection of the two curves indicate the point where the enemy must give up, or does it indicate something else?]

†12. What happens to equilibrium price and quantity if both supply and demand increase?

13. In the application to introducing a new supply source (as in Figure 2.5), what would happen if the initial equilibrium price P_0^* were below the import choke price F?

14. Show how the "incidence" of a per-unit tax on transactions depends upon the slopes of the supply curve and demand curve.

†15. a. In the early 20th century, there were many local opera and theatre companies and other local providers of musical entertainment. With the rise of mass media and duplicative technologies (such as television, radio, and recordings), many of these local services disappeared. What do you think happened to the demand for the services of performers with extraordinarily high charm or talent (the Luciano Pavorrotis, Britney Spearses, and Tom Cruises of their day)? What do you think happened to the equilibrium price of the services of the most exceptional individuals? How do you think the price of the services of performers of somewhat less talent changed?

b. Near the turn of the millennium, duplicative and transmission technology (the Internet, CDs) led to a further development: easy acquisition and duplication of music without paying the supplier. Assume that such piracy is cheap but not costless to consumers. Based on supply/demand analysis, what effect do you think this development had on the demand for the services of the very highest talent performers? Of performers with somewhat less talent?

II PREFERENCE, CONSUMPTION, AND DEMAND

3 Utility and Preference

As explained in the previous chapter, there are only two main methods of microeconomic analysis. The first is *finding an optimum*: what's the best thing to do? The second is *finding the equilibrium*: when everyone's actions are taken into account, what's the overall result? Here in Part Two of the book, we apply the first of these methods to analyze *the optimum of the consumer*. Specifically, what is the best bundle of goods for a consumer to purchase?

People in a market economy face two fundamental choices: how to earn an income, and how to spend it. Part Two deals with how income is spent, taking earnings (income) as given. Part Four will analyze the decisions that generate income – for example, whether or not to work overtime.

3.1   THE LAWS OF PREFERENCE

The economist thinks of the individual as aiming to *maximize utility*. The logic of utility analysis is the central topic of this chapter.

Theories or models are pictures that simplify reality. Irrelevant details are stripped away to concentrate on essentials. The economist's picture (theory) of preferences is based on two axioms:

1. *The Axiom of Comparison:* A person can compare any two baskets *A* and *B* of commodities. Such a comparison must lead to one of the three following results: he or she (i) prefers basket *A* over *B*, or (ii) prefers basket *B* over *A*, or (iii) is indifferent between *A* and *B*.
2. *The Axiom of Transitivity:* Consider any three baskets *A*, *B*, and *C*. If a consumer prefers *A* to *B*, and also prefers *B* to *C*, he or she must prefer *A* to *C*. Similarly, a person who is indifferent between *A* and *B*, and is also indifferent between *B* and *C*, must be indifferent between *A* and *C*.

Each of these axioms simplifies reality. The Axiom of Comparison does not permit a person to say "I just can't decide," even though that does sometimes happen. As for the Axiom of Transitivity, the Example that follows provides some indication as to when the axiom might or might not be valid.

EXAMPLE 3.1 TRANSITIVITY AND AGE

The psychologists Hinton Bradbury and Karen Ross[a] asked children of various ages, and also some adults, for their color preferences among square patches of red, green, and blue offered in a variety of sequences. In a fraction of cases transitivity was violated. A child choosing red over green, and then green over blue, might next time choose blue over red. As the table shows, the proportion of intransitive choices declined notably with age.

Intransitivity and age

Age	Number of subjects	% Intransitive choices
4	39	83%
5	33	82
6	23	82
7	35	78
8	40	68

9	52	57
10	45	52
11	65	37
12	81	23
13	81	41
Adults	99	13

Source: Adapted from Bradbury and Ross, Table 1.

COMMENT

At very low ages, transitivity failures might arguably be due to the limited reasoning abilities of young children. As another possible explanation, what appear to be intransitivities may only reflect that fact that younger persons are still exploring their needs and tastes. "Don't knock it until you've tried it" is a dangerous maxim, but has a degree of validity. Young children have more to learn, so it makes sense for them to be more strongly inclined toward experimenting with novelties. So supposing that Margie has chosen red over green and then chosen green over blue, she can try out blue only by violating transitivity, by choosing blue over red next time.

Although the tabulated percentages of intransitive choices steadily decrease with rising age, there is one exception: the sudden sharp increase at age 13. Perhaps the onset of puberty opens up new types of novelties calling for exploration.

[a] Hinton Bradbury and Karen Ross, "The Effects of Novelty and Choice Materials on the Intransitivity of Preferences of Children and Adults," *Annals of Operations Research*, 23(1990), 141–159.

The economist's laws of preferences are not "purely academic." Someone who violates them can be exploited by a clever swindler. Take the Axiom of Transitivity. Suppose Isaac prefers specific quantities of apples to bananas, and bananas to cherries, but (intransitively) also prefers cherries to apples. Imagine he initially has only cherries. The swindler offers him bananas in exchange for a small fee x. Since Isaac prefers the bananas to cherries, he is willing to make the exchange and pay the fee. Now holding bananas, Isaac would be willing to pay another fee y to obtain apples in place of the bananas. Last, holding only apples, he would be willing to pay a third fee z to obtain cherries instead. But now Isaac is back where he started, with cherries, but poorer by the dollar amount $x + y + z$!

The Axiom of Comparison and the Axiom of Transitivity taken together lead to the:

PROPOSITION OF RANK ORDERING OF PREFERENCES: A consumer can consistently rank all baskets of commodities in order of preference. This ranking is called "the preference function."

EXERCISE 3.1

Jane prefers basket A, consisting of one beer and one taco, to either (i) basket B, consisting of two beers alone, or (ii) basket T, consisting of two tacos alone. Comparing the last two baskets, suppose she would rather have two beers than two tacos. Do these facts indicate that the Axiom of Comparison and the Axiom of Transitivity apply for Jane, at least among the three combinations described? If they do apply, what is her rank ordering of preferences?

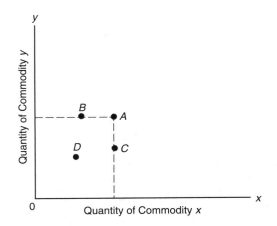

Figure 3.1. Alternative Consumption Baskets

Points *A*, *B*, *C*, and *D* represents different combinations, or baskets, of commodity *X* and commodity *Y*. If *X* and *Y* are both goods, then basket *A* is preferred to any of the other marked points.

ANSWER: As to the Axiom of Comparison, yes, the stated facts show that Jane can compare all three consumption baskets. As to the Axiom of Transitivity, the answer again is yes. Transitivity would tell us that if she prefers the mixed basket over two beers, and two beers over two tacos, she should prefer the mixed basket over two tacos. And we are told that she does. Her rank ordering is clearly first *A*, then *B*, then *T*.

Suppose now you are choosing among combinations of two commodities *X* and *Y*. The amounts *x* and *y* are scaled along the axes in Figure 3.1.[1] Four possible baskets are represented by the points *A*, *B*, *C*, and *D*. The Laws of Preference tell us only two things about this situation: (1) You can rank all four baskets; and (2) If, for example, you prefer basket *A* over *B* and prefer *B* over *C*, then you must also prefer *A* over *C*.

Since *A* contains more of both *X* and *Y*, and we usually think that "more is preferred to less," we might expect a consumer to definitely prefer basket *A* over basket *D*. But "more is preferred to less" is not an axiom of preference. The assertion is obviously false for commodities that are *bads* – such as garbage, pollution, risk, and exhausting labor. "More is preferred to less" is not an axiom; instead, it is the defining characteristic of what economists call a *good*.

> **DEFINITION:** A *good* is a commodity for which more is preferred to less; a *bad* is a commodity for which the reverse holds.

3.2   UTILITY AND PREFERENCE

The term *utility* was introduced by the British philosopher Jeremy Bentham. Bentham declared:

> Nature has placed mankind under the governance of two sovereign masters, *pain* and *pleasure*. . . . The *principle of utility* recognizes this subjection. . . . By the principle of utility is meant that principle which approves or disapproves of every action whatsoever, according to the tendency which it appears to have to augment or diminish the happiness of the party whose interest is in question.[2]

---

[1] Capital letters *X* and *Y* are used here to designate commodities, while lowercase letters *x* and *y* indicate particular quantities of each.

[2] J. Bentham, *An Introduction to the Principles of Morals and Legislation* (1823 edition), Chapter 1.

The modern economic theory of choice does not require us to agree with Bentham that humans seek only to gain pleasure and avoid pain. That is a question for psychology or perhaps philosophy. For economics, it is sufficient to say that the Axiom of Comparison and the Axiom of Transitivity Laws of Preference of the preceding section do generally describe actual behavior.

What modern economists call *utility* reflects nothing more than rank ordering of preference. The statements "Mary prefers basket *A* over basket *B*" and "Basket *A* has higher utility for Mary than basket *B*" mean the same thing. They both lead to the empirical prediction: If Mary is offered a choice between *A* and *B*, other things equal Mary will choose basket *A*. Conversely, if Mary is observed to choose *A* over *B*, economists infer that basket *A* has higher utility for her than basket *B*.

> **DEFINITION:** Utility is the variable whose relative magnitude indicates the direction of preference. In finding his or her preferred position, the individual is said to maximize utility.

Cardinal versus Ordinal Utility

Early economists thought that utility, like length or temperature, could be measured quantitatively. They would have regarded it as perfectly reasonable to construct a diagram like the upper panel of Figure 3.2, where an individual's utility is shown as a function of the amount consumed.

Some economists even believed it possible to add up these "util" numbers interpersonally: 5 of John Doe's utils could be added to 7 of Richard Roe's to give a total of 12 utils for the pair. On this basis, it was thought that correct public policies – how severely to punish crime, whether the rich should be taxed more heavily than the poor – could be scientifically chosen by summing the utils of everyone involved. (This seems to be what Bentham meant in recommending that public policy ought to aim at "the greatest good of the greatest number," a noble-sounding though hardly meaningful expression.) In deciding on length of jail terms, for example, Bentham would weigh the criminal's util loss from imprisonment against the util loss to prospective victims of the additional crimes he might commit if freed earlier. Economists today generally believe that comparing or summing the utilities of different people is meaningless, and cannot be used as a scientific basis for public policy.

A stronger case can be made that utility can be measured for a single individual. First, however, what does it means for a variable to be "quantitatively measurable"? Measurability does not require a unique way of scaling. Temperature can be measured, but a thermometer can be scaled to show degrees in Fahrenheit or else in Celsius. What makes temperature quantitatively measurable is that the Fahrenheit and Celsius scales differ only in zero point and unit interval: 32° Fahrenheit is 0° Celsius, and each degree up or down of Celsius corresponds to 1.8 degrees up or down of Fahrenheit. Similarly, altitude could be measured from sea level or from the center of the earth (shift of zero-point) and in feet or meters (shift of unit interval).

Quantitatively measurable variables such as temperature and altitude are *cardinal* magnitudes. The crucial property is that, regardless of shift of zero point and unit interval, the relative magnitudes of *differences* remain the same. Consider altitude: the height difference between the base and the peak of Mount Everest is greater than the height difference between the ground floor and roof of any manmade building. This remains true whether we scale altitude in feet or in meters and whether we measure from

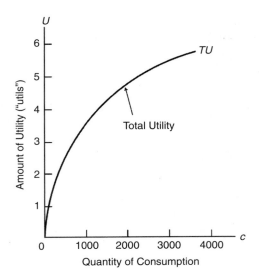

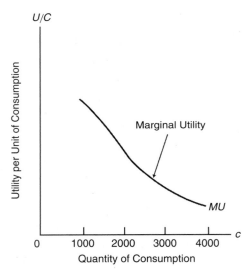

Figure 3.2. Cardinal Utility: Total and Marginal

The Total Utility curve TU in the upper diagram is a "cardinally measurable" utility function. Marginal Utility in the lower diagram can be derived from Total Utility, as explained in Chapter 2. As consumption rises, Total Utility increases but at a decreasing rate, and so Marginal Utility is positive but declining.

sea level or from the center of the earth. Looking at the upper panel of Figure 3.2, which pictures a cardinal utility function for an individual, it does not matter where we place the zero point or what unit interval is chosen for U. Regardless of these specifications, utility rises by more between 1,000 and 2,000 units of consumption than it does between 2,000 and 3,000 units.[3]

---

[3] *Mathematical Footnote*: Two utility scales U and U' are cardinally equivalent if measurements along the two scales are related by the linear equation:

$$U' = a + bU, \quad \text{for } b > 0$$

The constant a here represents the shift of zero point, and the constant b the change in unit interval. Consider three quantities U_1, U_2, and U_3 along the U scale, where the difference $U_3 - U_2$ exceeds the difference $U_2 - U_1$. Then $U'_3 - U'_2$ also exceeds $U'_2 - U'_1$, as can be verified by direct substitution. Thus for all cardinally equivalent scales, the *ranking of differences* is the same.

Utility in the upper diagram of Figure 3.2 is a *total* function of consumption *C*. The corresponding *Marginal Utility* function, following the discussion in Chapter 2, is the slope or rate of change of the Total Utility function, as shown in the lower panel of Figure 3.2. Since the Total Utility function as drawn in the upper panel rises throughout, Marginal Utility is always positive. But since the Total Utility curve increases *at a decreasing rate*, the Marginal Utility curve is falling as consumption increases. This property is called *diminishing Marginal Utility*.[4] In commonsense terms, you'd probably get more of a thrill from your first million dollars than from your tenth.

One possible way of measuring cardinal utility is by asking people "How happy are you?" Such surveys tend to confirm that Marginal Utility is positive, and that people's preferences are consistent with the principle of diminishing Marginal Utility.

EXAMPLE 3.2 INCOME AND HAPPINESS?

In a study by Richard Easterlin in 1994, American respondents were asked to rate themselves on a happiness scale.[a] As shown in Table 1, "life satisfaction" was reported as rising sharply with income. Table 2 is derived from a 1984 survey by the same author comparing satisfaction scores for 24 different nations, as related to per capita GNP.[b] The second study shows that, *across* different nations, greater average per capita incomes once again were associated with higher reported levels of satisfaction.

Table 1: Relative income and life satisfaction in the United States, 1994

Total household income (thousands)	"Very happy"	"Pretty happy"	"Not too happy"
Less than $10	16	62	23
$10–20	21	64	15
$20–30	27	61	12
$30–40	31	61	8
$40–50	31	59	10
$50–75	36	58	7
Greater than $75	44	49	6

Source: Adapted from Table 1 in Easterlin (2001).

Table 2: Absolute income and life satisfaction (across nations), 1984

GNP per capita	Number of nations	Median "satisfaction" score
< $2,000	1	5.5
$2,000–4,000	3	6.6
$4,000–8,000	6	7.0
$8,000–16,000	14	7.4

Source: Estimated visually from Easterlin (1995), Figure 3.4.

---

[4] *Mathematical Footnote:* Let utility be a function of consumption *c*. Since $U' = a + bU$, and *b* is positive, positive Marginal Utility according to the *U* scale ($dU/dc > 0$) implies positive Marginal Utility according to the U' scale ($dU'/dc = bdU/dc > 0$). Note that a change in zero point *a* does not affect Marginal Utility at all, and a change in unit interval *b* changes it only by the same positive multiplicative constant everywhere. *Diminishing* Marginal Utility according to the *U* scale ($d^2U/dc^2 < 0$) similarly implies diminishing Marginal Utility according to the U' scale.

COMMENT

Both tables suggest that utility, as measured by reported "satisfaction," consistently rises with income. That is, the Marginal Utility of income is positive. There is also an indication of *diminishing* marginal utility. In Table 2, for example, a comparison of the second and third rows shows that a doubling of per capita GNP is associated with only a small rise in national satisfaction level, from 6.6 to 7.0 – an improvement of only about 6%.

[a] Richard A. Easterlin, "Income and Happiness: Towards a Unified Theory," *The Economic Journal*, v. 111 (July 2001).

[b] Richard A. Easterlin, "Will Raising the Incomes of All Increase the Happiness of All?" *Journal of Economic Behavior and Organization*, v. 27 (1995).

Another possible indicator of utility is expected life span. It seems reasonable that, other things being equal, people who expect to live longer are happier. And we know that people do generally try to live longer. Life expectancy is a biological measure of well-being. Another biological measure is what students of evolution call *reproductive success* (*RS*): the offspring/parent ratio from one generation to the next at corresponding phases in the life cycle. (Thus, a population with $RS = 2$ would double in size each generation.) Evolutionists argue that the bodily form and the biochemistry and behavior of all living beings can be explained by the assumption that natural selection operates to maximize each organism's reproductive success in competition with all the others. Notice that maximizing reproductive success does not mean simply living as long as possible, or having as many offspring as possible; the point is to have the maximum number of offspring *surviving* into the next generation.

So, in a sense, reproductive success is what "Mother Nature" (that is, biological evolution) uses as its utility function for natural species. Does this biological utility measure have any relevance for modern human beings? That question will be taken up when the sources and content of people's preferences are examined later on in the chapter. But it is worth noting here that a utility scale can be analytically useful even if the organism involved does not *consciously* maximize it. Birds do not design their superb eyesight, or bats their excellent hearing. Mother Nature, by selecting these patterns for survival, is doing the designing. Yet if postulating that living organisms maximize reproductive success permits accurate predictions of bodily shape or of behavior, one can say that reproductive survival *RS* serves as a utility function. Similarly, human preferences may be described by utility functions even if individuals are unaware of pursuing any definite plan or goal.

EXAMPLE 3.3 PREFERENCES FOR BRIDES AMONG THE KIPSIGIS

The anthropologist Monique Borgerhoff Mulder studied the marital practices of the Kipsigis people of Kenya in the period 1940–1973.[a] In this polygynous society men had to buy wives. The "bridewealth" required to obtain a wife was generally a very substantial expenditure, around one-third of an average man's wealth. The bridewealth was paid in the form of cows, goats, and (after 1960) Kenyan shillings.

Early-maturing women commanded higher prices. The explanation offered by the author was that a man purchasing such a bride could anticipate higher reproductive success (*RS*). Not only is an early-maturing woman able to commence bearing children earlier, but she is likely to be in better health to begin with. The table here classifies 130 reported bridewealth payments (in "cow-equivalents") into upper, middle, and lower price groups – divided between early-maturing and late-maturing women. The first row, for example, shows that of the 46 cases where high prices were paid, 32 were on behalf of early-maturing women. The bottom row indicates that of the 42 brides for whom low prices were paid, 28 were on behalf of late-maturing women.

Bridewealth payments among the Kipsigis (cow equivalents)

	Early-maturing women	Late-maturing women
High price	32	14
Average price	19	23
Low price	14	28

Source: Estimated visually from Figure 5 in Borgerhoff Mulder.

[a] Monique Borgerhoff Mulder, "Early Maturing Kipsigis Women have Higher Reproductive Success than Late Maturing Women and Cost More to Marry," *Behavioral Ecology and Sociobiology*, v. 24 (1989).

For many purposes, however, it is not necessary to measure preferences cardinally. Instead, an "ordinal" concept of utility suffices. Under ordinal utility, a person may prefer basket A to basket B, and basket C to D, but need not be able to say "I prefer A over B *more* than I prefer C over D." If Total Utility is only an ordinal magnitude, whether Marginal Utility is positive or negative can still be determined, but not whether Marginal Utility is rising or falling. That last step would involve comparing utility differences. As will be seen shortly, ordinal utility suffices for analyzing most consumption choices.

Utility of Commodity Baskets

Figure 3.3 pictures a *cardinal* function $U(x, y)$ for two goods, X and Y. The quantities x and y are scaled along the two axes. If utility is cardinal, its magnitude (in "utils") can also be quantified as the height above the base plane. When $x = x_1$ and $y = y_2$, for example, utility is the height TT'. If the quantity of Y is held constant at $y = y_1$, how utility varies with x is shown by the curve PQR lying on the utility surface. If Y is held constant at $y = y_2$ instead, there is a similar curve STU; or if Y is held constant at $y = y_3$, we see the curve BVG. Each curve is shown as always rising (Total Utility increases as x increases); the Marginal Utility of X is therefore positive throughout. (X is a *good* rather than a *bad*.) Similarly, the rising curves OPB, WQV, and ARG show that the Marginal Utility of commodity Y is also always positive.

Typically, consumer preferences for goods are *interdependent*. (Your desire for another pound of butter varies with how much bread you will be eating.) In the illustration here, the Marginal Utility of X at the point T (i.e., when $x = x_1$ and $y = y_2$) is shown by the slope at point T along the curve STU. This is not necessarily the same as the Marginal Utility of X at the point V (where $x = x_1$ as before, but $y = y_3$), which is the slope at V along BVG. So the Marginal Utility of X may depend on the quantity of Y, and vice versa.[5]

[5] *Mathematical Footnote:* Where Utility $U(x, y)$ is a function of amounts consumed of both X and Y, the Marginal Utilities are defined as partial derivatives: $MU_x \equiv \partial U/\partial x$ and $MU_y \equiv \partial U/\partial y$. In general, the Marginal Utility

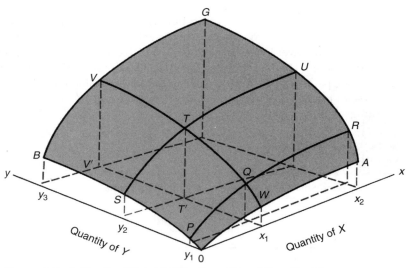

Figure 3.3. A Cardinal Total Utility Function of Two Goods

Utility is measured up from the base plane; the horizontal axes x and y represent quantities consumed of commodities X and Y. The curves OA, PR, SU, and BG along the surface show how Total Utility changes as x increases, holding y constant (at a different level for each curve). Similarily the curves OB, WV, and AG show how Total Utility changes as y increases, holding x constant.

The cardinal utility function of Figure 3.3 is pictured again in Figure 3.4. But now a different set of curves are drawn on the surface: CC, DD, and EE are contours connecting points of equal height on the "utility hill." These contours are therefore *curves of constant utility*, also called *indifference curves*.

Figure 3.5 pictures the same utility function again, but with the third vertical dimension suppressed. The indifference curves, contours of equal heights on the now invisible "utility hill," are shown in two dimensions as in a topographic map. The arrows in the diagram indicate the *preference directions*. (By assumption, X and Y here are both goods, so – as indicated by the arrows – "more is preferred to less" applies here to both X and Y.) The indifference curves, together with the preference directions, are all that are needed to determine how a consumer ranks baskets of goods.

The geometrical step of deleting the vertical utility dimension of Figure 3.4 corresponds to the shift from *cardinal* utility to *ordinal* utility. In terms of ordinal utility the only meaningful comparisons concern how baskets of commodities are *ranked*.[6] Two possible cardinal preference scales, U and U', are used to label the indifference curves of Figure 3.5, but the two scales are equivalent in the ordinal sense. Why? Because they give the same answers (i) as to which baskets are equal in utility (whether they lie along the same indifference curve) and (ii) as to how baskets that are unequal in utility should be ranked (what are the preference directions).

---

of each commodity will be a function of both x and y; that is, the cross-derivative $\partial^2 U/\partial x \partial y$ will not ordinarily be zero.

[6] *Mathematical Footnote:* If the two utility scales are only ordinally equivalent, all we can say is that $U' = F(U)$ and $dU'/dU = F'(U)$, where $F'(U) > 0$. Nevertheless, the positive derivative dU'/dU always preserves rankings of *magnitudes*. So if $U_1 > U_2$, then the same holds true on the U' scale: $U_1' > U_2'$.

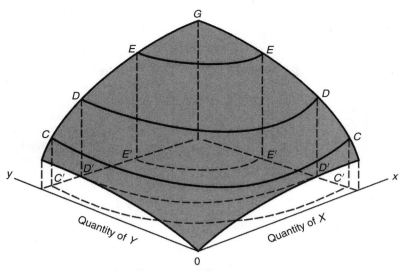

Figure 3.4. Cardinal Utility and Indifference Curves

The surface here is the same as in the preceding diagram, but the curves *along* the surface (*CC*, *DD*, *EE*) are contours that connect points of equal heights (levels of utility). The projections of these curves onto the base plane (the dashed *C′C′*, *D′D′*, *E′E′*) are indifference curves.

3.3 CHARACTERISTICS OF INDIFFERENCE CURVES

If *X* and *Y* are both *goods*, commodities for which more is preferred to less, then indifference curves drawn on *x,y* axes have four crucial properties.

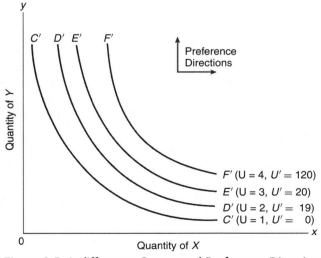

Figure 3.5. Indifference Curves and Preference Directions: Ordinal Utility

Here the cardinal (vertical) scaling of utility has been stripped away, leaving the indifference curves. These indifference curves, together with the preference directions, provide all the information needed to rank alternative consumption baskets in terms of *ordinal* utility.

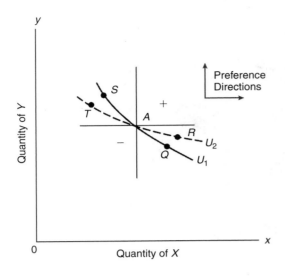

Figure 3.6. Properties of Indifference Curves

The preference directions indicate that every point in the + region is preferred to A, whereas A is preferred over every point in the − region. It follows that any indifference curve through A must have negative slope. Also, there can be only one indifference curve through A, because intersecting indifference curves violate transitivity of preference.

1. *Negative slope*: In the ordinal-utility diagram of Figure 3.6, each point corresponds to a particular basket of goods X and Y. Given the preference directions, starting with the basket represented by some point A, the consumer would prefer all points to the northeast (above and to the right) of A. Similarly, the consumer would prefer point A to all points that lie southwest (below and to the left) of A. It follows that all points *indifferent* to A must lie either southeast of A (like points R and Q) or else northwest of it (like points S and T). Thus an indifference curve passing through point A cannot lie within either the + or the − region shown in Figure 3.6. So any indifference curve cutting through A must necessarily have negative slope, like curves U_1 or U_2 in the diagram.[7]

2. *Indifference curves never intersect*: Assume tentatively that two indifference curves such as U_1 and U_2 do actually intersect at point A. This leads to a contradiction. Indifference curve U_1 states that the consumer is indifferent between baskets A and Q. Indifference curve U_2 states that the consumer is indifferent between A and R. By transitivity, the consumer must therefore be indifferent between Q and R. But R represents more of both commodities than Q. Since X and Y are both goods, more is preferred to less, and the consumer must prefer R over Q. But these two implications contradict one another. So the initial assumption is invalid; indifference curves cannot intersect.

3. *Coverage of indifference curves*: An indifference curve passes through each point in commodity space. In other words, between any two indifference curves another can always be drawn. The real number system has a corresponding property. Between any two numbers such as 17.4398 and 17.4399 there is always another

---

[7] *Mathematical Footnote*: In terms of calculus, along any indifference curve utility $U(x,y)$ is constant. So:

$$0 = dU \equiv \partial U/\partial x \, dx + \partial U/\partial y \, dy$$

Then the slope along the indifference curve is:

$$\left. \frac{dy}{dx} \right|_U = \frac{-\partial U/\partial x}{\partial U/\partial y}$$

Since $\partial U/\partial x$ and $\partial U/\partial y$ are both positive (X and Y are both *goods* with positive Marginal Utilities), the slope dy/dx is negative.

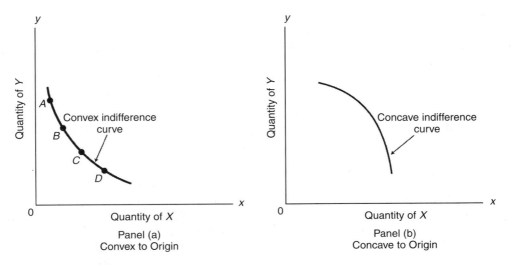

Figure 3.7. Convexity and Concavity

Between two goods, indifference curves must have negative slope. Curvature may be "convex to origin" as in panel (a), or "concave to origin" as in panel (b). The convex case is normally observed, even though concavity would not necessarily violate the laws of preference.

number such as 17.43987 larger than the first and smaller than the second. The coverage property is equivalent to the Axiom of Comparison, which says it is always possible to compare any baskets of commodities. It follows that any basket must lie on *some* indifference curve.[8] (A diagram can only show a selection of the indifference curves; to show them all, the picture would have to be solid black.)

4. *Indifference curves are convex to the origin*: The two panels of Figure 3.7 show the curvatures defined as "convex" and "concave" to the origin. The convex curve of Panel (a) represents the standard shape. A curve is convex if the straight line that connects any two points on it lies above the curve. For example, if the line segment *BC* in Figure 3.7(a) were plotted it would lie above the indifference curve. Correspondingly, a curve is concave if the straight line that connects any two points on it lies below the curve. In contrast with the previous three properties (negative slope, nonintersection, and coverage), convexity cannot be *proved* from the postulates of rational choice. Rather, it is based on the well-established empirical principle of "diversity in consumption," as will be discussed in Chapter 4.

As a commonsense justification for convexity, suppose Panel (a) of Figure 3.7 represents Sally's preferences for food *X* and entertainment *Y*. At point *A* she has plenty of entertainment but little food. To get a bit more food, we would expect her to be willing to sacrifice a fair amount of entertainment *Y*. The diagram shows her as just willing to move from *A* to *B*, giving up (say) 3 units of entertainment *Y* for just 1 unit of food *X*. At *B* her consumption is more diversified. Therefore, she should be less willing than before to give up entertainment for more food. This time she might be willing to give

---

[8] Psychological experiments indicate that below a certain threshold sensations cannot be distinguished from one another. This suggests that indifference curves in actuality have some "width." So indifference curves are an idealization rather than a precise picture of reality. But this is no more disturbing than the fact that the "lines" of Euclid's geometry, having length but no breadth, similarly could not ever actually be drawn in the real world.

up only 2 units of *Y* for 1 unit of *X*. Last, from *C* to *D*, perhaps she is willing to give up only 1 unit of her now scarce entertainment *Y* for 1 unit of food *X*. Thus, the picture in Panel (a) of Figure 3.7 seems to fit normal patterns of preference.

EXERCISE 3.2

(a) John claims that the two equations $xy = 100$ and $x + y = 20$ are both valid indifference curves for him. Can this be correct? (b) What about the curves corresponding to the equations $xy = 100$ and $xy = 200$?

ANSWER: (a) No. The curves corresponding to the two equations $xy = 100$ and $x + y = 20$ intersect at $x = 10$, $y = 10$. This violates the condition that his indifference curves cannot intersect (property 2). (b) The curves $xy = 100$ and $xy = 200$ do not intersect, and so satisfy property 2. You can use algebra or plot the functions to satisfy yourself that both curves have negative slope (property 1) and are convex toward the origin (property 4). So these two curves could both be valid indifference curves for the same person. (Since we are dealing with only two curves, property 3 – coverage – is not relevant here.)

EXAMPLE 3.4 CULTURES AND PREFERENCES

In a pioneering study, a team of two anthropologists and an economist used an ingenious technique to elicit indifference curves for human subjects of different cultural backgrounds.[a] The experimental subjects (all were Cornell University students or their spouses) came from the United States, France, Turkey, Chile, India, Cameroon, and Egypt.

The experimenters asked subjects to express preference ratios between alternative combinations, of shirts and (pairs of) shoes. For example, a subject might indicate a 7:4 preference ratio for the combination 4 shirts + 2 shoe-pairs as against another combination, 3 shirts + 0 shoe-pairs. Each subject expressed preference ratios between 1,176 paired combinations. From these reports a computer was programmed to generate a "best fit" pattern of indifference curves.

Although the computed indifference curves were almost always negatively sloped and convex in curvature, as would be expected, striking individual and cultural differences appeared. One male subject, for example, displayed a "tilt" toward shirts. That is, on a graph with shirts on the horizontal and shoes on the vertical axis, his indifference curves were quite steep. (He was very reluctant to give up shirts for more shoes.) Other individuals were much more balanced. In one case not only was the slope more like 1:1 (the subject was willing to exchange approximately one shirt per shoe-pair), but the indifference curves showed very little convexity – they were almost (though not quite) straight lines. Thus, for this individual shirts and shoes were (almost) perfect substitutes.

Turning to cultural differences, for the Americans the indifference curves tended to be more convex at low levels than at high. For small numbers of these clothing items, there was a strongly preferred ratio (close to 1:1). But when in a position to acquire relatively ample quantities, the American subjects were willing to tolerate a wider spread of ratios – so that combinations such as 4,2 or 3,3 or 2,4 were all almost equally preferred. A Chilean female subject, on the other hand, displayed such a strongly preferred ratio (again near 1:1) that divergence in either direction led to

Figure 3.8. Portfolio Preferences: Indifference Curves between a Good and a Bad

Mean return r on assets is a good, but riskiness of return s is a bad. The preference directions are therefore north and west (up and to the left), so the indifference curves slope upward.

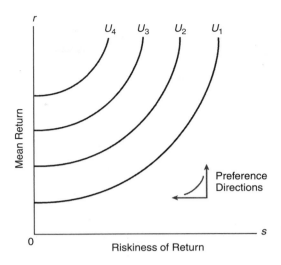

one commodity or the other (whichever was the more plentiful) becoming a "bad" for her.

[a] John M. Roberts, Richard F. Strand, and Edwin Burmeister, "Preferential Pattern Analysis," in Paul Kay, ed., *Explorations in Mathematical Anthropology* (M.I.T. Press, 1971).

3.4   MORE ON GOODS AND BADS

An important application of utility theory is to *portfolio selection* – how a person should balance wealth over assets such as stocks, bonds, and real estate. Portfolios have two main characteristics: (i) a *desired* feature in the form of average percent yield r and (ii) an *undesired* feature in the form of riskiness s. Figure 3.8 shows an investor's preferences over portfolios offering differing combinations of r and s. Note that the preference directions here are up and to the *left*. For the "good" feature r, more is preferred to less. But for the "bad" feature s, less is preferred to more. Given these preference directions, it is easy to see that the indifference curves must have *positive* slope.

Everyday experience also tells us that a commodity can be a good up to a point of satiation, beyond which it becomes a bad. Figure 3.9 pictures such a situation. Commodity Y, let us say shirts, is always a good. But commodity X (think of it as amounts of cake to be eaten in a short time period) is first a good and then a bad.[9]

Last, having more or less of some commodities can sometimes leave a person entirely indifferent. Amounts of such a neutral commodity neither add to nor detract from utility. In the indifference-curve picture of Figure 3.10, Y is a good but X is a neuter commodity.

---

[9] In *Roughing It*, Mark Twain describes a visit with the Mormon leader Brigham Young. After a harrowing day dealing with recriminations and jealousies among his multiple spouses, Young supposedly said to his visitor: "My friend, . . . don't encumber yourself with a large family . . . Take my word for it, ten to eleven wives is all you need." Presumably, Brigham Young found that, after the 11th, wives became a bad. [*Note:* This was probably a fictionalized account.]

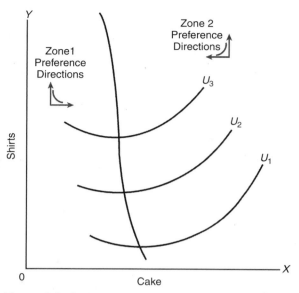

Figure 3.9. Satiation

In Zone 1 both commodities, X and Y, are goods, so the indifference curves have negative slope. Zone 2 is the region of satiation for Y; in this region the preference directions are north and west (up and to the left), and the indifference curves have positive slope. In this region an individual would have to be paid to eat another piece of cake.

EXERCISE 3.4

For each of the following possible algebraic utility functions, indicate whether each commodity is a good, a bad, or a neuter: (a) $U = xy$; (b) $U = x/y$; (c) $U = 2xy/y$.

ANSWER: (a) Since $U = xy$ rises as either x increases or y increases, both X and Y are goods. (b) Here U rises with x but falls as y increases, so X is a good and Y is a bad. (c) Here y cancels out, and the utility function becomes $U = 2x$. So X is a good, but Y is a neuter commodity (utility does not depend at all upon y).

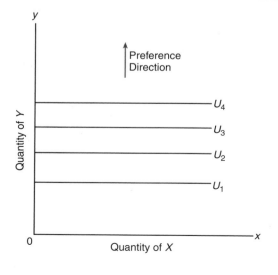

Figure 3.10. A Neuter Commodity

Y is a good, but X is a neuter commodity. The consumer does not care about having more or less of X. The only preference direction is up, and so the indifference curves are horizontal.

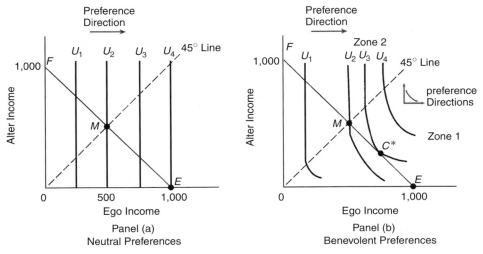

Figure 3.11. Preference and Utility

If Ego preferences are as pictured in panel (a), Alter income is a neuter commodity for me. Then I would never give charity to him. If panel (b) pictures Ego preferences, I may give charity, but only to someone poorer than myself. (Alter income is a good for me below the 45° line, but it is a neuter commodity for me above the 45° line.)

An Application: Charity

The following observations can be made about charity: (1) Not everyone contributes. (2) But a great many people do. (3) Almost always, contributors donate to persons poorer than themselves. Can we construct an indifference-curve picture consistent with these observations?

Figure 3.11 has axes "Ego's Income" and "Alter's Income" (where Ego is the person whose indifference curves are being described and Alter is any other person). Since we are dealing solely with Ego's preferences, Alter's feelings are not involved in the picture. Imagine first that Ego is completely unconcerned with Alter's well-being. For Ego, "Alter's Income" is a neuter commodity. This is the situation pictured in Panel (a) of Figure 3.11. Since "Ego's Income" is surely a good for Ego, the only preference direction is to the right. On these axes Ego's indifference curves are vertical.

With preferences as pictured in Panel (a), would Ego ever give charity to Alter? Suppose Ego is initially at point E in Panel (a) with an income of 1,000 units while Alter has an income of zero. Imagine that Ego can transfer income to Alter, dollar for dollar. In the diagram, this means Ego can move to any point along the line EMF with slope -1. But any such movement from point E must evidently put Ego on a lower indifference curve, and hence would not be undertaken.

Panel (b) of Figure 3.11 pictures a more interesting situation. Suppose Ego is benevolent, but only to *people poorer than herself*. The points where Alter is poorer than Ego all lie below the dashed 45° line (Zone 1 in the diagram). In this zone "Alter's Income" is a good for Ego. Since "Ego's Income" is of course always a good for Ego, the preference directions are north and east – up and to the right. Both commodities are goods, and the indifference curves have their usual negative slopes. So an Ego initially at E would now transfer some income to Alter, specifically an amount just enough to attain point

C^* along the line *EMF*. Why? Because C^* is the point along *EMF* where Ego can get onto her highest attainable indifference curve (U_3).

In contrast, suppose the initial situation is in Zone 2 of Panel (b), at some point above and to the left of point *M* along the line *EMF*. Since this range is above the 45° line, here Alter is richer than Ego. So Ego would be unwilling to transfer any income to Alter. As pictured, Ego is not actually malevolent to Alter. If she were malevolent her indifference curves in Zone 2 would have positive slope. (Alter's income would be a bad for Ego.) But Ego's indifference curves in the diagram are vertical in Zone 2, meaning that in this range Alter's income is merely a neuter commodity for Ego.

EXAMPLE 3.5 CHARITY AND INCOME

If people make charitable contributions mainly to recipients poorer than themselves, giving will be positively correlated with income. The table here extracts some data from a study of charitable contributions in 1994. Notice that the percentage of families making some contribution does indeed rise quite steadily with income. The average dollar amount in each bracket (taking into account the zero contributions of those not participating) also increases. As a percentage of family income, however, the rise is quite slow until very high income brackets are reached.

Charitable giving in 1994 – selected income levels[a]

Family income	% contributing	Average contribution, $	Average as % of income
$10,000–19,999	64	209	1.36
$30,000–39,999	80	474	1.37
$50,000–59,999	84	779	1.44
$100,000–124,999	92	1,846	1.71
$150,000–199,999	96	3,546	2.09
$500,000–999,999	97	27,491	4.15
> $1,000,000	100	244,586	4.88
Overall	75	960	2.14

Source: Data selected from Table 1 of Paul G. Schervish and John J. Havens, "Wealth and the Commonwealth: New Findings on Wherewithal and Philanthropy," *Nonprofit and Voluntary Sector Quarterly*, v. 30 (March 2001).

3.5   THE SOURCES AND CONTENT OF PREFERENCES

Why do people want some things and not others? Why are our desires for some goods easily satiated, for others not? How and why do tastes vary with age, ethnic origins, and circumstances?

Preferences are not always difficult to explain. It is easy to predict that iced drinks will be more popular in Georgia than in Alaska, that baby diapers will not be a big merchandising item in a retirement community, that pickled herring will sell best in Jewish neighborhoods and soul food in Harlem. But what are the bases for these commonsense judgments?

On the most fundamental level, human beings resemble other animals who seek (and so can be said to have preferences for) survival and comfort. We like to keep our skins intact, our body parts connected up, and our blood temperatures close to 98.6°F.

Physical considerations such as these broadly explain human desires for food, shelter, and protection against injury.

As already mentioned, evolutionary biologists contend that natural selection has shaped all our preferences, with the ultimate goal of maximizing reproductive success:

> Instead of a disorganized list of items that we may care to invest ourselves in, such as children, leisure time, sexual enjoyment, food, friendship, and so on, Darwin's theory says that all of these activities are expected to be organized eventually toward the production of surviving offspring.
> — Robert Trivers, *Social Evolution*, 1985, p. 21.

On the other hand, it is not immediately clear how evolutionary considerations translate into specific likes or dislikes for three-piece suits or Levi's, pizza or sushi, split-level houses or mobile homes. Cultural and accidental elements are also involved. Biological factors are particularly relevant for *interpersonal attitudes*, why we incline to help some people and refrain from helping others. The leading fact here is that people are especially keen to help their own children. This of course is consistent with the evolutionary need to maximize reproductive success. Organisms that help their own offspring rather than others' offspring have left more descendants over the generations. So it is not surprising that, other things being equal, people are especially inclined to aid and support their own biological offspring.

EXAMPLE 3.6 ARE STEPMOTHERS WICKED?

In fairy tales such as "Cinderella," stepmothers have a bad reputation. Might that possibly have some factual basis, at least in terms of statistical averages? Anne Case, I-Fen Lin, and Sara McLanahan compared food consumption in families with various patterns of biological and nonbiological children.[a] Concentrating upon the mother (the parent mainly responsible for food purchases and preparation), in a regression analysis they examined how family status related to family food expenditures. Some of the results are shown in the table.

Food consumption at home, 1972–1985, as related to family structure (mean = $4,305)

Variable	Adjustment of mean (dollars)
Child with adoptive mother	−204
Child with stepmother	−274
Child with foster mother and father	−365

Source: Extracted from Table 1 of Case, Lin, and McLanahan.

These data indicate, for example, that – holding constant other important variables such as family income and family size – replacing a single biological child with an adopted child is on average associated with a reduction of $204 on family food expenditures. With two adopted children in place of two biological children the difference would become $408, and so on.

The distinctions among the three different types of nonbiological children also make sense. On average we are not surprised that a nonbiological parent committing herself to formal adoption is likely to be more intensely concerned with that child than someone who remains merely a stepmother, and this consideration holds with even greater force when the comparison is with foster children (where parental care is in effect a hired service).

Apart from the fact that statistical averages paint an unjust picture of the many deeply loving and self-sacrificing nonbiological parents, a number of other considerations may also be involved. One is that families with nonbiological children are liable to have a number of other problems – for example, expenses connected with divorce and noncustodial child care – that may make it difficult for them to spend as much on children's food. Another is that aggregating food expenditures at the family level does not reveal possible *differential* treatment of biological and nonbiological children, and this is after all the crucial point (as brought out in the Cinderella story). And finally, the authors suggest, in view of the current problem of child obesity it is conceivable that lower expenditures on food may in many cases be on balance beneficial – so that the nonbiological mothers might be actually helping rather than slighting the children concerned.

[a] Anne Case, I-Fen Lin, and Sara McLanahan, "Household Resource Allocation in Stepfamilies: Darwin Reflects on the Plight of Cinderella," *American Economic Review*, v. 89 (May 1999).

The data in Example 3.6 suggest, without being necessarily fully convincing, that stepmothers slight children in their care. How about stepfathers? Suggestive evidence comes from England. In a sample of 29 babies fatally battered by male parents, 15 of the men involved (52%) were stepfathers – even though overall, fewer than 1% of such babies lived with their stepfathers. Thus the relative risk of fatal battery was over 15 times as great for stepfathers as compared with birth fathers![10] (Lest this give the wrong impression, it must be remembered that such child killings remain very rare. The great preponderance of stepfathers and stepmothers are loving and concerned parents.)

Biological influences upon parental choices may be reflected in subtler ways, as the following Example indicates.

EXAMPLE 3.7 LEGACIES

Debra S. Judge and Sarah Blaffer Hrdy[a] studied the legacies left in their wills by 1,538 male and female testators in Sacramento for the period 1890–1984. The table here illustrates some of their results for male and female testators who left both a surviving spouse and children.

Percent allocations

	Male testator	Female testator
% to spouse	69.8%	42.4%
% to children	21.7%	47.6%
Total	91.5%	90.0%

Apart from the obvious fact that decedents of both sexes left 90% or more of their estates to their immediate families – spouses or children – the feature of the table calling for explanation is that men left relatively more to their spouses, women relatively more to the children. The authors suggest a biological explanation. Since

[10] Martin Daly and Margo Wilson, *Homicide* (New York: Aldine de Gruyter, 1988), pp. 89–90. The fatality data are attributed to a study by P. D. Scott published in 1973.

men remain fertile longer than women, widows are less likely than widowers to be still of reproductive age. So a male testator could allocate wealth to his widow with considerable confidence that she will use the money only for the benefit of their joint biological offspring. But a widower is quite likely to remarry and have additional children with a new spouse. So when a woman leaves a legacy to her husband, the resources he inherits might well be converted to the benefit of the offspring of a later wife, possibly at the expense of her own offspring.

COMMENT

Although the biological explanation for leaving inheritances to offspring is plausible, it is not the only possibility. Arguably, it might be that the determining factor is not relatedness but rather simple *propinquity*, the fact that people get to love and identify with the children with whom they live until maturity. If people were forced to bring up one another's offspring rather than their own, perhaps decedents would leave their estates to their adoptive rather than to their birth children. And mothers giving relatively more to children than fathers do may similarly only reflect the fact that mothers spend more time with their children, hence are more closely bonded to them.

[a] Debra S. Judge and Sarah Blaffer Hrdy, "Allocation of Accumulated Resources among Close Kin: Inheritance in Sacramento, California, 1890–1984," *Ethology and Sociobiology*, v. 13 (1992).

Biologically founded preferences, such as benevolence toward one's children, are quite stable and permanent. In contrast, the kinds of tastes reflected in fashions are notoriously volatile. When it comes to skirt lengths or dance styles or popular songs, what is "in" this year is almost sure to be "out" next year. Somewhat intermediate between the two are long-lived cultural trends. Among these are, in the field of dress, the last century's movement toward light and informal attire, and in art, the movement away from realism and toward abstraction. In accordance with the analysis of Chapter 2, such changes in tastes increase the demand for some commodities, whose prices therefore tend to rise, while reducing the demand for other commodities, whose prices tend to fall.

EXAMPLE 3.8 MODERN ART AND THE TASTE FOR INNOVATION

Beginning in the latter half of the 19th century, new artistic movements such as impressionism and expressionism began to displace traditional representational styles in both critical and popular esteem. David W. Galenson and Bruce A. Weinberg[a] interpreted this development as a general increase in the demand for innovation, in turn associated with the ongoing drastic changes in technology, fashions, and morals that were taking place within society at large. An increase in the demand for artistic innovation would imply a comparative fall in the value that art purchasers placed upon pictorial works reflecting maturity and experience – as opposed to novelty and shock value.

Table 1 documents this change in the light of the ages at which French artists, born in various 19th-century cohorts, found their paintings achieving peak market values. The first cohort, born in the 1820s, received highest prices for paintings that were executed at the rather mature age of 46.6 years. But for the cohort born 60 years later, artists on average received their highest prices for paintings produced at the remarkably low age of 27.0 years.

Ages at which French artists' paintings achieved peak market value

Birth period	Peak age
1820–1839	46.6
1840–1859	37.0
1860–1879	28.8
1880–1900	27.0

Source: Adapted from Galenson and Weinberg, Table 4.

[a] David W. Galenson and Bruce A Weinberg, "Creating Modern Art: The Changing Careers of Painters in France from Impressionism to Cubism," *American Economic Review*, v. 91 (Sept. 2001).

SUMMARY   In choosing a preferred consumption basket, a person is said to maximize utility.

Preferences over different baskets of goods are assumed to obey two fundamental laws: (1) the Axiom of Comparison (a person can compare all possible pairs of consumption baskets) and (2) the Axiom of Transitivity (a person who prefers basket A to B, and prefers B to C, will prefer A to C). These two laws together imply that a person can rank all conceivable consumption baskets in order of preference.

If differences in utility, moving from one basket to another, can be measured, then utility is said to be a *cardinal* magnitude and Marginal Utility can be defined. Common-sense evidence indicates that, beyond a certain level, the Marginal Utility associated with income generally or with any commodity in particular begins to decline. But for many purposes in economics it suffices to merely ask whether the consumer prefers one basket over another, without measuring the size of the difference. If so, an *ordinal* concept of utility is being used. Indifference curves require only ordinal utility.

Each indifference curve connects baskets that the consumer views as equally desirable. Between pairs of goods, indifference curves have four properties: (1) each has a negative slope; (2) they do not intersect; (3) some indifference curve goes through each point; (4) each indifference curve is convex (a straight line connecting any two points on an indifference curve lies above the curve).

"More is preferred to less" is the defining characteristic of a commodity that is a *good*. For a *bad*, less is preferred to more.

Human preferences, and notably our desires to help our own offspring, are in part the outcome of the evolved history of the human species. But a host of historical and cultural and accidental factors, not yet fully understood, are also involved in generating our tastes and desires.

QUESTIONS

[†]The answers to daggered questions appear at the end of the book.

For Review

[†]1. Bill is offered a choice between a ski trip to Aspen and four cases of Cutty Sark whiskey. Which of the following possible responses violate the laws of preference?

    a.   "They're so different, I can't choose."

  b. "I don't care, you choose for me."

  c. "Whichever I choose, I know I'll be sorry."

2. Name a commodity that is a good for many people, but is a bad for you. Name a commodity that is a good for you, but only up to a point; after that it becomes a bad.

3. Draw possible indifference maps between the following:

  a. Two goods.

  b. A good and a bad.

  c. A good and a neuter.

  d. A good and a commodity that is a good up to a point, but then becomes a bad.

†4. What do modern economists mean by the term *utility*?

5. Given a "cardinal" (quantitatively measurable) Total Utility function, show how a corresponding Marginal Utility function is derived.

†6. What can be said about the Marginal Utility function if Total Utility is given only in "ordinal" terms?

7. What are the four essential properties of indifference curves between two goods? Explain the justification for each of the four properties.

†8. Which of the following requires only *ordinal* utility, which requires *cardinal* utility, and which requires *interpersonal comparability* of cardinal utilities?

  a. Indifference curves can be drawn.

  b. A Marginal Utility function can be used to see numerically how Total Utility changes as consumption of a good increases.

  c. It can be determined which person is most desirous of receiving a particular prize.

†9. In suppressing the "cardinal" dimension of the utility hill so as to picture preferences only in terms of indifference curves, why is it necessary also to indicate the preference directions?

For Further Thought and Discussion

†1. Why isn't it possible to give an exact meaning in utility terms to the expression "greatest good of the greatest number"?

†2. An example of an ordinal measure is the military rank system. A sergeant has more authority than a private, a lieutenant more than a sergeant, and so on. Give another example of an ordinal scale of magnitude.

3. Since you probably would not want to eat pickles and ice cream together, does it follow that your indifference curves between these two goods are concave rather than convex?

†4. For "His Income" and "My Income" regarded as goods, what shape for the indifference curves would correspond to the Golden Rule ("Love thy neighbor as thyself")?

†5. In surveys of income and happiness (see Example 3.3), a puzzling discrepancy has been noted. Although higher income is associated with higher reported happiness *at a moment in time*, this conclusion does not seem to hold for comparisons *over time*. Even though wealth has risen over the years in the United States all across the scale, so that both rich and poor have higher incomes than before, reports on happiness do not average higher than before. The most natural explanation of this paradox is that happiness is more powerfully affected by relative income status than by absolute income. The poor consume more than before, but are still on the bottom of the heap and so still feel just as unhappy. How would you draw the preference map to picture this situation?

6. In Example 3.4 on "Cultural Differences," sketch patterns of indifference curves with the preferences described, putting shirts on the horizontal axis and shoes on the vertical axis.

7. An economics student offered dessert tells his friend and classmate, "The Napoleon would increase my utility more, but the fresh fruit is better for me, so I'll take the fresh fruit." Does this comment reflect an accurate understanding of utility theory?

8. How could a confidence man exploit someone whose preferences violate the Axiom of Comparison? The Axiom of Transitivity?

4 Consumption and Demand

This chapter analyzes consumer decisions. Your choice among different consumption bundles, if you are rational, will depend upon your *preferences* (what you want to do) and your *opportunities* (what you are able to do). And, in a market economy, opportunities will in turn depend upon your income and upon the prices you face. Individual consumption choices respond to all three of these variables: preferences, incomes, and market prices.

THE OPTIMUM OF THE CONSUMER[1]

The Geometry of Consumer Choice

Dealing for simplicity with only two goods, Figure 4.1 shows the baskets of goods X and Y that a consumer with a given income can afford (the shaded triangle). The upper boundary of the shaded area, the *budget line KL*, shows the baskets attainable by a person who spends all of his or her income on the two goods X and Y.

Suppose that Mary's income is $I = \$100$ and that the market prices are $P_x = \$2$ and $P_y = \$1$. Spending all of her income on X, Mary could buy $x = 100/2 = 50$ units. This would put her at point L in the diagram. At the other extreme she could buy $y = 100/1 = 100$ units of good Y (point K). More generally she could afford any combination of X and Y lying on her budget line – the straight line between points K and L.

Prices are usually quoted in terms of money. But it is useful to pierce the veil of money to focus upon the underlying *real* magnitudes. Think of prices and incomes as measured in terms of some standard real good, what economists call a "numeraire" – say, corn. Then the prices P_x and P_y represent amounts of the numeraire (corn) that must be paid to obtain a unit of X or of Y. Similarly, income I is the total amount of the numeraire good available for spending.

If a person spends all of his or her income on goods X and Y, the following equation holds:

$$P_x x + P_y y = I \tag{4.1}$$

Unless indicated to the contrary, it will be understood that the variables x and y cannot be negative. Symbolically: $x \geq 0$, $y \geq 0$. On this understanding, equation (4.1) is the algebraic equivalent of the budget line KL in Figure 4.1. At the vertical intercept (where $x = 0$), point K corresponds to buying I/P_y units of Y. Similarly, at the horizontal intercept (where $y = 0$), point L corresponds to buying I/P_x units of X.

Allowing also for the possibility that some income might not be spent, equation (4.1) becomes an *inequality*:

$$P_x x + P_y y \leq 1 \tag{4.1'}$$

This inequality, again on the understanding that x and y cannot be negative, is the algebraic equivalent of the consumer's opportunity set (the shaded region in Figure 4.1). If X and Y are both *goods* for the consumer (if the preference directions are to the north and east, as shown in Figure 4.1), the individual would clearly prefer baskets along the budget line KL to any in the interior. On the other hand, points in the interior

---

[1] The optimum of the consumer is sometimes rather carelessly referred to as the "equilibrium of the consumer." Such wording blurs the distinction between the two key analytical concepts of microeconomics: *finding an equilibrium* versus *finding an optimum*. An optimum is the best possible action available to a decision-maker. In contrast, an equilibrium represents a balance of the actions of many independent decision-makers, for example, the balance between the overall forces of supply and demand in a market. Individual consumer choice is an optimization problem, not an equilibrium problem.

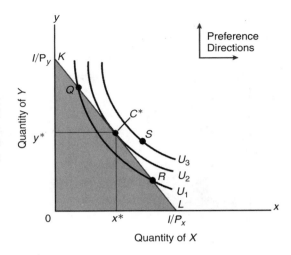

Figure 4.1. Optimum of the Consumer

The shaded region OKL is the consumer's market opportunity set; it is bounded by the horizontal and vertical axes and the budget line KL. The optimum is the point on the budget line KL that lies on the highest attainable indifference curve (point C^* on indifference curve U_2).

might become relevant if other constraints limited the available choices – for example, rationing in wartime (as will be discussed in Chapter 5).

The *slope* of the budget line KL, defined as "rise over run" (see Chapter 2), is the vertical intercept of the line KL (I/P_y) divided by the horizontal intercept (I/P_x). Since an increase in x is associated with a decrease in y, the sign is negative:

$$\text{Slope of budget line} \equiv \left.\frac{\Delta y}{\Delta x}\right|_I \equiv -\frac{I/P_y}{I/P_x} \equiv -\frac{P_x}{P_y} \tag{4.2}$$

In the notation here, Δx and Δy represent small changes in x and y. (The vertical bar with subscript "I" signifies that the slope is measured along a curve or line where income I is held constant.)[2]

EXERCISE 4.1

Suppose the price of apples is $P_a = 10$, the price of beer is $P_b = 2$, and Sam's income is $I = 100$. (a) If Sam consumes only these two goods, what is the equation of his budget line? With beer on the vertical axis, what are the intercepts? What is the slope? (b) What would happen if, with income unchanged, the price of apples were halved? (c) What if, with the original prices unchanged, income doubles?

ANSWER: (a) The equation of the budget line is $10a + 2b = 100$. The vertical b-intercept is $100/2 = 50$; the horizontal a-intercept is $100/10 = 10$. The slope is $-50/10 = -5$. (b) If P_a is halved, the equation of the budget line becomes $5a + 2b = 100$. The a-intercept becomes 20 instead of 10; the b-intercept is unchanged. Geometrically, the budget line swings out to the right from the unchanged vertical intercept, with a new flatter slope equal to $-50/20 = -2.5$. (c) If income doubles while the original prices are unchanged, the equation of the budget line becomes $10a + 2b = 200$. Both intercepts double. Geometrically, the budget line retains the old slope $-100/20 = -5$ but shifts outward parallel to itself.

---

[2] *Mathematical Footnote:* In terms of calculus, the derivative dy/dx replaces the ratio $\Delta y/\Delta x$ of finite increments. Along the straight line $P_x x + P_y y = I$, with income I held constant, standard calculus techniques show that the derivative is $dy/dx = -P_x/P_y$. (In this case the derivative is the same as the slope defined in terms of finite increments, as always holds for a straight line.)

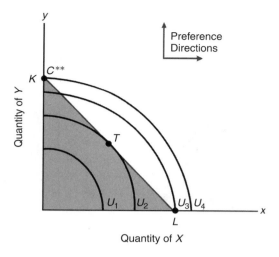

Figure 4.2. Concave Indifference Curves and Corner Solution

If the indifference curves have the usual negative slope but are concave to the origin, the best attainable position along the budget line *KL* must be a *corner solution*, at one or the other axis. Here the optimum of the consumer, C^{**} on the *y*-axis, lies on indifference curve U_4.

Now we want to locate the consumption basket that maximizes utility. In Figure 4.1, along the budget line *KL* the consumer attains the highest indifference curve U_2 at point C^* – the consumption basket containing x^* units of commodity *X* and y^* units of commodity *Y*. Although there are baskets preferred to (on a higher indifference curve than) C^*, any such bundle lies above the line *KL*; it would therefore require spending more than the income *I* available. And the points *Q* and *R* along *KL*, though attainable, lie on a lower indifference curve.

At the optimum point C^* the indifference curve U_2 is *tangent* to the budget line. For less desired combinations such as *Q* and *R* along *KL*, the indifference curve cuts through (and so is not tangent to) the budget line.

As described in Chapter 3, convexity is one of the essential features of indifference curves. That is, a line connecting any two points on an indifference curve lies above the curve, so the curve bulges toward the origin. Convexity is not a necessary inference from the Laws of Preference, but is founded upon the empirical principle of "diversification in consumption." Suppose indifference curves were not convex but concave, as in Figure 4.2 Again there is a tangency between the budget line *KL* and indifference curve U_2 (at point *T*). But now the tangency is not the optimum for the consumer. Indeed, *T* is the *least preferred* basket attainable along the budget line *KL*: a consumer who moves in either direction from *T* can get onto higher indifference curves such as U_3 or U_4. In Figure 4.2 the true optimum is at C^{**}, where all of the available income is spent on the single good *Y*. Such an outcome is called a *corner* optimum, as opposed to the *interior optimum* C^* in Figure 4.1 At a corner solution you would devote all your income to purchasing one good, buying none of the other. But people never limit themselves to consuming only a single good – they diversify their consumption. That is why, on observable empirical grounds, concave indifference curves must be rejected.

Consider, however, the following situation. Suppose you like Beluga caviar (it is a good for you), but it's so expensive you feel you can't afford to buy any. In Figure 4.3, suppose that *X* is caviar and *Y* is "everything else." The diagram illustrates how, with indifference curves of normal convex curvature, the consumer can still attain a corner optimum at C^{**} where consumption of *X* is zero. The upshot is that convex indifference curves are consistent *both* with interior solutions, as in Figure 4.1, and with corner solutions, as in Figure 4.3. In contrast, if indifference curves were concave, *only* corner solutions would be possible.

Figure 4.3. Convex Indifference Curves and Corner Solution

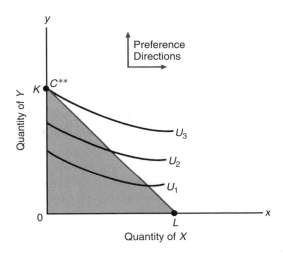

If indifference curves are convex to the origin, the optimum of the consumer may be *either* in the interior or at a corner. Here the optimum along the budget line KL is the corner solution C^{**}.

CONCLUSION

The optimum of the consumer is the point on the budget line that touches the highest attainable indifference curve. With convex indifference curves, the optimum can be an *interior solution* where positive amounts of both commodities are bought. Or it can be a *corner solution*: the budget line reaches the highest attainable indifference curve along an axis, so that one of the commodities is not bought at all.

Optimum of the Consumer (Cardinal Utility)

This section interprets the optimum of the consumer in terms of Marginal Utility (MU). Recall that, as discussed in Chapter 3, one can speak of larger or smaller MU only when utility is a "cardinal" variable. In addition, *diminishing* Marginal Utility is assumed: for any good X, as the amount of X increases, MU_X falls (refer back to Figure 3.2).[3]

If two goods X and Y are consumed in positive amounts, the consumer is at an interior optimum when the following Consumption Balance Equality is satisfied:

$$\frac{MU_x(\text{when } x > 0)}{P_x} = \frac{MU_y(\text{when } y > 0)}{P_y} \quad \begin{array}{c}\text{Consumption Balance Equality} \\ \text{(interior solution)}\end{array} \quad (4.3)$$

The explanation is immediate. For any good, Marginal Utility divided by price is *Marginal Utility per dollar* spent. At the optimum, the last dollar spent on X must yield the same satisfaction as the last dollar spent on Y.

EXERCISE 4.2

An apple costs 50 cents and a nectarine costs 25 cents each. Mary initially buys 10 apples and 5 nectarines. At this point suppose her Marginal Utility for an apple is 3 units of utility (utils) and for a nectarine is 1 util. Is Mary at an optimum? (Assume she is willing to accept fractional quantities.)

---

[3] *Mathematical Footnote*: Marginal Utility corresponds to the derivative dU/dx. The assumption here is that $dU/dx > 0$, but $d^2U/dx^2 < 0$. That is, Marginal Utility is a positive but decreasing function of x.

ANSWER: For an interior optimum, her Marginal Utility per dollar spent must be equal for the two goods. In terms of equation (4.3), $3/0.50 = 6$ exceeds $1/0.25 = 4$. So her MU_a/P_a for apples exceeds her MU_n/P_n for nectarines; hence Mary is not at an optimum. She should shift some of her spending from nectarines to apples. Giving up one nectarine means a sacrifice of 1 util, but that leaves 25 more cents to spend on apples. At a price of 50 cents, the extra 25 cents buys half an apple, yielding $3/2 = 1.5$ additional utils in place of the 1 util sacrificed.

What about the possibility of a corner solution? Suppose that commodity Z is Beluga caviar, whose price is so high that its MU_z/P_z remains lower than MU_y/P_y even for the very first unit of caviar bought. At such a corner optimum a Consumption Balance *Inequality* holds, as shown in Equation (4.3′):

$$\frac{MU_z(\text{when } z = 0)}{P_z} < \frac{MU_y(\text{when } y > 0)}{P_y} \quad \begin{array}{l}\text{Consumption Balance} \\ \text{Inequality (corner solution)}\end{array} \quad (4.3')$$

If (4.3′) is satisfied, at the optimum the consumer will be consuming *only* the numeraire good Y.

EXERCISE 4.3

For Andrew, the Marginal Utility of bread is $MU_b = 30 - b$. The Marginal Utility of wine is $MU_w = 40 - 5w$. (That Andrew's MU_b depends only on the quantity b, and his MU_w only on the quantity w, is a special assumption made for illustrative purposes only.) (a) Suppose the prices are $P_b = 1$ and $P_w = 5$, and his income is $I = 40$. Find the consumption optimum for Andrew. (b) What if his income were instead $I = 10$?

ANSWER: (a) Here the budget equation (4.1) is $b + 5w = 40$. Any interior solution must satisfy the Consumption Balance Equality $(30 - b)/1 = (40 - 5w)/5$. Solving the two equations simultaneously, the solution is $b^* = 25$, $w^* = 3$ (an interior solution). (b) Now the budget equation becomes $b + 5w = 10$. Solving simultaneously with the Consumption Balance Equality leads algebraically to $b^* = 20$, $w^* = -2$. But a negative consumption quantity is economically impossible. The best Andrew can do is move to the corner solution, where he sets $w^* = 0$, allowing him to buy $b^* = 10$ units of bread.

Consider now *three* commodities X, Y, and Z. For an interior solution it is simple to add an additional equality to the Consumption Balance Equality:

$$\frac{MU_x(x > 0)}{P_x} = \frac{MU_y(y > 0)}{P_y} = \frac{MU_y(z > 0)}{P_z} \quad \begin{array}{l}\text{Consumption Balance} \\ \text{Equality (interior} \\ \text{solution, three goods)}\end{array} \quad (4.4)$$

But now suppose that, at the optimum, commodities X and Y are bought but Z is not.

Figure 4.4. Consumption Optimum for Robinson Crusoe

Crusoe's opportunity set, the shaded region, is bounded by his Production-Possibility Curve for producing combinations of fish and bananas for his own consumption. His consumption optimum is the tangency point C^* (an interior solution).

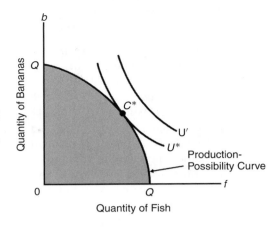

Then an *equality* holds as between commodities X and Y but an *inequality* with regard to Z:

$$\frac{MU_x(x > 0)}{P_x} = \frac{MU_y(y > 0)}{P_y} > \frac{MU_y(z = 0)}{P_z} \qquad \begin{array}{l} \text{Consumption Balance} \\ \text{Equality/Inequality} \\ \text{(mixed solution,} \\ \text{three goods)} \end{array} \qquad (4.4')$$

This is the condition for a mixed interior/corner solution. Marginal Utility per dollar is equalized for the two commodities X and Y that are consumed in positive amounts: $MU_x/P_x = MU_y/P_y$. Commodity Z is not bought at all, because even for the very first unit that might be consumed, MU_z/P_z is less than $MU_x/P_x = MU_y/P_y$.

Generalizing these results:

> **ANALYTIC OPTIMUM PRINCIPLE (CARDINAL UTILITY): For all goods consumed in positive quantities, at the optimum the Consumption Balance Equality holds (Marginal Utility per dollar is the same for each). For any good not consumed at all, its Marginal Utility per dollar must be smaller, even for the very first unit, than the Marginal Utility per dollar of the goods consumed in positive quantities.**

A digression: The analysis so far has dealt only with *market* opportunities. But even an individual isolated from markets needs to choose among alternative possible consumption baskets. Figure 4.4 shows how Robinson Crusoe might choose among differing combinations of fish and bananas. In the absence of markets, Robinson's opportunity set (the shaded region) is bounded not by a market budget line but by the "Production-Possibility Curve" shown in the diagram. The Production-Possibility Curve will be taken up in more detail in Chapter 13, but note that its curvature represents a kind of *diminishing returns in production*. (As Robinson tries to catch more fish, he has to sacrifice increasing amounts of bananas, and conversely if he tries to produce more bananas.) The diagram illustrates an interior solution where Robinson's optimum is at the tangency point C^*.

EXAMPLE 4.1 SMART ANTS

Ant colonies, like some primitive foraging tribes (see Example 2.11), must meet their nutritional needs without dealing in markets. Ants do not go through rational thinking processes – or, at least, we humans do not give them credit for doing so. Instead, as explained in the preceding chapter, efficient patterns of behavior tend to be selected for evolutionary survival by Mother Nature.

The biologist Adam Kay studied the foraging choices of the ant species *Dorymyrmex smithi.*[a] These ants forage for proteins and carbohydrates as nutrients. In the experiment six colonies were provided with a certain amount of 6% casein solution each day "for free," to see if that would affect their foraging choices between sources of casein (a protein) and sources of sucrose (a carbohydrate). A control group of six colonies were treated the same way except that, as a kind of placebo, plain water replaced the 6% casein solution.

The first data column shows the average choices of the control group, which can be taken to represent the normal foraging pattern for these ants. (The foraging options were controlled so that the ants could go to casein sources, to sucrose sources, or to sources representing a 50:50 mixture of the two nutrients.) The last column shows the choices of the groups receiving the casein supplement.

As can be seen, under normal conditions the ants divided their efforts fairly evenly between sucrose (carbohydrate) and casein (protein). But given the casein supplementation, they chose to devote more effort to seeking sucrose.

COMMENT

The ants' behavior was consistent with diminishing Marginal Utility. The "free" casein supplement reduced the Marginal Utility of protein relative to carbohydrate, so they shifted their foraging effort away from casein and toward sucrose.

Ant choices – proteins versus carbohydrates collected (% of total)

	Only water provided	Casein supplement provided
Sucrose only	20%	48%
Mixture	48%	37%
Casein only	32%	15%

Source: Estimated visually from Kay, Figure 2.

[a] Adam Kay, "The Relative Availabilities of Complementary Resources Affect the Feeding Preferences of Ant Colonies," *Behavioral Ecology*, v. 15 (1993).

Optimum of the Consumer (Ordinal Utility)

The preceding analysis assumed "cardinal" (measurable) utility. But, as indicated in the preceding chapter, in economics the weaker assumption of "ordinal" utility usually suffices.

The crucial idea is to think in terms of the ratio at which a person is *just willing to substitute* a small amount of Y for a small amount of X in his consumption basket. This ratio is called the *Marginal Rate of Substitution in Consumption* (MRS_C). The

Figure 4.5. Marginal Rate of Substitution in Consumption (MRS_C) and the Price Ratio (P_x/P_y)

At point A, MRS_C, the absolute value of the indifference-curve slope, is approximated by the ratio $AD/DB = 5/2$. The price ratio P_x/P_y is the absolute value of the budget-line slope. In the diagram, this slope is $AD/DG = 5/3$. Since the two slopes are unequal, point A cannot be an optimum for the consumer.

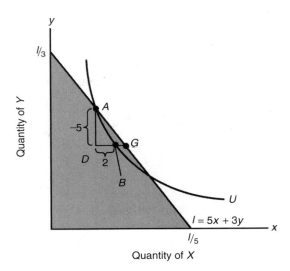

expression "just willing to substitute Y for X" means "a substitution of Y for X that leaves the consumer indifferent." So MRS_C is defined as:

$$MRS_C \equiv -\frac{\Delta y}{\Delta x}\bigg|_U \qquad (4.5)$$

The vertical bar with the subscript "U" indicates that the ratio is evaluated holding utility constant. Since constant utility is what defines an indifference curve, MRS_C corresponds to *the slope at a specified point along an indifference curve*. Because MRS_C is defined as positive whereas normal indifference curves have negative slope, the ratio on the right-hand side of (4.5) is preceded by a minus sign.)[4]

In Figure 4.5, suppose Ellen is initially at point A, holding the basket $x = 3$, $y = 15$. Consider the alternative basket $x = 5$, $y = 10$ represented by point B. Since baskets A and B lie on the same indifference curve, they are equally preferred. In moving from A to B, the change in Y is $\Delta y = -5$ and the change in X is $\Delta x = +2$. The ratio $-5/2$, the slope of the line connecting points A and B, therefore approximates (after reversing the sign) Ellen's MRS_C in the neighborhood of points A and B. (The smaller the changes considered, the better the approximation.)

MRS_C represents the ratio at which the consumer is *willing* to substitute Y for X. To find the consumption optimum, one must also know the ratio at which the market *permits* the two goods to be traded. That rate of exchange is the price ratio P_x/P_y.

Returning to Figure 4.5, suppose the prices are $P_x = 5$ and $P_y = 3$. Then it is possible to exchange 5 units of Y in the market for 3 units of X. But Ellen was willing to give up 5 units of Y for 2 units of X. So, although she was willing to move from A to B, the market permits a movement to point G on a higher indifference curve. Ellen should therefore make the trade. In fact, it is always possible to make an advantageous exchange, one way or the other, whenever there is any discrepancy between MRS_C and P_x/P_y – between the rate at which the consumer is *willing* to make such substitutions and the rate at which the market permits trades. This principle can be expressed as the *Substitution*

---

[4] *Mathematical Footnote*: The definition of MRS_C in the text is expressed in terms of finite changes Δx and Δy. Using calculus this ratio becomes the derivative $dy/dx|_U$.

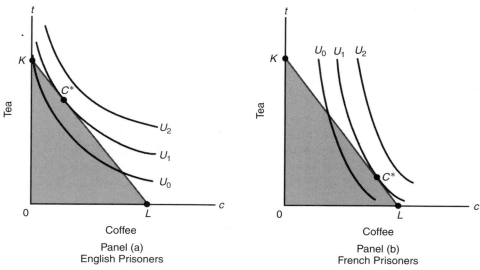

Figure 4.6. Coffee versus Tea in a P.O.W. Camp

English and French P.O.W.s had differing tastes for tea versus coffee. An efficient smuggling system equalized the price ratio P_c/P_t in the two sectors of the camp. At these prices the English optimum C^* involved relatively heavy consumption of tea, whereas the French optimum C^* was more heavily weighted toward coffee.

Balance Equation, which holds for any interior optimum:

$$MRS_c = P_x/P_y \quad \text{Substitution Balance Equation (interior optimum)} \quad (4.6)$$

Equation (4.5) was an *identity*, a definition of MRS_C, as indicated by the identity sign ($\equiv$). But equation (4.6) is a *conditional equality*, and so the equals ($=$) sign is used.[5] The relation between MRS_C and the price ratio in (4.6) is not determined by definition. Rather, it is the condition that must obtain at an interior optimum.[6]

EXAMPLE 4.2 PRISONERS OF WAR: TEA VERSUS COFFEE

As a prisoner of war in Germany and Italy during World War II, the economist R. A. Radford found that highly active markets functioned in the camps.[a] Cigarettes generally served as the numeraire (or standard good), so that prices for other goods were quoted in terms of cigarettes. A shirt might cost 80 cigarettes, washing services 2 cigarettes per garment, and so forth.

In the section for British prisoners, tea was preferred to coffee. In the French section, coffee was preferred to tea. The two panels of Figure 4.6 illustrate the situations of typical British and French prisoners. Owing to an efficient smuggling trade between the sections, the coffee-tea price ratio P_c/P_t was about the same for both groups of prisoners. But for the British prisoners, the tangency point C^* (where

---

[5] In this text, as in scientific writing generally, the ordinary = sign can optionally be used for identities when no confusion is likely to arise.

[6] *Mathematical Footnote*: Equation (4.6) is derived easily from equation (4.3), the Consumption Balance Equality in terms of Marginal Utilities. After simple transpositions, the left-hand side of equation (4.3) can be written as the ratio of Marginal Utilities and the right-hand side as the ratio of prices. Since MRS_C equals the ratio MU_x/MU_y, making that substitution immediately yields equation (4.6).

$MRS_C = P_c/P_t$) was well over toward the tea axis; for the French prisoners the optimum C^* lay toward the coffee axis.

---

[a] R. A. Radford, "The Economic Organization of a P.O.W. Camp," *Economica*, v. 12 (1945).

For *corner solutions*, the Substitution Balance Equation becomes an inequality instead. If the consumer buys none of commodity X, it must be that:

$$MRS_c < P_x/P_y \quad \text{when } x = 0 \quad \text{Substitution Balance Inequality} \qquad (4.6')$$

(A corresponding equation holds if the consumer buys none of the other commodity, Y.) Summarizing:

ANALYTIC OPTIMUM PRINCIPLE (ORDINAL UTILITY): If the optimum of the consumer is an interior solution along the budget line, with positive amounts of both commodities bought, then MRS_C, the Marginal Rate of Substitution in Consumption, must equal the price ratio P_x/P_y. This corresponds to the geometrical tangency of the budget line and indifference curve. But when the best attainable position along the budget line is at a corner (along one of the axes), it will generally be impossible to set MRS_C equal to P_x/P_y. Reducing consumption of one or the other commodity to zero brings MRS_C and P_x/P_y as near to equality as possible.

A more intuitive terminology is sometimes useful to avoid the awkward expression "Marginal Rate of Substitution in Consumption." Suppose Y stands for the numeraire commodity (e.g., corn) serving as standard of value. Then the MRS_C between X and Y can be interpreted as good X's *Marginal Value MV_x* in terms of the numeraire commodity. Thus MV_x is the consumer's "marginal willingness to pay" for X, in units of the numeraire good Y.

Recall that, by definition, the numeraire good Y has price $P_Y \equiv 1$. Then for any nonnumeraire good X, in Marginal Value terminology the Substitution Balance Equation and Inequality become:

$$MV_x = P_x \quad \text{when } x > 0 \quad \text{Substitution Balance Equation}$$
$$\text{(interior optimum)} \qquad (4.7)$$
$$MV_x < P_x \quad \text{when } x = 0 \quad \text{Substitution Balance Inequality}$$

The consumer will increase purchases of any good X as long as its Marginal Value MV_x exceeds its price P_x, both measured in terms of the numeraire good Y. If equality can be achieved, the individual is at an interior solution. But if MV_x remains less than P_x even when $x = 0$, the optimum is along the Y axis (corner solution).

EXERCISE 4.4

Edgar's preferences are represented by the Marginal Rate of Substitution $MRS_C = 2y/x$. His income is $I = 180$. The market prices are $P_x = 3$ and $P_y = 1$. (a) What is his optimal consumption basket? (b) Express the result in terms of Marginal Value (MV).

ANSWER: (a) The Substitution Balance Equation (4.6) provides one of the equations needed: $MRS_C = 2y/x = P_x/P_y$, or $2y = 3x/1$. The consumption optimum must

> also satisfy the budget equation $P_x x + P_y y = I$; this becomes here $3x + y = 180$. When these two equations are solved simultaneously, the solution is $x^* = 40$, $y^* = 60$. (b) Since $P_y = 1$, equation (4.7) can be written $MV_x = 2y/x = P_x$, or $3x = 2y$. Substituting $P_x x$ into the budget equation above leads to $2y + y = 180$. The solution is the same as before: $y^* = 60$, $x^* = 40$.

An important implication of the analysis is that, despite differences of tastes, *at interior solutions everyone ends up with the same* MRS_C – or, equivalently, the same *Marginal Value* MV_X. In our P.O.W. example the French prisoners' preferences inclined toward coffee and the British prisoners' preferences toward tea. Nevertheless, once each group adapted to the ruling prices, on the margin a French prisoner was no more willing than an English prisoner to give up a unit of tea for a unit of coffee. Thus, even though utility is "subjective," as a result of trade the "objective" price ratio between two goods in the market measures the *marginal* preference ratio for everyone consuming both goods.

4.2   COMPLEMENTS AND SUBSTITUTES

Certain commodities go well together and tend to be consumed in combination: bread and butter, shoes and socks, CD players and CD discs. Such pairs of goods are called *complements*. Other commodity-pairs go poorly together and tend to be used to the exclusion of one another: for example, butter and margarine, shoes and sandals, CDs and DVDs. Such pairs are called *substitutes* or *anticomplements*. (Pairs of goods that are on the borderline, neither complements nor anticomplements, are said to be *independent* in consumption.)

Consider two commodities that consumers might regard as perfect substitutes. A person may be completely indifferent between 2 nickels and 1 dime, 20 nickels and 10 dimes, 200 nickels and 100 dimes, and so on. Then the preference map will look like Panel (a) of Figure 4.7: the indifference curves are parallel straight lines. For two goods that are close but not quite perfect substitutes, such as Jonathan apples and Granny Smith apples, the indifference curves would be almost linear, as in Panel (b).

The observable characteristic of close substitutes is that *a small change in relative prices* brings about *large changes in relative consumption*. Suppose Roger has the preferences pictured in Panel (b), and initially faces a steep budget line like SS' in the diagram. The steep budget line means that Granny Smith apples are expensive compared to Jonathan apples. Roger's best consumption bundle is S^*, where he mostly buys inexpensive Jonathan apples. An only moderately flatter budget line such as FF' in the diagram (representing a slightly lower relative price of Granny Smiths) leads him instead to the drastically different consumption bundle F^*, where he now chooses mostly Granny Smith apples.

The extreme opposite case is *perfect complementarity*. Here the consumer wants to buy goods in some fixed ratio (for example, one left shoe for each right shoe). Panel (a) of Figure 4.8 shows the right-angled indifference curves implied by perfect complementarity. The slope of the dashed line through the "elbows" represents the desired ratio of the two commodities. (For right and left shoes this would be 1:1, or a slope of 45°.) Moving away from the extreme case, when two goods are strong though not perfect complements – examples include bagels and cream cheese, electricity and electric appliances, and roads and automobiles – the indifference map would be as in

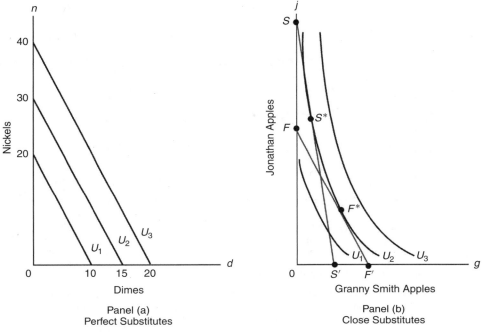

Figure 4.7. Substitute Commodities

The indifference curves of Panel (a) are parallel straight lines, indicating that the two commodities (nickels and dimes) are prefect substitutes. If the price ratio in the market, represented by the slope of the budget line, differs from the slope of the indifference curves, the consumer will go to a corner solution. In Panel (b) the indifference curves have a slight degree of normal convex curvature, indicating that the two commodities (Granny Smith apples and Jonathan apples) are close, though not perfect, substitutes. A relatively small change in the price ratio (from the slope of line SS' to the slope of line FF') causes a relatively large change in consumption (from S^* to F^*), though not a total switch from one good to the other.

Panel (b). If two goods are complements, then large changes in price ratios lead to only small shifts in relative quantities bought. In Panel (b), along the steeper budget line SS', the optimum solution S^* differs little from the optimum F^* along the much flatter budget line FF'.

EXERCISE 4.5

Suppose Evelyn's Marginal Rate of Substitution in Consumption between wine and bread is $MRS_C = w/b$. For another commodity pair, roses and daisies, it is $MRS_C = (r/d)^2$. Which pair are closer substitutes in Evelyn's utility function?

ANSWER: Plotting a few points, you can verify that the indifference curves for wine versus bread are more tightly "curled," as in Figure 4.8(b), whereas for roses versus daisies the indifference curves are relatively flat, as in Figure 4.7(b). Evelyn finds roses and daisies to be closer substitutes for one another than wine and bread.

The Examples that follow provide clues as to when commodities are likely to be complements, or conversely to be substitutes.

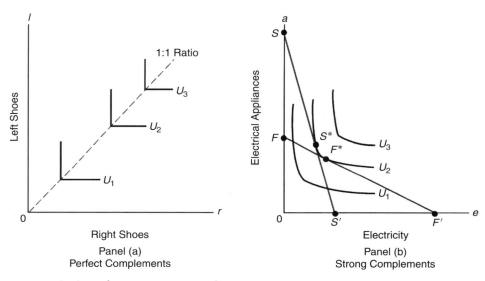

Figure 4.8. Complementary Commodities

The right-angled indifference curves of Panel (a) indicate that the two commodities (right shoes and left shoes) are perfect complements. A change in the price ratio has no effect on the quantity ratio chosen, which will always be 1 : 1 at the best attainable "elbow" point. In Panel (b) the indifference curves are nearly, but not quite, right-angled: the commodities (electricity and electrical appliances) are strong, though not perfect, complements. Here a relatively large change in the price ratio (from the slope of line SS' to the slope of line FF') induces only a relatively small change in the quantity ratio (from S^* to F^*).

EXAMPLE 4.3 RATS

A team of psychologists and economists investigated how rats responded to changes in "price ratios" of desired goods.[a]

In the first experiment, the rodents were given unlimited amounts of water and rat chow. They could obtain two other commodities – root beer and Collins mix – by pressing one of two levers. A rat's "income" was the total number of lever presses allowed per day. The "price" was the number of presses required per milliliter of fluid. The experimenters varied the price ratio by increasing one price and simultaneously reducing the other in such a way that each rat remained approximately on the same indifference curve. Root beer and Collins mix proved to be substitutes for these rats: just as in Figure 4.7, Panel (b), the consumption ratio shifted substantially when the price ratio changed even by a small amount.

In a second experiment, unlimited food and water were no longer provided, but instead became the two commodities "bought" by pressing the appropriate lever. When the price ratio between water and rat chow was varied (again holding "real income" approximately constant), the picture was more like Figure 4.8, Panel (b): the consumption ratio remained about the same. So food and water were strong complements.

COMMENT

When unlimited amounts of water and rat chow are provided, root beer and Collins mix are not "essential" nutrients for the rats. Since the proportions consumed seemed hardly to matter, the rats responded mainly to the relative "prices" of the two fluids. In contrast, water and food are both essential to life. Forced to choose between these essentials, the rats, despite changing price ratios, probably could not diverge much from the physiologically necessary proportionality between water intake and food intake.

[a] J. H. Kagel, H. Rachlin, L. Green, R. C. Battalio, R. L. Basmann, and W. R. Klemm, "Experimental Studies of Consumer Demand Behavior Using Laboratory Animals," *Economic Inquiry*, v. 13 (March 1975).

4.3 THE CONSUMER'S RESPONSE TO CHANGING OPPORTUNITIES

If *preferences* do not change, the optimum of the consumer can vary only in response to changes in *opportunities*. A person's market opportunities depend on two elements: (1) his or her income and (2) commodity prices. This section examines how optimal consumption choices vary in response to changes in income only. (Among other applications, this question could be important in studying what would happen if the government were to redistribute income from some people to others.)

The Income Expansion Path

Consider a simplified world of only two commodities X and Y. In Figure 4.9 the consumer's original optimum is at point Q, where the budget line KL is tangent to indifference curve U_0. (Point Q here corresponds to point C^* in Figure 4.1.) If income rises from I to I' while prices are held constant, the budget line shifts outward parallel to itself, from KL to $K'L'$. (The slope of the budget line, $-P_x/P_y$, is the same for KL and $K'L'$.) The new optimum position is at point R, where the budget line $K'L'$ is tangent to the higher indifference curve U_1. And a further increase in income from I' to I'' shifts the budget line further outward to $K''L''$, with the optimum at the tangency position S on indifference curve U_2.

More generally, as income varies while prices and tastes remain unchanged, an entire curve is traced out connecting all the different optimum positions like Q, R, and S. This curve is the *Income Expansion Path* (IEP). Each different price ratio generates a different Income Expansion Path. In particular, Figure 4.9 shows how a smaller ratio P_x/P_y (implying flatter budget lines) would be associated with a new Income Expansion Path (IEP') that lies below the original one.

EXERCISE 4.6

William's Marginal Rate of Substitution in Consumption is $MRS_C = y/x$. The market prices are $P_x = 5$ and $P_y = 1$. (a) What is the equation of his Income Expansion Path, and what does the curve look like? (b) How would the Income Expansion Path change if the price of X fell to $P_x = 4$?

ANSWER: (a) From the Substitution Balance Equation (4.6), $MRS_C = y/x = P_x/P_y = 5/1 = 5$. So the equation for the Income Expansion Path is $y = 5x$, which is a ray out of the origin with slope 5. (b) With $P_x = 4$, the equation of the Income Expansion Path would be $y = 4x$ (a flatter ray out of the origin, with slope 4).

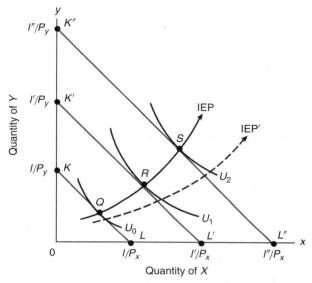

Figure 4.9. Derivation of the Income Expansion Path

As income increases from I to I' to I'', with prices P_x and P_y held constant, the budget line shifts outward from KL to $K'L'$ to $K''L''$. The tangency defining the consumer optimum correspondingly shifts from Q to R to S. The Income Expansion Path (IEP) shows all the optimum consumption bundles for the consumer as I varies, with prices remaining the same. For a smaller price ratio P_x/P_y (the corresponding flatter budget lines are not shown in the diagram) the IEP lies further down and to the right, as indicated by the dashed IEP' curve.

What shapes are possible for the Income Expansion Path? Consider Figure 4.10. In both panels the original optimum is at point Q, where indifference curve U_0 is tangent to budget line KL. Now let income increase, so that the budget line shifts to $K'L'$. In Panel (a) the new tangency point R lies northeast of Q: the Income Expansion Path has positive slope. This means that, given increased income, the consumer would buy more of both X and Y. When this holds, X and Y are both said to be "superior" goods.

In Panel (b) the new tangency R lies northwest of Q, meaning that at higher income the consumer chooses more Y but less X. Here Y remains a superior good. But X, whose consumption falls when income rises, is an *inferior* good. Since Y would be called superior in the situation of either Panel (a) or Panel (b), it is convenient to have a terminology that distinguishes the two cases. For the situation of Panel (a), X and Y can be termed "normal superior goods." For the situation of Panel (b), where X is inferior, the "partner" good Y might be called *ultrasuperior*. Less of the inferior good being purchased, once income rises, means that the amount spent upon the ultrasuperior partner exceeds the increase of income.

Last, a third type of curve (not shown in Figure 4.10) could be drawn for the case where Y is inferior and X ultrasuperior. In that third diagram the slope of the Income Expansion Path would again be negative, but the upward utility direction along the Income Expansion Path (as shown by the arrowhead) would point to the southeast rather than northwest.

CONCLUSION

For two goods X and Y, a positively sloped Income Expansion Path indicates that consumption of both goods rises as income grows. Then X and Y are called normal

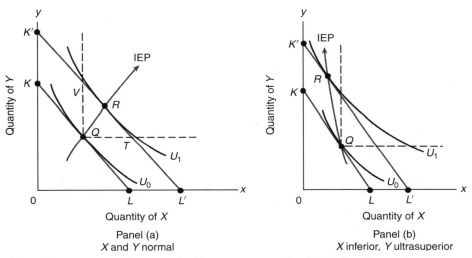

Figure 4.10. Income Expansion Paths: Superior and Inferior Goods

The outward shift of the budget line (from KL to $K'L'$) represents an increase in income I, with prices held constant. In Panel (a) the Income Expansion Path (IEP) points north and east. Here both X and Y are normal superior goods. In Panel (b) the IEP points north and west; here X is an inferior good, and Y is an ultrasuperior good.

superior goods. If instead the Income Expansion Path has negative slope, one of the goods must be inferior. The other good must of course be superior, but more specifically may be called ultrasuperior – because more than 100% of the increment of income now goes to purchasing it.

EXERCISE 4.7

(a) George's preferences are described by the condition $MRS_C = y/x$. Are goods X and Y both normal for him, or is one of them inferior? (b) What if his preferences are given by $MRS_C = y$?

ANSWER: (a) When $MRS_C = y/x$ the Substitution Balance Equation (4.6) is $y/x = P_x/P_y$. Solving for y, the equation of the Income Expansion Path is $y = P_x x/P_y$. Since P_x and P_y are both positive constants, the IEP has positive slope, as in Panel (a) of Figure 4.10. Then X and Y are normal superior goods. (b) If $MRS_C = y$, the equation for the IEP becomes $y = P_x/P_y$. So the Income Expansion Path is a horizontal line on x,y axes. This means that 100% of any income increase will be spent on good X. Here X is a superior good. Good Y, while not inferior, is just on the borderline of being so.

EXAMPLE 4.4 HOW MUCH ARE CHRISTMAS GIFTS WORTH?

Would you rather get a gift of $20 in cash, or two neckties that cost $10 each? Economic analysis suggests that cash is better. You can use the cash to buy the two ties, if you like, but you don't have to. Perhaps you are already satisfied with the ties you now own. If so, your marginal "willingness to pay" for additional ties could be less than the store price.

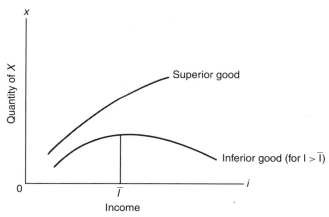

Figure 4.11. Engel Curve

For any good X, the Engel Curve shows the quantity purchased as a function of income. For a superior good, the Engel Curve has positive slope. An inferior good has negative slope; however, a good cannot be inferior over the entire range of income.

Joel Waldfogel surveyed 86 economics students about their holiday gifts.[a] The students were asked how much they would have been willing to pay in cash for the gifts received, in comparison with their guess as to how much the donors had actually paid. On average, givers had paid a total of $438.20, whereas as recipients the students would have been willing to pay on average of only $313.40 for those items – about 71.5% as much.

In Figure 4.10, Panel (a), the vertical axis represents cash and the horizontal axis represents noncash gifts; both commodities are assumed to be normal superior goods. If the pregift optimum was at point Q, a cash gift would move the recipient to the vertically higher point V. The cash gift would in effect increase income; the recipient would likely want to spend some of the cash to move to the tangency optimum point R. (This could mean, for example, spending $10 of the $20 gift on one tie but using the remaining $10 to buy something else.) But the gift in noncash form, assuming it is nonreturnable, moves the recipient from point Q to point T – which is less preferred than point R.

COMMENT

Does that mean that donors should always give cash? Not necessarily! A noncash gift may signal that the donor cares enough to devote time and thought to what the recipient desires or needs. Even if the choice itself misses the mark, the recipient may value the expression of concern that lies behind it.

[a] Joel Waldfogel, "The Deadweight Loss of Christmas," *American Economic Review*, v. 83 (December 1989), pp. 1328–1336.

The Engel Curve

The Income Expansion Path shows how consumption baskets (combinations of goods) change as income rises of falls. The *Engel Curve* pictures the effect of income changes upon a single good X.[7] Two possible Engel Curves are shown in Figure 4.11. The

---

[7] Ernst Engel (1821–1896), German statistician.

Figure 4.12. Food versus Cigarettes in a P.O.W. Camp

After a halving of cigarette and food rations, the typical P.O.W. was forced from an initial position like Q^* to a less preferred outcome Q'. Under these circumstances it was observed that P_f/P_c, the price of food in terms of cigarettes fell. Since $P_f/P_c = MRS_C$ at the consumer's optimum, we know that MRS_C (the absolute value of the slope of the indifference curve) must have been less at lower incomes. That is, cigarettes were relatively more preferred at lower levels of income.

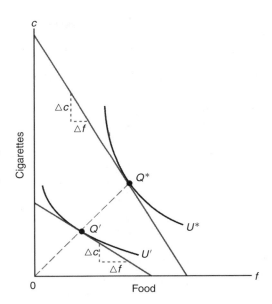

upward-sloping curve represents a superior good (the quantity bought always increases as income rises). The hill-shaped curve shows a good that is initially superior, but beyond a certain level of income becomes inferior. Lower-quality cuts of meat, for example, might be a superior good for poorer people but an inferior good for the wealthy. [*Note*: a good X cannot be inferior over its entire range, as that would require positive purchases of X even when income I is zero – which is impossible.]

EXAMPLE 4.5 LUXURIES VERSUS NECESSITIES IN A P.O.W. CAMP

Goods mostly bought by wealthy people are commonly called luxuries. Goods whose consumption does not vary very much between rich and poor are sometimes termed necessities – even if, strictly speaking, they are not essential for life. On these definitions, standard food items like bread or breakfast cereals are necessities. Although richer people can afford to and generally do buy more bread than poorer people (that is, bread is usually not an inferior good), the *proportion* of the budget spent on bread tends to fall as income rises.

In the prisoner-of-war economy described above, R. A. Radford[a] made interesting observations about necessities and luxuries. As the Germany economy worsened toward the end of the war, the Allied prisoners suffered severe privation. In August 1944 rations for food and cigarettes were cut in half from an already low level. Unexpectedly, after the rations were reduced, the price of food, as measured in terms of cigarettes, fell. Thus cigarettes proved to be more of a "necessity" (by the standard definition above) than food.

COMMENT

Figure 4.12 shows the implied shape of prisoners' indifference curves between cigarettes C and food F. At point Q', where income is very low, the indifference-curve slope (Marginal Rate of Substitution in Consumption) $MRS_C = -\Delta c/\Delta f$ is less than at the higher income level (point Q^*).

---

[a] R. A. Radford, "The Economic Organization of a P.O.W. Camp," *Economica*, v. 12 (1945).

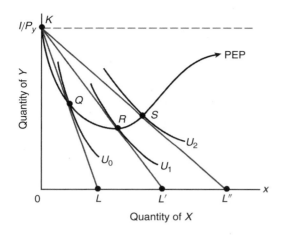

Figure 4.13. Derivation of the Price Expansion Path

A fall in the price of good X (with income I and the price of the other good Y held constant) tilts the budget line outward (from KL to KL' to KL''). The optimal consumption bundle shifts from Q to R to S. The Price Expansion Path (PEP) connects all such optimum positions; the arrowhead on the PEP curve indicates the direction of utility improvement.

Price Expansion Path and Demand Curve

The previous section dealt with changes in income. This section discusses changes in price. More specifically, how does the consumer's best choice respond when a specific price P_x changes, holding income and prices of other goods constant?

In Figure 4.13 the optimum is initially at Q where the budget line KL is tangent to indifference curve U_0. Now let the price of X fall. The intercept of the budget line along the vertical Y-axis is unchanged at I/P_y. But since the intercept of the budget line with the horizontal X-axis is I/P_x, the budget line swings outward to a new position like KL'. The consumer's new optimum is at point R where KL' is tangent to a higher indifference curve U_1. A further decline in P_x leads to further outward tilting of the budget line, to the position KL''; here the optimum is at S on the still higher indifference curve U_2.

The curve connecting all the optimum positions like Q, R, and S is called the *Price Expansion Path* (PEP). Just as there was a different Income Expansion Path for each different price ratio P_x/P_y, there is a different PEP for each possible level of income.

EXERCISE 4.8

Robert's Marginal Value for good X (his "marginal willingness to pay" in terms of the numeraire commodity Y) is given by $MV_x = y$. His income is $I = 120$. (a) What is the equation for his Price Expansion Path and what is its shape? (b) How would his Price Expansion Path change if income increased to $I = 150$?

ANSWER: (a) The Substitution Balance Equation (4.7) here becomes $MV_x = y = P_x$. The budget line is $P_x x + P_y y = I$, or (since $P_y \equiv 1$) $P_x x + y = 120$. The two equations need to be combined into a single equation involving x and y (since the Price Expansion Path is drawn on x,y axes). Eliminating P_x between the two equations, the Price Expansion Path is $y(x + 1) = 120$. This Price Expansion Path has a y-intercept of 120. Like the Price Expansion Path of Figure 4.13, it slopes down from the y-intercept; unlike that curve, it never curls up again but approaches (without ever intersecting) the horizontal axis. (b) If income is $I = 150$, the equation of the Price Expansion Path becomes $y(x + 1) = 150$. The intercept on the y-axis is higher and the curve shifts generally to the right.

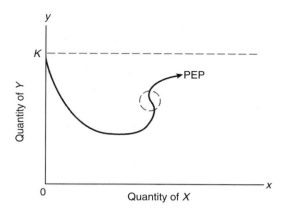

Figure 4.14. Price Expansion Path: Giffen Case

The Price Expansion Path (PEP) can have a segment where it curls back up and to the left (the circled region): less of X is purchased as its price declines. In this range X would be called a "Giffen good."

Leaving aside the details of verification, here are some properties of the Price Expansion Path:

1. As price P_x falls, income I held constant, the consumer attains higher utility. In Figure 4.13, the arrowhead indicates the direction of increasing utility along the Price Expansion Path.
2. When the Price Expansion Path slopes downward, as in the range between Q and R in Figure 4.13, the consumer responds to a fall in P_x by choosing more X but less of the numeraire good Y. Where the Price Expansion Path has a positive slope, as in the range between R and S in the diagram, reducing P_x induces the consumer to buy more of *both* X and Y.
3. Point K in Figure 4.13 is associated with a price P_x so high that the consumer buys none of good X at all. (This is the "choke price" for X.) The Price Expansion Path must also lie everywhere below the dashed horizontal line at height K in the diagram.
4. The Price Expansion Path *may* even have a section that curls upward and to the left (the circled region in Figure 4.14), in which a lower P_x causes the consumer to buy less of good X! When this condition applies, the commodity is called a "Giffen good"[8] for this consumer. The Giffen property can only hold over a limited range. With negatively sloped indifference curves and positive preference directions, the Price Expansion Path cannot move up and to the left very long and still enter regions of higher utility.

Most important of all, the data summarized by the Price Expansion Path can be replotted to show the relation between price P_x and the quantity of X bought. This is the consumer's *demand curve* for X, as shown in Figure 4.15. Panel (a) pictures the normal (non-Giffen) situation. Panel (b) pictures a situation where the Giffen property holds over a limited range – corresponding to the limited range in which the Price Expansion Path curls up and to the left in Figure 4.14.

---

[8] Sir Robert Giffen, British statistician and economist (1837–1910).

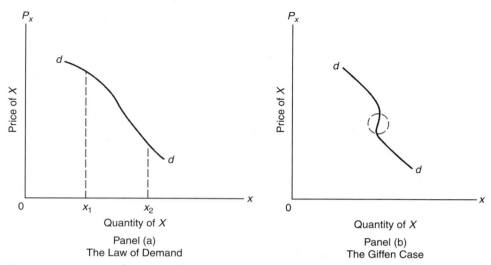

Figure 4.15. Demand Curves: The Law of Demand versus the Giffen Case

Panel (a) pictures a negatively sloped individual demand curve, satisfying the Law of Demand: as the price falls, more of X is purchased. In Panel (b) the demand curve has the exceptional "Giffen" property. In the small circled region (corresponding to the circled region in Figure 4.14) more of X is bought as P_x rises. The Giffen property can hold, if at all, only over a limited range of prices.

EXERCISE 4.9

In the preceding exercise, given the individual's Marginal Value $MV_x = y$ and income $I = 120$, the Price Expansion Path equation $y(x + 1) = 120$ was derived. What is the individual demand curve associated with this Price Expansion Path? Is X a Giffen good?

ANSWER: The derivation of the Price Expansion Path in Exercise 4.8 used the Substitution Balance Equality $y = P_x$ and the budget equation $P_x x + y = 120$. To derive the demand curve, which is a relation between x and P_x, starting from the same two equations, y needs to be eliminated. Omitting the algebraic details, the result is $P_x(x + 1) = 120$, or $x = 120/P_x - 1$. This is the equation of the demand curve for good X. Since this demand curve has negative slope throughout, X is not a Giffen good.

The Giffen condition violates the "Law of Demand," that a lower price always induces consumers to buy more. So the Law of Demand does not follow strictly from the pure logic of rational consumer choice. Like convexity of indifference curves, its justification is empirical observation. Giffen goods are rarely if ever encountered in the real world.

Figure 4.16 shows how a change in income affects the demand curve. If X a normal superior good, higher income shifts the demand curve to the right (more of X is desired at each price). If X is an inferior good, higher income shifts the demand curve to the left (less is desired at each price).

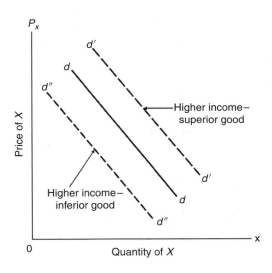

Figure 4.16. The Demand Curve: Effect of Income Changes

If X is a superior good (whether normal or ultrasuperior), a rise in income implies larger purchases of X at each price P_x— the demand curve shifts to the right (from dd to $d'd'$). If X is an inferior good, as income increases less is purchased at any given price; the demand curve shifts to the left (from dd to $d''d''$).

EXERCISE 4.10

For the individual of Exercise 4.9, how would the demand curve shift if income rose from $I = 120$ to $I = 150$?

ANSWER: With $I = 120$ the demand equation was $P_x(x + 1) = 120$, or equivalently $x = 120/P_x - 1$. With $I = 150$, the same technique yields $x = 150/P_x - 1$. With increased income the demand curve has shifted to the right. This shows that X is a superior good.

4.4 INCOME AND SUBSTITUTION EFFECTS OF A PRICE CHANGE

The effect of price changes upon consumer demand may be separated into two components.

1. A fall in P_x increases the consumer's real income. He or she could buy the same bundle of goods as before, and have something left over. If X is a superior good, the consumer will use some of the excess to buy more X. This is called the *income effect* of the fall in P_x.
2. Furthermore, at the lower P_x the Substitution Balance Equation tells us that even if real income or utility had remained the same, more X would have been purchased. This is called the *pure substitution effect* of the price change.

Continuing to think in terms of a fall in price, Figure 4.17 pictures the "Hicks[9] decomposition" of the income and substitution effects. Suppose Harriet is at an initial optimum position Q on indifference curve U_0. When P_x falls, the new optimum is at S on her higher indifference curve U_1. Now, keeping the lower price P_x, imagine taking away just enough income to leave Harriet on the old indifference curve U_0. This leads to the dashed budget line MN parallel to KL' and just touching indifference U_0 at point R. Since Q and R are on the same indifference curve, real income is unchanged. So

---

[9] Sir John R. Hicks, contemporary British economist.

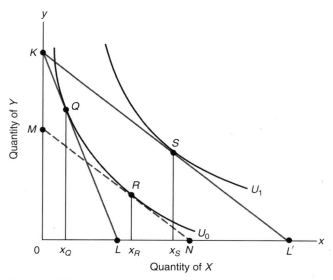

Figure 4.17. Income and Substitution Effects: Hicks Decomposition

A fall in price P_x, with income and P_y held constant, shifts the budget line from KL to KL' so that the consumption optimum changes from Q to S. Because S lies on a higher indifference curve, there has been an increase in real income. The income effect of the price change can be separated from the pure substitution effect by constructing an artificial budget line MN parallel to KL' and tangent to the original indifference curve U_0. At the tangency point R, utility is the same as at Q. The income effect of the price change is therefore $x_S - x_R$ and the pure substitution effect of the price change is $x_R - x_Q$.

this procedure isolates the *pure substitution effect* of the price change. The increased purchases of X due to the substitution effect alone is the distance $x_R - x_Q$.

The *income effect* of the price change is the movement from R to S. The increased amount of X purchased due to the income effect is $x_S - x_R$. So the overall change from Q to S has been divided into two movements: from Q to R (the pure substitution effect) and then from R to S (the income effect). Notice that, in the case pictured, the two effects reinforce one another. A price reduction increases consumption of X for two reasons: the *pure substitution effect* makes X a better buy for Harriet (in comparison with the numeraire good Y), and the *income effect* has enriched her so that she can now buy both more X and more Y.

Looking at the substitution effect alone, it is important to note that the quantity change and price change are in opposite directions. Why? Because the pure substitution effect involves movement *along* an indifference curve, and indifference curves have negative slopes.

The direction of the income effect can go either way, depending upon whether X is an inferior good or a superior good. In Figure 4.17, X was a superior good. Had X been inferior instead (so that a rise in income would decrease consumption of X), point S would lie to the northwest of R instead of to the northeast. The income effect and substitution effect would then no longer reinforce one another. As before, the pure substitution effect would be the positive difference $x_R - x_Q$. But now the income effect would be a negative difference $x_R - x_S$. Even with a negative income effect the Law of Demand would continue to hold if the new optimum S were to the right of the original

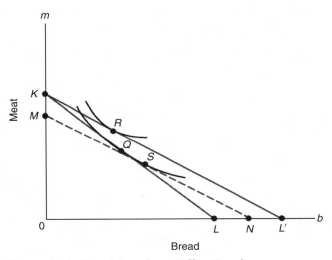

Figure 4.18. Conditions for a Giffen Good

At the initial high bread price the budget line is KL and the optimum is at Q. A fall in the price of bread shifts the budget line to KL'. The consumer is sufficiently enriched to prefer buying less bread and more meat at point R. The movement from Q to R consists of a small substitution effect (Q to S) and a large negative income effect (S to R). For this Giffen result to occur, bread must be strongly inferior.

optimum Q. Conceivably, however, such an abnormal (negative) income effect could be so great that S along the higher indifference curve U_1 lay to the left of Q. This would mean that a reduction in price reduced the quantity bought. This is the underlying explanation for the Giffen case.

An Application: How Can the Giffen Case Come About? How Likely Is It?

Giffen goods violate the Law of Demand. Here is an example commonly given. Suppose poverty forces you to live mainly on bread (the cheapest source of calories) and to consume little meat (a desired but more expensive food). Since you spend most of your income on bread, a fall in the bread price makes you richer in real terms. But when you are richer you can afford to buy more meat instead, so your consumption of bread might fall!

Referring back to Figure 4.17, which illustrated the decomposition of the income and substitution effects of a price change, a Giffen good must have the following properties:

1. It must be inferior, so that the income effect of a price change is negative.
2. It must account for a large fraction of the budget. This makes the "perverse" income effect large in magnitude. (It has to be large if it is to overcome the pure substitution effect.)

These properties are illustrated in Figure 4.18. Initially the consumer chooses a mixed basket along budget line KL indicated by point Q. When the price of bread P_b falls, the budget line swings outward to KL'. At the new optimum position R the individual chooses *less* bread! Although the pure substitution effect here is (as always) in the normal direction – involving movement from Q to S along the artificial dashed budget line MN – the income effect from S to R is "perverse" in direction and sufficiently large in magnitude to overwhelm the substitution effect.

EXAMPLE 4.6 WAS BREAD A GIFFEN GOOD?

Some historians have suggested that bread was a Giffen good for English rural laborers at the end of the eighteenth century.

A study by Roger Koenker casts doubt on this claim.[a] In the late eighteenth century, the limited transportation network in Britain meant that prices differed considerably across communities. These differences, as well as changes over time, provided data for estimating the demand for bread.

The demand function of a typical English rural laborer household was estimated as follows:

$$\text{Quantity of bread} = 0.40 + 0.41 \text{ Family size} + 0.024 \text{ Weekly expenditures} \\ - 0.35 \text{ Bread price} + 0.57 \text{ Meat price}$$

Here bread quantity was measured in loaves per week, bread price in pence per loaf, and meat price in pence per pound. Weekly spending (in pence per week) was used as the measure of overall income.

The negative coefficient (-0.35) for bread price shows that bread was not a Giffen good for these consumers. Indeed, the positive coefficient for weekly spending (income) suggests that both bread and meat were normal superior goods. (As the text showed, although an inferior good can be a Giffen good, a superior good cannot be.) The positive coefficient on the meat price means that an increase in the price of meat increased consumption of bread, suggesting that bread and meat were substitutes. Consumers, buying less meat in response to the higher meat price, bought more bread.

COMMENT

Recall that a person's demand for a good can have the Giffen property only over a limited range of prices. So averaging over different individuals and averaging over time could mask any Giffen effects: *some* individuals, in *some* periods, might still have been Giffen consumers. But if the Giffen effect is so easily lost by averaging, it is unlikely to be substantively important.

[a] Roger Koenker, "Was Bread Giffen? The Demand for Food in England circa 1790," *Review of Economics and Statistics*, v. 59 (1977).

4.5   FROM INDIVIDUAL DEMAND TO MARKET DEMAND

The *market demand curve* shows the aggregate quantity demanded by all consumers together, as a function of the price. Geometrically, the market demand curve is obtained by summing the individual demand curves horizontally, as Figure 4.19 illustrates.

Suppose there are only two consumers, whose individual demand curves are d_1 and d_2. At price P_x the first consumer will buy x_1 units and the second consumer will buy x_2 units. The total quantity demanded is then $x_1 + x_2$, which corresponds to point A on the market demand curve. Repeating this process for every possible price generates the entire market demand curve D.

More generally, with N consumers:

$$X \equiv \sum_{i=1}^{N} x_i \tag{4.8}$$

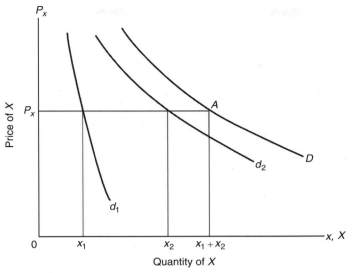

Figure 4.19. Individual and Aggregate Demand

Here d_1 and d_2 are the demand curves for two individuals. If these are the only two potential purchasers of the good, the overall market demand curve D is the horizontal sum of d_1 and d_2.

The market demand X is the sum of the demands of all N consumers in the market, where i indexes the consumers from 1 to N. (The uppercase letter X here symbolizes the *aggregate* market quantity.)

Note that the market demand curve in Figure 4.19 has a flatter slope than each of the individual demand curves. If price falls, the overall increase in the market quantity will ordinarily be much greater than the increase in the purchases by any single consumer. The *percentage* increase in X along the aggregate demand curve D, however, need not exceed the *percentage* increase along the individual demand curves. (This point will be considered further when the concept of elasticity is taken up in the next chapter.)

An implicit assumption of the foregoing analysis is that all consumers are charged the same price P_x. If they pay different prices, a market demand curve in the ordinary sense cannot be constructed.

CONCLUSION

The market demand curve is the *horizontal* sum of the individual demand curves.

EXERCISE 4.11

Adam's demand curve for commodity X is $x_A = 10 - 2P_x$. Betty's demand is $x_B = 10 - 3P_x$. They are the only two consumers in the market. What is the market demand curve? Compare the slopes along the individual demand curves with the slope of the market demand curve.

ANSWER: Remember that it is the *quantities demanded* that must be summed (not the prices). So the market demand equation is $X = x_A + x_B = 20 - 5P_x$. Since demand curves are drawn with price on the vertical axis, the slope (rise over run)

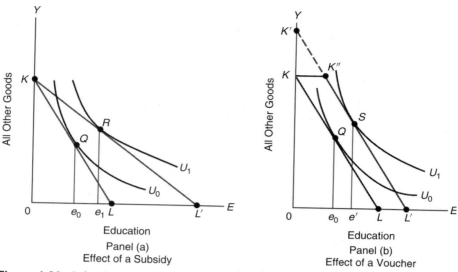

Figure 4.20. Subsidy versus Voucher

In Panel (a) a subsidy to consumers of education reduces its price; the budget line shifts from KL to KL'. At the new optimum R, the quantity of education purchased will be greater (unless it is a Giffen good in this range, which is highly unlikely). In Panel (b), the "voucher" amount KK' is a gift of income that is spendable only on education. The budget line shifts to the right, from KL to $K'L'$, except that the consumer cannot consume in the range between K' and K'' (because the full amount of the voucher would not then be spent on education). The new optimum at S will involve buying more education, so long as it is not an inferior good.

---

is $-\Delta P_x/\Delta x$. Specifically, Adam's demand equation implies that a quantity change of, say, $\Delta x_A = 1$ is associated with a price change of ΔP_x of $-1/2$. So the slope of Adam's demand curve is $-1/2$, the slope of Betty's demand curve is $-1/3$, and the slope of the market demand curve is $-1/5$. Thus, as in the diagram of Figure 4.19, the market demand curve is flatter than either of the individual demand curves.

4.6   AN APPLICATION: SUBSIDY VERSUS VOUCHER

Governments often try to encourage people to consume more of a particular good, for example, education. One method is to subsidize producers or consumers of education. (Free public education is of course an extreme kind of subsidy.) Here we shall explore a much-disucssed alternative, vouchers.

In Figure 4.20, E represents education and Y represents "all other goods." Panel (a) shows the effect of a subsidy. The original (unsubsidized) tangency optimum is at Q on indifference curve U_0. A subsidy acts like a reduction in price; it rotates the budget line from KL outward to KL'. The new optimum is at R on indifference curve U_1. Apart from the unlikely possibility that education is a Giffen good, the subsidy will increase the amount of education consumed. In the diagram, the increase is the distance $e_1 - e_0$ on the horizontal axis.

Panel (b) of Figure 4.20 shows the effect of a voucher. The initial optimum Q on indifference curve U_0 is the same as before. A voucher is a gift of income spendable *only*

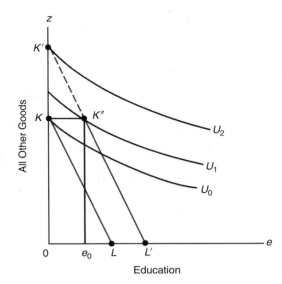

Figure 4.21. Corner Solution and Voucher

The initial optimum is the corner solution at K; no education is purchased. A voucher gift of income in the amount KK' leads to a new optimum at K''. (The consumer would prefer a corner solution at point K', but this is unattainable.) The voucher leads to increased consumption of education, provided only that education is a good rather than a bad for this individual.

on the voucher good – here, education. The distance KK' on the vertical axis represents the amount of the voucher, so the consumer's budget line shifts outward from KL to $K'L'$. But since the gift can only be spent on education, the consumer is not allowed to move to any point on the dashed segment $K'K''$. Therefore the effective new budget constraint is the kinked line $KK''L'$. In Panel (b) the new optimum is at S on indifference curve U_1, with increased consumption of education ($e' > e_0$).

So far a subsidy appears to differ little from a voucher. The subsidy works through a price change, the voucher through an income change. But the voucher has an especially strong effect upon those consumers who would otherwise have chosen little or no education. In Figure 4.21 the individual is initially at a corner solution at point K on indifference curve U_0, spending nothing on education. Even a large subsidy, swinging the budget line outward from point K, may have little or no effect upon the amount of education chosen. But the voucher moves the entire budget line outward to $K'L'$ (of which only the solid range $K''L'$ is effective). The new optimum is at K''. The consumer would prefer K' to K'', but K' is not available since the voucher amount can be spent only on education. At K'' the individual spends the entire voucher amount on education, and spends just as much on other goods as before.

CONCLUSION

For persons who had previously not consumed the voucher commodity at all (or who consumed an amount less than the voucher provides), vouchers almost always increase consumption. The only exception would be where the voucher commodity was regarded as a *bad* rather than a good; in that case, the voucher would remain unused.

For either subsidies or vouchers, this analysis is incomplete in at least two respects. First, the market price of the good was assumed to remain constant throughout. If a voucher or subsidy were to increase the desired consumption of education, for example, the enlarged demand by beneficiaries of the subsidy or voucher would tend to raise its price – thus possibly reducing the purchases of those not benefiting from the subsidy or voucher. Second, the taxes collected to finance the subsidy or voucher would reduce the spendable income of some or all consumers. So these other individuals might spend less on the commodity. A full analysis needs to take these secondary effects into account.

EXAMPLE 4.7 BUT DO VOUCHERS REALLY HELP?

Low-income housing has been subsidized in the United States since the 1930s. At first the subsidy mainly took the form of public housing projects. Since the early 1980s, vouchers have been increasingly used.

For families who receive them, vouchers are a big help. But not all eligible families are granted vouchers. If the voucher program raises the price of housing, those low-income households who do not receive vouchers could end up worse off.

A study by Scott Susin suggests that this indeed occurred.[a] He found that vouchers conferred a very large benefit upon recipients. But, allowing for the consequent rise in housing prices, the cost imposed upon nonsubsidized poor households was even greater.

As shown in the table, the average annual benefit covered 69% of the rental cost for the 1.3 million households receiving vouchers. But low-income families that did not get vouchers faced an increase of about 16% in their housing expense.

Benefits and costs of housing vouchers (1993)

	Households receiving vouchers	Low-income unsubsidized households
Average monthly rent	$537	$443
% effect on housing cost	−69%	+16%
Number of households	1.3 million	9.6 million
Annual benefit	+$5.8 billion	−$8.2 billion

Source: Adapted from Susin, Table 9 (p. 145).

This adverse effect might have been avoided by reforming the voucher program to spread the benefit more widely, instead of providing very large per-family benefits to a small fraction of low-income families.

[a] Scott Susin, "Rent Vouchers and the Price of Low-Income Housing," *Journal of Public Economics*, v. 83 (2002).

SUMMARY   The optimum of the consumer involves the interaction of *preferences* (indifference curves) with *market opportunities* (budget line). The consumer's optimum occurs where the budget line bounding the opportunity set touches the highest attainable indifference curve. This solution can be either an interior optimum (both goods are consumed) or else a corner optimum (only one good is consumed). In an interior solution the budget line is tangent to an indifference curve. In a corner solution the highest attainable indifference curve meets the budget line along one or the other axis.

Analytically, the budget equation for an individual with income I, who can buy good X at price P_x and good Y at price P_y, is:

$$P_x x + P_y y = I$$

The cardinal concept of utility allows the Marginal Utilities of goods to be defined. If goods X and Y are bought but good Z is not, the optimum of the consumer can be expressed as the Consumption Balance Equation/Inequality:

$$\frac{MU_X\,(x > 0)}{P_x} = \frac{MU_y\,(y > 0)}{P_y} > \frac{MU_z\,(z = 0)}{P_z}$$

Using the more general concept of ordinal utility, the rate at which the consumer is *willing* to substitute one good for the other (the slope along the indifference curve) is compared to the rate at which the market *permits* such exchanges (the price ratio). The Marginal Rate of Substitution in Consumption (MRS_C) is the slope of the indifference curve, with sign adjusted to be positive. If both goods X and Y are consumed, then the Substitution Balance Equation holds:

$$MRS_C = P_x/P_y$$

If good X is consumed but good Y is not, the Substitution Balance Inequality holds:

$$MRS_C > P_x/P_y$$

Suppose good Y is the numeraire commodity with price fixed at $P_y = 1$. Then the Marginal Rate of Substitution between X and Y can be expressed, in a more intuitive terminology, as the Marginal Value of X in terms of Y, symbolized as MV_X.

Goods that are strong *complements*, such as bread and butter, tend to be consumed together. Consequently, a large change in the price ratio between them causes only a small change in the ratio in which they are consumed. Close *substitutes*, such as Dell and HP computers, tend to be consumed to the exclusion of one another. Consequently, even a small price shift may lead to a big change in the ratio in which they are bought.

As income increases, with prices held constant, the budget line shifts parallel to itself and outward from the origin. The optimum positions attained, for given prices P_x and P_y, are shown by the Income Expansion Path (IEP). If both X and Y are normal superior goods, the Income Expansion Path has positive slope. The data described by the Income Expansion Path can also be plotted as an Engel Curve showing how the quantity of X bought varies with income.

As price P_x falls, with I and P_y held constant, the budget line tilts outward while retaining the same intercept on the y-axis. The optimum positions attained are represented by the Price Expansion Path (PEP).

Since a fall in P_x, with I and P_y held constant, implies an increase in real income (higher utility), a price change has both a *pure substitution effect* and an *income effect* upon consumption of X. The substitution effect shows that, as P_x falls, a consumer always buys more of X. The income effect can go either way: it is positive for a superior good, and negative for an inferior good.

Market demand is aggregated from individual demands by summing, at each price, the quantities bought by all the consumers. The slope of the market demand curve is always flatter than the slopes of the individual demand curves.

Government may attempt to increase consumption of a good by means of a subsidy or a voucher. A subsidy works like a reduction in price in inducing consumers to purchase more of the good. A voucher works like an increase in income, except that the enlarged income can be spent only on the voucher good. A voucher is therefore particularly effective for consumers who would otherwise have bought very little of the good, or none at all.

QUESTIONS

†The answers to daggered questions appear at the end of the book.

For Review

1. What is the meaning of the expression "the optimum of the consumer"?
2. In a situation with just two goods, how does the amount of income affect the shape of an individual's market opportunity set? How do the prices of the two goods affect the shape?
†3. a. What is the "budget line"?
   b. What is its equation?
   c. What determines the slope of the budget line?
†4. What is the geometrical condition for the optimum of the consumer? (Distinguish between a corner solution and an interior solution.)
5. If indifference curves were concave, why would the consumer's optimum never be in the interior?
†6. a. What is the Consumption Balance Equation that expresses the optimum of the consumer? Relate this to the Substitution Balance Equation.
   b. Do the equations hold for an interior solution, a corner solution, or both?
7. Explain the relation between Marginal Value and Marginal Rate of Substitution. What are the differences between them?
8. Give examples of pairs of goods that are strong complements, versus pairs that are close substitutes. What observable market characteristic distinguishes them?
9. Characterize a normal good, an inferior good, and an ultra-superior good. Give examples of each. For two goods, which of the above must they be if the Income Expansion Path has positive slope? What can you say if the Income Expansion Path has negative slope?
10. Prove that if X and Y are goods rather than bads, the Income Expansion Path never points down and to the left.
†11. a. A positively sloped Income Expansion Path implies what shape for the Engel Curve?
   b. What can you say about the Engel Curve for an inferior good?
12. Show how an individual's demand curve can be derived from the Price Expansion Path.
13. Is there a utility-increasing direction along the Income Expansion Path? Along the Price Expansion Path?
†14. What does the Law of Demand say about the shape of the Price Expansion Path?
15. How does the Hicks decomposition separate the "income effect" and the "substitution effect" of a price change?
16. Using the Hicks decomposition, show that the Giffen condition (a price decrease reduces consumption of the good) can hold only for an inferior good.
17. How is the market demand curve derived from knowledge of individuals' separate demand curves? Can individual demand curves be determined from knowledge of the market demand curve?
†18. "As compared with a simple subsidy, the voucher scheme is particularly effective for consumers who would otherwise have chosen little or none of the commodity." Illustrate and explain.

19. In Exercise 4.11, we can rewrite Adam's demand equation as $P_x = 5 - (x_A/2)$ and Betty's as $P_x = (10/3) - (x_B/3)$. Can we conclude that the price in the market demand curve for a given quantity x is the sum of Adam's demand price at x and Betty's demand price at x, $P_x = (25/3) - (5x/6)$?

For Further Thought and Discussion

†1. a.   Describe an experiment that might reveal an individual's Marginal Rate of Substitution in Consumption between two goods.

    b.   Describe how an experiment might reveal Marginal Utility for either good.

2. Why is diminishing Marginal Utility necessary if the Consumption Balance Equation is to express an optimum? Why is decreasing Marginal Rate of Substitution in Consumption necessary if the Substitution Equivalence Equation is to express an optimum? Is decreasing Marginal Utility also necessary?

†3. a.   Why can the Giffen condition hold only over a limited range of the Price Expansion Path?

    b.   Could the Price Expansion Path ever circle around and rejoin itself at its starting point on the y-axis?

†4. a.   How does a change in the price of a good tend to shift the position of the Income Expansion Path?

    b.   How does a change in income tend to shift the position of the Price Expansion Path?

5. Let an individual's demand curve cut the vertical price axis at some finite "choke price" P_x^o. Show the equivalent situation in terms of the individual's indifference curves and budget line. Must the consumer's optimum then be a corner solution at price P_x^o?

†6. "I think *I* could be a good woman if I had five thousand a year" – Becky Sharp, in Thackeray's *Vanity Fair*. Can you give an economic interpretation?

†7. Consider a pair of commodities such as bread and butter, which are strong complements, versus another pair such as butter and margarine, which are close substitutes. Which pair is more likely to have a member that is an inferior good? Explain.

†8. Why is the income effect of a price change usually small compared to the substitution effect?

9. "Since 1900, real income has increased tremendously, yet the average number of children per family has decreased." Consider the following possible explanations, and illustrate in terms of market opportunity sets and indifference curves of families between number of children and "all other goods."

    a.   Children are an inferior good; since we're richer now, we want fewer of them.

    b.   Children are not an inferior good; however, it has become more expensive to bear and raise children.

    c.   Children are not an inferior good, nor have they become relatively more expensive. What has happened is that tastes have changed; couples today want smaller families than couples did in 1900.

†10. In the comparison of subsidy versus voucher in the text, the price of the good was assumed to remain unchanged. Would it be correct to anticipate some change of price? In which direction is this likely to go? Show the effect upon the market opportunity set.

11. Still another consideration is that government spending on subsidies or vouchers must ordinarily be financed by taxes, say on income. Show the effects upon a consumer's market opportunity set of a tax-financed subsidy and of a tax-financed voucher.

†12. The following is sometimes given as an example of a Giffen situation. A person with only $100 available must make a 1,000-mile train trip. He prefers first-class travel to coach travel, but his first priority is to complete his trip. Suppose first-class travel costs 20 cents per mile and coach costs 5 cents per mile. Then it can be verified that he will travel 333 1/3 miles in first class and 666 2/3 miles in coach. Now let the price of coach travel rise to 10 cents per mile. Then the traveler cannot afford any first-class miles at all if he is to complete his trip, so the amount of coach travel will rise from 666 2/3 to 1000 even though its price has doubled!

    a.   Is coach travel an inferior good here? (What would happen if the travel budget were to rise above $100?)

    b.   Under what circumstances will the traveler choose a corner solution with only coach travel? With only first-class travel?

†13. a.   If two commodities are perfect substitutes, is it true that the consumer's optimum will almost always be a corner solution?

    b.   Will it ever not be?

14. How would you draw a consumer's opportunity set for three goods X, Y, and Z? What would you call this, instead of a budget line?

15. The discussion in Example 4.4 suggests some possible rationales for noncash gifts. Can you think of any others?

16. If X and Y are normal superior goods, verify that an increase in income tends to shift the Price Expansion Path (PEP) to the right.

17. In Exercise 4.9, what happens at $P_x = 120$? [*Hint:* This is the individual's "choke price."]

18. In Exercise 4.11, the market demand equation $X = x_A + x_B = 20 - 5P_x$ is invalid if $P_x \geq 10/3$. Why? [*Hint:* What is the choke price for each individual?]

†19. At a given price ratio, variations in income generate an Income Expansion Path (IEP). If the price ratio were different, we know that a different IEP curve would be generated. For the same individual, could these two IEP curves ever cross?

†20. What is the effect of an increased price of one good when the two goods the consumer can buy are perfect substitutes?

21. Suppose a gasoline tax is imposed, taking the form of a fixed number of cents per gallon (the same for regular and for premium gas). Consider the following arguments. (1) While we would expect the quantity demanded of both premium and regular gasoline to fall after the tax is imposed, there should be a *relatively smaller* effect for the premium quality, since a fixed number of cents is a smaller *proportionate* tax for the premium gas. (2) On the contrary, since premium gasoline is more of a "luxury" good, and regular gasoline more of a "necessity" good, we'd expect a *relatively bigger* effect for the premium quality. Is one or the other of these arguments totally wrong, or is it a matter of which of two valid arguments is the stronger? Analyze each argument separately and explain.

5 Applications and Extensions of Demand Theory

A tax on gasoline will raise its price. By the Law of Demand, gasoline consumption will fall. But how much? And a fall in consumer incomes will likely discourage gasoline usage, but to what extent? This chapter describes the measures that economists use to quantify how consumers respond to changes in price and changes in income. Other questions addressed include: (1) Why are consumers' demands sometimes very sensitive to changes in price or in income, sometimes not? (2) What is the effect of *nonprice* constraints upon choice, for example rationing in wartime?

<h2>5.1   THE ENGEL CURVE AND THE INCOME ELASTICITY OF DEMAND</h2>

For any good X, the change in consumption (Δx) due to a change in income (ΔI) could be measured by the ratio $\Delta x/\Delta I$. This ratio is the slope of the Engel Curve (see Section 4.3 in the preceding chapter) over the relevant range.[1] But there is a difficulty with the simple ratio $\Delta x/\Delta I$: it is sensitive to the units of measurement. If commodity X is butter, the numerical value of $\Delta x/\Delta I$ varies depending on whether the amount of butter is stated in ounces or pounds or tons, and whether income is quoted in dollars or cents. The concept of *elasticity* eliminates this difficulty by expressing the variables in proportionate (percentage) terms.

> **DEFINITION:** The income elasticity of demand is the proportionate change in the quantity purchased divided by the proportionate change in income.

Let ϵ_x (where ϵ is the Greek letter *epsilon*) symbolize the income elasticity of demand for commodity X; this definition is represented by the first ratio in equation (5.1). The other expressions are equivalent algebraic forms:

$$\epsilon_x \equiv \frac{\Delta x/x}{\Delta I/I} \equiv \frac{\Delta x/\Delta I}{x/I} \equiv \frac{\Delta x}{\Delta I}\frac{I}{x} \tag{5.1}$$

EXERCISE 5.1

Sally's income and purchases of apples A over two successive years are shown below. Assuming nothing else has changed, and in particular that the *price* of apples remains the same, compute her implied income elasticity for apples.

	Year 1	Year 2
Income	$10,000	$11,000
Apples purchased	100	116

ANSWER: The change in income is $\Delta I = \$1,000$, and for apples $\Delta a = 16$. The formulas for income elasticity in equation (5.1) also require a numerical value for income itself, and the question arises of whether to use $I = \$10,000$ or $\$11,000$ or

---

[1] *Mathematical Footnote:* In calculus notation this slope is $\partial x/\partial I$. (The partial derivative symbol indicates that other independent variables, such as the price P_x, are being held constant.) *Note:* Henceforth, the text will not provide Mathematical Footnotes that merely indicate how the Δ notation for finite changes could be replaced with differential notation (∂ or d).

Figure 5.1. Engel Curve and Unitary Income Elasticity

The straight-line Engel Curve ADB has income elasticity of 1, because the slope along the curve is the same as the slope of a ray from the origin to any point on the curve. The nonlinear Engel Curve CDE, tangent at point D to ADB, therefore also has an income elasticity of 1 for small changes in the neighborhood of point D. In the range CD the slope along curve CDE is less than the slope of a ray from the origin to the curve, so $\epsilon_x < 1$. Correspondingly, $\epsilon_x > 1$ in the range of CDE between D and E.

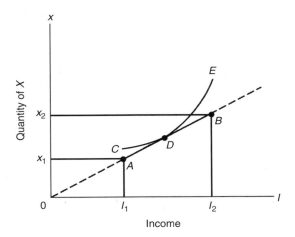

something in between. The most convenient approximation is the average of the two: $I = \$10{,}500$. Similarly for apples, the average is $a = 108$. Substituting these averages for I and a into equation (5.1) yields the income elasticity:

$$\epsilon_a = \frac{16}{1{,}000} \frac{10{,}500}{105} = 1.556$$

So Sally's income elasticity for apples is 1.556. A 1% increase in her income would increase her purchases of apples by 1.556%.

Income elasticity is illustrated geometrically in Figure 5.1. Consider the Engel Curve depicted by the straight line ADB drawn through the origin. Since the curve has positive slope, X is a superior good: more is purchased as income rises. By the geometry of similar triangles, the percentage increase in income I between points A and B is the same as the percentage increase in quantity x.[2] In equation (5.1), the first numerator is the percent change in quantity and the first denominator is the percent change in price. Since these percentages are equal, the income elasticity is $\epsilon_x = 1$ everywhere along the line ADB. The same holds along *any* straight-line Engel Curve through the origin.

Now consider the positively sloped but nonlinear Engel Curve CDE drawn tangent to ADB at point D. Along CDE the income elasticity of demand does not remain constant. Nevertheless, at the tangency point D the income elasticity along CDE is the same as along ADB. Why? The second formula for ϵ_x on the right-hand side of equation (5.1), $(\Delta x/\Delta I)/(x/I)$, involves the slope $\Delta x/\Delta I$ and the ratio x/I. At the point of tangency, the curves CDE and ADB have the same slopes. And they also have the same x and I. So any nonlinear Engel Curve CDE has income elasticity $\epsilon_x = 1$ in the neighborhood of its tangency with a straight line drawn through the origin.

---

[2] *Mathematical Footnote:* By similar triangles, $x_2/x_1 = I_2/I_1$. So $(x_2 - x_1)/x_1 = (I_2 - I_1)/I_1$. We could equivalently use x_2 and I_2 in the denominators, or else the averages $(x_1 + x_2)/2$ and $(I_1 + I_2)/2$.

In the range CD along the curve CDE, CD is flatter than AD. That means that x increases with income, but less than proportionately. Consequently, in this range the income elasticity along CDE is less than 1: $\epsilon_x < 1$. Reversing the argument, $\epsilon_x > 1$ in the range DE where x rises more than proportionately than income.

For any positively sloped Engel Curve that is a straight line through the origin, the income elasticity is $\epsilon_x = 1$. But such lines can be drawn from very nearly vertical to very nearly horizontal. So what corresponds geometrically to income elasticity is not the steepness of the Engel Curve, but rather *the steepness as compared with a line through the origin.*

PROPOSITION: An Engel Curve with positive slope has income elasticity greater than, equal to, or less than 1 depending upon whether the slope *along* the Engel Curve is greater than, equal to, or less than the slope of a ray drawn from the origin *to* the curve.

EXERCISE 5.2

The following equations correspond to four possible Engel Curves: (a) $x = I/8$; (b) $x = 5 + I/10$; (c) $x = -75 + I/2$; (d) $x = 30 - I/40$. Determine the slope and the income elasticity for each curve at the point $I = 200$, $x = 25$. (e) In which of these cases is the commodity an inferior good? (f) What if the equation for the Engel Curve were $x = 5 + I/8$?

ANSWER: (a) The slope $\Delta x/\Delta I$ all along the curve $x = I/8$ is 1/8. The income elasticity is $\epsilon_x = (\Delta x/\Delta I)(I/x) = (1/8)(200/25) = 1$. (b) The slope of $x = 5 + I/10$ is 1/10, and so $\epsilon_x = (1/10)(200/25) = 0.8$. (c) The slope is $\frac{1}{2}$, and $\epsilon_x = (\frac{1}{2})(200/25) = 4$. (d) The slope is $-1/40$, and $\epsilon_x = (-1/40)(200/25) = -0.2$. (e) Commodity X is inferior only in case (d), where the income elasticity is negative. (f) This was a trick question! The equation given is perfectly possible for an Engel Curve, but the specific point $I = 200$, $x = 25$ does not lie on the curve. So the question cannot be answered.

EXAMPLE 5.1 INCOME ELASTICITIES IN NEW ZEALAND

Using a sample of 3,487 New Zealand households in the period 1981–1982, David E. A. Giles and Peter Hampton calculated income elasticities for various categories of consumer expenditure.[a]

Category	Effect of income on expenditures (income elasticities)	
	Lowest income group	Highest income group
Food	0.63	0.84
Housing	1.22	1.80
Household operation	0.66	0.85
Clothing	1.29	0.98
Transportation	1.50	0.90
Tobacco and alcohol	2.00	0.85

Source: Giles and Hampton, Table 3 (p. 458).

For the low-income group, the income elasticity for "Tobacco and Alcohol" is surprisingly high. This has possibly disturbing implications for social policy. It suggests that increased income in the hands of the poor might largely be devoted to "undesirable" commodities such as tobacco and alcohol. (On the other hand, perhaps it is overly paternalistic to disapprove of poor people deriving some solace from smoking or drinking.)

COMMENT

The comparative income elasticities shown for Food versus Tobacco and Alcohol here are consistent with the reported observation in Example 4.5, "Luxuries versus Necessities in a P.O.W. Camp." In the P.O.W. case, a 50% cut in both cigarette and food rations led to a *fall* in the price of food as compared to cigarettes. In other words, the P.O.W.'s, extremely low-income consumers, were attempting to shift consumption away from food and toward cigarettes as their real income fell even further.

[a] David E. A. Giles and Peter Hampton, "An Engel Curve Analysis of Household Expenditures in New Zealand," *Economic Record*, v. 61 (March 1985).

It is sometimes useful to distinguish between elasticity *at a point* and elasticity *over some range or arc* along a curve. The definition in equation (5.1) covers both cases. Arc elasticity is a kind of average of the point elasticities within the range considered. As the intervals Δx and ΔI shrink toward zero, the arc elasticity approaches the point elasticity along the curve.

A person's income elasticities over all the commodities consumed are connected by an important condition:

PROPOSITION: The weighted average of an individual's income elasticities equals 1, where the weights are the proportions of the budget spent on each commodity.

If only two commodities X and Y are consumed, their respective weights in the consumer's budget are $k_x \equiv P_x x / I$ and $k_y \equiv P_y y / I$. So for this simplest case the proposition becomes

$$k_x \epsilon_x + k_y \epsilon_y = 1 \qquad (5.2)[3]$$

---

[3] *Mathematical Footnote:* It is easy to justify the proposition in the simple two-good case of equation (5.2). Substituting the definitions of k_x, k_y, and the two income elasticities, the left-hand side of (5.2) is:

$$\frac{P_x x}{I} \frac{\Delta x}{\Delta I} \frac{I}{x} + \frac{P_y y}{I} \frac{\Delta y}{\Delta I} \frac{I}{y} = \frac{P_x \Delta x + P_y \Delta y}{\Delta I}$$

The numerator here is the changed expenditure on the two goods taken together, while the denominator is the change in income. Since the two must be equal (assuming that all income is spent), the right-hand side of equation (5.2) must equal 1.

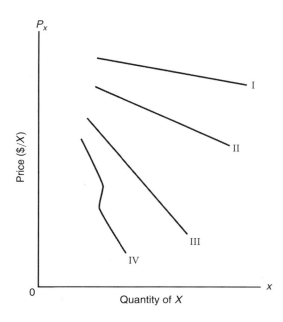

Figure 5.2. Alternative Demand-Curve Slopes

The four demand curves represent different responses of quantity purchased to changes in price. Since demand curves are conventionally drawn with price on the vertical axis, a greater response is represented by a flatter demand curve. Curve IV has a region that represents the exceptional Giffen case.

EXERCISE 5.3

Suppose there are just two goods, bread and wine. If bread accounts for 95% of the budget and has income elasticity $\epsilon_b = 0.9$, what can you say about the income elasticity ϵ_w for wine?

ANSWER: Equation (5.2) here becomes $(0.95 \times 0.9) + 0.05\,\epsilon_w = 1$. Solving, the income elasticity for wine must be $\epsilon_w = 2.9$.

It follows that a good that accounts for a very large fraction of a person's budget must have an income elasticity close to 1. Conversely, if a good has extremely high income elasticity, like wine in the exercise above, you can be confident that it constitutes only a small portion of the budget.

5.2   THE DEMAND CURVE AND THE PRICE ELASTICITY OF DEMAND

A direct measure of the consumer's response to a change in price would be the ratio $\Delta x/\Delta P_x$. This ratio is the *reciprocal* of the slope along the demand curve.[4] The Law of Demand tells us that the demand curve has negative slope. Figure 5.2 illustrates demand curves with flatter and steeper negative slopes; the steeper the curve, the smaller is the absolute magnitude of $\Delta x/\Delta P_x$.

Like the direct measure $\Delta x/\Delta I$ of sensitivity to changes in income, the direct measure $\Delta x/\Delta P_x$ of a good's sensitivity to changes in price has the disadvantage of being affected by the units of measurement. The responsiveness of quantity to price, $\Delta x/\Delta P_x$, could numerically be made to appear either great or small – depending upon whether quantity

---

[4] Economists conventionally draw demand curves with price P_x on the vertical axis. So the slope of the demand curve is $\Delta P_x/\Delta x$; the reciprocal of the slope is $\Delta x/\Delta P_x$.

x were measured in tons or pounds or ounces, or price P_x in dollars or cents. To avoid this difficulty, economists again use an *elasticity* measure defined in terms of proportionate changes. Specifically, the ratio of the proportionate change in quantity to proportionate change in price is called the *price elasticity of demand*. (The expression "elasticity of demand," standing alone, always refers to the price elasticity of demand.) Only in terms of such proportionate changes, independent of units of measurement, could one meaningfully say, for example, whether the demand for automobiles is more or less sensitive to price than the demand for bananas.

DEFINITION: The price elasticity of demand is the proportionate change in quantity purchased divided by the proportionate change in price.

In equation (5.3), η_x (where η is the Greek letter eta) symbolizes the price elasticity of demand for commodity X. The first ratio corresponds to the definition above; the other expressions are algebraically equivalent forms:

$$\eta_x \equiv \frac{\Delta x/x}{\Delta P_x/P_x} \equiv \frac{\Delta x/\Delta P_x}{x/P_x} \equiv \frac{\Delta x}{\Delta P_x}\frac{P_x}{x} \tag{5.3}$$

Since $\Delta x/\Delta P_x$ is normally negative, so is the price elasticity η_x. Conventionally, a demand curve is said to be "elastic" if $\eta_x < -1$, that is, if the elasticity measure exceeds unity in absolute value. In the opposite case, if η_x has an absolute value less than unity, the demand is said to be "inelastic." But since elasticity generally varies along a demand curve, it is rarely advisable to describe an entire demand curve as elastic (or inelastic). Rather, one should say that demand is elastic (or inelastic) *in the neighborhood of some given price-quantity point.*

EXERCISE 5.4

The following equations represent different possible curves for commodity X: (a) $x = 240 - 30P_x$; (b) $x = 320 - 50P_x$; (c) $x = 20 + 25P_x$. What are the associated price elasticities in the neighborhood of the point $x = 120$, $P_x = 4$?

ANSWER: From equation (5.2), $\eta_x = (\Delta x/\Delta P_x)/(x/P_x)$. In each case, the value of the denominator is $x/P_x = 120/4 = 30$. Inserting the appropriate numerator ratio, (a) $\eta_x = -30/30 = -1$; (b) $\eta_x = -50/30 = -5/3$; (c) $\eta_x = -25/30 = +5/6$. (Since the price elasticity is positive in the last case, this is a situation where the Law of Demand fails: at a higher price more is purchased rather than less.)

EXAMPLE 5.2 THE DEMAND FOR OPIUM

An alternative to interdicting the supply of narcotic drugs (see Chapter 2, Section 2.1) is to legalize the drug traffic but subject it to heavy taxation. Or the government might monopolize the business and charge steep prices.

How effective might high prices be for discouraging consumption of narcotics? That depends upon the elasticity of demand. A study by Jan C. van Ours examined the demand for opium in the Dutch East Indies in the period 1932–1938 when its consumption was legal – the supply being provided by a government monopoly.[a]

The author estimated the elasticity of demand for opium in this period to be around −0.7 with respect to overall *consumption*, and around −0.4 with respect to *number of users*. That is, a 1% increase in price was associated, other things equal, with a 0.7% decrease in the total consumed and a 0.4% decrease in the number of regular users. (It follows, of course, that those continuing to consume did not decrease their usage by the full 0.7%.)

COMMENT

To the extent that these data might be applicable to narcotics today, they suggest that a 50% increase in price would reduce consumption by around 35%. But as a practical problem, prices much higher than those currently being paid in the street would encourage illegal smuggling – with the result that, just as before, costly interdiction would be required. Perhaps the argument for legalization should not be based upon any expectation of actually *reducing* drug consumption by means of higher prices. A more practical goal might be to make the legal price about the same as the current effective street price.

Unfortunately, removing the risks and stigma of illegality would certainly, if the price were to remain about the same, *increase* consumption of narcotics. So a considerable rise in narcotics usage would have to be anticipated after legalization. As against this, society would gain by saving the resources now dissipated in the effort to interdict illegal supplies.

[a] Jan C. van Ours, "The Price Elasticity of Hard Drugs: The Case of Opium in the Dutch East Indies, 1932–1938," *Journal of Political Economy*, v. 103 (April 1995).

It is often thought that addictive commodities are necessarily characterized by low price elasticity: a consumer who is "hooked" cannot be very sensitive to price variation. And indeed, in the preceding Example the indicated demand for opium was in the inelastic range, though not extremely so. The next Example considers the elasticity of the demand for tobacco.

EXAMPLE 5.3 COLLEGE STUDENTS' DEMAND FOR CIGARETTES

Frank J. Chaloupka and Henry Wechsler studied how cigarette prices influenced the smoking choices of students at 140 American four-year colleges and universities.[a] Owing to differing state and local taxes, and other varying influences upon supply or demand, at any moment of time cigarette prices differ from region to region. These differences provide the price variation needed for estimating demand elasticity.

The authors calculated the overall price elasticity of demand for cigarettes to be in the elastic range, around $\eta = -1.4$. Higher prices reduced consumption through two approximately equal effects: smaller per capita usage by smokers, and fewer people choosing to smoke. This suggests that a 10% price increase would lead to about a 7% reduction in the proportion of college students smoking, and also to about a 7% reduction in cigarettes consumed per smoker.

These elasticities are somewhat higher than the figures for opium in the preceding Example. One explanation is that the cigarette study dealt only with students. Elasticity of demand is likely to be higher for young persons, whose habits are not yet so firmly ingrained. In fact, the authors quote various estimates indicating that, for adults, the elasticity of demand for cigarettes is considerably smaller – around

$\eta = -0.4$. So higher cigarette prices for young people are likely, owing to their effect upon habit formation, to reduce not just current use but lifetime patterns of consumption.

[a] Frank J. Chaloupka and Henry Wechsler, "Price, Tobacco Control Policies and Smoking among Young Adults," *Journal of Health Economics*, v. 16 (1997), pp. 359–373.

The Law of Demand says that a reduction in the price of good X will increase the quantity consumed. But if price falls and quantity increases, there are offsetting effects upon $E_x \equiv P_x x$, the consumer's *total spending* on good X.

The price elasticity can tell us whether the price effect or the quantity effect dominates. Suppose η_x is numerically greater than 1 (that is, $\eta_x < -1$), so that demand is "elastic." Then from the first ratio in equation (5.3), the proportionate change in quantity $\Delta x/x$ exceeds in magnitude the proportionate change $\Delta P_x / P_x$ in price. So, if demand is elastic, after a price decrease the rising quantity outweighs the falling price in proportionate terms – meaning that total spending on X increases. Correspondingly, if $\eta_x > -1$ (if demand is "inelastic"), total spending E_x decreases as P_x falls. And it follows that if $\eta_x = -1$ ("unitary" demand elasticity), spending remains constant for small changes in P_x up or down.

PROPOSITION: If a consumer's demand for X is *elastic*, a reduction in price P_x will lead to increased spending $E_x \equiv P_x x$ on commodity X. If demand is *inelastic*, a price reduction decreases E_x. If the demand elasticity is *unitary*, E_x remains the same.

EXERCISE 5.5

Robert's demand curve for good X is given by the equation $x = 100 - 2P_x$. (a) What is the elasticity of demand at the point $x = 20$, $P_x = 40$? (b) If price falls from $P_x = 40$ to $P_x = 35$, what happens to total spending E_x and what does this imply about the elasticity of demand? (c) Compute the elasticity to verify the answer.

ANSWER: (a) Along the demand curve $x = 100 - 2P_x$, the ratio $\Delta x/\Delta P_x$ (the reciprocal of the demand-curve slope) is a constant equal to -2. Using the second expression for η_x from equation (5.2):

$$\eta_x \equiv \frac{\Delta x/\Delta P_x}{x/P_x} = \frac{-2}{20/40} = -4$$

(b) At $P_x = 40$ the quantity is $x = 100 - 2(40) = 20$ and so total spending on X is $E_x = 800$. At $P_x = 35$, quantity is $x = 100 - 2(35) = 30$, so total spending is $E_x = 1{,}050$. Since spending is higher at the lower price, demand is elastic. (c) Since $\Delta x/\Delta P_x = -2$, taking the midpoint values for x and P_x, implies $x/P_x = 25/37.5 = 0.667$. So the elasticity is $-2/(0.667) = -3$, confirming that demand is elastic in this interval.

The logical relationship among price, elasticity of demand, and total spending on any good X can be expressed in another way that will be useful in later chapters. First, *Marginal Expenditure* can be defined as usual for a marginal magnitude:

$$ME_x \equiv \Delta E_x/\Delta x \tag{5.4}$$

It then follows that:

$$ME_x \equiv P_x(1 + 1/\eta_x) \qquad (5.5)$$

(The proof is provided in a footnote.)[5]

For elastic demand ($\eta_x < -1$), in equation (5.5) the expression in parentheses is positive, so Marginal Expenditure is also positive. By similar reasoning, Marginal Expenditure is negative when demand is inelastic ($\eta_x > -1$). Marginal Expenditure is zero for unitary demand elasticity ($\eta_x = -1$). And, of course, if $\eta_x = -1$ consumers will spend the same amount of dollars on X no matter what the price; Marginal Expenditure is zero.

Notice that what is *spending* from the consumer point of view is *revenue* from the viewpoint of the sellers. Using this re-interpretation, equation (5.5) will be important when the supply side of the market is taken up in later chapters.

5.3   THE CROSS-ELASTICITY OF DEMAND

The amount of butter that consumers buy depends not only upon the price of butter but also upon prices of related goods like bread and cheese. Once again, it is convenient to use a unit-free measure of demand responsiveness. The *cross-elasticity of demand* is defined as:

$$\eta_{xy} \equiv \frac{\Delta x/x}{\Delta P_y/P_y} \equiv \frac{\Delta x}{\Delta P_y}\frac{P_y}{x} \qquad (5.6)$$

In Chapter 4, Section 4.2, *complements* in demand (such as bread and butter) were defined by the following property: a large change in the price ratio between the two goods brings about only a small change in the ratio of consumption. For *substitutes* in demand (such as bread and margarine) a small change in relative prices causes a large change in relative consumption. The concept of cross-elasticity can quantify these ideas. Complements such as bread and butter can be expected to have negative cross-elasticity ($\eta_{xy} < 0$): a reduction in the price of bread tends to increase the quantity of butter purchased. Between *substitutes* such as butter and margarine, the cross-elasticity of demand is typically positive ($\eta_{xy} > 0$): a reduction in the price of butter will tend to decrease the quantity of margarine purchased.

EXAMPLE 5.4 DEMAND ELASTICITIES FOR PHARMACEUTICALS

A study by Sara Fisher Ellison and colleagues analyzed demand elasticities for four closely related drugs during the late 1980s.[a] The compounds Cephalexin, Cefadroxil, Cephradine, and Cefaclor fall generally under the heading of cephalosporins, a type of anti-infective drug. Two of the compounds (Brand 1 and Brand 3) went off patent during the period of study: hence generic competitors were able to enter the field. So

---

[5] *Mathematical Footnote*: ΔE, the change in total expenditure associated with small changes Δx and ΔP_x is approximately the sum of two components: $\Delta E_x \equiv P_x \Delta x + x \Delta P_x$. (This approximation is more accurate the smaller are the changes Δx and ΔP_x.) Dividing through by Δx:

$$\frac{\Delta E_x}{\Delta x} \equiv ME_x \equiv P_x + x\frac{\Delta P_x}{\Delta x} \equiv P_x\left(1 + \frac{x}{P_x}\frac{\Delta P_x}{x}\right)$$

The final step is to notice that the last fraction on the right is the reciprocal of the demand elasticity η_x defined in equation (5.3), which leads directly to the expression in the text above.

the researchers were able to compare the price elasticities with regard to "generic competition" as against "therapeutic competition" – the first of these being the competition between branded and generic versions of the same compound, and the second the competition between similar yet pharmaceutically distinct compounds.

Each cell of the table here shows a price elasticity. The cells along the main diagonal are the "own-price" elasticities. Thus, the entry at the upper left is the demand elasticity of Brand 1 with regard to the price of Brand 1. The value shown is negative (−0.38), as of course is to be expected. Reading down the column, the next entry is the demand elasticity of Brand 1 with regard to the price of its generic competitor – the generic version of the same compound. Since Brand 1 and Generic 1 are certainly good substitutes, the positive entry here (0.79) is consistent with expectations. As shown in the next cell down, Brand 1's therapeutic competitor Brand 3 is not so close a substitute – the figure shown is positive but smaller (0.52). Finally the entry for Generic 3 is even smaller (0.21). This makes sense, since Generic 3 differs from Brand 1 not only in being generic but also in being a different pharmaceutical compound.

| Drug | Demand elasticities of two pharmaceuticals | | | |
	Brand I	Generic I	Brand 3	Generic 3
Brand 1	−0.38	1.01	−0.20	−0.21
Generic 1	0.79	−1.04	−0.09	−0.10
Brand 3	0.52	0.53	−1.93	1.12
Generic 3	0.21	0.23	2.00	−2.87

Source: Adapted from Ellison et al. (1997), Table 7, p. 441.

Also, the own-price elasticities are greater for the generics than for the branded products. This is understandable, since buyers of generic products are likely to be more price-sensitive than purchasers of branded products. In addition, though the reason is unknown, compound 3 has (in both its branded and generic versions) notably higher own-price elasticity than compound 1.

[a] Sara Fisher Ellison, Iain Cockburn, Zvi Griliches, and Jerry Hausman, "Characteristics of Demand for Pharmaceutical Products: An Examination of Four Cephalosporins," *RAND Journal of Economics,* v. 28 (1997), pp. 426–446.

5.4 FITTING A DEMAND CURVE

Econometricians use historical data to estimate (to "fit") demand curves. Any such fitted curve is more or less artificial; a statistician can at best only approximate the true demand function.

Since econometricians normally care more about aggregate behavior in markets than about an individual's choices, the discussion in this section will use the upper-case symbols $X, Y, \ldots$ that represent *marketwide* quantities, rather than the lowercase symbols $x, y, \ldots$ which refer to *individual* purchases or consumption. In terms of these marketwide magnitudes, the elasticity formulas of equation (5.3) become:

$$\eta_x \equiv \frac{\Delta X / X}{\Delta P_x / P_x} \equiv \frac{\Delta X}{\Delta P_x} \frac{P_x}{X} \equiv \frac{P_x / X}{\Delta P_x / \Delta X} \tag{5.7}$$

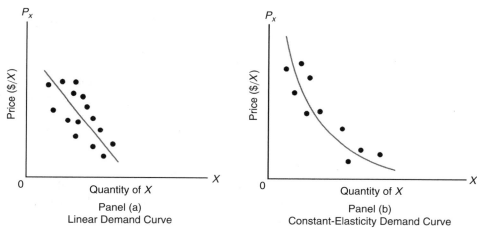

Figure 5.3. Constant-Slope and Constant-Elasticity Demand Curves

Simple functional forms are ordinarily assumed in attempting to estimate (to "fit") a demand curve to observed data (shown as heavy dots in the diagrams). The functional forms most commonly used are linear (constant-slope) demand as in panel (a) and constant-elasticity demand as in panel (b).

Constant Slope versus Constant Elasticity

To keep the statistical problems manageable, the econometrician often assumes that the demand curve has either *constant slope* or *constant elasticity*. Figure 5.3 compares the two. A demand curve with constant slope is a straight line. The demand curve with constant slope in Panel (a) "fitted" to the observed data (heavy dots) is the straight line best answering the question: "How do numerical changes of quantity respond to numerical changes of price?" The demand curve with constant elasticity in Panel (b) is convex (bowed toward the origin). It answers the question: "For these data, how do *proportionate* changes in quantity depend upon *proportionate* changes in price?"

A constant-slope (straight-line) demand curve such as DD' in Figure 5.4 does not have constant elasticity. First, from equation (5.7), the elasticity of demand must be zero at D' (the intersection with the horizontal axis) – since price P_x is zero there. Similarly, at point D (the intersection with the vertical axis), the value of X is zero and so the elasticity is infinite there. So, evidently, elasticity rises (increases in absolute value) moving northwest along a straight-line demand curve.

There is a neat geometrical method for finding the elasticity of demand at any point along demand curve DD' in Figure 5.4. Consider the last ratio on the right of equation (5.7). This corresponds graphically to dividing the *slope of a ray from the origin to the curve* (P_x/X) by the *slope of the curve itself* ($\Delta P_x/\Delta X$). So, for the elasticity at any point like T, divide the (positive) slope of OT by the (negative) slope of DD'. In the diagram OT is steeper than DD', so the absolute value of the ratio exceeds 1; that is, demand is elastic at point T ($\eta_x < -1$). This geometric technique also applies to estimating the elasticity along a nonlinear demand curve such as FF' in Figure 5.4. The elasticity in the neighborhood of point T along FF' is the slope of OT divided by the slope of DD' (the tangent line to FF' at point T).

A direct corollary is that at the *midpoint* of a linear demand curve, elasticity is always unitary ($\eta_x = -1$). In Figure 5.4, at the midpoint M along DD' the positive

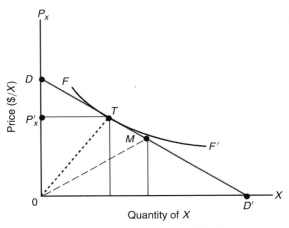

Figure 5.4. Graphical Measure of Elasticity

Elasticity at a point T along a linear demand curve DD' is the slope of a ray OT from the origin to point T divided by the slope of the demand curve. In the situation pictured, OT is steeper (its slope is larger in absolute value) than DD', so at T the demand is elastic ($\eta_x < -1$). Elasticity always equals -1 at the midpoint M along a linear demand curve like DD' (since OMD' is an isosceles triangle). For a nonlinear demand curve such as FF', the demand elasticity at point T is identical with the elasticity at T along the tangent straight-line demand curve DD.

slope of OM is numerically equal to the negative slope along DD'. (That is, OMD' is an isosceles triangle.)

EXERCISE 5.6

Consider the market demand curve $P_x = 30 - X/4$. What is the elasticity of demand when $X = 60$? (b) When $X = 120$? (c) When $X = 0$?

ANSWER: (a) The slope of this linear demand curve is $-1/4$, so elasticity at any point is equal to $(P_x/x)/(-1/4)$ or $-4P_x/x$. At the point $X = 60$, the price is $P_x = 30 - 60/4 = 15$, so elasticity at that point is $-4(15/60) = -1$. ($X = 60$ is the midpoint.) (b) At $X = 120$, $P_x = 0$ and so elasticity has to be zero. (c) At $X = 0$, elasticity is negative infinite.

Whereas the demand curve DD' in Figure 5.4 had *constant slope*, the demand curve EE' in Figure 5.5 has *constant elasticity*. Specifically, as drawn this constant elasticity is $\eta_x = -1$. This can be verified using the graphic rule described above to compare the *slope of a ray from the origin to the curve* with the *slope along the curve itself*. The geometrical construction shows that points F, G, and H are midpoints of the corresponding tangent lines $F'F''$, $G'G''$, and $H'H''$.

General Demand Functions

A demand curve of constant slope is a straight line. It can be written as a linear equation:

$$X = A + BP_x \qquad (5.8)$$

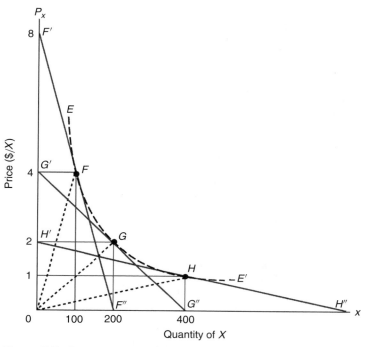

Figure 5.5. Constant-Unit-Elasticity Demand Curve

EE' is a demand curve with a constant elasticity of -1. At point F the ray OF and the tangent line segment F'' form an isosceles triangle, and similarly for points G and H along the curve.

Here A and B are constants, and B is normally negative in accordance with the Law of Demand.

Taking into account other variables that affect demand, such as income I and the prices of related goods like Y and Z, leads to a *generalized* demand function in linear form:

$$X = A + BP_x + CI + DP_y + EP_z + \cdots \qquad (5.9)$$

Here A is a constant term. B is the slope along the demand curve, normally negative. C, the coefficient attaching to income, is the slope of the Income Expansion Curve: it is positive when X is a superior good, and negative when X is inferior. The sign of D is negative if X and Y are complements and positive if the two goods are substitutes. The sign of E will similarly depend upon whether X and Z are complements or substitutes. The dots indicate that an indefinite number of other variables might also be used in the estimation.

When an econometrician statistically fits a demand function, the equation should be interpreted with caution outside the range of the original data. Taken to extremes, a fitted equation may give absurd results. For example, equation (5.9) might seem to imply that X could be positive even when $I = 0$. But of course, people cannot buy positive amounts of good X when they have zero income I.[6]

---

[6] Apart from the possibility of borrowing or lending, a topic to be taken up in Chapter 14.

For constant-elasticity demand curves, the equation is:

$$X = a P_x^b \qquad (5.10)$$

Here a is a positive constant and b is a negative constant. In fact, b is the constant elasticity of demand.[7]

Taking logarithms, equation (5.10) becomes:

$$\log X = \log a + b \log P_x \qquad (5.10')$$

So the statistician, in practice, would find a constant-elasticity demand curve by fitting a straight line to the logarithms of price and quantity.

The generalized constant-elasticity demand function can be written:

$$x = a \ P_x^b \ I^c \ P_y^d \ P_z^e \ldots \qquad (5.11)$$

(As before, the dots indicate possible other variables.) In logarithmic form, this becomes:

$$\log X = \log a + b \log P_x + c \log I + d \log P_y + e \log P_z + \cdots \qquad (5.11')$$

Here b is the demand elasticity with respect to the price of X itself (η_x), c is the income elasticity (ϵ_x), d is the cross-elasticity with good Y (η_{xy}), and e is the cross-elasticity with good Z (η_{xz}).

Lastly, the econometrician may find that some mixed form best explains the data: a constant-slope response for some of the explanatory variables, and a constant-elasticity response for others.

EXERCISE 5.7

William always spends exactly half his income on food F. (a) Express this observation in terms of a demand curve. (b) What can you say about his income elasticity ϵ_f and price elasticity η_f for food?

ANSWER: (a) The assertion is that, for William, $E_f \equiv P_f f = I/2$. As a demand curve, this can be written as follows:

$$f = 0.5 \ I/P_f = 0.5 \ I \ P_f^{-1}, \quad \text{or} \quad \log f = \log 0.5 + \log I - \log P_f$$

Evidently, this is a constant-elasticity demand function like (5.11), though with only price P_f and income I as variables. (b) Comparing William's demand function with equation (5.11), his income elasticity is $c = c_f = 1$ and his demand elasticity is $d = \eta_f = -1$.

EXAMPLE 5.5 DEMAND FOR COFFEE

Coffee supply often shifts drastically owing to crop fluctuations in the exporting nations, notably Brazil. Since demand for coffee is relatively stable, these supply changes provide the data needed to estimate demand functions. Cliff J. Huang, John

---

[7] *Mathematical Footnote:* If $X = a P_x^b$, then:

$$\eta_x \equiv \frac{dX/dP_x}{X/P_x} = \frac{ba P_x^{b-1}}{X/P_x} = \frac{bX/P_x}{X/P_x} = b$$

J. Siegfried, and Farangis Zardoshty examined the U.S. demand for coffee from 1963 to 1977, a period when instant coffee was becoming a major force in the market.[a]

For regular coffee the researchers found that the elasticity of demand was nearly the same at high prices as at low prices. As explained in the text, this justified using a logarithmic (constant-elasticity) equation form. The equation that best fit the data was:

$$\log C = -0.16 \log P_c + 0.51 \log I + 0.15 \log P_t - 0.009T + \text{constant}$$

Here C represents the quantity of coffee demanded, I is income, P_c and P_t are the prices of coffee and tea, and T is time. (Certain additional variables used by the authors are omitted here.) So the price elasticity for coffee appears to be -0.16, which means that the demand is quite inelastic. The income elasticity is 0.51, so coffee is a superior good. Since the cross-elasticity 0.15 is positive, tea, as expected, is a substitute for coffee. Finally, the time coefficient is negative, indicating that consumption of regular coffee was subject to a declining trend.

For instant coffee, the researchers found rather different results. First of all, the logarithmic form of the equation was inappropriate since the elasticity of demand proved not to be constant. Elasticity was high at high prices and low at low prices, a pattern more consistent with a linear demand curve. The price elasticities for instant coffee ranged from -0.89 at the highest prices down to -0.02 at the lowest prices observed. There was no time trend, suggesting that the overall downward tendency of coffee consumption was offset by increasing appreciation of the convenience of instant coffee – owing in part, perhaps, to the growing fraction of married women working away from home.

---

[a] Cliff J. Huang, John J. Siegfried, and Farangis Zardoshty, "The Demand for Coffee in the United States, 1963–1977," *Quarterly Review of Economics and Business*, v. 20 (Summer 1980).

5.5   DETERMINANTS OF RESPONSIVENESS OF DEMAND TO PRICE

Why is demand for some commodities highly sensitive to price (highly elastic), whereas demand for others is not? Here are some possible explanations.

1. *Availability of substitutes:* Demand for a commodity will be more elastic the more numerous and the closer the available substitutes. This explanation turns on *the substitution effect* of a price change, as pictured in Figure 4.18 of the previous chapter. In Figure 5.6, Panel (a) shows two goods that are close substitutes, such as butter and margarine. Here a fall in P_x, which tilts the budget line from KL to KL', leads to a large change in an individual's consumption of X. (So x_1 is considerably greater than x_0.) Panel (b) shows two goods that are close complements, such as ink jet cartridges and computer copy paper. At the lower price, here the new quantity x_1 is only a little larger than x_0.

2. *Luxuries versus necessities:* Demand for a "luxury" tends to be more elastic than demand for a "necessity." Recall that, for a luxury, consumption increases substantially as income rises, whereas, for a necessity, rising income brings about only a small increase in consumption. Thus the argument runs in terms of *the income effect* of a price change. A reduction in price enriches the consumer in real terms, and such an enrichment will affect purchases of luxuries more than purchases of necessities.

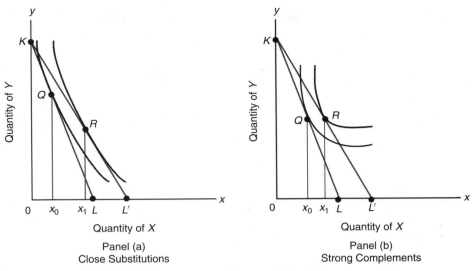

Figure 5.6. Closeness of Substitutes and Demand Elasticity

In Panel (a) the two goods are close substitutes. A decrease in P_x shifts the budget line from KL to KL' and leads to a relatively large change in consumption of X (from x_0 to x_1). In Panel (b) the two goods are poor substitutes (strong complements): a decrease in P_x leads to only a small change in the amount of X purchased.

3. *High-priced versus low-priced goods:* Along a linear demand curve, elasticity is higher at higher prices. At the choke price where the consumer no longer purchases the good at all – the vertical intercept of the demand curve – elasticity is infinite. So if demand for a good is approximately linear, elasticity will tend to be high near the choke price. (For constant-elasticity demand curves there is no choke price; these demand curves never intersect either axis.)

The "importance" fallacy: Another purported explanation of high and low price elasticities is sometimes encountered in textbooks: it has been termed "the importance of being unimportant." The idea is that if commodity X represents only a small (unimportant) fraction $k_x = P_x x / I$ of people's budgets, demand for X will be inelastic. (For example, if the price of salt falls, you are unlikely to buy much more salt.) And the same argument would seem to imply, of course, that a commodity that is important in people's budgets should tend to have highly elastic demand. Once again, the argument here is based on the income effect: if the price of an "important" commodity falls, the consumer is a lot richer in real terms, and so can buy much more of the commodity.

But this argument is wrong. It is true that if X is important in Mary's budget and its price falls, we can expect Δx, the *absolute* increase in Mary's consumption, to be large. But elasticity concerns not the absolute change Δx but the *proportionate* change $\Delta x / x$. Since for an important commodity Mary's consumption x was very likely large to begin with, the *percentage* change $\Delta x / x$ after a reduction in price need not be large.

EXERCISE 5.8

Mary consumes only cheese and wine. Her demand functions for the two products have the constant-elasticity forms $c = 0.99\, I/P_c$ and $w = 0.01\, I/P_w$. (a) How important is each commodity for her; that is, what percentages of her budget are accounted for by cheese and wine, respectively? (b) What are the demand elasticities?

ANSWER: (a) The demand equations imply that $P_c c = 0.99\ I$ and $P_w w = 0.01\ I$. Mary spends 99% of her income on cheese and only 1% on wine, so the two goods differ in "importance" by a ratio of 99:1. (b) Still, as follows directly from the fact that her total expenditures on each good remain the same regardless of price (so long as her income is unchanged), her demand elasticities for cheese and for wine are identical: $\eta_c = \eta_w = -1$!

Yet it is true that the demand for salt is inelastic. If "unimportance" is not the reason, what is? Actually, all three of the valid explanations listed above apply. Salt has no close substitutes (#1 above), it is a necessity rather than a luxury (#2), and its price is usually very low (#3). These reasons suffice; there is no need to call upon the fallacious "unimportance" argument.

5.6   MULTIPLE CONSTRAINTS – RATIONING

The market opportunity set was described in Chapter 4 (see Figure 4.1). If preference directions are up and to the right (that is, if commodities X and Y are both *goods*), the consumer's optimum will be along the budget line – the northeast boundary of the opportunity set. But, as noted in Chapter 4, other constraints such as rationing in wartime may prevent the individual from attaining this ideal optimum position.

Historically, rationing in wartime or other periods of scarcity has taken one of two forms: *coupon rationing* or *point rationing*.

Coupon Rationing

In World War II most of the nations at war imposed coupon rationing for "essential" commodities. Since the major purpose of rationing was to prevent rich persons from absorbing a disproportionate fraction of these "essential" goods, coupons were mainly distributed on a per capita or per family basis.[8]

Figure 5.7 depicts a consumer's choices when gasoline G is rationed. In each panel the vertical dashed line indicates the ration limit R_g. Suppose Panel (a) represents Joan's situation. Notice that the ration limit R_g is *not binding* upon her choices. Though the dashed vertical line does "truncate" her opportunity set (the shaded area), making unavailable some of the area along and under the budget line KL, her consumption choice C^* is unaffected – since, at the ruling prices, the amount of gasoline she wants to purchase is less than what the ration permits her to buy.

In Panel (b) the ration limit R_g is tighter; now the ration constraint *binds*. Here Joan's best achievable point is T. Although forced to consume less of G than desired, she partially compensates by consuming more of the other unrationed good Y. Even so, her best achievable combination at point T leaves her on a lower indifference curve than the original optimum C^*.

---

[8] Rationing has also been used for purposes other than equalizing consumption. In Nazi Germany, smaller rations were assigned to Jews than to Aryans. During the period 1917–1921 in revolutionary Russia, formerly upper-class or middle-class citizens were subjected to more stringent food rationing than individuals of proletarian origin.

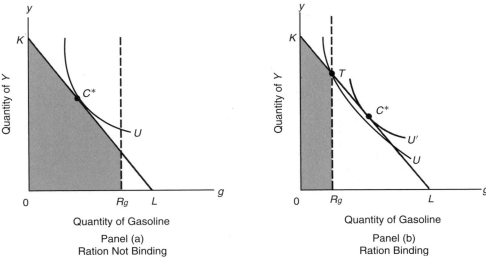

Figure 5.7. Rationing of One Commodity

Possible ration limits R_g upon purchases of gasoline are shown as vertical dashed lines. In Panel (a) the ration limit truncates the market opportunity set, but the consumer's preferences are such that the limit is not actually binding. In Panel (b) the ration limit is binding. The consumer's best attainable combination is at point T, where less gasoline is purchased but more of the other commodity Y.

EXERCISE 5.9

Richard's Marginal Value for gasoline G in terms of the numeraire good Y – that is, the absolute slope of his indifference curve on the g and y axes – is $MV_g = 2y/g$. The prices are $P_g = 3$ and $P_y = 1$, and his income is $I = 180$. (a) In the absence of rationing, what is his optimal consumption basket? (b) What if gasoline is subject to a ration limit $R_g = 50$? (c) What happens if the ration is tightened to $R_g = 20$? (d) Returning to the original ration limit $R_g = 50$, what if his income doubles to $I = 360$?

ANSWER: (a) The data here correspond to Exercise 4.4 of the previous chapter. When the Substitution Balance Equation (in the form $MV_g = P_g/P_y$) and the budget equation ($P_g g + P_y y = I$) are solved simultaneously, Richard's optimum consumption basket C^* is $g = 40$, $y = 60$. (b) The ration limit $R_g = 50$ is not binding, so Richard's consumption decision remains unchanged. (c) Since the ration limit $R_g = 20$ now binds, Richard can consume no more gasoline than $g = 20$. But this permits him to spend the remainder of his income upon good Y, so $y = 120$. (d) At the higher value of I, Richard's C^* optimum would be $g = 80$, $y = 120$. Had Richard been that affluent, the original ration limit $R_g = 50$ would have been binding. In that case his best consumption basket would have been $g = 50$ and $y = 120$.

In Figure 5.8, *both* commodities G and Y are subject to rationing. In Panel (a), although the opportunity set is now truncated at both ends, neither ration is binding: the originally preferred consumption basket C^* remains attainable. In Panel (b) the Y-ration is binding but the G-ration is not. Panel (c) shows the opposite situation. Finally,

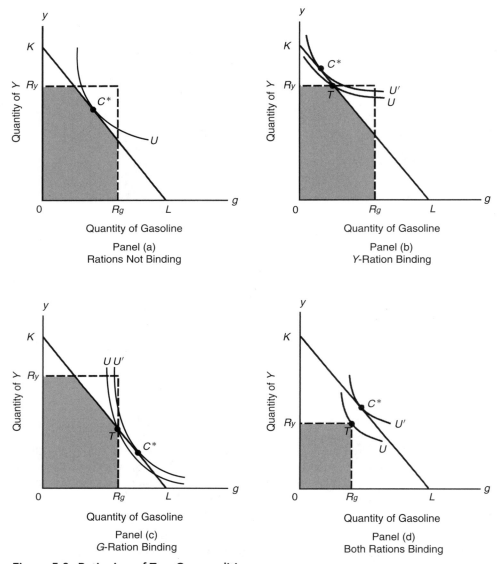

Figure 5.8. Rationing of Two Commodities

Here the ration limits are R_g and R_y (the vertical and horizontal dashed lines). In Panel (a) the ration limit truncates the market opportunity set at both ends, but the consumer's preferences are such that the limit is not actually binding for either good. In Panel (b) only R_y is binding, whereas in Panel (c) only R_g is binding. In Panel (d) both ration constraints are binding, so at the best attainable position T the consumer is left with unspent income.

Panel (d) illustrates a situation where *both* ration limits are binding. In this last case the consumer is left with unspent income.

Point Rationing

Coupon rationing as just described is a crude technique. It does not guarantee that poor people will receive the good, but merely limits the consumption of the rich in the hope that more will be left for the poor. Furthermore, goods do not go where they are wanted most. Suppose tea and coffee are both rationed. Alfred may not care very much for tea, yet, once his coffee ration is used up, he may consume tea for lack of anything better. Similarly Barbara, who only barely tolerates coffee, may find herself ingesting the stuff once her tea ration is exhausted.

The obvious solution would be to let Alfred and Barbara exchange tea and coffee coupons. Historically, such a market solution has rarely been permitted by rationing authorities, seemingly because it comes too close to exchanging coupons for money.[9]

In the later years of World War II, several countries adopted more sophisticated "point rationing" schemes. Instead of ration coupons, each individual (or in some cases, each family) was granted a periodic *ration-point total N*. Like cash, ration points could be spent as desired. The authorities assigned ration-point prices p_x and p_y to commodities, generally differing from the money prices P_x and P_y. To buy an item, the consumer had to pay *both* the money price and the point price. Thus, the maximum amount of good X that a consumer could purchase was the smaller of I/P_x and N/p_x. The ordinary income-budget equation is now supplemented by a point-budget equation, so a consumer faces a two-fold constraint:

$$
\begin{array}{ll}
P_x x + P_y \leq I & \text{Income constraint} \\
p_x x + p_y y \leq N & \text{Point constraint}
\end{array}
\tag{5.12}
$$

These expressions are both *inequalities*, which means that part of the available money income, or some of the available point total, may be left unspent.

Two possibilities are shown in Figure 5.9. In Panel (a) point income is so large, relative to ordinary cash income, that only the money income constraint binds. This could be the situation of a poor person. Panel (b) represents the opposite case: a rich person for whom cash income is so ample that only the point constraint binds.

EXERCISE 5.10

(a) Dennis has cash income $I = 180$ and faces money prices $P_x = 3$ and $P_x = 1$. He also has $N = 400$ points; the point prices are $p_x = 4$ and $p_y = 2$. Is his effective opportunity set illustrated by either panel of Figure 5.9? (b) What if his point total were $N = 200$ instead?

ANSWER: (a) His money income budget line has x-intercept $180/3 = 60$ and y-intercept $180/1 = 180$. His point budget line has x-intercept $400/4 = 100$ and y-intercept $400/2 = 200$. So the picture is like Panel (a) of Figure 5.9: only money income binds for Dennis. (b) Here the point budget line has shifted inward. The x-intercept becomes $200/4 = 50$ and the y-intercept $200/2 = 100$. Now only points are binding, so the picture is like Panel (b) of Figure 5.9.

Last, it may be that money income I limits consumption over *part* of the opportunity set, whereas elsewhere point income N is binding. In Figure 5.10 the income budget line KL is steeper than the point budget line GH: $P_x/P_y > p_x/p_y$. So commodity X is relatively expensive in terms of ordinary income, whereas commodity Y is expensive in

---

[9] Recall that a major motive for wartime rationing is to equalize consumption despite wealth differences. Allowing exchange of coupons for money partially defeats this purpose – even though, since the exchange would be voluntary, both rich and poor benefit thereby (at least in their own eyes). The authorities seem to have feared that poorer people, if permitted to sell their coupons, would cut back on the rationed essentials of life and spend more on frills and luxuries.

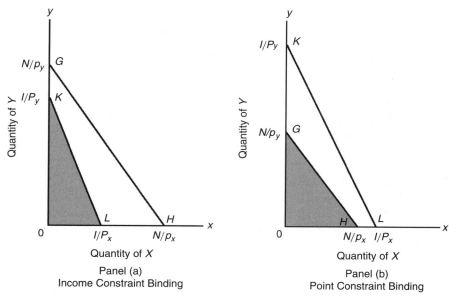

Figure 5.9. Point Rationing – Only One Constraint Binding

Consumption is subject to an income constraint I as well as a ration-point constraint N. Commodity X is more expensive in terms of income, and commodity y is more expensive in terms of points. The income budget line KL is, therefore, steeper than the point budget line GH. In Panel (a) the point total N is so large that only income is binding; Panel (b) represents the opposite case.

terms of points. It follows that consumers who particularly like commodity X tend to find the income constraint binding; those more interested in consuming Y would tend to find the point constraint binding.[10]

Figure 5.10 also illustrates how optimum positions vary with personal preferences. Albert's highest attainable indifference curve U_A is at the tangency with the point constraint line GH in its effective (solid) range GM. Betty's highest attainable indifference curve U_B is at the intersection point M. And Charles's highest indifference curve is at the tangency along the income budget line KL in its effective (solid) range ML. For Albert, only the point constraint is binding; he ends up not spending all his money income. For Charles, only the income constraint is binding and he ends up not spending all his points. Betty spends all her income and all her points.

EXERCISE 5.11

(a) Helen has money income $I = 200$ and faces money prices $P_x = 3$ and $P_y = 1$. She has $N = 400$ available points, the point prices being $p_x = 2$ and $p_y = 4$. Show that her two budget lines intersect, find the point of intersection, and determine whether it corresponds to Figure 5.10 or to the reverse situation where the point constraint is steeper than the money income constraint. (b) If her preferences are represented by $MV_x = y/x$, to which of the three types of tangencies in Figure 5.10 does her consumption optimum correspond?

---

[10] The opposite case, where the two budget lines intersect but GH is steeper than KL, can be analyzed in a corresponding way.

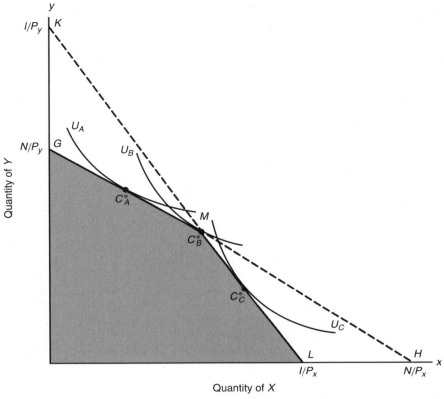

Figure 5.10. Point Rationing – Both Constraints Possibly Binding

The point constraint limits consumption in the range GM (the solid portion of the line GH), and the income constraint in the range ML (the solid portion of KL). Albert's highest attainable indifference curve U_A is at the tangency point along GM (only the point constraint is binding). For Charles, the highest attainable indifference curve U_C is along ML (only the income constraint is binding). Betty's highest attainable indifference curve U_B is at the intersection: for her, both constraints are binding.

ANSWER: (a) Simultaneously solving the budget equations for income ($P_x x + P_y y = I$) and for points ($p_x x + p_y y = N$), the intersection is at $x = 40$, $y = 80$. The absolute slope $P_x/P_y = 3$ of the income constraint exceeds the absolute slope $p_x/p_y = 0.5$ for the point constraint, so this is like the situation pictured in Figure 5.10. (b) If the highest attainable indifference curve is at the intersection point M, it must be that the indifference-curve slope at M is *steeper* than the slope of the point constraint (line GH) and *flatter* than the slope of the income constraint (line KL). Helen's absolute indifference-curve slope at M is $MV_x = y/x = 80/40 = 2$. Since the slope of the point constraint is 0.5, and that of the income constraint is 3, the condition just stated does indeed hold. So Helen's consumption optimum is at the intersection $M = (40,80)$, where both constraints are binding.

EXAMPLE 5.6 WARTIME POINT RATIONING

Cheese and canned fish were among the commodities rationed by points during World War II in the United States. L. A. Epstein compared the 1942 (prerationing) purchases of different income groups with the quantities that were purchased during 1944 when rationing was effective.[a]

Average weekly purchases by housekeeping families in cities (lb.)

Income	$1,000 or less	$1,000–2,000	$2,000–3,000	$3,000–4,000	Over $4,000
1942					
Cheese	0.26	0.57	0.64	0.81	1.03
Canned fish	0.21	0.36	0.56	0.44	0.37
1944					
Cheese	0.24	0.33	0.44	0.49	0.52
Canned fish	0.06	0.12	0.17	0.22	0.28

Source: Adapted from Epstein, p. 1148.

The last three columns show that, in 1944 for the three highest income groups, the consumption patterns in 1944 were almost identical. In that year the richest group consumed 0.52 pounds of cheese and 0.28 pounds of canned fish – very little more than the two next-richest groups in the adjoining columns. Consumers in these income brackets were in the situation pictured in Panel (b) of Figure 5.9. Purchases of both cheese and canned fish was almost entirely limited by points, so income being a little higher or lower made little difference.

What of price changes? In this period the money price of canned fish relative to cheese approximately doubled between 1942 and 1944. For the *lowest* income group, the fish/cheese consumption ratio fell from 0.21/0.26 = 0.81 in 1942 to 0.06/0.24 = 0.25 in 1944, showing strong sensitivity to price disparities. (Fish and cheese were evidently close substitutes for these consumers.) But for the *highest* income group the fish/cheese consumption ratio for 1942 remained almost unchanged in 1944. The reason was, as indicated above, that dollar prices were simply not binding upon the consumption decisions made by families in the upper income ranges.

[a] L. A. Epstein, "Wartime Food Purchases," *Monthly Labor Review*, v. 60 (June 1945), p. 1148.

Time as well as income may constrain consumption. Activities such as playing a round of golf, watching a movie, or eating a meal absorb time as well as cash. As society becomes more affluent, the time constraint will grow in importance. People finds themselves wealthier, but increasingly harried for lack of time to do everything they can financially afford.

EXAMPLE 5.7 GASOLINE AND WAITING TIME

In the spring of 1980 there was an "oil crisis." A quirk of government regulation required certain Chevron gasoline stations in California to charge from 16 to 21 cents per gallon less than competing stations. As would be expected, long lines formed at the low-priced Chevron pumps. Motorists could then choose to wait in line for the cheap gasoline, or else avoid delay by purchasing more expensive gasoline elsewhere.

Robert Deacon and Jon Sonstelie surveyed customers at a low-priced Chevron station and at two neighboring stations, a Mobil and a Union, where prices were uncontrolled.[a] The table shows some of the data collected for 109 Chevron customers and 61 non-Chevron customers.

Average values of variables

	Chevron	Non-Chevron
Gallons purchased	11.6	8.8
% weekend customers	31.2	26.2
% with passengers	7.3	18.0
% employed full-time	67.9	83.6
% housewives	5.5	3.3

Source: Adapted from Deacon and Sonstelie, p. 636.

As can be seen, average purchases were larger at the stations where waiting in line was required. For consumers who will be waiting a long time in line, it makes sense to hold off refilling until the fuel gauge reads (say) 10% rather than 25%. The Chevron customers, the ones more willing to wait in line, were also more likely to be purchasing on weekends (where time pressures are normally less severe) and more likely to be housewives. Conversely, the non-Chevron customers (those who preferred not to wait) were more likely to be employed full time or to be carrying passengers.

Calculating in terms of the size of purchase and the minutes spent in line, the authors were also able to estimate gasoline purchasers' value of time. The average Chevron customer saved $1.94 by waiting in 14.6 minutes, implying an average time value of $7.97 per hour. But this value differed by type of customer, ranging from $3.52 to $5.39 per hour for part-time workers up to $11.26 to $17.26 per hour for those fully employed and reporting income over $40,000.

[a] Robert T. Deacon and Ron Sonstelie, "Rationing by Waiting and the Value of Time: Results from a Natural Experiment," *Journal of Political Economy*, v. 93 (August 1985).

SUMMARY   Elasticity is a unit-free measure of how a change in one variable is associated with a change in another variable.

1. The response of quantity demand to changes in income is measured by the income elasticity of demand for commodity X, denoted ϵ_x. It is the percent change in the quantity of X purchased, divided by the percent change in income I. Income elasticity is positive for superior goods, and negative for inferior goods.

2. The response of quantity demand to changes in price is measured by the price elasticity of demand for good X, denoted η_x. It is the percent change in the quantity of good X purchased, divided by the percent change in the price of good X. The Law of Demand implies that price elasticity is negative. Demand is said to be *elastic* if $\eta_x < -1$; a fall in the price of the good then leads to increased spending on that good. Demand is *inelastic* if $\eta_x < -1$; a fall in the price of the good then leads to lower spending on that good. Demand is *unitary* elasticity when $\eta = -1$; a fall in the price the good leaves spending unchanged.

3. The cross-elasticity of demand η_{xy} is the percent change in the quantity demanded of good X, divided by the percent price change of a different good. If the

cross-elasticity is positive, the two goods are *substitutes*. If the cross-elasticity is negative, the two goods are *complements*.

The additional spending on a good induced by a small increase in the quantity sold is Marginal Revenue to the seller, and equals $P_x(1 + 1/\eta_x)$

Demand functions are commonly estimated (fitted) from data using either a constant-slope (linear) form or a constant-elasticity form. Price elasticity changes along a linear demand curve, increasing in absolute value moving northwest along the curve.

Demand elasticity is high: (1) if the good has close substitutes; (2) if the good is a luxury (a strongly superior good); (3) if the price is high, that is, near the consumer's choke price. However, it is not in general true that an "important" good (one accounting for a large proportion of the consumer's budget) tends to have high elasticity, or that an "unimportant" good tends to have low price elasticity.

Consumption opportunities may be constrained by factors other than market price, for example by limitations of time or by rationing in wartime. If good X is rationed by *coupon*, the ration may or may not be binding – depending upon the consumer's income and preferences. If the ration is binding, the consumer will in part compensate by buying more of other commodities. Under *point rationing*, either points alone may be binding, or dollars alone may be binding, or both may be binding.

QUESTIONS
[†]The answers to daggered questions appear at the end of the book.

For Review

1. What is the general definition of all elasticity measures? Why is the income elasticity of demand considered a more useful measure than the simple slope along an Engel Curve? Why is the price elasticity of demand considered a more useful measure than the simple slope along a demand curve? Are elasticity measures always better than the simple measures? (See question 2.)

[†]2. Consider this paradox: Income elasticity is supposed to measure the responsiveness of consumption to changes in income. But income elasticity is unity along *any* Engel Curve that is a straight line through the origin, whether very steep or very flat. Since Engel Curves of different steepness surely show different responses of consumption to income, how can they all be characterized as having the same income elasticity?

3. True or false: "Income elasticity is unity at any point along an Engel Curve such that the tangent at that point extends through the origin." Explain.

4. True or false: "Since income elasticities must average out to unity, any commodity accounting for a very large fraction of income expenditure must have an income elasticity close to 1." Explain.

[†]5. a. What is meant by elastic demand and inelastic demand?

   b. How can elasticity at a point along a linear demand curve be determined by inspection?

   c. Along a nonlinear demand curve?

[†]6. Let the demand curve be $P = A - BG$, where A and B are positive constants.

   a. What is the elasticity at $G = 0$?

   b. At $G = A/B$?

   c. At $G = A/(2B)$?

7. If the demand curve is $PG = 100$, what is the price elasticity of demand at $G = 10$? At $G = 50$? At $G = 100$?

8. What is the analytical form of a demand function that is *linear* in both income and price? What is the analytical form of a demand function that has *constant elasticities* with respect to both income and price? Explain the economic meaning of each form.

†9. If a single "all-important" commodity absorbs all of the individual's income, what is its price elasticity? What is its income elasticity?

†10. Gasoline rationing was proposed in 1973 and again in 1979 as a remedy for the energy crisis. If all persons are given identical rations, compare the opportunity sets of a wealthy and a poor consumer for gasoline consumption versus "all other goods." Would permitting sale of coupons be a good idea?

For Further Thought and Discussion

1. "On average over all goods, income elasticity must be unity." Prove this proposition.

†2. a. Consider the demand curve $PG = 100$. What happens to the elasticity of demand as price falls? What happens to "importance" (share of the consumer budget spent on G) as price falls?

   b. Apply the previous questions for the demand curve $P^2 G = 100$.

   c. For the demand curve $P^{1/2} G = 100$.

   d. What can you infer about the relation between elasticity and "importance"?

†3. The American economist Irving Fisher argued in 1891 that a poor community will hardly distinguish quality grades of a commodity like beef, while a rich community would. "In the country districts of 'the West' all cuts of beef sell for the same price (about 10 cents per lb.). In the cities of the West two or three qualities are commonly distinguished, while in New York a grocer will enumerate over a dozen prices in the same beef varying from 10 to 25 cents per lb." [Irving Fisher, *Mathematical Investigations in the Theory of Value and Prices* (New Haven: Yale University Press, 1925), p. 74.]

   a. Construct the implied indifference curves, at low and high levels of income, between low-quality beef and high-quality beef.

   b. Why should different beef qualities be better substitutes at low incomes than at high incomes? What would you anticipate about the price elasticity of demand for low-quality beef in poor versus rich communities? For high-quality beef?

4. Name some goods you expect to have elastic demand and some with inelastic demand. Justify your choices.

†5. Tickets to a sports match are available only on a black-market basis. Professor G, calling from out of town, gives purchasing instructions to his secretary: "If the price is $30 each, buy one ticket for me; at $20 each, buy two; if it is $10, buy three." The secretary says: "Prof, there must be something wrong here. You're saying you'd be willing to pay more in total for two tickets than for three!" Is the secretary correct? Explain.

†6. For a commodity with snob appeal, consumers might be willing to buy more at a higher price than at a lower price (violation of the Law of Demand). Is this possible or likely? Explain.

†7. If uninformed consumers judge quality by price, they may also be willing to buy more at a higher than at a lower price. Is this possible or likely? Explain.

8. What could cause a commodity's Engel Curve to become steeper, while remaining linear through the origin? [*Hint*: What if the purchased quantities were to double at each income level?]

9. From the numbers shown in Figure 5.5, can you figure out what is the fixed total spending $E_x \equiv P_x X$ associated with demand curve EE'?

10. Suppose that a good X has a close substitute Y and a distant substitute Z. Do you expect the cross-elasticity of demand for X with respect to the price of Y to be positive or negative? The cross-elasticity of demand for X with respect to the price of Z? Which elasticity do you expect to be larger?

†11. In wartime rationing situations it is generally illegal to buy another person's ration allowances for cash, or to exchange ration coupons.

    a.   Is there any justification for this?

    b.   Are there adverse consequences of forbidding such exchanges?

III | THE FIRM AND THE INDUSTRY

6 The Business Firm

Part II of this text analyzed consumer choices – the demand side of the market for goods and services. Part III now deals with the supply side. This chapter explains the nature of business firms and the relations among entrepreneurs, owners, and managers. The chapter then describes the firm's cost and revenue functions and its profit-maximizing level of production.

6.1   WHY FIRMS? ENTREPRENEUR, OWNER, MANAGER

Business firms are artificial creations, organized to produce goods and services for the market. But individuals or groups can produce for the market without creating a firm. So if firms are not essential, why are they formed?

Firms exist to take advantage of team production while minimizing costs of contracting. All but the simplest production processes call for team effort. Manufacturing typically requires machine operators, inspectors, and clerks together with nonlabor inputs such as electricity, materials, and buildings. The same holds for mining, transportation, retail sales, and so forth. Still, team production could take place without forming a firm. A movie could be produced via a *multilateral contract* specifying the types and quantities of inputs to be provided, at stated places and times, by the producer, director, actors, camera operators, and so on. The contract would also need to define each person's financial obligations and rewards. Such multilateral deals do occur. But the high costs of negotiation and enforcement make them rare. If instead a firm produced the movie, only *bilateral contracting* would be required. Each resource-owner would need only to contract with the firm itself, on a one-to-one basis.

Yet people can really deal only with other human beings. Some person or group, *management*, is needed to act in the name of the firm. Management must necessarily be granted some discretion – for example, to decide how many workers to employ. So forming a firm replaces a set of highly specific contracts among team members with a more general contract that grants management leeway for dealing with suppliers, employees, and customers.

Management differs from *ownership*. The owners of a firm are "the residual claimants," those legally entitled to the firm's income or assets after all contractual payments are made. Although combining ownership and management has advantages, larger firms usually divide the two functions. Owners, instead of managing the firm themselves, authorize someone else to negotiate and enforce the firm's contracts with other resource-suppliers.

But who monitors the managers? Ultimately, it is up to the owners to do that monitoring themselves. This inescapable decision-making aspect of firm ownership is called *entrepreneurship*. Even though firms are set up to reduce costs of contracting, the owners (if there are more than one) must still contract among themselves to set up the firm. If owners do not themselves manage the firm, then the owners must contract with the managers.

The corporate form is a specific type of contract among multiple owners of a firm. It has been hugely successful, thanks to two key features: *limited liability* and *transferable shares*. Limited liability means that the contractual obligations of the corporation are not personal obligations of the individual owner or owners. A supplier owed money can sue the corporation, but cannot sue any individual stockholder. Shares may become valueless (at worst), but the rest of the owner's assets are safe. And transferability make it possible for any individual stockholder who needs cash, or who is dissatisfied with corporate practices or policies, to exit by selling his or her stock.

These two features are connected. Under unlimited liability, were a stockholder with a good credit rating to sell out to another with shakier financial standing, the firm's creditors would surely object. But if liability is limited anyway, creditors don't care who the owners are.

Why would creditors ever deal with a firm whose owners have only limited liability? Banks that lend to the firm, and workers paid only at the end of the month, must worry about the money owed them. The same holds for consumers who make advance payments: you become a creditor of a corporation such as American Airlines when you buy an airline ticket. So, it may appear, financiers and suppliers and consumers should all prefer to deal with companies whose owners have *unlimited* liability in the event of default.

Other things equal, this is true. But no one is forced to do business with corporations on a limited-liability basis. Indeed, banks, before lending to a small corporation, often insist that the owners back up the corporation's credit by accepting personal liability for its debts. People deal with corporations on limited liability terms because – despite the risk – on balance they expect to gain thereby. It is up to the corporation to offer terms favorable enough so that, despite limited liability, suppliers and customers are willing to do business with it.

What types of people are likely to become owner/entrepreneurs, residual claimants? Consider farming. The landowner might possibly be the owner/entrepreneur, hiring labor at a contractually fixed wage. Alternatively, the working farmer might be the owner/entrepreneur, leasing the land at a contractually fixed rent. Similarly, in a software firm, the entrepreneur might be the programmer, the financial officer, or the person with the innovative idea.

All these possibilities occur, but a few general principles apply. One is the *need for monitoring.* It is easier for a working farmer to know the quality of the land than it is for the landowner to check how hard a farm laborer is working. So agricultural enterprises are more often owned by working farmers than by absentee landlords.[1] A small restaurant is more likely to be owned by the cashier or the chef or the food buyer, each of whom might otherwise be in a position to cheat or shirk, than by the landlord of the building or the supplier of the silverware. More generally, inputs whose provision can easily be checked for quantity or quality tend to be bought or rented under contract, whereas owners are more likely to provide those goods or services that are difficult to monitor. A second factor is the *distribution of risk.* Since residual claimants are more exposed to the hazards of doing business, someone very averse to risk is likely to prefer fixed contractual payment instead. Corporate bonds (nonownership investments) are typically owned by trust funds and other risk-averse investors, whereas corporate shares (ownership investments) are generally held by investors willing to accept risk.[2]

---

[1] Hence the proverb: "The best fertilizer is the owner's footprint in the soil."

[2] In farming and some other businesses, under "share-cropping" arrangements landowner and worker each receive a percentage of the crop. So each side must monitor the other, which might be costly. The advantage of share-cropping is that the risks of crop failure and of price fluctuations can be divided between the parties.

Economic Profit versus Accounting Profit

Individuals maximize utility, but what do firms maximize? Economists usually assume that the firm maximizes its *profit* – the difference between *Total Revenue* and *Total Cost*.

A firm's revenue is its receipts from sales. Cost is a more complicated concept. The economic cost of any activity, its "opportunity cost," is the value of the *best foregone alternative*. To attract inputs necessary for production, the firm must pay each resource-owner an amount sufficient to warrant sacrificing his or her next best opportunity – whether that be some other employment of the resource or choosing to retain it for "reservation uses" (as will be explained in more detail in Chapter 12).

The concept of *economic profit* tells the firm whether it should remain in business, or instead shut down. If economic profit is positive, owners of the firm will want to remain in business. And from the viewpoint of the economy as a whole, positive economic profit means that the value consumers place upon the firm's production (Total Revenue) exceeds the value that suppliers attach to the best alternative uses (Total Cost). In contrast, if economic profit is negative the owners of the firm would want to shut it down. And for the economy as a whole, negative economic profit indicates that the resources would be more productive elsewhere.

Accounting profit is a measure used for quite different purposes, among them controlling fraud and computing tax liabilities. In contrast to economic profit, accounting profit does not deduct the alternative opportunity value of the owners' self-supplied services. A shopkeeper's accountant might report annual revenue of $96,000 and expenses of $64,000 – so that the accounting profit was $32,000. But if the shopkeeper could have clerked that year at a local supermarket for $42,000, and if there are no other costs that need be considered, the *economic* profit of the business is $96,000 − $64,000 − $42,000 = −$6,000, a negative number. So whereas the accountant would say the firm is making a profit (and the tax authorities will want to collect a slice), the shopkeeper would do better by shutting down. (We set aside other possible considerations, such as the satisfaction of running one's own business.) Failure to allow for alternative uses of the entrepreneur's self-supplied resource makes accounting profit exceed economic profit.

The costs taken into account by the concepts of economic profit and accounting profit also diverge. Suppose the firm owns a building that has risen or fallen in value. In estimating accounting profit the accountant would deduct an annual depreciation figure based upon the *historical* cost of the building. But for estimating economic profit, the relevant cost is what some other party would pay for the property today. If in the meantime the building has risen in price, the accountant's measure of depreciation would understate the true cost of operating the business. Or of course, if the building has declined rather than grown in value, the bias would go the other way.

The Separation of Ownership and Control

Some critics claim that in modern corporations the economist's standard assumption that firms maximize economic profit is false. Instead, they allege, managers can run things pretty much their own way – even though theoretically they are merely employees of the owners (the stockholders), are supervised by elected Boards of Directors, and are subject to legal constraints. Supposedly, this especially applies to very large firms, whose ownership may be so highly diffused that any one person or family owns only a small fraction of the shares. If so, though collectively the stockholders elect the directors and thus indirectly choose the managers, each shareholder may be individually powerless.

Still, there are limits to managerial control. If shareholders were literally powerless, management could do whatever it wished, even dissipate the value of the firm by enormous executive salaries and expense accounts. But managers do not quite have a license to steal. Shareholders can and do sue executives for violating the contract setting up the firm (the corporate charter) or the managers' contract with the firm. And although it might not pay small stockholders to monitor management, large stockholders may be motivated to do so. The 2002 merger of Hewlett Packard and Compaq was publicly opposed by members of the Hewlett family, although the deal was eventually approved by a close shareholder vote. So at least some owners do indeed monitor corporate managers.

An additional check on managerial control arises when outsiders stand ready to supplant a self-serving or inefficient management. If the firm's earnings are less than they should be, the company's stock price will be low. An outside group might then try to take over the firm, buying shares at their current low prices or else challenging existing management in a proxy contest for control.

EXAMPLE 6.1 MERGERS AND TAKEOVERS

When management of a corporation performs poorly for shareholders, the stock price tends to fall. An outside group could attempt to gain control by (i) purchasing shares in the open market, (ii) making a tender offer to stockholders for a controlling block of shares, or (iii) winning shareholder support in a proxy fight. Or possibly, the *threat* of a takeover contest may lead existing management to negotiate a transfer of power, usually by merging the firm with the outsiders' corporation.

If the general market opinion is that the new management will run the company more profitably, a successful takeover will lead the stock price to increase. Factoring out movements of the stock market as a whole, Michael C. Jensen and Richard S. Ruback calculated the "abnormal" stock price effect attributable to the takeover itself.[a] Table 1 summarizes some of their estimates, which integrated several studies based mainly on pre-1980 data.

Table 1 Abnormal stock price changes

Takeover classification	Price change (%)
Successful takeovers	
Tender offer	30
Mergers	20
Proxy contests	8
Unsuccessful takeovers	
Tender offers	−3
Mergers	−3
Proxy contests	8

Source: Adapted from Jensen and Ruback, Tables 1 and 2, pp. 7–8.

Evidently, shareholders profited from *successful* takeovers; this suggests that previous management had not maximized profits for the shareholders. Shareholders gained little if anything after *unsuccessful* takeover attempts. The low returns may reflect disappointment by investors that a potentially more effective management had failed to gain control. Or the takeovers may have failed because the stockholders doubted that the challenging group would do any better.

A later study by George Andrade, Mark Mitchell, and Erik Stafford examined the frequency of hostile takeovers since 1973.[b] The first column of Table 2 shows that in 1973–1979 hostile bids took place for 8.4% of the stocks listed on the New York Stock Exchange, the American Stock Exchange, or Nasdaq. Of these, 4.1%, around half, were successful. The middle column shows a sharp jump in the frequency of hostile bids during the 1980s, and the last column reveals an even more drastic dropoff in the 1990s. One important reason for the decline is the adoption of antitakeover defenses, among them "poison pills" and "golden parachutes" (see Example 6.2). An alternative explanation is that the takeover threat has historically done its job, so that managements on average have now become more responsive to the interests of stockholders.

Table 2 Merger bids and "abnormal" stock returns

	1973–1979	1980–1989	1990–1998
% Hostile bids	8.4	14.3	4.0
% Successful hostile bids	4.1	7.1	2.6
% Gain to target firms	16.0	16.0	15.9
% Gain to acquirer firms	−0.3	−0.4	−1.0

Source: Adapted from Andrade et al., Table 1 and Table 3.

Table 2 also confirms that shareholders in target firms consistently gained from successful takeovers. (The "abnormal return" tabulated here is the percent gain on the stock in the 3-day period surrounding the merger announcement.) But acquirer firms seem to come out, on average, a bit behind! It may be that many takeovers are motivated by nonpecuniary considerations such as empire-building or power-seeking. Or, alternatively, the takeover business may be so competitive that (at least on average) large profits cannot be earned.

[a] Michael C. Jensen and Richard S. Ruback, "The Market for Corporate Control: The Scientific Evidence," *Journal of Financial Economics*, v. 11 (1983), pp. 5–50.

[b] George Andrade, Mark Mitchell, and Erik Stafford, "New Evidence and Perspectives on Mergers," *Journal of Economic Perspectives*, v. 15 (2001), pp. 103–120.

Managements have sometimes been able to secure state legislation to restrict takeover attempts. Also, the Boards of Directors of most large corporations have adopted a variety of antitakeover provisions, usually with stockholder approval. Whether these defenses on balance help or hurt shareholders has been the subject of much debate.

EXAMPLE 6.2 TAKEOVER DEFENSES, CORPORATE GOVERNANCE, AND STOCK PRICES

Paul A. Gompers, Joy L. Ishii, and Andrew Metrick created an index based on 24 different corporate governance provisions, all associated with defending management against takeovers, and related this index to the level and movements of stock prices.[a]

The table shows, for a sample of about 1,500 corporations, the percentages that adopted a selection of antitakeover provisions as of 1998.

Selected corporate governance provisions (1998)

Provision	Percentage	Description of provision
Blank check	87.9	Preferred stock over which board has wide authority to determine voting, conversion, and other rights
Classified board	59.4	Directors serve overlapping terms (so board cannot be overturned all at once)
Golden parachutes	56.6	Generous compensation for management if forced out in a takeover
Indemnification	24.4	Protects officers from lawsuits based on their conduct
Poison pill	55.3	Gives stockholders, other than takeover bidder, rights to purchase stock at steep discount after change of control.
Supermajority	34.1	Supermajority (beyond that specified in state law) required for takeovers

Source: Selected and adapted from Gompers, Ishii, and Metrick, Table 1.

The authors' index of corporate governance was essentially the number of such antitakeover measures adopted by a corporation. (So high values of the index represent greater freedom of action for management.) To test how corporate governance affects stock prices, they compared a hypothetical portfolio of stocks in the lowest 10 percent of the index (strongest shareholder rights) with an opposite portfolio of stocks in the highest 10 percent (weakest shareholder rights). The group with strong shareholder rights included well-known companies such as IBM, Wal-Mart, and Du Pont; the group with weak shareholder rights included companies such as NCR, Kmart, and Time Warner. They found that during the 1990s, the first portfolio earned 23.3 percent per year, but the second only 14 percent. The difference did not seem to reflect different levels of riskiness between the two portfolios, or the performance of just a few firms in either portfolio, or different industrial compositions of the two portfolios. These results suggest that antitakeover provisions have on average harmed shareholders.

COMMENT

Nevertheless, stockholders usually voted to approve these changes in corporate charters. Or at any rate, the shareholders had elected directors who adopted such provisions. This seeming paradox is the subject of continuing discussion and debate among economists and policy-makers.

[a] Paul A. Gompers, Joy L. Ishii, and Andrew Metrick, "Corporate Governance and Equity Prices," National Bureau of Economic Research Working Paper 8449 (2001).

The critique of the profit-maximizing model need not go so far as to claim that shareholders are powerless. Perhaps management provides a minimum level of profits, enough to head off lawsuits or takeover contests. But beyond this, critics contend, entrenched managers can pursue their own goals rather than those of owners. Managers may seek power (empire-building), publicity in the form of a corporate image, amenities like luxurious offices, or a stable environment without risk of unpleasant surprises. Stockholders may sometimes be able to verify that such abuses occurred, at least after the fact. If such an entrenched manager unexpectedly relinquishes control – in the extreme case, if he or she dies suddenly, then the stock price should jump.[3]

The incentives for managers to shirk on their duties to shareholders can arguably be reduced by compensation packages (including salaries, options, and possible other payments) that reward good performance.

EXAMPLE 6.3 CEO COMPENSATION

Paul L. Joskow and Nancy L. Rose studied the association between compensation received by chief executives and firms' success in the period 1970–1990.[a] CEO pay packages in that period were typically designed to reflect profitability in the current and in the two previous years. The averaging tends to minimize the role of random or accidental elements in any single year.

CEO compensation contracts, the authors found – including salary and bonuses, other company benefits, and especially stock options – allowed for both the *market rate of return* accruing to stockholders (reported earnings divided by share price) and the firm's *accounting rate of return* (reported earnings divided by book value of the firm's equity). In the 1980s, for example, an increase in the current market return on company shares from 15 to 25% over a three-year period raised CEO compensation on average by around 4.7%. A similar calculation in terms of accounting rates of return (which were typically smaller than stockmarket returns in this bull-market period) was associated with a compensation increase of 11.7%.

COMMENT

In view of the conceptual superiority of economic profit as opposed to accounting profit, it may seem surprising that Boards of Directors tied CEO compensation to reported corporate earnings, which is closer to accounting profit than to economic profit. But economic profit is calculated in terms of alternative opportunities, which are not directly measurable. In contrast, accounting data are generated under established rules and standards, and hence are more objective – even if conceptually less meaningful. Also, managers are commonly compensated in terms of year-to-year earnings *changes*. Despite the conceptual flaws, it is reasonable to assume that year-to-year increases or decreases in accounting earnings typically correlate well with increases or decreases of true economic profit.

---

[a] Paul L. Joskow and Nancy L. Rose, "CEO Pay and Firm Performance: Dynamics, Asymmetries, and Alternative Performance Measures," National Bureau of Economic Research Working Paper No. 4976 (December 1994).

---

[3] Armand Hammer, the long-time chief executive of the Occidental Petroleum Corporation, died in 1990. Since Hammer was 92 years old, this was not totally unexpected, but as the death was due to a home accident there was some surprise. Hammer had often been accused of abusing his executive position for personal advantage. On the day after Hammer's death, the New York Stock Exchange was flooded with "buy" orders for Occidental shares. The stock ended the day up about 9% – an increase in market value of over $550,000,000. This might be interpreted as convincing support for the allegations against Hammer. But the increase was completely reversed the next day, and in the week following there were no abnormal changes in the stock price. So it is not clear after all that stock investors regarded Hammer's management as exploitive.

No doubt managers sometimes serve their own interests at the expense of the owners. But does this problem make the hypothesis that firms maximize profit unworkable? Overall, economists have found that viewing firms as maximizing profit has proved to be more useful than alternative assumptions.

6.2   THE OPTIMUM OF THE FIRM IN PURE COMPETITION

Economic profit, symbolized here as Π,[4] is the difference between the firm's Total Revenue and Total Cost – or, for short, between its Revenue R and Cost C. The cost concept is of course economic cost rather than accounting cost. And Revenue for the firm is price P times output q. In symbols:

$$\Pi \equiv R - C \tag{6.1}$$

$$R \equiv P \times q \tag{6.2}$$

This chapter deals with a *competitive* or "price-taking" firm. By definition, a competitive firm views the market price P as constant, regardless of its own output. (While never literally true, this may approximate reality if the firm produces only a small fraction of the output in its industry.)

A hump-shaped Total Revenue curve was pictured in Figure 2.10 of Chapter 2. In the upper panel, R first increases as output q rises, but then decreases. The reason is that there are two offsetting forces. R is the product $q \times P$, but as quantity q rises price P tends to fall. However, the picture in Figure 2.10 does not apply to the price-taking firm of this chapter.[5] The assumption here is that price P is constant regardless of the firm's own output, so Total Revenue R rises in proportion to output. For a competitive firm the Total Revenue curve R is not hump-shaped, but is instead a ray out of the origin with slope P, as shown in the upper panel of Figure 6.1.

The Total Cost function, which was briefly described in Chapter 2 (see Figure 2.11), is shown again here as the curve C in the upper panel of Figure 6.1. Note that Cost may be positive even when $q = 0$. The reason is Fixed Cost, for example rent that has to paid for use of a building even when nothing is produced. So Total Cost is the sum of Fixed Cost (F) and Variable Cost (F):

$$C \equiv F + V \tag{6.3}$$

Apart from the positive vertical intercept F in the diagram, Total Cost curves have the following typical features:

1. At low output, cost rises with quantity but at a decreasing rate, owing to the advantages of large-scale production.
2. At high output, however, cost rises with quantity at an increasing rate, reflecting the Law of Diminishing Returns.

---

[4] Π is the Greek upper-case letter "pi."
[5] The picture in Figure 2.10 would apply to a *monopoly* firm, to be studied in Chapter 8.

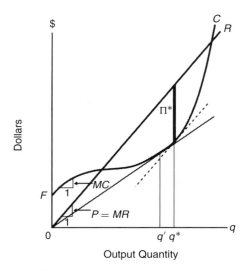

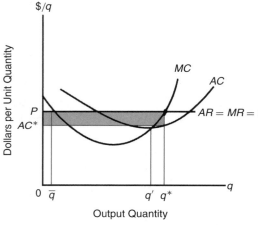

Output Quantity

Figure 6.1. Optimum of the Competitive Firm

The profit-maximizing output is q^* in the upper diagram, where the vertical difference between the Total Revenue curve R and the Total Cost curve C is maximized. The maximized profit is Π^*. At q^* the slopes along curves R and C are equal, so in the lower diagram the Marginal Revenue curve MR and the Marginal Cost curve MC intersect at output q^*. At output q' in the upper diagram, a ray from the origin is tangent to the Total Cost curve, which means that Average Cost equals Marginal Cost. Thus, in the lower diagram q' lies at the intersection of the MC and AC curves, where Average Cost is at a minimum.

EXAMPLE 6.4 SCALE ECONOMIES IN ELECTRIC POWER DISTRIBUTION

John E. Kwoka, Jr. analyzed the cost structure of electric power distribution in a report produced for the American Public Power Association.[a] Distribution costs fall into two main categories: "wire" costs (providing the physical network for movement of electricity) were around 60%, and "supply" costs (marketing and administrative functions such as packaging and selling power, billing, and servicing accounts) were around 40% of the total.

The table here shows that, in terms of customer numbers, wire costs and supply costs both displayed economies of scale (falling Average Cost), but only up to a point. Economies of scale were more evident for the physical or wire aspect of the business: unit costs started high, reached a minimum at about 1,470,000 customers, and then turned upward. Unit supply costs were more uniform: they fell less sharply to begin with, reached a minimum at about 530,000 customers, and rose moderately thereafter. The difference is understandable. Wire costs involve big physical investments that must be spread over a large clientele to become economical, whereas costs of billing are more proportional to customer numbers.

Average costs per KWH, by number of customers

Number of customers ('000s)	Unit wire costs (cents/KWH)	Unit supply costs (cents/KWH)
1	1.741	1.035
5	0.9666	0.633
10	0.868	0.583
50	0.782	0.542
100	0.763	0.537
500	0.688	0.530
1000	0.635	0.531
1500	0.620	0.539
2000	0.640	0.552
3000	0.788	0.596
5000	1.520	0.752

Source: Adapted form Kwoka, Table 5.

[a] John E. Kwoka, Jr., "Electric Power Distribution Costs: Analysis and Implications for Restructuring," A Report to the American Public Power Association (2001).

Looking at the Revenue side in more detail, Average Revenue AR and Marginal Revenue MR were defined in Chapter 2 as:

$$MR \equiv \frac{\Delta R}{\Delta q} \quad \text{and} \quad AR \equiv \frac{R}{q} \tag{6.4}$$

(As before, the Δ symbol indicates small changes of the variable.)

Geometrically, MR is the *slope* of the TR curve. For the competitive (price-taking) firm assumed here, the slope is a constant equal to the market price P, as suggested by the small triangle drawn along the curve in the upper panel of Figure 6.1. Since Marginal Revenue is constant and equal to P, in the lower panel MR becomes a horizontal line at height P.

Total Revenue and Total Cost are measured in dollars,[6] so the vertical axis in the upper panel of Figure 6.1 is scaled in dollar units. But Average Revenue and Marginal Revenue, and Average Cost and Marginal Cost, have the dimension *dollars per unit quantity* (like price itself), so the vertical axis of the lower panel is scaled in units of $/q$. [*Caution:* As already explained in Chapter 2, it is a mistake to plot average or marginal curves in a "total" diagram where the vertical axis is scaled in dollars. And do not plot total curves in an "average-marginal" diagram where the vertical axis is scaled in dollars per unit of output ($\$/q$).]

From the definition of Average Revenue above, since $R \equiv Pq$ it follows also that $AR \equiv P \equiv R/q$. That is, Average Revenue AR is the same as price P.[7] Since price is

---

[6] As mentioned in Chapter 2, Revenue and Cost can be interpreted as *dollars per unit time.*
[7] Assuming each unit of the product is sold at the same price, as necessarily holds under perfect competition.

constant here, the *AR* curve in Panel (b) must be a horizontal line at the level of *P*. Thus, for a price-taking firm the *AR* curve and the *MR* curves *coincide*, as a horizontal line at height *P*. (This is an example of Proposition 2.2c of Chapter 2: When the average function is constant, the marginal function is equal to it.) Last, note that the horizontal line $P = AR = MR$ can be interpreted as the *demand curve* d faced by this single firm.

EXERCISE 6.1

A firm faces a horizontal demand curve at the market price $P = 25$, independent of its own output q. What are the equations for Total Revenue, Marginal Revenue, and Average Revenue?

ANSWER: Total Revenue is $R = 25q$. Since $\Delta R / \Delta q$ – the increase in R per unit increase in q – is always 25, we know that Marginal Revenue is a constant with equation $MR = 25$. And since $R/q = 25$, Average Revenue is also constant with equation $AR = 25$.

Turning to the cost side, Marginal Cost *MC* and Average Cost *AC* are:

$$MC \equiv \frac{\Delta C}{\Delta q} \quad \text{and} \quad AC \equiv \frac{C}{q} \tag{6.5}$$

In the upper panel of Figure 6.1, *MC* is the slope along the Total Cost curve (note the small illustrative triangle drawn along the curve). As plotted in the lower panel, *MC* first declines (corresponding to the region where *C* rises at a decreasing rate) but eventually begins to rise (corresponding to the region where *C* rises at an increasing rate).

The shape of the Average Cost curve *AC* in the lower panel can be derived similarly. In the upper panel, $AC \equiv C/q$ corresponds to the slope of a ray drawn from the origin to the *C* curve. At $q = 0$ this ray is vertical, so *AC* is infinite at the vertical axis. As output increases, the slope of the ray falls until output reaches q'. This is the point of minimum *AC*. Thereafter, the slope of the ray rises as q increases.

From Propositions 2.2a, b, and c of Chapter 2 we know that when *AC* is falling, *MC* lies below it; when *AC* is rising, *MC* lies above it; and when *AC* is constant (at a minimum), $MC = AC$. Accordingly, the lower panel of Figure 6.1 shows that *MC* lies below *AC* for outputs less than q', that *MC* cuts (equals) *AC* at q' (where *AC* is at a minimum), and that *MC* is greater than *AC* for outputs greater than q'.

In the upper panel the maximum profit Π^* occurs at q^*, where the Total Revenue curve *R* and Total Cost curve *C* are parallel. (The parallelism is suggested by the dashed line drawn tangent to the *C* curve at $q = q^*$.) Since *MR* is the slope of the *R* curve, and *MC* is the slope of the *C* curve, it follows that in the lower panel *MR* and *MC* are equal (the *MR* and *MC* curves intersect) at q^*. So the firm maximizes profit by choosing the output at which Marginal Revenue = Marginal Cost. And since we are dealing with a competitive (price-taking) firm for which $MR = $ Price $= AR$, this condition takes on the specific form

$$MC = MR = P \quad \text{Maximum-Profit Condition, Competitive Firm} \tag{6.6}$$

But there is an important qualification. Setting $MC = MR$ maximizes profit *only if the MC curve cuts the MR curve from below*. Notice that, in the lower panel of Figure 6.1, the *MR* and *MC* curves intersect twice. But at the left-hand intersection (where

$q = \bar{q}$), MC cuts MR *from above.* Since to the right of that intersection MR exceeds MC, economic logic tells us that it pays to produce more units until the right-hand intersection is reached where MC cuts MR *from below.*[8]

> **PROPOSITION:** The profit-maximizing output for the firm occurs where Marginal Cost equals Marginal Revenue, provided that the Marginal Cost curve cuts the Marginal Revenue curve from below.

EXERCISE 6.2

A firm faces price $P = 38$, independent of its output q. Marginal Cost is $MC = 2 + (q - 10)^2$. (a) At what output or outputs does Marginal Cost (MC) equal Marginal Revenue (MR)? (b) At what output does the MC curve cut the MR curve from below? (c) What is the most profitable level of output?

ANSWER: (a) Marginal Revenue here is $MR = P = 38$. Setting $MC = MR$ implies $2 + (q - 10)^2 = 38$. There are two algebraic solutions: $q = 16$ and $q = 4$. The MC and MR curves intersect at both these outputs. (b) By plotting some points it can be verified that MC cuts MR from below only at the larger output $q = 16$. (c) The most profitable output is $q = 16$.

The *size* of economic profit at the profit-maximizing output q^* is represented in the upper panel of Figure 6.1 as the bold vertical line-segment Π^* between the Total Revenue curve and the Total Cost curve. In the lower graph, profit *per unit* is the vertical distance between Average Revenue and Average Cost. The definition of total profit directly implies that $\Pi \equiv (AR - AC) \times q$. That is, profit Π equals the difference between Average Revenue and Average Cost, multiplied by the level of output. So, in the lower panel the maximized profit is the shaded rectangle with area $(P - AC) \times q^*$.

Table 6.1 illustrates hypothetical revenue and cost data for a competitive firm. Price is constant at $P = 60$, so Average Revenue AR and Marginal Revenue MR also equal 60 throughout. The Total Revenue column (R) is $R = 60q$. The cost function is assumed to be $C = 128 + 69q - 14q^2 + q^3$. This formula was used to compute values in the Total Cost column C. These Total Revenue and Total Cost functions reflect the general shapes pictured in the upper panel of Figure 6.1, and the average and marginal functions would resemble those in the lower panel.

Applying the method of approximating marginal quantities from discrete or tabular data recommended in Chapter 2, consider the approximate Marginal Cost at $q = 7$ in Table 6.1. The cost increment due to the "last" unit produced (that is, between $q = 6$ and $q = 7$) is $268 - 254 = 14$. [We can think of this as the Marginal Cost at $q = 6\frac{1}{2}$.] The cost increment from the "next" unit produced (that is, between $q = 7$ and $q = 8$) is $296 - 268 = 28$. (We can think of this as the Marginal Cost at $q = 7\frac{1}{2}$.) Our recommended approximation for Marginal Cost at $q = 7$ is then the average of

---

[8] *Mathematical Footnote:* Maximizing $\Pi \equiv R - C$ with respect to q by differentiating and setting equal to zero, the *first-order* condition for a maximum is $dR/dq = dC/dq$, or $MR = MC$. The *second-order* condition for a maximum is $d^2\Pi/dq^2 < 0$, or $d^2R/dq^2 < d^2C/dq^2$. So MR must be falling relative to MC, meaning that MC must cut MR from below. (The left-hand intersection of MC and MR in the lower panel, which violates the second-order condition for an optimum, corresponds to the output that *minimizes* profit.)

Table 6.1 Hypothetical revenue and cost functions: competitive firm –
$R = 60q$, $C = 128 + 69q - 14q^2 + q^3$

q	P AR MR	R	C	Recommended approximation of marginal cost	MC (exact)	AC	VC	AVC
0	60	0	128	–	69	∞	0	–
1	60	60	184	45	44	184.0	56	56
2	60	120	218	26	25	109.0	90	45
3	60	180	236	13	12	78.7	108	36
4	60	240	244	6	5	61.0	116	29
5	60	300	248	5	4	49.6	120	24
6	60	360	254	10	9	42.3	126	21
7	60	420	268	21	20	38.3	140	20
8	60	480	296	38	37	37.0	168	21
9	60	540	344	61	60	38.2	216	24
10	60	600	418	–	89	41.8	290	29

these two, specifically Marginal Cost $= 21$ as shown in the table.[9] Last, the *true* Marginal Cost at integer values of q is shown by the column labeled "*MC* (exact)," based on the equation $MC = 69 - 28q + 3q^2$ derived by calculus.[10]

With $P = 60$, setting the true Marginal Cost equal to price leads to the correct profit-maximizing solution $q^* = 9$.[11] At $q^* = 9$, Total Revenue is 540 and Total Cost is 344; hence the maximized profit is $\Pi^* = 196$. (Using our recommended approximation method and linearly interpolating, a very similar solution would be obtained.)

EXERCISE 6.3

Suppose Total Revenue remains $R = 60q$ as in Table 6.1, but the Total Cost function becomes $C = 10 + 5q^2$. (a) How does this Total Cost function differ from that pictured in the upper panel of Figure 6.1? (b) How does Marginal Cost differ from that pictured in the lower panel of Figure 6.1? (c) What is the profit-maximizing output, and what is the associated profit?

ANSWER: (a) Plotting several points and sketching, the *C* curve here always rises at an increasing rate (whereas in Figure 6.1 the *C* curve initially rises at a decreasing rate). (b) The points fit the equation $MC = 10q$. (This is also the exact Marginal Cost that can be obtained by calculus.) Unlike the *MC* curve in Figure 6.1, here *MC* is a straight line through the origin with positive slope. (c) Since $MC = 10q$ and $MR = P = 60$, setting $MC = MR$ leads to a profit-maximizing solution at $q^* = 6$. (Here the *MC* curve intersects the *MR* curve only once.) At this output, $R = 6 \times 60 = 360$ and $C = 10 + (5 \times 6^2) = 190$, so profit is $\Pi^* = 360 - 190 = 170$.

---

[9] Failure to use our recommended method – for example, taking the Marginal Cost as the cost increment associated either with the "last" unit or with the "next" unit produced – can lead to considerable error, as was illustrated in Chapter 2.

[10] *Mathematical Footnote:* $C = 128 + 69q - 14q^2 + q^3$. Then $MC \equiv dC/dq = 69 - 28q + 3q^2$.

[11] *Mathematical Footnote:* The second-order condition should also be checked. Setting $MC = 69 - 28q + 3q^2 = 60$ yields two algebraic solutions: $q^* = 9$ and $q = 1/3$. The incorrect solution, $q = 1/3$, violates the second-order condition for a maximum.

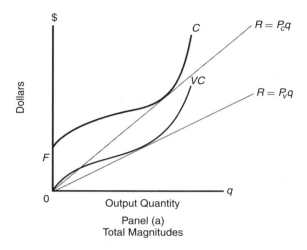

Panel (a)
Total Magnitudes

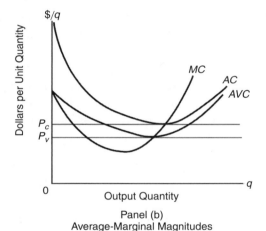

Panel (b)
Average-Marginal Magnitudes

Figure 6.2. The Cost Function

In the upper diagram, Total Cost C rises with output, first at a decreasing rate but ultimately at an increasing rate. The curve VC showing Total Variable Cost lies below the curve C by the amount of the fixed cost F. In the lower diagram the Marginal Cost MC curve cuts first through the low point of Average Variable Cost AVC, and then through the low point of Average Cost AC. The firm will shut down if in the long-run price is less than P_C. If price is below P_V, the firm produces nothing even in the short run.

The last two columns of Table 6.1 show *Total Variable Cost VC* and *Average Variable Cost AVC*. From equation (6.3) and the definition of the average concept, it follows that

$$VC \equiv C - F \quad \text{and} \quad AVC \equiv VC/q \equiv (C - F)/q \tag{6.7}$$

In comparing the curves of Total Cost and Total Variable Cost in the upper panel of Figure 6.2, note that VC is everywhere lower than C by a constant vertical distance equal to F.

Marginal Cost MC, Average Cost AC, and Average Variable Cost AVC are shown in the lower panel of Figure 6.2. At $q = 0$, $AC \equiv C/q$ is necessarily infinite, but

$AVC \equiv (C - F)/q$ generally is not.[12] Notice that as q increases, AC and AVC converge. The difference between them, the term F/q, becomes ever smaller as q rises.

Marginal Cost was defined as the slope of the Total Cost curve C. Since at any given output the VC curve has the same slope as the C curve, MC is also the slope along VC. In other words, the level of fixed costs does not affect Marginal Cost.[13]

Following are some other important features of Figure 6.2:

1. *At $q = 0$*, Marginal Cost (MC) equals Average Variable Cost (AVC). In Table 6.1, note that as q approaches zero, MC and AVC approach one another.[14]
2. MC is related to AVC in the same way as to Average Cost (AC). That is, when AVC is falling, $MC < AVC$; when AVC is rising, $MC > AVC$, and when AVC is constant (at its minimum level), $MC = AVC$. So MC cuts through the minimum points of both AC and AVC.
3. The minimum of AVC is to the left of the minimum of AC. This must hold if the rising MC curve is to cut the minimum points of both AC and AVC.

In Table 6.1, both MC and AVC equal 20 when $q = 7$; hence this is the minimum of AVC. And both MC and AC equal 37 at $q = 8$, so this output minimizes AC.[15]

The Shutdown Decision

Even when a competitive firm satisfies the condition $MC = MR = $ Price, and even if the MC curve in the lower panel of Figure 6.2 cuts the horizontal price line $MR = P$ from below, Total Revenue may be less than Total Cost. The best possible positive output might still generate a loss (profit Π is negative). So should the firm go out of business? (A multiproduct firm should ask whether it should exit from this particular line of business.) For this "shutdown decision," the *minimum* values of Average Cost and of Average Variable Cost are crucial.

Whether the firm should shut down depends on whether the decision involves the short run or the long run. As will be explained below, the economic meaning of the "short run" is not a period of time but rather refers to a decision situation in which certain choices – in this case, amounts of some of the inputs – are not subject to revision. In meeting a temporary surge in demand, the factory and machinery might be considered fixed. Then the desired increase in output has to be achieved by changing only some of the inputs, for example using more overtime labor. In the "long run," however, all inputs can be varied.

In the *short run*, then, a firm should continue to produce if Total Revenue exceeds Total Variable Cost:

$$R \geq VC, \text{ or equivalently } P \geq AVC \quad \text{No-Shutdown Condition, short run}$$

$$(6.8a)$$

---

[12] *Mathematical Footnote:* C/q must be infinite at $q = 0$. But at $q = 0$, $(C - F)/q$ is the difference between two infinite magnitudes, C/q and F/q, and so it is not in general infinite.

[13] *Mathematical Footnote:* Since $C \equiv VC + F$ and F is a constant, the derivative $MC \equiv dC/dq$ is the same as $d(VC)/dq$.

[14] *Mathematical Footnote:* At $q = 0$, $AVC = 0/0$ is indeterminate. But applying L'Hôpital's Rule, the limit (as $q \to 0$) of VC/q equals the limit of $d(VC)/dq$. So MC and AVC coincide at $q = 0$.

[15] *Mathematical Footnote:* To find the exact minimum of AVC, differentiate $AVC = q^2 - 14q + 69$ and set the derivative equal to zero. The solution is $q = 7$. To find the minimum of AC, differentiate $AC = q^2 - 14q + 69 + (128/q)$. A cubic equation is obtained, but the only root in the relevant range is $q = 8$.

In Figure 6.2, the firm should continue operating in the short run if price exceeds P_V, the minimum of Average Variable Cost (AVC). The idea is that if the firm's long-run expectations warrant staying in business (or, for a multiproduct firm, warrant remaining in a particular line of activity), it pays to keep operating (to produce positive output) in the short run. Total Revenue covers the Total Variable Cost, with possibly something over to meet some of the Fixed Cost.

But in the long run, a firm should continue to operate only if *all* its costs are covered. So the long-run No-Shutdown Condition is

$$R \geq C, \text{ or equivalently } P \geq AC \quad \text{No-Shutdown Condition, long run} \quad (6.8b)$$

In Figure 6.2 the lowest price meeting the long-run No-Shutdown Condition is P_C.

PROPOSITION: A price-taking firm maximizes profit by producing that output where Marginal Cost = Marginal Revenue = Price (provided that Marginal Cost cuts Marginal Revenue from below, that Price $\geq$ Average Variable Cost in the short run, and that Price $\geq$ Average Cost in the long run).

EXERCISE 6.4

Using the data of Table 6.1, what are the short-run and long-run shut-down prices P_C and P_V?

ANSWER: The minimal Average Variable Cost occurs at about $q = 7$, where $AVC = 20$. So the short-run shutdown price is $P_V = 20$. The minimum Average Cost occurs at about $q = 8$, where $AC = 37$. So the long-run shutdown price is $P_C = 37$.

Fixed costs are sometimes confused with "sunk costs." Suppose an aircraft assembly plant had bought a wing-stamping machine for a certain model of airplane. It financed the machine by a noncancellable bank loan, to be paid off in annual $1,000,000 installments over several years. Sales are slow, and the company is considering abandoning this line of business. Since the annual installment remains payable whether or not any wings are produced, the annual $1,000,000 is surely not a variable cost of production. But is it a fixed cost from the point of view of the abandonment decision? The crucial principle to remember is that, for there to be an economic cost, a resource must have alternative uses. For simplicity, suppose there are no other uses whatsoever for this machine.[16] Since the firm cannot avoid the $1,000,000 annual commitment even by permanently abandoning this line of business, the outlay is "sunk" and should not enter into the calculation.

To summarize, fixed costs, although applicable only for the long-run decision, are actual economic costs. So-called "sunk costs," in contrast, are irrevocably lost to the firm. They are irrelevant to any present or future decisions, and so are not economic costs at all.[17]

---

[16] That of course is an extreme assumption. Almost always there is some minimal alternative use, if only to break up the machine for scrap metal.

[17] The treatment of "sunk costs" is one of the differences between economic profit and accounting profit. The annual $1,000,000 installment would be counted as a cost in calculating *accounting* profit.

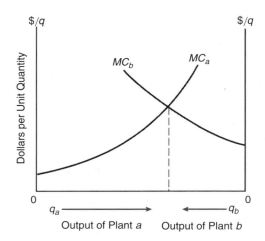

Figure 6.3. Division of Output between Plants

A firm with two plants should divide any given output q in such a way that Marginal Costs in the two plants, MC_a and MC_b, are equal.

An Application: Division of Output among Plants

Suppose a firm can divide output q between factories in Albany (plant a) and Buffalo (plant b):

$$q_a + q_b \equiv q \tag{6.9}$$

By a straightforward extension of equation (6.6), the optimizing rule is:

$$MC_a = MC_b = MR \equiv P \tag{6.10}$$

In words, the firm should divide its production to make the Marginal Costs in the different plants equal. Furthermore, both Marginal Costs should be set equal to Marginal Revenue. (For a price-taking firm, of course, Marginal Revenue is identical with price P.)

Figure 6.3 depicts the first of the above equalities, the optimal division of output between two plants. The firm's *total* output q is taken as given in the diagram; q is indicated by the horizontal distance between the two vertical axes. The Albany output q_a is measured in the usual way, as the distance to the right of the left-hand axis. The Buffalo output q_b is measured in the opposite direction, as the distance to the left of the right-hand axis. Then the equality $MC_a = MC_b$ occurs at the intersection of the

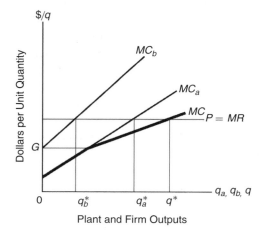

Figure 6.4. Optimal Outputs with Two Plants

The firm's Marginal Cost curve MC is the horizontal sum of the plant MC_a and MC_b curves. In setting firm output q^* where $MC = P$, the corresponding plant outputs q_a^* and q_b^* are such that $MC_a = MC_b = P$.

two Marginal Cost curves. Assuming both Marginal Cost curves rise throughout as illustrated here, this is indeed the best division of the given output q between the two plants.

What if the MC_a and MC_b curves, each an increasing function of its own plant output, never intersect? This means that, for the specified total output q, one plant's Marginal Cost is *always* higher than the other's. Then the plant with the lower Marginal Cost should produce all the output.

EXERCISE 6.4

(a) Suppose the Marginal Cost functions for the two plants are $MC_a = 5 + 2q_a$ and $MC_b = 40 + q_b$. If the total output is $q = 25$, how should the outputs be divided? (b) What if the total output were $q = 15$?

ANSWER: (a) Setting the Marginal Costs equal implies $5 + 2q_a = 40 + q_b$. Making use of $q_a + q_b \equiv q = 25$ and substituting, the solution is $q_a = 20$, $q_b = 5$. (b) For $q = 15$, setting the Marginal Costs equal would indicate a negative output for plant b. This is impossible. The explanation, which can be verified by sketching, is that the MC_a and MC_b curves do not intersect when the required total output is $q = 15$. The best solution is to assign all output to the lower-cost plant in Albany, that is, to set $q_a = 15$ and $q_b = 0$. At $q_a = 15$ the Albany plant's MC_a is only 35, whereas MC_b is *never* less than 40.

Now consider the second part of equation (6.10). Output q cannot be taken as given, but must be chosen so that MC_a and MC_b both equal $MR = \text{Price}$. In Figure 6.4 the bold curve MC represents the *firm's* Marginal Cost function. It is the horizontal sum of the separate MC_a and MC_b curves.[18] Thus, setting $MC = P$ as illustrated in the diagram also implies setting $MC_a = MC_b = P$ in accordance with equation (6.10). The overall optimal firm output q^* and the separate optimal plant outputs q_a^* and q_b^* can be read off along the horizontal axis.

EXERCISE 6.5

Using the Marginal Cost data of the previous exercise, suppose the market price is $P = 45$. (a) Find the optimal outputs for the separate plants and for the firm as a whole. (b) What is the equation for the *firm's* MC curve in Figure 6.4?

ANSWER: (a) The conditions $MC_a = MC_b = P = 45$ imply $q_a = 20$ and $q_b = 5$, so $q = 25$. (b) The trick here is to remember that we are *summing quantities*. The separate plant Marginal Cost equations can be written $q_a = (MC_a - 5)/2$ and $q_b = MC_b - 40$. Summing over quantities, and remembering that the firm's MC is defined in terms of the equated values of $MC_a = MC_b$, we have $q = (MC - 5)/2 + MC - 40$. Solving, $MC = 2/3 \times (q + 42.5)$. As a check, setting this MC equal to $P = 45$ does confirm the solution $q = 25$.

---

[18] Notice that the MC_b curve for the higher-cost plant does not enter into the horizontal summation until MC_a equals the minimal (initial) level of MC_b. (For a somewhat similar geometrical construction see Figure 2.5, "Introduction of an Import Supply.")

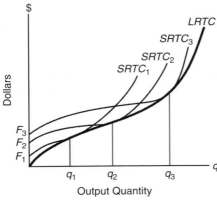

Figure 6.5. Short-Run and Long-Run Cost Functions

In the upper diagram, *LRTC* is the Long-Run Total Cost function showing the cost of producing any output q when all inputs are allowed to vary. The Short-Run Total Cost curve, *SRTC*, applies when the fixed input is held constant at a level appropriate for small-scale production (q_1); similarly, $SRTC_2$ and $SRTC_3$ are associated with the higher levels of fixed cost appropriate for medium-scale production (q_2) and large-scale production (q_3). The corresponding average and marginal curves are shown in the lower diagram. At output q_1, $SRAC_1 = LRAC$ (the curves are tangent) and $SRMC_1 = LRMC$ (the curves intersect); similar conditions hold for output levels q_2 and q_3. At any point, the Total Cost curves and the Average Cost curves are never higher in the long run than in the short run. (Note that no such statement can be made for the Marginal Cost curves.)

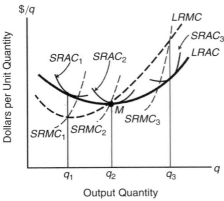

6.3   COST FUNCTIONS

Short Run versus Long Run

This section goes more deeply into the distinction between the long run and the short run. The fundamental difference has to do with *the range of inputs taken as fixed*. This is not a yes/no contrast but rather a matter of degree. The longer the planning horizon, the greater the extent of costs that are variable rather than fixed.

In a manufacturing firm, toward the variable end are expenses for electric power, materials, and labor. Toward the fixed end are costs associated with ownership or leasing of real estate and machinery. Suppose a machine breakdown called for an hour-long reduction in output. Some electric power would be saved. But little else could be changed; for this output decision, almost all costs are fixed. If output were to be cut back over a period as long as a day, casual labor might also be laid off. Over a period such as a month more workers could be discharged (their wages would become a variable cost), and some leased equipment such as trucks could be returned. Last, if the firm planned to reduce output permanently, it could sell off machinery and reduce its real-estate commitments.

For simplicity in the following discussion, unless otherwise indicated "long run" will mean that *all* costs are variable; "short run" will mean that *some* costs are fixed. So there is a single Long-Run Total Cost curve *LRTC*, as shown in the upper panel of Figure 6.5.

Furthermore, this curve goes through the origin: at zero output, $LRTC = 0$. (In the long run all costs are variable, so no costs are incurred if nothing is produced.)

The Long-Run Total Cost function shows the *lowest cost* of producing any given level of output. Why the lowest cost? Because, when *all* costs are variable, at any output q the firm is free to choose the best (the most economical) mix of all resources employed.

Three different Short-Run Total Cost functions are shown in the upper panel of Figure 6.5. $SRTC_1$ is associated with a low fixed cost F_1. This level is assumed optimal for the relatively small rate of output q_1. If the lowest cost of producing output q_1 is with fixed cost F_1, then the Short-Run Total Cost as given by curve $SRTC_1$ at q_1 must equal the Long-Run Total Cost at q_1. Any other output will call for a different level of optimal fixed cost. The Short-Run Total Cost curve $SRTC_1$ must therefore lie above the Long-Run Total Cost for all outputs other than q_1. Then the curve $SRTC_1$ is necessarily tangent to $LRTC$ at output q_1.

Operating along $SRTC_1$ is fine for small outputs. But at larger outputs the curve $SRTC_1$ rises steeply. So moderately large levels of production are cheaper along the curve $SRTC_2$, where $SRTC_2$ represents the short-run costs associated with a somewhat higher fixed cost F_2 that is best for output q_2. Last, $SRTC_3$ is associated with a fixed cost F_3 that is optimal for the large output q_3. It represents the best of the three situations for high output, but the worst for low output. Notice that the $LRTC$ curve in the diagram is a *lower envelope* of all the $SRTC$ curves.

[*Caution*: Here is a common mistake. Consider a retail store. Since short-run adjustments involve increasing only *some* of the inputs (say, the number of salespeople), whereas long-run adjustments may involve increases in *all* inputs (including, perhaps, floor space), one might think that short-run costs of increasing output must necessarily be lower than long-run costs. Isn't it cheaper to increase sales by expanding only the workforce than by expanding both the workforce and the floorspace? Expressed this way, the fallacy is evident. The store will expand its floorspace (incur a higher fixed cost) only when doing so is *less* costly (involves lower expense overall) than expanding output by increasing variable costs (the sales force) alone.]

Let us now translate from the total units in the upper panel of Figure 6.5 to average-marginal units in the lower panel. Recall that $SRTC_1$ lies above $LRTC$ everywhere except at the tangency point where $q = q_1$. It follows that the corresponding Short-Run Average Cost curve $SRAC_1$ lies above the Long-Run Average Cost curve $LRAC$ everywhere except at q_1. A similar argument applies for the relation between $SRAC_2$ and $LRAC$ and so forth. The upshot is that $LRAC$ is a lower envelope of the $SRAC$ curves, just as $LRTC$ is a lower envelope of the $SRTC$ curves.

Notice that $SRAC_1$ is tangent to $LRAC$ at a point where both curves slope down. The minimum of the $SRAC_1$ curve therefore lies to the right of (at a greater output than) the tangency at $q = q_1$. For $SRAC_3$ the reverse holds; the minimum of $SRAC_3$ is to the left of $q = q_3$. A famous economist once made the following error. In the belief that the $LRAC$ curve, representing the least-cost way of producing any output q, must go through *the minimum points* of all the $SRAC$ curves, he asked his Research Assistant to draw the $LRAC$ accordingly. Experimenting with the curves will show that it is geometrically impossible to draw an $LRAC$ curve through the minimum points of the $SRAC$ curves and still have $LRAC$ lie everywhere *below* these curves. The principle to hold onto is that Long Run Average Cost is the lowest possible unit cost of producing any given level of output.

What about short-run and long-run Marginal Costs? At the tangencies of the $SRTC$ and $LRTC$ curves in the upper panel of Figure 6.5, both the *levels* and the *slopes* of the curves in contact are equal. Since the marginal function is always the slope of the corresponding total function, at output q_1 Short-Run Marginal Cost $SRMC_1$ equals Long-Run Marginal Cost $LRMC$; at q_2, $SRMC_2 = LRMC$; and at q_3, $SRMC_3 = LRMC$. This leads to the relation among the various short-run and the long-run marginal curves shown in the lower panel. Notice that the $LRMC$ curve is generally flatter than the $SRMC$ curves. This feature will play a role in the distinction between the short-run and long-run *supply functions of the firm*, to be discussed in the next chapter.

PROPOSITION: Given the market price P, a competitive firm makes the best long-run adjustment (selects the correct level of the fixed input) and the best short-run adjustment (selects the profit-maximizing output q) by satisfying the conditions Long-Run Marginal Cost = Short-Run Marginal Cost = Price. (Assuming that the MC curves cut the price line from below, and that the no-shutdown conditions are met.)

EXERCISE 6.5

A firm's Long-Run Total Cost curve is $LRTC = q^2$. The Short-Run Total Cost curve is $SRTC = 2B + q^4/(8B)$, where B represents the level of the input "fixed" in the short run, for example, the number of machines. Suppose $B = 4$, so that $SRTC = 8 + q^4/32$. Then it can be shown by calculus (or approximated by tabulating) that the associated Marginal Costs are $LRMC = 2q$ and $SRMC = q^3/8$. (a) At what output are $LRTC$ and $SRTC$ tangent? (b) What can you say about the Marginal Cost functions $LRMC$ and $SRMC$ at this output? (c) At what price P is $B = 4$ the best level of fixed input for the firm? (d) How does the overall picture here differ from the cost function diagrammed in Figure 6.5?

ANSWER: (a) At a point of tangency the curves must touch and have equal slopes. If $LRTC$ and $SRTC$ touch, it must be that $LRTC = SRTC$. So $q^2 = 8 + q^4/32$. This condition is met at $q = 4$. Since the marginal functions correspond to the slopes of the total functions, is it true that, at $q = 4$, $LRMC = SRMC$? Direct substitutions in the $LRMC$ and $SRMC$ equations show that indeed $2 \times 4 = 4^3/8$. So the $LRTC$ and the $SRTC$ curves associated with $B = 4$ are tangent at $q = 4$. (b) In (a) above, $LRMC = SRMC$ held true at $q = 4$. Calculus or plotting verifies that $SRMC$ is steeper than $LRMC$. In other words $LRMC$ and $SRMC$ intersect at $q = 4$, but are not tangent to one another there. (c) At $q = 4$, $SRMC = LRMC = 8$. So when $P = 8$, choosing $B = 4$ allows the firm to meet both the short-run and long-run conditions for optimal output: $LRMC = SRMC = P$. (d) The main difference is that the $LRTC$ curve here rises throughout at an increasing rate. This implies that both $LRAC$ and $LRMC$ have positive slopes throughout, and are not U-shaped as in the diagram. (But the short-run $SRAC$ curves all have the usual U-shape.)

The continuous $LRAC$ "envelope" curve in the lower panel of Figure 6.5 in effect assumes that the fixed input can take any value whatsoever in the range of interest. What if the fixed inputs come in discrete lumps? Using the notation of the preceding exercise, at the extreme imagine that the fixed input can take on only one of the two distinct values $B = 1$ or $B = 2$. Then the envelope would have a discontinuous appearance, somewhat as illustrated in Figure 6.6. Below the "crossover" output $\hat{q}$ the $LRAC$ runs

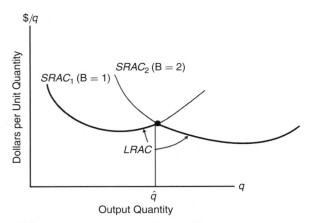

Figure 6.6. Short-Run and Long-Run Average Costs with Discrete Fixed Input

Here the fixed input can only take on one of the two levels $B = 1$ or $B = 2$, and the *SRAC* curves are drawn accordingly. The *LRAC* curve runs along the lower edges of the two *SRAC* curves.

along the $SRAC_1$ curve, and afterward along the $SRAC_2$ curve. (In Figure 6.6 the very lowest point along *LRAC* occurs with the larger fixed input $B = 2$, but the reverse is also possible.)

Is the concept of fixed costs meaningful? Commonsense tells us that a firm, intending to halt production for an hour, will not sell off its buildings and machinery with the intent of buying them back an hour later. But is this consistent with our analytical models? Why should a firm continue to incur any needless "fixed" costs, even for an hour? If machines and buildings are not needed, even for an instant of time, why not sell them off and then buy them back?

Transaction costs, a topic that came up earlier in the chapter in exploring the reasons why firms exist at all, are part of the answer. The cost and difficulty of negotiating and executing complex contracts make it impractical to sell and rebuy a factory building in an hour. But a somewhat subtler consideration is also involved: *specialization of resources to the firm.* Machinery may have been made to order and buildings partitioned or remodeled to the firm's specifications. Since such highly specialized assets are of lesser use to other firms, they may have little or no resale value. So, even if transaction costs were zero, the firm could not advantageously sell off such assets to meet a temporary reduction of output. (And knowing that resale value will be low, firms will be less ready to acquire highly specialized resources for a temporary production increase.) Even if the firm had leased rather than bought such resources, cancelling the lease can be costly. The owner of a building remodeled for a particular tenant, for example, will surely insist upon steep cancellation penalties.

Much the same applies for employees. Suppose a worker has received specialized job training of value only within the firm. If the firm bears the cost of the training, it would be reluctant to lay off the worker for fear of having to train a replacement. And the worker would be reluctant to bear the cost of training without some long-term job protection. So there may be an element of fixity in employing human as well as nonhuman inputs.

If transaction costs were absent, and if only unspecialized resources were used in production, one would not need to distinguish between the long run and the short run.

Transaction costs and specialization force a firm to choose between responding to a decline in demand in a short-run way or in a long-run way. In the short-run response, appropriate for a *temporary* reduction of output, the firm holds its specialized (or high-transaction-cost) resources fixed and continues to count spending on them as a cost of doing business. Thus, a loss may be incurred in the short run (Average Cost may exceed price): the firm should accept a temporary loss rather than dispose of a resource that it would shortly rebuy or rehire. The long-run response, appropriate for a *permanent* decline in output, is to dispose of the resource. Hence its cost is no longer fixed. (Any accounting loss suffered in the disposition of specialized inputs is "sunk," the result of a possible past error of judgment, and thus not a cost at all.)

Corresponding considerations apply to an *increase* in demand. A firm that regards the increase as temporary will hesitate to acquire additional specialized or high-transaction-cost inputs, in view of the penalties incurred when the time comes to dispose of them. If the demand change is believed to be permanent, however, incurring additional fixed costs is justifiable, in order to increase production at lower unit cost along the Long-Run Average Cost curve.

CONCLUSION

Inputs may be held fixed in the face of a temporary demand fluctuation for two reasons: (1) to avoid round-trip transaction costs associated with selling and rebuying (or firing and rehiring) inputs, and (2) to save the costs of specializing inputs to the firm. Holding some inputs fixed makes sense if the firm is dealing with a *short-run* fluctuation in demand. If the firm regards the demand change as permanent, it will make a *long-run* response, varying the amounts of all inputs.

Rising Costs and Diminishing Returns

Throughout this chapter, both Marginal Cost and Average Cost were pictured as (eventually) rising functions of output. These characteristics must apply if the firm operates under competitive price-taking conditions.

What if instead Marginal Cost (MC) were falling throughout? Recall that the profit-maximizing condition Marginal Cost = Marginal Revenue = Price is valid only if the MC curve cuts the MR curve *from below*. Since competitive conditions dictate a horizontal $MR \equiv P$ curve, an ever-falling Marginal Cost curve cannot cut Marginal Revenue from below. So a competitive optimum cannot be found.[19]

What if *Average* Cost (AC) falls throughout? Then any firm getting a sufficiently large output lead over other firms could produce at lower cost, thus driving its competitors out of business. So falling Average Cost can create a "natural monopoly," as will be discussed in Chapter 8. [*Question*: If Marginal Cost always declines with output, does Average Cost necessarily decline? If Average Cost falls everywhere, must Marginal Cost also fall? *Answer*: Verify that Average Cost falling throughout does not necessarily imply that Marginal Cost falls throughout. On the other hand, a negatively sloped Marginal Cost curve dictates that the corresponding Average Cost curve declines throughout.]

Marginal Cost and Average Cost curves that eventually rise are associated with the famous Law of Diminishing Returns, a topic to be covered in more detail in Chapter 11. That "law" is a technological principle that explains, for example, why it is impossible

---

[19] If MC cuts the constant $MR = P$ from above, by producing more output the firm could increase its profit forever – which is impossible.

to grow all the world's food in a flowerpot. The principle can be stated as follows: If one or more productive inputs are held fixed, then additional production requires that the other (variable) inputs be increased at an increasing rate. Thus, holding constant the amount of soil in the flowerpot, the attempt to grow more food – if successful at all – requires ever-rising additions of labor, fertilizer, and so forth. Of course, rising amounts of inputs imply rising costs. Thus, *diminishing returns* (marginal and average) translate into *rising costs* (marginal and average).

The Law of Diminishing Returns applies in the *short run*, defined by the condition that one or more inputs are held fixed by the firm. Figure 6.5 shows the Short-Run Marginal Cost and Short-Run Average Cost curves as eventually rising. It also shows the Long-Run Marginal Cost and Long-Run Average Cost curves as rising. Can these shapes be justified?

If it were literally true that in the long run *all* inputs were variable, the Law of Diminishing Returns would not apply. It would be possible to choose the best resource combination, and then expand or contract output by proportionately increasing or decreasing all the inputs together. Then the Long-Run Average Cost curve would be horizontal; the Long-Run Marginal Cost curve would also be horizontal and equal to Long-Run Average Cost (Proposition 2.2c of Chapter 2). But varying all inputs together is not actually possible. Some inputs, and in particular entrepreneurship, may not be readily expandable. Also, a firm is often associated with some more or less unique productive opportunity. A mining company, for example, may be exploiting a particular ore deposit. It could raise output by using more labor and machines, but the firm cannot duplicate the ore body itself. So, in any economically possible long run, the Law of Diminishing Returns ultimately applies: Long-Run Marginal Cost and Average Cost curves must eventually rise.

EXAMPLE 6.5 SCALE ECONOMIES – NUCLEAR VERSUS FOSSIL FUELS

David R. Kamerschen and Herbert G. Thompson, Jr. compared the costs of generating electric power from nuclear versus fossil fuels.[a] Using 1985 data, they found that normal U-shaped Long-Run Average Cost curves applied for both types of plant. For fossil fuels the minimum occurred at about 10,000 GWH (million kilowatt-hours), at a unit cost of about 3.7 cents per KWH (kilowatt hour). For nuclear plants the minimum occurred at about the same scale of output, but the unit cost was lower – about 2.5 cents per KWH. The table summarizes some of their data.

Average costs of power generation – nuclear versus fossil fuels

	Unit cost (cents/KWH)	
Output (GWH)	Fossil fuels	Nuclear fuel
5,000	3.90	2.60
10,000	3.75	2.55
15,000	3.78	2.58
20,000	3.80	2.60
25,000	3.85	2.70
30,000	3.90	2.80

Source: Estimated visually from Kamerschen and Thompson, Figure 3, p. 21.

Despite the lower costs of nuclear generation, no U.S. utility has ordered a nuclear power plant for over 25 years. The reason is that environmental concerns. and public fears of Chernobyl-type incidents, have made it difficult – almost impossible, it seems – to gain the necessary political and regulatory approvals. The authors comment that growing anxieties about "greenhouse effects" and other forms of pollution associated with coal and oil may make nuclear power more acceptable in the future. On the other hand, increasing concerns about terrorism cut the other way.

COMMENT

Around half of the fossil fuel plants, and the great majority of the nuclear points studied, were located in the range of falling Long-Run Average Cost. As indicated in the text, this could not be a profit-maximizing solution for competitive firms. However, electric power utilities generally exercise some regional monopoly power, and are accordingly usually subject to government regulation. The price-quantity optimum for monopolistic firms, and the principles on which such firms are regulated, will be analyzed in Chapter 8.

[a] David R. Kamerschen and Herbert G. Thompson, Jr., "Nuclear and Fossil Fuel Steam Generation of Electricity: Differences and Similarities," *Southern Economic Journal*, v. 60 (July 1993).

6.4   AN APPLICATION: PEAK VERSUS OFF-PEAK OPERATION

Many industries must deal with sharp variations between peak demands and off-peak ("slack") demands. Telephones are more heavily used during business hours than during evenings or weekends, local transit demands are greatest in the morning and afternoon commuting hours, restaurants are busiest at mealtimes. In arid areas water is more intensely demanded in summer than in winter. A firm facing peak and off-peak demands must decide how to divide its efforts between the two.

Assume for simplicity that the peak and slack periods are of equal duration. Under pure competition the firm would be a price-taker in both markets. The peak price P_p would exceed the off-peak price P_o. In a city served by competing restaurants, for example, dinner (peak period) prices are generally higher than lunch (slack period) prices. But, by assumption, in each market the price will be independent of the firm's own output (as shown by the horizontal price lines in Figure 6.7).

It is essential to distinguish between the "common costs" and the "separable costs" of serving the two types of demand. *Common* costs apply to both peak and off-peak service. For a restaurant they can include the cost of renting and maintaining the premises, of dishes and silverware, of management and accounting services, and so on. *Separable* costs are those incurred to serve only one market or the other. Some waiters could be hired only to serve lunch, others only to serve dinner. (The distinction between common and separable costs is quite apart from our earlier distinction between fixed and variable costs. Common costs can be fixed or variable, and the same holds for separable costs.)

EXAMPLE 6.6 PEAK VERSUS OFF-PEAK OPERATION: WATER SUPPLY

In urban water supply, especially in the arid west of the United States, the major peaking problem is seasonal. In the summer months precipitation and stream flow are low, and demand for irrigation and other uses is high. Darwin C. Hall estimated the costs of providing water for Los Angeles in the winter and summer seasons.[a] The table here shows Marginal Costs in terms of "billing units" (BU) – 748 gallons (100 cubic feet).

Marginal cost per billing unit of water, city of Los Angeles

	Winter ($)	Summer ($)
Supply		
Capital	1.38	1.28
Operation and maintenance	0.63	0.90
Transmission and treatment		
Capital	0.00	0.08
Operation and maintenance	0.01	0.01
Distribution and tank storage		
Capital	0.00	0.30
Operation and maintenance	0.00	0.00
TOTALS	2.02	2.67

Source: Hall, selected from Tables 1 and 2 (pp. 86–87).

Since the greater summer demand determines the need for capacity, the marginal capital requirements for Transmission and treatment and for Distribution and tank storage are considered separable costs and assigned entirely to summer production. (It is puzzling however that the capital costs for the "supply" category are higher for winter than for summer.) Also, since Los Angeles purchases water from outside sources in the winter (when it is cheap) and stores it for use during the summer, certain increased storage expenses are incurred that are listed under the category of operation and maintenance.

[a] Darwin C. Hall, "Calculating Marginal Cost for Water Rates," *Advances in the Economics of Environmental Resources*, v. 1 (1996), pp. 77–94.

The analysis that follows deals only with "short run" solutions and makes simplifying assumptions about costs. (1) For *common variable costs*, Marginal Common Cost (*MCC*) is assumed constant at the level *M*, which means that Average Common Cost (*ACC*) also always equals M. In the diagram, therefore, the *MCC* and *ACC* curves coincide as a horizontal line of height *M*. (2) *Separable variable costs*, illustrated by the curves for Marginal Separable Cost (*MSC*) and Average Separable Cost (*ASC*) in the diagram, are assumed identical for both periods. (However, although *the cost function* is the same, the firm will typically choose different on-peak and off-peak levels of output *q along the cost function*. Even if it costs the same to serve any given number of meals, a restaurant may employ more waiters at peak dinner hours.)

It turns out there are two differing types of possible situations, called the "stable-peak" and "shifting-peak" cases.

Stable-Peak Solution: In Figure 6.7 for the off-peak market, the Marginal Common Cost (*MCC*) may be regarded as already having been incurred to meet the larger peak demand. (The restaurant has scaled its dining capacity to serve the larger dinner market.)

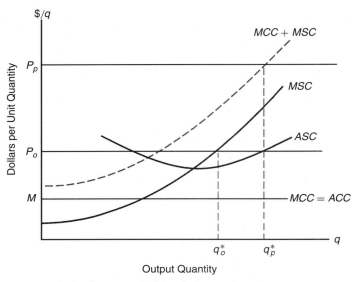

Figure 6.7. Peak versus Off-Peak Operation, I

In the peak-demand period, the price-taking firm will set the sum of the Marginal Common Cost and the Marginal Separable Cost ($MCC + MSC$) equal to the peak-period price P_p. In the off-peak period only the separable costs are incurred, so the firm should set MSC equal to the off-peak price P_o. Peak-period output is q_p^* and off-peak output is $q_o^* < q_p^*$.

So the off-peak period is a "by-product." If so, only its separable costs are relevant for the off-period output decision. The off-peak period marginal cost is then $MC_o =$ Marginal Separable Cost (MSC), and the optimal off-peak output q_o^* is determined by the condition $MC_o = MSC = P_o$. In the diagram, the restaurant produces q_o^* lunch meals at the point where the rising MSC curve cuts the horizontal P_o price line. However, *both* the common and the separable variable costs are incurred in meeting the larger peak demand. So the peak-period Marginal Cost is higher: it is the *vertical sum* $MC_p = MCC + MSC$ (the dashed curve). The optimal on-peak output q_p^* is determined by the condition $MC_p = P_p$, where the dashed curve intersects the horizontal P_p price line. It follows that $q_p^* > q_o^*$ – more meals are served at peak than at slack hours.

Shifting-Peak Solution: The other possibility is pictured in Figure 6.8. Here the procedure outlined above – setting the peak output by the condition Marginal Common Cost + Marginal Separable Cost $= P_p$ and the slack output by the condition Marginal Separable Cost $= P_o$ – leads to a paradoxical "shifting peak" result. That is, the indicated peak output q_p^* would be *less* than the slack output q_o^*. The restaurant would serve more meals at lunch than at dinner! Something is wrong. The mistake was to assume that the Marginal Common Cost MCC is always incurred for the peak demand only. That assumption was valid in Figure 6.7. There the price difference $P_p - P_o$ was sufficiently great to warrant incurring some additional common cost MCC of serving only the on-peak market. But when the price difference is small, and in particular if $P_p - P_o < MCC$, incurring the Marginal Common Cost cannot be warranted by service to the peak trade alone. In this situation, as pictured in Figure 6.8, the last units of common cost can profitably be incurred only *for serving both markets together*.

It follows that, if $P_p - P_o < MCC$, the peak and off-peak outputs q_p and q_o must be equal. But equal at what level? The answer is that the relevant or "joint" Marginal Cost

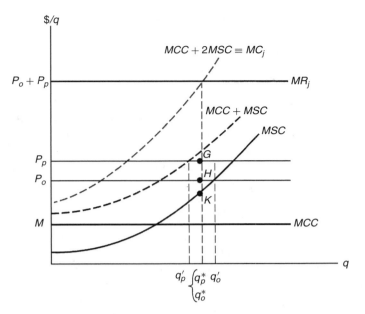

Figure 6.8. Peak versus Off-Peak Operation, II

Here, if the common costs are charged solely to the peak-period demand (by setting $MCC + MSC = P_p$ for the peak period and $MSC = P_o$ for the off-peak period, as in Figure 6.7), a paradoxical result is obtained. The off-peak quantity supplied (q'_o) would be larger than the peak-period quantity (q'_p), which cannot be correct. This paradox occurs when $p_p - P_o < MCC$ – when the price difference between periods is less than the Marginal Common Cost. In this case the profit-maximizing solution is to produce the same in each period, setting $q^*_p = q^*_o$ at the level of output where $MCC + 2MSC = P_p + P_o$. At this output the combined prices just suffice to cover the Marginal Separable Costs and the Marginal Common Cost.

MC_j for serving the two markets together is the vertical summation $MC_j = MCC + 2MSC$ (the dotted curve). As for the demand side, the joint Marginal Revenue MR_j is the sum $MR_j = P_p + P_o$ (the dotted horizontal line). The correct q^*_p and q^*_o, now equal to one another, are determined by the intersection of the dotted MC_j and MR_j.

> **PROPOSITION:** For a price-taking firm facing peak and slack markets of equal duration, and assuming Marginal Common Cost (MCC) is constant, there are two classes of "short run" solutions: (a) *Stable-Peak:* If MCC is less than the price difference $P_p - P_o$, peak output is determined by setting the peak-period Marginal Cost MC_p equal to the peak-period price P_p – where MC_p is the sum of the Marginal Common Cost MCC plus the peak period's Marginal Separable Cost$_p$. Off-peak output is determined by the condition $MC_o = MSC_o = P_o$. Thus $q^*_p > q^*_o$ – more is produced on-peak than off-peak. (b) *Shifting-Peak:* If the Marginal Common Cost exceeds the price difference $P_p - P_o$, the profit-maximizing peak and off-peak outputs are equal, determined by setting the joint Marginal Cost MC_j equal to the price difference: $MC_j = MCC + 2MSC = P_p + P_o$.

As an interpretation of the "shifting-peak" case, notice that at the correct joint output $q^*_p = q^*_o$ in Figure 6.8, each period's price yields some excess over the Marginal Separable Cost. In the diagram the distance GK, the vertical difference $P_p - MSC$, can be regarded as the "contribution" of the marginal on-peak sale toward covering the common cost *MCC*. Similarly, the smaller distance *HK*, the vertical difference $P_o - MSC$, is the "contribution" of the marginal off-peak sale toward this common cost. By construction in the diagram, the sum of the distances *GK* and *HK* exactly equals Marginal Common Cost – so that, at the optimal joint output, the aggregate of the two "contributions" exactly covers the Marginal Common Cost.

Since the off-peak market is less profitable, the firm may consider abandoning it entirely. Whether it should do so can be determined by extending the short-run "No Shutdown Condition" discussed earlier. The firm should abandon the off-peak market if, in Figure 6.7, the horizontal off-peak price line P_o were to lie below the *minimum* of the Average Separable Cost (*ASC*) curve. Then, even at the profit-maximizing output, the firm's total off-peak separable costs exceed the total revenue received from its off-peak customers.

SUMMARY   Business firms are artificial economic units organized for team production. When many separate resource-suppliers are involved, creating a firm reduces transaction costs. Members of the team need only contract with the firm itself (bilateral contracting) rather than with one another. The owners of a firm are entitled to the residual rewards that remain after contractually agreed payments to other resource-suppliers. Costs of monitoring performance, and differing preferences for risk, help explain why some suppliers are employed on a contractual basis while others become the owners of the firm (residual claimants).

A firm's goal is to maximize economic profit – the difference between revenue and economic cost. Its Total Revenue equals price times quantity: $R \equiv PQ$. For a competitive (price-taking) firm, price P is assumed constant, so that $P \equiv$ Average Revenue $\equiv$ Marginal Revenue.

Accounting costs count only contractual payments as expenses, but economic costs also include opportunity costs. In addition, accountants value assets (before depreciation) at their historical acquisition cost, whereas economic profit measures asset depreciation by loss of current market value.

Marginal Cost is the added cost of producing a unit of output. Marginal Cost may initially be falling, but at sufficiently high levels of cost will rise with output. Average Cost is Total Cost divided by output. Variable Cost is Total Cost minus Fixed Cost.

Average Cost and Marginal Cost must ultimately rise with output because of the Law of Diminishing Returns. With some inputs held fixed, eventually at least, additional output requires increasing increments of the variable inputs.

Some inputs that are fixed in the short run become variable in the long run. At any output, Short-Run Total Cost is at least as great as Long-Run Total Cost; similarly, Short-Run Average Cost is at least as great as Long-Run Average Cost. Short-Run responses, which hold some inputs fixed, are appropriate for demand changes that the firm expects to be temporary.

A firm in a competitive industry maximizes profits by setting that level of output at which Marginal Cost equals price. The firm will shut down in the short run if the going price is less than the minimum of Average Cost.

Firms often deal in markets with distinct peak-period and slack-period demands. If there is a sufficient gap between the peak-period and the slack-period prices, the profit-maximizing peak output is determined by the condition that the sum of Marginal Common Cost + Marginal Separable Cost equals the (higher) peak-period price. Output in the off-peak period satisfies the condition that the Marginal Separable Cost alone equals the (lower) off-period price. Output in the off period is smaller. In that "stable peak" case the peak period alone bears the common cost. But if the price gap is not so great, the peak period alone cannot bear the full Marginal Common Cost, since off-peak output would exceed on-peak output. The solution is to have the same quantity sold in both periods, at prices reflecting the marginal "willingness to pay" of the on-peak and off-peak demanders. But the sum of the prices charged must cover the full Marginal Cost of supplying both periods: the Marginal Common Cost + the sum of the two Marginal Separable Costs.

QUESTIONS

†The answers to daggered questions appear at the end of the book.

For Review

1. Why is most productive activity carried out by firms rather than simply by individuals who contract mutually with one another?

†2. Partnership firms are generally small and managed directly by their owners. Why? How does the corporate form facilitate the organization of larger enterprises?

†3. a. What is meant by economic profit?
   b. Is profit maximization an appropriate goal for owners? For managers?
   c. What tends to happen if owners are not also managers?

4. What would be the effect upon the firm's decisions of a 50% tax upon economic profit? Upon accounting profit?

5. How will an increase in a firm's fixed costs affect its Marginal Cost curve? What will be the effect of such an increase in fixed costs on the firm's supply curve?

†6. Consider a firm with Marginal Cost $MC = 10 + 5q$, Average Variable Cost $AVC = 10 + 2.5q$, and fixed costs of $250.
   a. What is the firm's Total Cost function?
   b. If the market price for the firm's output is $50 per unit, what is the firm's profit-maximizing output?
   c. Is it making an economic profit?

†7. a. If Marginal Cost falls throughout, does Average Cost necessarily fall?
   b. If Average Cost falls throughout, does Marginal Cost necessarily fall?

8. If Marginal Cost MC is rising throughout, will the Average Cost curve AC necessarily be rising? If AC is rising throughout, is MC necessarily rising?

†9. When will a firm respond to changes in economic conditions by a short-run adjustment? When by a long-run adjustment?

†10. Evaluate the following reasoning: In the short run a retail store can increase some of its inputs, such as salespeople, but not others, such as floor space. Since increasing some inputs costs less than increasing all inputs, short-run marginal cost is less than long-run marginal cost.

11. Show why no Long-Run Average Cost curve can satisfy both of the following conditions:
   a. It shows the lowest cost at which any given output can be produced (i.e., it is a lower envelope of the Short-Run Average Cost curves).
   b. It shows the lowest-cost output at any given level of the fixed input (i.e., it goes through the minimum points of all the Short-Run Average Cost curves).

   Which of the two conditions is the correct one?

12. Is the firm's Total Cost curve necessarily rising, or can it have a falling range? Is the firm's Average Cost curve necessarily U-shaped, or can it be rising throughout (or falling throughout)? What about the Average Variable Cost curve? For each allowable shape of the Average Cost and Average Variable Cost curves, show the implied shape of the Marginal Cost curve.

13. In Figure 6.3, how should output be allocated if both Marginal Cost curves fall throughout? What if one is rising and the other falling?

14. How should the *LRMC* curve be drawn in Figure 6.6?

15. Microprocessors for computers are produced in "fabs," large high-tech factories which can require billions of dollars of fixed investment. Do you expect there will be a range of declining average cost in the microchip industry? How does your answer relate to Example 6.4 on scale economies in electric power distribution?

For Further Thought and Discussion

1. What types of production that take place in the household are not delegated to firms?

†2. A Mafia leader was on trial for directing his enforcers to break the legs of anyone defaulting on a debt owed him. The leader readily admitted the fact, but explained,

> We provide a valuable service to borrowers who do not have good enough credit standing to obtain loans from banks. In the interests of full disclosure, we always inform our borrowers that we will break their legs if they default. We have found that borrowers would very likely fail to exercise due diligence in their use of the borrowed funds if we allowed them to walk away from their loans whenever unable to pay. Indeed, it would be impossible to carry on our business if we allowed something like a declaration of bankruptcy to cancel the debts owed us.

Answer the following, and explain briefly in each case.
   a. Is this type of business a "valuable" service to borrowers?
   b. Would it be efficient to permit contracts in which borrowers agreed in advance that their legs would be broken if they failed to repay?
   c. Does it follow that this form of contract enforcement should be legalized?

†3. In railroading, about two-thirds of costs are said to be fixed and only one-third variable. If so, *AVC* is approximately one-third of *AC*. It would therefore always be financially advantageous for railroads, it has been argued, to take on *additional* traffic even at a price lower than Average Cost. Is this argument valid? Explain.

†4. a. Why will a firm ever keep any inputs fixed in the face of changing economic conditions?
   b. What determines which inputs are held fixed, and which varied?

5. Compare the effect upon a competitive firm's output of a tax of $1 per unit upon output versus a license fee of $200 payable each year regardless of output.

6. Consider the most efficient way of dividing output between two plants (as in electricity load dispatching). If the Marginal Cost curves are rising, when will one of the plants not be operating? What can be said if one or both of the Marginal Cost curves are falling?

†7. What is wrong with the following reasoning on the part of a factory manager:

> My plant is working steadily at its most efficient output. Nevertheless, I could always meet a short-run surge in demand simply by running the machines a little faster and deferring maintenance. So in the short run my Marginal Cost is practically zero.

†8. Electric utilities commonly keep their most modern and efficient generating equipment, characterized by a low ratio of fuel input to power output, working around the clock.

Older equipment still on hand is used only to meet periods of higher load. What does this imply about the shape of the Short-Run Marginal Cost curve for generation of electricity?

†9. An urban rapid-transit line runs crowded trains (200 passengers per car) at rush hours, but nearly empty trains (10 passengers per car) at off hours. A management consultant makes the following argument:

The cost of running a car for one trip on this line is about $50 regardless of the number of passengers. So the per-passenger cost is about 25 cents at rush hour but rises to $5 per passenger in off hours. Consequently, we had better discourage off-hour business.

a.   Is there a fallacy in the consultant's argument?
b.   "Commutation tickets" (reduced-price, multiple-ride tickets) sold by some transit systems are predominantly used by rush-hour riders. Are such tickets a good idea?

7 Equilibrium in the Product Market – Competitive Industry

The preceding chapter was devoted to an *optimization* problem: in a competitive industry, what level of output maximizes the firm's profits? For example, how many shoes will a footwear manufacturer want to produce? This chapter moves on to the *equilibrium* problem. Looking now at the industry as a whole, we ask when shoe prices will be high and when they will be low. What about the quantities produced and consumed?

The answers of course depend upon supply and demand. Chapter 4 analyzed how the *market demand curve* for a good was derived from the consumption choices of individuals. Similarly, this chapter will show how the separate decisions of the different firms lead to an industry's *market supply curve*. Together, the market demand curve and the market supply curve determine the equilibrium price and the overall quantities produced and consumed.

Later in the chapter Consumer Surplus will be introduced as a measure of the gains to buyers from market exchange, and Producer Surplus as a measure of the gain to suppliers. The analysis will be extended to demonstrate how "hindrances to trade" – such as transaction taxes – affect market equilibrium and prevent full achievement of the benefits of exchange.

7.1   THE SUPPLY FUNCTION

From Firm Supply to Market Supply: The Short Run

For a competitive (price-taking) firm, the preceding chapter showed that the price P of its product is necessarily identical to its Marginal Revenue (the additional revenue per additional unit sold). The key proposition derived was that a competitive firm, under appropriate conditions, maximizes profit by setting output so that Marginal Cost equals price: $MC = P \equiv MR$.

The firm's supply curve s_f, pictured in Figure 7.1, showing how a firm's output q responds to different levels of price P, basically runs along its MC curve. However, the "No-shutdown conditions" discussed in the preceding chapter must also be taken into account. The diagram depicts the firm's *short-run* supply curve, applicable when some inputs are held fixed. The No-Shutdown condition then dictates zero output whenever the market price (P) is less than the minimum (P_V) of Average Variable Cost AVC. So s_f in the diagram is a broken curve. For prices below P_V the supply curve lies along the vertical axis. Then, at $P = P_V$, the supply curve skips to the right (dotted line) to point K. Last, for all higher prices the supply curve is identical to the rising branch of the MC curve.

EXERCISE 7.1

Let a firm's cost function be as shown in Table 6.1: $C = 128 + 69q - 14q^2 + q^3$. Find the supply function for this firm, using the exact formula for Marginal Cost: $MC = 69 - 28q + 3q^2$.

ANSWER: The firm's supply curve is based on the rule Marginal Cost = Price, which implies $P = 69 - 28q + 3q^2$. The equation is valid, however, only for P greater than or equal to P_V, the minimum of Average Variable Cost. (For P less than P_V, the best output is $q = 0$.)

The next step is to find P_V. From the equation for Cost it follows that Average Variable Cost $\equiv (C - F)/q = 69 - 14q + q^2$. Marginal Cost ($MC$) and Average Variable Cost (AVC) always intersect at the minimum of the Average Variable Cost curve.

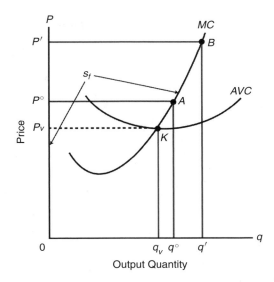

Figure 7.1. Supply Function of a Competitive Firm: Short Run

At product prices less than P_V, the minimum of Average Variable Cost AVC, the firm's best output is $q = 0$ (the firm's supply curve s_f runs along the vertical axis). Above this price, s_f coincides with the Marginal Cost curve MC.

Setting $MC = AVC$, $69 - 28q + 3q^2 = 69 - 14q + q^2$. Solving algebraically, MC and AVC intersect at $q = 7$ where $MC = AVC = 20$ (as was also indicated in Table 6.1). So the supply function is:

$$\begin{cases} P = 69 - 28q + 3q^2, & \text{for } P \geq 20 \\ q = 0 & \text{otherwise} \end{cases}$$

Any specific good is typically produced only by a limited group of firms, the industry associated with that commodity. The industry's supply curve, the market supply curve for that good, is the horizontal sum of the individual firms' supply functions. (Just as the overall market demand curve is the horizontal sum of the individual demand functions, as was shown in Chapter 4.)

EXERCISE 7.2

An industry consists of 100 identical firms. Each firm has the cost function of the preceding exercise: $C = 128 + 69q - 14q^2 + q^3$. What is the industry supply curve?

ANSWER: Let industry output be $Q \equiv 100q$, where q is the output of each firm. Going directly to the supply function of Exercise 7.1 and substituting $Q/100$ for q:

$$\begin{cases} P = 69 - 28(Q/100) + 3(Q/100)^2, & \text{for } P \geq 20 \\ Q = 0 & \text{otherwise} \end{cases}$$

There is one further consideration. By definition, in perfect competition each firm views the *product price* as given independently of its own output decision, but nothing has yet been said about *input prices.* Implicitly, the assumption has been that the competitive firm views these also as given. A single coal mine, in expanding output after a rise in coal price, may be able to hire more workers without causing the wages of coal miners to increase. But to analyze the *industry* supply that function, one must ask what would happen if all coal mines simultaneously expanded output. The wages of coal miners would surely rise, increasing costs of production for each and every firm. Similarly, a

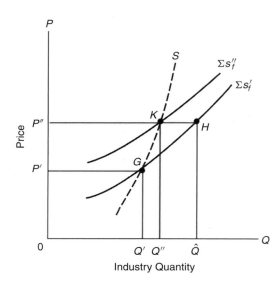

Figure 7.2. Industry Supply Function: Input-Price Effect

At price P' the industry will provide quantity Q', determining G as one point on the industry supply curve. If the product price rises to P'' but input prices remain unchanged, the new equilibrium would be at point H along curve $\Sigma s'_f$, which is the horizontal sum of the firms' separate supply curves at the initial input prices. However, normally the rise in industry output will force input prices upward. As firms' costs rise, their supply curves shift upward. The new equilibrium will be at point K along the curve $\Sigma s''_f$ that aggregates the firm supply curves at these higher input prices. The industry supply curve through points such as G and K is therefore steeper (less elastic) than the aggregate of the firms' supply curves.

single PC manufacturer could buy more memory chips without noticeably affecting their prices – but if the entire computer industry increased its output, the prices of memory chips would tend to rise.

In Figure 7.2, suppose that the price of coal was initially P' and that aggregate industry output was Q'. So P' and Q' define a point G on the industry supply curve S. For simplicity, suppose also that all firms have Marginal Cost curves like MC in Figure 7.1, and that $P > P_V$ (so that the region where firm supply curves run along the vertical axis can be ignored). The curve labelled $\Sigma s'_f$ is the *horizontal summation* of the individual firm s_f curves under the input-price conditions associated with industry output level Q'.

To find another point on the industry supply curve, we ask what happens if product price rises from P' to P''. It might be thought that the new higher output is found by moving along the curve $\Sigma s'_f$ to the output level Q at point H. If, however, the expansion of aggregate output raises miners' wage rates, each firm will discover that its entire Marginal Cost curve has shifted upward.

So the industry as a whole cannot expand output along the $\Sigma s'_f$ curve. Instead, at the higher wage for miners, the industry supply curve is $\Sigma s''_f$. The new quantity supplied is indicated by point K, where $\Sigma s''_f$ intersects the horizontal price line $P = P''$. The industry supply curve, the dashed curve S in the diagram, therefore runs through points G and K rather than through G and H. Curve S is steeper than the $\Sigma s'_f$ or $\Sigma s''_f$ curves because of the adverse effect on cost of an increase in the prices of inputs. An observer who failed to take this "input-price effect" into account would therefore predict too big a supply response of the industry to variations in output price P.

CONCLUSION

The short-run supply curve of a competitive firm, above the minimum of its Average Variable Cost curve, is identical to its Marginal Cost curve. The short-run supply curve of a competitive industry is the horizontal sum of the firms' supply curves, but only after allowing for the input-price effect that raises Marginal Cost curves as industry output rises (or lowers Marginal Cost curves as industry output falls). The input-price effect reduces the magnitude of the supply response to changes in output price, making the industry supply curve steeper than it would otherwise be.

Just as elasticity of demand measures how quantity demanded responds to changes in price, *elasticity of supply* measures the response of quantity supplied to price changes.

DEFINITION: Elasticity of supply κ is the proportional change in quantity supplied divided by the proportional change in price:

$$\kappa \equiv \frac{\Delta Q/Q}{\Delta P/P} \equiv \frac{\Delta Q}{\Delta P} \cdot \frac{P}{Q} \qquad (7.1)$$

Recall that elasticity of demand is, apart from the exceptional Giffen case, always negative. In contrast, elasticity of supply is normally positive.[1]

Since elasticity is defined in terms of proportionate changes, it is independent of the units of measurement. As explained in Chapter 5, this allows us to meaningfully say, for example, that steel is more (or less) elastically supplied than cotton. So the conclusion about the responsiveness of an individual firm versus the industry as a whole to price changes, can be expressed:

PROPOSITION: The input-price effect normally makes the industry's short-run supply curve less elastic than the separate firms' short-run supply curves.

Long-Run and Short-Run Supply

In the firm's short-run supply function pictured in Figure 7.1, some input or inputs were held fixed. For a coal mine, the number of shafts might be such a fixed input. Facing a temporary product price increase, the firm might find it inadvisable to open new shafts – or to close existing shafts if the price of coal momentarily falls. But if the firm believes the price of coal has permanently changed, it will want to adjust *all* of its inputs in choosing its long-run optimal output q.[2]

In Figure 7.3 the firm's long-run supply function Ls_f is discontinuous, like the short-run supply function s_f in Figure 7.1. The long-run supply curve must take into account the long-run No-Shutdown condition. So for the firm to remain in business, price P must be greater than P_C, the minimum of its Long-Run Average Cost curve. The supply curve Ls_f therefore runs along the vertical axis up to P_C, then skips to the right (dotted line), and thereafter overlies the curve of Long-Run Marginal Cost $LRMC$.

Suppose the product price is initially P°, so that the firm produces the amount q° – the level of output at which $LRMC = P^\circ$. Now let the market price jump to P'. A firm that regards the price change as temporary will choose output q_S, where $SRMC = P'$. But a firm that expects the price change to be permanent will set output at q_L, where $LRMC = P'$.

---

[1] For supply as for demand, *cross*-elasticities may be important. The cross-elasticity of supply would reflect, for example, how output of mutton would respond to changes in the price of wool. Only the direct price elasticity of supply will be taken up here.

[2] How rapidly it pays to move to the optimal long-run level of the fixed factor depends upon the durability and the resale value of the fixed equipment specialized to the firm. Suppose the firm reduces output. If resale value is relatively high, the firm may sell off the excess equipment and move to the correct scale almost immediately. But if resale value is very low, it may pay the firm to retain the equipment until it wears out. (Note that it may or may not take a long period of *calendar time* to make a long-run scale adjustment.)

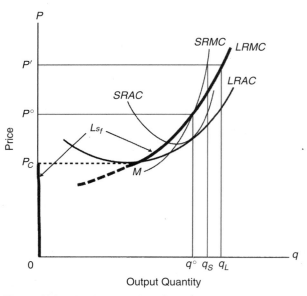

Figure 7.3. Firm's Long-Run Supply Function

The firm's long-run supply function Ls_f runs along the vertical axis (zero quantity supplied) up to P_C, the minimum level of the Long-Run Average Cost curve $LRAC$. Above this price, the supply function coincides with the Long-Run Marginal Cost $LRMC$.

EXERCISE 7.3

Using the data of Exercise 6.5 of the preceding chapter, suppose Long-Run Total Cost is $LRTC = q^2$ and Short-Run Total Cost is $SRTC = 2B + q^4/(8B)$, where B is the amount of the "fixed" input. For Marginal Costs use the exact calculus formulas $LRMC = 2q$ and $SRMC = q^3/(2B)$. (a) If $B = 4$, find the firm's short-run supply curve. (b) Find its long-run supply curve. (c) At what price and output do these supply curves intersect, and what is the significance of this intersection? (d) What happens if price rises to $P = 27$, temporarily or permanently?

ANSWER: (a) The short-run supply curve is given by the condition $SRMC = P$, or $P = q^3/8$. (b) The long-run supply curve is similarly given by $LRMC = P$, or $P = 2q$. (c) The curves intersect at $q = 4$, $P = 8$. The intersection signifies that if the fixed input can be varied, $B = 4$ is its optimal level. The short-run supply curve for $B = 4$ and the long-run supply curve both dictate the same output, $q = 4$. (d) If price rises to $P = 27$ and the firm regards the change as temporary, it would respond along the Short-Run Marginal Cost curve, setting $q^3/8 = 27$. The new short-run optimal output would be $q = 6$. But if the firm regards the price change as permanent, it would make a long-run response and choose output where $LRMC = 2q = 27$, so that $q = 13\frac{1}{2}$. The long-run output response is greater.

For convenience, long-run versus short-run has been interpreted as a simple dichotomy. But it's really a matter of degree. Some inputs lie toward the fixed end of the spectrum, others toward the variable end, and still others are in between. Similarly, some price changes are regarded as highly permanent, others as relatively transitory. *How permanent* the price change is considered to be, and *how fixed* the various inputs are, determine the extent to which the firm adjusts production in response to a price change. Within the industry as a whole, different firms will in their mix of fixed versus variable costs, and also in their estimates about the permanence of a price change. Consequently, any historical price change is likely to elicit, over time, a mixture of short-run and long-run firm responses.

EXAMPLE 7.1 COTTON SPINDLES

Cotton spinning in the United States has historically been a highly competitive industry. Originally located mainly in New England, in the 20th century the industry gradually shifted toward the southern states to take advantage of cheaper labor and a warmer climate.

Comparing the South and New England, the table here shows the average variation of "spindle hours" by calendar quarters during the midcentury period (1945–1959). Spindles are essential for spinning, so spindle hours are a measure of output. Changes in spindle hours (variations in output) may be due either to changes in hours per spindle or to changes in the number of spindles. The first of these, "Variation in Hours per Spindle," reflects firms' short-run adjustments to the price changes taking place quarter by quarter. "Variation in Active Spindles" represents firms' long-run adjustments as they alter amounts of fixed equipment.

Changes in cotton spindle hours, per quarter 1945–1959

Area	Average variation in hours per spindle (%)	Average variation in active spindles (%)
Southern states	90.5	9.2
New England	76.5	21.8

Source: U.S. Census data cited in G. J. Stigler, *The Theory of Price*, 3rd ed. (New York: Macmillan, 1966), p. 144.

Cotton prices were generally falling in this period. In addition, irregular quarter-by-quarter changes in demand were taking place. The table suggests that firms usually interpreted these demand changes as temporary. That is why hours per spindle (short-run response) varied so much more than the number of spindles (long-run response). In particular, Southern firms responded to demand changes almost exclusively by adjusting variable inputs (hours per spindle). These firms felt little need to adjust their long-run position. But in the declining region, New England, firms more frequently made long-run adjustments by disposing of fixed spindle equipment.

The industry long-run supply curve, like the industry short-run supply curve, is the horizontal sum of the corresponding firm supply curves. An additional element operating in the long run is the *entry-exit effect*. In long-run equilibrium every firm in the industry must earn non-negative economic profit, which means that price must cover Long-Run Average Cost: $P \geq LRAC$. Any firm that cannot meet this condition will eventually go out of business. And conversely, if there are profit opportunities within an industry, outside firms – whether newly organized, or now operating in some other industry – will eventually enter.

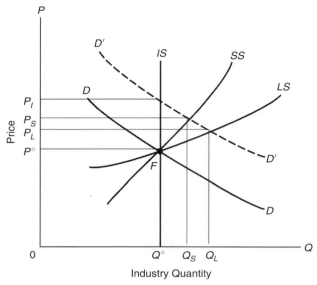

Figure 7.4. Market Response to Change in Demand

The initial demand curve is *DD* and equilibrium is at point *F* (price P° and output Q°). In the "immediate run" an upward shift in the demand curve from *DD* to *D'D'* has no effect on output because, by assumption, the quantity Q° cannot be immediately changed (the supply curve is the vertical line *IS*). The entire effect is therefore upon price, which rises to P_I. In the "short run" (i.e., if firms can vary output but believe the demand change is temporary), the upward sloping supply curve *SS* is relevant; aggregate quantity increases to Q_S and price declines from P_I to P_S. In the "long run" (if firms believe the demand change is permanent), the relevant supply curve is *LS*; quantity sold increases to Q_L, and the price falls from P_S to P_L.

Exit and entry affect the industry's long-run supply curve. If an indefinitely large number of essentially identical firms always stand ready to enter or leave, the long-run industry supply curve will be highly elastic. At the extreme, the supply curve is horizontal (infinitely elastic). Even a tiny price increase attracts an indefinitely large number of firms, and the reverse holds for a price decrease.

Such extreme conditions are unrealistic. The most important reason is that firms are not identical. If (as seems reasonable) new entrants typically have higher costs than firms already in the industry, the long-run supply curve will have positive slope. [*Note:* Although potential entrants may be higher-cost firms, that does not mean they are necessarily less efficient. Their *economic* costs may be higher in this industry only because they have more favorable alternative opportunities for operating in some other industry.]

Supply tends to be more elastic in the long run. First, the response of each individual firm to changes in price is likely to be larger, since Long-Run Marginal Cost curves rise less steeply than Short-Run Marginal Cost curves. Second, changes in the number of firms (entry and exit) work in the same direction. So a high coal price leads in the long run to each firm mining more coal, and also leads to an increase in the number of coal-mining firms. The converse holds for a low coal price.

Figure 7.4 illustrates the effect of "length of run" on the supply-demand equilibrium. The initial equilibrium is represented by price P° and quantity Q° along demand curve

DD. Suppose the demand for coal shifts upward to $D'D'$. The vertical curve labeled I_S is the *immediate-run* supply function. Think of it as representing a time interval so short that production has no chance at all to respond. Since the quantity produced is fixed, price is determined by the intersection of supply curve I_S with demand curve $D'D'$ at the level P_I. If the demand change lasts long enough for coal mines to adjust their variable inputs, for example the number of miners, quantity will respond – as indicated by the positive slope of the *short-run* supply curve SS. In the new short-run equilibrium, price P_S exceeds the initial price P^o, but is lower than the immediate-run price P_I. Last, the *long-run* supply curve L_S (which allows coal-mining firms to "unfix" the fixed inputs by opening new shafts, acquiring new machinery, and so on) is still more elastic. Consequently, the long-run equilibrium price P_L is lower still, though remaining higher than the original P^o.

CONCLUSION

If an industry has an upward-sloping supply curve, after an increase in demand both price and quantity will rise. But in moving from the immediate run to the short run to the long run, the *price* increase is progressively moderated whereas the *quantity* increase is accentuated. And similarly for a decrease in demand, the longer the run the smaller the change in price and the greater the change in quantity.

External Economies and Diseconomies

In examining an industry's response to changes in demand, it is useful to distinguish between (1) influences that are *internal* to the separate firms and (2) those that are internal to the industry as a whole but *external* to the separate firms.

The internal influences that limit individual firms' responses to a price change are summarized by their short-run and long-run cost functions, whose rising shapes reflect "internal diseconomies of scale." (There may be an initial range of falling average and marginal costs, or "internal *economies* of scale," but in the neighborhood of equilibrium, firms' Marginal Cost functions must be rising.)

The "input-price effect" pictured in Figure 7.2 above is an *external diseconomy* of scale. The upward shift of the individual firm's cost function is due not to the firm itself, but to the overall level of industry output.

External economies and diseconomies can be either *pecuniary* (monetary) or *technological*. The input-price effect is a "pecuniary" diseconomy: industry output impacts upon individual firm costs through financial considerations, the prices that must be paid to resource suppliers. Pecuniary externalities are almost always diseconomies. A "technological" externality, which can go either way, occurs when changes in industry output directly affect a firm's physical possibilities of production. Think of farming on marshy land. To increase production, farmer A must drain his land. But his pumping drains the lands of neighboring farmers $B, C, D, \ldots$, reducing their costs of production – and vice versa. So these farming operations involve a technological *external economy* of scale. On the other hand, suppose the farm lands are too dry rather than too wet. To irrigate, each farmer pumps water from underground wells. Doing so drains water from neighbors' wells, thus raising their irrigation costs. This would represent a technological *external diseconomy*.

Figure 7.5 illustrates an external economy. The original industry price-quantity equilibrium is at point G. When product price rises from P' to P'', the $\Sigma s'_f$ curve (the

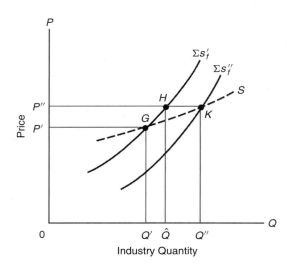

Figure 7.5. Industry Supply Function: External Economy

An external economy makes each firm's cost of production fall as industry output expands, and therefore flattens the industry supply curve. (Note that the picture here is the reverse of Figure 7.2.)

horizontal sum of the firms' *MC* curves above the shutdown price) indicates an equilibrium at point *H* with industry output *Q*. But the assumed technological external economy lowers each firm's *MC* curve, and so the horizontal sum of the firms' *MC* curves shifts down to $\Sigma s''_f$. The new equilibrium is at point *K*, where output is *Q''*. Thus the supply curve runs through points *G* and *K*: the external economy makes the industry supply curve *S* more elastic than the separate supply curves of the component firms. (Whereas Figure 7.2 pictured an external *diseconomy*, Figure 7.5 illustrates an external *economy* of scale.)

Favorable externalities can be so powerful as to make the industry supply curve slope downward. This can occur even though individual competitive firms still operate in the range of rising Marginal Cost, so that all the individual *firm* supply curves necessarily slope upward. In Figure 7.6, starting from the initial equilibrium at point *F*, suppose demand increases from *D'* to *D''*. Momentarily at least, product price *P* rises. Then firms expand output, so industry output must also increase. But thanks to the assumed strong external economy, the horizontal sum of the firms' *MC* curves shifts downward from

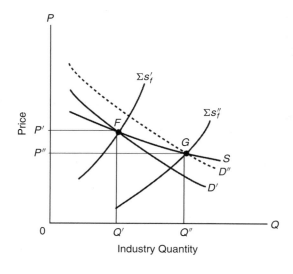

Figure 7.6. Negatively Sloped Supply Function Due to External Economies

The initial demand curve is *D'* and the industry supply curve is $\Sigma s'_f$; the equilibrium is at point *F*. An upward shift in the demand curve to *D''* temporarily raises price; firms begin to respond along their individual supply curves. However, the external economy means that increased industry output reduces firms' costs of production, shifting the sum of the firm's supply curves downward from $\Sigma s'_f$ to $\Sigma s''_f$. If the external economy is sufficiently strong, as shown here, the new equilibrium at *G* represents larger quantity at lower price. Thus, the industry's supply curve *S* is negatively sloped.

$\Sigma s'_f$ to $\Sigma s''_f$. The new equilibrium at point G has higher quantity but lower price! So the industry supply curve through points F and G has negative slope. External economies of scale partly explain why computers, CD players, and other electronic devices have all fallen in price despite huge increases in demand. Rapidly growing output in these industries has generated huge numbers of ideas that spread from firm to firm. The more production, the more ideas, and the lower the costs all around.

EXERCISE 7.4

A small island contains a plum-producing industry consisting of 100 identical farms, each with Marginal Cost $MC = 10 + 8q - Q/10$, where q is a single farm's own output and Q is the industry output. (a) Does this cost function reflect an external economy or diseconomy? (b) Is the external effect here pecuniary or technological? (c) What is the equation for the industry supply curve? (d) Which diagram in the text pictures this situation?

ANSWER: (a) As can be seen from the equation, larger industry output Q reduces each firm's Marginal Cost. So this situation represents an external economy. (b) The question has not provided the information necessary to answer this. Each firm's Marginal Cost fell as industry output Q grows, but there are different possible reasons. Larger aggregate plum shipments could induce the local ferries to invest in more efficient vessels, lowering transport rates. For the plum industry, that would be a *pecuniary* external economy. But if Marginal Cost fell with Q because of improved soil drainage, as described in the text, that would be a *technological* external economy. (c) Since each farm sets Marginal Cost = Price, its supply function is $P = 10 + 8q - Q/10$. Substituting $Q \equiv 100q$, the industry supply curve is $P = 10 + 8Q/100 - Q/10 = 10 - 0.02Q$. (d) The situation is like the picture in Figure 7.6: the industry supply curve has negative slope.

CONCLUSION

In a competitive industry, the "internal" effects (how changes in a firm's output affect its own costs) must be *diseconomies* in the neighborhood of equilibrium, since the firm's optimum requires that Marginal Cost slope upward. The "external" effects (how changes in industry output influence firms' cost functions) are of two types – pecuniary and technological. Pecuniary effects are normally *diseconomies*, since rising industry output tends to raise the input prices faced by individual firms. But technological externalities can be *economies or diseconomies*; increases in industry output can have either favorable or unfavorable effects upon the production functions of the individual firms.

7.2   FIRM SURVIVAL AND THE ZERO-PROFIT THEOREM

Competition tends to reduce economic profit to zero.[3] A profit opportunity in an industry induces new firms to enter, so industry output grows and product prices fall. This squeezes profit from above. And increased output also raises resource prices (the

---

[3] *Accounting profit* (see Chapter 6) must be positive if the firm is to survive, since accounting profit does not deduct the opportunity costs of inputs supplied by the firm's owners.

input-price effect), pressing upon profit from below. Profit in a competitive industry is thus continually squeezed by pressure from above and from below.

Entry stops (long-run equilibrium is attained) when no firm still outside the industry can earn a profit within it. It follows that the *marginal firm*, just on the borderline of entering or leaving the industry, can earn only negligibly more within the industry than outside. For such a marginal firm, economic profit (excess of revenues over the best alternative foregone) is zero.

But it doesn't follow that, in long-run equilibrium, firms with lower costs than the marginal firm earn positive economic profits. *All* firms in the industry earn zero economic profit in the long run!

To have lower cost of production than the marginal firm, an "inframarginal" firm must have access to some superior productive resource. But then every firm in the industry will want to bid for that special resource, raising its price. Consider copper mining. If a marginal firm working a thin copper ore just breaks even, it might be thought that firms exploiting richer ores will be earning large profits. But all firms in the industry can bid against one another for the right to work the richer ore. So, in the long run, the price of such a special input will rise to the point where economic profit is eliminated even for inframarginal firms. Similarly, if a software firm employs a brilliant programmer who can code faster than anyone else, other firms will want to hire that programmer, increasing his wage and reducing the profits of the firm that employs him.

If the mining firm itself owns the richer ore deposit, its *accounting profit* may indeed be high. But that firm could lease or sell the right to exploit that ore deposit to another firm. It should therefore charge itself, as an economic cost of its mining operations, the highest bid an outsider would make for the right to work its ore. So, as a mining firm, its *economic profit* will be zero in long-run equilibrium. (Similarly, if the brilliant programmer owns the firm himself, the forgone opportunity to work for a high wage at another firm is part of the economic cost of being in his own business.)

> **PROPOSITION:** In the long run, economic profit for any firm in a competitive industry is zero.

Of course, in an ever-changing world long-run equilibrium may never come about. But the *tendency* toward zero economic profit, stemming from downward pressure on product prices and upward pressure on input prices, is always operating.

EXAMPLE 7.2 ECONOMIES OF SCALE AND THE SURVIVOR PRINCIPLE

Firms choosing wrong levels of fixed inputs will have higher production costs. In the long run, if they are to survive in the industry, such firms must shift to a more appropriate scale. The *survivor principle* draws inferences about firms' cost functions from changes in the proportions of large and small producers in an industry.

The survivor principle was applied to medical practice by H. E. Frech III and P. Ginsberg,[a] who compared the market shares of physicians engaged in solo versus joint practice for the years 1965 and 1969. A later study by William D. Marder and Stephan Zuckerman[b] extended the results through 1980. The table shows that between 1965 and 1980 the market share accounted for by solo or two-physician practices declined, whereas larger-sized groups gained steadily. But it seems that by 1980 the decline in one- or two-physician practices had tapered off.

Market share by group size, medical practice

Group size	1965	1969	1975	1980
1–2	84.69%	78.25%	68.67%	67.45%
3–7	8.37%	11.53%	13.31%	13.14%
8–25	4.30%	5.09%	8.53%	7.78%
26–99	1.33%	3.00%	5.08%	4.66%
100+	1.31%	2.12%	4.42%	6.97%
Total	100%	100%	100%	100%

Sources: Frech and Ginsberg, p. 30; Marder and Zuckerman, p. 167.

The data in the table can be interpreted quite differently, depending on whether a *static* or *dynamic* viewpoint is adopted. From the static point of view, even in 1980 most of the market consisted of single-physician or two-physician groups. This suggests that small size must indeed be the most efficient in medical practice. On the other hand, these sizes declined relative to all others. So it appears that, *on the margin*, larger firms have been more profitable. New entrants have found it profitable to form larger groups, whereas exiting firms have come disproportionately from the one-to-two-physician category.

A possible explanation is that in any period there is an efficient *mixture* of firm sizes. Even though one-physician and two-physician firms may on the whole be most efficient, in recent years there may have been relatively too many firms of these sizes. So market shares have shifted in favor of the larger groups.

[a] H. E. Frech III and P. Ginsberg, "Optimal Scale in Medical Practice: A Survivor Analysis," *Journal of Business*, v. 47 (January 1974), p. 30.

[b] William D. Marder and Stephan Zuckerman, "Competition and Medical Groups: A Survivor Analysis," *Journal of Health Economics*, v. 4 (June 1985), p. 167.

7.3 THE BENEFITS OF EXCHANGE: CONSUMER SURPLUS AND PRODUCER SURPLUS

One of the most important principles of economics is *The Fundamental Theorem of Exchange*:

PROPOSITION: Trade is mutually beneficial.

Voluntary exchange benefits all parties involved. An alternative, mistaken view might be called "the exploitation theory" – the idea that what one side gains in exchange is a loss to the other side. The proof of the Fundamental Theorem of Exchange, and disproof of the exploitation theory, is elementary. In voluntary exchange between rational persons, both sides must expect to gain. True, owing to mistakes or trickery, one or both participants might lose out. However, if beliefs are not systematically mistaken, the proposition remains true.

But *how much* does each side gain from trade? As explained in Chapter 3, economists do not generally believe it possible to compare one person's utility with another person's. So it would be helpful to have a way of measuring the benefits of trade in objective units, independent of subjective utilities. Consumer Surplus and Producer Surplus are such measures. In Figure 7.7 the market supply-demand equilibrium is at price P^*

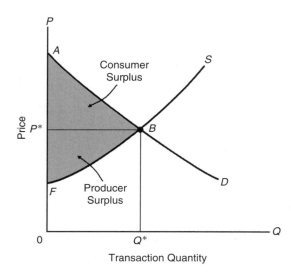

Figure 7.7. Consumer Surplus and Producer Surplus

At the transaction quantity Q^*, Consumer Surplus is the area that lies below the demand curve D and above the equilibrium price P^*. It is the difference between the aggregate willingness to pay for the quantity Q^* (the roughly trapezoidal region $OABQ^*$) and the amount actually paid (the rectangle OP^*BQ^*). The Producer Surplus is similarly the area above the supply curve S and below the price P^*.

and quantity Q^*. Consumer Surplus CS is represented by the upper shaded area lying beneath the demand curve D and above the horizontal line P^*B. Producer Surplus PS is the corresponding lower shaded area lying above the supply curve S and below the horizontal line P^*B.[4]

Consumer Surplus measures the advantage to buyers of being able to buy Q^* units at price P^*, when they would have been willing to pay higher prices (as shown by the height of the demand curve) until the transaction quantity Q^* is reached. Producer Surplus similarly measures the gain to producer-sellers from receiving a price as high as P^* when they would have been willing to supply up to Q^* units at lower prices.

The concepts of *demand price* (height of the demand curve at any quantity) and *supply price* (height of the supply curve at any quantity) are useful here. For any individual the demand price for good X is equivalent to *Marginal Value MV_x* as defined in Chapter 4 – a person's willingness to pay, in units of the numeraire good, for an additional unit of commodity X. Similarly, for the market as a whole the demand price at any specified quantity is the height of the market demand curve at that quantity. In Figure 7.7, for the first unit purchased the demand price is OA, meaning that at least one consumer in the market has a Marginal Value that high. But the equilibrium price is only P^*, so that the consumer gains Consumer Surplus of $OA - OP^* = AP^*$ on the first unit bought. Now extend this argument to all successive units. At the transaction quantity $Q = Q^*$ the sum of the successive demand prices, representing consumers' *aggregate willingness to pay* for quantity Q^*, is the roughly trapezoidal area $OABQ^*$. But the amount that consumers actually pay is only the rectangle OP^*BQ^*. So the upper shaded (roughly triangular) area AP^*B is the Consumer Surplus – the difference between aggregate willingness to pay and actual aggregate payments. A corresponding argument applies for Producer Surplus, which can be regarded as the difference between sellers' aggregate receipts OP^*BQ^* and the minimum aggregate payment $OFBQ^*$ they would have been willing to accept – the area FBP^*.

---

[4] The names of these measures are somewhat misleading. The benefits stem *from trading*, not from consuming or producing. Instead of Consumer Surplus and Producer Surplus one should, properly speaking, refer to Buyer Surplus and Seller Surplus.

EXAMPLE 7.3 LOTTO AND CONSUMER SURPLUS

In November 1984 the United Kingdom initiated a weekly National Lottery. Over half the adult population have participated. Each ticket costs £1. There are a variety of prizes, but on average 45% of the revenue is paid out to winners. So, in a sense. the "price of participation" is £0.55 – the difference between the cost of the ticket and the average reward.

Under certain conditions a "rollover" or "double rollover" occurs, which increases the size of the prizes and thus, in effect, reduces the price of participation. As would be expected, for drawings where such a lower price obtains, more lottery tickets are typically purchased. A study by Lisa Farrell and Ian Walker used these data on price and quantity to estimate the Consumer Surplus attributable to the lottery.[a] The table here shows some of their results.

UK Lotto – consumer surplus

	Revenue (£ million)	Consumer surplus (£/draw)	Consumer surplus (£ million)
Regular draw	65	0.49	32
Rollover	78	0.53	41
Double rollover	98	0.68	67

Source: Adapted from Farrell and Walker, Table 4 and text.

The top number in the middle column, £0.49, means that on average buyers would have been willing to pay £1.49 for a lottery ticket priced at £1. (The consumer on the margin would have been willing to pay only a trifle above the price of £1, but other buyers would have been willing to pay even more.)

COMMENT

It may seem curious that, over and above paying £1 for a ticket returning on average only £0.45, Lotto customers would have been willing to spend even more. Evidently, Lotto tickets are not a very good investment, a topic to be taken up in Chapter 15. A plausible explanation of why they are purchased is that Lotto-type games generally involve only small stakes and yield an entertainment value, over and above the rather inadequate monetary return. Or, players might not realize that these bets lose many on average.

[a] Lisa Farrell and Ian Walker "The Welfare Effects of Lotto: Evidence from the UK," *Journal of Public Economics*, v. 72 (1999).

An Application: The Water-Diamond Paradox

A vital commodity such as water may be very cheap. Diamonds, which meet only a frivolous human desire, are expensive. To understand how this can come about, *both supply and demand* need to be taken into account.

Diamonds are valuable because they are so rare. Thinking in terms of Consumer Surplus and Producer Surplus helps clarify the issue. Figure 7.8 illustrates what the supply and demand curves for water (S_w and D_w) might look like, in comparison with the corresponding curves for diamonds (S_d and D_d), when scaled in terms of a common physical unit – say, gallons. It is only because of the tremendously disparate

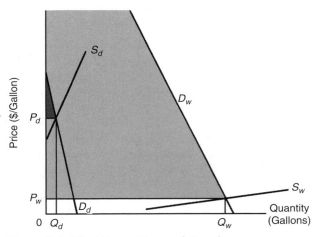

Figure 7.8. The Water-Diamond Paradox

Water is "more valuable" than diamonds in the sense that consumers' aggregate willingness to pay (total area under the demand curve) is greater. However, the supply of water is so enormous, in comparison to demand, that the market value of water (rectangle of width Q_w and height P_w) is small. Purchasers of water therefore derive a huge Consumer Surplus (shaded region). For diamonds demand is smaller, but quantity on the market is smaller still. Compared to the area under the demand curve, the market value of diamonds (rectangle of width Q_d and height P_d) is large and Consumer Surplus is therefore small.

quantities available that the price of water is so low. Municipal water services typically provide consumers with about 150 gallons (five-eighths of a ton) per capita per day, at a price of around 3 cents per hundred gallons. Diamonds, if they were ever accessible in such quantities, would be "cheap as dirt." But for the scanty supply actually available, consumers are willing to pay steep prices. Gem-quality diamond prices run upward from $1,000 per carat, which comes to around $20,000,000 per gallon!

In the diagram the market value of water, $P_w Q_w$, is the flat unshaded rectangle lying just above the horizontal axis. In the terminology of Adam Smith, this is water's *value in exchange* for the quantity Q_w. What Adam Smith called the *value in use* (the total worth to consumers, their total willingness to pay for the same quantity) includes also the huge lightly shaded area lying above the market price P_w and below the demand curve D_w. The additional area, the difference between value in use and value in exchange, is the Consumer Surplus for that quantity of water. For diamonds, in contrast, Consumer Surplus is only the small dark area under the D_d curve and above P_d. So the value in use of water is enormous in comparison with its value in exchange (market value); hence Consumer Surplus is huge. But the value in exchange of diamonds almost equals its value in use; Consumer Surplus is small.

An Application: Benefits of an Innovation

An innovation may be useful in either of two ways: it can reduce costs of production, or it can improve the product in the eyes of consumers. A cost-reducing innovation shifts the supply curve downward, whereas a product-improving innovation shifts the demand curve upward. (Some inventions work both ways: transistors are cheaper to produce than the vacuum tubes they replaced and are also far more reliable and versatile.)

Figure 7.9 illustrates a product-improving innovation. The initial equilibrium at point E^o is associated with price P^o and quantity Q^o. The innovation shifts the demand

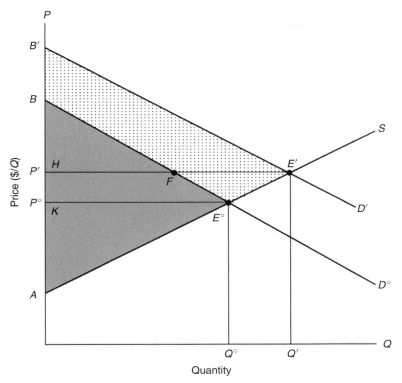

Figure 7.9. Benefits of an Innovation

A quality-improving innovation shifts the demand curve upward from $D°$ to D'. The market equilibrium correspondingly moves from $E°$ to E'. The combined PS and CS, initially the triangle $ABE°$, now becomes the larger triangle $AB'E'$, where the stippled area shows the combined gain. PS alone increases from $AE°K$ to $AE'H$. The higher price is reflected in a reduction in CS corresponding to the trapezoidal area $HFE°K$, but this is smaller than the gain in CS represented by the larger trapezoidal area $BFE'B'$.

curve up from $D°$ to D', leading to the new equilibrium point E' at P', Q'. The shaded area shows the combined Consumer Surplus (CS) and Producer Surplus (PS) in the initial situation. Consumer Surplus is the portion of the shaded triangle lying above price $P°$; Producer Surplus is the portion lying below $P°$. The innovation that shifts demand upward to D' increases the combined Consumer Surplus and Producer Surplus by the stippled area, where Consumer Surplus and Producer Surplus are now measured in comparison with the new price P'. Producer Surplus necessarily increases. But the change in Consumer Surplus is more complex. Although Consumer Surplus is greater overall, some of the *former* Consumer Surplus has now been transferred to Producer Surplus.

7.4 TRANSACTION TAXES AND OTHER HINDRANCES TO TRADE

The preceding section analyzed the benefits of trade. Taxes levied upon exchange transactions reduce these benefits; as do other market interventions such as price ceilings and price floors. The adverse effect of such hindrances to trade can be quantified in terms of Consumer Surplus and Producer Surplus.

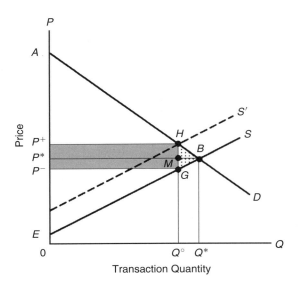

Figure 7.10. Effects of a Transaction Tax on Consumer Surplus and Producer Surplus

An "add-on" transaction tax shifts the supply curve upward from S to S'. At the new equilibrium, the quantity exchanged falls from Q^* to Q^o. The gross price paid by consumers rises from P^* to P^+; the net price received by sellers falls from P^* to P^-. The upper shaded area is a transfer from Consumer Surplus, and the lower shaded area is a transfer from Producer Surplus; the two transfers together constitute the tax collections. The small dotted areas represent losses of Consumer Surplus and Producer Surplus that are not balanced by tax collections.

Transaction Taxes

Figure 7.10 illustrates an "add-on" tax as described in Chapter 2 (see especially Figure 2.6) – a tax quoted as an addition to the seller's stated price. Recall that imposition of the tax requires distinguishing between the *gross price* P^+ paid by buyers and the *net price* P^- received by sellers. Before imposition of the tax, the equilibrium price is P^* and the quantity is Q^*. The tax leaves the industry supply curve defined in terms of the *net price* P^- unchanged. But defined in terms of gross price P^+ the supply curve shifts upward from S to S'. The equilibrium quantity exchanged falls from Q^* to Q^o. At this new equilibrium quantity, the gross price P^+ is higher but the net price P^- is lower.

Both buyers and sellers are now worse off than before. The higher gross price paid by buyers reduces Consumer Surplus by the flat trapezoidal area P^+HBP^*. Since the price received by sellers falls to P^-, Producer Surplus shrinks by the area P^*BGP^-. The combined loss of Consumer Surplus and Producer Surplus is therefore the rectangular shaded area P^+HGP^- plus the stippled triangular area HBG.

These two areas have quite different economic significance. The rectangle corresponds to the government's tax receipts. So that area represents a *transfer* from buyers and sellers of the taxed commodity to the government. As an approximation, the gains and losses from this transfer might be regarded as cancelling out. (Whether it is better to leave the resources in the hands of individual buyers and sellers, as opposed to transferring control to the government, involves an arguable value judgment.[5]) That leaves the

---

[5] Such issues will be considered under the heading of "welfare economics" in Chapter 16.

dotted triangle HBG as the *net economic loss* to society, sometimes called "deadweight loss" or "efficiency loss." The loss stems from the reduced volume of mutually beneficial exchange.

PROPOSITION: Taxes on transactions reduce both Consumer Surplus and Producer Surplus. Some of the loss is a transfer from consumers and producers to the beneficiaries of government spending. But the reduced volume of trade also creates a deadweight or efficiency loss.

EXERCISE 7.5

The market demand curve for caviar is $P = 300 - Q$: the market supply curve is $P = 60 + 2Q$. As was shown in Exercise 2.5, using these data the initial equilibrium (simultaneous solution of the two equations) is $Q^* = 80$, $P^* = 220$. (a) If a tax of $T = 15$ is imposed on each jar of caviar, what is the new equilibrium? (b) What is the loss of Consumer Surplus? What is the loss of Producer Surplus? (c) What is the amount of the transfer (the tax collections)? (d) How great is the efficiency loss?

ANSWER: (a) This problem was solved in Exercise 2.5. The new equilibrium quantity is $Q^o = 75$, the gross price (paid by purchasers) rises to $P^+ = 225$, and the net price (received by sellers) falls to $P^- = 210$. (b) The original Consumer Surplus corresponds to the area ABP^* in Figure 7.10. Since the supply and demand curves here are linear, the area is a triangle with size $(300 - 220)(80)(\frac{1}{2}) = 3{,}200$. The new Consumer Surplus is the smaller area AHP^+, or $(300 - 225)(75)(\frac{1}{2}) = 2{,}812.5$. So the loss of Consumer Surplus is 387.5. Similarly, the old Producer Surplus (area EBP^*) was $(220 - 60)(80)(\frac{1}{2}) = 6{,}400$. The new Producer Surplus (area EGP^-) is $(210 - 60)(75)(\frac{1}{2}) = 5{,}625$, so the loss of Producer Surplus is $6{,}400 - 5{,}625 = 775$. (c) The transfer (tax revenue) represented by the rectangular area P^+HGP^- is $(225 - 210)(75) = 1{,}125$. (d) The remainder of the summed losses of Consumer Surplus and Producer Surplus is the efficiency loss, corresponding to the small dotted triangle HGB. Numerically it is $387.5 + 775 - 1{,}125 = 37.5$.

Supply Quotas

Taxes reduce trade through their effect on prices, by driving a "wedge" between the gross price P^+ paid by buyers and the net price P^- received by sellers. Other restrictions on trade, for example, consumption quotas (rationing of demand) or production quotas (rationing of supply), can also be analyzed in terms of lost Consumer Surplus and Producer Surplus.

Figure 7.11 illustrates a situation where government regulations dictate that only a fixed quota $\overline{Q}$ (less than the equilibrium quantity Q^*) of a good can be supplied to the market. Quotas have been imposed, for example, to control the supply of milk to urban consumers.

Under the usual quota arrangements, the reduced quantity $\overline{Q}$ is sold at "whatever price the market will bear," in this case $\overline{P}$ – which is the consumers' demand price at the quantity $\overline{Q}$. (There is no need here to distinguish between gross and net prices.) In comparison with the unregulated equilibrium P^*, Q^*, the quota both raises price and reduces the quantity exchanged.

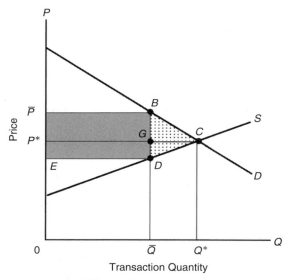

Figure 7.11. Effects of a Supply Quota Upon Consumer and Producer Surplus

Market supply is limited to the quota $\overline{Q}$, so price rises from P^* to $\overline{P}$. Consumer Surplus is reduced by area $\overline{P}BCP^*$. Producer surplus increases by the area $\overline{P}BGP^*$ minus the area GCD. If this difference is positive, sellers benefit from imposition of the quota. However, buyers and sellers, considered together, lose by the amount of area BCD, which represents the combined efficiency losses. [*Note*: There may be an additional loss of PS to the extent that individual firm production quotas are not assigned to the lowest-cost producers.]

Rectangle $\overline{P}BGP^*$ is part of the loss of Consumer Surplus. Like the tax receipts analyzed earlier, it is a kind of transfer – except that the benefit now goes to the suppliers of the good rather than to the government. (The suppliers retain the lower shaded area P^*GDE.) It follows that suppliers *may* benefit from the quota. They will benefit if their transfer gain (upper shaded area $\overline{P}BGP^*$) is larger than their deadweight loss from the reduced sales (lower dotted area GCD). Consumers, in contrast, suffer a transfer loss ($\overline{P}BGP^*$) plus a deadweight loss (BCG). Thus, buyers are surely worse off.

However, Figure 7.11 shows only a part – perhaps only a small part – of the efficiency loss from quotas. An additional loss of Producer Surplus, which cannot be shown in the diagram, occurs if firm-by-firm production quotas are not assigned to the lowest-cost producers. In practice, production quotas have usually been assigned on the basis of past sales ("grandfathering"). When a high-cost producer is granted a quota and a low-cost producer is not, the loss of Producer Surplus will be greater than shown in the diagram.

An Application: Import Quotas

Import quotas are partial production quotas, since only foreign supply sources are subject to restriction. Like tariffs, quotas are usually aimed to protect domestic producers of the product. Unlike tariffs, import quotas generate no revenue for the government.

Suppose for simplicity that the importing country's demand is not big enough for the quota to affect world prices of the product. Figure 7.12 then indicates the effect upon Consumer Surplus and Producer Surplus in the nation imposing the import quota.

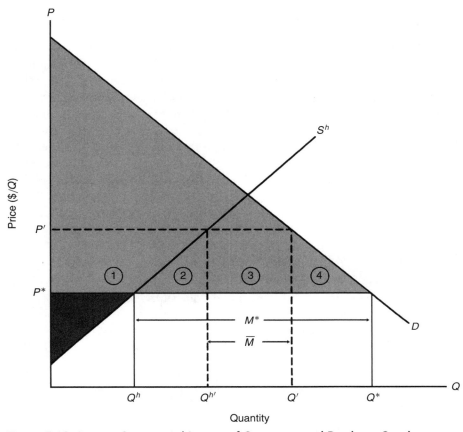

Figure 7.12. Import Quotas and Losses of Consumer and Producer Surplus

D is the country's demand curve for the product, and S^h is the "home supply curve." At the fixed world price P^* the country's total consumption is Q^*, of which Q^h is the amount domestically supplied; the horizontal difference $M^* \equiv Q^* - Q^h$ is the imported amount. The upper lightly shaded area is the Consumer Surplus in the home country, and the lower heavily shaded area is the Producer Surplus received by domestic suppliers. If the import quota $\overline{M} < M^*$ is imposed, the domestic price rises to P'. Domestic suppliers now provide a larger quantity $Q^{h'}$, but domestic consumption Q' is less than before. The four numbered areas all represent losses of Consumer Surplus. Area 1 is an increase in the Producer Surplus of domestic suppliers. Area 3 is a transfer gain to *foreign* suppliers. Area 2 is a "deadweight" loss to the domestic economy on the supply side, due to domestic production that is costlier than the import alternative. Area 4 is an efficiency loss on the demand side, because some previous consumers are frozen out of the market by the higher price P'.

As in Figure 2.5 of Chapter 2, D is the country's demand curve for the product and S^h is the "home supply curve". Figure 2.5 shows the amount that would be imported at each price as a *horizontal gap* between D and S^h. In the absence of an import quota, at the fixed world price P^* the country's total consumption is Q^*, of which Q^h is the amount domestically supplied. The imported amount is the horizontal gap $M^* \equiv Q^* - Q^h$ in the diagram. The upper lightly shaded triangle is the Consumer Surplus in the home country; the lower heavily shaded triangle is the Producer Surplus received by domestic suppliers.

Now suppose an import quota $\overline{M} > M^*$ is imposed. The domestic price must move up, as shown by P' in the diagram, to shrink the horizontal gap between D and S^h

to the quota amount $\overline{M}$. Domestic suppliers now sell a larger quantity than before ($Q^{h'} > Q^h$), but domestic consumption declines ($Q' < Q^*$).

The effects upon Consumer Surplus or Producer Surplus and Producer Surplus are indicated by the four numbered areas. All four represent losses of Consumer Surplus or Producer Surplus. Area 1 represents a transfer from Consumer Surplus to the Producer Surplus of the domestic suppliers. Area 3 is a transfer gain to those *foreign* suppliers who receive import quota assignments and can therefore benefit from the higher price P'. Area 2 represents a deadweight loss to the domestic economy on the supply side: extra costs are incurred in domestic production that could have been avoided by accepting imports instead. Last, area 4 is a deadweight loss on the demand side: consumers who were willing to pay more than P^* but less than P' for the product are now frozen out of the market.

EXAMPLE 7.4 IMPORT QUOTAS

Using data for the years around 1985, Robert C. Feenstra[a] analyzed the impact upon American consumers and foreign and domestic suppliers of several U.S. import quota programs. His analysis was more complex than the discussion in the text. Among other things, he allowed for the effects of the program upon world prices. Nevertheless, it is still possible to interpret his results in terms of Producer Surplus and Consumer Surplus.

For each group of products considered, the table provides estimates of two categories of annual losses: the U.S. deadweight loss (areas 1 and 4 in Figure 7.12) and the transfer gain to foreign suppliers (area 3).

Some costs of U.S. import quota programs ($billion/year)

	U.S. deadweight loss (areas 2 and 4)	Transfer to foreign suppliers (area 3)
Automobiles	0.7	5.0
Dairy	1.4	0.25
Steel	0.2	1.3
Sugar	0.1	0.8
Textiles & apparel	5.4	5.0

Source: Adapted from Feenstra, Table 1, p. 163.

COMMENT

A U.S. import quota on any commodity would tend to reduce its world price. That generates an additional deadweight loss, not listed in the table here: the loss to *foreign* suppliers who reduce production in response to reduced U.S. sales. Allowing for such changes in world prices, Feenstra estimated that foreign suppliers' deadweight losses were comparable in scale to the deadweight losses incurred by U.S. producers and consumers.

[a] Robert C. Feenstra, "How Costly Is Protectionism?" *Journal of Economic Perspectives*, v. 6 (Summer 1992).

Price Ceilings and "Shortages"

Prices are continually changing. A flood in Brazil will raise the price of coffee; good farming weather in the Midwest will reduce the price of wheat; advances in technology steadily reduce the price of computers. Those hurt by price changes often press the government to do something about it. Rising apartment rents lead to calls for rent control, falling wheat prices generate political pressures for agricultural price supports, and so forth.

Legislation that sets the price of a good below its market-clearing level creates a "shortage." A shortage differs from scarcity. Scarcity, meaning that some desires are unsatisfied, is always present. Diamonds are scarce, but there is no shortage; anyone willing to pay the price of a diamond can buy one. A shortage exists when goods are unavailable even to people willing to pay the price. In a city with rent controls, newcomers may be unable to find an apartment at all, regardless of willingness to pay. If changing conditions of demand and supply make the product more scarce, consumers are bound to be worse off, one way or the other. If the market is unimpeded, they suffer from a higher price. If the price is controlled they lose from the "shortages" created.

EXAMPLE 7.5 TWO SAN FRANCISCO HOUSING CRISES[a]

In the 1906 earthquake and fire, the city of San Francisco lost more than half its housing facilities in three days. Nevertheless, the first postdisaster issue of the *San Francisco Chronicle* did not report a housing shortage! Indeed, the newspaper's classified advertisements carried 64 offers of houses or apartments for rent, and only 5 advertisements for apartments or houses wanted. Of course, prices of accommodations had risen sharply in the meantime.

In contrast, in 1946 San Francisco was gripped by the national postwar housing shortage. In the first 5 days of 1946 newspapers carried only 4 advertisements offering houses or apartments for rent, but around 150 advertisements by persons seeking rentals. The explanation: after the 1906 catastrophe, no attempt was made to control rents. But in 1946, rents were frozen below the market-clearing price, leading to an excess of quantity demanded over quantity supplied.

COMMENT

San Francisco housing was much scarcer, in relation to the population seeking accommodation, after the 1906 earthquake and fire than in 1946. During the wartime period preceding 1946, housing supply had not decreased at all. But rising money incomes, the return of war veterans, and a growing number of families led to an upward shift in demand for housing. With rents frozen, a shortage ensued.

---

[a] Discussion based on M. Friedman and G. J. Stigler, *Roofs or Ceilings?* (Irvington-on-Hudson, NY: The Foundation for Economic Education, September 1946).

Figure 7.13 adapts the earlier Figure 7.4, omitting the "short run" supply curve SS. The initial equilibrium is at the price-quantity combination P^o, Q^o. An upward shift of demand in an unregulated market brings about a new long-run equilibrium P_L, Q_L. But suppose a ceiling prevents price from rising above P^o. At this ceiling price there is a perceived shortage equal to the horizontal distance $Q - Q^o = H$. Price, if it were

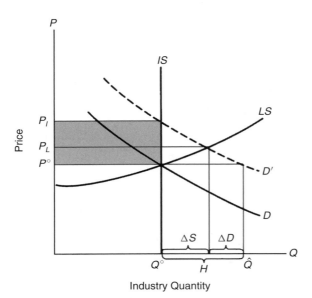

Figure 7.13. Effect of a Price Ceiling

An upward shift of demand in an uncontrolled market, from D to D', causes price in the "immediate run" to increase from P° to P_I. Producers benefit from a temporary windfall gain. Ultimately, the higher price will induce a larger supply; the long-run equilibrium price is P_L. However, if a ceiling is enforced at the initial price P°, the supply and demand adjustments are both blocked. The perceived "shortage" at the ceiling price is H. If price were permitted to rise to P_L, ΔD of the larger quantity demanded would be choked off by the higher price, and ΔS would be the supply increment provided.

allowed to rise, would jump to P_I in the "immediate run" – before quantity had time to adjust – but would eventually come back down as new supplies arrived. (The longer the period considered, the smaller the price increase and the larger the increase in quantity supplied.) At the new long-run equilibrium price P_L, the pictured interval ΔD is the long-run reduction in demand quantity and ΔS is the long-run increase in supply.

EXERCISE 7.6

Suppose demand is described by the equation $P = 300 - Q$. The long-run supply curve is $Q = P/2 - 30$ and the short-run supply curve is $Q = 36 + P/5$. It can be verified that the market is in long-run and short-run equilibrium at quantity $Q^\circ = 80$ and price $P^\circ = 220$. Now suppose the demand curve shifts to the right, becoming $P = 360 - Q$. (a) What happens in the immediate run? (b) What is the new short-run price-quantity equilibrium? (c) What is the new long-run equilibrium? (d) What would be the perceived "shortage" if a price ceiling prevented price from rising above its initial level $P^\circ = 220$?

ANSWER: (a) In the immediate run, quantity would be unchanged at $Q_I = 80$. The new equilibrium price is found by using the new demand condition: $P_I = 360 - Q_I = 280$. (b) Solving the new demand equation and the short-run supply equation simultaneously, the new short-run equilibrium is $P_S = 270$, $Q_S = 90$. Quantity rises only slightly above $Q_I = 80$, and correspondingly price falls by only a small amount from $P_I = 280$. (c) Solving the new demand equation and the long-run supply equation simultaneously leads to larger adjustments: $P_L = 260$, $Q_L = 100$.

(d) If price could not rise above $P = 220$ the quantity supplied would remain $Q = 80$, but the quantity demanded would be $Q = 360 - P = 140$. The perceived "shortage" would be $140 - 80 = 60$ units of output.

Returning to Producer Surplus and Consumer Surplus, it might be thought that a price ceiling causes only a transfer from sellers to buyers. That would be correct only in the "immediate run," and even then with one important qualification. The qualification is that, under rent controls, families who get apartments are not necessarily those who value the apartments the most. In terms of Figure 7.13, apartments might be rented to families who are willing only to pay P^o, while others willing to pay P_I or more do not obtain apartments. So even in the immediate run, a price ceiling can reduce Consumer Surplus.[6] And, as has been seen, the longer the run considered, the greater the loss of production that would have been forthcoming in the absence of a price ceiling.

Consumers who cannot buy desired commodities owing to price ceilings may compete for desired goods in other ways: by waiting in line (see Example 5.7), by fighting, by using political influence, and so forth. These forms of competition are wasteful because what consumers give up (for example, time spent waiting in line) does not provide any benefit to sellers.

EXAMPLE 7.6 INEFFICIENT HOUSING ALLOCATION IN NEW YORK CITY

Rent controls have been operative in New York City, with relaxations from time to time, since World War II. The city has accordingly been subject over the years to very serious "shortages." Large numbers of people have been unable to obtain apartments though willing to pay the legal controlled price.

A study by Edward L. Glaeser and Erzo F. P. Luttmer looked at a somewhat different consequence of rent controls, to wit, the effect on the *sizes* of apartments occupied.[a] An elderly widow in New York might be living in a seven-room rent-controlled apartment all by herself, while a struggling working-class family might have to pay as much or more for very cramped accommodations. Using a model of housing demand based upon demographic and income characteristics, the authors calculated what percentage of renters would under normal conditions have occupied apartments of different sizes (number of rooms). Comparing this calculation with the observed occupancy of apartments, they found that in New York City some 20.9% of the apartments are misallocated. As would be expected, the fraction is greatest in Manhattan (26.1%), where the rent controls are the most severely binding. In contrast, the misallocation was considerably less for comparable accommodations in two cities without rent controls, the figures being 7.0% for Chicago and 4.5% for Hartford, CT.

---

[a] Edward L. Glaeser and Erzo F. P. Luttmer, "The Misallocation of Housing under Rent Control," *American Economic Review*, v. 93 (2003).

Suppliers may try to evade price ceilings in more or less subtle ways. Unable to raise prices openly, firms can eliminate customary discounts and suspend off-price seasonal

---

[6] This loss in Consumer Surplus, when available supplies are not assigned to consumers whose demand prices are the highest, parallels the loss in Producer Surplus when supply quotas are not assigned to the lowest-cost producers.

sales, might offer less quality or variety, or might shift toward producing goods that happen to receive a better break from the price-control authorities. Supplies may be legally or illegally exported to more profitable foreign markets, leaving even less available for domestic consumers. Black markets may develop. In extreme cases, legitimate trade may disappear. A dramatic case was the great inflationary episode in post-World War II Germany.

EXAMPLE 7.7 REPRESSED INFLATION IN POSTWAR GERMANY[a]

Germany, like the other major belligerent countries in World War II, financed her war effort by inflationary expansion of money and credit – in effect, by printing money – while freezing prices. By the end of the war in 1945 the German money supply had risen about tenfold, while prices were still largely fixed at their 1936 levels. Meanwhile, available supplies had fallen sharply, owing to wartime bombing, territorial losses, punitive war reparations, and division of the nation into several zones of occupation.

In the early postwar years, the Allied occupation authorities in Germany continued the wartime price freeze. Prices were so drastically out of line with supply-demand reality that, over most of the economy, production for legal sale could take place only at financial loss. Industrial production in the first half of 1948 was only 45% of the 1938 amount, despite a larger population.

According to official statistics of the period, black markets accounted for only 10% of transactions. This figure was so low because in Germany the term black market was narrowly defined as the outright trading of goods for cash at illegal prices. Professional black-marketeers were regarded as disreputable individuals. In contrast, *everybody* engaged in a form of transaction known as "bilateral exchange" or "compensation trade." Such trade took place at entirely legal prices in money, with one catch: no one could acquire goods or services for money alone. In addition to the money price, every buyer had to provide "compensation" in real goods and services. Estimates are that one-third to one-half of all transactions took this form. Even the military occupation authorities engaged in it; the noon meal provided to German workers at the occupation administration was often a more important attraction than the monetary salary. Eventually money was effectively eliminated as a medium of exchange, and the economy suffered the inefficiencies of barter (as will be discussed in Chapter 14).

In June 1948 most price controls were removed. Contemporaneously, a drastic currency reform exchanged new marks for old, at a ratio of about one to ten. The effect was dramatic. Goods suddenly appeared on store shelves, and workers avidly sought jobs in order to buy the now available commodities. According to one observer: "It was as if money and markets had been invented afresh as reliable media of the division of labor."[b] The German postwar economic miracle was under way.

---

[a] Discussion based on J. Hirshleifer, *Disaster and Recovery: A Historical Survey*, The RAND Corporation, Memorandum RM-3079-PR (April 1963), pp. 83–112.

[b] Horst Mendershausen, "Prices, Money and the Distribution of Goods in Postwar Germany," *American Economic Review*, v. 39 (June 1949), p. 646.

So price ceilings cause at least three types of loss even in the immediate run: (1) the "wrong" (less highly valued) demands may be the ones satisfied; (2) irregular methods of acquiring goods, such as waiting in line, waste resources; (3) firms may evade the ceilings in ways that either are costly or reduce the value of the good to consumers. Even more important is the longer-run effect. Price ceilings discourage the development of additional supplies by producers.

SUMMARY   The supply curve of a competitive firm is its Marginal Cost curve, with two qualifications: (1) only the rising branch of the Marginal Cost curve is relevant, and (2) price must cover Average Variable Cost AVC in the short run ($P > AVC$) and cover Average Total Cost AC in the long run ($P > AC$).

The industry supply curve is the sum of the quantities offered at each price by all the separate firms. It is also necessary to allow for the "external effects" on firms' costs that stem from changes in industry-wide output, and to allow for entry into or exit from the industry.

External economies reduce a firm's costs as industry output rises; external diseconomies increase costs as industry output rises. If the industry-wide level of output affects only the prices that firms pay for required inputs, the external effects are *pecuniary*. These externalities make the industry supply curve less elastic than it would otherwise be. If industry wide output directly affects firms' production functions, the external effects are *technological*. Technological external effects can go either way, and might even be so strong as to make the industry supply curve slope downward.

In the *immediate run*, the quantity produced by an industry is constant (the supply curve is vertical), so a shift in demand affects only price. In the *long run* the supply curve is more elastic because (1) firms' Long-Run Marginal Cost curves are less steep than their Short-Run Marginal Cost curves, and (2) new firms enter in response to price increases (or old firms exit in response to price decreases).

In long-run equilibrium the marginal firm, just on the border of entry or exit, earns zero economic profit. But even "inframarginal" firms earn only zero profit in the long run. Whatever the especially desirable input that is responsible for a firm's low costs and positive profit, all firms in the industry can compete for that input. Eventually, it will command a price so high that its owner captures the entire benefit.

The Fundamental Theorem of Exchange states that voluntary trade is mutually beneficial. Consumer Surplus, the difference between buyers' aggregate willingness to pay and what they pay in the market, measures the benefit of trade to buyers. Producer Surplus, the difference between sellers' aggregate revenue and the minimum revenue at which they would be willing to offer the good, measures the benefit of trade to sellers.

Hindrances to trade such as transaction taxes, supply quotas, or price ceilings affect Consumer Surplus and Producer Surplus in two ways: (1) *transfers* of surplus from one group to another, and (2) *deadweight losses* caused by the reduced amount of exchange.

Following an increase in demand or a decrease in supply, a price freeze creates a "shortage" – an excess of quantity demanded over quantity supplied. By paying a lower price, consumers reap a transfer gain at the expense of suppliers. But the supply response that would have occurred in the long run is blocked; this is an efficiency loss to both producers and consumers. Consumer Surplus and Producer Surplus are also reduced when the limited supplies available are distributed inefficiently. Wasteful activities (such as standing in line to acquire the good) and deceptive moves by firms (such as subtly reducing quality) are additional sources of deadweight loss from price ceilings.

QUESTIONS

†The answer to daggered questions appear at the end of the book.

For Review

†1. At any rate of output, the industry long-run supply curve tends to be less steep than the short-run supply curve. Is it also necessarily more elastic? Explain.

†2. "In the long run, a firm could always produce twice as much simply by doubling the amount of every input employed. So in the long run there must be constant returns to scale." Evaluate.

3. Does elasticity of supply for an industry tend to be large or small if the firms' Marginal Cost curves are sharply upward-sloping? What is the effect on elasticity of supply if higher industry output greatly increases the hire-prices of inputs employed in the industry?

†4. If there are N identical firms and no "external" effects on input hire-prices, is the industry supply curve more or less steep than the firm supply curve? More or less elastic?

5. Explain the distinction between internal and external economies or diseconomies.

†6. a.   In long-run equilibrium, why does the marginal firm (the highest-cost firm in the industry) earn zero economic profit?

   b.   Why do the other "inframarginal" firms earn zero economic profit?

7. Consider the exceptional case of an industry with a downward-sloping supply curve. Starting from an initial equilibrium, will a decline in demand lead to a rise or a fall in price? To a rise or a fall in output? Explain.

8. If a tax is imposed upon some commodity, indicate the areas of the following: loss of Consumer Surplus, loss of Producer Surplus, tax collections (transfers of Consumer Surplus and Producer Surplus to government), and efficiency losses.

9. Under rent control, why would some individuals rent apartments of size or quality different from what they would have selected without rent control? Why would some individuals have trouble finding a place to rent?

†10. Normally, can external pecuniary effects override internal diseconomies of scale? Can external technological effects? What is the slope of the industry supply curve when external economies override internal diseconomies?

For Further Thought and Discussion

1. Apartments in New York City are subject to rent control. Apartment owners there often require tenants to purchase their furniture from them. Why?

†2. "In a competitive industry, for any firm there may be internal economies of scale over a certain range. But each firm must operate in the region where internal diseconomies of scale dominate." True or false? Explain.

3. Under what circumstances would you expect a rise in demand for an industry's product to be met primarily by a short-run output response by existing firms? By a long-run response by existing firms? By entry of new firms?

†4. Which of the following is a pecuniary effect, which a technological effect? Which is internal to the firm, which external to the firm (but internal to the industry)?

   a.   As the number of films produced rises, actors' salaries go up.

   b.   As fishing activity intensifies, each fisherman finds fish scarcer.

   c.   As new retail shops open, existing shops find customers scarcer.

   d.   Steel mills along a river use the water for cooling. But the greater the use, the warmer the water gets, so that the river becomes less effective for cooling.

†5. If at a certain equilibrium price every firm in the industry earns zero economic profit, doesn't that imply that a fall in market price would cause all firms to fail? Explain.

6. A number of techniques are available to cope with increased scarcity and higher world prices of petroleum. Analyze the following in terms of supply-demand responses in the short run and long run.
   a. Price freeze and "rationing by queue" (waiting in line for gasoline).
   b. Price freeze and rationing by coupon (nonsalable).
   c. Rationing by coupon (nonsalable) without a price freeze.
   d. A tax on all petroleum used.
   e. A tariff on imports of petroleum.

†7. In policy (c) above (rationing by coupon without a price freeze), suppose consumers were permitted instead to sell ration coupons to one another.
   a. Would this change elicit more supply?
   b. Would the limited supplies be reallocated to those with greater willingness to pay?
   c. Explain the consequences in terms of Consumer Surplus.

†8. Suppose a price ceiling is imposed on some good X, and that nonsalable ration tickets are all assigned to consumers who are unwilling to pay even the ceiling price. Would that mean that no one purchases good X? What if the tickets were made salable?

9. Suppose that, after a decline in demand for a product, a *floor* is placed under its market price. Then the problem arises of managing a surplus instead of a shortage. What are the disadvantages of a price floor? Do the disadvantages tend to increase over time, as in the case of managing a shortage? Would black markets tend to develop?

†10. Petroleum regulations in the United States froze prices of "old oil" coming from existing wells. The justification was that while producers had to be offered more to induce them to drill new wells, the output from existing wells would be forthcoming even at low prices. Is this argument correct?

11. The presence or even the threat of price freezes may induce firms to integrate vertically (to merge with "upstream" supplier firms or with "downstream" customer firms). Explain why.

†12. a. Analyze the effects of a subsidy upon Consumer Surplus and Producer Surplus.
   b. Taxes hinder trade, causing an efficiency loss. Does it follow that subsidies, which encourage trade, cause an efficiency gain?

13. If the Average Variable Cost curve rises throughout, does the short-run supply curve s_f have a discontinuity? [*Hint*: If Average Variable Cost rises throughout, its minimum lies along the vertical axis.]

14. In Exercise 7.3, no discontinuity appears in either the long-run or short-run supply curve. Why? [*Hint*: What are the long-run and short-run shutdown prices?]

A monopoly exists when an industry contains only a single firm. If a firm can drive out competitors because its costs of production are lower, it enjoys a *natural* monopoly. Not all monopolies, however, are natural. Governments often award monopoly privileges. Cities grant exclusive franchises to firms providing cable television. The Federal government confers patents that give inventors a monopoly for a period of years. And even without government aid, a firm may possess monopoly power owing to entry barriers – for example, if banks believe that financing a new competitor in the industry would be too risky.

In perfect competition, as studied in Chapter 7, the number of firms is large enough to make product price substantially independent of any single firm's level of output. Each competitive firm is a "price-taker." But a monopolist, facing the entire industry demand curve, must take account of its own influence upon price: it is a "price-maker." Geometrically, a competitive firm faces a horizontal demand curve, whereas a monopolist faces a downward-sloping demand curve.

Actually, the number of firms is economically significant only as a clue to behavior. By forming a *cartel,* as will be seen later in the chapter, a number of firms can sometimes get together and behave like a collective monopolist. On the other hand, even if only a single firm is active in the industry, such a firm may be unable to exploit its market as a monopolist if outside potential competitors stand ready to enter.

Sometimes firms produce unique products that nevertheless compete closely with one another – for instance, different brands of digital cameras. This market structure, called *monopolistic competition*, will be covered in Chapter 9. When there are more than one but only a few firms in an industry, the market structure is called *oligopoly* – competition among the few. Such firms may engage in "strategic" behavior, to be explored in Chapter 10.

8.1   THE MONOPOLIST'S PROFIT-MAXIMIZING OPTIMUM

Price-Quantity Solution

The upper panel of Figure 8.1 shows the monopolist's profit-maximizing optimum in terms of Total Cost C and Total Revenue R. The lower panel displays the corresponding average and marginal functions. Compare this diagram with Figure 6.1 for the competitive firm in Chapter 6. The upper panel of Figure 6.1 showed the Revenue curve R as a ray out of the origin, reflecting the fixed product price P. But here, in the upper panel of Figure 8.1, R is hump-shaped. Price now falls as the quantity sold increases, and beyond a certain point the revenue loss due to falling price outweighs the revenue gain from rising quantity. And whereas Average Revenue AR and Marginal Revenue MR coincided at the fixed price P in the lower panel of Figure 6.1, here in Figure 8.1 AR and MR both decline as the firm's output rises.

A monopolist firm can choose *either* product price P or industry output Q.[1] It cannot fix both. Once price P is set, the market demand function determines the quantity Q that can be sold at that price. Conversely, given any output Q, the market demand curve determines the price at which that quantity can be sold. (In this chapter, it is usually convenient to think of the monopolist as choosing output Q.)

---

[1] In Chapters 6 and 7 the lower-case symbol q represented *firm* output and the upper-case letter Q *industry* output. Since the monopolist is a single-firm industry, Q here denotes the output of both the firm and the industry.

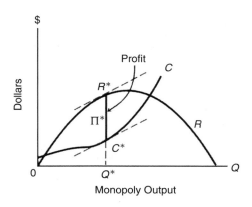

Figure 8.1. Monopolist's Profit-Maximizing Optimum

Maximum profit Π^* occurs at output Q^*, where the vertical difference between the Total Revenue curve R and the Total Cost curve C in the upper diagram is greatest. At this output the slopes of the R and C curves are equal (note the dashed tangent lines.) In the lower diagram, the curves of Marginal Revenue MR and Marginal Cost MC intersect at output Q^*. Profit in the lower diagram is represented by the shaded area, equal to Q^* times the difference between price P^* and Average Cost AC^* at that output.

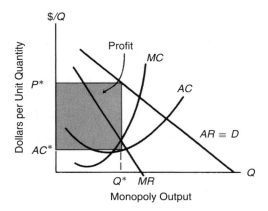

In the upper panel of Figure 8.1, the bold line-segment Π^* is the maximized profit – the excess of Total Revenue over Total Cost at the profit-maximizing output Q^* and price P^*. At this output the R and C curves are farthest apart, which means that the curves have equal slopes (as suggested by the dashed parallel tangent lines). So in the lower panel Marginal Revenue MR (representing the slope of the R curve) and Marginal Cost MC (representing the slope of the C curve) intersect at quantity Q^*. In the lower panel the Marginal Revenue curve always lies below the Average Revenue (demand) curve. This is an instance of Proposition 2.2a of Chapter 2: when an average magnitude is falling, the marginal magnitude must lie below it. (Notice that although the monopolist's optimal *quantity* is set at the output where MC and MR intersect, the optimal *price* is not at the height of the point where MC and MR intersect. Instead, the price P^* associated with the optimal output Q^* is found higher up, along the industry demand curve $AR \equiv D$). The maximized profit Π^* is shown in the lower panel by the shaded rectangle. The base of this rectangle is the optimum quantity Q^*; its height is the difference between P^* and Average Cost AC.

CAUTION

Do not confuse Marginal Revenue with *the price charged for the last unit sold*. In Figure 8.2, as sales increase from Q to $Q+1$ units, along the demand curve price falls slightly from P' to P''. The price received for the last unit is represented by the thin tall rectangle of height P'' and width $\Delta Q = 1$. But when output increases

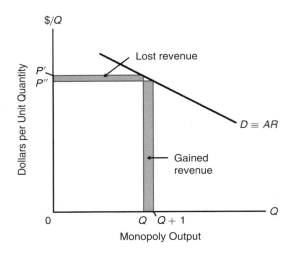

Figure 8.2. Marginal Revenue versus Price of the Last Unit Sold

The price of the last unit sold corresponds in revenue terms to the area of the tall shaded rectangle of width $\Delta Q = 1$ and height P''. To calculate Marginal Revenue we must subtract the area of the thin flat rectangle of height $P' - P'' \equiv \Delta P$ and width Q. This flat rectangle corresponds to the loss of receipts due to the reduced price on units that could have been sold at the higher price P'.

by one unit, price falls from P' to P'' on *all* the units sold. The revenue loss from this price reduction is represented by the flat thin rectangle of width Q and height $\Delta P \equiv P' - P''$. Marginal Revenue is the difference between the areas of the tall rectangle and the flat rectangle.

Symbolically, Marginal Revenue is:[2]

$$MR \equiv P + Q\frac{\Delta P}{\Delta Q} \tag{8.1}$$

Since $\Delta Q = 1$, the first term on the right-hand side is equivalent to the area of the tall rectangle $P \times (\Delta Q)$ and the second term to the area of the flat rectangle $Q \times (\Delta P)$. Because the demand curve normally slopes downward, $\Delta P/\Delta Q$ is negative. Thus we see again from equation (8.1) that Marginal Revenue MR must be less than price P.

In Figure 8.1 the cost functions (Total Cost C, Average Cost AC, and Marginal Cost MC) – though not the Revenue and demand functions – generally resemble the corresponding curves for the competitive firm in Figure 6.1.[3]

As before, profit Π is defined as:

$$\Pi \equiv R - C \equiv PQ - C \tag{8.2}$$

As shown in Figure 8.1, profit is at a maximum where MC equals MR:

$$MC = MR \equiv P + Q\frac{\Delta P}{\Delta Q} \quad \text{Monopolist's Maximum-Profit Condition} \tag{8.3}$$

As in Chapter 6, there are two qualifications: (1) the Marginal Cost curve must cut the Marginal Revenue curve from below. (2) The "No-Shutdown" conditions must hold: the firm will produce a positive output only if $P >$ Average Variable Cost in the short run

---

[2] *Mathematical Footnote:* Since Total Revenue is $R \equiv P \times Q$, Marginal Revenue is the derivative:

$$dR/dQ \equiv P + QdP/dQ$$

[3] There is one conceptual difference. Chapter 7 covered the topic of "external economies and diseconomies" – effects upon the *firm's* cost function due to changes in aggregate *industry* output. Since a monopolist firm is the entire industry, what would have been "external" effects in a competitive industry are all "internalized" into its cost function.

and if $P >$ Average Cost in the long run. (Henceforth in the chapter, unless indicated otherwise these conditions are assumed to be met.)

Converting the definition of the price elasticity of demand in Section 5.2 of Chapter 5 into the notation of this chapter:

$$\eta \equiv \frac{\Delta Q/Q}{\Delta P/P} \equiv \frac{\Delta Q}{\Delta P}\frac{P}{Q} \tag{8.4}$$

Equations (8.1) and (8.4) lead to an expression connecting Marginal Revenue MR and the price elasticity η:[4]

$$MR \equiv P(1 + 1/\eta) \tag{8.5}$$

Since elasticity η is ordinarily negative, we see again that Marginal Revenue is less than Price.

Recall from Chapter 5 that elasticity η generally varies along the demand curve. In fact, elasticity is infinite ($\eta = -\infty$) where any demand curve intercepts the vertical axis, and elasticity equals zero ($\eta = 0$) at its intercept with the horizontal axis. Chapter 5 noted that, when demand is elastic ($\eta < -1$), lower price is associated with higher Revenue $R \equiv P \cdot Q$. The reverse holds when demand is inelastic. So for levels of output at which demand is elastic, increased output leads to lower price but nevertheless to increased revenue for the firm: Marginal Revenue is positive.[5] And similarly, when demand is inelastic, Marginal Revenue is negative. But since Marginal Cost is never negative, and since Marginal Cost must equal Marginal Revenue at the monopolist's price-quantity optimum, the monopolist will never produce in the region of inelastic demand.

PROPOSITION 8.1: A profit-maximizing monopoly firm always chooses a price-quantity solution in the range of *elastic demand* along the market demand curve.

Another useful theorem is:

PROPOSITION 8.2: Given any *linear* demand curve $P = A - BQ$, Marginal Revenue is $MR = A - 2BQ$. (So the MR curve starts at the vertical intercept of the demand curve on the P-axis and then falls twice as fast as the demand curve.)[6]

COROLLARY: If the demand curve is a straight line, the Marginal Revenue curve bisects the horizontal distance between the vertical axis and the demand curve.

---

[4] *Mathematical Footnote:* To derive equation (8.5), start with (8.1) and divide both sides by P:

$$\frac{MR}{P} \equiv 1 + \frac{Q}{P}\frac{\Delta P}{\Delta Q}$$

Notice that the last term on the right is the reciprocal of the elasticity η in equation (8.4). Substituting and rearranging leads to equation (8.5).

[5] In equation (8.5), elastic demand means that the absolute value of η exceeds 1, so the negative $1/\eta$ term within parentheses will be between 0 and -1, leaving Marginal Revenue positive.

[6] In the linear demand equation $P = A - BQ$, the slope of the curve equals $-B$. Substituting on the right hand side of equation (8.3):

$$MR \equiv P + Q\Delta P/\Delta Q = (A - BQ) + Q(-B) = A - 2BQ$$

EXERCISE 8.1

A monopolist faces the demand curve $P = 10 - Q$. (a) What is the equation for Marginal Revenue? (b) If Marginal Cost is $MC = 1 + Q$, what are the profit-maximizing price and quantity? (c) What is the elasticity of demand at this solution?

ANSWER: (a) The demand curve is a straight line. So, from Proposition 8.2, $MR = 10 - 2Q$. (b) Setting $MC = 1 + Q$ equal to $MR = 10 - 2Q$, the solution is $Q = 3$, $P = 7$. (c) The slope of the demand curve is $\Delta P / \Delta Q = -1$, so from (8.4) the elasticity of demand at the monopolist's optimal output is:

$$\eta \equiv \frac{P}{Q} \frac{\Delta Q}{\Delta P} = \frac{7}{3} \times (-1) = -\frac{7}{3}$$

Since $\eta < -1$, demand is in the elastic range at the monopolist's optimum output.

Monopoly versus Competitive Solutions

Table 8.1, in comparison with Table 6.1 of Chapter 6, illustrates the differences between the monopolistic and competitive solutions. Suppose there are 100 competitive firms, so that $Q \equiv 100q$. If so, the cost data of the two tables correspond. (The Marginal Cost used here is the "exact" Marginal Cost of Table 6.1.)[7] On the revenue side, instead of the assumed $P = 60$ facing the competitive firm of Table 6.1, in Table 8.1 price declines with output: $P = 132 - 8(Q/100) = 132 - 0.08\,Q$. In accordance with Proposition 8.2 the monopolist's Marginal Revenue is $MR = 132 - 0.16\,Q$.

Table 6.1 indicated that each competitive firm, setting $MC = P$, would produce $q = 9$ when $P = 60$. So the industry output would be $Q = 900$.[8] (Notice that $Q = 900$ in Table 8.1 implies that $P = 60$, so the data in the two tables are consistent.) The monopolist *could*, of course, also set $MC = P$ and produce $Q = 900$. But to maximize profit it would set $MC = MR$ instead. In Table 8.1, this equality occurs at $Q^* = 700$, where $MC = MR = 20$. The result is a higher price, $P^* = 76$. The monopolist's Total Revenue is 53,200 and Total Cost is 26,800, so the maximized profit is $\Pi^* = 26,400$.

The last column of Table 8.1 shows the demand elasticity at various levels of output, computed using equation (8.5). At the monopoly optimum $Q = 700$, demand is elastic: $\eta = -1.36$ (as is consistent with Proposition 8.1 above). But for the competitive industry, at the equilibrium $Q = 900$ the elasticity is $\eta = -0.83$. So the competitive industry output would be in the *inelastic* range of demand. In other words, a competitive industry produces too much for its own good! (But, of course, the consumers benefit thereby.)

PROPOSITION 8.3: The monopoly output solution occurs where Marginal Cost = Marginal Revenue. Since competitive firms produce where Marginal Cost = Price, and since Marginal Revenue < Price, a monopolized industry charges a higher price and produces a smaller output than a competitive industry with the same cost and demand functions.

---

[7] *Mathematical Footnote*: In this verification the lower-case symbols refer to a single small firm and the upper-case symbols to the monopolist. Since the single large firm corresponds to 100 small firms, from the chain rule of calculus:

$$MC \equiv \frac{dC}{dQ} \equiv \frac{dC}{dc} \frac{dc}{dq} \frac{dq}{dQ} \equiv 100 \times mc \times 1/100 \equiv mc$$

[8] Setting aside possible "external" economies or diseconomies that might impact upon the firms' cost functions and thereby affect the industry supply curve.

Table 8.1 Hypothetical revenue and cost functions: monopolist
($P = 132 - 8Q/100$; $C = 100[128 + 69Q/100 - 14(Q/100)^2 + (Q/100)^3]$)

Q	P	R	MR	C	MC (exact)	η
0	132	0	132	12,800	69	$-\infty$
100	124	12,400	116	18,400	44	−15.5
200	116	23,200	100	21,800	25	−7.25
300	108	32,400	84	23,600	12	−4.5
400	100	40,000	68	24,400	5	−3.125
500	92	46,000	52	24,800	4	−2.3
600	84	50,400	36	25,400	9	−1.75
700	76	53,200	20	26,800	20	−1.36
800	68	54,400	4	29,600	37	−1.06
900	60	54,000	−12	34,400	60	−0.83
1,000	52	52,000	−28	41,800	89	−0.65

Last, one important qualification. Earlier on, this chapter distinguished between monopolies created by government license or franchise and "natural" monopolies arising from ability to produce at low cost. The governmentally protected monopolist need not fear entry of competitors, but may be subject to regulation (as will be discussed later in the chapter). On the other hand, a monopolist lacking government protection is limited by the threat posed by potential competitors. In particular, a monopolist that wants to deter entry *cannot set a price higher than the minimum Average Cost of the lowest-cost potential entrant.* So the threat of entry may prevent a monopolist from achieving the solution Marginal Cost = Marginal Revenue that would otherwise maximize its profit.

EXAMPLE 8.1 POTENTIAL ENTRY IN MONOPOLY AIRLINE MARKETS

Margaret A. Peteraf and Randal Reed studied air fares in monopoly markets, that is, in city-pairs served by only one airline.[a] There were 345 such city-pairs in 1984.

For these routes the average fare, excluding first class, was $0.213 per mile. In studying the effects of *potential* entry in each market, the authors allowed for several additional influences upon fares, such as length of trip, city populations at each end, and per capita incomes. They found that prices were indeed influenced by potential competitors, defined as airlines already serving at least one endpoint of the route.

Their results indicated that, in any given market, a 10% reduction in the average cost per seat-mile of the lowest-cost potential entrant would reduce the monopoly fare by about 2%. The authors suggested that the effect was even stronger than these data indicate, since very large airlines serving many locations tended to be disproportionately represented as the lowest-cost alternative. For example, although overall United Airlines does not have particularly low costs, it was the lowest-cost *alternative* carrier in 53% of the observations. Monopolists facing competition from low-cost carriers such as People Express and Southwest Airlines charged lower fares than did airlines whose primary competition was United Airlines.

---

[a] Margaret A. Peteraf and Randal Reed, "Pricing and Performance in Monopoly Airline Markets," *The Journal of Law and Economics*, v. 37 (April 1994).

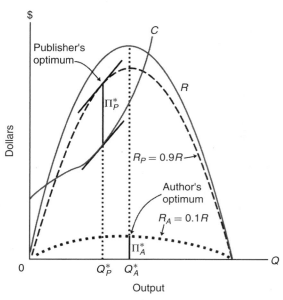

Figure 8.3. Author versus Publisher

Total Revenue from customers is shown by the R curve. Of this revenue, 10% goes to the author (R_A curve) and 90% to the publisher (R_P curve). Output Q_A^* maximizes the author's royalty income. The publisher's maximum profit Π_P^* occurs at output Q_P^*, where the distance between the R_P curve and the Total Cost curve C is at a maximum. The publisher prefers a smaller output (wants to set a higher price) than the author.

An Application: Author versus Publisher

Book prices are usually set by the publisher. But authors can negotiate with publishers over the retail price. As between author and publisher, which would prefer a lower price for the book?

Suppose authors' royalties are a straight percentage of the publisher's revenues from sales of the book, say 10%. Since normally only one firm publishes any title, this is a monopoly situation. $R \equiv P \times Q$ represents the consumer spending on the book, so (as illustrated in Figure 8.3) the author's revenue is $R_A \equiv 0.1R$ and the publisher's revenue after payment of royalties is $R_P \equiv 0.9R$.

The publisher's profit-maximizing output Q_P^* occurs where the slope along R_P equals the slope along the Total Cost curve C; the maximized profit Π^* at that output is indicated by the height of the upper bold line-segment in the diagram. The publisher's preferred output, however, is not ideal for the author. Since the author incurs no cost of production, her preferred output is Q_A^*, where R_A is greatest. That is, the author prefers the price that maximizes Revenue *without regard to production cost.* The largest possible royalty income for the author is shown by the lower bold line-segment Π_A^*. So the publisher prefers a higher price (implying fewer books sold) than the author does.

EXERCISE 8.2

The demand function for a certain text is given by $P = 20 - 0.0002Q$ and the publisher's Marginal Cost is $MC = 6 + 0.00168Q$. The author's royalty is 20% of Total Revenue. What is the publisher's preferred price-quantity solution? The author's?

> **ANSWER:** The publisher wants to set $MR_P = 0.8\ MR$ equal to Marginal Cost. Since $MR = 20 - 0.0004\,Q$, eight-tenths of this is $MR_P = 16 - 0.00032Q$. Setting $MC = MR_P$, the publisher's optimum is $Q = 5000$, $P = \$19$. The author wants to maximize royalty income, which requires that $MR = 20 - 0.0004\,Q = 0$. The author's optimum is $Q = 50{,}000$, $P = \$10$. Note the huge difference between the two solutions.

Now consider a more difficult problem: Given that the publisher sets the price of the book, what royalty rate would the author want? Let α signify the author's percentage royalty, rate. Then the author would want to maximize $R_A \equiv \alpha R \equiv \alpha P \cdot Q$. The publisher wants to maximize $R_P \equiv (1 - \alpha)R \equiv (1 - \alpha)P \cdot Q$.

To find her ideal royalty rate α, the author must recognize that the publisher will take this into account in choosing the output (number of copies of the book). This two-level optimization is rather tricky.[9] Rather than develop the equations involved, a specific illustration will be instructive.

EXERCISE 8.3

Using the data of the preceding Exercise, instead of the fixed 20% royalty, suppose the author can set the royalty rate α. (a) What is her best α, and what are the implications for quantity produced Q, for price P, and for the receipts accruing to author and publisher? (b) Same question, if the publisher can choose α.

ANSWER: (a) Using calculus, the best royalty rate for the author is around 36.9%.[10] The publisher will take that royalty rate into account in setting $MC = MR_P \equiv (1 - \alpha)MR$. At its profit-maximizing optimum the publisher would produce $Q = 3{,}428$ copies of the book, priced at $\$19.31$. Total consumer spending $P \times Q$ on the book will therefore be around $\$66{,}195$ – of which $\$24{,}426$ goes to the author and $\$41{,}769$ to the publisher. From this the publisher's production costs must be deducted. Total Variable Costs, obtained by aggregating the Marginal Cost function from $q = 0$ to $q = 3{,}428$, come to $\$30{,}439$.[11] So, even before allowing for any fixed cost, the profit to the publisher is only $\$11{,}330$. (b) The publisher would enjoy the highest profits if the royalty rate were zero, or if $\alpha = 0$. He then simply sets Marginal Cost equal to Marginal Revenue. This leads to the solution $P = \$18.65$, $Q = 6{,}731$, $R = \$125{,}555$, $C = \$78{,}439$, and $\Pi = \$47{,}115$.

In the preceding exercise, the publisher's maximized profit Π was $\$47{,}115$ in the absence of royalties but fell to only $\$11{,}330$ when the author set her preferred royalty

---

[9] It represents an instance of the "Stackelberg solution," discussed in Chapter 10.

[10] *Mathematical Footnote*: The author wants to choose the α that maximizes $R_A \equiv \alpha PQ$, knowing that the publisher will set $MC = MR_P$ in choosing output Q.

We can solve $MC = MR_P \equiv (1 - \alpha)\,MR$ to express Q in terms of α. In the demand function, P is a function of Q and so can also be expressed in terms of α. So αPQ reduces to a function of α. Taking the derivative and setting equal to zero gives the optimal $\alpha = 36.9\%$.

[11] *Mathematical Footnote*: This result can be obtained by integrating the Marginal Cost function:

$$\int_0^{3,428} (6 + 0.00168\,Q)\,dQ$$

Or, since the Marginal Cost function is a straight line, it could be found geometrically as the area of the trapezoid under the MC curve between $Q = 0$ and $Q = 3{,}428$.

rate – a difference of $35,785. At this ideal royalty rate her receipts were $24,426. Now suppose the publisher proposes a *lump-sum* payment as an alternative to a royalty. Shifting to zero royalty would mean a loss of $24,426 for the author while the publisher gains $35,785. So the publisher could offer a lump-sum payment somewhere between these two figures, and both parties would be better off.

In the negotiations between author and publisher the royalty rate would generally end up somewhere between zero and the percent the author would ideally prefer. But the same principle applies: whatever royalty rate is set, both parties could do better if the publisher made an appropriate lump-sum payment instead.

Nineteenth-century authors such as Charles Dickens and Anthony Trollope usually sold their manuscripts to publishers for fixed sums. Nowadays, however, the most common arrangement is a straight percentage royalty, or a combination of a lump-sum payment and a percentage royalty. Why? The probable explanation relates to differences in the information available to the parties. An author who is optimistic about prospective sales will tend to prefer a percentage, whereas an author who is pessimistic would take the lump-sum instead. If the author proposes a lump-sum payment, therefore, the publisher might suspect that the author has reason to believe the book will not be a big seller. Conversely, a publisher who is optimistic will favor a lump sum, leading the author to the suspect that a percentage royalty might be a better deal for her!

Another factor involved is risk. Under the lump-sum payment, the publisher bears all the risk. In contrast, a royalty is like a "share-cropping" arrangement for dividing the risk, as will be discussed when risk is taken up in later chapters.

Government agencies drawing tax revenues from racetrack betting are in some respects like authors seeking royalty income. Just as an author disregards the publisher's costs of production, a taxing agency bears none of the costs of running horse races. There is, however, one big difference: an author is not usually in a position to dictate the royalty rate, whereas the state generally can dictate the tax rate.

EXAMPLE 8.2 RACETRACK BETTING

Racetrack betting is an important source of tax income for several states in the United States. Of the total amount wagered by bettors (the *handle*), a fraction (the *takeout*) is withdrawn from the pari-mutuel pool and not paid out in winnings. The takeout percentage can be regarded as the price paid for the privilege of wagering. This takeout is divided between taxes paid to the government and revenues for the racing industry (payments to the track management, horse owners, etc.) Another source of receipts, *breakage*, is usually computed by rounding down winnings to the next lower 10 cents. If the pari-mutuel odds would have paid off $5.18 on a winning $2.00 bet, it is presumed that the bettor does not want to bother with the extra 8 cents. So the state kindly retains the odd amounts. For simplicity, breakage can be considered part of the takeout.

In accordance with the analysis in the text, since the state incurs no costs of production it would prefer that the track charge prices that maximize revenue (that set $MR = 0$). And since it can dictate that the track do so, a state that seeks to maximize its revenues should fix the takeout percentage where the demand for wagering has an elasticity $\eta = -1$. The track management, in contrast, would prefer somewhat higher prices so that demand is in the elastic range.

A 1982 study by W. Douglas Morgan and Jon David Vasché found the demand elasticity at California tracks to be in the elastic range, $\eta = -1.3$, suggesting that the takeout percentage was too high for the taxing authority – though possibly just right for the racetrack firms.[a] In recent years parimutuel wagering has been declining, probably owing to growing competition from other forms of entertainment. Increasing competition would be expected to lower total demand while raising demand elasticity. A 1992 study by Richard Thalheimer and Mukhtar M. Ali indicated that elasticity of demand has indeed been rising.[b] For the Louisville Downs racetrack specifically, they found a demand elasticity of $\eta = -1.88$ for the year 1987.

COMMENT

One ought not simply assume that the governments' sole goal is to maximize revenues. Political decision-makers must balance between having more tax revenue, keeping the tracks profitable, and pleasing bettors. In the recent period of declining demand, it appears that the racetrack firms have exerted increasing influence on government decisions.

[a] W. Douglas Morgan and Jon David Vasché, "A Note on the Elasticity of Demand for Wagering," *Applied Economics*, v. 14 (1982).

[b] Richard Thalheimer and Mukhtar M. Ali "Demand for Parimutuel Horse Race Wagering with Special Reference to Telephone Betting," *Applied Economics*, v. 24 (1992).

An Application: Monopolist with Competitive Fringe

Sometimes a single large firm in an industry coexists with many small firms (the "fringe"). Currently, Intel is the dominant producer of computer chips, though it shares the market with other relatively small chip manufacturers at home and abroad. Although such a large firm is not a sole seller in its industry and thus is not technically a monopolist, it cannot disregard the effect of its own output upon product price P. Therefore, it acts as a "price maker," setting output where $MC = MR$. Each of the small fringe firms is in contrast a "price taker," setting its output where $MC = P$. The question is, how do these decisions interact to determine the equilibrium of the industry?

The solution is easier to see geometrically than to spell out in words. In Figure 8.4, before choosing its output the large firm must consider how much output its fringe competitors will produce at each price. Its effective demand curve D' is therefore found by *horizontally subtracting* the supply curve S_F of the fringe firms from the overall market demand D. Associated with the D' curve is the large firm's effective Marginal Revenue curve MR'. The profit-maximizing solution sets $MC = MR'$ to determine the large firm's optimal output Q'.

The profit-maximizing price P^* is determined along D' for output Q'. At that price, Q'_F is the quantity supplied by the fringe firms. The overall amount provided to the market is $\hat{Q}$, the horizontal sum of Q' and Q'_F. As a check, the summed quantity $\hat{Q}$ is the overall amount demanded by consumers at price P^* along the original demand curve D.

8.2 MONOPOLY AND ECONOMIC EFFICIENCY

Monopoly, as compared to perfect competition, leads to higher prices and lower output. This makes consumers worse off, but owners of the monopoly firm better off. The

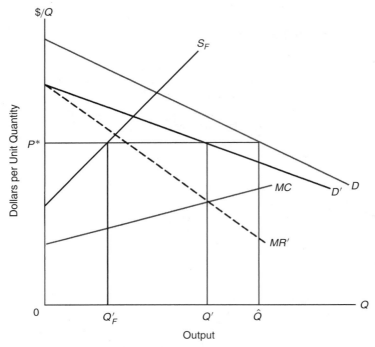

Figure 8.4. Monopolist with Competitive Fringe

D is the overall market demand curve. After horizontally subtracting the supply curve S_F of the price-taking fringe firms, the large firm has an effective demand curve D' and Marginal Revenue curve MR'. Setting Marginal Cost MC equal to MR' leads to the large firm's optimal output Q'. The corresponding fringe output is Q'_F. Industry output is $\hat{Q} = Q' + Q'_F$. Price P^* can be found along the D' curve at output Q' or along the D curve at output $\hat{Q}$.

concept of *efficiency loss* – that is, the net change in Consumer Surplus and Producer Surplus – introduced in the previous chapter provides a way of balancing the gains to some against the losses to others.

In Figure 8.5, a competitive industry with supply curve S would produce at Q_c, P_c where the supply and demand curves cross. Now suppose the industry is monopolized (without any changes in costs of production). The competitive supply curve S then becomes the Marginal Cost curve of the single large firm.[12] The monopolist chooses the level of output where Marginal Cost = Marginal Revenue, selling the amount Q_m at price P_m.

The shaded area in Figure 8.5 is the difference $P_m - P_c$ multiplied by the monopoly output Q_m. This area was part of Consumer Surplus under competition and is now captured by the monopolist as Producer Surplus; it is a *transfer* between Consumer Surplus and Producer Surplus, not an efficiency loss. The monopoly solution, however, also involves reduced levels of production and exchange, which do entail an efficiency loss. The lost Consumer Surplus is the upper dotted triangle in the diagram; the lost Producer Surplus is the lower dotted triangle. Overall, consumers lose both the shaded rectangle (transfer) and the upper dotted triangle (efficiency loss). The monopolist

---

[12] As explained in an earlier footnote, any "external" economies or diseconomies are already incorporated within the monopolist's Marginal Cost curve.

Figure 8.5. Monopoly and Efficiency Loss

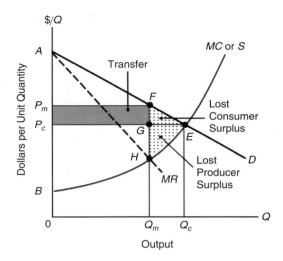

If there are no productive losses or gains from organizing the industry into a single large firm, the supply curve S of the competitive industry is identical with the Marginal Cost curve MC of the monopolist. The competitive equilibrium is at price P_c and quantity Q_c; the monopoly optimum is at the higher price P_m and smaller quantity Q_m. In comparison with the competitive outcome, the shaded area is a transfer from consumers to the monopolist (equal to the price difference times the quantity still produced). The upper dotted area is the loss of Consumer Surplus due to the reduction in quantity produced. The lower dotted area is the corresponding loss of Producer Surplus.

gains the shaded rectangle (transfer) but loses the lower dotted triangle (efficiency loss). Canceling out the transfer, the net efficiency loss is the dotted area.

CONCLUSION

In comparison with the competitive outcome, monopoly involves a transfer from consumers to suppliers. There is also an efficiency loss, the sum of the reductions in Consumer Surplus and Producer Surplus due to reduced trade.[13]

EXERCISE 8.4

Use the data of Exercise 8.1, and assume that the supply curve S under perfect competition would be the same as the monopolist's given Marginal Cost curve. Find (a) the competitive price-quantity solution and the associated Consumer Surplus and Producer Surplus; (b) the monopoly price-quantity solution and the Consumer Surplus and Producer Surplus under monopoly; (c) the efficiency loss.

ANSWER: (a) Using the demand equation $P = 10 - Q$ and supply equation $P = 1 + Q$, the competitive solution is $Q = 4.5$, $P = 5.5$. Referring back to Figure 8.5,[14] Consumer Surplus is the area of the right triangle AP_cE, which is numerically $(10 - 5.5) \times 4.5/2 = 10.125$. Producer Surplus is the area of the right triangle $(5.5 - 1) \times 4.5/2$, also equal to 10.125. (b) The monopoly solution was given in Exercise 8.1 as $Q = 3$, $P = 7$. In Figure 8.5, Consumer Surplus is the triangular area AP_mF, or numerically the monopoly output times half the distance AP_m, or $3 \times \frac{1}{2}(10 - 7) = 4.5$. Producer Surplus is the area $BHFP_m$ (a trapezoid in terms of the equations, though only approximately so as drawn in the diagram). The area of the trapezoid is the monopoly output times the average of the vertical distances BP_m and FH, or numerically $3 \times \frac{1}{2}[(7 - 1) + (7 - 4)] = 13.5$. (c) Since the sum of Consumer Surplus and Producer Surplus has fallen from 20.25 to 18, the overall efficiency loss is 2.25.

---

[13] One cannot, however, therefore conclude that monopoly should be abolished. (Any more than one could conclude from the analysis in Chapter 7 that taxes, which also reduce Consumer Surplus and Producer Surplus, should be abolished.) Other considerations need to be balanced against the efficiency loss.

[14] The pictured supply and demand curves are not linear, however, and so do not exactly match the specific equations used here.

An additional inefficiency may arise because of the *costs incurred in getting or keeping the monopoly privilege.* (A process called "rent-seeking," to be discussed further in Chapter 16.) If monopoly profits are $5,000 per day, the monopolist would be willing to spend up to $5,000 per day to acquire and retain the monopoly position. Geometrically in Figure 8.5, to maintain a monopoly the firm would, if necessary, spend any amount up to the value of the Producer Surplus, area $BHFP_m$.

The extent to which "rent-seeking" costs of contending for the monopoly are an efficiency loss depends upon the nature of the contest. Suppose the monopoly privilege is simply auctioned off by the government. Then, since running an auction consumes little in the way of resources, the additional efficiency loss can be negligible. (The amount the winning bidder pays is a transfer to the government, not a net loss to society.) Cable TV franchises are usually awarded in this way: local governments offer an exclusive franchise to whichever cable company makes the most attractive bid. Sometimes, however, the struggle for a monopoly is very costly. Chicago-style gang wars were attempts to gain monopolies over bootlegging and other criminal activities – a destructive activity for all concerned. Less picturesque, entirely lawful, but still often quite expensive, are contests in which a government agency awards prizes at its discretion. The Federal Communications Commission awards broadcasting channels, the Patent Office grants patents, and so on. The proceedings typically involve elaborate documentary submissions, hearings at which expensive lawyers and consultants plead their cases, and perhaps large costs secretly incurred to bring political pressures to bear.

What if a government official simply awards the monopoly to whoever offers the highest bribe? This is like an auction, so there would or no efficiency loss! Only a transfer is involved, in this case going to the private purse of the corrupt official. Note that illegal or immoral methods may involve an efficiency loss (gang war) or may not (bribery), just as legal and moral methods may or may not.

8.3   REGULATION OF MONOPOLY

Monopoly, as has been seen, can lead to economic inefficiency. In addition, excessive monopoly profits are commonly regarded as unfair to consumers. Policies for dealing with monopoly range from laissez faire at one extreme to trust-busting at the other. Monopolies are sometimes owned by government agencies. Railroads and telephone service, for example, are often government monopolies in Europe. This section discusses a different policy: *government regulation* of the monopoly's price, quantity, or quality of service. In the United States privately owned public utilities such as electric power and water, usually thought to be "natural" monopolies, are commonly regulated.

Regulation usually aims to limit the monopolist to a "normal" accounting profit, just adequate to attract the needed capital and other resources into the business. Normal profit in the accounting sense corresponds to zero *economic* profit, as explained in Chapter 6. And, as we saw in the preceding chapter, zero economic profit characterizes long-run equilibrium. So, in a sense, regulation aims at achieving the same result that would have occurred had competition been possible.

Figure 8.6 shows a monopoly firm with rising Average Cost and Marginal Cost curves. The diagram repeats the monopoly solution P_m, Q_m and the competitive solution P_c, Q_c seen earlier. It also shows also a zero-profit regulatory solution P_z, Q_z. Zero economic profit is equivalent to setting a price and associated output (determined along the consumers' demand curve) such that Average Cost = Average Revenue. In the

Figure 8.6. Regulation of Monopoly: Increasing Cost

The regulatory solution, fixing price so that the monopolist receives zero economic profit, is the price-output combination P_z, Q_z where the Average Cost AC and Average Revenue AR curves intersect. If this occurs in the range where AC rises, regulated output Q_z will be even greater than the competitive equilibrium output Q_c. In comparison with the competitive solution, the lightly shaded rectangle is a transfer from suppliers to consumers. The dotted area GHK is an efficiency loss due to excessive output. This negative Producer Surplus is larger than the heavily shaded area showing the gain of Consumer Surplus. Thus, overall the output increment $Q_z - Q_c$ is inefficient.

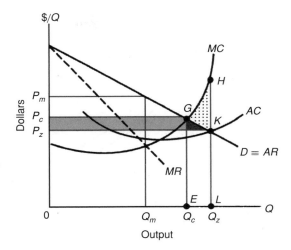

situation pictured the unregulated monopoly solution has – as compared to the efficient competitive outcome – too small an output and too high a price. But the regulatory correction overshoots the competitive ideal. The requirement that output be set where Average Cost = Average Revenue means that output in the industry is too great and price too low!

Output can be excessive because resources have alternative uses. As described earlier, an *efficient* outcome maximizes the sum of Consumer Surplus and Producer Surplus. At the competitive output Q_c in Figure 8.6, Consumer Surplus is the triangular area below the demand curve and above price P_c; Producer Surplus is the corresponding area above the MC curve and below price P_c. But for units between Q_c and the assumed regulatory output Q_z, MC lies *above* the demand curve. So this range of output involves an efficiency loss: the cost of providing the additional units is greater than their value to buyers.

Geometrically, when output rises from Q_c to Q_z the cost incurred on the additional output is $EGHL$ – the area under MC between Q_c and Q_z. The benefit to consumers is only $EGKL$ – the area under the demand curve. So the dotted area represents a net efficiency loss in comparison with the competitive ideal. Usually, however, one wants to compare regulated monopoly with *unregulated* monopoly, which also falls short of the ideal. This comparison is indeterminate. The unregulated monopoly produces too little, the regulated monopoly produces too much, and without more specific information it cannot be said which is the more efficient.

The analysis so far has dealt with a monopoly whose Average Cost curve AC was rising throughout the relevant range. Consider next a "natural" monopoly, where the Average Cost curve AC is falling (as in Figure 8.7). (Average Cost cannot fall forever, since that would violate the Law of Diminishing Returns, but may decline throughout the range of practical interest. If all firms have the same cost function, the firm producing the most would have lowest Average Cost. So ultimately only one firm is likely to survive.)[15]

---

[15] A falling Average Cost curve does not, strictly speaking, correspond to natural monopoly. A natural monopoly occurs when a single firm can produce any output at lower Average Cost AC than its competitors. A firm's Average Cost curve may fall throughout and still leave that firm with costs higher than its competitors'. Or Average Cost may be rising and yet the firm's Average Costs could remain lower than its competitors' costs.

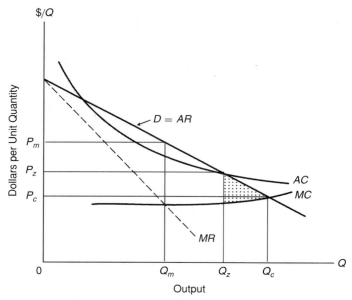

Figure 8.7. Regulation of Monopoly: Decreasing Cost

The regulatory solution (zero economic profit) occurs at P_z, Q_z where Average Cost AC equals Average Revenue AR. If this occurs in the range where Average Cost is falling, the regulated output Q_z is greater than the profit-maximizing monopoly output Q_m but is less than the ideally efficient output Q_c where Marginal Cost $MC = AR$. In comparison with the efficient outcome, the dotted areas represent losses of Consumer Surplus and Producer Surplus due to *insufficient* output.

Since in Figure 8.7 Average Cost AC falls throughout, Marginal Cost MC always lies below it (Proposition 2.2a of Chapter 2). It follows that, as shown in the diagram, the regulatory solution where $AC = AR$ (at output Q_z and price P_z) lies between the monopoly solution (output Q_m and price P_m) and the competitive solution (output Q_c and price P_c). So when Average Cost falls throughout, the regulatory solution improves over the unregulated monopoly: it comes closer to the competitive ideal. The dotted roughly triangular area shows the efficiency loss that remains, owing to a regulated output that is still "too small."

As shown in Figure 8.5, the competitive solution at Q_c maximizes the sum of Consumer Surplus and Producer Surplus. But notice that, in Figure 8.7, at Q_c Marginal Cost lies below Average Cost. So Average Cost exceeds price – violating the long-run No-Shutdown Condition! From an efficiency point of view, it is indeed better to have the utility produce the larger output despite any financial loss.[16] In principle, the loss could be covered by a lump-sum transfer of funds to the firm, from customers or from the government, that would leave Producer Surplus and Consumer Surplus unaffected.[17]

---

[16] The justification is as follows. The regulatory solution sets Average Cost = Price ≡ Average Revenue, so this is a breakeven situation. Nevertheless, efficiency calls for output to increase from Q_z to Q_c. In the region between Q_z and Q_c, the demand price (Marginal Value) always exceeds Marginal Cost. The amount consumers are willing to pay for the additional units exceeds the cost of providing those units.

[17] Where would the money come from? Perhaps from a government subsidy. Or the consumers themselves may be willing to pay lump-sum fees up front, to allow the firm to remain in business while still charging efficient low prices.

To prevent entry of competitors, the firm must charge a price below the minimum Average Cost of the lowest-cost potential entrant. That remains true even for a natural monopoly with falling Average Cost curve, as in Figure 8.7. Though only a single firm can ultimately survive in the industry, different firms may compete to be the single supplier. Such situations are described as "competition for the field" instead of "competition in the field".[18]

EXAMPLE 8.3 LONG-DISTANCE TELEPHONE SERVICE[a]

A 1982 consent decree between the American Telephone and Telegraph Co. (AT&T) and the U.S. Department of Justice ended AT&T's effective monopoly of long-distance telephone service in the United States. AT&T had benefited from regulatory decisions of the Federal Communications Commission (FCC) that let it erect barriers against potential entrants. The most important barrier was AT&T's refusal to allow new entrants to interconnect with AT&T's huge network of customer lines.

If only this barrier could be overcome, firms could profit from entry. The potential profits largely arose from the formula employed for dividing long-distance revenues between the local companies at each end and AT&T's Long Lines Division; the formula strongly favored the local companies. Though this formula was imposed by local regulators, AT&T had not historically opposed it, first, because AT&T itself owned many of the local operating companies, and second, because the "cross-subsidization" generated political support from these local companies for AT&T. But the artificially high long-distance rates were very attractive to potential outside competitors.

In the 1982 consent decree AT&T divested itself of ownership in the local service companies in order to concentrate on the long-distance market. By eliminating the burden of "cross-subsidization," the divestment helped AT&T meet the competition from MCI, Sprint, and other new long-distance providers. In addition, however, AT&T accepted restrictions designed to protect the new entrants from being driven out of business.

Since the consent decree became effective in 1984, the long-distance market has become more competitive. AT&T faced competition from other long-distance companies (primarily MCI and Sprint) and from large regional phone companies (primarily Qwest, SBC, and Verizon) that had been freed by regulators to offer long-distance service. In addition, numerous "resellers" act as wholesalers between these firms and the consumers. AT&T's share of interstate minutes declined from about 84% in 1984 to about 31% in 2002; the average price for long distance service fell by 43% between those dates.[b] Faced with such pressures, in 2004 AT&T announced that it is withdrawing from the consumer market for long-distance service.

---

[a] This discussion is based in part on Giles H. Burgess, Jr., *The Economics of Regulation and Antitrust* (1995), on Roger G. Noll and Bruce M. Owen, "The Anticompetitive Uses of Regulation: United States v. AT&T (1982)" in John Kwoka and L. White, eds., *The Antitrust Revolution: The Role of Economics* (1994), and on Nicholas Economides, "The Telecommunications Act of 1996 and Its Impact," *Japan and the World Economy*, v. 11 (1999).

[b] Economides, pp. 459–460, and Federal Communications Commission, *Statistics of the Long Distance Telecommunications Industry*, 2003.

---

[18] Harold Demsetz, "Why Regulate Utilities?" *The Journal of Law and Economics*, v. 11 (April 1968); William J. Baumol, "Contestable Markets: An Uprising in the Theory of Industry Structure," *American Economic Review*, v. 72 (March 1982).

CONCLUSION

If the Average Cost curve is rising in the relevant range, the regulatory zero-profit solution increases output beyond the monopolist's profit-maximizing solution. Such regulation is inefficient, leading to output that is "too large" in comparison with the monopolist's "too small" output. With a falling Average Cost curve, on the other hand, the regulatory zero-profit solution increases output insufficiently. The supposed inefficiency of monopoly may be exaggerated, however. The pressure of outsiders anxious to enter the industry limits the monopolist's ability to exploit consumers.

There is a further problem with regulation, not visible in Figures 8.6 and 8.7. Regulated firms may have little incentive to reduce costs. Indeed, if regulators always maintained the zero-profit condition Average Cost = Price, the firm's costs would not affect its profits. Any cost reduction would lead the regulator to lower the allowable price, with no gain for the firm. In practice, "regulatory lag" somewhat remedies the situation. When costs rise or fall, some time passes before the regulators adjust prices. So the regulated firm does not entirely lack incentive to reduce costs, though the incentive is weakened.

8.4   MONOPOLISTIC PRICE DISCRIMINATION

Until now it has been assumed that the monopolist quotes a single price. Sometimes a firm may use more complex *discriminatory* pricing schemes. A monopolist may divide the market, offering different prices to different classes of buyers (*market segmentation*). Or, for any given buyer, the monopolist may offer quantity discounts or in other ways charge different prices in accordance with the quantities purchased (*block pricing*). In the extreme a different price might be charged to each consumer for each unit taken; this is called *perfect price discrimination*.[19]

Market Segmentation

Suppose the monopolist divides the customers into two or more segments. Japanese auto manufacturers have been accused, for example, of "dumping" – charging lower prices for their cars abroad than in Japan. For market segmentation to work, the monopolist must control possible leakage between segments. If cars are priced at $25,000 in Japan and $20,000 in the United States, and if shipping costs are less than $5,000 per car, Americans could ship their $20,000 cars back to Japan and sell them for $25,000. So any price difference in excess of the shipping cost would tend to disappear.[20]

Dumping can be profitable because demand is generally more elastic in the competitive world market than in the home market. Figure 8.8 pictures a manufacturer who can charge separate prices P_1 and P_2 in markets 1 and 2. To maximize profit, the firm must equate the respective Marginal Revenues mr_1 and mr_2. (If not, profit could be increased by withdrawing some units from the market segment with low Marginal Revenue and selling them in the segment with high Marginal Revenue.) Furthermore, the firm will

---

[19] Price discrimination cannot exist under perfect competition. No consumer would pay more than the market-determined competitive price, and no firm would sell for less.

[20] Even with some leakage, the monopolist could profit from market segmentation.

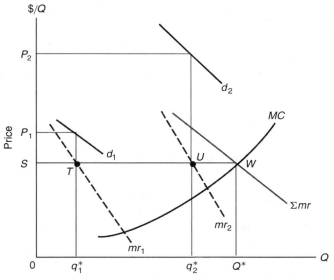

Firm Output and Segment Sales Quantities

Figure 8.8. Market Segmentation

The market consists of two segments with independent demand curves d_1 and d_2; the corresponding Marginal Revenue curves are mr_1 and mr_2. The Σmr curve is the horizontal sum of these separate Marginal Revenue curves. At the profit-maximizing output Q, $MC = MR = mr_1 = mr_2$. Of this total output, q_1 is sold to sector 1 at price P_1 and q_2 is sold to sector 2 at price P_2.

want to set Marginal Cost equal to $mr_1 = mr_2$. These conditions can be expressed:

$$MC = mr_1 = mr_2 \quad \text{Market-Segmentation Optimality Condition}^{21} \quad (8.6)$$

From Equation (8.5), and knowing that $mr_1 = mr_2$, it follows that:

$$P_1(1 + 1/\eta_1) = P_2(1 + 1/\eta_2) \quad (8.7)$$

So if demand is more elastic in market 1 (in algebraic terms, if $|\eta_1| > |\eta_2|$), the profit-maximizing monopolist will set a lower price in that market.

PROPOSITION 8.4: Under market segmentation, the segment with more elastic demand will be charged a lower price.

In Figure 8.8 notice the curve Σmr, the horizontal sum of mr_1 and mr_2. Equation (8.6) is satisfied at the intersection of the firm's Marginal Cost curve MC with Σmr at point W, which determines the optimal total output Q^*. The optimal quantities q_1^* and q_2^* for the separate markets can be picked off along the horizontal line from W to the vertical axis. Since $Q_1^* \equiv q_1^* + q_2^*$, the distances ST and SU sum to SW. The associated prices P_1 and P_2 are found along the respective demand curves d_1 and d_2.

---

[21] The technical qualification earlier, that MC must cut MR from below, here takes the following form: MC must cut the *horizontal sum* of the mr curves (the Σmr curve in Figure 8.8) from below.

As instances of market segmentation, movie theaters and buses often offer discounts to the elderly or to children (markets segmented by age). Vacation resorts charge different prices in season and off season, and prices usually vary by time of day at restaurants and movie theaters. Since, however, the costs of serving different classes of customers may differ, not all price variations are necessarily instances of monopolistic price discrimination.[22] Dinner prices at restaurants may be higher than lunch prices in part because waiters and other employees may demand premium pay for working in the evening. And retail chains may charge higher prices in high-crime neighborhoods becasue the costs of doing business are greater.

Discount coupons offered by supermarkets may also represent market segmentation: they let the store charge lower prices to those people willing to take the trouble of collecting coupons. Customers who are retired or unemployed have more free time, and so may be more able to shop around – making them more sensitive to discounts, or in other words making their demand more elastic. It is also sometimes thought that discount coupons are particularly aimed at poorer customers, who presumably have lower demand prices (less willingness to pay). But that does not follow. Market segmentation does not depend on the *heights* of the demand curves, but upon the demand *elasticities*. Poorer customers typically do have smaller demands but not necessarily more elastic demands.

EXERCISE 8.3

A monopolist has its domestic market protected by law from import competition. Its domestic demand curve is $P_d = 120 - q_d/10$. The firm can also export to the more competitive world market, where the price is $P_e = 80$ independent of its export quantity q_e. (So the firm is a "price-taker" in the world market.) Marginal Cost is $MC = 50 + Q/10$, where $Q \equiv q_d + q_e$. (a) Find the firm's profit-maximizing total output, and its division between the two markets. (b) Compare the prices and demand elasticities in the domestic market versus the world market.

ANSWER: (a) In accordance with equation (8.6), the firm sets $mr_d = mr_e = MC$. Since the domestic demand curve, $P_d = 120 - q_d/10$, is linear, the corresponding marginal revenue is $mr_d = 120 - q_d/5$. And since the export demand curve is horizontal, $mr_e = P_e = 80$. Equating the Marginal Revenues, $120 - q_d/5 = 80$, which implies a domestic output $q_d = 200$. Setting $MC = mr_e$ leads to $50 + Q/10 = 80$, which implies $Q = 300$. Since $Q = 300$ and $q_d = 200$, it follows that the export quantity is $q_e = 100$. (b) In the export market the price $P_e = 80$ is given. Using the equation for the domestic demand curve, $P_d = 120 - q_d/10$, since $q_d = 200$ the price is $P_d = 100$. The export demand curve is horizontal, so demand elasticity in that market is $\eta_e = -\infty$. In the domestic market, we can use equation (8.4), $\eta = (\Delta Q/Q)/(\Delta P/P)$, with quantity $q_d = 200$ and price $P_d = 100$. The value of $\Delta Q/\Delta P$ in the formula is the reciprocal of the slope of domestic demand curve, or -10. Substituting, the domestic demand elasticity is $\eta_d = (100/200) \times (-10) = -5$. As expected, price is higher in the domestic market where demand is less elastic.

---

[22] The differences between *on-peak and off-peak* prices, as analyzed in Chapter 6, are cost-based rather than discriminatory.

EXAMPLE 8.4 PAPERBACKS VERSUS HARDBACKS

In the book trade, typically a new title is introduced first in hardcover, possibly followed by a paperback edition. The physical form of the book, and the timing as well, segment the two markets. (Though sometimes the two versions are issued simultaneously.)

Sofronis K. Clerides, making use of a database representing essentially all the titles published in both hardback and paperback editions by Yale University Press in the period 1970–1995, asked whether the price difference between the two editions exceeded what could be explained in terms of differences in production costs.[a]

For the books studied, on average the prices were (in 1990 dollars) $39.16 for hardbacks and $17.04 for paperbacks. Marginal Costs were much lower, $2.95 and $1.74, demonstrating that the markets for book titles were much closer to monopoly than to perfect competition. (Of course, substantial fixed costs were also incurred in setting up a run of print for each book.)

Price discrimination between the two book types can be measured by comparing the differences between price and Marginal Cost (the "margins"). The table indicates that, in percentage terms, margins were lower on paperbacks. The margin would be expected to be smaller (that is, price should be nearer Marginal Cost) in the market segment with more elastic demand. The author obtained a relatively high elasticity estimate, $\eta = -3.9$, for the more competitive paperback market, so the low margin in that segment is consistent with expectations. Although it is reasonable to expect lesser elasticity in the hardback market, for that segment the obtained elasticity estimate was too extreme – strangely, it was actually in the positive range. (Selection effects may provide the explanation. Presumably, books of anticipated higher-than-average quality had both higher prices and higher sales, leading to a misleading statistical association.)

Paperbacks versus hardbacks

	Hardbacks	Paperbacks
Price	$39.16	$17.04
Marginal Cost	2.95 (7.5%)	1.74 (10.2%)
Price – Marginal Cost (= "margin")	36.21 (92.5%)	15.30 (89.8%)

Source: Adapted from Table 2 in Clerides.

[a] Clerides, Sofronis K. "Book Value: Intertemporal Pricing and Quality Discrimination in the U.S. Market for Books," *International Journal of Industrial Organization*, v. 20 (2002).

Block Pricing

Whereas in market segmentation the seller charges different prices to different customers, in *block pricing* the seller charges different prices to a single customer. For example, a 1-pound package of detergent might sell for $1.00 while a 2-pound package sold for $1.50. The seller is charging $1.00 for the first pound bought and $0.50 for the second pound.

Figure 8.9 shows the demand curve of a single consumer. Suppose that without price discrimination the monopolist would charge P^* for each unit sold. Consumer Surplus

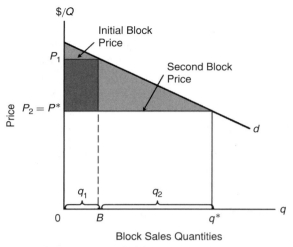

Figure 8.9. Two-Part Pricing

The monopolist faces the demand curve d for a typical consumer. P^* is assumed to be the profit-maximizing simple price for a monopolist. The monopolist can do better by charging a higher price P_1 on an initial block quantity B and charging $P_2 = P^*$ thereafter. This two-part pricing scheme allows the monopolist to capture the portion of Consumer Surplus represented by the rectangle lying within the shaded area.

would equal the entire shaded triangle. The monopolist, however, could charge as much as P_1 for the first block of q_1 units sold and then sell an additional q_2 units at the lower price P^*. The monopolist could thereby capture the dark-colored rectangle as revenue, rather than leaving it as Consumer Surplus. The rectangle is thus a transfer from the consumer to the monopolist.

The monopolist could not usually do this well. The high initial price reduces the disposable income the consumer could spend on buying additional units. (This is the "income effect of a price change" discussed in Chapter 4.) So only if the *income elasticity* of demand for this product is zero will the demand curve for additional units be totally unaffected. (The diagram implicitly makes this assumption.) Block pricing, therefore, cannot capture quite as much additional revenue for the monopolist as suggested in Figure 8.9.

Differences among consumers also limit the profitability of block pricing. The monopolist would like to use a different block price schedule for each buyer. But this is usually impractical. If the same price schedule is used for all, some consumers may be charged too high a price and others too low a price for maximizing the firm's profit. As another practical difficulty, block pricing entails higher transaction costs for the seller.

Discrimination via block pricing may seem quite common. Electric and water utilities often charge a high price for the first block consumed in any period, and a lower price thereafter. Utility price schedules often have four or five blocks, and also market segmentation of different classes of customers. Printing shops and furniture movers also commonly use declining-block prices. Indeed, wherever quantity discounts are encountered, block price discrimination may be suspected.

The suspicion, however, is not conclusive. As with market segmentation, observed price differences may reflect not discrimination but differences in costs. Electric utilities, for example, incur a lump-sum cost to connect a consumer to the main power line, a

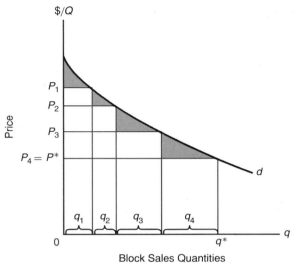

Figure 8.10. Four-Part Pricing

The monopolist charges P_1 for each of the initial q_1 units bought, P_2 for each of the additional q_2 units bought, and so on. This four-part pricing scheme leaves only the shaded area as Consumer Surplus.

cost that is essentially independent of electricity consumption. Similarly, a printing job not only consumes paper and ink but requires initial setting of the type. In such cases, charges to consumers should ideally include a lump-sum charge independent of use, plus a variable charge that increases with consumption. It may be more convenient to bill for the lump-sum component by charging an extra-high price on the first few units taken. So what appears to be discriminatory block pricing may be "cost-justified."[23]

Perfect Discrimination

At the logical extreme, *perfect price discrimination*, the monopolist charges a different price for each successive unit bought by each consumer. Figure 8.10 shows a four-part pricing schedule, an extension of the two-part schedule in Figure 8.9. (As in the previous analysis, the income elasticity of demand is assumed to be zero, so that higher prices paid for earlier units do not affect the consumer's willingness to pay for additional units.) Such a block schedule can transfer large portions of the Consumer Surplus to the seller; in Figure 8.10, only the small shaded areas remain as Consumer Surplus.

Carried to the limit, with different prices for each successive infinitesimal unit, essentially all the Consumer Surplus will be transferred from the buyer to the seller. So a perfectly discriminating monopolist can gain for itself all the advantages of trade.

Despite the seeming inequity when the seller captures all the benefits from trade, perfect price discrimination is efficient! For the last infinitesimal unit purchased by each consumer, the monopolist is charging a price equal to Marginal Cost. Thus, under perfect price discrimination as under perfect competition, the firm sets Marginal Cost equal to the price paid. And since each buyer's Marginal Value (demand price) then equals the seller's Marginal Cost of production, there can be no efficiency gain from producing either a larger or a smaller output.

---

[23] "Cost justification" is a legal defense for a pricing practice that might otherwise be unlawful.

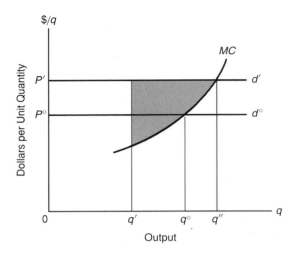

Figure 8.11. A Firm's Incentive to Chisel under a Cartel

If the competitive equilibrium price is P°, a price-taking firm would produce output q°. A cartel can drive price up only by having its members cut back production. If this firm's assigned production quota were q', and the cartel raised the price to P', the firm's gain from chiseling (increase in profit due to exceeding its quota) would be the shaded area. Note that, at the high price P', the firm would find it profitable to produce output q'', which is even greater than its competitive output q°.

8.5   CARTELS

A cartel is a group of firms behaving as a collective monopoly. Each firm in a cartel agrees to produce less than it would under unrestrained competition. The aim is of course to raise the price so that all can reap higher profits.

Cartels have an Achilles heel. However desirable the arrangement for the firms as a group, it pays any single firm to cheat. For the single firm illustrated in Figure 8.11, in perfect competition d° is its horizontal demand curve at the ruling price P°. Assuming the No-Shutdown Condition is met, under perfect competition the firm maximizes profits by producing output q° where $MC = P^\circ$.

A cartel can raise price over the competitive level only by reducing aggregate industry output – for example, by assigning production quotas to each cartel member. Suppose a firm agrees to hold its output down to q', and imagine that the cartel successfully raises price to P'. The incentive to chisel is evident. The new demand curve as viewed by the firm is d' – effectively horizontal, just like the d° curve before cartelization. This means that by charging a slightly lower price, any single firm can get as much business as it desires, taking away sales from others. Even at the old competitive price P° the firm would have liked to produce q°, more than the quota q'. (Cartel production quotas must be smaller than what competitive firms would have produced, else the market price could not have risen from P° to P'.) Once the cartel has raised price, the incentive to "chisel" is even greater. At price P' the firm would want to sell output q'. The additional profit capturable by a chiseler, assuming all the other firms abide by the cartel agreement, is indicated by the shaded area in the diagram.

Furthermore a cartel might not include *all* the producers in the industry. A firm outside the cartel will be essentially in the same position as illustrated in Figure 8.11 – except that, not being a member of the cartel at all, by producing at level q'' it isn't even cheating on an agreement. So if a cartel is ever successful, nonmembers do better than members! This fact makes cartels even less viable.

CONCLUSION

Cartels can raise prices above the competitive level only by cutting industry output. But at the higher prices, a member firm can profit by covertly producing even more than at the competitive equilibrium. Nonmembers can do the same and, since they need not disguise their actions, can gain even more. The added production of members and of nonmembers combine to subvert the cartel.

EXERCISE 8.4

Suppose 100 identical firms produce in an initially competitive market. Industry demand is $P = 10 - Q/200$; supply is $P = 1 + Q/200$. (a) Find the competitive equilibrium price, industry output, and firm output. (b) If the 100 firms formed an effective cartel, what would be the price-quantity solution for maximum aggregate profit? (Assume the industry supply curve is simply the horizontal sum of the firm Marginal Cost curves.) (c) At this price, what production quota would be assigned each firm? How much would each firm like to produce at the price set by the cartel?

ANSWER: (a) Equating supply and demand: $10 - Q/200 = 1 + Q/200$. The solution is $Q^o = 900$, $q^o = 9$, and $P^o = 5\frac{1}{2}$. (b) The demand curve is linear, so Marginal Revenue for the industry (the cartel) has double the slope of the demand curve, or $MR = 10 - Q/100$. Since the industry supply curve corresponds to the horizontal sum of the firms' Marginal Cost curves, Marginal Cost for the industry is $MC = 1 + Q/200$. The profit-maximizing solution for the cartel (where Marginal Revenue = Marginal Cost) is $Q' = 600$, $P' = 7$. (c) To achieve the monopoly price $P' = 7$, the typical firm's production must decline from $q^o = 9$ to a quota amount $q' = 6$. But at the monopoly price, each firm would like to set its output where Marginal Cost $= P'$, so that $1 + q/2 = 7$. This means that, instead of cutting back to $q' = 6$, each firm wants to expand output to $q'' = 12$.

In dealing with cartels, the laws of different nations vary considerably. Some countries treat cartel agreements as legally enforceable contracts. Other governments take a neutral position: the cartel agreement is lawful, but the courts will not enforce it. In the United States, with a few exceptions, cartels are outlawed as "conspiracies in restraint of trade." To be viable when illegal, a cartel would need to enforce its quotas in ways that are both *effective* and *secret* – an unlikely combination.

Even in the United States, the Webb–Pomerene Act allows American exporters to form a cartel for dealings in foreign markets. More important, the Federal government has encouraged or even insisted upon the formation of cartels aimed at raising prices of certain agricultural products.

EXAMPLE 8.5 PEANUTS

As described in Example 2.7 of Chapter 2, starting in the 1930s the U.S. government fixed "support prices" for crops with the aim of helping depressed farmers. The initial intention was to buy surpluses in high-production years and then sell them in years of low production, at little or no net cost to the government. But political pressures kept the support prices so high that surpluses accumulated. The Federal agencies attempted to dispose of undesired inventories by diverting them to secondary markets, most importantly "dumping" them abroad (at a financial loss to the taxpayers). These approaches in turn became excessively costly or unfeasible in terms of international diplomacy, so the next step was "supply management." Typically, to "earn" the right to a support price, an industry was required to form a cartel that would limit supply – usually, by establishing marketing quotas for each supplier. Of course prices could be maintained above competitive levels only because the force of law ruled out both above-quota production and the entry of nonmember suppliers.

Randall R. Rucker and Walter N. Thurman studied how such supply management programs affected the peanut industry.[a] Peanuts are used for two main purposes: there is an "edible" market (for direct consumption) and a "crush" market (for peanut oil, cake, and meal). An important feature of the industry is that there are better substitutes for crush (corn oil, cottonseed oil, canola oil, etc.) than for edible peanuts.

From 1949 to 1977 the main supply management technique was acreage allotment: only peanuts grown on "allotted acres" were eligible for the edible market support price. The government's excess accumulations were diverted mainly into crush, so a huge price gap developed between the two branches of the market. But over this period the per-acre yields on allotted acres tripled, as growers employed fertilizers and more sophisticated farming techniques to increase output from their privileged acres.

Once again the government – having to buy at the high support price and sell at the unsupported crush price – suffered heavy losses. So from 1977 on the government has imposed "poundage quotas" which quantitatively limit supply on the edible market. A supplier could produce over-quota, but only for sale in the crush market. This last feature increased the political acceptability of the program, since it gave crushers a source of supply that would have disappeared had the U.S. production come to be devoted entirely to the high-price edible market.

---

[a] Discussion based upon Randal R. Rucker and Walter N. Thurman, "The Economic Effects of Supply Controls: The Simple Analytics of the U.S. Peanut Program," *Journal of Law and Economics*, v. 33 (October 1990), pp. 483–516.

So some cartel agreements have been supported or even dictated by government agencies. As for the anticartel activities of other branches of government, it is often unclear whether these are well-designed or effective.

EXAMPLE 8.6 ANTITRUST AND PRICES

The Antitrust Division of the U.S. Department of Justice is responsible for prosecuting cartels illegally fixing prices. If antitrust prosecutions are effective, detection of a price-fixing conspiracy and indictment of its members should be followed by lower prices.

For 25 accused industry cartels indicted between 1970 and 1985, Michael Sproul examined price movements after indictment.[a] In each case he compared the change in price to change in a closely related industry – for example, the price movement of potash (indicted) was compared with nitrogen fertilizers (not indicted). The evidence was mixed. The table indicates that for the period before 1976, prices in most cases rose rather than fell after the indictment. In 1976 the legal penalties for price-fixing were increased, but even then prices more frequently rose rather than fell after indictment.

Indicted industry cartels – price movements after indictment

	Number of cases	Prices rose	Prices fell	Unclear or mixed
Before 1976	10	7	1	2
After 1976	15	9	1	5

Source: Estimated visually from Sproul, Figure 2 (pp. 747–748).

Two explanations come to mind: (1) The government may have been harassing innocent firms, so that prosecutions served only to raise the costs of doing business. Or (2) penalties were insufficiently severe to induce the firms to abandon the conspiracy.

The second explanation is not well supported by the tabulated data, since the after-1976 period (with its heavier penalties) looks similar to the before-1976 period. However, when the author directly examined the effect of *severity* of penalties – for example, whether jail terms were imposed – harsher punishments did seem more likely to lead to price reductions.

Overall, the study suggested that, at least so far as effects upon consumers are concerned, many antitrust cases alleging cartel behavior are unjustified.

---

[a] Michael F. Sproul, "Antitrust and Prices," *Journal of Political Economy*, v. 101 (August 1993).

A famous cartel is the Organization of Petroleum Exporting Countries (OPEC). The members of that cartel were and are sovereign governments rather than private firms. Nevertheless, over time its power has generally declined, owing to chiseling and to increased production by nonmembers of OPEC.

EXAMPLE 8.7 THE OPEC[a]

Before 1960, international oil companies such as Royal Dutch Shell and Standard Oil of New Jersey were often accused of acting as a cartel aimed at keeping prices high. If so they failed – as became evident later on when the Organization of Petroleum Exporting Countries (OPEC) came into existence and *really* raised prices! In fact, it was the attempt of the major companies to cut oil prices that led the oil-exporting nations to establish the OPEC. (At what must have been a low point for intelligent foreign economic policy, the U.S. State Department actively encouraged formation of the OPEC cartel!)

Starting about 1960, the main OPEC nations solidified their control over pricing and production, in effect expropriating the private companies whose efforts had discovered and developed their oil resources. Thereafter private oil companies operating in OPEC countries received only what amounted to handling fees for extraction and marketing services. In 1973, for example, the Saudi Arabian government took all but about $0.60 of the $2.59 price per barrel.

The problem for the OPEC was and is to limit production. In fact, most OPEC members have *not* been holding back production. To the extent that the cartel has been viable, it is only because a few major producers, notably Saudi Arabia and Kuwait, have limited their own production.

The petroleum trade since formation of the OPEC has gone through several dramatic phases. After Egypt and Syria attacked Israel in 1973, the Arab countries dominating OPEC halted the previous rising trend of oil exports, aiming to influence the diplomatic policies of the Western nations. Oil prices moved sharply upward. By January 1974 the price more than quadrupled to $11.65 per barrel. During this period the cartel was extraordinarily successful. Presumably, agreement upon foreign policy issues (mainly, opposition to Israel) helped to limit the chiseling that would otherwise have tended to undercut the cartel.

For some years afterward OPEC's power gradually weakened. Although the official price rose from $11.65 per barrel at the beginning of 1974 to $13.00 five years later (an increase of about 12%), the U.S. dollar depreciated about 38% over the same period. Thus, by January 1, 1979, the *real* price of OPEC crude oil was down from its peak.

But then, starting in 1979, another round of price increases was triggered by the revolution that paralyzed production in Iran. The official OPEC price rose ultimately to $34 per barrel in late 1981. But by 1985 maintaining these high prices required increasingly severe production cutbacks by the major OPEC producers – in particular, Saudi Arabia. Owing to OPEC cutbacks and rising non-OPEC production, the OPEC share of the world market, which had been 56% in 1973, fell to only 30% in 1985.

After 1985 Saudi Arabian production began to rise, along with the exports of other OPEC members. In consequence, despite a moderate upward trend in non-OPEC output, the OPEC fraction of the world market has recovered to about 40% in recent years. The price, still at about $28 per barrel in 1985, has since ranged between $15 and $25 per barrel – apart from a sharp temporary jump due to Iraq's occupation of Kuwait and the first Gulf War in 1990–1991.

In some periods the cartel has been hugely successful, thanks in large part to the Middle East wars of 1973 and 1990–1991 and the Iranian revolution of 1979. In the interludes between these historical shocks, two factors worked against the cartel. First, consuming nations began to use oil more economically and shift toward substitute fuels. Second, the high prices encouraged non-OPEC oil exporters such as Britain, Russia, and Mexico to expand their production and exports.

---

[a] The data on prices and production used here have been collected from several sources including *International Economic Report of the President*, Washington, DC: U.S. Government Printing Office, February 1974, pp. 110–111; *Los Angeles Times* (March 15, 1983), p. 1; M. A. Adelman, *The Genie out of the Bottle: World Oil since 1970* (M.I.T. Press, 1995), especially Figure 6.1 (p. 144), A. F. Alhajji and David Huettner, "OPEC and Other Commodity Cartels: A Comparison," *Energy Policy*, v. 28 (2000), and Energy Information Administration, *Monthly Energy Review* (July 2003).

8.6   NETWORK EXTERNALITIES

A person's demand for a good is usually independent of how much others buy. Sometimes, however, a person values a good more highly the greater the number of other people buying it. Such goods are said to exhibit positive network externalities.

The network effect upon demand may be due to direct interaction among consumers. Telephone service would be valueless if no one else had a phone, and in general becomes more useful as the number of subscribers rises. Or, the source of the externality may be informational. If John thinks Mary is a wise shopper, and Mary has just bought a Sony CD player, John is more likely to buy it. Or last, preference for conformity, as in the world of fashion, generates positive network effects. Men may prefer to wear trousers with cuffs only because most other men do.[24]

Demand for a Network Good

In Chapter 4, aggregate industry demand for a good was derived by horizontally summing the separate demand curves of the individual consumers. But a different technique is needed for a network good, where any one person's demand depends also upon the aggregate demand.

---

[24] Nevertheless, some consumers are contrarians, averse to conformity. For them, the network effect would be negative.

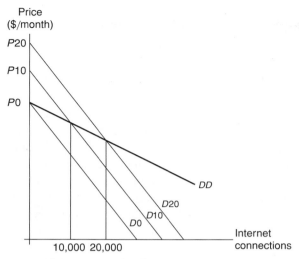

Figure 8.12. Network Effects and Market Demand

The horizontal axis measures the number of consumers connecting to the Internet. The more steeply sloped curves show, for any specified price, the numbers of consumers desiring to connect as a function of the number of others they expect to be connected. Owing to the network effect, $D10$ lies to the right of $D0$, $D20$ to the right of $D10$, and so on. For consistency however, expectations must be correct. The market demand curve DD, based upon such confirmed expectations, passes through the point on $D0$ (where no other people are expected to be connected), the point on $D10$ (where 10,000 others are expected to be connected), and so forth. So DD is flatter (more elastic) than the curves $D0$, $D10$, and $D20$, etc.

In Figure 8.12 the horizontal axis measures the number of consumers connecting to the Internet. The Internet would provide useful informational services even if no other consumer were connected, so a typical person would be willing to pay something even as the sole user. But when others connect, added services such as e-mail become possible. The curve $D0$ is the horizontal summation of the individual solo demand curves, which would be applicable if each potential user believes no one else will be connected. The curve $D10$ is the demand when everyone expects that 10,000 consumers will be connected, the curve $D20$ is the corresponding summation when each potential buyer expects that 20,000 people will be connected, and so forth. Owing to the network effect, $D10$ lies to the right of $D0$, $D20$ to the right of $D10$, and so on.

To find the market demand, assume that consumers' expectations are correct and therefore consistent with what actually happens, at least in the long run. The "confirmed expectations" demand curve DD will pass through the point on $D0$ where no people are connected, the point on $D10$ where 10,000 people are connected, and so on. As is geometrically evident, curve DD is flatter (more elastic) than the curves $D0$, $D10$, and $D20$. Thus, a positive network effect increases the responsiveness of demand to price changes.

The diagram also reveals a "chicken-and-egg" or start-up problem. The "choke prices" $P0$ for demand curve $D0$, $P10$ for $D10$, $P20$ for $D20$, etc. are indicated on the vertical axis. The choke price for the $D0$ or solo demand curve is also necessarily the choke price for the overall demand curve DD. If costs of production dictate that the price cannot be lower than $P0$, the market is not viable at all. Although under some conditions positive numbers of potential buyers would pay prices above $P0$, no point of "confirmed expectations" lies above that price. Lack of a critical mass of buyers often holds up the introduction of innovative products. To make the market viable, either consumers must more highly value the new product (that is, the confirmed-expectations demand curve DD must rise) or else production costs must fall.

Monopoly or Competition?

As indicated in the preceding chapter, falling Average Costs AC (increasing returns to scale) often leads to natural monopoly. Other things equal, the largest firm can always produce more cheaply than smaller firms. Network effects may also cause natural monopoly, but the reason lies on the demand side rather than the supply side. Now the leading firm gains not from falling Average Cost but because consumers are willing to pay more for its brand. So, although several firms may initially struggle for market dominance, only one firm will eventually survive. (As a qualification, however, if consumers have varied preferences, a smaller enterprise may survive to serve a "niche market.")

Network effects and returns to scale may operate in opposite directions. The demand-side network externality favoring natural monopoly may be opposed on the supply side by decreasing returns to scale in production (rising Average Cost curves). So, although a network effect on the demand side may suggest that all personal computers should be suppled by a single producer, it appears that rising costs in manufacturing have allowed many producers of personal computers to survive.

An important source of network externalities is the convenience of a common standard or format. The format or standard itself could be the basis for a monopoly. But if no one owns that standard, the producing firms can constitute a competitive industry. The more firms adhering to a given format (in cell phones or compact disks or computer operating systems), the more acceptable that format is to consumers. So there is pressure toward convergence upon a single standard. Yet multiple standards do sometimes survive. For one thing, consumers' preferences may differ, and some may be willing to pay more to retain their favorite standard. Or, rising costs on the supply side may offset the advantage of rising consumer acceptance on the demand side.

Human languages can also be regarded as alternative formats or standards. In the competition among languages, whichever is the most popular and widespread is at an advantage. Yet multiple languages persist. One reason is that not everyone prefers the same language. Another factor is the cost of switching. This relates to the next topic, lock-in.

The Lock-in Issue

Network effects might possibly lock an industry into an inferior technology. A technologically inferior brand might have been the first to enter the market, thus gaining a network advantage great enough to attain a monopoly. Or, many firms may be in the market, but all follow a single format that might possibly be technologically inferior. In recording tapes, Betamax was unable to made headway against VHS. In keyboard layouts, QWERTY dominates over Dvorak.

But some analysts regard these examples as largely mythical. Betamax may have lost out not because it entered the field late – actually, Betamax preceded VHS in the market – but because its product was inferior to VHS. And the Dvorak keyboard does not appear to be notably superior to QWERTY.

EXAMPLE 8.8 QWERTY AS INEFFICIENT LOCK-IN?

The standard English keyboard layout is called QWERTY, after the pattern of letters on the upper-left of the keyboard. At a glance, QWERTY seems to be an inefficient layout. Some very frequently typed letters (such as "a") require an awkward finger stretch, while less important letters (such as "j") have a better, more central location. The best-known alternative layout, the Dvorak keyboard dating to 1936, was invented to remedy these and other deficiencies. The Dvorak International Corporation still actively promotes that keyboard. Nevertheless, QWERTY has maintained its dominance. This situation appears to have the earmarks of an inefficient lock-in.

The usual explanation is that QWERTY gained an early lead. The first successful touch typist, Frank McGurrin, used a QWERTY machine to win a series of typing contests beginning in 1888. Since then, alternative keyboards have faced a chicken-and-egg problem. At any moment of time almost all typists are trained on QWERTY, so there is little demand for other keyboards. And it doesn't pay for typists to train on alternative keyboards, when they will almost certainly end up using QWERTY.

Although superficially appealing, this explanation does not really hold water. True, it may not pay for an individual QWERTY typist to learn the Dvorak keyboard. But a major corporation such as General Motors, which over many decades has employed tens of thousands of typists, could have easily bought Dvorak keyboards and trained typists to use them. Had the huge benefits claimed by Dvorak enthusiasts (for example, a 75% speed increase reported in an often-cited 1944 U.S. Navy study) been valid, these gains would have swamped the switching costs. In fact, though Dvorak keyboards have been commercially available for many years, no major employer of typists has ever switched over.

As explanation, the economists S. J. Liebowitz and Stephen E. Margolis have contended that this historical story is largely a myth, and that the Dvorak layout is not demonstrably superior to QWERTY.[a] Reviewing the U.S. Navy study cited by Dvorak supporters, Liebowitz and Margolis found it poorly designed and biased. (It appears that the tests were conducted by Lt. Cdr. August Dvorak, holder of the patent on the Dvorak keyboard.) The report was never endorsed by the Navy, and a later study by the U.S. Treasury Department did not support changing over to Dvorak.

Later comparative tests have usually shown a small superiority for Dvorak. The most significant recent study was conducted by Leonard J. West, timing the subjects by having them repeatedly type the most common English-language digraphs (two-letter combinations such as "th th th th").[b] To overcome the difficulty that most subjects have prior experience using QWERTY, the typists actually used QWERTY keyboards. But, to achieve the effect of typing on a Dvorak keyboard, instead of "th" the typists were asked to type "kj" – which is where "th" would appear on the Dvorak keyboard. This was done for all the common digraphs, and in both directions to avoid bias. The overall result was a small (4%) speed advantage for Dvorak, close to the average of previous studies.

Despite the ingenuity of the West experiment, the objection remains that speed in repetitively typing digraphs ("th th th") may not be much of an indicator of speed and accuracy in typing regular text. Earlier studies were also subject to a variety of flaws and objections. So, in view of the substantial costs of switching, it remains in doubt whether QWERTY's persisting dominance of the market – in spite of a

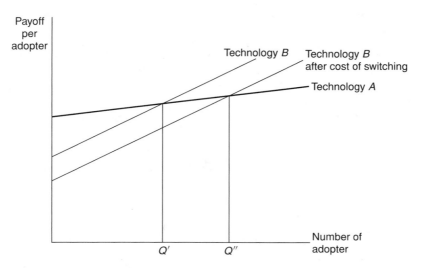

Figure 8.13. Network Technology and Switching Cost

For each technology, the horizontal axis shows the number of adopters and the vertical axis the payoff per adopter. If the market is small (if there are only a few users), technology A is the better choice. For more than Q' users, technology B would be better. But with technology A initially in place, allowing for the cost of switching means that no individual or small group can profitably adopt B until the number of potential adopters reaches point Q''. Within the range between Q' and Q'' there is lock-in.

seeming small speed superiority of the Dvorak keyboard – represents an instance of inefficient lock-in.

[a] S. J. Liebowitz and Stephen E. Margolis (1990), "The Fable of the Keys," *Journal of Law and Economics*, v. 33 (April 1990). For a case in favor of the Dvorak keyboard, see Jared Diamond (April 1997), "The Curse of QWERTY," *Discover Magazine*.

[b] Leonard J. West, "The Standard and Dvorak Keyboards Revisited: Direct Measures of Speed," Santa Fe Institute Working Paper 98-05-041 (1998).

In evaluating whether lock-in is economically inefficient, it is essential to allow for the cost of switching. Retaining a currently dominant format makes economic sense if it is too costly to switch to an alternative – even if that alternative would indeed have been hypothetically superior starting from a blank slate. The problem is illustrated in Figure 8.13. The horizontal axis shows the number of adopters of one technology or the other, and the vertical axis shows the payoff per adopter. Initially the market is small, there are few users, and technology A is the better choice. But then the industry grows. At point Q' crossover occurs, and technology B becomes better – or rather, would have been better starting from a clean slate. But no individual or small group can profitably adopt B until the number of adopters reaches point Q''. Within the range between Q' and Q'' there is lock-in, but it is not inefficient. Only beyond Q'' is lock-in inefficient.

Inefficient lock-in is possible for two related reasons. People might be myopic and choose – or expect others to choose – only on the basis of a short-sighted calculation: that if technology A is better today, it will continue to be better in the future. Or, even if all can look ahead and realize that demand is sufficient to make technology B better, switching from A to B calls for coordinated action that may be impossible to achieve.

Despite these difficulties, a variety of market forces will always be at work to overcome inefficient lock-in. For example, there would be a payoff to inventors who find ways of reducing switching costs.

> **CONCLUSION**
>
> Network effects may lock the market into a technology that, although superior initially, becomes inferior once demand grows beyond a certain size. Market forces at work, however, tend to overcome lock-ins. No conclusive examples of inefficient lock-in have yet been demonstrated.

SUMMARY   A monopoly exists when an industry consists of a single firm. Sometimes a monopoly is conferred by a governmental license or franchise. A "natural" monopoly occurs when one firm can produce more cheaply than any larger number. Or a firm that is not a natural monopolist may succeed in erecting barriers against competitors.

A competitive firm is a "price-taker," whereas a monopolist is a "price-maker." The monopolist can set either industry price P or industry output Q – not both. A monopolist maximizes profits by setting output such that Marginal Cost = Marginal Revenue, where Marginal Revenue MR is less than price. This can be seen from the expression $MR = P(1 + 1/\eta)$, where elasticity (η), is negative.

Compared to a competitive industry, the higher price and lower output under monopoly are associated with an *efficiency loss* (reduction in Consumer Surplus and Producer Surplus) as well as a *transfer* from consumers to the monopolist. An additional efficiency loss may arise from "rent-seeking" – the struggle to gain and maintain a monopoly positon.

Regulation of monopoly commonly aims to reduce price to the lowest level that attracts and retains the resources employed in the industry. Since no economic profits are then earned, Average Revenue must equal Average Cost. If the monopolist's Average Cost curve is rising, the intersection of Average Cost and Average Revenue overshoots the competitive equilibrium: there will be an efficiency loss due to *excessive* production in this industry. For levels of output where Average Cost is falling, the regulated solution lies between the monopolist's profit-maximizing output and the competitive outcome.

Price discrimination may allow a monopolist to earn even higher revenue.

(1) Under *market segmentation*, the monopolist sets overall Marginal Cost of production equal to the Marginal Revenue in each segment. So higher prices will be charged in segments with less elastic demands.

(2) Under *block pricing*, the monopolist charges different unit prices for different quantities sold.

(3) Under *perfect discrimination* the monopolist charges the maximum each consumer would be willing to pay for each successive unit. The monopolist then gains all the advantage of trade: Consumer Surplus is zero. Surprisingly, however, there is no efficiency loss.

Cartels are associations of firms in an industry that act collectively like a monopolist. But each member is motivated to "chisel" (produce beyond quota), and producers outside the cartel are induced to increase their production.

When consumers value a good more highly the greater the number of other people using it, the good exhibits positive network externalities. Network effects work in a way somewhat parallel to falling Average Costs, making it possible for an initially leading firm to end up as a monopolist. And, although the issue remains subject to debate, network effects might also lock an industry into a leading firm's inferior technology.

QUESTIONS

†The answers to daggered questions appear at the end of the book.

For Review

†1. If a monopolist sells 1,000 portable ultrasonic ghost repellents she will receive $48 per unit. If she sells only 999 units, she will receive a price of $50 per unit. Is the marginal revenue for unit 1,000 greater than, equal to, or less than $48?

†2. Why will a monopolist's profit-maximizing rate of output always be in the region of elastic demand?

†3. A monopolist initially maximizes profits by selling 1,000 panes of glass a year. A salesman then offers to rent a machine that reduces the firm's Marginal Cost by $10 at each level of output. Should the firm be willing to pay more or less than $10,000 rent (as a lump sum) per year for the machine?

4. Why is monopoly power over price smaller as elasticity of demand increases?

†5. "Monopoly is a bad thing for consumers, but a good thing for producers. So, on balance, we can't be sure that monopoly is responsible for any loss in economic efficiency." Analyze.

6. A competitive industry may have its equilibrium in the range of inelastic demand. Then the industry would receive more revenue if its output were smaller. Does it follow that such a competitive industry is producing "too much" of the good in terms of efficient use of resources?

†7. Monopoly firms are accused of pursuing "nonprofit goals" to a greater degree than competitive firms. Why might a monopolist be any less interested in profit than a firm in a competitive industry?

8. Compare the profit-maximizing conditions for simple monopoly, market-segmentation monopoly, and perfect-discrimination monopoly. Why is only the last of these said to be efficient?

†9. In making efficiency comparisons between a monopolized and a competitive industry, the Marginal Cost function of the monopolist was said to correspond to the supply function of the competitive industry. Explain why.

10. When will zero-profit regulation of a monopoly lead to too high a price from an efficiency point of view? Too low a price?

11. Show how behavior of a cartel's members may threaten its survival. Show how behavior of outsiders may threaten it.

For Further Thought and Discussion

†1. Movie theaters often offer price discounts to the young.
   a.   Is there likely to be a "leakage" problem in this form of market segmentation?
   b.   Sometimes youth discounts are explained in terms of differing elasticities of demand. Is this likely to be correct?

†2. Explain whether there is a contradiction between the following assertions: (1) the oil industry is an effective monopoly (cartel), and (2) higher prices for petroleum products will do little to discourage demand?

3. Is it better (more efficient) to have a monopolized industry, or no industry at all?

†4. a. In comparison with a simple monopolist, does a perfectly discriminating monopolist possibly or necessarily produce more output?

 b. Does a market-segmentation monopolist?

 c. A multipart pricing monopolist?

†5. Market segmentation is more common in the sale of services (e.g., discrimination by income for medical services, by age for transportation services) than in the sale of manufactured goods. Why?

†6. a. Are supermarket discount coupons a form of market segmentation? If so, how is "leakage" controlled?

 b. Do consumers who choose to use the coupons have a more elastic demand for grocery products? Explain.

7. Physicians often charge poorer customers lower fees for medical services. They usually explain this as a charitable gesture. Alternatively, can this be an example of market segmentation?

8. It has been said that sellers' cartels are more effective in dealing with government agencies as buyers, owing to the public records of transactions in which governments engage. Explain. How might the contention be tested?

9. Governments sometimes auction off the right to monopolize a commodity. (The *gabelle*, or salt monopoly, of pre-Revolutionary France was an example.) Show in a diagram the maximum amount the government could expect to acquire by auctioning off a monopoly. Is this likely to generate more or less income for the government than the most lucrative excise tax the government might impose?

†10. The following contentions about the demand and supply for narcotic drugs are widely believed: (1) that demand is highly inelastic – hooked users are practically forced to buy drugs, no matter what the price; (2) that the supply side of the market is dominated by a cartel consisting of a few major providers ("Colombian drug lords"). Is there a contradiction between these two beliefs? Explain.

11. Show that with price discrimination across two markets, the lower price corresponds to the more elastic demand. [*Hint:* Figure 5.4 shows how to graphically determine the elasticity along a demand curve.]

12. A monopolist selling a durable good may sometimes be unable to charge more than the competitive price, because it is in competition with itself. Having initially sold some units at a price P' exceeding its Marginal Cost MC, at any point thereafter it will want to sell additional units at a slightly lower price P'', and so on down to $P = MC$. Knowing this in advance, buyers will be unwilling to pay more than $P = MC$ to begin with. How could such a monopolist escape this trap?

†13. It has been argued that libraries have very inelastic demand for hardback editions of books, and that this inelasticity leads to high prices of certain academic and specialty hardbacks. Is this argument consistent with the evidence discussed in Example 8.4 on Paperbacks versus Hardbacks?

†14. If an organization like the Mafia effectively monopolized illegal activity, would you expect to observe less crime than under competitive free entry into this "industry"?

9 Product Quality and Product Variety

The text so far has focused on how prices and quantities are determined in markets. But firms also can get to choose the *nature of the products* they offer to consumers. Television networks can air comedies or dramas or news programs, farmers can grow different strains of wheat, barbers can cut hair in different styles, automobile manufacturers can offer sedans or sports utility vehicles.

Firms have two main dimensions of choice in determining the nature of the product: what level of quality to offer, and how much variety. *Quality*, to be taken up in the first section of the chapter, is something that all consumers want and agree on. Durability, reliability, and safety are always desirable. In contrast, *variety*, the topic of the second section of the chapter, is a matter of taste. Some people like red roses, some pink, some white; some prefer conservative clothing, others want flash and novelty.

9.1   QUALITY

Products vary in many quality dimensions. For simplicity, suppose all consumers are seeking some single service feature from a product. For light bulbs it might be lumens of light output, for hard disks it might be gigabyte capacity, for gasoline it might be mileage.

EXAMPLE 9.1 USED-CAR PRICES

As cars age, their quality deteriorates. Operating costs rise, and reliability falls off. In addition, consumers may suffer a loss of psychological satisfaction as the vehicle's style becomes unfashionable. B. Peter Pashigian, Brian Bowen, and Eric Gould examined how these factors affected used-car prices in the 1990s.[a]

Although all cars fall in value over time, there are differences in the *annual rate* of price decline with age. The tabulated data show that intermediate passenger cars fell around 22% in value the first year, an additional 16% the next year, and so forth. In contrast, for pick-up trucks the annual price decrease remained close to 13% per year over the entire range of vehicle life considered (up to 5 years). Also, compare the old-style Volkswagen bus and the new-style vans. For the Volkswagen the initial rate of value decline was only 13%, with even smaller rates of decline later on. (It appears that some consumers derive contrarian satisfaction from owing such a "classic" machine.) The newer-style vans suffered a much larger first-year price decline of around 22%, tapering off in following years.

The authors' interpretation was that the new type of van was valued more for its current stylishness. When no longer quite new, such cars go out of fashion and their prices fall off rapidly.

Annual percentage price declines by age, selected vehicle types

	1–2 years	2–3 years	3–4 years	4–5 years
Intermediate cars	22	16	14	13
Pickup trucks	13	13	13	13
New vans	22	14	12	11
VW buses	13	12	11	12

Source: Estimated visually from Pashigian et al., Figure 2 (p. 287).

---

[a] B. Peter Pashigian, Brian Bowen, and Eric Gould, "Fashion, Styling, and the Within-Season Decline in Automobile Prices," *Quarterly Journal of Economics*, v. 38 (October 1995).

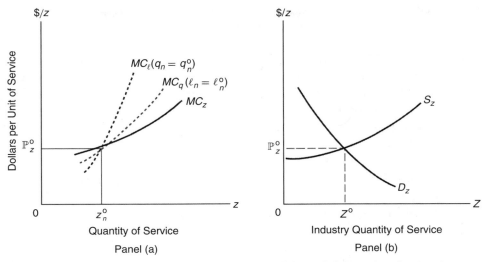

Figure 9.1. Marginal Cost of Quantity versus Quality, and the Market for Service

In Panel (a) the dashed and dotted curves MC_ℓ and MC_q show the Marginal Cost of producing more service output by increasing *quality* of product and *quantity* of product, respectively. Panel (b) shows market equilibrium at price $\mathbb{P}_z^o$ and service amount Z^o. The industry supply curve, S_z, is the horizontal sum of the firm's MC_z curves.

Quality under Competition and Monopoly

The key idea in analyzing quality is to distinguish between the *product* that is sold in the market and what consumers are really interested in – the underlying *service*. Consumers buy gasoline, but they are really interested in the road mileage they can get from the gasoline. The quality of an offered good is the service provided per physical unit. For gasoline, it would be miles per gallon (mpg). So service (mileage) is quantity (gallons) times quality (mpg).

Suppose there are a fixed number N of competitive firms, say oil refineries. The nth refinery produces quantity q_n gallons of gasoline at quality (mpg) level ℓ_n. So that firm's output of the *service* z_n can be written

$$z_n \equiv \ell_n \times q_n \tag{9.1}$$

A refinery producing $q_n = 1,000,000$ gallons of gasoline per day, at quality level $\ell_n = 20$ miles per gallon, is effectively generating $z_n = 20,000,000$ units of mileage service for consumers.

How about price? If users are fully informed, the price of each firm's product will reflect its quality. Although consumers pay a direct dollar price P_n for the physical product of firm n, what underlies that price is the *price of the service*, denoted $\mathbb{P}_z$. The prices of different brands must reflect the product quality offered:

$$P_n \equiv \ell_n \times \mathbb{P}_z \tag{9.2}$$

If one brand of gasoline has 10% better mpg than another brand, and assuming mpg is the only dimension of quality, then in equilibrium the price of the superior-quality brand must be 10% higher.

What determines the underlying price $\mathbb{P}_z$ of the service? Under conditions of pure competition, the answer, as usual, is supply and demand. In Panel (b) of Figure 9.1, the height of the demand curve D_z shows what consumers are willing to pay for amounts of service Z (mileage) offered on the market. The supply curve S_z shows, for each price $\mathbb{P}_z$, the amounts of service (mileage) that the firms in aggregate are willing to provide.

Chapter 6 showed how the competitive firm determines its profit-maximizing output q by setting the Marginal Cost of its *product* equal to market price P. But when products can differ in quality, in effect each firm chooses the profit-maximizing amount of the *service* (mileage) to offer. It does so by setting the Marginal Cost MC_z of the service it generates equal to $\mathbb{P}_z$, the going market price of the service:

$$MC_z = \mathbb{P}_z \tag{9.3a}$$

The firm's Marginal Cost of service MC_z depends upon both the *quantity* q_n it produces and the level of *quality* ℓ_n that it chooses to offer. Panel (a) of Figure 9.1 shows an initial situation where firm n provides quantity q_n^o (gallons of gasoline) at quality ℓ_n^o (mpg). The service output (mileage) generated is thus $z_n^o \equiv q_n^o \times \ell_n^o$.

The diagram shows three different Marginal Cost curves. The dotted curve MC_q shows the cost of providing more mileage by *varying quantity alone* (holding quality constant at ℓ_n^o). The dashed curve MC_ℓ shows the cost of providing more mileage by *varying quality alone* (holding quantity constant at q_n^o). Last, the third Marginal Cost curve MC_z shows the balanced (lowest-cost) way of generating additional units of the service. Quality and quantity are shown as balanced at service output z_n^o, where the firm's chooses quality ℓ_n^o and quantity q_n^o. At that point it is equally costly to generate another small unit of service by expanding quantity as by improving quality, so all three Marginal Cost curves intersect.

PROPOSITION: For any amount of service generated, the firm's quality and quantity choices are correctly balanced when the Marginal Cost of expanding service by increasing quantity (MC_q) and the Marginal Cost of expanding service by improving quality (MC_ℓ) are equal. The true (lowest) Marginal Cost MC_z of providing the service is the same as MC_q and MC_ℓ *when these are equal.*[1]

EXERCISE 9.1

Suppose a firm's cost function is $C = q\ell^2 + q^2\ell$. Initially the firm chose $q = \ell = 10$, so its service output is $z \equiv q\ell = 100$. (a) As an approximation of Marginal Cost, how much more will it cost to expand service output to $z = 101$: (i) by increasing q only, (ii) by increasing ℓ only, and (iii) by the lowest-cost (balanced) increase in q and ℓ? (B) What is the incremental cost of a bigger increase in service output, form $z = 100$ to $z = 200$?

ANSWER: (a) At the initial $q = \ell = 10$, the cost of producing $z = 100$ was $C = 10(10^2) + 10^2(10) = 2,000$. (i) Holding quality fixed at $\ell = 10$, producing $z = 101$ requires that $q \equiv z/\ell = 101/10 = 10.1$. The associated cost is therefore $C = 10.1(10^2) + 10.1^2(10) = 2,030.1$. The cost increment is approximately $MC_q = 30.1$.

---

[1] *Mathematical Footnote:* In terms of derivatives, the Marginal Costs of expanding service produced by providing more quantity or by providing more quality are:

$$MC_q = \frac{dC}{dq}\frac{dq}{dz} \quad \text{and} \quad MC_\ell = \frac{dC}{d\ell}\frac{d\ell}{dz}$$

(ii) Owing to the algebraic symmetry of the cost function, MC_ℓ is also 30.1. (iii) To produce $z = 101$ with a *balanced* increase of quantity and quality, again the symmetry of the cost function means that q and ℓ must remain exactly equal. The solution is $q = \ell = 10.05$ approximately. The associated Total Cost is about 2,030.075, so Marginal Cost of the service, MC_z, is approximately 30.075. As expected, a balanced increment of quality and quantity is cheaper than expanding z by raising either q alone or ℓ alone. (b) Although the difference between 30.1 and 30.075 is small, the disparity is magnified for larger changes. To produce $z = 200$ while holding quality fixed at $\ell = 10$ means that $q = 20$, the Total Cost being 6,000. To produce $z = 200$ while holding quantity fixed at $q = 10$ means that $\ell = 20$, so again the Total Cost is 6,000. In contrast, a balanced increase of quality and quantity to $q = \ell = 14.142$ generates a service output of $z = 200$ at a substantially lower cost of 5,656.9.

This principle of balance enters into the firm's profit-maximizing choice, which now involves the condition (9.3a) together with:

$$MC_z = MC_q = MC_\ell \tag{9.3b}$$

In Panel (a) of Figure 9.1, at the service price $\mathbb{P}_z^o$ the firm's profit-maximizing service output is z_n^o.[2]

In line with the analysis in Chapter 6, the MC_z curve is the *firm's supply curve for the service*. Summing horizontally over all the firms in the industry leads to the industry supply curve S_z (the aggregate amounts of the service Z provided at each price $\mathbb{P}_z$),[3] as pictured in Panel (b) of the diagram.

Firms in a competitive industry need not all produce the same level of quality. Depending upon their cost functions, some could specialize in high-quality products and others in low-quality products. The key point is that, since consumers are really buying the underlying service, quality differences will be fully reflected in higher or lower prices.

EXAMPLE 9.2 PRICE AND QUALITY: SHOPPING HOURS IN QUEBEC

In July 1990 the Quebec laws governing retail hours were relaxed, and a number of stores began to remain open on Wednesday evenings and on Sundays. This represented improved quality of retail service. Georges A. Tanguay, Luc Vallée, and Paul Lanoie studied how the change affected supermarkets' price margins for several standard commodities.[a]

Taking chicken as an example, for the period when the earlier law was in effect the authors estimated the relation between the stores' costs and the prices charged consumers by the equation:

$$P = 1.68 \, C^{0.851}$$

Here P is the retail price of chicken per kilogram and C is the store's wholesale cost per kilogram. The equation means, for example, that when the store's cost was $1.50

---

[2] The qualifications to the $MC = P$ rule covered in Chapter 6 also apply here: (i) the MC_z curve must be rising and (ii) $\mathbb{P}_n \geq AC_z$ (the No-shutdown condition).

[3] Setting aside possible "external" economies and diseconomies, and also changes in the number of firms (entry or exit), as discussed in Chapter 7.

per kilogram, the estimated average retail price for chicken was $P = 1.68(1.50^{0.851}) = \$2.37$.

For the period after the closing law was relaxed, the multiplicative constant rose from 1.68 to 1.76. This meant that, under the more relaxed law, when the store's cost was $1.50 per kilogram the average retail price would now be $2.49. So the longer shopping hours appear to have raised the stores' average margin, given a wholesale cost of $1.50 per kilogram, from $0.87 to $0.99 – about 12%. Similar results were obtained for other products: beef, bananas, apples, and onions. Presumably the higher margins reflected consumers' willingness to pay for the increased convenience of the extended shopping hours.

Margins might possibly also have increased owing to higher operating costs in keeping stores open longer. But, the authors found, costs per kilogram appeared to rise very little, if at all. True, there are additional costs incurred in staying open longer hours, but on the other hand the stores were able to manage their inventories better. For one thing, there was less wastage of perishable produce. So it appears that the increase in price margins was indeed due to the improved quality of service offered to consumers.

---

[a] Georges A. Tanguay, Luc Vallée, and Paul Lanoie, "Shopping Hours and Price Levels in the Retailing Industry: A Theoretical and Empirical Analysis," *Economic Inquiry*, v. 33 (July 1995).

So far only competitive industries have been studied. What about monopoly and quality? Chapter 8 showed that a monopolized industry would provide a *smaller quantity* of product than a competitive industry. Is there any reason to expect it to offer *lower quality* as well?

Taking laundry detergent as an illustration, suppose quality can be defined in terms of cleaning power per ounce. Again, the crucial point is to appreciate that the firm, whether a monopolist or a competitor, is really providing consumers with levels of service Z. Since the consumers' demand for service is surely negatively sloped, a monopolist would offer a smaller service output Z than would a competitive industry. In fact, the familiar monopoly equation will apply. The monopolist will set its Marginal Cost equal to its Marginal Revenue, both now defined in terms of amounts of service:

$$MC_z = MR_z \qquad (9.3c)$$

The only question is, will this smaller Z be associated with *both* lower quality (weaker detergent) and less quantity (fewer pounds of detergent)? Or would the change be only in one dimension? Or might the quality actually improve, accompanied by an even greater cut in quantity?

The answer is already evident in equation (9.3b), which indicated that changes in service output are best achieved by balanced adjustments of both quantity and quality. In fact, equation (9.3b) applies for any type of firm, whether a competitor or a monopolist. Consequently, the smaller service output Z of the monopolized industry should logically involve *some combination of reduced quantity and lower quality*. The monopolist would produce a weaker detergent, and produce fewer pounds.

CONCLUSION

A monopolist produces a smaller service output Z than a competitive industry, and generally does so by some combination of reduced quantity and lower quality.

Figure 9.2. A Quality-Improving (Cost-Reducing) Invention

A monopolist is considering an innovation that costlessly doubles the quality of its product. Since the horizontal axis represents amount of service Z, the original Total Cost curve C_z^o shifts to C_z' – service output is doubled at each level of cost. Fully informed consumers are interested only in amount of service, and so the Total Revenue function R is unchanged. The monopolist will necessarily increase profits by adopting rather than suppressing the invention. In the situation pictured, the profit comparison is $\Pi' > \Pi^o$. Consumers also benefit, because more service is produced to be sold at a lower price.

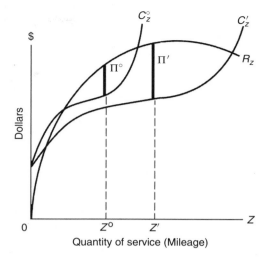

Quantity of service (Mileage)

An Application: Suppression of Inventions

Monopolists are sometimes accused of suppressing useful inventions. A useful invention is a discovery permitting production of a higher-quality product at given cost, or of a given quality of product at lower cost. As will be seen, if buyers are adequately informed it is never profitable for a monopolist to suppress such an innovation.

Consider gasoline, where as before consumers are interested only in the service generated (road mileage). Suppose the monopolist discovers how to produce its existing quality of gasoline at half the cost. Obviously, it will never suppress (fail to make use of) such a cost-reducing discovery. Now suppose instead that the discovery lets the firm double the quality (mpg) with no increase in production costs. To the firm, such a quality-improving invention is equivalent to the cost-reducing invention. The firm would not suppress either invention.

Figure 9.2 illustrates the equivalence of cost-reducing and quality-improving inventions. Suppose the invention doubles quality ℓ (miles per gallon) of gasoline without changing the cost of producing the physical product (gallons of gasoline). Assuming consumers are fully informed, the demand curve for mileage service remains unchanged. (Consumers don't care about gasoline as such, they will only pay for what concerns them – mileage.) So it follows that the Total Revenue curve, showing $R_z \equiv \mathbb{P}_z Z$ as a function of Z, remains unchanged. On the cost side, although the Total Cost curve in terms of *gasoline output Q* would remain unchanged, here it is *service output Z* that is shown on the horizontal axis. Since $Z \equiv Q \times \ell$, the doubling of quality ℓ shifts the Total Cost curve of producing Z from C^o to C' – a horizontal stretching to the right by a factor of 2. So a quality-improving invention is indeed equivalent to a cost-reducing invention.

The profit-maximizing level of service output was Z^o before the invention and became Z' after the invention. The associated profits are Π^o and Π'. (The postinvention profits are of course larger.) In the situation illustrated, the monopolist's profit-maximizing service output increases ($Z' > Z^o$) but does not quite double ($Z' < 2Z^o$). This means that, although the firm generates more service output, it does so while actually producing fewer gallons of gasoline. So consumers benefit from the invention,

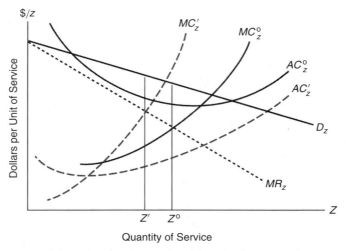

Figure 9.3. A Quality-Improving (Cost-Reducing) Invention Adverse to Consumers

A quality-improving invention is equivalent to a reduction in the Average Cost of producing the service, and so the new AC'_z curve lies everywhere below the original AC^o_z curve. Nevertheless, as shown here, there may be a range in which the new Marginal Cost MC'_z is higher than the original MC^o_z. As a result, the new $MC'_z = MR_z$ intersection may determine a profit-maximizing level of service z that is smaller than the initial level z^o. If so, consumers will be worse off for the invention.

which allows them to consume more service Z (mileage), and the firm saves cost by producing a smaller physical quantity Q of output (gallons).

It is also possible, if the revenue and cost curves have somewhat different shapes, that the service output Z that maximizes profits could *more than* double ($Z' > 2Z^o$). Consumers would then benefit even more. The firm would incur higher costs, but would nevertheless earn higher profits.

Last, although this may seem paradoxical, Figure 9.3 shows that it is also logically possible for the output of service in the postinvention solution to *fall* ($Z' < Z^o$). The monopolist does not suppress the invention, but the consumers end up worse off! This surprising possibility is more easily visualized in a diagram like Figure 9.3, a diagram in "average-marginal" units as opposed to the "total" units used in Figures 9.1 and 9.2. The demand curve, or Average Revenue curve, in terms of service output Z remains unchanged. Since this is a cost-reducing invention, the postinvention Average Cost curve AC'_z is lower throughout than the original Average Cost curve AC^o_z. Nevertheless, it is possible (as shown in the diagram) for the postinvention *Marginal* Cost curve MC'_z actually to be higher than the original Marginal Cost curve MC^o_z in the relevant range. If so, as shown in the diagram, the new intersection of Marginal Revenue and Marginal Cost can occur at some $Z' < Z^o$. In that case the firm's profit-maximizing output of service is smaller, the monopoly price is higher, and consumers lose out. Such a result requires very special shapes of the Marginal and Average Cost curves – specifically, there must be a range where Average Cost falls while Marginal Cost rises. This is probably very unusual.

The assumption that consumers are fully informed is essential to this entire analysis. If the invention really improves product quality but consumers do not believe that is the case, they will initially be unwilling to pay more for the higher-mileage gasoline. That would eliminate the monopolist's incentive to introduce the innovation. Still, the cost of informing consumers is a real economic cost. It is not really "suppression" when an invention, even though a genuine quality improvement, cannot be put on the market except at a cost – including the cost of convincing consumers that it really is a quality improvement – that is too great in comparison with the benefit received.

CONCLUSION

If consumers are fully informed, a quality-improving innovation is equivalent to a cost-reducing innovation. Neither would be suppressed by a profit-maximizing monopolist. Normally consumers also gain, except in exceptional circumstances.

Cartels and Quality

Chapter 8 showed that each member of a cartel is motivated to "chisel" – to produce beyond its assigned production quota. If firms can vary quality as well as quantity, then to remain effective the cartel would have to control cheating in both dimensions. But it is often difficult to define or measure quality unambiguously. This difficulty was what led to the "sandwich wars" among international airlines in the 1970s. In that period international cartel agreements fixed international coach fares. To limit quality competition, the agreements also banned full on-flight meals. However, the airlines were permitted to offer their customers sandwiches. The result: sandwiches grew more and more elaborate, eventually becoming sumptuous meals in themselves.

EXAMPLE 9.3 THE JAPANESE AUTO EXPORT CARTEL

With the aim of protecting manufacturers of American cars, in 1981 the United States induced Japan to limit its automobile exports to the United States. (In these negotiations little attention was paid on either side to the interests of U.S. consumers!)

The agreement effectively converted the Japanese auto industry into a highly profitable export cartel. Japanese auto manufacturers, previously unable or unwilling to agree on export quotas, had competed with one another in quoting relatively low prices for cars exported to the United States. Thanks to the "successful" American diplomatic prodding, Japan's Ministry for International Trade and Industry agreed to limit exports by assigning export quotas to the various Japanese auto manufacturers. The effect upon the profitability of Japanese auto companies was drastic. Corporate shares in Japanese auto firms rose by an average of around 24% in the single month when the arrangement was announced.[a]

The reduced numbers of Japanese cars available raised the U.S. prices of Japanese cars in comparison with those of American-made cars. But there was also a quality effect. Since the export controls limited only the *numbers* of Japanese cars sold in the United States, the cartelized Japanese exporters still competed with one another in the quality dimension. According to a study by Robert C. Feenstra, though the price index of Japanese cars in the United States rose by 48.3% in the period 1980–1985, the quality index also rose by 25.4%. So the increased quality offered to consumers of imported Japanese cars offset about half the observed price increase.[b]

---

[a] Arthur T. Denzau, "Made in America: The 1981 Japanese Automobile Cartel," Center for the Study of American Business, Washington University (August 1986).

[b] Robert C. Feenstra, "Quality Change under Trade Restraints: Theory and Evidence from Japanese Autos," Department of Economics, University of California, Davis (May 1986).

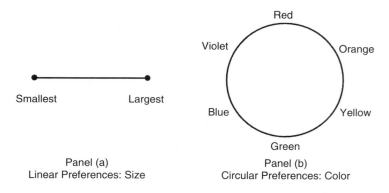

Figure 9.4. Linear versus Circular Preferences

For a characteristic such as *size*, individual consumer preferences range from smallest to largest. For a characteristic such as *color*, individuals' preferences may be thought of as distributed around a ring. For simplicity, assume the preference distribution is uniform over the linear range in the one case, or around the circle in the other case.

9.2   VARIETY

How do product markets respond to variations in consumer tastes or needs?

Just as quality has several possible dimensions, variety has many possible aspects. Manufacturers of women's dresses, for example, attempt to meet consumer requirements by offering many combinations of size, fabric, color, and cut.

Imagine a single dimension of variation – for example, clothing size or color. Sizes vary from large to small. Consumer size preferences can be imagined as distributed over a line-segment as in Panel (a) of Figure 9.4. A consumer preferring a small size can be regarded as located toward the left; a consumer preferring a large size toward the right.

Size has a lower limit and an upper limit. It will be more convenient here to think of a product attribute such as color, which can be illustrated as a ring in Panel (b) of the diagram. Imagine that as many people prefer red as yellow as green and so on. So consumers can be thought of as distributed uniformly around the color circle.

As a geographical analogy, the product characteristic (color) most desired by any consumer can be thought of as a specific point on the ring; call this point the consumer's *consumption locale*. Similarly, any variety produced and sold can be regarded as a *production locale*. The distance around the circle between the two locales measures the extent of imperfect matching between preferences and products. For example, a consumer looking for a true blue dress (consumption locale) may find that only greenish-blue or reddish-blue garments (production locales) are available on the market. The loss suffered from imperfect color matching is the economic equivalent of having to pay the cost of (metaphorically) "transporting" the good from point of sale to point of consumption.

The value of variety is illustrated in Figure 9.5. Here the limiting (highest) aggregate consumer demand function D_∞ represents the ideal case. Imagine there are an infinite

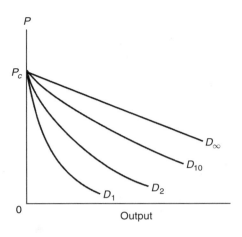

Figure 9.5. Aggregate Demand as Related to Number of Producing Plants

$D_1, D_2, \ldots, D_\infty$ show the rising aggregate effective demand, as viewed by a monopolist seller, achieved by increasing the number of plants (production locales) spaced evenly around the ring of Figure 9.4. Effective demand increases with the number of plants, because consumer preferences are better matched (there is less wastage in transport costs). However, demand grows at a decreasing rate.

number of production locales spread evenly around the ring ($N = \infty$), so every consumer can be located at a production locale. Then there are no "transport" losses, so consumer desires for the product are fully reflected in the D_∞ demand curve. At the opposite extreme, curve D_1 shows the aggregate demand when there is only a single production locale at some arbitrary point on the circle. Here the most distant consumer must pay for shipment halfway around the ring. The *average* loss of value (transport cost) per consumer then corresponds to a quarter-circle of circumference about the ring. Similarly, D_2 is the effective demand curve with two production locales, located 180° apart. The average consumer is then separated by an eighth-circle from the nearest production locale, and so forth. Note that the curve of aggregate demand shifts upward, *but at a decreasing rate*, as the number of production locales rises – that is, as the assortment of products on the market more closely approximates the distribution of consumer preferences.

EXAMPLE 9.4 RELIGION: THE VALUE OF VARIETY

In countries with an established church, religion is somewhat like a monopoly. At the extreme, if all other religions were prohibited, there would be only one "production locale." But most countries, with or without an established church, are characterized by varying degrees of competition among different sects and denominations.

Laurence R. Iannaccone studied the religious worship records of Protestant denominations in several Western countries where Protestants constituted the major religious group.[a] The table relates weekly religious attendance to the "degree of concentration" of church membership. Concentration could range from 100% (if there was only one church) to practically 0% (if each person had his or her own denomination).

The table indicates that high concentration is associated with low religious attendance. The range is from the United States (2% concentration, 43% attendance) to Denmark (94% concentration, 3% attendance). It appears that consumers have varied preferences for religions, as they have for clothing or automobiles. So a single predominant religion will be a "poor fit" for many consumers, who in consequence opt out of religious observance.

In addition, with more competition religious organizations will likely strive harder to meet the needs of present and prospective members.

Religious attendance and concentration (Protestant denominations)

	% attendance	Concentration (%)
United States	43	2
Canada	31	3
Netherlands	27	10
Switzerland	25	21
W. Germany	21	23
Australia	21	18
New Zealand	20	21
Britain	14	40
Norway	8	85
Sweden	5	72
Finland	4	92
Denmark	3	94

Source: Estimated visually from Iannaconne, Figure 1 (p. 158).

[a] Laurence R. Iannaconne, "The Consequences of Religious Market Structure," *Rationality and Society*, v. 3 (April 1991)

Product Variety under Monopoly

A monopolist must decide on the profit-maximizing assortment of products to offer consumers. Its first problem is *how many* varieties to produce. In the geographical metaphor this becomes the number N of distinct production locales (manufacturing plants) to establish around the ring of Figure 9.4. (A nearly production source is, for a consumer, analogous to a product that closely matches his or her needs.) The next decisions for the monopolist are *how much* of each variety to produce (the scale of output at each production plant) and *what prices* to charge.

An increase in the number of varieties (production locales around the ring) reduces the average gap between what the consumer wants and what he or she finds in the market. The smaller the average gap, the higher will be the average price consumers will be willing to pay. (Consumers would be willing on average to pay more if shirts were offered in sizes 28, 30, 32, ..., 50 rather than only Small, Medium, and Large.) What prevents carrying this process to the limit – attaining the D_∞ demand curve – is *economies of scale*. Over some range, Average Cost per plant may fall as plant output expands. So the monopolist must balance the savings in production costs from offering fewer varieties against the additional revenue that a more varied assortment of products would make possible.

Suppose that costs of production are the same regardless of location around the ring, and that consumers are uniformly distributed around the ring. Then the firm should locate its producing plants (whatever their number) evenly around the circle. The price at the factory (the so-called "f.o.b. price") must then also be identical at each producing

Figure 9.6. Monopoly Total Revenue and Total Costs, as Related to Number of Plants

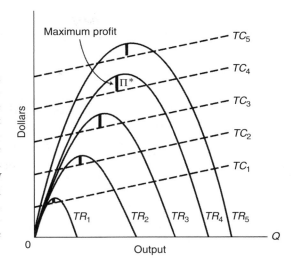

The aggregate Total Revenue curves TR_1, TR_2, ... correspond to the aggregate demand curves (curves of Average Revenue) D_1, D_2, ... in the previous diagram. As the number of plants N rises, Total Revenue TR_N also rises *but at a decreasing rate*. The Total Cost curves TC_1, TC_2, ... show the aggregate cost of producing any output Q with 1, 2, ... plants. Under the assumption of an identical linear cost function each plant, TC_N shifts upward by a constant amount as N rises (because an additional Fixed Cost is incurred each time a new plant is brought into production). The bold vertical segments show the highest achievable profit for each N; the greatest of these is the profit maximum Π^*, which occurs here at $N = 4$.

plant. Continuing with the geographical metaphor, each consumer will pay the f.o.b. price *plus* the transport cost from the nearest plant.

Figure 9.5 showed how demand is affected by the number of production locales – in this case, the number of plants N that the monopolist distributes around the preference ring. Now consider the cost side. Suppose the production costs for the monopolist's nth production plant is:

$$C_n = A + Bq_n \tag{9.4}$$

Here A is the fixed cost of each plant, and B is the constant Marginal Cost.

Let the number of identical plants be N, so that aggregate output is $Q \equiv Nq_n$. Then overall Total Cost is:

$$TC_N = NC_n = N(A + Bq_n) = NA + BQ \tag{9.5}$$

How Total Cost varies with the number of plants N is shown by the dashed lines TC_1, TC_2, ... in Figure 9.6. Since a fixed cost of A is incurred per plant, the Total Cost of producing any aggregate output Q rises as the *number* of plants N increases. However, the Marginal Cost remains B per unit wherever that unit is produced.

Figure 9.6 also shows Total Revenue functions for different numbers of plants. The Total Revenue curve with only one producing plant (corresponding to demand curve D_1 in the previous diagram) is TR_1; similarly TR_2 is the Total Revenue curve with two plants (corresponding to D_2), and so on.

For any given number of plants N, the monopolist chooses the f.o.b. price P^m and the associated quantity Q^m by using the familiar condition Marginal Cost = Marginal Revenue. For each possible number of plants N, the firm's profit Π is the maximum vertical distance between the TR_N and TC_N curves, shown in the diagram by bold line-segments. As plotted, Π initially increases as N rises. (The bold line-segment between the TR_2 and TC_2 curves is longer than the segment between the TR_1 and TC_1 curves.) This means that the revenue gain from better matching of products to consumers' desires exceeds the increased cost arising from a larger number of production locales. But the gains from increasing N taper off. Meanwhile costs rise steadily as N grows, because an additional fixed cost A is incurred for each additional plant. There will, consequently, be an optimum number of plants. In Figure 9.6 the largest profit Π^* is achieved at $N = 4$: having exactly four production locales represents the best compromise between production costs and transport costs.

Blending Monopoly and Competition – Monopolistic Competition

What happens to overall variety when competitors can enter, producing closely similar products? Assume now a number of firms, with free entry and exit. Furthermore, suppose each firm produces just a single variety of product. So a monopolistic element remains in the picture: each firm is the sole supplier of its own particular product.

The market structure representing such a mixture of monopolistic and competitive elements is called "monopolistic competition." Each firm offers a unique product that best satisfies its "clientele": those customers whose preferences (consumption locales) closely match its product (production locale). A city, for example, may have a dozen supermarkets closely competing in many respects. Yet any single store, given its geographical location and other possibly unique features, may face a downward-sloping demand curve. That is, it might be able to raise prices slightly without losing *all* of its customers. So each firm under monopolistic competition is a "price-maker," not a "price-taker." Still, the store is not a monopolist. If it raises prices, customers can switch to some more or less similar store (some nearby production locale).

How do the assortment of products and their associated prices under monopolistic competition compare with the monopoly situation? The question can be separated into two parts: (i) *If* the range of products offered were the same, would prices be lower (and the quantities offered therefore larger) under monopoly or under monopolistic competition? (ii) Which of the two market structures will offer consumers more varieties to choose from?

In Figure 9.7 the demand curve D_N and the associated Marginal Revenue MR_N represent the situation of a monopolist with N plants. Since each plant serves a fraction $1/N$ of the total demand, a single plant's share of the overall demand is $D_n \equiv D_N/N$. Similarly, Marginal Revenue for each plant is $MR_n \equiv MR_n/N$. If $N = 4$, the per-plant D_n and MR_n curves would represent a quarter of the quantities along the corresponding D_N and MR_N curves. Given the assumed constant Marginal Cost $MC = B$, in the diagram the profit-maximizing solution is Q_N^* for a monopolist controlling all the plants. This translates into production of q_n^* at each of its separate plants. Thus aggregate output Q_N^* must satisfy $MC = MR_N$. Or equivalently, the per-plant output level q_N^* satisfies $MC = MR_n$. Either approach determines the same monopoly price P^m.

Now suppose the industrial structure changes from monopoly to monopolistic competition. Each of the monopolist's production plants has become an independent firm. Increased competition, it can be anticipated, will lead to greater output and lower f.o.b. prices. But how does this work out?

In Figure 9.8 the independent firm's *perceived* demand curve d_n is more elastic (flatter) than the monopolist's per-plant demand curve D_n. The curve d_n is more elastic than D_n because, by lowering price relative to its neighbors, each firm can win some customers away from them. (Whereas, when the industry was one single firm, the monopolist

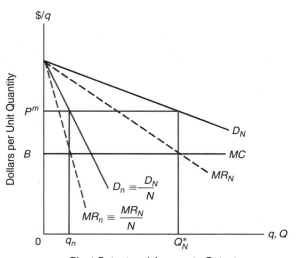

Figure 9.7. Monopoly Solutions: Aggregate and Plant

For a given number of plants N, the monopolist's effective aggregate demand curve is D_N. Curve $D_n = D_N/N$ is the pro rata *plant* demand curve. MR_N and $MR_n = MR_N/N$ are the associated Marginal Revenue curves. Marginal Cost is assumed to be constant at the level B. The profit-maximizing aggregate output is Q_N^* (where $MC = MR_N$), and plant output is q_n^* (where $MC = MR_n$). Of course, $Q_n^* = Nq_n^*$. For either the plant or the firm solution, the same profit-maximizing price P^m is found along the associated demand curve.

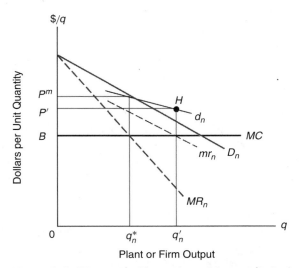

Figure 9.8. Monopoly Plant versus Monopolistic-Competition Firm, at Monopoly Solution

The solution for the monopoly plant, where $MC = MR_n$ at output q_n^* and associated monopoly price P^m is the same as in the preceding diagram. However, once the monopoly plant becomes an independent firm, at price P^m the firm's perceived demand curve is d_n. This curve is more elastic than the pro rata demand curve D_n, because the firm can win customers from its neighbors if it lowers its price. The firm will therefore attempt to achieve the solution H at output q_n', where Marginal Cost MC cuts the curve mr_n.

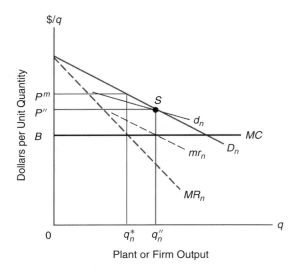

Figure 9.9. Monopoly Plant versus Monopolistic-Competition Firm, at Monopolistic-Competition Equilibrium

Curve mr_m is the Marginal Revenue associated with the *perceived* (flatter) firm demand curve d_n. With N firms, point S in the diagram represents a monopolistic-competition equilibrium. Each firm is maximizing profit since $MC = mr_n$. This outcome is consistent with equilibrium of the industry as a whole, because the combination of output q_n'' and price P'' constitutes point on the pro rata demand curve D_n. Price is lower and output greater than in the monopoly case.

would not allow its separate plants to cut price at one another's expense.) Corresponding to the *more elastic* firm demand curve d_n is a *higher* perceived Marginal Revenue curve mr_n.[4] The firm in Figure 9.8 therefore maximizes profits at point H, producing output q_n', where $mr_n = MC \equiv B$. Since the firm produces an output q_n' that exceeds the monopoly per-plant output q_n^*, it would have to set an f.o.b. price P' lower than the monopoly price P^m.

Figure 9.8 suggests, correctly, that the output of a firm under monopolistic competition is greater than the per-plant output of an ordinary monopolist. The argument as presented, however, is flawed: the solution with output q_n' sold at price P' is *not possible as an overall equilibrium of the industry*. Since the firms are assumed identical, no single firm can sell more than its pro rata share of the overall demand – the D_n curve in the diagram. The flatter d_n demand curve is therefore an illusion (just as the strictly horizontal demand curve faced by the firm in pure competition is an illusion). Any single firm can hope that, if it cuts price, it can expand output along d_n. And indeed, *if* its competitors kept their prices unchanged, it could do so. But in equilibrium the N identical firms will all charge the same price. So if a firm cuts its price, others will do the same; sales per firm will expand less than expected. The firms all together will move along the steeper pro rata demand curve D_n curve rather than along their "illusory" d_n curves.

The final equilibrium is represented in Figure 9.9 by point S on the pro rata demand curve D_n. The firm still perceives an "illusory" demand curve d_n and its relatively flat associated mr_n curve. Now, however, the firm's optimum $MC = B = mr_n$ leads to the price-quantity combination P'', q_n'', which lies along the pro rata demand curve D_n. So the firm's solution is now consistent with its pro rata share of the overall consumer demand. Each firm's output, though not as large as Figure 9.8 had suggested, still exceeds the output the monopolist would set at each of its plants ($q_n'' > q_n^*$). And the price to consumers is lower ($P'' < P^m$).

---

[4] Since $MR \equiv P(1 + 1/\eta)$, as the demand elasticity η becomes greater (takes a larger negative value), Marginal Revenue is higher – approaching P as η goes to $-\infty$.

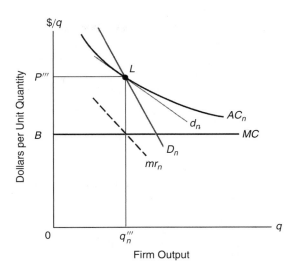

Figure 9.10. Long-Run Equilibrium: Representative Firm in Monopolistic Competition

The short-run equilibrium conditions of the preceding diagram continue to hold: $MC = mr_n$, and the representative firm's price-output combination at L lies on the true pro rata demand curve D_n. The additional long-run condition is that entry or exit takes place until the representative firm earns zero profit (price equals Average Cost AC_n).

What about long-run equilibrium, for which entry and exit have to be taken into account? Depending upon the fixed costs, in the short-run equilibrium of Figure 9.9 the typical firm might either be earning an economic profit (which would induce new firms to enter) or suffering an economic loss (which would induce some old firms to exit). Let us assume that the short-run equilibrium is profitable, so that new firms enter. The true pro rata demand curve $D_n \equiv D_N/N$ then shifts inward (to the left); so does the illusory d_n as viewed by an existing firm.[5]

Figure 9.10 shows the long-run solution for the representative firm as point L. Here all three equilibrium conditions are satisfied: (1) each firm chooses the level of output that maximizes profits ($MC = mr_n$); (2) the aggregate quantity that firms supply equals the quantity that consumers demand (the firm's price-output combination is consistent with the pro-rata demand curve D_n); and (3) no firms want to enter or exit (each firm earns zero economic profit). (The zero-profit condition is represented in the diagram by the tangency of the firm's perceived demand curve d_n with its Average Cost curve AC_n at point L.) So the equilibrium output is Q_n''' and price is P_n'''. At this equilibrium, total industry output is greater than what would be produced by a monopolist who owned all the different plants. Price under monopolistic competition is therefore lower than under monopoly.

EXAMPLE 9.5 ADVERTISING AND COMPETITION

The competitive element in monopolistic competition is greater, and the monopolistic element smaller, the greater the elasticity of demand. One influence upon elasticity is the degree to which consumers know prices. If consumers are poorly

---

[5] This shift is due to dividing the aggregate demand curve D_N horizontally by a larger N. However, a larger number of varieties allows a better match to consumer desires. So as N rises, D_N will also rise (see Figure 9.5). However, in the ratio D_N/N that defines the D_n curve, the numerator rises less than the denominator. When the number of firms increases from 2 to 3, N increases by 50%. But, in general, consumers' demand prices will increase by a smaller percentage. So the D_n curve must, at least eventually, shift inward as N rises. The same holds for the d_n curve.

informed and do not know they can get better prices elsewhere, the demand curve facing each firm is less elastic – so firms can charge higher prices.

A natural experiment to test this hypothesis arose in New York in 1979. Because of a strike, the three major newspapers in New York City (the *Times*, *Post*, and *Daily News*) suspended publication from August 10 to October 5. A newspaper in neighboring Long Island, *Newsday*, continued publishing. Lacking their regular newspapers, shoppers in New York City had less access to supermarket food advertisements in comparison with residents of the suburban areas served by *Newsday*.

Amihai Glazer studied prices for six products (peaches, grapes, lettuce, watermelon, chicken, and ground beef) in Queens County within New York City, in comparison with neighboring Nassau County outside the city.[a] He found that over the period August 14–18, the first week of the strike, prices in Queens supermarkets increased by 3.4% more than in Nassau supermarkets. In contrast, over the period August 23–October 6, which saw the reappearance of the *Post* in New York City, Queens prices changed by about 8.8% less than in Nassau.

These differential price changes were observed for supermarkets, which do normally advertise in newspapers, but were not observed for prices charged by small fruit and vegetable stores, which do not generally advertise in newspapers.

Another study by Jeffrey Milyo and Joel Waldfogel examined changes in Rhode Island liquor prices after a Supreme Court ruling in 1996 permitting advertising of liquor prices.[b] Once advertising was allowed, stores cut prices of advertised liquors about 20%. But prices of other products, at both advertising and nonadvertising stores, did not change.

---

[a] Amihai Glazer, "Advertising, Information and Prices – A Case Study," *Economic Inquiry*, v. 19 (October 1981).

[b] Jeffrey Milyo and Joel Waldfogel, "The Effect of Price Advertising on Prices: Evidence in the Wake of 44 Liquormart," *American Economic Review*, v. 89 (December 1999).

A second question is: under monopolistic competition will consumers be offered *more variety* (in comparison with a multiplant monopolist)? In terms of the ring model, would the number of independent firms (each serving its own clientele) under monopolistic competition be greater or smaller than the number of separate production locales under monopoly? It turns out that the result could go either way. When the plants operated by a monopolist become independent competing firms, the per-plant profit declines. But these profits may still be positive. If so, new firms will *enter*, increasing the variety offered to consumers. On the other hand, when the separate plants become independent firms, what was a positive per-plant monopoly profit could turn into a per-firm loss. If so, some firms would *exit*, reducing variety.

CONCLUSION

Under monopolistic competition, aggregate output is greater and price is lower than under multiplant monopoly. But the number of independent firms under monopolistic competition, each offering its own unique variety, could be either larger or smaller than the profit-maximizing number of varieties offered by a monopolist producer. Thus, though consumers benefit from a lower price under monopolistic competition, they may or may enjoy not a better assortment of varieties.

EXAMPLE 9.6 CUSTOMIZATION IN THE U.S. ECONOMY

In recent years the United States has seen an astounding increase in the range of product varieties offered consumers. A study by W. Michael Cox and Richard Alm documented this development,[a] as summarized in the table.

Product choices in the U.S. economy

Product type	Early 1970s	Late 1990s
Vehicle models	140	260
Vehicle styles	654	1,212
Personal computer models	0	400
Software titles	0	250,000
Websites	0	4,000,000+
Movie releases	267	458
Airports	11,261	18,292
Amusement parks	362	1,174
McDonald's menu items	13	43
National soft drink brands	20	87
Milk types	4	19
Levi's jean styles	41	70
Running shoe styles	5	285
Women's hosiery styles	5	90
Contact lens types	1	36
Bicycle types	8	31

Source: Selected from Cox and Alm, Exhibit 1.

Variety has increased not only for new products such as computers but even for long-established goods and services including movie releases, soft-drink brands, women's hosiery, bicycles, and milk.

The authors emphasize that, by failing to allow for the value of variety, standard national income measures such as GNP drastically understate the real increases in consumer well-being that have taken place in recent decades.

[a] W. Michael Cox and Richard Alm, "The Right Stuff: America's Move to Mass Customization," Federal Reserve Bank of Dallas, *1998 Annual Report.*

In the preceding Example, most of the tabulated products and services are probably generated by industries whose market structures more closely fit the monopolistic competition model than the pure monopoly model. So, though a direct test is unavailable, there is ground for doubting – despite the theoretical possibility – that monopolies offer more variety.

SUMMARY   Firms can sometimes choose the characteristics of the product offered to consumers, including product *quality* and product *variety.*

Quality refers to a characteristic like durability or reliability that is unambiguously desirable. Firms then effectively offer consumers some underlying service z generated by the product, with z equal to the physical output times the quality per unit of output.

In a competitive market, supply and demand for the service will determine its implicit price $\mathbb{P}_z$. The firm will set its Marginal Cost of providing service equal to that price: $MC_z = \mathbb{P}_z$. In doing so it will balance generating more service by increasing quantity q and by improving quality ℓ. Varying production conditions can cause different firms to produce goods of differing qualities. In any case, the price of the nth firm's product must be proportional to its quality: $P_n = \ell_n \times \mathbb{P}_z$.

A monopolistic firm would set $MC_z = MR_z$. So it would produce a smaller amount of the desired service than a competitive industry, and would generally do so by reducing both the quantity and the quality offered.

A monopolist would always adopt an invention that reduces cost without hurting quality. Also, *if* consumers are fully informed, a monopolist would always adopt an invention that improves quality without raising production costs. If, however, consumers are initially imperfectly informed, firms have to consider whether it is worth while building a reputation for producing a superior product.

The problem of *variety* arises when consumer tastes are distributed over some dimension such as size or color. A monopolist would choose a product assortment and associated prices and quantities so as to maximize its overall profit.

Under monopolistic competition, each variety is produced by an independent firm. Each separate firm has some monopoly power (faces a demand curve that is not perfectly elastic). The competitive element in monopolistic competition is provided by firms producing similar though not identical products, to whom customers can transfer their business. In comparison with ordinary monopoly, monopolistic competition leads to greater aggregate output and lower price, but may not lead to more product variety.

QUESTIONS

†The answers to daggered questions appear at the end of the book.

For Review

1. How does monopolistic competition differ from pure competition? From pure monopoly?
2. In monopolistic competition, why is the firm's perceived demand curve flatter than the true demand curve?
3. Why is the firm's perceived demand curve in monopolistic competition analogous to the horizontal demand curve faced by the firm in pure competition?
†4. If a monopolist normally produces a smaller quantity of a product than a competitive industry, is it correct to presume that the monopolist would normally also offer a product of lower quality?
†5. a. Would a monopolist ever suppress an invention that lowered the cost of producing its product without reducing quality?
   b. Would it ever suppress an invention raising quality with no increase of cost?
   c. Will consumers in either case necessarily be better off if the invention is adopted?
6. What conditions make it more profitable for a firm to produce high-quality rather than low-quality products?
†7. What is the trend toward "mass customization" in recent decades? What does it imply for the ability of GNP to measure real increases in consumer well-being?

†8. A common criticism of markets is that sellers spend resources on advertising, an allegedly wasteful use of resources, which they recover by raising prices to consumers. Do advertising expenditures necessarily lead to higher prices? Why or why not?

For Further Thought and Discussion

†1. Some analysts assert that there is "excessive competition" among hospitals. Allegedly, too many hospitals acquire expensive diagnostic machinery such as CAT scanners, which remains idle much of the time. These analysts propose that in each community just one or a very few hospitals should obtain such devices; anyone validly needing to use them could be directed to those hospitals. Comment, in the light of the discussion in the text, about the quality of service likely to be provided by monopolized versus competitive industries.

†2. Is there a reason to expect monopolistic competition (rather than pure competition) to emerge when the desired commodity is really a single "quality" characteristic contained in the marketed good? Explain.

3. Would the price-quantity equilibrium under monopolistic competition tend to lie between that achieved under pure monopoly on the one hand, and pure competition on the other? Explain.

†4. Suppose that every peach looks good in the store, but half of them turn out to be inedible. Given that fact, suppose the consumers' demand curve for peaches on the shelf is $P = 100 - 2Q$. What would the demand curve be if all peaches were good?

†5. Could a quality-improving invention in a competitive industry ever reduce consumer welfare?

†6. It is sometimes argued that only relatively high-quality products can "bear the cost" of shipment to distant locations. Thus, California oranges shipped to New York are (on average) better quality than those consumed by Californians at home. Does this follow from the analysis in this chapter? [*Hint*: Does it cost much more to ship high-quality oranges than low-quality oranges?]

†7. Would imposition of a fixed per-unit tax (e.g., 10 cents per gallon of gasoline) tend to increase or decrease the equilibrium quality of gasoline (miles per gallon) offered on the market?

8. Mr. A says: "A monopolist will produce a product of higher quality, since cut-throat competition must lead to a decline in quality." Mr. B says: "A monopolist produces a smaller quantity of product than would a competitive industry, and by the same logic will also produce a product of lesser quality." Is either correct, or are they both wrong?

†9. In an attempt to reduce tobacco production and thereby raise prices received by tobacco farmers, a government program introduced in 1933 allotted quotas to farmers that fixed the number of acres that could be planted. Over the years production expanded anyway, since the farmers responded by applying more fertilizer, irrigating more intensively, etc. In 1965 the program was reformed, replacing acreage limitations with quotas that fixed the number of pounds that each farmer could sell. Would you expect the original and the reformed programs to have different effects upon the quality of tobacco produced by American farmers? Explain.

†10. Suppose that in an initial period firms choose machinery and product designs that commit them to a particular level of quality for five rather than two years. Explain why this increases the firm's incentives to produce a high-quality product.

†11. We stated in Section 9.1.2 that a quality-improving invention need not lead the monopolist to reduce Q, the amount of physical product produced. Prove this. [*Hint*: Convert Figure 9.2 (where the vertical axis is in "total" units) to a diagram like Figure 9.3 (where

the vertical axis is in "average-marginal" units). The stretching of the Total Cost curve from C_z^o to C_z' in the "total" diagram implies that the MC_z curve in the "average-marginal" diagram is lower over some range. A lower MC_z, together with a (nearly) level MR_z, means that the profit-maximizing service output Z could be *more than twice* the preinvention amount.]

[†]12. Explain why the various D_N curves in Figure 9.5 eventually become parallel to the D_∞ curve. [*Hint*: Transport costs can be regarded as a *tax* upon consumption, but the tax is effective only for consumers who are not "choked out" of the market.]

[†]13. Example 9.1 indicated a decline in the average selling price for used cars as the age of the car being sold increases. Suppose that we can observe the selling prices only of used cars that the owner wants to get rid of. Do you think that the decline in average selling price with age is a good measure of the decline in quality of the average car (whether sold or not) as it ages?

10 Competition Among the Few: Oligopoly and Strategic Behavior

An industry that consists of only a small number of firms is called an oligopoly. If there are just two firms, the term duopoly is used. Oligopoly stands between pure competition (many suppliers) and pure monopoly (a single supplier).

Facing only a few competitors, each firm is in a "strategic" situation. In choosing its own price or output, it needs to consider how its rivals will individually react.[1] The best price for firm A to charge depends on what firms B and C are charging, and similarly the best choices for B and C depend upon what firm A does. This chapter introduces the *theory of games*, the method used by economists to predict the likely outcomes when decision-makers find themselves engaged in strategic choices.[2]

10.1   STRATEGIC BEHAVIOR: THE THEORY OF GAMES

A game, in the mathematical sense, is a way of picturing social interactions. Two distinct elements must be kept in mind: (a) the pattern of payoffs, and (b) the protocol of play. The *pattern of payoffs* reflects the mix of shared versus opposed interests. If a particular outcome is good for John, is it also good for Mary? Or can John make himself better off only by making Mary worse off? The other element, the *protocol of play*, corresponds to the "rules of the game." Do the parties take turns, or do they move simultaneously? Can a chosen move be revoked? Are the players allowed to communicate? Both elements, the pattern of payoffs and the protocol of play, enter into all game-theory solutions.

Patterns of Payoffs

Table 10.1 is an illustrative *payoff matrix* reflecting Paul Revere's famous ride. The redcoats had to come by land or by sea, and their choice could be observed from the steeple of Boston's Old North Church. Paul Revere's task was to carry the message (signalled by lanterns in the church steeple – "One if by land, two if by sea") to the American defenders at Lexington and Concord. In Table 10.1 the rows represent possible Attacker (British) strategies; the columns represent Defender (American) strategies. In each cell, the paired numbers are the payoffs: the first number is the payoff to the Row player, the second the payoff to the Column player. If Defender correctly matches the point of attack, Attacker loses 10 and Defender gains 10. But if Defender makes the wrong choice, Attacker gains 25 and Defender loses 25. Notice that in this table the numbers vary from cell to cell, but within each cell they add up to a fixed sum (zero). Such a pattern of payoffs, representing a situation of totally divergent interests,

Table 10.1 Zero-sum game: land or sea?

		Defender's choice of strategy	
		Land	Sea
Attacker's choice of strategy	Land	−10, +10	+25, −25
	Sea	+25, −25	−10, +10

---

[1] Monopolistic competition (discussed in the preceding chapter), like oligopoly, falls between pure competition and pure monopoly. But in monopolistic competition there are, by assumption, enough firms so that no supplier has to consider the possible reactions of any *single* competitor.

[2] The path-breaking book on the theory of games, by the mathematician John Von Neumann and the economist Oskar Morgenstern, is titled *Theory of Games and Economic Behavior*.

Table 10.2 Mutuality of interests: the coordination game

		B's choice of strategy	
		Right	Left
A's choice of strategy	Right	+15, +15	−100, −100
	Left	−100, −100	+10, +10

is called a "constant-sum game." (Or in this case, more specifically a "zero-sum game," since the winner's gain exactly equals the loser's loss.)

Table 10.2 pictures the opposite extreme, a pure Coordination Game. Here the players' interests are in complete accord. Imagine two cars moving in opposite directions on an otherwise empty highway. Each driver can choose to drive on the right or to drive on the left. If they coordinate their choices to both choose Right, by assumption they obtain their best payoffs 15,15. Coordinating on Left is (as assumed here) not quite so good, with payoffs 10,10. (Perhaps the drivers find it easier to drive on the right.) But the crucial point is that if they fail to coordinate, each loses 100 (the cars crash). Once again the numbers may vary from cell to cell, but now within each cell the payoffs are identical for the two players. Their interests are in complete harmony.

Complete harmony of interests and total divergence of interests are the extreme cases. Intermediate situations can blend opposed and parallel interests in many different ways. An important class of situations, the Prisoners' Dilemma, is illustrated in the payoff matrix of Table 10.3.

Starting with Panel (a), suppose the police have apprehended two men, accomplices in a crime, but the evidence against them is weak. Lacking a confession, the authorities will be able to impose only a minor penalty. But if either prisoner confesses, conviction on a major count is guaranteed. Isolating the prisoners from one another, the district attorney offers to let either one go free in return for his turning state's evidence – provided that the other does not also do so. (If both confess, each will receive a reduced punishment.)

In Panel (a) each prisoner has the strategy options Confess or Don't Confess. The degree of shared interests is indicated by the identical second-best payoffs (−1 each) in the upper-left cell and their identical second-worst payoffs (−24 each) in the lower-right cell. But the prisoners also have opposed interests, as shown in the other two cells: the best outcome for each (0) goes along with the other's very worst outcome (−36).

Table 10.3 The Prisoners' Dilemma: two versions

		Months of imprisonment	
		Don't confess	Confess
Panel(a)	Don't confess	−1, −1	−36, 0
	Confess	0, −36	−24, −24
		Rank-ordered payoffs	
		Small output	Large output
Panel(b)	Small output	3, 3	1, 4
	Large output	4, 1	2, 2

Table 10.4 Farm drainage as a public good: a Prisoners' Dilemma

	Pump	Don't pump
Pump	2, 2	−3, 5
Don't pump	5, −3	0, 0

The "dilemma" here is that *each does better confessing, regardless of what his accomplice does* – even though they could gain by both refusing to confess.

Panel (b) of Table 10.3 is equivalent to Panel (a), except that the numbers in the cells indicate only the *rank* ordering of the outcomes. For each player 4 is best, 3 second best, 2 next, and 1 is worst. Any situation described by this rank ordering of payoffs corresponds logically to a Prisoners' Dilemma.

The rank-ordered pattern of payoffs in Panel (b) can be applied to chiseling in cartels (Chapter 8). If both firms abide by the cartel agreement and restrict output, the outcome is the second-highest payoff for each: 3,3. But, *regardless of what the other firm does*, each does better violating the agreement. If firm A abides by the agreement and limits its output, firm B can gain its best outcome of 4 by producing without restriction. And if firm A is a violator and does not limit its output, firm B does better for itself if it also produces without restriction (payoff of 2 rather than 1).

International armaments represent another Prisoners' Dilemma situation. All countries together might be better off in a disarmed world. But if other nations disarm, a single armed nation could successfully attack any of the others. And when all others are armed, no single nation is likely to expose itself by disarming unilaterally. The upshot is that all nations, or at rate the great majority of nations, continue to arm themselves.

An Application: Public Goods – Two-Person versus Multiperson Prisoners' Dilemma

A commodity is called a public good if its consumption by any one person does not reduce the amount available to others. If a public good is provided to *any* consumer, that makes it available to *every* consumer. A radio signal intended for receiver A can equally well be picked up by receivers B, C, D, ... An Internet website intended for one class of customer can equally well be visited by anyone else.[3]

Imagine a group of farmers attempting to improve marshy soil by drainage. In pumping excess water from his own field, each individual farmer finds himself also partially draining his neighbors' fields – he is providing them with a public good. In that case it may not pay any single farmer to pump even if, were everyone to pump, all would be better off.

In Table 10.4 the *rank ordering* of the payoffs is consistent with Panel (b) of Table 10.3. So this situation is once again a Prisoner's Dilemma. For each farmer the strategy options are Pump and Don't Pump. Numerically, the table sets the per-farmer cost of pumping at 8, while the per-farmer benefit is 5 multiplied by the number of pumpers.

---

[3] A radio broadcast could be coded to exclude undesired users, and a website might require a password. When such exclusionary devices are effective, the commodity is no longer a public good.

Table 10.5 Farm drainage as a multiperson Prisoners' Dilemma

	Number of other farmers pumping				
Farmer A's choices	0	1	2	3	4
Pump	−3	2	7	12	17
Don't pump	0	5	10	15	20

So each farmer is individually better off choosing Don't Pump, even though the resulting 0,0 payoffs are worse for both sides than the 2,2 achievable if they were both to pump.

Table 10.5 shows how the logic of the Prisoners' Dilemma extends to more than two decision-makers. As before, for any single farmer A the choices are Pump and Don't Pump. The columns represent the number of other farmers, apart from A, who might also be pumping (and thereby helping to provide the public good). Under the assumptions here, the payoffs are such that Don't Pump always remains the better choice for farmer A *regardless of the number of others who are pumping*. And since farmer A is typical of all the others, no single farmer will provide the public good of drainage. So Table 10.5 represents a Multiperson Prisoners' Dilemma.

The Prisoners' Dilemma payoff pattern is a kind of social trap. All the farmers would benefit from an enforceable contract whereby each would provide his share of pumping, in consideration of everyone else doing the same. But each individual farmer has an incentive to cheat on such a contract. Later chapters will deal with Prisoners' Dilemma and other possible social traps, together with ways of escaping them.

Pure Strategies

In game theory a *solution* is a prediction of the strategies that rational players will select in the light of opponents' possible choices. Solutions depend upon both the pattern of payoffs and the protocol of play.

For a given pattern of payoffs, the protocol ("rules of the game") can vary in many ways. Consider one possible difference in the rules: whether the parties move *simultaneously* or *in sequence*. If the players move sequentially, the rules must also specify who goes first and who goes last. [*Note:* Simultaneity in game theory refers not to clock times but to equivalent states of information. Choices are considered simultaneous even if A makes his choice first in time, provided that B has to make her decision without knowing A's.]

SEQUENTIAL PLAY In the Coordination Game (Table 10.2) under the sequential protocol of play, whoever moves first should choose Right. The second mover will then rationally match the first mover's choice, so the solution is the strategy-pair (Right, Right) with payoff 15 to Row and 15 to Column.

The solution concept just employed is called the "perfect equilibrium."[4] Each player makes a rational decision, on the assumption that the opponent will choose rationally when it comes to his or her turn.

---

[4] Or, more explicitly, the "subgame-perfect equilibrium" concept.

Table 10.6 The Entry-Deterrence game

		Player B (monopolist)	
		Resist	Tolerate
Player A (potential entrant)	Enter	−10, 30	20, 80
	Stay out	0, 100	0, 100

With regard to sequential-move solutions, two important questions are: (1) Who does better, the first mover or the second mover? (2) Are the results "efficient?" That is, does some other pair of choices yield payoffs better for both parties, or at least better for one side without being worse for the other?

In the Land or Sea game of Table 10.1, if the protocol calls (say) for Row as Attacker to move first, there are two perfect equilibria: (Land, Land) and (Sea, Sea), each with payoffs −10,+10. The advantage is to the second mover. Although "biased" in this sense, the result remains efficient. No other strategy combination yields a better outcome for both players.

In the general Prisoners' Dilemma pattern pictured in Panel (b) of Table 10.3, the perfect equilibrium leads to payoffs 2,2 regardless of who moves first. So there is neither a first mover advantage nor a last mover advantage in Prisoner's Dilemma games. But here the perfect-equilibrium solution is not efficient. If both players were instead to choose Don't Confess, their payoffs would be 3,3 rather than 2,2.

Up to now all the illustrations have been of *symmetrical* games: each player's situation is the mirror image of the other's. Table 10.6, the Entry-Deterrence game, represents an *asymmetrical* situation. Suppose a monopoly currently exists, but a competitor threatens to enter. If entry occurs, the incumbent monopolist could Resist (by waging a price war to drive out the newcomer) or else might Tolerate the intrusion (so as to retain a share of its former monopoly profit).

Suppose the protocol is sequential, with the potential entrant (Row) moving first. Under the numerical assumptions here, the perfect-equilibrium strategy-pair is (Enter, Tolerate) – with payoff 20 to the new entrant and payoff 80 to the former monopolist. But suppose the monopolist were to threaten the potential competitor: "If you enter I will resist, which means you will get −10 rather than +20. So you had better stay out." If this threat were *credible*, Row should rationally stay out. Under the protocol assumed here, however, the threat is *not credible*. Given that entry has occurred, the monopolist loses by carrying it out. To make such a threat credible, the monopolist would have to somehow change either the payoffs or the rules of the game.

Here is one possibility. The monopolist might say: "You are not the only potential entrant I will be facing. I expect to be dealing repeatedly with potential competitors like you. This means that the payoff numbers in Table 10.6 are incorrect – they don't tell the full picture. Because, if I give in to you now, others will expect me to do the same. To achieve a tough reputation and thereby deter others, I will simply have to resist if you enter." The monopolist is saying that the (Enter,Tolerate) payoffs are not 20,80 but perhaps something more like 20,0. If these were indeed the payoffs, the monopolist would rationally respond to Enter with Resist. Knowing this, the Row player should rationally choose Stay Out. (Possible disagreement or uncertainty about the payoffs will be taken up in the Information chapter that follows.)

Table 10.7 Profits in duopoly

		Output of firm B		
		Zero	Small	Large
Output of firm A	Zero	0, 0	0, 1500	0, 2000
	Small	1500, 0	1300, 1300	800, 1400
	Large	2000, 0	1400, 800	500, 500

EXERCISE 10.1

Table 10.7 shows the payoffs (profits) for duopolists who can each choose among the *three* strategies Zero, Small, or Large levels of output. (i) The protocol is sequential: firm A moves first, then firm B. Find the perfect equilibrium. Is there a first-mover or last-mover advantage? Is the solution efficient for the two firms together? (But recall that an efficient outcome for the two firms could hurt consumers.) (ii) Answer the same questions, but now assume that after firm B responds to A's initial choice, firm A can then *revise* its own decision. (Thus firm A has both the first move and the last move.)

ANSWER: (i) A's best choice is Large output. B would respond with Small, and the payoffs are 1400,800. The first mover has the advantage. The solution is efficient, since no other cell yields higher payoffs for both firms. (ii) It might seem here that firm A would benefit from having both the first move *and* the last move. But not so! Firm B should ignore A's initial choice, which makes no difference for the final outcome. Instead, firm B should act as if its own choice were the first move, and choose Large. The final outcome would be the strategy-pair (Small, Large) with payoffs 800,1400. (So what is involved here is really not a *first-move advantage* but rather a *last-move disadvantage*.)

SIMULTANEOUS PLAY   Under the simultaneous-move protocol each player must make his or her choice without knowing what the opponent has decided to do. In the Prisoners' Dilemma of Table 10.3, the Row player did better choosing the less cooperative strategy (Confess) *no matter what Column chose*. This means he does not have to know what choice Column might be making in order to pick his own best move. And Column can reason in exactly the same way. In game-theory terminology, in Table 10.3 the less cooperative strategy *dominates* the other strategy for both players. So the (Confess, Confess) strategy-pair is a *dominant equilibrium*.

To see what happens when one side has a dominant strategy but the other doesn't, consider the Entry-Deterrence game in Table 10.6. Tolerate does not always give Column a strictly higher payoff than Resist. But Tolerate always yields *at least as much* and sometimes more. So it is natural to extend the previous reasoning and say that Column should always choose even such a "weakly dominant" strategy. Row, in contrast, has no dominant strategy. But, making the inference that Column will choose her weakly dominant strategy (Tolerate), Row's best move is clearly Enter. So the solution is (Enter, Tolerate).

When neither side has a dominant strategy, a broader solution concept for the simultaneous-move protocol is the *Nash equilibrium*. (A dominant equilibrium, if it exists, will also be a Nash equilibrium.) To find the Nash equilibrium, look for a cell in the payoff matrix such that, even if the opponent's strategy were revealed, neither party would benefit from a unilateral change of move. In Table 10.2, for example, there is no dominance. But the (Right, Right) and (Left, Left) strategy-pairs are both Nash equilibria. If either of these were somehow arrived at, neither player would ever want to deviate into a $-100, -100$ payoff situation.

EXERCISE 10.2

Using Table 10.7, now assume a simultaneous-move protocol. Are there one or more dominant equilibria? Nash equilibria?

ANSWER: By inspection, there is no dominant equilibrium. But the strategy-pairs (Large, Small) with payoffs 1400,800 and (Small, Large) with payoffs 800,1400 are both Nash equilibria.

Mixed Strategies

Returning to Table 10.1, that payoff matrix has no dominant equilibrium. Furthermore, if the players are restricted to using only the "pure strategies" shown, there is no Nash equilibrium either. But a Nash equilibrium does exist in "mixed strategies." A player choosing a mixed strategy in effect tosses a coin (the coin having known probabilities, not necessarily even, of coming up one way or the other) and moves accordingly.

Let Attacker (Row) play Land with probability p_R; let Defender (Column) play Land with probability p_C. That implies that Row plays Sea with probability $1 - p_R$ and Column plays Sea with probability $1 - p_C$. Given these probabilities and the payoff numbers in Table 10.1, it is possible to calculate the average or "expected" payoff for each of the two possible strategies, for each player. For example, when Row plays Land he will receive -10 if Column plays Land and 25 if Column plays Sea. So the expected payoff is $(-10)p_C + 25(1 - p_C)$. Similarly, Row's expected payoff from playing Sea is $25 p_C - 10(1 - p_C)$.

The essential idea of mixed strategies is: Keep the opponent in doubt! With this aim, Column as Defender wants to choose a p_C that makes neither Land nor Sea a clearly superior choice for the attacker. So she will choose a p_C that makes Row's average payoff the same whichever strategy he chooses. Setting $(-10)p_C + 25(1 - p_C)$ equal to $25 p_C - 10(1 - p_C)$, her solution is $p_C = 0.5$. By corresponding reasoning, the solution for Row is $p_R = 0.5$. So, the prediction is, the players will each randomly mix the two pure strategies on a 50:50 basis.

More generally, the solution depends upon the payoff numbers, so it will not generally involve a 0.5, 0.5 mixture. For a payoff matrix in the general symmetric form of Table 10.8, algebra shows that the mixed-strategy equilibrium has Row choosing his first (top) strategy with probability p_R and Column choosing her first (left-hand) strategy with probability p_C in accordance with:

$$P_R = P_C = \frac{d - c}{a - b - c + d} \tag{10.1}$$

Table 10.8 General symmetric payoff matrix

	Left	Right
Top	a, a	c, b
Bottom	b, c	d, d

One might think that mixed strategies are a "purely academic" idea with no practical application. On the contrary, mixed strategies can be observed whenever intelligent play involves keeping the opponent guessing.

EXAMPLE 10.1 MIXED STRATEGIES IN TENNIS

Tennis serves are usually aimed to the receiver's left or right. (Center serves are unusual, at least in championship play.) Since the server needs to keep the receiver guessing, rational play dictates a mixed strategy. The best mixture will depend upon many factors: whether the players are right-handed or left-handed, possible weaknesses of forehands or backhands, individual peculiarities of play, the current point score, the direction of the sun, possible referee bias, and more.

Despite these complications, the *test* of an optimal mixed strategy is that all the pure strategies being played must on average be equally profitable. (If they were not, it would pay to choose the more profitable option more often.) In particular, for the player with the service, serves to the left and serves to the right should have equal success rates.

Mark Walker and John Wooders obtained data on all first serves in 10 important professional tennis matches – most of them final championship matches.[a] If the players were choosing rationally, in a given match there might be a large disparity between the percentages of left and right serves, but left and right serves should have been, on average, equally likely to win points.

Mixed strategies in championship play

Match	Server	Mixture (%)		Win rates (%)	
		Left	Right	Left	Right
74 Wimbledon	Rosewall	93	7	71	60
80 Wimbledon	Borg	37	63	70	66
80 US Open	McEnroe	61	39	61	56
82 Wimbledon	Connors	84	16	67	53
84 French	Lendl	37	63	73	69
87 Australian	Edberg	25	75	63	71
88 Australian	Wilander	26	74	80	63
88 Masters	Becker	63	37	72	65
95 US Open	Sampras	56	44	61	85
97 US Open	Korda	63	37	73	63
Average of differences		39.0%		10.4%	

Source: Adapted from Walker and Wooders, Table 1.

The results reported here refer to the service choices of the ultimate match winner when the score was at "deuce." The left-right mixtures are percentages that sum to 1, since center serves (only about 6%) were not counted. The win rates for both left serves and right serves are all well above 50%, reflecting the advantage at tennis of having the serve. (Winning was defined here as gaining the point, whether earned on the initial service as an ace or only after additional strokes.) The imbalance between left and right service proportions was sometimes very great. Rosewall at Wimbledon in 1974 served left 93% of the time. That was the extreme, but the percent differences between the proportions of left and right serves were generally quite large – averaging about 39%. In contrast, the *win rates* for the two types of service were close together, diverging on average by only around 10%.

The authors' interpretation was that, unconsciously perhaps, championship tennis players appreciate the need to mix their strategy choices, and do so in a way close to the theoretical optimum.

---

[a] Mark Walker and John Wooders, "Minimax Play at Wimbledon," *American Economic Review*, v. 91 (December 2001).

In warfare as in tennis, it is essential to keep the opponent in doubt. Military writers sometimes advise generals always to go round the enemy's flanks, never to make a frontal attack. But that cannot be right, since then the enemy could leave his center bare and place all his strength on the flanks. General William Tecumseh Sherman, in his march through Georgia in 1864, usually preferred to attack the Confederates on one or the other flank. But at Kennesaw Mountain he made an unsuccessful frontal attack, a choice criticized by military historians. The critics failed to realize that, to remain unpredictable, Sherman had to follow a mixed strategy – which dictated that he make frontal attacks some of the time.

CONCLUSION

In the *sequential-play* protocol, the perfect equilibrium concept has each player make a rational (payoff-maximizing) choice on the assumption that the opponent will do the same when it comes to his or her turn. A perfect equilibrium always exists, though it may not be unique. In the *simultaneous-play* protocol, a dominant strategy – one that is better in the strong or weak sense no matter what the opponent does – should be chosen if available. A *dominant equilibrium* exists if even only player has such a strategy available (since then the other player can predict what his opponent will do). In the absence of a dominant equilibrium, the *Nash equilibrium* concept applies. At a Nash equilibrium, no player has an incentive to alter his or her decision, given the other's choice. There may be one, several, or no Nash equilibria in pure strategies. If mixed strategies – probabilistic mixtures of pure strategies aimed at keeping the opponent guessing – are also permitted, a Nash equilibrium always exists.

10.2   DUOPOLY – IDENTICAL PRODUCTS

Apart from the discussion in the preceding Chapter 9 ("Product Quality and Product Variety"), most of the analysis in the text has assumed that firms in an industry are offering identical products. The same simplifying assumption is used here in this section of the chapter. Section 10.3, which follows, will then take up the more realistic assumption that the products offered by competing oligopolists vary from firm to firm.

Table 10.9 Duopoly solutions, industry demand curve:
$P = 100 - (q_1 + q_2)$, **zero cost of production**

	q_1	q_2	Q	P	Π_1	Π_2
Symmetrical						
Collusive	25	25	50	50	1,250	1,250
Cournot	$33\frac{1}{3}$	$33\frac{1}{3}$	$66\frac{2}{3}$	$33\frac{1}{3}$	$111\frac{1}{9}$	$1,111\frac{1}{9}$
Competitive	50	50	100	0	0	0
Asymmetrical						
Stackelberg	50	25	75	25	1,250	625
Threat	50	0	50	50	2,500	0

For a *monopolist* providing a single uniform product, the same profit-maximizing optimum can be achieved either by choosing the most profitable price or the most profitable quantity. (Because along the industry demand curve, the chosen price will determine the quantity that can be sold and vice versa.) But in oligopoly or duopoly, it makes a difference whether the firms engage in quantity competition or price competition. These will be taken up in turn.

Quantity Competition

Consider two duopolists producing an identical product. Firm 1 chooses a level of output q_1 and firm 2 chooses q_2. Suppose the industry demand curve is $P = 100 - Q$, where industry output Q is the sum of the two firm outputs: $Q \equiv q_1 + q_2$. And imagine, for extreme simplicity only, that the Total Cost, Average Cost, and Marginal Cost functions are all zero throughout. (This unlikely assumption might be approximated by a situation where each firm owns a mineral spring gushing forth costlessly in unlimited volume.)

A monopolist would set Marginal Revenue equal to Marginal Cost. Numerically, here, the $MR = MC$ condition would be $100 - 2Q = 0$,[5] implying $Q = 50$. The monopolist, though able to produce any amount without cost, would offer only $Q = 50$ units at price $P = 50$. Its Total Revenue would be $R \equiv P \times Q = 50 \times 50 = 2,500$. And, since costs are zero, the monopolist's profit is $\Pi = R = 2,500$.

What happens when the industry is a duopoly instead? Table 10.9 summarizes several of the possible outcomes.[6]

The upper part of the table shows possible symmetrical outcomes for firms operating under a simultaneous-move protocol. First, the *Collusive solution* occurs when the two firms act together as a collective monopolist or cartel, sharing the gain equally. (By assumption, the "chiselling" problem has somehow been solved.) Since joint profit is maximized when $Q = 50$ and $P = 50$, the firms' separate outputs are $q_1 = q_2 = 25$. The profits are $\Pi_1 = \Pi_2 = 50 \times 25 = 1,250$.

If the firms cannot collude, several other possibilities arise. Skipping to the third line of the table, the opposite extreme is the *Competitive solution*. This holds if the firms behave as price-takers, each using the decision rule Marginal Cost = Price. Since Marginal Cost = 0, a price-taking firm would be willing to produce an indefinitely large amount at any price P even infinitesimally greater than zero. So, in effect, the

---

[5] Recall that if $P = A - BQ$, then $MR = A - 2BQ$.
[6] The discussion here is based in part on M. Shubik, "Information, Duopoly, and Competitive Markets: A Sensitivity Analysis," *Kyklos*, v. 26 (1973), p. 748.

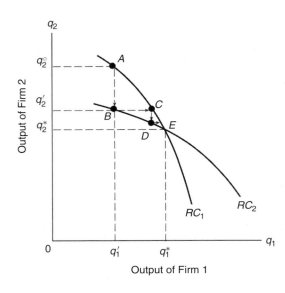

**Figure 10.1. Duopoly Reaction Curves –
Identical Products, Quantity Competition**

Given any output q_2 of firm 2, firm 1 can determine its profit-maximizing output q_1. Considering
all possible levels of q_2, a Reaction Curve RC_1 for the
first firm is defined. Similar reasoning (based on taking q_1 as given) leads to the construction of RC_2,
the Reaction Curve of the second firm. The intersection of the two Reaction Curves determines the
Nash–Cournot equilibrium. A hypothetical dynamic
process $A \to B \to C \to D \to \cdots$ suggests how the
equilibrium at E might eventually be attained.

competitive supply curve runs along the horizontal axis with equation $P = 0$. Combining this with the demand curve $P = 100 - Q$ implies that at competitive equilibrium
$P = 0$ and $Q = 100$. Revenue and profit will be zero for both firms.

On the second line of the table, lying between the Collusive and the Competitive
outcomes, is the *Cournot solution*. Here the underlying assumptions are as follows:
(1) Each firm recognizes that increasing its own output will reduce the market price
P. (2) However, in making its own output decision each firm assumes its competitor's
output is *fixed*. That is, each decision-maker chooses the highest available payoff *given*
the decision of the other. (The Cournot solution corresponds therefore to the Nash
equilibrium in game theory.)

The rationale for the Cournot solution goes as follows. For any output q_2 chosen
by the second firm, the first firm has some profit-maximizing q_1. In effect, firm 1 is a
monopolist over the *remaining* demand not satisfied by the second firm's output q_2.
Plotting firm 1's optimal q_1 as a function of all of its rival's possible outputs leads to the
Reaction Curve RC_1 shown in Figure 10.1. Firm 2 has a corresponding Reaction Curve
RC_2. The Reaction Curves are mutually consistent only at the point of intersection,
which therefore defines the Cournot equilibrium. (When the firms are both on their
Reaction Curves, each is responding optimally to the other's decision, so neither will
want to change.) The Nash–Cournot solution lies between the two extremes represented
by the Collusive and Competitive solutions.

Figure 10.1 also illustrates a possible dynamic process leading to the Cournot equilibrium. Suppose firm 2 initially produces q_2°. The curve RC_1 indicates that firm 1 will
then want to produce q_1' in response (point A in the diagram). But if firm 1 produces
q_1', firm 2 reacts by moving to point B on its Reaction Curve RC_2 to produce q_2'. Firm 1
responds further by moving to point C; firm 2 then moves to point D, etc. The result is
that both firms end up at the intersection of the two Reaction Curves.[7]

---

[7] There will be a stable equilibrium if the "cobweb" of dynamic reactions spirals inward (as shown in the diagram)
rather than outward. If the labels of the two RC curves were interchanged, there would be an outward rather
than an inward spiral – in which case one of the firms would end up with a sole monopoly of the industry.

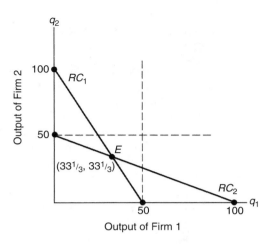

**Figure 10.2. Linear Reaction Curves –
Identical Products, Quantity Competition**

The straight-line Reaction Curves correspond to the data of Exercise 10.3. The firm's demand curves are $P_1 = P_2 = 100 - q_1 - q_2$, and production is assumed costless ($MC_1 = MC_2 \equiv 0$).

EXERCISE 10.3

Use the numerical assumptions of Table 10.5 to find the equations for the Reaction Curves RC_1 and RC_2. Verify that their intersection is indeed the Cournot solution shown in the table.

ANSWER: If firm 1's output q_1 is given, the demand equation for firm 2 is $P = (100 - q_1) - q_2$, with firm 2 regarding q_1 as constant. Since this is a linear demand equation, firm 2's Marginal Revenue is $MR_2 = (100 - q_1) - 2q_2$. To obtain firm 2's best choice of q_2 as a function of firm 1's different possible choices of q_1, set $MR_2 = MC_2$. Since Marginal Cost MC_2 is zero, the equation becomes $100 - q_1 - 2q_2 = 0$, so that $q_2 = 50 - q_1/2$. This is the equation for RC_2. Similar reasoning yields $q_1 = 50 - q_2/2$ as the equation for RC_1. Solving the two Reaction Curve equations simultaneously, the solution is $q_1 = q_2 = 33\ 1/3$, as shown in Table 10.9 and pictured in Figure 10.2.

Zero Marginal Cost is of course an extreme assumption. The exercise that follows employs a more normal Marginal Cost function.

EXERCISE 10.4

Use the same industry demand function $P = 100 - Q$ as before, where $Q \equiv q_1 + q_2$. But now suppose the firms' Marginal Cost functions are $MC_1 = 20 + q_1$ and $MC_2 = 20 + q_2$. Find the Reaction Curves and the Cournot solution.

ANSWER: For firm 1, setting $MR_1 = MC_1$ implies $100 - 2q_1 - q_2 = 20 + q_1$, which reduces to $80 - 3q_1 = q_2$. This is the equation for RC_1. By similar reasoning, firm 2's Reaction Curve is $80 - 3q_2 = q_1$. Solving simultaneously, the equilibrium outputs are $q_1 = q_2 = 20$. Therefore $Q = 40$, the equilibrium price is $P = 60$, and profits are $\Pi_1 = \Pi_2 = 600$. (The positive costs of production make the outputs and profits smaller than for the corresponding Cournot solution in Table 10.9.)

EXAMPLE 10.2 PIONEER OLIGOPOLY EXPERIMENT

The economist Lawrence E. Fouraker and the psychologist Sidney Siegel jointly conducted one of the first controlled economic experiments.[a] The experiment simulated a duopoly situation. Each subject, paired with an unknown counterpart, was asked to choose an output. The profit earned depended upon the quantities offered by the two sellers together. One group of trials was conducted under conditions of complete information: each subject knew the counterpart's output choice and profit schedule. A second group of trials was conducted under incomplete information: each subject knew only the quantity decision of the other player.

There were 28 trials – 14 for each of the two informational conditions. In the complete-information case, 5 results were closest to the Collusive solution, $7\frac{1}{2}$ to the Cournot solution, and $1\frac{1}{2}$ to the Competitive solution. (The fraction represented a tie.) In the incomplete-information case, all 14 trials most closely approximated the Cournot solution.

COMMENT

This experiment suggests that the Nash–Cournot solution, where each participant takes as given the quantity decision of the other, is likely to describe outcomes in oligopoly situations – especially in the absence of additional information. Consistent with the Nash–Cournot model, the subjects usually failed to achieve the Collusive arrangement. On the other hand, they seemed aware of how their separate output decisions would affect price, and so were usually able to avoid the disastrous Competitive outcome.

The sensitivity of the experimental observations to the informational conditions was also an important finding. Later studies showed that other details of the market process – for example, whether prices are secretly negotiated or openly posted – affect how closely the final outcome approaches the collusive or the competitive end of the spectrum of possibilities.[b]

---

[a] L. E. Fouraker and S. Siegel, *Bargaining Behavior* (New York: McGraw–Hill, 1963).

[b] Charles R. Plott, "Industrial Organization Theory and Experimental Economics," *Journal of Economic Literature*, v. 20 (December 1982).

In the lower portion of Table 10.9 the firms' payoff functions remain symmetrical, but the *protocol* is asymmetrical. Suppose that firm 1 moves first and is aware of the other firm's Reaction Curve RC_2. These conditions correspond to the Stackelberg[8] solution in the table, the first mover having the advantage.

More specifically, suppose the leader (firm 1) sets an output and commits to it. If so, the follower (firm 2) does best by choosing the corresponding point along its Reaction Curve RC_2. Of course, the leader will choose that output q_1 which, when combined with the follower's correctly predicted output q_2, leads to the most profitable outcome for itself.

---

[8] Heinrich von Stackelberg, 20th-century German economist.

EXERCISE 10.5

Verify the Stackelberg solution shown in Table 10.9.

ANSWER: Since firm 1 is the leader, it chooses the most profitable output for itself, knowing that firm 2 will respond along its Reaction Curve RC_2. In Exercise 10.3 firm 2's Reaction Curve was found to be $q_2 = 50 - q_1/2$. Substituting in the industry demand curve, $P = 100 - (q_1 + q_2)$, leads to the net demand curve facing firm 1: $P = 50 - q_1/2$. Since this is linear, the Marginal Revenue equation for the Stackelberg leader is $MR_1 = 50 - q_1$. Setting $MR_1 = MC$, where $MC = 0$ as assumed here, the leader's optimal output is $q_1 = 50$. The other values shown in Table 10.9 for the Stackelberg solution can then be verified.

Last, the Threat solution in Table 10.9 has the leader respond to entry by carrying out a threat to make q_1 so big as to lower the price to zero. Seeing no way to make a profit, the second firm would stay out. Here the leader firm does as well as if it had the sole monopoly of the industry.

As in the Entry-Deterrence Game (Table 10.6), such a threat is not *credible* under the protocol and payoff assumptions used. The symmetrical Collusive solution is also not achievable under these assumptions, owing to the "chiselling" problem. These solutions might, however, be realized under protocols not considered here, for example ones in which a threatener can guarantee to carry out his threat. The threatener might, for example, post a bond to be forfeited if he fails to follow through. (One's reputation can sometimes serve as such a bond.) But posting a bond or staking one's reputation would then have to be listed as additional strategy options, making for a different game.

Price Competition

Rather than just supplying quantities to the market, firms more usually compete by quoting prices to consumers.[9] It turns out that *price competition is more severe than quantity competition*. The reason is that, if the products are identical, a firm that quotes a price lower than its competitor's takes away not just part of the market but *all* of it.

Suppose that Marginal Cost is $MC = 0$ for both firms, and that firm 1 quotes some positive price P_1. Firm 2 will then set its P_2 just a trifle lower. But then firm 1 can go still lower, and so on – until the final stopping-point where $P_1 = P_2 = 0$! More generally, when duopolist firms choose prices, the Nash outcome (called the Bertrand[10] solution, analogous to the Cournot solution under quantity competition) is the same as the Competitive equilibrium: $P_1 = P_2 = MC$. The following exercise uses the more realistic nonzero Marginal Cost of Exercise 10.4 to obtain a solution that involves positive prices P_1 and P_2.

---

[9] To illustrate the distinction, a shareholder can sell stock by placing a *market order* for a specific number of shares with his broker. Placing a market order means that the seller will accept whatever is the current market price. Alternatively, the shareholder can place a *limit order* that specifies a minimum acceptable price.

[10] Joseph L. F. Bertrand, 1822–1900, French mathematician.

EXERCISE 10.6

Using the same data as in Exercise 10.4, find the Nash–Bertrand solution.

ANSWER: Each firm will undercut the other's price as long as it gains from so doing. So in equilibrium they must charge the same price $P_1 = P_2 = P$. Furthermore, these prices must be equal to the respective Marginal Costs MC_1 and MC_2. The condition $MC_1 = P$ becomes $20 + q_1 = 100 - q_1 - q_2$. The corresponding equation for firm 2 is $20 + q_2 = 100 - q_1 - q_2$. Solving simultaneously gives $q_1 = q_2 = 26 \ 2/3$. Since total output is $Q \equiv q_1 + q_2 = 53 \ 1/3$, the equilibrium price is $46 \ 2/3$. This checks with the numerical values of MC_1 and MC_2.

The preceding exercise illustrates the assertion that price competition is more severe than quantity competition. The outcome under price competition is less favorable for the firms but more favorable for the consumers (output is larger and price is lower) than the corresponding Cournot solution for quantity competition obtained in Exercise 10.4.

Consider next the Stackelberg solution, assuming price is the decision variable and the firms have the same costs of production. The follower (second mover) will always do better than the leader (first mover). If the leader sets a price leaving him any profit at all, the follower will quote a price a bit lower and take away all the business. Since neither firm will want to be the Stackelberg leader, we would not expect to observe Stackelberg equilibria under these conditions.

In contrast, the asymmetrical Threat solution is still valid when price is the decision variable. Here firm 1 as leader would announce that if firm 2 attempts to do any business at all, by either matching or undercutting the leader's price, firm 1 will quote a price so low as to drive out its competitor. If firm 2 believes this threat, it may as well stay out of business completely. Firm 1 gains all the profit, as shown on the bottom line of Table 10.9. Once again, however, to make such a threat credible either the payoff structure or the protocol of the game, or both, must have changed.

EXAMPLE 10.3 STANDARD OIL AND JOHN D. ROCKEFELLER

"Predatory" price-cutting corresponds to the Threat solution of Table 10.9, with price rather than output as the decision variable. A ruthless firm with sufficient resources might always stand ready to wage a price war to drive out any competitors. Having achieved a reputation for doing so, such a predator would not need to execute its threat very often. Occasional punishment meted out to foolish interlopers would suffice to deter others.

John D. Rockefeller's old Standard Oil Company – dissolved in 1911 as a result of a landmark antitrust decision – is often described by historians as a predator. Standard Oil had acquired, before that date, substantial monopoly power in oil refining through merger and acquisitions. It is widely believed that these mergers and acquisitions were mainly secured by predatory price-cutting. But a study by John S. McGee[a] demonstrated that Standard Oil rarely if ever started costly price wars to achieve its monopoly. Rather, it bought out its competitors.

However, Elizabeth Granitz and Benjamin Klein[b] showed that the competitors were willing to sell out at prices favorable to Standard Oil only because of indirect pressures that Standard exerted through railroad rates. Before the 1870s, the three major railroads that transported petroleum products from the Pennsylvania oil regions had repeatedly attempted to form a cartel. The familiar chiselling problem led in each case to breakdowns and rate wars. Standard Oil found an innovative way to enforce the railroad cartel. Once the roads had agreed upon shipment quotas, Standard served as an "evener." If any single railroad secretly cut prices, its traffic would visibly increase. So Standard would simply reduce its own shipments on that road. For its services to the cartel as an evener, Standard was given preferential shipping rates. In 1874–1979 Standard received a 10% rebate, plus a commission on *all* shipments (not just on Standard's own oil) received through Standard's pipeline collection network. For example, while the regular rate in 1878 for shipments to New York was $1.70 per barrel, Standard paid only $1.06. This handicap induced many of the independent oil refiners to sell out to Standard.

The discovery of new fields in Ohio (1885) and especially in Texas (1901) weakened Standard's position. Several new refiners entered, other railroads were transporting oil, and Standard had no established transport network in the new areas. So Standard lost its effective monopoly of the petroleum industry.

---

[a] J. S. McGee, "Predatory Price Cutting: The Standard Oil (NJ) Case," *Journal of Law and Economics*, v. 1 (October 1958).

[b] Elizabeth Granitz and Benjamin Klein, "Monopolization by 'Raising Rivals' Costs': The Standard Oil Case," *Journal of Law and Economics*, v. 39 (April 1996).

CONCLUSION

When duopolists produce identical products, the possible outcomes depend upon the nature of the payoffs (as determined by the market demand curve and the firms' cost functions) and the protocol of play, together with the assumed behavior of the decision-makers. If *quantity* is the decision variable and the simultaneous-move protocol applies, at one extreme the firms may behave as a joint monopolist (the Collusive outcome) and at the other extreme as price-taking competitors (the Competitive outcome). The Nash solution is the intermediate Cournot equilibrium: each firm chooses optimally, given the other firm's production quantity. When *price* is the decision variable instead, the Nash solution is called the Bertrand equilibrium: each firm chooses a profit-maximizing price, given the other's price. Price competition is more severe than quantity competition, and so leads to worse outcomes for the firms (but better outcomes for the consumers). For the sequential-move protocol, the Stackelberg leader (the first mover) is at an advantage under quantity competition but at a disadvantage under price competition.

An Application: "Most-Favored-Customer" Clause[11]

Oligopolists might collude by offering buyers price guarantees. Imagine that only two firms, A and B, sell steel in a small country. For simplicity, suppose each firm considers only two possible price quotations, High and Low. The profit payoffs of Table 10.10

---

[11] This analysis is based largely upon Steven C. Salop, "Practices That (Credibly) Facilitate Oligopoly Coordination," in Joseph E. Stiglitz and G. Frank Mathewson, eds., *New Developments in the Analysis of Market Structures* (Cambridge, MA: M.I.T. Press, 1986).

Table 10.10 The Prisoners' Dilemma: oligopoly profits

		Firm 2 price	
		High	Low
Firm 1 price	High	100, 100	−10, 140
	Low	140, −10	70, 70

indicate that the duopolists are once again caught in a Prisoners' Dilemma. If both choose High, each firm can attain its second-best outcome (numerically, a profit of 100). Yet for either firm Low yields higher profit *regardless* of what the other does. So the two are likely to end up at their next-to-worst outcome – the Prisoners' Dilemma equilibrium strategy-pair (Low, Low) yielding a profit of 70 each.

Each firm could charge the high price provided the other did the same. But suppose such agreements are illegal or unenforceable. The "Most-Favored-Customer" clause is a subtler way of achieving the same effect. Imagine that the duopolist "generously" guarantees each customer that, if it were ever to offer a reduced price to anyone else, the first customer would get the same low price. It may seem that the firm's clientele ought to be happy about the Most-Favored-Customer clause. But notice in Table 10.11 how the payoffs have changed in comparison with Table 10.10. The assumption here is that, if the firm were ever to cut price, the cost of carrying out its guarantee would be 50 units. Thus, for each firm the profit from pricing Low when its competitor is pricing High falls from 140 to only 90. Thus the strategy-pair (Low, Low) with payoffs 70,70 is no longer a dominant equilibrium. True, it remains a Nash equilibrium, but so is the mutually more profitable strategy-pair (High, High) with payoffs 100,100. The firms are likely to be able to coordinate on this superior solution.

This is an instance of a more general paradox often encountered in strategic situations. A player is sometimes better off sacrificing an opportunity. Here the "sacrifice" – arranging to lose rather than to gain profit by cutting price – makes it likely that neither firm will want to cut price.

A different arrangement with somewhat similar consequences is the Meet-or-Release clause. The seller would guarantee a buyer who has not yet taken delivery that any lower price on the market will be matched, else the customer is released from the obligation to buy. (The Most-Favored-Customer clause guarantees that buyers will get the advantage of the seller's own later price cuts, if any; Meet-or-Release guarantees that buyers will get the advantage of *other* firms' lower prices.) The Meet-or-Release clause has the side effect of encouraging the buyer to report when competitors cut prices, thus reducing the likelihood of secret discounts and chiselling.

Table 10.11 The "Most-Favored Customer" clause

		Firm 2 price	
		High	Low
Firm 1 price	High	100, 100	−10, 90
	Low	90, −10	70, 70

One ought not, however, jump to the conclusion that the Most-Favored-Customer clause or the Meet-or-Release clause or similar arrangements are used only to keep prices high. They may have other uses, for example, to protect buyers from price discrimination. Therefore, such clauses are not conclusive evidence of anticompetitive collusion.

10.3 DUOPOLY – DIFFERENTIATED PRODUCTS

In the preceding analysis the duopolists provided identical products. That assumption simplified the analysis, since in equilibrium the firms' prices have to be the same. Moving on now to the more typical situation in which the products differ, in equilibrium the prices need not be equal. Nevertheless, the same underlying forces operate.[12]

Quantity Competition

Previously, the assumed industry demand function was:

$$P = 100 - q_1 - q_2 \tag{10.2}$$

To allow for differentiated products, let s be an index of the *similarity* of the two firms' distinct products, where s ranges from 1 (the products are indistinguishable) down to 0 (the products are so different neither has any effect upon the market for the other). As a numerical illustration, the demand functions might be:

$$P_1 = 100 - q_1 - sq_2 \quad \text{and} \quad P_2 = 100 - sq_1 - q_2 \tag{10.3}$$

When $s = 1$, equation (10.3) reduces to the preceding (10.2). In the opposite limiting case where $s = 0$ instead, the two firms are not competing at all. They would be independent monopolists, each in its own industry.

Under *quantity competition*, the exercise that follows illustrates the nature of the solution.

EXERCISE 10.7

In equations (10.3) suppose $s = \frac{1}{2}$, and for simplicity assume again that costs of production are zero throughout. (i) Find the firms' Reaction Curves and the Nash–Cournot solution. (ii) What happens as s approaches 0? (iii) What happens as s approaches 1?

ANSWER: (i) Following the same reasoning as in Exercise 10.3, the Marginal Revenues now become $MR_1 = (100 - sq_2) - 2q_1$ and $MR_2 = (100 - sq_1) - 2q_2$. Setting $s = \frac{1}{2}$, the Marginal Revenues equal to the zero Marginal Costs, and solving, the Reaction Curves become:

$$q_1 = 50 - q_2/4 \quad \text{and} \quad q_2 = 50 - q_1/4$$

The Reaction Curves intersect at $q_1 = q_2 = 40$ and the implied equilibrium prices are $P_1 = P_2 = 40$. (ii) As s approaches zero, the two demand curves become less

---

[12] In the analysis here the oligopoly firms are producing products of fixed, although distinct, characters. The issues taken up in Chapter 9, as to the types of products (*quality* and *variety*) offered on the market, also arise under oligopoly. These topics are set aside here.

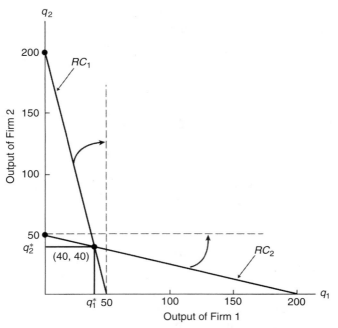

Figure 10.3. Linear Reaction Curves – Differing Products, Quantity Competition

The Reaction Curves correspond to the data of Exercise 10.7. The products are no longer identical, and the demand curves are $P_1 = 100 - q_1 - sq_2$ and $P_2 = 100 - sq_1 - q_2$, where s (the coefficient of similarity) is $\frac{1}{2}$. As $s \to 0$, the Reaction Curves swing toward the respective dashed horizontal and vertical lines, showing the optimal outputs if each firm were an independent monopolist.

and less interdependent. At the limit where $s = 0$ the two firms would be separate monopolists each producing $q_1 = q_2 = 50$ at prices $P_1 = P_2 = 50$. (iii) As s approaches 1, the firms' demands become more and more interdependent. At the limit where $s = 1$ the same solution as in Exercise 10.3 is obtained: $q_1 = q_2 = 33\ 1/3$ and $P_1 = P_2 = 33\ 1/3$.[13]

The results of the preceding exercise are illustrated in Figure 10.3. As s approaches 0 the Reaction Curve RC_1 pivots about the horizontal intercept at $q_1 = 50$ to become more and more vertical. RC_2 would similarly pivot about the vertical intercept at $q_2 = 50$ to become more and more horizontal. Thus, if the firms were independent monopolists ($s = 0$) the intercept values would indicate the respective outputs. (Although omitted from the diagram to avoid excessive clutter, as s approaches 1 the two Reaction Curves would pivot in the opposite directions, approaching limiting shapes corresponding to the RC_1 and RC_2 equations of Exercise 10.3.)

Price Competition

What would happen if *price* were the decision variable instead? Figure 10.4 pictures the outcome under price competition for the demand data of Exercise 10.7. The crucial point is that the Reaction Curves now *slope upward*. In quantity competition, when

---

[13] Although with nonidentical products the prices P_1 and P_2 do not have to be the same, they equal one another in this exercise since the cost and the demand conditions are completely symmetrical.

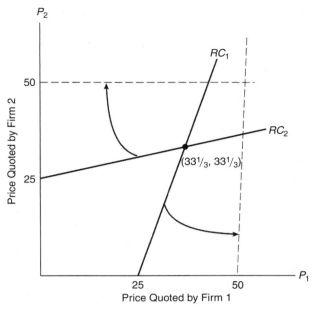

Figure 10.4. Linear Reaction Curves – Differing Products, Price Competition

The Reaction Curves are based on the data of Exercise 10.7, but the firms are assumed to compete in terms of price rather than quantity as the decision variable. The Reaction Curves now have positive slopes: each firm rationally raises price if the competitor does and similarly follows a price reduction – but by less than 1:1 in either case. As the similarity index approaches $s = 0$, the Reaction Curves swing toward the respective and vertical dashed lines, indicating the optimal prices if each firm were an independent monopolist.

firm 1 produces more, firm 2 will rationally produce less. But in price competition, if firm 1 raises its price, firm 2 benefits by raising its own price.

The slopes of the Reaction Curves, however, indicate that each firm responds by less than 1:1 to a price change on the part of its competitor (else there could be no equilibrium). Also, as suggested in the diagram, as s approaches 0 the Reaction Curves pivot toward the limiting horizontal and vertical dashed lines at $P_1 = P_2 = 50$ (the price solutions when the two firms are independent monopolists). For the data of Exercise 10.7 the solution is $P_1 = P_2 = 33\ 1/3$, which implies outputs $q_1 = q_2 = 44\ 4/9$.

Note that, consistent with the result for identical products, outputs are greater and prices lower under price competition than under the quantity competition.

CONCLUSION

When duopolists produce differentiated products, the Cournot and Bertrand solutions will be a function of s, the *index of similarity* between the two products. At one extreme $(s = 1)$ the firms produce identical products. At the other extreme $(s = 0)$ the two firms are independent monopolists. For intermediate values of s, when *quantity* is the decision variable the Reaction Curves slope downward. When *price* is the decision variable the Reaction Curves slope upward. So for differentiated as for identical products, price competition is more severe than quantity competition; the outcomes are less favorable to the firms and more favorable for the consumers.

This last conclusion suggests the question: Why do oligopoly firms more typically engage in price competition, when they would do better collectively under quantity competition? The answer turns upon the fact that consumers are interested only in the prices quoted, not the quantities manufactured by the suppliers. So suppliers trying to compete on a quantity basis, simply offering produced quantities for sale, would have to rely upon some kind of market or auction mechanism to translate the quantities offered into the prices that the consumers need to see. Market mechanisms are necessarily imperfect, as will be discussed in Chapter 14. Rather than rely upon them, more usually oligopolist firms find it more profitable to quote prices directly to consumers.

10.4   OLIGOPOLY, COLLUSION, AND NUMBERS

What circumstances help oligopolists to collude? First and most obviously, firms can more easily police one another the fewer of them there are. Second, secret price cuts are more likely to be offered to large than to small buyers. A chiselling deal with a single big customer could be kept quiet; trying to get the same increase of business from 10 small customers is stretching secrecy too far. Third, enforcement of collusion should be much easier if firms' products are identical – since, otherwise, price cuts can take the hard-to-penetrate guise of better quality. (However, even where the physical commodity is the same for all firms, it may be possible to chisel by offering better credit terms or delivery.) Fourth, the more unstable the conditions of the industry, the harder it will be to negotiate and maintain agreements.

An Application: The "Kinked" Demand Curve

In the early 1900s, prices in the American steel industry were remarkably stable. The industry had few firms and so fit the pattern of an oligopoly. The *kinked demand curve*, representing a kind of partial collusion, was proposed to explain why such oligopolies might be characterized by unusually stable prices.

Figure 10.5 pictures a single oligopolist firm initially charging price $\overline{P}$. If that firm tried to expand sales by cutting price, then (allegedly) all the other oligopolists will meet the price cut – so the original price-cutter sells very little more at the lower price. In other words, in the region below the initial $\overline{P}$ the firm's demand curve is steep. What if the firm were to raise its price? Then, allegedly, competing oligopolists would not meet the price increase, so the firm loses a lot of sales. Above $\overline{P}$, therefore, the firm's demand curve is relatively flat.[14]

This hypothesis is not a complete theory. It does not say how the original price $\overline{P}$ was determined. But it has a testable implication: the prices arrived at by oligopolistic sellers should be relatively stable.

In Figure 10.5, notice that the kink in the firm's demand curve generates a *vertical jump* in the corresponding Marginal Revenue curve. This is evident geometrically in the special case where the two branches of the demand curve are straight lines. For any linear demand curve, the Marginal Revenue curve bisects the horizontal distance from the demand curve to the vertical axis. With two separate linear branches of the demand curve, there must then be a vertical break or jump in the Marginal Revenue curve, as shown.

For the price $\overline{P}$ to be optimal for the firm, Marginal Cost must equal Marginal Revenue at $\overline{q}$. Geometrically, the MC curve must cut through the vertical jump of MR.

---

[14] The argument presumes differentiated products, since only then could any price divergence persist.

Figure 10.5. Kinked Demand Curve: Nonidentical Products

Suppose the firm currently produces output $\overline{q}$ at price $\overline{P}$. If the firm cuts its price, the other oligopolists will meet the price reduction, so the price cutter's sales gain will be small. If the firm raises price, the others will not follow the increase and the sales loss will be large. These assumptions define a kink in the firm's demand curve d that is associated with a *vertical jump* in the Marginal Revenue curve MR. The equilibrium price will be relatively stable, because even after small changes in the demand and cost curves, the MC curve likely continues to cut through the vertical jump of the MR curve.

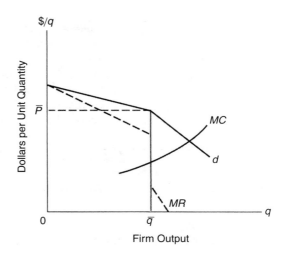

Suppose cost conditions were to change. If the effect on Marginal Cost is not too large, the MC curve might shift up or down but continue to intersect MR within the vertical gap in MR. So the firm will continue to produce $\overline{q}$ at price $\overline{P}$. And similarly, a change in demand for the firm's product could shift the demand curve a little to the right or to the left. But if its rivals continue to follow the assumed pattern of reaction, the changed demand curve will still be kinked at $\overline{P}$. If the demand shift is not too great, the MC curve will once again cut through the vertical jump of MR. If so, while the firm's output $\overline{q}$ may change, its price $\overline{P}$ will remain the same.

EXAMPLE 10.4 OLIGOPOLY AND PRICE RIGIDITY

Some Canadian market areas are served by only a single daily newspaper (monopoly), whereas others are served by several (oligopoly). Timothy C. G. Fisher and Jerzy D. Konieczny compared the frequency of price changes in these two types of markets during the period 1965–1990.[a]

The newspapers typically quoted different prices for various classes of customers: single copy (newsstand) sales, weekly carrier sales, mail subscriptions, and so forth. The table indicates that, consistently across all these classes, newspaper prices in oligopoly markets changed less frequently than monopoly prices. And, as follows logically, the oligopoly price changes – when they did take place – were on average larger.

Price changes for Canadian daily newspapers

Category	Average time between changes (mos.)		Average price change (%)	
	Monopoly	Oligopoly	Monopoly	Oligopoly
Single copy	40.5	41.8	26.2	29.0
Weekly carrier	21.9	25.9	13.1	16.6
Carrier	22.0	29.0	12.8	16.3
Dealer	37.1	42.0	25.5	30.2
Mail rate	21.9	26.6	20.5	28.0

Source: Selected from Fisher and Konieczny, Table 1.

In this generally inflationary period, any price fixed in nominal dollar terms was gradually eroding in real value. As a result, the price changes tabulated typically represented attempts to catch up with inflation. To avoid the costs and disruption of frequent changes, the newspapers compensated for the gradual decline in real value by making only occasional discrete upward adjustments. But any paper making such an adjustment risked losing customers. The oligopolist newspapers, facing competitors in the same market, were evidently more reluctant to raise prices.

[a] Timothy C. G. Fisher and Jerzy D. Konieczny, "The Relative Rigidity of Oligopoly Pricing," *Economics Letters*, v. 49 (July 1995).

Oligopoly and Numbers

Even in the absence of collusion, oligopoly prices would be lower the larger the number of competitors. How this comes about can be illustrated by extending the data of Exercise 10.3, for the case of quantity competition with identical products, to allow for increasing numbers of firms N.

Under the conditions of Exercise 10.3 each firm has zero costs. The market demand curve is $P = 100 - Q$, where Q is the sum of the quantities produced by the oligopoly firms. Thus:

$$Q \equiv q_1 + q_2 + \cdots + q_N \tag{10.4}$$

Now define Q_{-1} as the sum of all the outputs *except* that of firm 1, so that:

$$Q \equiv q_1 + Q_{-1} \tag{10.5}$$

And let q_o represent the output of each and every firm other than firm 1, all assumed to make identical choices.

Then the industry demand curve can be written:

$$P = 100 - [q_1 + (n-1)q_o] \tag{10.6}$$

Since this is a linear demand curve, firm 1's Marginal Revenue MR_1 is:

$$MR_1 = 100 - (n-1)q_o - 2q_1 \tag{10.7}$$

Setting this Marginal Revenue equal to firm 1's $MC_1 = 0$ leads algebraically to the condition:

$$q_1 = 50 - \frac{N-1}{2}q_o \tag{10.8}$$

This is the Reaction Curve for firm 1, responding to the quantity choices of any typical other firm.

Given that the firms are identically situated, their outputs must be equal. So it must be that q_1 equals q_o. Making the substitution and solving algebraically leads to the results (where q now signifies the output of any single firm):

$$\begin{cases} q = \dfrac{100}{N+1} \\[2mm] Q = 100\dfrac{N}{N+1} \\[2mm] P = \dfrac{100}{N+1} \end{cases} \qquad (10.9)$$

For two firms ($N = 2$), this confirms the Exercise 10.3 result that each firm has output 33 1/3. Aggregate output is 66 2/3 and price is 33 1/3. With $N = 3$, each firm has output $q = 25$, aggregate output rises to $Q = 75$, and price falls to $P = 25$.

This special case illustrates the general forces at work. As the number of oligopoly firms in a given market increases, each single competitor will produce less. But, in aggregate, all the firms together will produce more. So as N increases the outcome moves in the direction of the solution under perfect competition.

EXAMPLE 10.5 CONCENTRATION AND MARKET PRICES IN SWEDEN

Marcus Apslund and Richard Friberg studied how retail grocery food prices in local Swedish markets responded to the number of competing stores during the period 1993–1997.[a] The data were based upon twice-annual surveys conducted by the Pensioners' National Organization. The results reported here indicate that a larger number of stores was indeed associated with lower prices.

Retail food prices in Sweden

Number of stores	Median price
1	103.9
2	102.9
3	101.8
4	101.7
5	100.8
...	...
10	97.8
15	96.3
20	93.2

Source: Selected from Apslund and Friberg, Table 3.

Although the tabulated differences might appear small, competition in retailing services can narrow only the *margin* between stores' food acquisition costs and what consumers pay. The retail margin often accounts for only a small fraction of the product's cost to consumers.

Apart from the price effect, consumers also gain convenience and variety (as discussed in Chapter 9) as the number of retail stores in a local market increases.

---

[a] Marcus Apslund and Richard Friberg "Food Prices and Market Structures in Sweden," *Scandinavian Journal of Economics*, v. 104 (December 2002).

SUMMARY   Oligopoly is competition among a small number of firms in an industry. With small numbers, the best action for each competitor depends upon what the others are doing. So the firms are involved in strategic situations, as studied in the theory of games.

In game theory the outcome depends upon the *pattern of payoffs* and the *protocol of play* (the "rules of the game"). Payoffs may range from completely opposed interests (a "constant-sum game") to completely parallel interests; most economic situations fall in between. An important protocol distinction is between sequential-move versus simultaneous-move play. (When one player moves later than the other, but without knowledge of the opponent's choice, the two moves are considered simultaneous.)

For sequential-move play the *perfect equilibrium* solution assumes that each player chooses rationally, in the belief that players moving later will also play rationally. A perfect equilibrium always exists, though it may not be unique.

In simultaneous-move play there may be a *dominant equilibrium*, where one or both players has a strategy that is best no matter what the other player does. A more general solution concept is the Nash equilibrium, in which no player can gain by revising his or her choice even after knowing the opponent's choice. A Nash equilibrium may or may not exist in pure strategies, but if not it will exist for probabilistically mixed strategies.

In the payoff context known as the Prisoners' Dilemma, the players could mutually gain from cooperating. But rational self-interested choices lead to a less cooperative outcome, which is a dominant equilibrium in simultaneous play and is also a perfect equilibrium in sequential play. The problem of "chiselling" in oligopoly is a typical Prisoners' Dilemma.

Oligopolists can engage in price competition or quantity competition. Price competition is more severe, since at stake are not fractions of the market but the whole market. In equilibrium, however, price differences can persist only if the oligopolists' products differ. Under quantity competition the Nash equilibrium is called the Cournot solution; under price competition it is called the Bertrand solution.

For oligopolists producing differentiated products, one particular type of assumed strategic interaction leads to a "kinked" demand curve for any single firm. If the other producers will meet any price cut, the firm's demand curve below the current price will be steep; if the others will not meet any price increase, above the current price the firm's demand curve will be flat. The effect is to discourage price changes.

With increasing numbers of firms in an industry, the Nash–Cournot (and Nash–Bertrand) solutions, as would be expected, move in the direction of the outcomes in pure competition.

QUESTIONS

[†]The answers to daggered questions appear at the end of the book.

For Review

1. What is strategic behavior? Why are suppliers more likely to engage in strategic behavior when there are only a few of them?

[†]2. What is the "Prisoners' Dilemma"? Do the participants in this game have an unexploited mutual gain from trade, and if so, why?

†3. Distinguish oligopoly from monopolistic competition.

†4. Justify the statement in the text that the Cournot oligopoly outcome is a special case of the Nash equilibrium in the theory of games.

5. Explain the Cournot solution to the duopoly problem.

6. Why is collusion more likely if the firms expect to remain in the industry in the future?

7. Diagram the Reaction Curves for the asymmetrical Stackelberg and Threat cases (letting output be the decision variable).

†8. a.   Why does a "kinked" demand curve tend to lead to rigid prices?

   b.   How might a "kinked" demand curve for any single oligopolist result from the behavior of others designed to enforce a collusive agreement?

†9. In American football, the quarterback of the team on offense can call a running play or a passing play. If the team on defense knew which kind of offensive play would be called, it could prepare for the play and have a better chance of defeating it. If the quarterback follows an optimal mixed strategy, on average do you expect the offense to benefit more on passing plays or on running plays? How does your answer relate to Example 10.1 on mixed strategies in tennis?

For Further Thought and Discussion

1. It seems strange that different duopoly solutions are obtained depending on whether price or quantity is the decision variable. Which outcomes are different, and why?

†2. Under the Cournot model, in making its output decision each duopolist firm assumes that the other's output is fixed. Over time, however, each would surely learn that this assumption about the other's behavior is not valid. What would then be likely to happen?

†3. In deterring entry, a monopolist faces the problem of making his threat – that he will always produce enough to drive out the entrant – credible. The difficulty lies in the fact that, once a newcomer has entered, it may be more profitable to share the market than to engage in a costly price war. How might a monopolist make his threat more credible?

†4. Can a kinked demand curve arise under homogeneous duopoly? If so, what would be its shape?

5. Do small numbers inevitably imply cartel-like collusion?

†6. Consider the argument that "predatory price cutting" to enforce the Threat solution will rarely be observed because the symmetrical Collusive solution is typically better for both parties.

   a.   Is this necessarily correct? Is it ever correct?

   b.   Under what circumstances will predatory price cutting be likely to emerge, if ever?

7. Construct a payoff table in which two duopolist firms both offer consumers a Meet-or-Release clause. Show that this permits them to escape from the Prisoners' Dilemma in order to charge higher prices.

8. Verify that there are no dominant strategies in the payoff matrices shown in Tables 10.1 and 10.2.

†9. For the payoffs shown in Tables 10.1 and 10.2, under the sequential protocol:

   a.   Who has the advantage, first mover or last mover?

   b.   Are the results "inefficient" in the sense introduced in Chapter 7 (that is, is there another outcome whose paired payoffs are better for at least one party without being worse for the other)?

†10. (Mathematically challenging) Using the values of Exercise 10.7, but assuming price competition, justify the shapes of the Reaction Curves in Figure 10.4 What happens when s approaches 0? When s approaches 1?

11. Discuss sources of possible "outward spiral" in the duopoly cobweb of dynamic reactions.

12. In price competition with a Stackelberg leader, the text describes the solution with zero costs of production. What if costs are positive? (To isolate the leader versus follower distinction, assume the two firms' cost functions are identical.) Is the leader still at a disadvantage? Will it necessarily earn a profit of zero?

13. Using the Marginal Cost functions for Exercise 10.4, find the Collusive and the Competitive solutions.

11

Dealing with Uncertainty – The Economics of Risk and Information

Up to now consumers have been assumed to be entirely aware of their incomes and personal preferences, and suppliers fully informed as to the technology and costs of production. Although assuming complete certainty is not realistic, most of the results obtained so far – for example, that demand curves are negatively sloped – hold even when people are less than perfectly informed. Nevertheless, uncertainty is often crucial. Without uncertainty there would be no insurance industry, no need for consultants, no litigation, no advertising, no reason to engage in scientific research.

Another crucial aspect of uncertainty is that some market participants are likely to be better informed than others. A jeweler usually knows a lot more about the quality of a diamond offered for sale than do potential buyers. This chapter introduces the tools necessary to deal with imperfect information and with unbalanced distributions of knowledge.

11.1   DECISIONS UNDER UNCERTAINTY

Expected Gain versus Expected Utility

Suppose an airline must decide whether to send off a flight from Los Angeles to Chicago, despite being unsure about the weather at O'Hare Airport in Chicago by the time the flight arrives. The plane already has 100 people aboard. If the flight is dispatched and O'Hare is open, suppose the airline will gain $40,000. If the airline holds the flight until the weather clears, the disruption in the schedule will make its gain smaller, say only $20,000. But if the flight departs and finds Chicago snowed under, returning the plane to Los Angeles and reboarding the passengers later on will cause a loss of $30,000. Suppose also that the airline estimates that the chance of O'Hare Airport being closed is 25%. What should the airline do?

As a first step the airline might ask, which of the possible actions would maximize its *mathematical expectation* (or *expected value*) – the probability-weighted average – of its dollar gain. The mathematical expectation of gain if the flight is dispatched would be:

$$\text{Expected Gain if Dispatch} = (0.75 \times \$40,000) + (0.25 \times -\$30,000)$$
$$= \$22,500$$

And since by assumption there is no uncertainty if the flight is held:

$$\text{Expected Gain if Delay} = \$20,000$$

So, in terms of mathematical expectation of gain, the airline should dispatch the plane.

The general rule for choosing among different actions on the basis of mathematical expectation of gain is:

For any single action that might be undertaken, take the value of each possible outcome, multiply it by the probability of that outcome occurring, and sum all these products. The result of that calculation is the *expected value* of that particular action. Repeat the calculation for each of the available actions, and select the action with greatest expected value.

Algebraically, suppose state 1 occurs with probability π_1, state 2 with probability π_2, state 3 with probability π_3, and so forth. (The probabilities, when all possible states are counted, necessarily sum to 1.) Consider some specific action a_i. The values associated with action a_i in the possible states (numbered from state 1 to state S) can be denoted

$V_{i1}, V_{i2}, \ldots, V_{iS}$. So the expected value of taking action a_i can be written:

$$E[V(a_i)] = \pi_1 V_{i1} + \pi_2 V_{i2} + \cdots + \pi_S V_{iS} \qquad (11.1)$$

And the decision rule is: Among all the available actions $a_1, a_2, \ldots$, choose the action that yields the highest $E[V(a_i)]$.

Risk Aversion

If a decision, like that of the airline here, will be repeated many times over, achieving the highest dollar gain *on average* makes sense. The "law of large numbers" cancels out the risk. But sometimes situations arise in which risk cannot be ignored.

Suppose Helen has two job offers. A job in Iowa pays a straight salary at a rate of $40 an hour. (At 2,000 hours a year, that would be $80,000). A job in Nebraska offers a lower assured salary of $30, but there's a possibility of an annual bonus equivalent to $20 an hour. Suppose Helen thinks there is a 60% chance she will get the bonus. Then the expected per-hour compensation on the riskier job is $(0.4)(\$30) + (0.6)(\$50) = \$42$. If she cared only about the mathematical expectation of dollar income, she would take the risky job in Nebraska. But choosing a job is not an action that will be repeated many times, and furthermore it might involve a large fraction of her lifetime wealth and income. So Helen might be willing to pay something to avoid the risk of ending up with low income in the bad state of the world. If so, she could be well advised to take the job with the guaranteed salary of $40 an hour.

A way of expressing her possible willingness to sacrifice income to avoid risk is to describe her as desiring to maximize *expected utility* rather than *expected income*.

Using the "cardinal" utility interpretation of Chapter 3, a person associates a utility number with each level of income.[1] *Expected utility* is the probability-weighted average of the utilities attached to all the possible outcomes. Suppose the utilities that Helen assigns to different possible weekly incomes are $U(\$30) = 2$, $U(\$40) = 3$, and $U(\$50) = 3.5$. Then her expected utility for the riskier job is $(0.4)(2) + (0.6)(3.5) = 2.9$. Since this is less than $U(\$40) = 3$, Helen should choose the job with the fixed salary.

For any action a_i, the mathematical expectation of utility is:

$$E[U(a_i)] = \pi_1 U_{i1} + \pi_2 U_{i2} + \cdots + \pi_S U_{iS} \qquad (11.2)$$

The decision rule is: Choose the action a_i with highest expected utility. Equation (11.2) is identical to equation (11.1), except that the cardinal utility values are entered into the calculation instead of the dollar measures of gain.

In Figure 11.1 the horizontal axis represents income I and the vertical axis represents utility U. The utility function shown is concave: it becomes flatter at higher incomes. Since utility is rising with income at an always-decreasing rate, this decision-maker has *diminishing marginal utility of income*. It is diminishing marginal utility of income that leads to risk aversion.

In the diagram, points A, B, and C represent Helen's assumed utilities $U(\$30) = 2$, $U(\$40) = 3$, and $U(\$50) = 3.5$. As previously calculated, for the risky job 2 her expected

---

[1] As explained in Chapter 3, "ordinal" utility only ranks the outcomes, telling us in this case only that the individual prefers more income to less. "Cardinal" utility means that the decision-maker can quantitatively scale the desirability of different levels of income. The justification for using cardinal utility in dealing with choices under uncertainty is discussed in more advanced economic treatises.

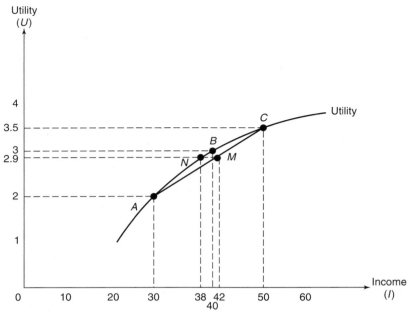

Figure 11.1. Certainty-Equivalent Income

Points *A* and *C* are the possible outcomes of Helen's risky job; point *B* represents the safe job. Since the probability of the good outcome *C* is 0.6, the expected utility of the risky job is shown by point *M*, 6/10 of the distance from *A* towards *C*. Since *M* is lower on the utility scale than point *B*, Helen should prefer the safe job. The sure salary that would give Helen the same utility as the risky job is shown by point *N*, whose vertical coordinate is the same as point *M*.

utility is 2.9. To find the expected utility geometrically, connect points *A* and *C* with a line segment. Since the probability of the good outcome *C* is 0.6, on this line find the point 6/10 of the distance from *A* towards *C*. Call this point *M*. The height of *M* is necessarily $(0.4)(2) + (0.6)(3.5) = 2.9$, confirming the previous calculation. Geometrically, point *M* lies lower on the utility scale than point *B*, which represented the 3.0 utility of the safe job 1. So the geometry confirms that, given Helen's degree of risk aversion, she would prefer the safe job in Iowa.

What sure salary would give Helen the same utility as the risky Nebraska job? That is shown by point *N*, which has the same height as point *M*. Point *N* corresponds to a weekly salary of $38. So Helen is indifferent between receiving $38 for sure and receiving $30 with probability 0.4 and $50 with probability 0.6. In other words, $38 an hour is the *certainty-equivalent* for Helen of the risky salary. The difference between $38 and $(0.4)($30) + (0.6)($50) = $42 is the *risk premium*. Helen is willing to give up income of $4 an hour in income to avoid the risk entailed by the Nebraska job.

[*Note:* It would be wrong to infer that Helen would never accept any risk. A risk-averse person *will* accept a risky option, if the terms are sufficiently favorable. That is, if the difference in expected income exceeds his or her risk premium. Or put another way, if the riskier option is associated with a higher certainty-equivalent income.]

The concave curve in Figure 11.1 was associated with diminishing Marginal Utility of income, which is the normal case. (Compare Chapter 3, Figure 3.2.) It is also possible to construct a utility function that is not concave but instead convex (becoming steeper

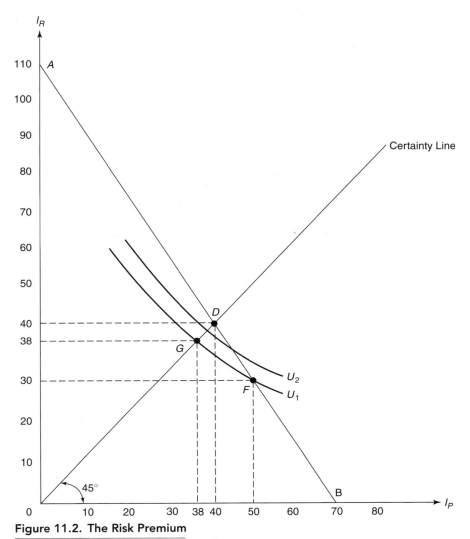

Figure 11.2. The Risk Premium

The horizontal axis measures income I_P under Prosperity; income I_R under Recession is shown on the vertical axis. Line AB shows all the possible combinations of state-contingent incomes in Prosperity and Recession whose expected value is the same as the sure income represented by point D along the certainty line. The risky job offer is represented by point F along AB. Point F lies on the same indifference curve as point G, lower down on the certainty line. The monetary difference between point F and point G is the risk premium – the additional expected income that Helen requires to make her indifferent between the risky job and the job with guaranteed income.

moving to the right). Then the decision-maker has *increasing* Marginal Utility of income. Such a person, over a certain range at least, prefers a risky option over a safe one with the same average income. The risk premium is negative; that is, the person is willing to sacrifice some sure income in order to incur the risk. Last, if the utility function is neither concave nor convex but is instead a straight upward-sloping line (*constant* Marginal Utility of income), the individual is risk-neutral and the risk premium is zero.

As a different way of representing risk aversion, now think in terms of two distinct "states of the world" such as Prosperity and Recession. In Figure 11.2, income in the

Prosperity state, denoted I_P, is measured along the horizontal axis. Income in the Recession state, I_R, is scaled along the vertical axis. (These are the *state-contingent incomes*.) Any given level of expected income is associated with a straight line such as AB whose slope reflects the probabilities of the different states. Suppose the probability of Prosperity is π_P and of Recession is $\pi_R \equiv 1 - \pi_P$. Then for some specific expectation of income $E[I]$, the equation of the line is:

$$E[I] = \pi_R I_R + \pi_P I_P \qquad (11.3)$$

With I_P on the horizontal axis and I_R on the horizontal axis, the slope of the line is $-\pi_P/\pi_R$. The line shows all the possible probabilistic combinations of state-contingent incomes in Prosperity and Recession associated with any given mathematical expectation of income.

Returning to Helen's situation, if the bonus will be paid only in the Prosperity state of the world, for the risky job Helen's expected income is $E[I] = (0.4)(\$30) + (0.6)(\$50) = \$42$. In Figure 11.2 the line AB reflects this expected income. The probabilistic income combination represented by her risky job in Nebraska ($I_R = \$30$ and $I_P = \$50$) appears as point F. Were Helen able to choose among all possible income combinations with an expectation of $42, then line AB would be a *budget line*, just like those discussed in Chapter 4. The only difference is that Chapter 4 dealt with a consumer choosing between ordinary goods such as shoes and hats, whereas here the two "goods" are amounts of the respective state-contingent incomes. Indifference curves such as U_1 and U_2 between the various income combinations can also be drawn on axes I_R and I_P.

A person whose earnings are the same in Prosperity and Recession receives those earnings with certainty. Any such sure income would be a point on line OC – the "certainty line." The certainty line necessarily has a slope of $45°$, reflecting the fact that $I_R = I_P$. In the diagram, the sure salary of $40 associated with Helen's riskless job offer in Iowa is shown as point D. D lies on a higher indifference curve than does point F. This shows, in another way, that Helen's risk-aversion leads her to prefer a guaranteed income of $40 over the risky income combination at point F – even though point F lies on the budget line representing a higher expected income of $42.

The risk premium can also be shown in Figure 11.2. Point G lies on the same indifference curve as point F, but G lies on the $45°$ certainty line and so represents riskless income. The difference between the expected income at point F ($42) and the expected income at point G ($38) is the risk premium – how much more expected income Helen would require to bear the risk associated with accepting the risky job in Nebraska over the riskless job in Iowa.

Risk-Bearing and Insurance

Joe has wealth of $300,000. One-third of his wealth is tied up in an Old Master painting worth $100,000. With probability 40%, art thieves will steal his painting this year. (This unrealistically high probability figure is used here for numerical convenience only.)

For Joe the two states of the world are "Painting stolen" (state S) and "Painting not stolen" (state N). Joe's initial situation or *endowment* is represented by point E in Figure 11.3, consisting of his possible contingent wealth levels $W_N = \$300,000$ (measured on the horizontal axis) and $W_S = \$200,000$ (measured on the vertical axis). Joe is initially in a risky position, off the $45°$ certainty line. Suppose, however, that for a

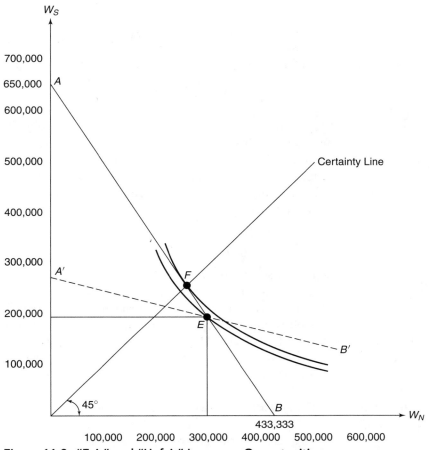

Figure 11.3. "Fair" and "Unfair" Insurance Opportunities

The horizontal axis measures wealth W_N in the state of the world "Painting not Stolen"; wealth W_S in the state "Painting Stolen" is shown on the vertical axis. Point E represents Joe's initial situation, off the certainty line. With insurance at "fair" rates, Joe could move anywhere along budget line AB. His optimal point is F on the certainty line, where he fully insures against his potential loss. The line $A'B'$ represents an "unfair" insurance opportunity, so Joe's indifference curve tangency would necessarily lie below and to the right of the 45° line. This means that Joe would not fully insure.

premium of $40,000 Joe can buy insurance in the amount of $100,000 (the "indemnity") against the risk of theft.

At this point it is useful to define a "fair"[2] gamble or insurance contract.[3]

DEFINITION: A gamble is *fair* if the mathematical expectation of net gain, $E[G]$, is zero.

Suppose the probability of winning is π and of losing is $1 - \pi$, and let the winning payoff be a wealth gain of H and the losing payoff be a wealth loss of F. So a gamble is

---

[2] "Fair" in probability theory is only a technical term. It does not mean moral or just.
[3] Whether a contract is a gamble or insurance depends upon the point of view. A risk-reducing insurance arrangement for a purchaser is a risk-increasing gamble for the insurance company.

fair if:

$$E[G] = \pi H + (1 - \pi)(-F) = 0$$

From this equation it follows immediately that, as a condition for a fair gamble:

$$\frac{H}{F} = \frac{1 - \pi}{\pi} \tag{11.4}$$

That is, the ratio of payoffs must be inversely proportional to the ratio of probabilities.

On this definition the offered insurance contract is a fair gamble. As Joe sees it, the gamble "succeeds" if the painting is stolen. If Joe "loses" the gamble (the painting is not stolen) he is out the $40,000 premium. If he wins, his net gain on the contract is $60,000 (the $100,000 indemnity, less the $40,000 premium that the insurance company keeps). That the premium is fair is shown by:

$$\frac{H}{F} = \frac{\$60,000}{\$40,000} = 1.5 = \frac{0.6}{0.4} = \frac{1 - \pi}{\pi}$$

Since $E[G]$ – the mathematical expectation of income gain or loss – is zero for fair gambles, it follows that all fair gambles or fair insurance contracts leave the individual's mathematical expectation of income unchanged. Referring back to Figure 11.3, the line AB represented all possible combinations of state-contingent incomes for Helen with a mathematical expectation of $42. Figure 11.4 here represents a similar situation for Joe. The mathematical expectation of his endowment in dollar terms is $(0.6)(\$300, 000) + (0.4)(\$200, 000) = \$260, 000$. So his budget line has the equation $0.6W_N + 0.4W_S = \$260, 000$.

If Joe accepts the offered fair insurance contract, he would move along this budget line to the 45° certainty line, ending up with wealth $260,000 for sure. If he fails to insure, he will remain in a risky position southeast of the 45° line.

This analysis now allows a more precise definition of risk aversion:

DEFINITION: A person is risk averse if, offered a choice of fair gambles (or fair insurance contracts), he always prefers to end up at a position on the 45° certainty line.

It follows that an individual endowed with any given amount of *riskless* wealth or income would never accept a fair gamble. Doing so would move him away from the 45° line. If instead his endowment already contains some risk, so that his initial position lies off the 45° line, he would accept a gamble tending to offset the risk inherent in his endowment. That is what insuring means.

This definition has an important implication for the shape of the indifference curves. If Joe is risk-averse, as shown in the diagram he would move along the budget line to the tangency position F on a higher indifference curve. More generally, risk aversion means that the individual would end up at a certainty position along any fair-gamble budget line, whenever offered such an opportunity. So the individual's indifference curves must all be tangent to fair-gamble budget lines precisely where each such line crosses the 45° line out of the origin.

But what if, as is more common, an insurance contract is "unfair" in probability terms? After all, insurance companies have costs of doing business, so on average must do better than break even on the coverage they offer. In Figure 11.3 the hypothetical dashed budget line $A'B'$ is flatter than the fair budget line AB – that is, the H/F ratio of equation (11.4) is numerically smaller than the fair ratio $(1 - \pi)/\pi = 0.6/0.4 = 1.5$. Along $A'B'$ the tangency with Joe's indifference curve would necessarily lie to the southeast of the 45° line. This means that Joe would not fully insure.

The diagram has been constructed so that at Joe's endowment, point E, an indifference curve is tangent to the budget line $A'B'$ – meaning that Joe maximizes utility there and will stand pat with his initial gamble. If instead the tangency point falls between point E and the certainty line he will want to go only part of the way in purchasing insurance – "underinsuring" – in order to bear part of the risk himself. And a tangency lying along $A'B'$ in the opposite direction from the certainty line would mean that Joe finds the insurance terms so attractive that he would like to buy more insurance. He might do so by buying a second painting with the intention of also insuring that one.

EXAMPLE 11.1 RISK AVERSION AND EXECUTIVE STOCK OPTIONS

Stock options are rights to purchase corporate shares at a specified "exercise price." A stock option may pay off handsomely if the company's stock rises above the exercise price, but is worthless otherwise. In recent decades Boards of Directors have increasingly been granting executives stock options as part of their "pay packages." The idea is that the options will motivate executives to take actions that will benefit the corporation and lead therefore to a higher stock price. (Or so the company's directors presumably hope.) Since stock options are so risky, the valuation that an executive places upon this form of pay will depend importantly upon his or her overall financial situation and degree of risk aversion, together with the underlying riskiness of the stocks themselves.

Brian Hall and Kevin J. Murphy estimated certainty-equivalent values for an executive offered a 10-year nontradable stock option with an exercise price of $30.[a] The row headings of the table represent differing assumptions as to the executive's degree of risk aversion r (a theoretical measure called the "constant of relative risk aversion") and as to his or her exposure to risk (measured by the percent of the executive's personal wealth already held in the form of the company's stock). As each of these factors increases, the certainty-equivalent of a stock option decreases as compared with straight cash.

The column headings show various assumed levels of the stock price at the time of granting an option with the fixed exercise price of $30. If the exercise price is below the current stock price the option is already "in the money" – that is, it has an immediate conversion value in addition to its option value. Such an option is of course also less risky. The data in the cells show the value of an option to buy a single share. The first data cell shows that for an executive with the stated characteristics ($r = 2$, and 50% of wealth already in company stock), if the current stock price is $15 an option to buy a share 10 years from now at the exercise price of $30 is worth only $2.50 today. Moving to the right in any row, the option values increase – simply because the stock is already worth more today. But moving down the columns, the option values decrease as the executive's risk aversion r rises, and also decrease as the executive's risk exposure (proportion of wealth already held in company stock) grows.

The key conclusion is that the value of stock options for executives, after allowing for risk aversion, is typically considerably less than might at first appear.

Certainty-equivalents of an option to buy a share at $30

Current stock price	$15	$30	$45	$60
$r = 2$, 50% in stock	2.5	12	22	32
$r = 2$, 67% in stock	2.0	8	17	25
$r = 3$, 50% in stock	1.8	7	13	22
$r = 3$, 67% in stock	0.6	3	9	15

Source: Estimated visually from Hall and Murphy, Figure 2 (p. 42).

---

[a] Brian Hall and Kevin J. Murphy, "Stock Options for Undiversified Executives," National Bureau of Economic Research Working Paper No. 8052, December 2000.

11.2 THE VALUE OF INFORMATION

If you will be getting better information before you have to lock in your decision, it may pay to defer making a final choice. Suppose you see an ad for a computer, at a special price today of $800. The sale is for one day only. If you wait for tomorrow, you are unsure what the price will then be. Let's say you estimate there is a two-thirds chance the price will rise to $950, but a one-third chance the price will decline to $700.

Should you buy today or wait? Suppose you are risk-neutral, which means you only need to take into account the mathematical expectation (the probability-weighted average) of the dollar amounts. If you wait, the expected price is $(1/3)(\$700) + (2/3)(\$950) = \$866.67$, which exceeds the $700 you would pay for the computer today. So if you were sure you wanted the computer, even at a price of $950, you should buy it today at the sale price of $800.

But now suppose your *demand price* (see Chapter 7), the most you would be willing to pay for the computer, is $P_d = \$810$. So if you buy today your Consumer Surplus will be $810 − $800 = $10. If you wait and the price falls to $700, you would buy the computer and receive a larger Consumer Surplus, $810 − $700 = $110. But if the price rises to $950 you would not buy at all, in which event Consumer Surplus is zero. Thus, if you wait, the mathematical expectation of your Consumer Surplus is $E(CS) = (1/3)(\$110) + (2/3)(\$0) = \$36.67$. Since this exceeds the $10 Consumer Surplus on an immediate purchase, on average waiting is better than buying the computer today. And waiting is better even though today's price is lower than the mathematical expectation of tomorrow's price.

How can this be? Postponing the decision gives you the *option* of varying your final action in accord with information you will receive tomorrow. Since the future is never entirely knowable, option value enters into the worth of any durable asset. When buying a car today, an element in its value is that you could resell it if used-car prices rise – or if not, you can retain it for continued use.

It is option value that makes information useful. Acquiring knowledge is worthwhile only if it might change a decision you would otherwise have made. Continuing with the example, now suppose your willingness to pay for a computer exceeds $950. If so, as seen above, you should buy the computer today at the sale price of $800, which is less than the expected later price of $866.67. But suppose you can subscribe to a marketing service that can reliably tell you today whether the price tomorrow will be $700 or $950. If the report arrives in time so that you could still buy at the sale price today, how much would you pay for that information?

The reasoning goes as follows. Your demand price P_d is some value greater than $950. If you don't invest in the information you should buy the computer today, paying $800. Your Consumer Surplus would be $CS = P_d - 800$. If you do buy the information, with probability 1/3 the marketing service will report that the future price will be $700. If so, you will wait to buy the computer tomorrow, paying $700. Or, with probability 2/3 you will learn that tomorrow's price will be $950 – but in that case you will buy the computer today at its sale price of $800. Thus, the mathematical expectation of Consumer Surplus due to having the information about future prices would be $E[CS] = (1/3)(P_d - 700) + (2/3)(P_d - 800) = P_d - \$766.67$. If you do not subscribe to the service, you will buy the computer today so that Consumer Surplus is $P_d - \$800$. The difference is the value to you of the information, which is the maximum you would be willing to pay to subscribe to the marketing service: $33.33.

In terms of symbols, let the two possible states of the world be s_1 and s_2. Let CS° denote the expected Consumer Surplus of the best *uninformed* action; CS' is the expected Consumer Surplus of the best *informed* action. For simplicity suppose that the number of actions matches the number of states, and that a_1 is the better action in state 1 and a_2 is the better action in state 2. Suppose f is the probability you attach to state 1, so that $1 - f$ is the probability of state 2. Let $CS(a_1|s_2)$ signify Consumer Surplus when the action is a_1 and the state of nature is s_2. Similar interpretations apply to $CS(a_1|s_1)$ and so on.

In the absence of information, the chosen action cannot be adapted to the state of nature. Therefore, whichever of a_1 or a_2 generates a higher benefit should be chosen. Let it be a_1. Then:

$$CS^\circ = f CS(a_1|s_1) + (1 - f)CS(a_1|s_2)$$

Given the information, however, the chosen action can be adapted to the state of the world, so:

$$CS' = f CS(a_1|s_1) + (1 - f)CS(a_2|s_2)$$

Since by assumption a_2 is the better action in state s_2, CS' must exceed CS. The difference represents the worth of the information, the most you should be willing to pay for the marketing service.

On the other hand, if your decision would not be affected the information has no value to you. For example, suppose your willingness to pay for a computer is only $600. Then you wouldn't buy the computer at today's price of $800, you wouldn't buy it if the price later rose to $950, and you wouldn't buy it if the price later fell to $700. So you gain nothing from learning whether the price will be $950 or instead $700.

11.3 ASYMMETRIC INFORMATION

Adverse Selection – The Lemons Problem

In any transaction the better-informed party has an advantage. Suppliers usually know more about their product than do buyers. A patient may not know which physician or dentist is the best qualified, a prospective buyer may not know that a used car has a

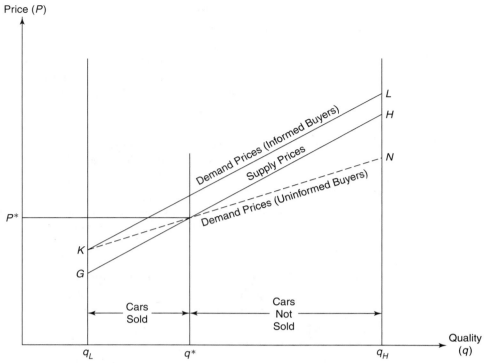

Figure 11.4. The "Lemons" Problem

GH shows the reservation supply prices of the existing owners of used cars, ranked upwards from the lowest-quality car to the highest-quality car. *KL* shows what the corresponding demand prices of the potential buyers would be, if buyers were perfectly informed about quality. Assuming equal numbers of owners and potential buyers, each wanting to sell or to buy a single unit, all the cars would be sold. But when buyers can observe only the *average* quality of the cars currently offered, their demand prices for any quantity on the market are shown by the lower curve *KN*. Point *N* is the buyers' demand price for a car of average quality in the entire population of cars. *KN* intersects *GH* at quantity q^* between q_L and q_H. In equilibrium only the cars with quality below q^* will be sold. The equilibrium price is P^*, where the reservation price of the marginal seller equals the reservation price of the marginal uninformed buyer.

broken transmission, an employer cannot be certain how well an applicant will perform on the job. All such instances create a problem of *adverse selection*. Low-quality goods or services ("lemons") may destroy the market for high-quality goods ("peaches").[4]

Consider used cars. The potential seller, Sally, may know that her car stalls intermittently, that the air-conditioning frequently fails on hot days, or that the car accelerates poorly on mountains. But potential buyers, like Bob, do not generally know about these problems. Were customers fully informed, good cars would sell at a higher price than bad cars. But if buyers cannot determine a car's condition before purchase, good cars and bad cars end up selling at the same price. That is the heart of the problem.

In Figure 11.4 the horizontal axis represents used-car quality q; the vertical axis represents price P. Suppose the qualities of all the cars offered for sale are distributed

---

[4] George A. Akerlof, "The Market for Lemons: Quality Uncertainty and the Market Mechanism," *Quarterly Journal of Economics*, v. 84 (1970), pp. 488–500.

evenly from a low of q_L to a maximum of q_H. For simplicity, let there be equal numbers of existing owners and potential buyers, each wanting to sell or to buy a single unit.

The rising curve GH shows the reservation supply prices of the existing owners, ranked upward from the lowest-quality car to the highest-quality car. It is drawn for convenience as a straight line. The curve KL (also drawn for convenience as a straight line) shows what the corresponding demand prices of the potential buyers would be, *if* buyers were perfectly informed about quality. Since KL lies entirely above GH, by assumption here every available car has at least one customer willing to pay more for it than the reservation price of its present owner: Bob, for example, is willing to pay Sally enough so that she would want to sell the car. So ideally, all the cars should be sold.

But buyers are not perfectly informed. Suppose Bob and other buyers can observe only the *average* quality of the cars currently offered for sale at the going price. The curve KN shows the demand prices that buyers would offer for the *average* visible quality in the market, starting from the bottom. Since at the low end only the single car of lowest quality (q_L) is on the market, at that point the average quality in the market and the actual quality of the single offered car are identical. That is why the KL and KN curves coincide at point K. But when price is so high that *all* the cars are offered for sale, the height of point N is the buyers' demand price for a car of average quality in the overall population of cars – halfway between q_L and q_H. So the height of point N is half the vertical distance between points K and L.

As drawn, KN intersects the GH curve at the quantity q^* between q_L and q_H. In equilibrium all the cars below q^* will be sold, at a price P^* that equates the reservation prices of the marginal seller and the marginal buyer. For the marginal seller, say Sally, the reservation price is the minimum she will take to part with the car. For the marginal buyer, say Bob, it is the maximum he is willing to pay for the *average* quality of the cars in the market, that is, the average of qualities ranging from q_L to q^*. Cars of quality higher than q^* are not sold. They are worth more to their present owners than any potential buyer, knowing only the average quality of cars in the market, is willing to pay.

So long as point K (showing what some buyer would pay for the lowest-quality car) lies above point G (showing what that car's owner would be willing to accept), the lowest-quality lemons will always remain in the market. What of the highest-end peaches? The diagram shows that they might be frozen out of the market. But this is not inevitable. If the gap between the buyers' demand prices and the sellers' reservation prices is sufficiently great, the mutual advantage of trade is large and the KL curve lies considerably above the GH curve. In that case even the KN curve could lie always above GH, so that in the diagram no interior q^* intersection would exist. But for the peaches to remain on the market, owners of the highest-quality cars must be willing to sell them for no more than cars of merely average quality.

EXAMPLE 11.2 ADVERSE SELECTION IN DENTAL INSURANCE

Adverse selection is a serious problem for the insurance industry. People who face the greatest risks, or are the most likely to make claims, are the ones most anxious to buy insurance. But these are the very people that the insurance companies are least happy to welcome as customers.

Martin Godfried, Hessel Oosterbeek, and, and Frank Van Tulder examined the role of adverse selection in the purchase of dental insurance in the Netherlands.[a] In 1995 the Netherlands government decided to exclude dental services from the standard health insurance package covering 60% of the Dutch population. Individuals, formerly automatically covered, now had to choose whether or not to purchase dental insurance.

If voluntary dental insurance has to be offered on the same terms to all, regardless of the condition of teeth, adverse selection is inevitable. Conversely, adverse selection will be moderated to the extent that insurers can charge differential rates. For some time after the policy change in the Netherlands, private insurance suppliers were under political pressure to charge the same rates to everyone regardless of the condition of their teeth. Moreover, no applicants were to be refused. In these circumstances, adverse selection could be expected.

Statistically, the authors found poorer quality of teeth raised the probability of becoming insured. Also, individuals who customarily visited dentists more frequently were found to be more likely to choose insurance. Among those who chose to insure after the change in policy, 93% customarily visited the dentist twice a year. Among those who chose not to insure, it was only 82%. So people whose teeth were of poorer quality, or people more anxious about dental health, were indeed more likely to purchase the insurance.

---

[a] Martin Godfried, Hessel Oosterbeekand, and Frank Van Tulder, "Adverse Selection and the Demand for Supplemental Insurance," *De Economist*, v. 149 (2002), pp. 177–190.

EXAMPLE 11.3 RACEHORSES CAN BE LEMONS

Credible information about quality helps overcome the lemons problem. For thoroughbred racehorses in the United States, auction houses provide information as to quality, where quality refers to potential race earnings. Horses offered for sale may or may not be "certified." Certification means that the horse has been physically inspected by the auction house and found to be in good shape. A noncertified horse could be of any level of quality. Understandably, owners seeking to sell high-quality horses arrange to have them certified.

Bradley S. Wimmer and Brian Chezum examined a sample of 3,376 thoroughbreds born in 1993.[a] Overall, the average price in noncertified sales was $13,268 compared to $93,437 in certified sales. That certification was a reliable process is evidenced by the fact that average race earnings turned out to be $48,475 for horses sold in certified sales, as compared to $27,188 for horses in noncertified sales.

The most definitive test for adverse selection is to compare the prices of certified as against uncertified horses when all other publicly determinable factors – age, pedigree, and so forth – are held constant. The authors estimated that, for an average-quality horse in terms of observable attributes, the expected price would be $88,259. But the additional fact that the horse was sold on a noncertified basis reduced the expected price to $9,253 – almost 90% less!

Some breeders also enter their own horses in races. These owners have a very strong motivation to retain their best horses. Buyers, aware of this, are reluctant to pay high prices for the horses those breeders offer for sale. Consequently, noncertified horses sold by racing-intensive breeders received lower prices than noncertified horses offered by breeders who less commonly race their own horses.

---

[a] Bradley S. Wimmer and Brian Chezum, "An Empirical Examination of Quality Certification in a 'Lemons Market,'" *Economic Inquiry*, v. 41 (2003), pp. 279–291.

Table 11.1 Price versus cost in each of two periods

	Case 1		Case 2	
	Low quality	High quality	Low quality	High quality
Price	4	13	4	7
Cost of production	4	5	4	6

Conveying Quality through Reputation

Any firm may claim to offer a high-quality product, so how can consumers know which ones are telling the truth? A *reputation* may make it profitable to produce a high-quality product even in the face of initial consumer ignorance.

Taking account of reputation requires thinking of the future as well as of the present. To keep things simple, assume that firms and consumers are concerned with only two periods. Assume also that the firm decides in the first period what quality to produce and cannot profitably modify its decision in the second period. Customers are willing to pay a premium price for superior quality, but can only determine quality after an initial purchase. So the firm's reputation is established in the first period.

In Table 11.1, the numbers for price and for cost of production apply for each of the two periods. High quality is more highly valued by consumers, but also involves higher cost of production. To begin with, assume consumers have pessimistic expectations, and so are willing to pay in the first period only the low-quality price ($4).

Suppose the firm aims to maximize the *sum* of profits (Price minus Cost of Production) over the two periods.[5] Then, in Case 1 it would do better producing the high-quality product. A low-quality firm just breaks even: its production cost of $4 in each period just equals the price in that period. A high-quality firm suffers a $1 loss in the first period. But having earned a good reputation, its second-period profit of $13 − $5 = $8 outweighs the first-period loss.

In Case 2 the numbers do not warrant production of the high-quality product. The firm's cost in the first period is higher by $2, but the second-period gain is only $1.

EXERCISE 11.1

Instead of consumers holding pessimistic beliefs about the products offered in the first period, suppose instead they are optimistic (they initially believe they are buying from a high-quality firm). (a) For Case 1 of the table, which type of firm does better? (b) Same question, for Case 2.

ANSWER: (a) In Case 1, a high-quality firm has total profit $8 + $8 = $16; a low-quality firm has total profit $9 + $0 = $9. As before, here the high-quality firm does better. (b) In Case 2, a high-quality firm has total profit $1 + $1 = $2; a low-quality firm has profit of $3 + $0 = $3. As before, here the low-quality firm does better. So, in this example, whether consumers are initially optimistic or pessimistic does not affect the *relative* profitability of high-quality products versus low-quality products.

---

[5] Chapter 15, which covers the economics of time, will show that future benefits and costs are normally *discounted* relative to the present. For simplicity here, second-year benefits and costs have not been discounted.

Returning to Case 1 in Table 11.1, assume now that, since producing the high-quality product is more profitable regardless of consumer beliefs, consumers will plausibly expect the firm to produce a high-quality product. (This is an instance of the concept called "rational expectations." The idea of rational expectations is that each individual and firm makes predictions about what others will do that are consistent with the incentives that these other firms and individuals face.) Specifically, here, under rational expectations the consumers would be willing to pay $13 each period and the firm's profits would be $16, just as under the optimistic assumption of Exercise 11.2. In Case 2, however, the optimistic assumption is shown to be mistaken, since under that assumption profits are greater for a firm supplying the low-quality product. So rational expectations dictate that, under the conditions of Case 2, the firm will indeed offer the low-quality product.

CONCLUSION

Even in the face of initial consumer ignorance, market forces can support production of high-quality products. Depending upon the specific demand and cost conditions, it may pay a high-quality firm to accept a temporary loss while building a reputation, thereby gaining future business. But in other circumstances it would be unprofitable for a firm to incur the extra costs of establishing a reputation for high quality.[6]

EXAMPLE 11.4 RESTAURANT HYGIENE

Restaurant patrons can observe cleanliness in the dining area, but might wonder about what goes on back in the kitchen. Since any restaurant could claim to have good kitchen hygiene, mere assertions to that effect have to be discounted.

In Los Angeles County, eating establishments had been subject to inspection by the Department of Health Services for a number of years. As of December 1997 restaurants were required, in a number of cities within the county, to publicly display grade reports rating their hygiene as A, B, or C. A study by Ginger Zhe Jin and Phillip Leslie investigated whether the public displays tended to raise hygienic standards.[a]

As shown in the table, there was indeed a noticeable rise in hygiene scores in the period surrounding the new requirement. In the first half of the period, through the second quarter of 1997, the average scores were consistently between 75 and 76. In the second half of the period, starting with the third quarter of 1997, the scores were all above 80 – ranging up to and even slightly beyond 90.

The authors also investigated the effect of the A, B, or C grades upon restaurant prices and volume of business. Price and quantity data were not available separately, but taxation statistics provided useful information about revenue (price times quantity). Mandatory posting was associated with a 5.7% increase in revenue for an A-rated restaurant, a 0.7% revenue increase for a B-rated restaurant, and a 1% decrease for a C-rated restaurant. Thus consumers were evidently attending to the posted ratings.

Another question was whether the better information made available by the ratings improved the overall market for restaurant services. This indeed appeared to be the case. Despite the higher average level of quality evidenced by the rise in the hygiene ratings, the price index for restaurant meals in Los Angeles actually

---

[6] The more important the future relative to the present, the more attractive it is to produce a higher-quality product. If a reputation lasts for many years, even a small annual future advantage (profit improvement) could justify incurring a considerable first-period loss.

fell – relative to restaurant price indexes in other regions, and relative to price indexes for other retail goods in Los Angeles. Presumably, restaurant patrons, being better informed, were able to shift their patronage to restaurants representing "better buys" in terms of price as related to quality.

The effects of grade cards on restaurant hygiene score in Los Angeles

Quarter	Hygiene score
1996	
Q1	75.62
Q2	75.37
Q3	75.03
Q4	75.27
1997	
Q1	75.81
Q2	75.31
Q3	83.99
Q4	81.82
1998	
Q1	86.69
Q2	90.26
Q3	89.85
Q4	90.30

Source: Adapted from Table 1 in Jin and Leslie (2003).

[a] Ginger Zhe Jin and Phillip Leslie, "The Effect of Information on Product Quality: Evidence from Restaurant Hygiene Grade Cards," *Quarterly Journal of Economics*, v. 118 (2003), pp. 409–451.

Do Prices Signal Quality? Information as a Public Good

In the lemons situation consumers were assumed to be unable to distinguish qualities of used cars on the market. Now suppose instead that, for branded products, some consumers know the quality of each brand while others do not.

Imagine that brands X and Y of a particular product such as cell phones may differ in quality. If none of the consumers knows which brand is better, prices P_X and P_Y would have to be the same. But if some consumers know that X is better, their market choices would tend to raise P_X over P_Y. Then an initially ignorant consumer, observing that X is now selling for a higher price, would rationally conclude that X must be the higher quality brand. Thus, market prices tend to reveal quality differentials.

This process works out if informed consumers incur no extra costs in discovering which brand is better. But if the information can only be obtained at a cost, consumers who spend nothing on collecting information, merely observing the quality-revealing price differential, are better off than consumers who have incurred the costs of collecting the information. Since the information revealed by the price is visible to all, it is a *public good* in the sense of Chapter 10. As in all public goods, each individual is tempted to let others bear the cost of providing it. The paradox is that if all consumers reason in this way, no one would collect the needed data, and all the consumers would remain ignorant.

Table 11.2 Should you pay for information?

	Pay	Don't pay
	Value of paying or not paying	
Pay	7, 7	2, 10
Don't pay	10, 2	0, 0
	Rank-ordered payoffs for chicken	
Pay	3, 3	2, 4
Don't pay	4, 2	1, 1

Using uses the game-theoretic concepts introduced in the preceding chapter, Table 11.2 is a payoff matrix for two consumers considering whether to pay for information about quality. Panel (a) shows the specific numbers used for this example, while Panel (b) shows the rank ordering of the payoffs. Comparison of the rank orderings with those in Table 10.3 reveal that this situation is *not* a Prisoners' Dilemma. Instead it follows a different pattern – called by game theorists the Chicken game. Whereas in Prisoners' Dilemma the bottom row and the right-hand column are *always* the more desirable choices, in Chicken each party's preferred action depends upon the other player's decision. Specifically, if the other party is paying for information, you do best by not paying. Instead, you can observe the price without incurring any cost. But if the other party is not paying, then by assumption you would be better off buying the information yourself rather than remain ignorant.

In contrast with Prisoners' Dilemma, there is no dominance equilibrium in Chicken. Instead there are two Nash equilibria in pure strategies: (Pay, Don't Pay) with payoffs 3,5 and (Don't Pay, Pay) with payoffs 5,3. Both of these are asymmetrical; in Chicken-type games there is no symmetrical solution in pure strategies. However, Chapter 10 showed how to find a *mixed-strategy* equilibrium. Using the formula of equation (10.1), here $a = 7, b = 10, c = 2$, and $d = 0$. Then Row's probability choice p_R for his first (top) strategy and Column's p_C for her first (left-hand) strategy are given by the symmetrical solution:

$$p_R = p_C = \frac{0 - 2}{7 - 10 - 2 + 0} = 0.4$$

So each decision-maker would choose Pay with probability 40% and Don't Pay with probability 60%.

But this symmetrical mixed-strategy solution is inefficient. With 16% probability both consumers pay for the information, the payoffs summing to 14. Or, with 36% probability, neither pays. Both are then ignorant about the product quality, and the summed payoffs are 0. Last, with probability 48% either of the two asymmetrical outcomes (in which only one of the consumers buys the information) occurs; the summed payoffs are 12. Calculation shows the overall expectation (probability-weighted average) of the summed payoffs for the mixed-strategy solution to be 8, or 4 per player. In contrast, as just seen, the asymmetrical solutions have summed payoffs of 12, or 6 per player.

As always, it is possible to find a contract that rescues the parties from social traps such as Prisoners' Dilemma or Chicken. For example, the individuals could agree to divide the cost of acquiring the information, or to take turns in doing so. So if information about quality is inadequately available in markets, that failure must be due to the difficulty of entering into a suitable contract.

Conveying Information – Advertising

Again assuming two brands X and Y, another quality-revealing force operates on the supply side of the market. The manufacturer of the superior brand, brand X, has a motive to publicize that information through advertising. But, although brand X can claim to be better, so can brand Y. How can the consumer know which one to believe?

Brand X has one advantage: the truth is often more intrinsically credible than a lie. True facts and logically valid inferences are, to a degree, self-evident. If so, then brand X's ads will, other things equal, be more convincing.

But suppose readers of ads simply cannot tell whether X or Y is lying. Even so, ads may have an effect. Suppose the prices P_X and P_Y are initially the same. Imagine that consumers, observing the ads placed by brands X and Y, are still totally in doubt and so buy the two brands in equal quantities. But, on average, purchasers of brand X will have better experiences with the product. They are likely to recommend X to their friends, and to buy more X themselves in the future. The opposite will hold, of course, for brand Y. So, in the long run at least, this reputation effect means that *advertising will pay off more for the higher-quality brand*.[7] Consequently, better brands are likely to advertise more heavily. Consumers can therefore, to a degree, expect that a heavily advertised product is likely to be of better quality.

But this is only part of the story. An important force operates in the other direction. The low-quality manufacturer can likely produce at lower cost. The high unit returns associated with low production costs make it more profitable to advertise heavily. In effect brand Y can try to look as much as possible like the high-quality brand X not only in what it says in its ads, but in the scale of its advertising.

A firm producing an inferior brand has two main options. It can adopt a hit-and-run strategy, aiming at quick sales and then a quick exit. Alternatively, to find a permanent niche in the market, it is likely to cut its price in order to offer consumers a low-price low-quality alternative to brand X. So, in the long run, we can indeed expect that prices tend to reveal quality.

11.4 HERD BEHAVIOR AND INFORMATIONAL CASCADES

One can gain useful information by observing the actions of others. If your tastes resemble other people's, a crowded restaurant is likely to be a good place to eat, and a popular movie is likely to be good entertainment.

Suppose a number of individuals face the same choice problem, for example which movie to go to. But imagine that each person can observe the decisions of those preceding him or her. Let everyone be risk-neutral so that the calculation can run in terms of the mathematical expectation (the probability-weighted average) of monetary gains and losses.

Imagine the choice concerns a fork in the road. Let action a be taking the left branch and action b taking the right branch. In state of the world A only the left branch leads to your desired destination; in state B the right branch does. Matching the action to the state of Nature yields a payoff of 1, whereas a mismatch has payoff -1.

Before making a decision, suppose each person receives an imperfect private signal, either α or β. For example, a signal can be a hazy recollection of what an old tour book

---

[7] Phillip Nelson, "Advertising as Information," *Journal of Political Economy*, v. 82 (1974), pp. 729–754.

said. Signal α has some probability $p > \frac{1}{2}$ of being observed when the state is A; signal β has the same probability $p > \frac{1}{2}$ when the state is B. So p is the probability that the observed signal, α or β, is correct. For a person with no other information, action a is evidently better if the person sees signal α, and action b if the person sees signal β.

Imagine that Aaron, the first individual in the sequence, follows this rule. By assumption, everyone after Aaron knows what Aaron did (which branch of the fork he chose). If they believe that Aaron acted rationally, these successors can all infer Aaron's signal perfectly from his decision. If he chose action a, he must have seen signal α; if he chose b, he must have seen signal β.

Now consider the next individual in sequence, Barbara. If she observes that Aaron chose a, and if Barbara's own private signal is α, then she should choose, a herself. As Barbara sees it, there have now been two α signals, one inferred from Aaron's actions and the other that she herself observed; both signals favor action a. If, however, Barbara's private signal is β, then the signal inferred from Aaron's action and her own private signal point in opposite directions. So she should be exactly indifferent between a and b. In that case, suppose Barbara tosses a fair coin.

The third individual, Clarence, knows the actions of his predecessors. He faces one of three possible situations: both Aaron and Barbara chose a, both chose b, or their choices diverged.

If Aaron chose a and Barbara chose b, then Aaron must have seen an α signal and Barbara a β signal. If so the two predecessor actions balance out, and no information is conveyed to Clarence. He therefore will decide on the basis of his own signal, choosing a if he observes α and b if he observes β.

If both Aaron and Barbara chose a, Clarence should also choose action a *regardless of his own personal signal*. The reasoning is as follows. First, if Aaron rationally chose a, he must have seen signal α. As for Barbara, she must have chosen action a either because she saw α herself or because she saw β and then tossed a coin which happened to come up in favor of action a. More likely than not she saw α, since if she had seen β her action would have depended on the coin flip, which could have led her to choose b instead of a. Even if Clarence observed β, the fact that Aaron observed α is enough to make Clarence indifferent between a and b. Since he infers that Barbara probably saw α, Clarence unambiguously prefers a. Of course, if Clarence observes α, he prefers a even more strongly. So Clarence's action does not depend on his signal.

A corresponding argument applies, in the other direction, if Aaron and Barbara had both chosen action b.

So Clarence's choice does not convey any information to later observers. If the fourth person, Donna, observes Clarence choosing a, she is in the same position informationally as Clarence. Donna also chooses a. But this means that *her* action is uninformative too. And Edward, Francine, and so forth all take the same action as well.

This situation, in which individuals decide based upon observing others without regard to their own signals, is called an *information cascade*. No later series of signals can break the cascade. One's own private signal, being imperfect, after a certain point, cannot outweigh the public information represented by the aggregate of all the prior actions.

Once an informational cascade starts, information stops accumulating. Later private signals never join the public pool of knowledge. And, supposing that obtaining a private signal involves some cost, people will rationally stop paying for them. So once the cascade begins not only public information but also private information will no longer accumulate.

Nevertheless, cascades are fragile, as they rest upon only a small amount of public information – the actions of a few decision-makers early in the sequence.

Cascades may break because of "leakage" of private signals. To the extent that not just predecessors' actions but also the signals they observed are known, a cascade is less likely to begin and more likely to end. Another factor is the *weight* of one's private information. An individual who receives a very powerful signal, which she knows to be more informative than the signals received by predecessors, may rationally deviate and possibly break the cascade. But most important is the arrival of information about whether action *a* or action *b* was more successful. Later decision-makers usually can observe, to a degree, not just the *actions* of their predecessors but the *results* of those actions. So information tends to accumulate, over time, about the true state of the world. That helps explain why cascades seldom go on forever.

Not all commonality of behavior stems from herd effects. Producers or consumers may all choose to do the same thing simply because doing so is best for one and all. Or, it may make sense for everyone to buy the same good or service because of returns to scale in production or consumption.

EXAMPLE 11.5 FADS AND CASCADES IN TELEVISION PROGRAMMING

Television programming seems to run in cycles. In some years reality shows predominate, at other times comedies or dramas or westerns. One possible explanation is that the public taste itself runs in cycles. If viewers currently are in the mood to watch comedies, that is what the networks will show. But another possibility is a herd effect or cascade: executives in the various networks might be imitating one another. One or two networks having taken the lead by introducing reality shows, a cascade gets under way that other networks are inclined to follow.

A study by Robert E. Kennedy of program introductions and cancellations by ABC, CBS, and NBC between September 1961 and October 1989 provides some support for the cascade interpretation.[a] During this period the selection process began 12–18 months before each fall season. After looking at a great many program ideas, each network chose about 150 programs to be developed into scripts, and from these about 30 to develop into pilot episodes. The network then evaluated the pilots and chose seven to ten for inclusion in the fall schedule. All three networks announced their schedules in early May each year.

Through word of mouth, each network knows early on what pilot programs the other networks are developing. Later in the process, information about each network's strengths, weaknesses, and portfolio of pilots gradually becomes accessible to rivals. And finally, once broadcasts actually begin, their relative success in attracting viewers is visible to all.

After classifying all prime-time television program introductions into 15 categories, the author estimated whether a network was more likely to introduce programs in a particular category when rival networks were doing so, and to cancel programs in a particular category when other networks were cancelling theirs. Imitation turned out to be common. For example, if NBC increased its introductions of dramas by 10 percentage points, CBS increased its new hours of drama by 2.3 percentage points. Cancellations showed a similar pattern.

> But was such imitation profitable? For each category of television programs, the author measured "trendiness" as the percentage change in the hours of programming in that category from one year to the next. On average, nontrendy introductions outperformed trendy introductions. For example, programs in the top third on the trendiness scale lasted an average of 1.82 years; programs in the bottom third of trendiness lasted longer, an average of 2.29 years. Similarly, programs in a trendy category had, on average, lower ratings than nontrendy programs. So, it appears, in this period herding behavior had been carried beyond what could rationally be justified.
>
> ───────────────────────────────
>
> [a] Robert E. Kennedy, "Strategy Fads and Competitive Convergence: An Empirical Test for Herd Behavior in Prime Time Television Programming," *Journal of Industrial Economics*, v. 50 (2002), pp. 57–84.

11.5   COPYRIGHT, PATENTS, AND INTELLECTUAL PROPERTY RIGHTS

The laws of most nations recognize several types of private property rights in information, among them copyrights, patents, trademarks, and trade secrets. The central problem with intellectual property (IP) rights is the need to balance two conflicting ends: inducing the *creation* of novel ideas and promoting their widespread *use*. By allowing creators to charge a price for their product, IP rights reward and therefore encourage creation of new ideas. But the prices charged discourage use of the same ideas. Patent royalties provide incentives to inventors but may freeze out some potential uses of the invention.

The various forms of intellectual property rights represent different compromises between the ends of promoting the creation and the dissemination of valuable new ideas. A *patent* requires the public disclosure of the invention and grants to its owner the right for a period of years to exclude others from making, using, offering for sale, selling, or importing the invention. *Trade secrets* (such as the formula for Coca-Cola) are not disclosed to the general public, but are to some extent protected against theft. The disadvantage of trade secrets, as opposed to patents, is that the owner has no protection against anyone who comes up with the same idea independently.

A *copyright* gives its owner the exclusive right, again for a limited period, to make and distribute copies of a literary, musical, or artistic work. There is an important procedural difference between patent and copyright. The U.S. Patent Office awards a patent only after careful investigation that the invention is novel (the invention is not the same as any previously described or known to the public), useful (the invention functions for its intended purpose), and nonobvious (the invention would not be self-evident to a person of ordinary skill in the art.). In contrast, copyrights are granted automatically – simply by registration.

A copyright does not protect *ideas* but only a particular *expression* of them. So though anyone can use the ideas in this book, another author cannot extensively copy the exact words in it. But it is difficult to maintain this distinction in any consistent way. Unauthorized translation of a work, though surely a different expression of its ideas, would almost always be considered an infringement of copyright. Expressions further removed from the original, for example summaries or parodies, may or may not be considered infringements.

Three main policy issues are involved in the economics of copyright and patent. (1) Are IP rights given out too freely, or not freely enough? In the case of patents, should the

Table 11.3 Creation without copyright –
a Prisoner's Dilemma

	Author #2	
Author #1	Create	Don't create
Create	2, 2	−3, 5
Don't create	5, −3	0, 0

criteria of originality and utility be interpreted more or less stringently? (2) A related question concerns scope. Should the Wright Brothers have been granted a broad patent covering all powered flight, or only a narrow patent on powered flight using wings warped by wires for control purposes?[8] (3) When granted, are the rights too strong, or too weak? For example, should "fair use"[9] be permitted without charge?

One confusion should be cleared away. A patent or a copyright is a property right, not a "monopoly" in the sense used in economic analysis. An intellectual property right, like any property right, must grant some special power to the owner. But that property right becomes a monopoly only if close competitors are absent. Consider a patent for a new rose variety. Thousands of rose varieties have been invented, and hundreds are in the market. So, although the patent protects against unauthorized use of that unique variety, there is no monopoly. (These cases, of unique yet closely competing products, fall under the heading of *monopolistic competition* as discussed in Chapter 9 above.) Or consider a patent for a new type of bottle-opener. Again, dozens of designs for bottle-openers are on the market, so there is no monopoly. On the other hand, a sufficiently broad patent could have monopoly implications. If the Wright brothers had been granted a patent on all powered flight, they would have had a stranglehold over the aircraft industry.

Thinking for concreteness of copyright, in the absence of legal protection authors would face a *public good* problem like that discussed in Chapter 10 and earlier in this chapter. The payoffs in Table 11.3 here are, by assumption, identical to the Prisoners' Dilemma payoffs of Table 10.4 that dealt with draining marshy soil as a public good. Here, instead of two farmers there are two potential authors. Instead of Pump and Don't Pump, the strategy options are Create and Don't Create. If one author chooses Create, the other can free-ride by copying – which, by assumption, yields the highest payoff (namely, 5). The creative author, having invested time and effort to little or no avail, gets the lowest payoff (−3). If both choose Create the payoffs are 2,2; if both choose Don't Create, the payoffs are 0,0. Here Don't Create is better for a player regardless of what the other player does. As before the equilibrium is the inefficient (Don't Create, Don't Create) strategy-pair with payoffs 0,0.

The authors might escape this trap by signing a binding contract not to copy. That could be feasible if there were only two potential authors, but not when there are many. As an alternative to such a contract, copyright law, by making unauthorized copying illegal, enables both authors to create and thus achieve the efficient (2,2) payoffs.

But this analysis is too extreme. It implies there would be little or no creative activity in the absence of copyright. Yet books, symphonies, and other compositions were created

---

[8] They were awarded only the narrow patent.
[9] Under the copyright law in the United States, anyone can copy copyrighted material without the permission of the original author, if the amount copied is limited and if the purpose falls into specified categories such as criticizing or parodying the copyrighted work.

before copyright laws existed and would undoubtedly be created today even if copyright were abolished.

There are several possible reasons. (1) Some people are willing to create without material reward, simply for the pleasure and glory. (2) Original composition may yield *indirect* material gains. Wolfgang Amadeus Mozart (1756–1791) was paid a pittance for the operas, concertos, and symphonies he composed. He was hoping for an indirect reward, appointment as a salaried musician to a European court or church. (His predecessors Franz Joseph Haydn and Johann Sebastian Bach found such positions, but Mozart never realized his hopes). (3) The original creator can profit from a *time advantage* over imitations. Paris and Milan high-fashion designs are rapidly copied, yet command a steep premium while still new. Original digital recordings may reap substantial revenues before unauthorized digital copies become widely available. (This was one of the arguments used by the defense in the Napster litigation.)

EXAMPLE 11.6 THE NAPSTER STORY[a]

Digital technology has made it possible to produce essentially perfect copies of CD recordings at extremely low cost. As a result, it is technologically possible for consumers to copy recordings without compensating the original creators. In January 2000, MP3.com began making musical works available for copying via its Internet computer servers. (MP3 had purchased single copies, but had not purchased licenses to reproduce them, claiming an exemption for "fair use.") Major record companies and artists then sued MP3 for copyright infringement.

MP3 lost its case and went out of business. But then Napster was initiated as a peer-to-peer network for transfer of downloaded recordings. The "fair use" defense was stronger for Napster than for MP3, since Napster was not directly selling services to anyone. But Napster also lost in court and was forced to go out of business as well.

At the date of writing the recording industry has so far won the major legal battles, yet may still lose the war. The reason is that, in part with the help of successors to Napster such as Gnutella and Kazaa or even without any special help, it is becoming increasingly feasible to transfer recordings from computer to computer without payment to copyright holders. The copyrights, though upheld in court, may turn out to be impossible to enforce.

The recording industry has tried a number of strategies in defense. One is encryption, which is subject to attack by hackers. Prices have also been reduced, and there have been experiments with new marketing techniques such as subscription services. Another device is to package additional features such as interviews and photos together with legitimate copies. Industry leaders have also, perhaps with some degree of success, appealed to customers' sense of ethics. For all these reasons the recording industry will not be totally going out of business. However, the number of recorded new compositions and new performances or their quality may well fall off.

As an impending development, rising hard-drive capacities of personal computers and continuing improvements in transmission speeds and bandwidth seem bound to threaten the business of selling recorded motion pictures.

---

[a] For a description of the legal history, see Peter K. Yu, "The Escalating Copyright Wars," *Hofstra Law Review*, v. 32 (2004).

Table 11.4 Creation without copyright – a chicken game

	Create	Imitate
Create	7, 7	2, 10
Imitate	10, 2	0, 0

Last, a fourth explanation for the continued creation of original compositions even in the absence of copyright protection is that the situation may not really be a Prisoners' Dilemma. Though freely copyable compositions are public goods, the choice situation facing potential creators may be better reflected by the payoff environment of Chicken.

Just as Table 11.3 repeated the Prisoners' Dilemma payoffs of Table 10.5, Table 11.4 here repeats the Chicken payoffs of Table 11.2. But instead of paying to acquire information as a public good, here the issue is whether to create information as a public good or to imitate an existing creation. The logic is essentially the same. The idea is that, although copying is preferred when there is something to copy (Imitate is a player's best choice if the other player chooses Create), if the other player produces nothing you would rather choose Create.

Imagine a theatrical entrepreneur who wants to produce live musicals. If he can put on a revival of *Oklahoma* or *Guys and Dolls* without paying royalties, that would be ideal. But if no musicals are available for reviving, to present something to the public he would have to commission one himself. Or imagine that Paris and Milan stop creating original dress designs. Then a dress manufacturing firm previously specializing in knockoffs might find it profitable to begin creating its own designs.

Since Table 11.4 is numerically equivalent to Table 11.2, the solutions are the same. In particular, the symmetrical mixed-strategy equilibrium is $p_R = p_C = 0.4$. It is possible also to interpret this mixed-strategy solution nonprobabilistically. Instead of saying the game has only two players, each choosing a 40:60 strategy mix, we can say there are many players – of whom 40% choose Create and the other 60% choose Imitate. So in the absence of rights in intellectual property we would expect to see a decrease in intellectual creative activity, but not its complete elimination.

The preceding discussion emphasized the role of legal protection for encouraging intellectual creation. But what of the other side of the picture, the spread and use of such ideas as are created? Without copyright fewer musical recordings may be produced, but those that are produced will be more accessible. When it comes to life-saving or life-enhancing pharmaceutical drugs, striking a proper balance between having new medications and allowing for their widest possible use is a highly important issue.

EXAMPLE 11.7 PHARMACEUTICALS – CREATION VERSUS UTILIZATION

If patents on pharmaceutical drugs were eliminated, generic competitors for already-developed medications (see Example 5.4) would rapidly enter. To meet the competition the branded products would have to come down in price, and consumers would benefit. On the other hand, manufacturers' incentives to undertake the costly research needed to develop new drugs – according to some estimates, as high as $800,000,000 per genuinely new drug ("new chemical entity" or NCE) – would fall off correspondingly. So consumers, though benefiting in the short run, would very likely suffer later on from a deficiency of new drugs.

James W. Hughes, Michael J. Moore, and Edward A. Snyder attempted to quantify these conflicting considerations. They estimated the aggregate Consumer Surplus under the two alternative policies – having drug patents or not.[a]

In their calculations the authors took into consideration a great many factors including the years of useful life per new drug, the period of exclusivity if patented (the number of years before generic competitors could enter), the market share retained by branded products after generic entry, and the fraction of drug profits allocated to research. In allowing for all of these, the authors balanced the benefit to consumers of lower current prices (the static gains) against the loss to consumers of reduced future availability of new drugs (the dynamic losses).

Balancing the present against the future is a topic that will be taken up in Chapter 15 that deals with the economics of time. For a variety of reasons – among them the brevity of human life, the fact that resources grow over time, and the presence of risk – markets discount the future relative to the present, and the far future relative to the near future. The authors calculated the Present Values of current and future benefits from abolition of patents, using a range of discount rates ranging from 1% to 5% per annum. The table here shows that at the extremely low 1% discount rate, which weights the future relatively heavily, the benefit from abolishing drug patenting is far less than the loss. The benefit/cost ratio is only 0.15. As the discount rate rises the balance swings in the other direction. But only at the extremely high 5% discount rate, associated with very heavy discount of future benefits, does the gain/loss ratio for abolition of patents rise above unity, to 1.11.

What the authors regard as the most accurate assumption, a discount rate of 2%, is associated with a cost/benefit ratio of 0.33. So, they conclude, although the short-run gain in Consumer Surplus due to lower prices for drugs would be quite substantial, the long-run loss from abolition of patents and consequent reduced future availability of drugs would be even greater – around three times as great.

Benefits and costs of abolishing pharmaceutical patents (present values of consumer surplus, 2001 dollars, billions)

Discount rates	1%	2%	3%	5%
Static (current) gains	882	840	800	727
Dynamic (future) losses	5760	2501	1454	673
Gain/loss ratio	0.15	0.33	0.56	1.11

Source: Adapted from Hughes, Moore, and Snyder, Table 6.

[a] James W. Hughes, Michael J. Moore, and Edward A. Snyder, " 'Napsterizing' Pharmaceuticals: Access, Innovation, and Consumer Welfare," National Bureau of Economic Research Working Paper No. 0229 (October 2002).

SUMMARY   For frequently repeated and independent decisions, the Law of Large Numbers in effect cancels out risk. Then it is possible to choose the best action on the basis of maximizing one's average (expected) dollar gain. But for nonrepeatable choices involving large fractions of the decision-maker's resources, individuals averse to risk are willing to sacrifice expected gain to in order to avoid very bad outcomes. Analytically, the individual is then maximizing expected utility rather than expected dollar gain. Risk aversion is equivalent to diminishing marginal utility of income.

A "fair" gamble or insurance contract is one for which the mathematical expectation of net gain is zero. If already in a riskless position, a risk-averse decision-maker would always reject such a gamble or contract. On the other hand, if initially in a risky income situation – for example, facing a risk of theft – such a decision-maker will accept gambles or contracts that offset his or her initial risk. Indeed, a risk-averse decision-maker would be willing to accept even some "unfair" gambles or insurance contracts, provided they tended to offset the riskiness of his or her endowed income combination. This is typically the case when insurance is purchased.

It sometimes pays to delay taking action until further information becomes available. But for the information to be of value, it must be that different messages or signals might lead to different optimal actions. As one example, a consumer may delay deciding whether to buy a good, even if the expected price is expected to rise. The delay reflects the option value of being able to buy the good only if its price turns out to be low.

When sellers know more than do potential buyers about the characteristics of a good, a "lemons" problem may emerge. Owners of low-quality items are more eager to sell than are owners of high-quality items, and that makes potential demanders less eager to buy. As a result only low-end items may appear on the market, ranging up to some critical level of quality. Above that quality level the "peaches" (better-quality items) may never be available for purchase.

People can sometimes infer quality from the price of the good itself. An ignorant but rational consumer who knows that informed consumers are willing to pay more for a better product may conclude that higher-priced goods are of higher quality. But these informed consumers, if they have incurred cost in evaluating product quality, are providing a kind of public good. If the payoff situation is a Prisoners' Dilemma, no one will be willing to incur the cost. But if the payoffs correspond to the pattern of Chicken, there will be a mixed-strategy equilibrium in which with some positive probability each decision-maker makes the investment in information.

Owing to anticipation of repeated sales, other things equal, producers of high-quality goods can expect to profit more from advertising than producers of low-quality goods. If so, the fact that a product is advertised may signal quality (regardless of what the ads actually say). But such an inference is not entirely reliable, since a bad product is likely to be cheaper to produce. Then the seller, even with little hope of repeated sales, may find it pays to advertise.

People who know they are imperfectly informed can try to gain information by observing others' actions. When others in aggregate are likely to have better information than one single person can advantageously acquire, the result may be an informational cascade. If a crowded restaurant is likely to be a good place to eat, and a popular movie to be good entertainment, then any one person has an incentive to follow the choices of others rather than to rely on his private information. Once an informational cascade starts, information stops accumulating. But informational cascades are fragile, leading sometimes to short-lived fads.

Intellectual property (IP) rights encourage the creation of inventions and novel ideas by permitting creators to reap some return from their efforts. But holders of IP rights are likely to make the new ideas available only for a price, which discourages their use and dissemination. The laws covering various forms of intellectual property – patent, copyright, trademarks and so on – balance these factors in different ways. In the absence of IP rights the creation of new ideas would be a public good. The payoff pattern is likely to fall into the Chicken category, so that a certain amount of creative activity would continue to take place, though less than would occur under strong intellectual property rights.

QUESTIONS

†The answers to daggered questions appear at the end of the book.

For Review

1. Explain graphically why a convex utility function implies a preference for greater risk.
†2. Why do insurance companies require medical tests before agreeing to sell an individual a life insurance policy?
3. a.   Describe a benefit and a cost to consumers of drug patents.
   b.   Are patents more likely to be desirable if consumers place high value on long-term costs and benefits?
†4. Do the following increase or decrease the certainty-equivalent associated with a gamble? The risk premium?
   a.   High risk (variability).
   b.   High risk aversion.
   c.   High expected value.
†5. Would a risk-averse individual who is endowed with riskless wealth ever accept a fair gamble?
†6. What is another word for the acquisition of a gamble that offsets endowed risk?
†7. Why might an individual underinsure?
†8. Theorists who study financial economics have developed models that have been very successful in determining the value of financial options. For example, a call option gives the holder the right (but not the obligation) to purchase a stock at a prespecified price during a prespecified time period. Why is a call option valuable? Discuss in relation to the value of information.
9. What is adverse selection? How does it affect the price that consumers are willing to pay for a product whose quality is not observable at the time of purchase?
10. Suppose that the quality of a product is not observable to consumers at the time of purchase. How can reputation encourage a firm to produce a high-quality product?
†11. What can impair the credibility of price as a signal product quality? Despite this problem, can high product price work as a signal?
†12. Why would a high-quality brand have a higher marginal benefit from advertising than a low-quality brand?
†13. Employers are often skeptical of job applicants who have "gaps" in their resumes – periods of time during which the individual had no employment. Explain why based on informational cascades.

For Further Thought and Discussion

1. You want to find out whether there is a lemons problem in the market for houses. How, if at all, could you use the following information to answer the question?
   a.   Repair rates for homes owned by the original buyer compared to houses which have been resold.
   b.   The fraction of houses resold in each year after purchase.
2. A firm spends money on advertising attempting to persuade consumers of the brand name of its grapes. Should consumers conclude that its grapes have better quality than grapes sold by other firms?

3. Suppose that consumers are willing to pay as much as $8,000 for a good used car but only $2,000 for a "lemon." Each owner of a good used car will sell only if the price exceeds $4,000; each owner of a lemon will sell only if the price exceeds $600. Buyers cannot tell if a used car is a lemon or not, and 20% of all used cars are lemons. In equilibrium, which cars are sold, and at what prices?

4. Some mortgage companies offer mortgages without asking the borrower anything about her income or nonhouse assets. Why do such loans have higher interest rates?

5. Medford University offers each new faculty hired a choice: he or she can get a tenured job, or else choose a series of shorter-term (e.g., 3 or 5 years) contracts at a higher salary level designed to compensate for the decreased job security. What is likely to be the outcome of this "menu" plan if faculty members differ in quality, that is, in ability to find a job elsewhere?

6. Why is it usually incorrect to call a patent award a "monopoly"?

†7. John argues, "Sure, I don't like risk. But if I always choose the option with higher expected value, over the long run the wins and losses will more or less cancel out, except that I'll end up getting a higher payoff on average. So it is irrational to be averse to risk." Do you agree?

†8. Investment advisors typically recommend that individuals diversify, by placing portions of one's invested wealth into different asset classes (such as bonds, domestic stocks, and foreign stocks). Suppose that there are two asset classes A and B, which are similar in variability and expected payoff; sometimes A does better and sometimes B. Which investment strategy do you think is riskier, placing all your invested wealth in asset A, or dividing it equally between assets A and B?

†9. Many employees invest for retirement by using their retirement plans to buy stocks in their own companies. Is this likely to be a good decision if the employee is risk-averse?

†10. You are trying to decide how much to offer for a television set being sold at a garage sale. One of the other shoppers mentions to you that the reason for the sale is that owner is planning on moving to another country and cannot bring anything with him. How does this news affect the amount you should be willing to offer? How is this related to the problem of adverse selection?

11. The evidence on restaurant hygiene in Los Angeles (Example 11.4) suggests that regulation forcing conspicuous public display of hygiene scores caused restaurants to improve their hygiene. Even without such regulation, a private ratings agency could have gone into the business of inspecting restaurants and offering grades. If customers valued hygiene, hygienic restaurants might have been willing to pay the ratings agency to provide evaluations, in order to win more business. Does the absence of conspicuous private hygiene ratings prior to the regulation indicate that customers did not value hygiene very much?

†12. Consider a setting like that in Section 11.4 in which individuals with private information make decisions in sequence. Suppose, however, that Aaron possesses a signal that is slightly more accurate than Barbara's. In other words, his signal probability is $q > p$, where p is Barbara's signal probability. Suppose that Aaron chooses action a. What will Barbara do? How many individuals must make decisions before a cascade forms?

†13. During the rise of the personal computer industry, IBM allowed competitors to produce compatible PCs whereas Apple maintained a proprietary design. What are some possible advantages of permitting imitation by competitors?

IV FACTOR MARKETS AND INCOME DISTRIBUTION

12 The Demand for Factor Services

The text so far has concentrated on markets for final products: cars, cameras, hair-cuts, and so forth. Here in Part Four the emphasis shifts to the markets for productive inputs such as land, labor, and machines. The *demand side* of the markets for these "factors of production" is the topic of this chapter: firms decide upon the amounts of land, labor, and other productive services to hire. On the *supply side*, the topic of the following chapter, owners of land or machines decide where to put their assets to use, and workers (owners of their labor power) decide where and how much to work.

12.1 PRODUCTION AND FACTOR EMPLOYMENT WITH A SINGLE VARIABLE INPUT

The Production Function

A mining firm, in order to extract ore, has to employ land (the mine itself) together with labor, buildings, electric power, gasoline, and machines. The technological relation between such inputs and the firm's output is called the *production function*. It can be expressed:

$$q \equiv \Phi(a, b, c, \ldots) \tag{12.1}$$

This equation says that the output quantity q depends in some specified way upon the amounts a, b, c, ... of the resource inputs A, B, C, ...[1]

Suppose all inputs are held fixed except for the amount of a single variable factor A. Then the production function can be written in the simpler form:

$$q \equiv q(a) \tag{12.2}$$

This equation says that q depends algebraically only upon the single variable a. The amounts b, c, ... of the fixed inputs B, C, ... no longer directly appear – but the levels at which these inputs are held fixed do affect the shape of the $q(a)$ function.

EXERCISE 12.1

Suppose the underlying production function makes use of two inputs A and B. Specifically, let equation (12.1) take the form $q = 6a^{1/2}b^{1/4}$. What would be the form of equation (12.2) if the quantity of input B were held fixed at $b = 1$? At $b = 16$?

ANSWER: Substituting $b = 1$ in equation (12.1), equation (12.2) becomes $q = 6a^{1/2}$. For $b = 16$, equation (12.2) becomes $q = 12a^{1/2}$.

Diminishing Returns

The Law (or Laws) of Diminishing Returns explain why costs of production rise as output grows, that is, why the Total Cost, Average Cost, and Marginal Cost functions as shown in Chapter 6 must, at least eventually, all rise as the firm increases output.

---

[1] In the notation here A, B, C are the *names* of factors of production; the lower-case symbols a, b, c signify specific *amounts* of those factors.

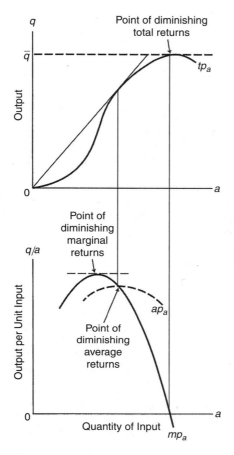

Figure 12.1. The Laws of Diminishing Returns

The upper panel shows the Total Product function for factor A, tp_a. The lower panel shows the corresponding Average Product function ap_a and Marginal Product function mp_a. Diminishing *marginal* returns set in first (the mp_a curve reaches its peak), then diminishing *average* returns set in (the ap_a curve reaches its peak), and finally diminishing *total* returns set in (the tp_a curve reaches its peak, at output $\bar{q}$).

Let the only variable factor be A. As a (the amount used of factor A) increases, the Total Product tp_a (which is the quantity produced, so that $tp_a \equiv q$), the Average Product ap_a (which is quantity per unit of input, so that $ap_a \equiv q/a$), and the Marginal Product mp_a (which is the change in quantity per unit change of input, so that $mp_a \equiv \Delta q/\Delta a$) all eventually rise:

THE LAWS OF DIMINISHING RETURNS: If the amount a of input A increases, with other inputs held fixed, the rate of increase of Total Product q – that is, the Marginal Product mp_a – eventually begins to fall. This is the point of *diminishing marginal returns*. As the input amount increases further, Average Product ap_a also begins to fall. This is the point of *diminishing average returns*. And as use of input A rises further, even Total Product may fall. (An extreme overabundance of input A could be counterproductive.) This would be the point of *diminishing total returns*.

Figure 12.1 illustrates the Laws of Diminishing Returns. The upper panel shows the Total Product curve tp_a. The lower diagram shows the corresponding curves for Marginal Product mp_a and Average Product ap_a. The diagram confirms that diminishing marginal returns set in first, then diminishing average returns, and then (possibly) diminishing total returns.

EXERCISE 12.2

A firm's Total Product function is $tp_a \equiv q = 100a^2 - a^3$. The Average Product function is then $ap_a \equiv q/a = 100a - a^2$. It can be shown algebraically[2] that the Marginal Product function is $mp_a \equiv \Delta q/\Delta a = 200a - 3a^2$. (Or the same result can be obtained by calculus.) (a) When do diminishing marginal returns set in? (b) Diminishing average returns? (c) Diminishing total returns?

ANSWER: (a) *Diminishing marginal returns* set in where the mp_a function reaches a maximum. It can be determined by plotting the function (or by calculus) that Marginal Product reaches its maximum at $a = 33\,^1/_3$. (b) Average Product reaches a maximum (*diminishing average returns* set in) at $a = 50$. (c) Total Product reaches a maximum (*diminishing total returns* set in) at $a = 66\,^2/_3$.

EXAMPLE 12.1 NEW MEXICO ONIONS

In dry climates such as New Mexico, onions, a water-intensive crop, need irrigation. M. S. Al-Jamal, T. W. Sammis, S. Ball, and D. Smeal studied the relation between inputs of water and crop yield (the "water production function") in an experiment at the Fabian Garcia Research Center in Las Cruces, NM.[a]

One of their studies estimated the relationship as:

$$\text{Yield} = -7809.28 + 693\,\text{Water} - 1.164\,\text{Water}^2$$

The negative squared term implies that, as more water is increasingly applied, Marginal Product and Average Product and even Total Product must eventually fall.

The table shows a selection of their data for the year 1995. Total Product is measured in kilograms per hectare, and water in centimeters (cm) applied (including natural rainfall). The last two columns on the right calculate the Average Product and Marginal Product for various amounts of water applied. (Following the recommended approximation method of Chapter 2, Section 2.2, the marginal estimates are placed at the midpoints of the intervals.) The table indicates that, consistent with the discussion in the text, diminishing marginal returns set in before diminishing average returns. (As can be seen, diminishing marginal returns hold here from the beginning – the Marginal Product of water is declining throughout.)

---

[2] *Mathematical Footnote*: Algebraically, Δq is the difference between $q(a + \Delta a)$ and $q(a)$, so that:

$$\Delta q = [100(a + \Delta a)^2 - (a + \Delta a)^3] - [100a^2 - a^3]$$

Carrying out the algebraic expansion, simplifying, and dividing through by Δa leads to:

$$\frac{\Delta q}{\Delta a} = 200a - 3\,a^2 + (\text{several terms involving } \Delta a)$$

Since marginal calculations deal with small changes, to a good approximation the terms involving Δa can be neglected, leading to the expression in the text.

Water input and onion crop, New Mexico 1995

Water (cm)	Total product (kg/ha)	Average product (per cm of water)	Marginal product (at mid-interval)
86.8	39,665	457.0	
			475.4
109.1	50,267	460.7	
			343.3
131.3	57,888	440.9	
			192.5
153.5	62,162	405.0	
			123.6
175.7	64,906	369.4	

Source: Adapted from Table 2 of Al-Jamal et al. (2000).

[a] M. S. Al-Jamal, T. W. Sammis, S. Ball, and D. Smeal, "Computing the Crop Water Production Function for Onion," *Agricultural Water Management*, v. 46 (2000), pp. 29–41.

From Production Function to Cost Function

The cost functions described in Chapter 6 reflect the underlying production function together with the prices of inputs. There are two ways the firm might pay to use a resource: by purchasing it or hiring it. A business firm can own its trucks or lease them as needed; a farmer might either buy or rent the land he cultivates. (Labor, of course, cannot be purchased but only hired.) In this chapter it will be more convenient to think of the firm as always hiring inputs.[3] The rental rates or "hire-prices" of inputs A, B, C, ... will be denoted h_a, h_b, h_c, ...

To begin with, suppose the firm is a price-taker (has no "monopsony power") in its input markets. This means that the hire-prices of factors of production can be taken as constants in calculating costs of production.

For any given combination of inputs, the firm's Total Cost is:

$$C \equiv h_a a + h_b b + h_c c + \cdots \tag{12.3}$$

When some factors are held fixed – say, all but input A – Total Cost can be divided into a fixed component F and a variable component V:

$$C \equiv F + V \equiv F + h_a a \tag{12.3'}$$

The Variable Cost, the spending on input A, is $V \equiv h_a a$. Fixed Cost F corresponds to spending on the nonvarying inputs B, C, and so forth.

Suppose the production function (12.2) is $q = \sqrt{a}$, all other factors being fixed. Since then $a = q^2$, in equation (12.3') the firm's cost of producing any output q becomes $C = F + h_a q^2$.

---

[3] A firm that decides to purchase rather than hire a needed input is making an *investment* decision. Investment decisions involve choices between present and future, a topic taken up in Chapter 15.

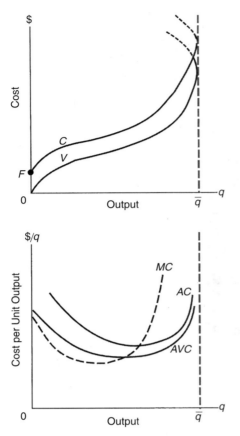

Figure 12.2. From Production Function to Cost Function

Multiplying the horizontal axis of the previous diagram by the constant hire-price h_a shifts the dimension from units of input (a) to units of Variable Cost ($h_a a$). Rotated $180°$ and flipped over, the tp_a curve of the previous diagram becomes the Total Variable Cost V curve in the upper diagram. The mp_a curve of the previous diagram becomes the Marginal Cost curve MC in the lower diagram; the ap_a curve becomes the Average Variable Cost curve AVC.

More generally, if $q \equiv q(a)$ is the production function, the inverted function is $a \equiv a(q)$.[4] So the cost function can be written:

$$C \equiv F + h_a a(q) \tag{12.4}$$

Thus Total Cost depends upon the fixed cost F, the hire-price h_a, and (after inversion) the production function $q = q(a)$.

In Figure 12.2, the shape of the Total Variable Cost curve V in the upper panel reflects the shape of the tp_a curve of Figure 12.1 – rotated $180°$ and flipped over. The dashed *vertical* bound on the right of Figure 12.2 represents the same maximum output $\overline{q}$ as the dashed *horizontal* bound $\overline{q}$ in Figure 12.1. Note also that the Total Cost curve C lies above the Variable Cost curve V by the amount of the Fixed Cost F.[5]

The Marginal Cost (MC) and Average Cost (AC) curves of Figure 12.2 look like upside-down versions of the mp_a and ap_a curves of Figure 12.1. For the marginal curves the reason is evident from the relation between Marginal Cost MC and Marginal

---

[4] *Mathematical Footnote*: As a technical qualification, it is sometimes impossible to uniquely invert $q \equiv q(a)$ so as to write $a \equiv a(q)$. This complication will be ignored here.

[5] The firm would always ignore the dotted upper branches of the C and V curves. These correspond to the range in Figure 12.1 where tp is a *declining* function of input amount a. It would never pay the firm to produce any given output at greater cost if it can do the same at lower cost.

Product mp_a:

$$MC \equiv \frac{\Delta C}{\Delta q} \equiv \frac{h_a \, \Delta a}{\Delta q} \equiv \frac{h_a}{\Delta q / \Delta a} \equiv \frac{h_a}{mp_a} \qquad (12.5)$$

So *Marginal Cost* MC *necessarily increases as Marginal Product* mp_a *decreases.* (Recall that since the firm is a price-taker in the factor market, hire-price h_a is assumed constant.) Thus, the Law of Diminishing Marginal Returns (which states that as use of an input rises, Marginal Product eventually declines) explains why the MC curve must eventually rise.

A corresponding inverse relationship holds between Average Product ap_a and Average Variable Cost $AVC \equiv V/q$. As ap_a falls, AVC rises:

$$AVC \equiv \frac{V}{q} \equiv \frac{h_a a}{q} \equiv \frac{h_a}{q/a} \equiv \frac{h_a}{ap_a} \qquad (12.6)$$

Taking into account fixed costs as well, for Average Cost the relationship is:

$$AC \equiv \frac{C}{q} \equiv \frac{F + h_a a}{q} \equiv \frac{F}{q} + \frac{h_a}{ap_a} \qquad (12.7)$$

Since F/q on the right-hand side (Average Fixed Cost) shrinks towards zero as q rises, the AC curve converges toward the AVC curve. So both curves must eventually rise as a continues to increase.

EXERCISE 12.3

Suppose the firm's short-run production function, corresponding to equation (12.2), is $tp_a \equiv q \equiv 2\sqrt{a}$. Let the hire-price be $h_a = 4$, and the fixed cost $F = 50$. (a) Find the Total Variable Cost function V and the Total Cost function C. (b) Relate Marginal Cost MC to Marginal Product mp_a. (c) Relate Average Variable Cost AVC and Average Cost AC to Average Product ap_a.

ANSWER: (a) Inverting the production function, $a = q^2/4$. So Total Variable Cost is $V \equiv h_a a = 4a = q^2$ and Total Cost is $C \equiv F + V = 50 + q^2$. (b) Since $C = 50 + q^2$, direct tabulation (or calculus) shows that Marginal Cost is $MC \equiv \Delta C/\Delta q = 2q$. And since Total Product is $q = 2\sqrt{a}$, it follows that $mp_a \equiv \Delta q/\Delta a = 1/\sqrt{a}$. From equation (12.5), $MC \equiv h_a/mp_a = 4/mp_a$, which can be directly confirmed: $h_a/mp_a = 4\sqrt{a} = 2q = MC$. (c) Using equation (12.6), $AVC \equiv h_a/ap_a = 4/ap_a$. And equation (12.7) becomes $AC = 50/q + 4/ap_a = 25/\sqrt{a} + 4/ap_a$.

The Firm's Demand for a Single Variable Input

The production function is a technological relation between inputs and outputs. But in deciding upon the amounts of factors to employ, the firm must go beyond technology and consider financial variables as well – in particular, the factor hire-prices $h_a, h_b, h_c, \ldots$.

Dealing with a single variable input A, the assumption that the firm is a price-taker in the factor market means that the horizontal line in Figure 12.3 at hire-price h_a can be regarded as the supply curve s_a of the resource to the firm. Just as the price-taking (nonmonopolist) firm in the product market faces a *horizontal product demand curve d*

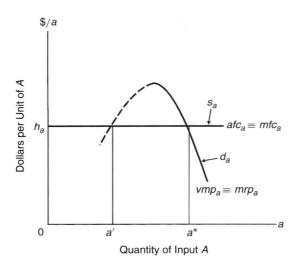

Figure 12.3. Optimal Factor Employment: Price-Taking Firm in Both Factor Market and Product Market

The horizontal line, showing the supply curve s_a to the price-taking firm at hire-price h_a, is the curve of Average Factor Cost (afc_a) and also of Marginal Factor Cost (mfc_a). If the firm is a price-taker in the product market as well, the Value of the Marginal Product (vmp_a) curve coincides with the Marginal Revenue Product (mrp_a) curve. The firm's demand curve d_a for input A is then the downward-sloping branch of the $vmp_a \equiv mrp_a$ curve.

(as shown in the lower panel of Figure 6.1 in Chapter 6), here s_a is the *horizontal input supply curve* facing a price-taking (nonmonopsonist) firm in the factor market.

In deciding whether to employ an additional unit of input A, the firm must balance the hire-price h_a to be paid against the benefit to be gained. This benefit has two elements: the additional physical output, and what that added output generates in the way of revenue.

Assume to begin with that the firm is also a price-taker in the product market. Then each additional unit of output can be sold at the given product price P. Combining product price and Marginal Product leads to the concept called *Value of the Marginal Product*.

> **DEFINITION:** The Value of the Marginal Product for input A, vmp_a, is the product price P times the physical Marginal Product mp_a:
>
> $$vmp_a \equiv P \times mp_a \quad \text{Definition of } vmp_a \qquad (12.8)$$

The Example that follows illustrates how changes in the price of the product can affect the demand for an input used in production.

EXAMPLE 12.2 THE PRICE OF RICE AND THE PRICE OF SLAVES

Peter C. Mancall, Joshua L. Rosenbloom, and Thomas Weiss studied South Carolina probate records to estimate the prices of slaves in the period 1722–1809.[a] During this period the major agricultural activity in South Carolina was rice cultivation using slave labor – an inhumane system, but nevertheless subject to the laws of economic logic.

The text indicates that product prices (P) affect the Value of the Marginal Product (vmp) of a factor. The table shows that upward movements in the price of rice were indeed associated with upturns in slave prices, reflecting increased planter demand for slave labor – and conversely for downward movements in the price of rice. (For other historical reasons, during this period slave prices were tending to rise.) As would be expected, high prices for rice were also associated with increased imports of slaves.

Slaves and the price of rice in South Carolina			
Period	Rice price (cents/lb)	Slave price (real $/adult male)	Slaves imported
1722–1729	1.40	164.16	11,600
1730–1739	1.64	175.43	21,150
1740–1749	1.18	149.17	1,950
1750–1759	1.56	167.74	16,497
1760–1769	1.58	154.30	21,840
1770–1779	1.87	245.70	18,866
1780–1789	3.15	343.50	19,200
1790–1799	2.73	197.20	19,991
1800–1809	3.81	393.20	30,195

Source: Adapted from Mancall et al., Tables 2 and 5.

[a] Peter C. Mancall, Joshua L. Rosenbloom, and Thomas Weiss, "South Carolina Slave Prices, 1722–1809," National Bureau of Economic Research Historical Paper 123 (March 2000).

The vmp_a curve in Figure 12.3 has the same general shape as the mp_a curve in the lower panel of Figure 12.1, since the only change is multiplication by a constant product price P. The vertical axis, however, differs. In Figure 12.1 the vertical axis is scaled in *output* per unit of input (q/a); in Figure 12.3 it is scaled in *dollars* per unit of input ($\$/a$).

Turning to the employment decision, whenever vmp_a exceeds hire-price h_a the firm can profitably employ an additional unit of A. And if $vmp_a < h_a$, the firm would do better hiring fewer units. So for a firm that is a price-taker in both its product market and the factor market, the optimal employment of input A is given by the equality:

$$vmp_a = h_a \quad \text{Factor Employment Condition for a Price-Taking Firm[6]} \quad (12.9)$$

It can happen, however, that this equality is satisfied at two or more input levels, for example a' and a^* in Figure 12.3. So something more is needed. A secondary condition for an optimum is that the vmp_a curve must be *falling* relative to the horizontal line associated with the current hire-price h_a;[7] this occurs only at a^* in the diagram.[8] A firm that used only a' units of input would be missing out on the profitable range in the diagram where the revenue increment vmp_a exceeds the cost h_a.

---

[6] Equation (12.8) is a definitional *identity*, whereas equation (12.9) is an *equality* that holds only when the firm has chosen the profit-maximizing employment of the factor.

[7] Recall from Chapter 6 that the output optimum for the price-taking firm occurs at $MC = P$, provided that the MC curve cuts the horizontal line at price P *from below*. Here the input optimum occurs where $vmp_a = h_a$, provided that the vmp_a curve cuts the horizontal line at hire-price h_a *from above*.

[8] *Mathematical Footnote*: The conditions above correspond to the first-order and second-order conditions for a profit maximum. The firm chooses the amount of A to maximize profit $\Pi = R - C \equiv Pq - h_a a - F$ (where F stands for fixed costs representing expenditures on inputs other than A). Differentiating Π with respect to a and setting the derivative equal to zero leads to the first-order condition:

$$P \frac{dq}{da} = h_a \quad \text{or} \quad P \times mp_a = h_a$$

This corresponds to equation (12.9). Taking the second derivative of Π, the *second-order* condition for a maximum is:

$$P \frac{d^2 q}{da^2} < 0 \quad \text{or} \quad \text{(since } P \text{ is a positive constant)} \quad \frac{d^2 q}{da^2} < 0$$

This means that to have a profit maximum, the Value of the Marginal Product $vmp_a \equiv P \times mp_a$ must be falling.

Constructing the firm's demand curve for input A requires that the firm satisfy the Factor Employment Condition for all possible levels of the hire-price h_a.

CONCLUSION

For a firm that is a price-taker in both factor and product markets, the demand curve for a single variable input A is the downward-sloping range along the vmp_a curve.

EXERCISE 12.4

Suppose the firm's Total Product function is $q = 2\sqrt{a}$ as in Exercise 12.3. Let the product price be $P = 60$ and let the input hire-price be $h_a = 4$. (a) Find the equation for the vmp_a curve. (b) Find the optimal input amount a^*. (c) What is the associated output q^*? (d) What is the firm's demand curve equation for the input?

ANSWER: (a) Exercise 12.3 showed that if $q = 2\sqrt{a}$ then $mp_a = 1/\sqrt{a}$. Thus, $vmp_a \equiv (P)(mp_a) = 60/\sqrt{a}$. (b) The optimal input amount a^* satisfies the condition $vmp_a = h_a$, or $60/\sqrt{a} = 4$, which implies $a^* = 225$. (Here no other value of the input satisfies the condition.) (c) The associated output is $q^* = 2\sqrt{a^*} = 2\sqrt{225} = 30$. (d) Since vmp_a here slopes down throughout, the demand curve is identical with the vmp_a curve. The equation is $h_a = 60/\sqrt{a}$.

What if the employing firm were instead a monopolist in its product market? A copper-mining enterprise, for example, might face a downward-sloping demand curve for copper ore. Then its additional revenue from an additional unit of input would no longer be the *value* of the physical Marginal Product (the price P of copper ore). Instead the additional revenue would be the *Marginal Revenue MR* – where $MR < P$ (as illustrated in Figure 8.1). The revenue gain from an additional unit of input A is defined as the *Marginal Revenue Product mrp_a*:

DEFINITION: Marginal Revenue Product mrp_a equals Marginal Revenue MR times physical Marginal Product mp_a:

$$mrp_a \equiv MR \times mp_a \quad \text{Definition of } mrp_a \quad (12.10)$$

Since Marginal Revenue is less than price P for a monopoly firm, its mrp_a curve always lies below the vmp_a curve, as shown in Figure 12.4. For a monopolist, the profit-maximizing input employment occurs where the mrp_a curve – *not* the vmp_a curve – intersects the horizontal input supply curve s_a.[9] It follows that the monopoly firm's demand curve d_a for input A is given by the Marginal Revenue Product curve mrp_a rather than by the Value of Marginal Product curve vmp_a.

For a price-taking firm in the product market, Chapter 6 showed that Marginal Revenue is simply the product price P. It follows that for such a firm vmp_a and mrp_a are

---

[9] *Mathematical Footnote*: The firm maximizes $\Pi \equiv R - C \equiv Pq - h_a a - F$ as before, but now recognizes that P decreases with output q – and so, indirectly, decreases with the input a. Differentiating and setting equal to zero, the first-order condition is:

$$P\frac{dq}{da} + q\frac{dP}{dq}\frac{dq}{da} = h_a \quad \text{or} \quad \left(P + q\frac{dP}{dq}\right)\frac{dq}{da} = h_a$$

The element in parentheses is Marginal Revenue. So the condition can be expressed:

$$MR \times mp_a \equiv mrp_a = h_a$$

Figure 12.4. Optimal Factor Employment: Monopolist in Product Market

The firm is a price taker in the input market, as indicated by the horizontal supply curve s_a at the level of the going hire-price h_a. However, here the firm has monopoly power in the product market. Since at any output the product price exceeds Marginal Revenue, the Value of the Marginal Product ($vmp_a \equiv P \times mp_a$) lies above the Marginal Revenue Product ($mrp_a \equiv MR \times mp_a$). The firm's optimum is at the intersection of s_a and mrp_a, leading to employment a^* of input A. The downward-sloping branch of the mrp_a curve is also the firm's demand curve for input A.

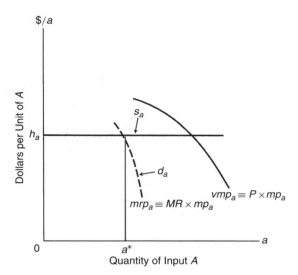

identical: $vmp_a \equiv mrp_a$. So the Factor Employment Condition, expressed in terms of mrp_a, is a general condition that holds both for monopolists and for price-taking firms:

$$mrp_a = h_a \quad \text{General Factor Employment Condition} \qquad (12.11)$$

Again, as a technical qualification, the mrp_a curve must cut the horizontal input supply curve s_a *from above*.

CONCLUSION

For a firm that faces a given hire-price h_a, the optimal use of input A occurs where $mrp_a = h_a$. And since the firm's demand curve for input A must satisfy the Factor Employment Condition for every possible hire-price h_a, its demand curve for a single variable input A is the mrp_a curve. (Except that if the mrp_a curve has an upward-sloping branch, the demand curve consists only of the downward-sloping branch.)

The firm's *output* decision studied in Chapters 6 and 8, and its *input* (resource employment) decision studied in this chapter, are logically connected. To see how this works out with a single variable factor, start with equation (12.5) – $MC \equiv h_a/mp_a$. Now divide both sides by Marginal Revenue MR to obtain:

$$\frac{MC}{MR} \equiv \frac{h_a}{(MR)(mp_a)} \equiv \frac{h_a}{mrp_a} \qquad (12.12)$$

So $MC = MR$ – the Maximum-Profit Condition of Chapter 8 – implies the Factor Employment Condition of this chapter: $mrp_a = h_a$.

12.2 PRODUCTION AND FACTOR EMPLOYMENT WITH SEVERAL VARIABLE INPUTS

In some ways, a firm hiring multiple inputs resembles a consumer choosing an assortment of goods and services. Consumers purchase goods to obtain utility; firms employ resources to generate output and revenue.

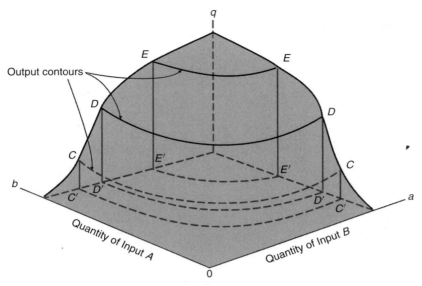

Figure 12.5. Output as a Function of Two Inputs

Output q, measured vertically, is shown as a function of input quantities a and b. Curves CC, DD, and EE are contours of equal height (output) along the three-dimensional surface. The curves $C'C'$, $D'D'$, and $E'E'$ are the projections of these contours in the base plane.

The Production Function

With two variable inputs, say labor and machines, the production function of equation (12.1) reduces to:

$$q = \Phi(a, b) \tag{12.13}$$

The three-dimensional "output hill" of Figure 12.5 (compare the "utility hill" in Figure 3.3) illustrates such a production function. Product quantity q is on the vertical axis and the input amounts a and b appear on the two horizontal axes. The curves CC, DD, EE, etc. are equal-output contours known as *isoquants*. Each isoquant represents all the combinations of input amounts a and b that generate a given output q. Figure 12.6 shows these isoquants in a two-dimensional diagram.

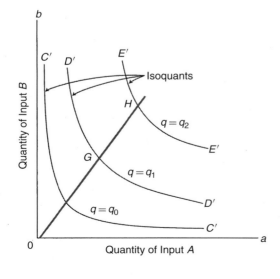

Figure 12.6. Isoquants of Output

The projections $C'C'$, $D'D'$, and $E'E'$ in the base plane of the previous diagram are shown here as isoquants (curves of equal output) in a contour map, without the overlying vertical dimension. Each isoquant is associated with a definite quantity of output (q_0, q_1, or q_2).

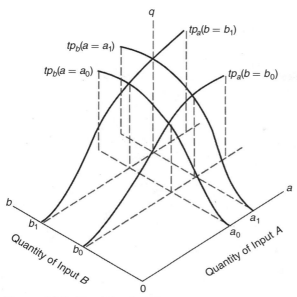

Figure 12.7. Total Product Functions

Total Product curves are drawn along an output hill. The Total Product curves for input A, designated tp_a, hold constant the amount of the other input, B. However, the heights of the tp_a curves depend upon the specific constant values assumed for b in each case; similarly the tp_b curves depend on the values assumed for a.

In Figure 12.7 the Total Product curves along the surface of the output hill indicate how output q changes as one input increases, with the other input held constant. Figure 12.1 showed only one Total Product curve tp_a, corresponding to the single variable factor A. But now there are two whole families of Total Product curves – tp_a and tp_b. Along each of the tp_a curves, output q is a function of the input amount a. Similarly, along each tp_b curve output q is a function of b.

In the diagram the labelling $tp_a(b = b_0)$, for example, identifies the Total Product curve for input A when input B is held fixed at the specific level $b = b_0$. Notice that the entire tp_a curve shifts upward as the amount of B increases. Similarly the entire tp_b curve shifts upward as the amount of A increases. (More acreage enables a given number of farm workers to produce more, and vice versa.)

In Figure 12.8, the two families of Total Product curves are displayed again, but now as a pair of two-dimensional diagrams. Here each separate curve resembles the tp_a curve of Figure 12.1, with the general shape dictated by the Laws of Diminishing Returns. As is consistent with the three-dimensional picture of Figure 12.7, the highest tp_a curve in Panel (a) of Figure 12.8 corresponds to the largest amount of input $B(b = b_2)$ and the lowest curve corresponds to the smallest amount of $B(b = b_0)$. The same considerations apply also for the other input, as shown in Panel (b).

Associated with these families of Total Product curves are corresponding families of Marginal Product curves,[10] as pictured in Figure 12.9.

Now consider what happens when the factors are all changed together in the same proportion (this is called a *change of scale*). In the three-dimensional diagram of

---

[10] *Mathematical Footnote*: With two or more variable inputs, the Marginal Product of any single input such as A becomes a *partial* derivative:

$$mp_a \equiv \lim_{\Delta \to 0} \frac{F(a + \Delta a, b) - F(a, b)}{\Delta a} \equiv \frac{\partial q}{\partial a}$$

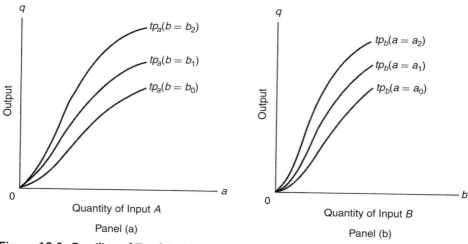

Figure 12.8. Families of Total Product Curves

Panel (a) shows tp_a curves like those drawn along the output hill of Figure 12.7, but on q,a axes; the tp_b curves are similarly shown on q,b axes in Panel (b).

Figure 12.5, that would correspond to moving upward in some particular direction out of the origin along the surface of the output hill. If in that direction the surface at first grows steeper, then in that range there would be *increasing returns to scale*. The Laws of Diminishing Returns, however, eventually apply even when all controllable factors increase together. So ultimately there will be *decreasing returns to scale*. The output hill must eventually flatten out.

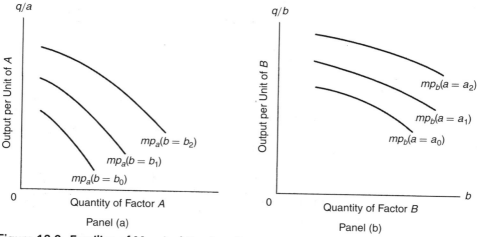

Figure 12.9. Families of Marginal Product Curves

The Marginal Product curves mp_a and mp_b are derived from the corresponding Total Product curves of Figure 12.8. Only the ranges where the curves have negative slope (where the Marginal Product of each factor is a decreasing function of its own quantity) are illustrated here.

EXAMPLE 12.3 MISSOURI CORN

An agricultural experiment in Missouri, reported by John Ambrosius, studied how corn yield (bushels per acre) changed as two inputs (number of plants per acre and pounds of nitrogen per acre) were varied.[a] Reading across any single row, the table shows selected points on the Total Product curve tp_a for plants per acre – with nitrogen input per acre held constant along the row. Reading down any column, points are shown on the tp_b curve for nitrogen input – holding fixed the number of plants per acre. If these points were plotted in a diagram like Figure 12.8, the entire tp_a curve would shift upward as b increased, and the tp_b curve would shift upward as a increased.

Bushels of corn per acre (Q)

	Number of plants per acre (a)				
Nitrogen per acre (b)	9,000	12,000	15,000	18,000	21,000
0	50.6	54.2	53.5	48.5	39.2
50	78.7	85.9	88.8	87.5	81.9
100	94.4	105.3	111.9	114.2	112.2
150	88.9	107.1	121.0	130.6	135.9

Source: Adapted from Ambrosius, as cited in Doll et al., p. 89.

Diminishing returns apply here even to *proportionate variation* in both inputs together. For example, doubling both inputs from the combination (9,000, 50) to the combination (18,000, 100) does not double corn output, which rises from 78.7 to only 114.2.

[a] John Ambrosius, "The Effects of Experimental Size upon Optimum Rates of Nitrogen and Stand for Corn in Missouri" (1964), cited in J. P. Doll, V. J. Rhodes, and J. G. West, *Economics of Agricultural Production, Markets and Policy* (Homewood, IL: Richard D. Irwin, 1968).

The "Missouri corn" Example suggests why decreasing returns to scale must always eventually hold. In that experiment, nitrogen and number of plants per acre were the two controlled inputs. The amounts of other potentially controllable inputs, among them labor input, were held constant. But even if labor and other controllable inputs were also increased in proportion, other aspects of the environment that affect plant growth – such as the Earth's gravity, or the oxygen content of the atmosphere – cannot be experimentally manipulated. Thus it is impossible to vary literally all inputs. This means that the essential condition underlying the Laws of Diminishing Returns, the fixity of one or more inputs, is inescapable. So even when all controllable variables are increased in proportion, there must eventually be diminishing returns to scale.

The Example that follows employs the Cobb–Douglas production function, an algebraic form that has proved useful in economic analysis. For two inputs A and B the function is:

$$q \equiv \kappa a^{\alpha} b^{\beta} \qquad \text{Cobb–Douglas production function} \qquad (12.14)$$

(The Greek letters κ (kappa), α (alpha), and β (beta) here are given constants.)

In the Cobb–Douglas equation, it can be shown that if the sum of the exponents, $\alpha + \beta$, exceeds one, there will be increasing returns to scale. Then a doubling of both inputs will more than double output.[11] If the sum of the exponents exactly equals 1 there will be constant returns to scale. Decreasing returns to scale hold if the sum is less than 1. Under constant returns to scale, if a factor's hire-price equals its Marginal Product then each exponent also equals the fractional share of total output going to that factor.[12]

EXAMPLE 12.4 AGRICULTURAL PRODUCTION IN CANADA

Christina Echevarria estimated agricultural production functions for provinces of Canada in the period 1971–1991.[a] A Cobb–Douglas function was used, under the assumption of constant returns to scale. The independent variables were the traditional three basic factors of production: land, labor, and capital:

$$Y_t = A_t K_t^{\alpha} L_t^{\beta} N_t^{\gamma}$$

Here Y_t is the value added each year in the province's agricultural sector. K_t, L_t, and N_t are estimates of the amounts of capital, land, and labor inputs employed in agriculture each year. Annual changes in A_t, "total factor productivity," represent the output growth not accounted for by changes in the amounts of the inputs. Presumably, A_t reflects general technological progress. Over the period studied total factor productivity grew about 0.35% per year.

The table shows a selection of the results for Canada as a whole and for several provinces. Notice that in British Columbia labor's share is high, consistent with the fact that agriculture in that province concentrates on labor-intensive commodities such as dairy products and fruit. By contrast, in the prairie state of Saskatchewan, large-scale grain production is land-intensive and labor's share is relatively small.

Agricultural production in Canada – Cobb–Douglas shares

Province	Share of land (γ)	Share of labor (β)	Share of capital (α)
Saskatchewan	0.2217	0.2954	0.4830
Quebec	0.1240	0.4308	0.4452
British Columbia	0.0956	0.6530	0.2514
Canada (Average)	0.1597	0.4138	0.4265

Source: Echevarria, selected from Table 3.

[a] Christina Echevarria, "A Three-Factor Agricultural Production Function: The Case of Canada," *International Economic Journal*, v. 12 (Autumn 1998).

---

[11] Let $\kappa = \alpha = \beta = 1$. Since $\alpha + \beta > 1$, there should be *increasing* returns to scale. To verify this, suppose the initial (a,b) input combination is $(10,20)$. Now imagine that the inputs double to $(20,40)$. Then output increases from $q = 200$ to $q = 800$ – not a doubling but a quadrupling!

[12] *Mathematical Footnote:* From equation (12.14), the Marginal Product for factor A is the partial derivative:

$$\frac{\partial q}{\partial a} = \alpha \kappa a^{\alpha-1} b^{\beta} = \alpha \frac{q}{a}$$

So if each unit of factor A receives its Marginal Product mp_a, then $h_a a = mp_a a = \alpha q$. The owners of factor A in aggregate receive the fractional share α of the total output q.

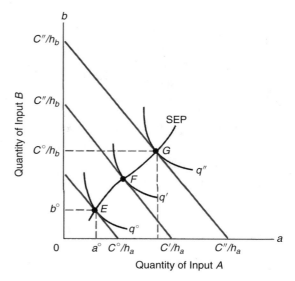

Figure 12.10. Scale Expansion Path

Along any isocost line, the tangency with an output isoquant represents the largest output attainable at that cost. Each such tangency shows the best factor proportions for that level of cost and output. The Scale Expansion Path (SEP) connects all these tangency positions.

Factor Balance and Factor Employment

The question of *factor balance* asks what are the best input proportions at any given level of cost or output. This is a preliminary to asking about factor employment – the actual amounts of inputs to hire at any given set of factor hire-prices.

Consider a specific level of Total Cost, say $100. Suppose the hire-price of labor A is $h_a = \$1$ per man-hour and the hire-price of a machine is $h_b = \$2$ per machine-hour. If the firm used only one or the other, for $100 it could hire either 100 units of labor or 50 machines. More generally, the firm could employ any combination of inputs A and B whose cost comes to $100.

For two variable factors, A and B, Figure 12.10 pictures *isocost lines* C°, C', C'', ... At a specified level of cost, say C°, equation (12.3) takes the form $C^\circ \equiv h_a a + h_b b$. The intercepts are C°/h_a on the horizontal axis and C°/h_b on the vertical axis. Since C° cancels out in taking the ratio of "rise over run," all the isocost lines have the same slope $-h_a/h_b$.

The diagram also shows output isoquants q°, q', q'', ... Along isocost C° the highest attainable isoquant q° is found at the tangency point E with coordinates a°, b°. At cost level C°, therefore, the firm maximizes output by using the input combination a°, b°. Equivalently, the input combination a°, b° is the cheapest way of producing output q°.

Figure 12.10 resembles Figure 4.1 in Chapter 4, which illustrated the optimum of the consumer. Instead of indifference curves now there are isoquants, and the isocost lines look like the budget line of the earlier diagram. But there is an important difference. The consumer, constrained by a given level of spendable income, had a single budget line. But a firm is not restricted to a single isocost line. A firm *decides* how much cost to incur. It may be profitable to incur higher costs to produce more output. Consequently, the analysis must consider the tangencies E, F, G, ... associated with all possible cost levels C°, C', C'', ...

The curve passing through all these tangencies is called the *Scale Expansion Path* SEP. The Scale Expansion Path shows the best combination of inputs at each level of cost. The optimum of the firm must lie somewhere along the Scale Expansion Path.

In Chapter 4 the consumer's optimum condition was expressed in equation 4.5 as an equality between the product price ratio P_x/P_y (the absolute slope of the consumer's budget line) and the Marginal Rate of Substitution in Consumption MRS_C (the absolute slope of the indifference curve). MRS_C was defined as the ratio at which a person was *just willing to substitute* a small amount of Y for a small amount of X in the consumption basket. In other words, MRS_C is the ratio leaving the consumer indifferent (at the same level of utility). Correspondingly here, the *Marginal Rate of Substitution in Production* MRS_Q is defined as the amount of input B that can be substituted for a small change in input A – while leaving the firm "indifferent" in the sense of generating the same output q. Also, just as MRS_C was shown in Section 4.1 of Chapter 4 to equal the ratio of the Marginal Utilities, here MRS_Q is equivalent to the ratio of the Marginal Products.[13] Thus:

$$MRS_Q \equiv -\left.\frac{\Delta b}{\Delta a}\right|_q \equiv \frac{mp_a}{mp_b}\text{[14]} \tag{12.15}$$

Since the slope of the isocost line is $-h_a/h_b$, the tangency condition is:

$$\frac{mp_a}{mp_b} = \frac{h_a}{h_b} \tag{12.16}$$

This leads immediately to the firm's Factor Balance Equation, the analog of the Consumption Balance Equation 4.3 in Chapter 4:

$$\frac{mp_a}{h_a} = \frac{mp_b}{h_b} \quad \text{Factor Balance Equation}^{\text{[15]}} \tag{12.17}$$

Inputs are in balance when the Marginal Products per dollar are equal for all resources employed. If this condition were violated, the firm could increase output at the same level of overall cost by substituting toward the more economical input – the one with higher Marginal Product per dollar.

When the Factor Balance Equation is satisfied, the firm's input combinations at each level of output are shown by the Scale Expansion Path of Figure 12.10. But beyond the question of factor balance, answered by the Scale Expansion Path, the firm has to

---

[13] Imagine that at an assumed initial output level $q = 20$ the Marginal Products are $mp_a = 2$ and $mp_b = \frac{1}{2}$. A unit reduction of $A(\Delta a = -1)$ would reduce output by 2 units, which could be recouped if input B were increased by 4 units ($\Delta b = +4$). So the slope of the isoquant is $\Delta b/\Delta a = +4/-1 = -4$, and MRS_Q equals the absolute value 4. (This argument holds if Δa and Δb represent small changes, so that mp_a and mp_b can be regarded as remaining approximately constant.)

[14] The notation of the middle expression indicates that a small change in a is substituted for a small change in b in such as way as to hold q constant.

[15] *Mathematical Footnote*: The Factor Balance Equation generalizes in a direct way for any number of inputs A, B, C, ... employed in positive amounts. So, with a third input C:

$$\frac{mp_a\,(a > 0)}{h_a} = \frac{mp_b\,(b > 0)}{h_b} = \frac{mp_c\,(c > 0)}{h_c}$$

If, however, the current hire-prices are such that some input (say D) is not employed at all, its ratio of Marginal Product per dollar is related to the others by an *inequality*:

$$\frac{mp_a\,(a > 0)}{h_a} = \frac{mp_b\,(b > 0)}{h_b} > \frac{mp_d\,(d = 0)}{h_d}$$

That is, for the optimal employment of D to be zero, its Marginal Product per dollar must be less than that of other inputs, even for the very first unit of D. (Note the parallel with the Consumption Balance Inequality of Chapter 4.)

Figure 12.11. Total Revenue and Total Cost Functions

Each point on the Scale Expansion Path of the previous diagram is associated with a particular level of cost and output. This information permits plotting the Total Cost curve C. Also, each level of output is associated with a level of revenue $R = P \times Q$. This information permits plotting the Total Revenue curve R. The profit-maximizing output q^* determines the firm's optimal factor employments as shown in the preceding diagram.

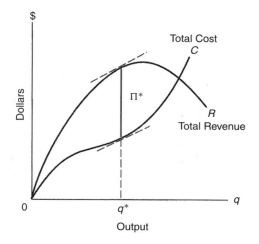

determine the actual amounts – not just the ratios – of the factors to be used. That requires some additional information.

Figure 12.10 indicated that output q° can be produced at a cost of C°, output q' can be produced at cost C', and so on. This information leads directly to the Total Cost curve C shown in Figure 12.11. To construct the curve of Total Revenue $R \equiv P \times q$, the needed information as to how P varies with q is provided by the firm's demand function.

In Figure 12.11 profit is maximized at output q^*, where the difference between Total Revenue and Total Cost is greatest – as shown by the maximized profit Π^*. (The R curve pictured in Figure 12.11 applies to a firm with monopoly power. For a price-taking firm, P would be a constant and R would be a straight line out of the origin.) Last, the optimal output q^* tells on which isoquant in Figure 12.10 (or equivalently, on which isocost line) the firm should operate to determine the best combination of inputs.

The exercise that follows illustrates the solution process.

EXERCISE 12.6

A firm's production function has the Cobb–Douglas form $q = a^{0.5}b^{0.5}$. Using calculus, it can be shown that the Marginal Product functions are $mp_a = 0.5q/a$ and $mp_b = 0.5q/b$. Suppose the demand function for the firm's product is $P = 100 - q$. (This firm has monopoly power in its product market.) The input prices are $h_a = 4$ and $h_b = 1$. (a) Find the equation of the Scale Expansion Path (SEP). (b) Derive the Total Cost and Total Revenue equations. (c) Find the profit-maximizing output. (d) Find the optimal input employments a^* and b^*. (e) What is the maximized profit?

ANSWER: (a) The Factor Balance Equation can be written:

$$\frac{0.5q/a}{4} = \frac{0.5q/b}{1}$$

From this it follows that $b = 4a$. This is the equation of the Scale Expansion Path. (b) Substituting $b = 4a$ into the production function equation leads to $q = (a^{0.5})(4a)^{0.5} = 2a$. Total Cost is $C = h_a a + h_b b = 4a + b$. Since $q = 2a$ and $b = 4a$, it follows that Total Cost is $C = 4q$. This is the Total Cost function. Using the given demand function, Total Revenue is $R \equiv P \times q = 100q - q^2$. (c) For the cost function $C = 4q$, Marginal Cost is $MC = 4$. Since the demand curve $P = 100 - q$ is linear, Marginal Revenue is $MR = 100 - 2q$. Equating Marginal Revenue to Marginal Cost, the profit-maximizing output is $q^* = 48$. (d) Since $q = 2a$, it follows that $a^* = 24$. And since $b = 4a$ it follows that $b^* = 96$. (e) Total Cost is $C = 4q = 4(48) = 192$. Total Revenue is $(100)(48) - 48^2 = 2,496$. So profit is $\Pi^* = 2,304$.

The Firm's Demand for Inputs

Since inputs are used jointly, the firm's demands for them will be interrelated. How much labor the firm will want to hire depends upon the amount of machinery used, and vice versa.

First, making use of the Factor Balance Equation, equation $(12.5) - MC \equiv h_a / mp_a -$ can be extended to obtain:

$$\frac{h_a}{mp_a} = \frac{h_b}{mp_b} = MC \qquad (12.18)$$

This is a valid generalization because, when the firm uses the optimal input proportions as dictated by the Factor Balance Equation, it is equally costly to expand output by hiring a small extra amount of A, or by hiring a small extra amount of B, or by any mixture of the two.

Dividing through by MR:

$$\frac{MC}{MR} = \frac{h_a}{mrp_a} = \frac{h_b}{mrp_b} \qquad (12.19)$$

So when a firm maximizes profit by equating Marginal Cost to Marginal Revenue, it automatically satisfies the Factor Employment Conditions:

$$\begin{cases} mrp_a = h_a \\ mrp_b = h_b \end{cases} \text{ Factor Employment Conditions} \qquad (12.20)$$

These equations parallel equation (12.11), which applied for a single variable input. But in the multi-input case, Marginal Product mp_a and therefore also Marginal Revenue Product mrp_a will generally also depend upon the amount of the *other* input B employed. Similarly, of course, mp_b and mrp_b will vary with the amount of input A.[16]

Two inputs are said to be *complementary* if increased use of one raises the Marginal Product of the other. Examples of complementary input pairs are ships and sailors, computers and programmers, bosses and secretaries. If instead one input has no effect at all upon the Marginal Product of the other input, the two are said to be *independent*. Handcraftsmen and mass-production machines may be such a pair. (A firm might offer customers both a machine-produced line of goods and also a premium hand-made line, the two produced entirely separately.) It is even possible that increased use of one input would reduce the Marginal Product of the other. If so, the two inputs

---

[16] *Mathematical Footnote*: If $q = \Phi(a, b)$, the Marginal Products or partial derivatives $\partial q / \partial a$ and $\partial q / \partial b$ will in general both be functions of a and b. Geometrically, in Figure 12.7 the slope along the Total Product curves tp_a in the a-direction $(\partial q / \partial a)$ varies both as a increases and also from one curve to the next as b increases. And similarly for the slope along the tp_b curves $(\partial q / \partial b)$.

are *anticomplementary*.[17] Inputs that closely substitute for one another tend to be anticomplementary. Employing more male waiters, for example, might reduce the need for (that is, lower the marginal productivity of) female waitresses and vice versa.[18] Normally, however, factors are complementary in production, especially when large categories such as land and labor are considered.

EXAMPLE 12.5 THE BLACK DEATH

In the years 1348–1350 between a fourth and a third of the population of Western Europe died of the Black Death (bubonic plague). The reduced labor supply led to sharp wage increases. "The increase [in English farm wages] due to the plague is 32 percent for the threshing of wheat, 38 percent for barley, 111 percent for oats in the eastern counties. In the middle counties the percentages of rise are 40, 69, 111; in the south, 33, 38, 75; in the west, 26, 41, 44; in the north, 32, 43, and 100."[a]

The consequent shift in the wage/rent ratio led to shifts in the relative employments of labor and land and consequently to changed patterns of land uses. For England, the table shows some results reported by David D. Haddock and Lynne Kiesling.[b]

Land use in essex before and after the Black Death (mean acreage)

Date	Arable	Meadow	Pasture	Wood	Total acreage	% arable
1272–1307	243	8	11	7	269	90.2%
1377–1399	164	10	28	14	216	76.1
1461–1485	143	16	30	20	209	68.4

Source: Adapted from Haddock and Kiesling, Table 1.

Of the land uses tabulated, "arable" (land devoted to crops) is the most labor-intensive, so would be hit the hardest by the reduced labor supply. The table shows that the percentage of land used for arable did drop sharply between the pre-epidemic years (1272–1307) and the postepidemic years (1377–1399). The decline continued into the period 1461–1485, owing in part to recurrences of plague throughout these centuries. The total amount of land employed fell as well. Evidently, land and labor were complements in production. With less labor available, and its hire-price very high, the Marginal Product of land fell so drastically that large areas were simply abandoned.

COMMENT

The feudal system is far removed from the economists' model of a competitive labor market. Feudal economic relationships are, in principle, dictated solely by custom

---

[17] *Mathematical Footnote:* Whether factors are complements or anticomplements is indicated by the sign of the second cross-derivative of the production function. In the normal complementary case, $\partial(\partial q/\partial a)/\partial b \equiv \partial^2 q/\partial a \partial b$ is positive. Independence corresponds to a zero cross-derivative, and anticomplementarity to a negative cross-derivative.

[18] Anticomplementary inputs should not be confused with *interfering* inputs. With anticomplementary factors, hiring more of input A reduces mp_b, and vice versa, but does not reduce the Total Product of either factor. But for interfering factors, Total Product actually declines. (Such a situation might arise if a mining firm in an undeveloped country attempted to employ members of two hostile tribal groups.) A firm would never rationally employ two interfering inputs in the same productive process. It should use only one of them, to the exclusion of the other.

and status. Nevertheless, the forces of supply and demand did operate. Wages rose relative to land rents, to the disadvantage of the high-status land-owning classes. An attempt in the reign of Richard II to return to the old feudal status relationships led to the Peasants' Revolt of 1381, which almost overthrew the monarchy. The agricultural laborers demanded the end of serfdom, of feudal dues and services, of governmental monopolies, and of restrictions on what they could buy or sell. In short, the peasants wanted laissez faire – so that marketplace revisions of economic status could proceed in their favor without government interference.

[a] H. Robbins, "A Comparison of the Effects of the Black Death on the Economic Organization of France and England," *Journal of Political Economy*, v. 36 (August 1928), p. 463.

[b] David D. Haddock and Lynne Kiesling, "The Black Death and Property Rights," *Journal of Legal Studies*, v. 31 (June 2002).

Figure 12.9 pictured two *complementary* inputs A and B. Notice that as the amount of input B increases from b_0 to b_1 to b_2, the mp_a curves shift up. Similarly, as input A rises from a_0 to a_1 to a_2, the mp_b curves shift up. This stacking would be reversed if the two inputs were anticomplements.

The firm's demand curve for a single variable input A is, as noted above, the downward-sloping range along the Marginal Revenue Product curve mrp_a. But with more than one input, matters are more complicated.

To derive the firm's demand curve for one of the two inputs, say input A, suppose that at point G in Figure 12.12 the Factor Employment Conditions in Equations (12.20) are met. At the initial hire-prices h_a^o and h_b^o the firm employs a^o units of A and b^o units of B. Now let the hire-price of A fall from h_a^o to h_a'. If the quantity of the other input B were unchanged, the diagram indicates that the firm would want to employ $\hat{a}$ units of input A – since that is where $mrp_a(b = b^o)$ equals h_a. But suppose inputs A and B are *complementary*. If so, the increase from a^o to $\hat{a}$ is not the full adjustment. Greater use of input A increases the Marginal Product of input B, so all the mrp_b curves will shift up. This leads to increased use of input B, which makes input A more productive (now the mrp_a curves shift up), making the firm desire to hire still more of A. Such a "reverberation" process must, however, reach a limit. There is some increased employment of both inputs that restores the equalities of equation (12.20). The restored equalities can be expressed more explicitly as:

$$\begin{cases} mrp_a(b = b') = h_a' \\ mrp_b(a = a') = h_b^o \end{cases} \tag{12.20'}$$

The upshot, in Figure 12.12, is that the demand curve d_a goes not through points G and L, but through points G and K. So the firm's demand curve for input A, when A and B are complementary, is flatter (more elastic) than the mrp_a curves.

If the inputs are *independent* in production rather than complementary, the interaction effect disappears. A change in the hired amount of one input does not change the Marginal Product of the other. The initial adjustment to a change in the hire-price is the full adjustment.

What about anticomplementary inputs? One might think that since d_a is flatter than the mrp_a curves in the complementary case and since d_a is the same as the unique mrp_a

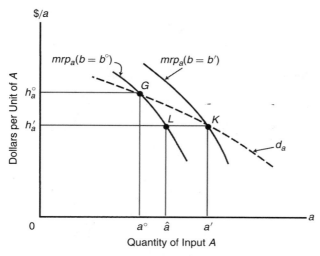

Figure 12.12. Firm's Demand Curve for an Input

At the initial hire-price h_a° the Factor Employment Conditions are met by employments $a = a^\circ$ and $b = b^\circ$. Thus, mrp_a $(b = b^\circ)$ equals h_a° at point G; this is one point along the firm's demand curve for input A. If the hire-price of A falls to h_a', increased employment of A to the amount $\hat{a}$ will be indicated by a movement along $mrp_a(b = b^\circ)$ to point L. But this movement throws the employment condition for input B out of equality, if there is any complementarity (or anticomplementarity) between A and B. Restoring the equality for input B raises the Marginal Product of input A. The Factor Employment Condition can only be reestablished at a point such as K, where h_a' equals $mrp_a(b = b')$ – with b' representing the optimal increased amount of input B. The firm's demand curve d_a is therefore flatter than the slope of the mrp_a curves for input A.

curve when the inputs are independent, then d_a would be steeper than the mrp_a curves in the anticomplementary case. Not so. In the anticomplementary as in the normal complementary case, the firm's demand curve for a factor is flatter than the mrp curves, as illustrated in Figure 12.12.

CONCLUSION

Given either complementarity or anticomplementarity between inputs, the demand curve for any input is flatter (more elastic) than the Marginal Revenue Product curves. One important implication: the employment of a variable input is more sensitive to hire-price changes in the long run, when the amounts of the "fixed" factors can be varied.

Another result follows directly from this analysis: factor demand curves *always* slope downward. That is, there can be no such thing as a "Giffen factor" (see Chapter 4, Section 4.4). A reduced hire-price h_a can never lead to smaller employment of A. For a single variable input, since the input demand curve d_a is the *negatively sloped* portion of the vmp_a curve, a fall in h_a must increase the firm's use of input A. Allowing for possible interactions with some other input B either leaves d_a unchanged (the independent case), or otherwise makes the firm's demand curve for the factor flatter. This flattening means that a fall in h_a causes the firm to use even more of input A. So a positively sloped factor demand curve, implying a *decrease* in desired use of A after a fall in the hire-price h_a, is impossible.

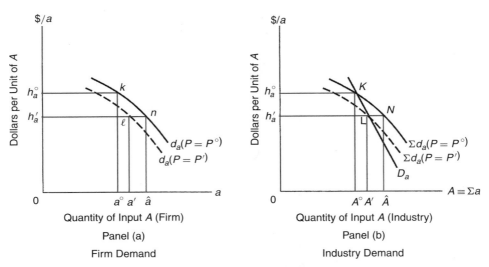

Figure 12.13. Demand for an Input: The Product-Price Effect

Panel (a) pictures a firm's demand for input A; Panel (b) pictures industry demand. At an initial hire-price h_a^o and product price P^o, point k in Panel (a) lies on the firm's demand curve for input A. In Panel (b) the solid curve $\Sigma d_a(P = P^o)$ is the horizontal sum of these firm demand curves. When factor price falls to h_a', each firm aims to expand use of A from a^o to $\hat{a}$ – the corresponding industrywide summations in Panel (b) are A^o and $\hat{A}$, But as firms use more of input A, industry-wide output also rises, reducing product price to P'. Thus, each firm's demand curve will fall to a position such as the (dashed) curve $d_a(P = P')$ in Panel (a); the dashed summation curve in Panel (b) will move similarly. The new point on the industry factor demand curve in Panel (b) will be L. Thus, the product-price effect tends to make the industry demand curve for a factor steeper (less elastic).

12.3   THE INDUSTRY'S DEMAND FOR INPUTS

The question here is how to combine the individual firms' demands into the overall demand for an input by a competitive industry.[19] The short answer is that the industry's demand will be the horizontal sum of the firms' separate demands for that input. This is basically correct, but there are complications to take into account.

Consider first the short run, with a single variable input. In Figure 12.13, Panel (a) pictures a typical firm and Panel (b) pictures the industry as a whole. Suppose that, at some given initial hire-price h_a^o for an input like labor, the equilibrium product price was $P = P^o$. In Panel (a), the curve labelled $d_a(P = P^o)$ is the firm's demand curve for labor when $P = P^o$. (This curve corresponds to the curve d_a derived in the previous diagram.) Given this product price and a hire-price of h_a^o for labor, the firm would employ a^o workers (point k). If the hire-price falls to h_a', the firm would employ $\hat{a}$ workers (point n).

The first complication is the *product-price effect.* Although product price P is unchanged when a single competitive *firm* adjusts its output, for the industry as a whole price P will decline when output Q increases and will rise if Q decreases.

---

[19] If the industry is *monopolized*, the industry demand for an input is of course identical with the single firm's demand. (The analysis here will not cover intermediate cases such as oligopoly and monopolistic competition.)

As a first step, the firms' separate $d_a(P = P^\circ)$ curves can be summed horizontally to obtain the industry curve labelled $\Sigma d_a(P = P^\circ)$ in Panel (b). At the initial input price h_a°, the industry uses A° units of input (point K). What happens if the hire-price falls to h_a'? Looking only at the curve $\Sigma d_a(P = P^\circ)$, it appears that the industry would want to use $\hat{A}$ units of labor (point N). But as the firms use more labor, industry output necessarily rises. This means, given a normally- sloping demand curve, that the equilibrium product price must fall, say to $P = P'$. And since the Value of Marginal Product for input a, vmp_a, is $P \times mp_a$, for each and every firm vmp_a ends up lower than before. So in Panel (a) the firm's demand curve for labor shifts down from the original $d_a(P = P^\circ)$ curve to the new dashed curve $d_a(P = P')$.

It follows that the horizontal sum of the firm demand curves also shifts down – as indicated by the dashed curve $\Sigma d_a(P = P')$ in Panel (b). The upshot is that at the lower hire-price h_a', a typical firm uses not $\hat{a}$ units of labor but only a' units (point ℓ). The industry as a whole uses not A units but only A' units (point L). So the *true* demand D_a is drawn through point K (for $h_a = h_a^\circ$) and point L (for $h_a = h_a'$): the industry demand curve is steeper (less elastic) than the simple horizontal sum of the firms' demand curves.

EXERCISE 12.7

Suppose all firms have the same production function $q = 2\sqrt{a}$; let the initial product price be $P = 60$. The price-taking firm's demand for input A was found in Exercise 12.4 to be $h_a = 60/\sqrt{a}$. Suppose that the industry consists of 1,000 identical such firms, and that the market demand curve for the product is given by the equation $P = 90 - Q/1,000$. (a) What is the equation corresponding to the curve labelled $\Sigma d_a(P = P^\circ)$ in Figure 12.13? (b) What is the industry demand equation for input A? (c) Compare the effect on the firm and on the industry of a fall in the hire-price of A from $h_a^\circ = 4$ to $h_a' = 3$.

ANSWER: (a) The firm's demand equation $h_a = 60/\sqrt{a}$ implies $a = 3,600/h_a^2$. Summing horizontally for 1,000 identical firms, $A \equiv 1,000a = 3,600,000/h_a^2$. (b) The industry demand equation corresponds to the curve D_a in Panel (b) that allows for the interaction between input price h_a and product price P. Since $Q \equiv 1,000q$, the *product* demand curve $P = 90 - Q/1,000$ can be written as $P = 90 - q$. Exercise 12.3 showed that $mp_a = 1/\sqrt{a}$. Since each price-taking firm sets $vmp_a \equiv P \times mp_a = h_a$, it follows that $(90 - q) \times (1/\sqrt{a}) = (90 - 2\sqrt{a}) \times (1/\sqrt{a}) = h_a$, or $a = 8,100/(h_a + 2)^2$. So, since $A \equiv 1,000a$, the industry's demand equation for labor is $A = 8,100,000/(h_a + 2)^2$. (c) Using the *firm's* demand function $a = 3,600/h_a^2$, when the hire-price falls from $h_a = 4$ to $h_a = 3$, employment rises from $a^\circ = 225$ to $\hat{a} = 400$. But as industry hiring expands beyond the initial $A^\circ = 225,000$, the product price P falls. At the new equilibrium, using the *industry's* input demand function $A = 8,100/(h_a + 2)^2$, employment rises only to $A = 324,000$ for the industry as a whole, or to $a = 324$ for the typical firm. At the new equilibrium, product price has fallen from $P^\circ = 60$ to $P' = 54$.

There is also an "entry-exit effect." A fall in the hire-price of any input tends in the short run to increase profits in the industry, so new firms are likely to enter. With more firms in the industry, in Panel (b) the dashed summation curve Σd_a for factor A would shift to the right. (Correspondingly, after an increase in any hire-price, exit of firms

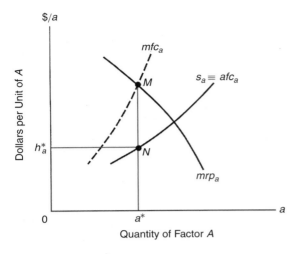

Figure 12.14. Monopsony in the Factor Market

The rising supply curve of A to the firm, s_a, is also a curve of Average Factor Cost afc_a. The curve of Marginal Factor Cost mfc_a will then lie above afc_a, as shown here. The optimum factor employment for the firm is a^*, where the mfc_a and mrp_a curves intersect (point M). The associated hire-price h_a^* is the price along the s_a curve at this level of employment.

would shift the summation curve to the left.) The overall consequence is to make the industry demand curve D_a flatter (more elastic) than would otherwise be the case.

CONCLUSION

After a fall in hire-price h_a, industry-wide output increases and so product price falls – thus lessening the firms' incentive to hire more of the cheapened input A. This *product-price effect* makes the industry demand curve steeper than the simple aggregate of the individual firm demand curves for the factor. On the other hand, the *entry-exit effect* cuts in the opposite direction. A fall in h_a increases firms' profits, inducing new firms to enter and thereby flattening the industry demand curve for input A.

12.4 MONOPSONY IN THE FACTOR MARKET

Just as a monopolist is a sole seller in a market, a *monopsonist* is a sole buyer. If everyone in a small town works for a single enterprise, that firm has monopsony power in its local labor market. Just as a product-market monopolist faces a downward-sloping demand curve, a factor-market monopsonist faces an input supply curve that is upward-sloping.

The curve labeled $s_a \equiv afc_a$ in Figure 12.14 shows the supply of factor A to a monopsonist. At any employment level the wage h_a, or equivalently the Average Factor Cost $afc \equiv h_a a/a$, is the height of the supply curve. As the diagram shows, the corresponding Marginal Factor Cost curve $mfc_a \equiv (\Delta h_a a)/\Delta a$ rises *faster* than afc_a. The reason is that Marginal Factor Cost consists of two elements: the hire-price paid to the "extra" unit *plus* the additional payments to the previous units:

$$mfc_a \equiv \frac{\Delta C_a}{\Delta a} \equiv h_a + a\frac{\Delta h_a}{\Delta a} \tag{12.21}$$

Turn now to the monopsonist's employment decision. The optimal quantity to hire, a^*, is found where Marginal Factor Cost mfc equals Marginal Revenue Product mrp (point M in the diagram). At that point the marginal expense of hiring one more unit equals the firm's marginal benefit from the extra revenue:

$$mfc_a = mrp_a \quad \text{Factor Employment Condition for a Monopsonist} \quad (12.22)$$

Note that the hire-price is *not* the height of point *M*, but the height of point *N* in the diagram.

EXERCISE 12.8

Suppose the firm of Exercise 12.5, with production function $q = 2\sqrt{a}$, has monopoly power in its product market (faces demand curve $P = 90 - q$) and also has monopsony power in the factor market. Specifically, let the supply curve of factor A to the firm be $h_a = 1 + a/75$. What is the firm's profit-maximizing use of input a, and its profit-maximizing output?

ANSWER: Using the Factor Employment Condition for a monopsonist, the firm sets $mrp_a \equiv MR \times mp_a = mfc_a$. Marginal Revenue is $MR = 90 - 2q$. Marginal Product here is $mp_a = 1/\sqrt{a}$. With a linear factor supply curve or Average Factor Cost curve, the curve of Marginal Factor Cost is also linear and rises twice as fast. Thus, $mfc_a = 1 + 2a/75$. The condition $mrp_a = mfc_a$ can be expressed either in terms of the variable q or the variable a. Working for convenience in terms of q, the equation becomes $(90 - 2q) \times (2/q) = 1 + (q^2/2)/75$, which simplifies to $q^3 + 750q = 27,000$. The firm's optimal output is $q^* = 21.9$ and the optimal level of input is $a^* = 120.2$.

EXAMPLE 12.6 MONOPSONY IN PROFESSIONAL BASEBALL

Before some recent reforms, labor-market monopsony was an important feature of several professional sports. A legal quirk, perhaps based upon the idea that sports are a pastime rather than a business, permitted employers to form buyers' cartels. In baseball the most important cartel instrument was the "reserve clause," which effectively made the player the exclusive property of the team that first signs him up, or to which he is traded. A player refusing to accept the wage offer of his assigned employer was forbidden to play for any other team in the cartel.

Gerald W. Scully investigated the effect of the reserve clause in major-league baseball.[a] He anticipated that if the buyers' cartel was an effective monopsony, the wage rates for players, h_a, would be less than their Marginal Revenue Products, mrp_a (compare Figure 12.14).

But first, differences in player *quality* must be considered. Using 1968 and 1969 data, Scully estimated "gross" mrp_a by calculating the player's contribution to gate receipts and broadcast revenues. In this period, however, employers were incurring large costs for player development (on the order of $300,000) before knowing how successful the athlete would become. Allowing for this and certain other expenses led to "net" mrp_a estimates for players of different qualities. Under competition, average wage rates at any quality level should tend to equal this net mrp_a. If on the other hand the situation is one of monopsony, average wages should fall short of net mrp_a.

The table here indicates that, for "mediocre" players, during this period salary exceeded net mrp_a – and indeed, net mrp_a was negative. But for "average" and especially for "star" players, net mrp_a was far higher than the salary received. So this evidence suggests considerable monopsony power.

Quality versus pay of baseball players

Quality group	Net *mrp* ($)	Salary ($)
Hitters		
Mediocre	−30,000	17,200
Average	128,300	29,100
Star	319,000	52,100
Pitchers		
Mediocre	−10,600	15,700
Average	159,600	33,000
Star	405,300	66,800

Source: Scully, p. 928.

Thus, contrary to common opinion among fans and sports writers, in the period studied it appears that star players were not "overpaid." They received far less than their economic worth to employers.

Since the time of Scully's analysis, legislation and judicial decisions have weakened the reserve clause in professional sports. In consequence, stars' salaries have risen.

In a later study Paul M. Sommers and Noel Quinton[b] examined the earnings of "free agents" – players who are free to play for whichever club offers the best salary. For free-agent hitters the average mrp_a was estimated at $521,923 while teams incurred an average of $827,393 in salaries, benefits, and development costs. Free-agent pitchers had an average mrp_a of $259,658, while teams paid an average of $257,600. So though the data suggest hitters were "overpaid," the figures for pitchers approximated what would be expected under competitive conditions.

[a] Gerald W. Scully, "Pay and Performance in Major League Baseball," *American Economic Review*, v. 64 (December 1974).

[b] Paul M. Sommers and Noel Quinton, "Pay and Performance in Major League Baseball: The Case of the First Family of Free Agents," *Journal of Human Resources*, v. 17 (Summer 1982).

12.5   AN APPLICATION: MINIMUM-WAGE LAWS

When it comes to analyzing the economic impact of minimum-wage laws, there are two conflicting approaches. The first approach assumes that low-wage labor markets are mainly competitive. Large numbers of demanders and suppliers interact to determine the levels of employment and wages. The second approach is based on the premise that employers typically have monopsony power.

The *competitive model* is illustrated in Figure 12.15. Let the commodity be a certain grade or class of labor L, whose hire-price is the wage rate w. At the intersection of the supply and demand curves, the equilibrium wage is w_c and employment is L_c. Now suppose a legal minimum wage w^o is imposed, at a level higher than w_c. At the higher wage w^o the labor offered on the market is now the amount L_s, larger than L_e, but the labor demanded is only L_d. So there will be an *unemployment gap*, the difference between the quantity offered and the quantity demanded at the legal wage, shown as $BC = L_s - L_d$. The *disemployment effect* of the minimum wage, the number of workers who lose jobs, is the smaller amount $FE = L_c - L_d$. When a minimum

Figure 12.15. Minimum Wage: Competitive Model

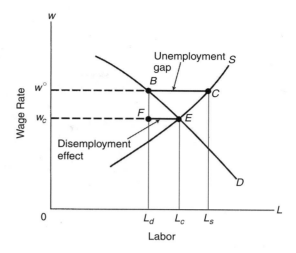

The competitive equilibrium point E is associated with wage w_c and employment L_c. A wage floor (minimum wage) at the level w^o reduces employment to L_d. The quantity FE is the reduction in employment. At the higher wage, L_s units of labor are seeking employment, so the perceived "unemployment gap" is the larger quantity BC.

wage is set higher than the market equilibrium wage, therefore, the competitive-market model would clearly predict some *disemployment* of those previously working and an even larger amount of *unemployment* – since at the higher wage more workers will be seeking employment.

EXERCISE 12.9

Suppose the demand function for labor is $D = 240 - 20w$, and let the supply function be $S = -60 + 80w$. (a) What is the competitive equilibrium wage? The level of employment? (b) If a minimum wage $w^o = 5$ is imposed, determine the amount of disemployment and compare it with the level of unemployment.

ANSWER: Solving the equation $240 - 20w = -60 + 80w$, the market equilibrium wage rate is $w_c = 3$. The associated level of employment is found by substituting $w = 3$ in either the demand or supply equation. The answer is $D = S = 180$. (b) If a minimum wage $w^o = 5$ is imposed, the quantity demanded is $240 - 20(5) = 140$; the quantity supplied is $-60 + 80(5) = 320$. Since employers want to hire only 140 workers, as compared with the unregulated solution the amount of *disemployment* is $180 - 140 = 40$. But because so many more workers seek employment at the higher wage w^o, the *unemployment* gap is much larger, namely, $340 - 140 = 200$.

The *monopsony model* has rather different implications, as shown in Figure 12.16. According to this model, a single employer is typically dealing with many individual workers. Employment is initially L_m; at this employment level the Marginal Revenue Product (*mrp*) curve intersects the Marginal Factor Cost (*mfc*) curves. The wage $w_m < mrp$ is determined along the labor supply curve S. An effective minimum-wage law *replaces the market supply curve by a horizontal line at the level of the minimum wage* (in the range where the market supply curve S lies below the level of the minimum wage). The monopsonist employer is forced to become a *price-taker* at the minimum wage,

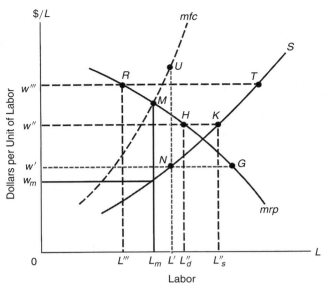

Figure 12.16. Minimum Wage: Monopsony Model

Under monopsony, the optimality condition $mfc = mrp$ determines the wage w_m at employment L_m. If a minimum wage were imposed at the relatively low wage w', the optimality condition is satisfied at employment L' – both wage and employment would rise slightly. At an intermediate minimum wage w'', employment would be L''_d. Here there is a considerable increase in both wage and employment; nevertheless, a perceived "unemployment gap" HK arises, because at wage w'' the offered labor supply is L''_s. At a sufficiently high minimum wage such as w''', employment falls to L''' as in the competitive model.

wherever the market supply conditions would otherwise have permitted establishing a monopsony hire-price lower than the legally imposed floor.

Three classes of possibilities are illustrated in Figure 12.16. First, suppose the minimum wage is only a little higher than w_m, for example w' in the diagram. Then the *effective* supply curve to the firm is horizontal at the level w' until the S curve is reached at point N. In this range the Marginal Factor Cost (mfc) also equals w'. If the monopsonist firm could hire as many units as desired at wage w', it would employ the quantity associated with point G, where $w' = mrp$. But this is impossible. Beyond point N the effective supply curve of labor to the firm rejoins the original S curve, because at wage w' the laborers are unwilling to supply more than L' units. It follows also that, beyond employment L', the effective Marginal Factor Cost leaps upward discontinuously to rejoin the original mfc curve (at point U). Since the mrp curve in the diagram passes through this vertical discontinuity of the mfc curve, the firm will find it optimal to employ L' workers at wage w'. Note that, relative to the unregulated outcome L_m, the minimum-wage law here has *increased* employment! Nor is there any perceived unemployment at the legally imposed wage.

Second, consider a somewhat higher, intermediate level of minimum wage, w''. As before the monopsonist firm is forced to become a price-taker until the supply curve S is reached (at point K). But then the condition $w'' = mrp$ implies that the firm would want to employ no more than L''_d units (at point H). This employment is also greater than the L_m of the unregulated monopsony solution; no disemployment takes place.

At wage w'', however, the offered labor supply is L_s'', more than the firm wants to hire. The resulting unemployment gap is indicated by the distance NK in the diagram. So there is no disemployment – indeed, employment actually increases – yet there is unemployment!

Last, w''' represents a high minimum wage, higher than the level at which the *mrp* and *mfc* curves intersect. Here employment would be reduced to L'''. Thus, a minimum wage as high as w''' would lead to the same qualitative implications as in the competitive-market model. Such a high minimum would generate some *disemployment*, as compared with L_m, and generate a larger *unemployment* gap represented by the distance RT in the diagram.

In applying this analysis it is important to appreciate that labor skill and quality vary across a spectrum. Although many unskilled workers might previously have been earning less than the imposed minimum wage, highly skilled workers were likely earning well above it. So minimum-wage laws would affect high-wage and low-wage workers differently.

Using the *competitive* model, low-skilled (low-wage) workers would be affected as in Figure 12.15. Their wage rates would rise, but some will lose their jobs. In contrast, for the higher-skilled workers, the market equilibrium wage w_c is likely to be already above the new minimum wage w^o – there will be no direct effect.

What if instead the *monopsony* model of Figure 12.16 applies? Then: (1) For very low-skilled workers the imposed minimum wage would be effectively at a high level, like w''' in Figure 12.16, so their wage rates would rise but their employment would fall. (2) For medium-skilled workers, the minimum wage might be more like w' or w'', in which case *both* the wage rate and employment could increase. (3) For very high-skilled workers, the imposed minimum wage would be relatively low, even lower than w_m in Figure 12.16. For such workers there would be no direct effect on wages or employment.

Which of these models is the more correct picture is still debated by economists. The federal minimum-wage laws in the United States are uniform over the entire country, making no distinctions for age, experience, or geography. In contrast, most European countries have at least youth differentials. In Great Britain, for example, the youth minimum is only about 30% of the adult minimum. In Canada, minimum-wage schedules are set by the provinces rather than by the central government, a procedure that automatically allows for variations in cost-of-living and other differences across geographical regions. The absence of differentials in the United States leads us to expect that the brunt of the disemployment effects, if any, will be suffered by low-wage areas such as Appalachia and by low-wage demographic groups such as "minorities" and youthful workers.

EXAMPLE 12.7 DO MINIMUM-WAGE LAWS REDUCE EMPLOYMENT?

Economists, at least up to recently, have believed that in most labor markets the evidence supports the competitive model. A minimum wage, set higher than the previous equilibrium level, would be expected to reduce employment among the affected low-wage groups. The table here indicates some of the results of a study by Donald Deere, Kevin M. Murphy, and Finis Welch dealing with minimum wage increases legislated in 1990 and 1991.[a]

Percent employment reduction after 1990–1 minimum wage Increases[*]

Age group	% low wage[1]	% employment change[2]
Men		
15–19	44.5	−15.6
20–24	14.2	−5.7
25–64	3.3	−2.4
65–69	14.0	−4.2
Women		
15–19	51.8	−13.0
20–24	19.0	−4.2
25–64	8.8	−0.3
65–69	21.0	+3.1

[1] Percentage of those employed in age group paid less than $4.25 between April 1, 1989 and March 31, 1990.

[2] Calculated as percent change in employment between year ending March 31, 1992 and year ending March 31, 1990, divided by percent employed in earlier period.

Source: Extracted from Deere, Murphy, and Welch, p. 48.

The table shows that age-sex groups with the highest proportions of low-wage workers – most notably the 15–19 age groups – generally suffered the largest proportionate reductions in employment. This is exactly what the competitive model would predict. (A possible exception was women 65–69, but only a small percentage of this group was employed to begin with.) The investigators also found large employment drops across other demographic groups with high proportions of low-wage workers, among them African-Americans and persons of Mexican descent.

Furthermore, the U.S. results confirming the competitive model have generally been supported by experiences with minimum wages in countries as different as Great Britain, Singapore, and Kenya.[b]

As an interesting exception, however, a study by David Card and Alan Krueger obtained results in conflict with the competitive model.[c] The competitive theory predicts that an increase in the New Jersey minimum wage would reduce employment of low-wage workers in New Jersey relative to the neighboring state of Pennsylvania, but if anything the opposite was found.[d]

COMMENT

As emphasized in Chapter 1, ongoing scientific debate in economics is healthy. Even seemingly well-established results, such as those concerning employment effects of minimum wage legislation, should be repeatedly tested. But these critiques must themselves be held to high scientific standards if they are to overcome a strong previous consensus of belief.

[a] Donald Deere, Kevin M. Murphy, and Finis Welch, "Sense and Nonsense on the Minimum Wage," *Regulation* (1995), No. 1.

[b] Deepak Lal, "The Minimum Wage: No Way to Help the Poor," The Institute of Economic Affairs, Occasional Paper 95 (1995).

[c] David Card and Alan Krueger, "Minimum Wages and Employment: A Case Study of the Fast-Food Industry in New Jersey and Pennsylvania," *American Economic Review*, v. 84 (September 1994).

[d] But see David Neumark and William Wascher, "The Effects of New Jersey's Minimum-Wage Increase on Fast-Food Employment: A Re-evaluation Using Payroll Records," National Bureau of Economic Research Working Paper 5224 (August 1995).

Regardless of their arguably adverse economic effects, minimum-wage laws have been politically popular. They appeal to humanitarian sentiments.

In both the competitive and monopsonist models, low-skilled and high-skilled workers are affected differently. If the competitive model is valid, the supposed "beneficiaries," very low-wage workers (largely teenagers and minorities) previously earning less than the minimum wage, may end up worse off. True, many will receive the benefit of an increased wage but others are likely to lose their jobs entirely. So for this main target group the good and bad effects are mixed.

If the monopsonist model is valid, the only group who definitely gain both in employment and in wages are the mid-skilled workers, as analyzed in the discussion of Figure 12.16.

In actuality the most powerful political pressure in the United States for higher minimum wages has come not from the low-wage or mid-wage "beneficiaries" but from labor unions, in particular the AFL-CIO. This may seem puzzling, since unions mainly represent relatively high-skilled workers, already earning above the legislated minimum. It has been argued, perhaps cynically, that a higher minimum wage – by increasing the cost of hiring *unskilled* workers – will make more jobs available for the skilled workers represented by the AFL-CIO.

Whether or not the union leaders reason this way, the argument would be valid only if skilled and unskilled labor were *anticomplements* in firms' production functions. If skilled and unskilled labor are (as perhaps is more normally the case) *complements* instead, disemployment of unskilled workers would reduce rather than increase the demand for the skilled workers represented by the AFL-CIO.

Two other possible economic justifications for minimum wage laws are of interest. (1) Even if labor markets are *competitive*, they are surely not *perfect*. So, at any moment of time, some workers – especially poorly informed ones – may be earning below-equilibrium wages. An imposed minimum, if set at a moderate level, might compensate for this informational disadvantage so as to move the labor market in the direction of equilibrium. (2) A more sophisticated argument, which goes beyond material covered in this text, takes into account worker *effort*. Conceivably there could be two distinct equilibria in labor markets: a *high-wage high-effort* equilibrium and a *low-wage low-effort* equilibrium. Workers and employers could both be trapped in a situation where a low wage was paid for low effort. Conceivably, all might benefit by minimum-wage legislation forcing the labor markets toward the high-wage high-effort equilibrium. (Or, of course, one or both sides might have preferred the low-wage low-effort equilibrium.)

SUMMARY   This chapter deals with the demand for inputs used in production.

Underlying a firm's demand for inputs is its production function – the technological relation between inputs to production and outputs. Production functions are subject to the Laws of Diminishing Returns. If some input A increases in amount while others are held fixed, a point is eventually reached where the *Marginal Product* of the varying input, $mp_a \equiv \Delta q/\Delta a$, begins to decrease. At some later point the *Average Product* $ap_a \equiv q/a$ begins to decrease. And, still later, the *Total Product* q may possibly begin to decrease.

The Laws of Diminishing Returns apply when some factors are increased relative to others. The consequences of changing all factors together are described as *returns to scale*. Returns to scale are increasing when proportionate expansions of all inputs lead to a more-than-proportionate rise in output. Constant and decreasing returns to scale are correspondingly defined. It is impossible, however, for a firm to increase literally all inputs in the same proportion. Consequently, decreasing returns are eventually observed, even when all *controllable* inputs are increased proportionately.

The firm's profit-maximizing use of a single variable factor depends upon both the *market structure in the product market* (whether the firm is a price-taking seller of its output or else a monopolist) and the *market structure in the factor market* (whether the firm is a price-taking buyer of inputs or else a monopsonist). A general form of the Factor Employment Condition that holds for all these cases is:

$$mfc_a = mrp_a$$

That is, to maximize profit the firm chooses the level of input such that Marginal Factor Cost $mfc_a \equiv \Delta C/\Delta a$ equals Marginal Revenue Product $mrp_a = \Delta R/\Delta a$. The Marginal Factor Cost concept allows for a possibly rising factor supply price when the employer is a monopsonist in the input market. The Marginal Revenue Product concept similarly allows for a possibly falling product demand price when the firm is a monopolist in the product market. In short, the firm operates where the cost of hiring one more unit of input equals the revenue it generates.

When the firm is a *price-taker in its product market*, the Value of the Marginal Product ($vmp_a \equiv P \times mp_a$) can be substituted for the Marginal Revenue Product ($mrp_a \equiv MR \times mp_a$) in the Factor Employment Condition. And if the firm is a *price-taker in the input market*, the Average Factor Cost or hire-price h_a can be substituted for Marginal Factor Cost $\Delta C/\Delta a$.

The firm's demand curve for input A can only be defined when it is a price-taker in the input market. The demand curve is then the downward-sloping branch of the mrp_a curve. Since $mrp_a \equiv MR \times mp_a$, input demand depends upon the marginal physical productivity of the input (mp_a) and also upon the revenue increment (MR) associated with the additional output.

When more than one input is variable, the analysis becomes more complex. With two variable inputs A and B, profit is maximized when the Factor Employment Condition simultaneously holds for both. For a firm that is a price-taker in the factor markets for both A and B, the conditions are:

$$\begin{cases} h_a = mrp_a \\ h_b = mrp_b \end{cases}$$

Inputs A and B are called *complements* if increased use of either raises the Marginal Product of the other, and *anticomplements* if the reverse holds. (If there is no interdependence, the inputs are called *independent* in production.) Both complementarity and anticomplementarity make the firm's demand curve for inputs flatter (more elastic) than would otherwise be the case.

The *industry's* demand for an input is based on summing the individual firms' demands, but there are several complications. First is the "product-price effect." When any hire-price h_a falls, the industry's increased use of A increases industry output Q. Since consumers' demand curves are downward-sloping, this reduces the product price P. This consideration weakens the firms' desires to use more of A, and thus tends to make the industry demand curve steeper (less elastic). (There is an analogous "input-price effect," working through the prices of related factors, that was not analyzed in the chapter.) Last is an "entry-exit effect." A reduction in h_a makes the industry more profitable, inducing entry by new firms. The entry-exit effect makes the industry demand for an input flatter (more elastic) than it would otherwise be.

Demand for an input A tends to be *greater* (1) where the employers are product-market price-takers rather than monopolists, (2) where the physical Marginal Product mp_a is high, and (3) where the additional output produced by employing A is highly valued by consumers. Demand for A tends to be *more elastic* (1) the more elastic are the consumers' demand curves and resource-owners' supply curves, (2) the less powerfully the Law of Diminishing Returns operates as employment of A increases, (3) the greater the complementarity between A and other inputs, and (4) the greater the exit-entry effect as the hire-price h_a changes.

Two contesting models, the competitive model and the monopsonist model, have been used in analyzing minimum-wage laws. If the competitive model is applicable, so that firms are price-takers in the input market for labor, a legally imposed minimum wage higher than the previous equilibrium will raise wages for those workers who remain employed, but will disemploy others. The perceived unemployment gap, the difference between the labor quantities supplied and demanded, will be even larger. (Since at the higher wage more workers will seek employment.) If the monopsony model applies, the effects are mixed. Over a certain range it is even possible that wages and employment may both increase. The consensus of economists has been that the evidence favors the competitive model, but the issue remains subject to continuing scientific investigation.

QUESTIONS

†The answers to daggered questions appear at the end of the book.

For Review

1. A firm's demand for an input depends upon the productivity of the input and also upon the demand for the firm's product. Explain.

†2. a. Does the curve of Marginal Revenue Product for input A, mrp_a, necessarily lie below the curve of Value of the Marginal Product, vmp_a? Explain.

  b. Which is the firm's demand curve for input A?

3. Why is $mrp_a = h_a$ the Factor Employment Condition for a price-taking firm in the *input* market? What if the firm is not a price-taker in the *product* market? Is this condition sufficient, or are there other subsidiary conditions that must be met?

†4. a. Is it ever rational to employ so much of an input as to be in the region of diminishing marginal returns?

  b. In the region of diminishing average returns?

  c. In the region of diminishing total returns?

†5. With two inputs A and B, explain why the conditions $mrp_a = h_a$ and $mrp_b = h_b$ lead both to the choice of optimal input proportions and to the optimal scale of output.

†6. a. With two factors of production, is the slope of the output isoquant equal (in absolute value) to the ratio of the Marginal Products? Explain.

  b. Interpret the absolute slope of the isocost line as a ratio.

7. Explain why, if two inputs are complementary, the demand curve for either is flatter than the Marginal Revenue Product curves. What if the inputs are anticomplementary?

†8. Is the input demand curve of a competitive industry necessarily less elastic than the summation of the demand curves of the separate firms?

9. True or false (explain in each case)? The economywide demand curve for input A will be more elastic:

   a. The more elastic is consumer demand for products that use input A.

   b. The weaker is the operation of the Law of Diminishing Returns as employment of A increases.

   c. The more elastic is the supply of inputs complementary to A.

†10. Suppose the factor market is competitive. If the quantity of an input employed increases, holding other inputs constant, eventually marginal cost must rise. Explain why.

†11. In the Cobb–Douglas production function, under what conditions are there increasing, constant, and decreasing returns to scale?

For Further Thought and Discussion

†1. a. Are there examples in this text providing empirical support for the Laws of Diminishing Marginal and Diminishing Average Returns?

   b. Would you expect to find any exceptions?

†2. Why might a firm hire positive amounts of two inputs that are anticomplementary?

3. Would you expect, typically, that different classes of labor (for example, skilled versus unskilled) are more or less likely to be complementary – in comparison with labor versus machines?

4. Assuming that labor organizations were interested only in the selfish gains of their members, would you expect them to oppose immigration?

†5. Historically, wages in the United States have been high relative to wages elsewhere. Does the chapter shed light on this phenomenon? Explain.

†6. Would you expect technological progress generally to raise wage rates?

7. How might a consumer boycott of grapes or lettuce work to the detriment of farm workers who specialize in farms raising these crops?

8. A minimum-wage law raises firms' *relative* demand for skilled labor versus unskilled. Would it tend to raise the *absolute* demand for skilled labor, if skilled and unskilled are complementary? If they are anticomplementary? How does your answer bear upon the attitudes of trade unions toward minimum-wage laws?

9. In Figure 12.12, after the initial adjustment from a^o to $\hat{a}$ in the anticomplementary case, do the mrp_b curves shift up or down? What is the direction of the effect upon the employment of B? Does that secondary effect shift the mrp_a curves up or down?

†10. It has been argued that a law that imposed a maximum work week of 35 hours (from a typical 40 hours) would increase employment, because businesses would have to hire more workers to get the same amount of work done. How would such a regulation affect the demand for labor as a factor of production?

†11. A single lily bulb could, in principle, reproduce to provide flowers to everyone in the world. Does this reproductive ability violate the law of diminishing returns?

13 Resource Supply and Factor-Market Equilibrium

The previous chapter surveyed the *demand side* of the markets for resource services. This chapter deals with the *supply side* – how people choose among possible uses of the productive assets they possess, and especially their labor power. The analysis then brings supply and demand together to show how prices and quantities are determined in the factor markets.

13.1   THE OPTIMUM OF THE RESOURCE-OWNER

In Chapter 4 the individual was assumed already endowed with a certain amount of income. But income does not come out of thin air. To earn income, owners of resources offer them for hire in the market. Or, alternatively, owners can retain the resources for personal *reservation uses*. A person's time, for example, considered as an owned resource, can be divided between market work and leisure. (In economics "leisure" does not mean merely lazing away the hours. It includes time devoted to biological necessities like sleep as well as socially valuable nonmarket activities such as homemaking and community service.)

Figure 13.1 shows a resource-owner's possible choices between income I and leisure R. The arrows (preference directions) indicate that income and leisure are both "goods" rather than "bads." Note the similarity with the choice situation of the consumer in Chapter 4, Figure 4.1. At the initial "endowment" position E in the diagram, the individual starts with $\overline{R}$ units of time available (24 hours per day, let us say) plus $\overline{I}$ dollars of income from other sources (possibly from gifts or property earnings).

Labor hours L plus leisure hours R add up to the total time available:

$$L + R = \overline{R} \tag{13.1}$$

In Figure 13.1 the shaded *opportunity set* for the resource-owner resembles the opportunity set of the consumer pictured in Figure 4.1 of Chapter 4. The upper-right boundary of the opportunity set is his or her *budget line*.[1]

Moving along the budget line from the endowment point E, a person who sells an hour of labor (thereby sacrificing an hour of leisure) receives an hourly wage or hire-price h_L. If the individual is a price-taker with respect to the wage rate, the budget line has constant slope $\Delta I / \Delta R = -h_L$.[2] (Depending upon the point of view, h_L can be regarded either as the price of an hour of labor or as the price of an hour of leisure.) So the equation of the budget line is:

$$I = \overline{I} + h_L L \tag{13.2}$$

That is, achieved income I equals endowed income $\overline{I}$ plus earnings from labor.

Substituting from equation (13.1), the budget equation can be written:

$$h_L R + I = h_L \overline{R} + \overline{I} \tag{13.2'}$$

---

[1] The opportunity set is also bounded on the right at $R = \overline{R}$, which means that no one can choose more than 24 hours of leisure a day. The vertical axis is a bound on the left saying that no one can choose to work more than 24 hours a day.

[2] Chapter 4 showed that if good x is plotted on the horizontal axis and good y on the vertical axis, then the slope is $\Delta y / \Delta x \equiv -P_x / P_y$. So in Figure 13.1 the slope is $\Delta I / \Delta R \equiv -h_L / P_I$, where P_I is the "price" of a unit of income. But since income is measured in units of the numeraire (in this case, in dollars), P_I necessarily equals 1. So the slope is $\Delta I / \Delta R \equiv -h_L$.

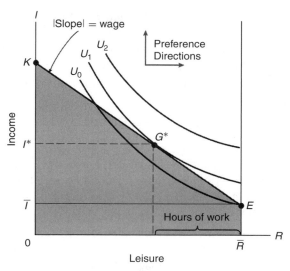

Figure 13.1. Optimum of the Resource Owner

The resource owner's preferences, as indicated by indifference curves U_0, U_1, U_2 ..., show that income I and reservation uses (or "leisure") R are both goods. The person with endowment at E has initial income $\overline{I}$ and leisure $\overline{R}$. The shaded area below the budget line EK is the opportunity set. The absolute slope of the budget line is the hire-price or wage at which the individual can obtain income by sacrificing leisure. The tangency point G^* is the resource owner's optimum position.

The right-hand side of this equation is a constant, showing the *potential* market value of the resource-owner's $(\overline{R}, \overline{I})$ endowment. The left-hand side of the equation indicates the range of leisure and income combinations that can be chosen within this constraint.

At the tangency optimum G^* in Figure 13.1, two conditions hold. First, the resource-owner is on the boundary of the opportunity set. Algebraically, this means that the equation of the budget line is satisfied. The economic interpretation is that neither income nor leisure is wastefully thrown away. Second, at the tangency G^* the indifference curve has the same slope as the budget line. Paralleling the concept of the Marginal Rate of Substitution in Consumption (MRS_C) in Chapter 4, the *Marginal Rate of Substitution in Resource Supply* (MRS_R) is the absolute value of the slope along an indifference curve drawn on R,I axes. And, again following the discussion in Chapter 4, MRS_R can be interpreted as a ratio of Marginal Utilities – the Marginal Utility of the reservation uses (MU_R) divided by the Marginal Utility of income (MU_I):

$$MRS_R \equiv \left. \frac{-\Delta I}{\Delta R} \right|_U \equiv \frac{MU_R}{MU_I} \tag{13.3}$$

Since the slope of the budget line is $\Delta I / \Delta R = -h_L$, the condition for a tangency optimum is:

$$MU_R = MU_I h_L \tag{13.4}$$

This says that the rational individual will work up to the point where his or her Marginal Utility of leisure exactly equals the Marginal Utility of income times the wage.

The convex curvature of the indifference curves of Figure 13.1 (the curves get flatter moving to the right) reflects the preference of individuals for "diversification" between income and leisure. People work less than 24 hours a day, but normally more than

0 hours. Nevertheless, an individual with sufficiently large endowment $\bar{I}$ or with unattractive opportunities might choose not to work for hire at all. At the other end of the income scale, a poor person might receive "welfare" benefits generous enough to discourage working in the market.[3] In terms of the geometry, an individual will prefer a zero-work corner solution if, at the endowment position E, the indifference curve U_0 in Figure 13.1 is steeper than the budget line EK.[4]

EXERCISE 13.1

Jane is endowed with $\bar{R} = 24$ hours of leisure per day and $\bar{I} = 40$ units of income (dollars) per day. Her Marginal Rate of Substitution in Resource Supply (the absolute slope of her indifference curve) is $MRS_R = I/R$. The market wage rate is $h_L = 10$. How many hours of labor will Jane supply, and what will she earn?

ANSWER: Jane's budget-line equation (13.1) is $10R + I = 10(24) + 40 = 280$. Using equation (13.4), she will set her $MRS_R = I/R = h_L = 10$. The solution is $R^* = 14$, $I = 140$. So she works $24 - 14 = 10$ hours per day and earns $10(\$10) = \$100$ per day from labor.

EXAMPLE 13.1 WHO DOES THE HOUSEWORK?

Despite "women's liberation," in married couples wives still do most of the housework. Joni Hersch and Leslie S. Stratton found that this is the case even when both spouses work outside the home.[a]

The table here is based on data from national surveys of families and households in 1987–1988 and 1992–1994. Overall, women – whether married, divorced, or never-married – consistently spent more time on housework than did men in the same categories. Since marriage involves a division of labor, married men spent fewer hours than never-married men on "typically female" home tasks (such as cooking) but more hours on typically male tasks (such as household repairs). The total hours that married and never-married men devote to housework are about the same, however. For women, in contrast, the shift from never-married to married status is associated with a large increase in total hours of housework.

Weekly hours spent on home production

	Women			Men		
Status	Married	Divorced, etc.	Never married	Married	Divorced, etc.	Never married
Total hours spent	29.8	27.8	21.2	17.7	21.6	17.9
"Typically female" tasks	25.1	21.9	17.2	8.6	14.0	12.0
"Typically male" tasks	1.7	2.6	1.9	6.6	4.9	3.8
Neutral tasks	3.0	3.3	2.0	2.4	2.6	2.1

Source: Adapted from Hersch and Stratton (2002), Table 1.

---

[3] Once again, this does not mean that the person merely lazes away the hours. A needy mother's "welfare" receipts may allow her to take better care of her children.

[4] The analytical condition for a corner solution at E is $MRS_R > h_L$ at $R = \bar{R}$. (Even when working zero hours, the slope of the indifference curve exceeds the market wage.)

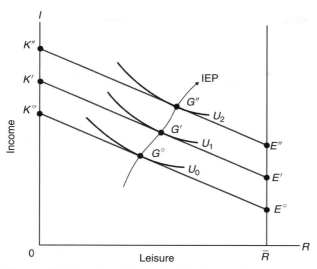

Figure 13.2. Income Expansion Path

As endowed income $\bar{I}$ rises, with the hire-price (wage) held constant, the budget line shifts upward parallel to itself. If I and R are both normal (superior) goods, the successive optimum positions G°, G', G'', . . . show that both more income and more leisure are chosen. Thus, the Income Expansion Path IEP has positive slope.

An economic explanation is that women have a comparative advantage in family activities, men in outside jobs. This is most obvious for child-bearing and child-rearing, especially at early ages. Furthermore, given this initial divergence, women are less likely to undertake the training needed to secure attractive and higher-paying positions in the outside world.

Other data indicate that the total number of working hours, taking housework and outside work together, is about the same for men and women. So a woman who shifts from never-married to married status, while likely increasing the hours she works at home, will also probably decrease the time she devotes to outside jobs.

[a] Joni Hersch and Leslie S. Stratton, "Housework and Wages," *Journal of Human Resources*, v. 37 (2002).

The optimum of the resource-owner is affected by (1) changes in endowed income $\bar{I}$ and (2) changes in the available hire-price (market wage) h_L.

(1) When endowed (nonlabor) income $\bar{I}$ rises, the individual's opportunity set expands. Figure 13.2 shows how the budget line shifts upward from $E^{\circ}K^{\circ}$ to $E'K'$ to $E''K''$. (The wage h_L being unchanged, all these lines are parallel.) Both income I and leisure R are, it is reasonable to assume, normal superior goods as defined in Chapter 4. (For example, someone who receives an unexpected inheritance will typically want to end up with both more spendable income and more leisure.) On this assumption, increases in property income would shift the optimum position G° in Figure 13.2 successively up and to the right to G' and G''. Connecting all these optimum positions generates a positively sloped *Income Expansion Path* (*IEP*).

(2) When the wage rate h_L rises, the initial budget line EK° in Figure 13.3 tilts up, pivoting around the fixed endowment position E. The associated optimum positions

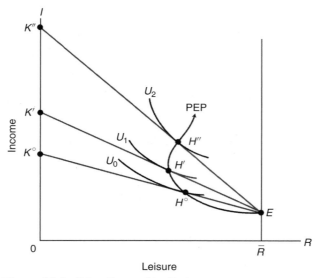

Figure 13.3. Price Expansion Path

As the wage or hire-price h_L increases, the budget line becomes steeper, rotating upward around E. The successive optimum positions are $H°$, H', H'', ... In an initial range where the wage rate is still low, increases in h_L lead to choice of more income but less leisure (i.e., more labor will be offered). In this range the Price Expansion Path PEP has negative slope. A range *may* be reached where further increases in h_L lead to less labor being offered – the PEP curve may "bend backward" for sufficiently high h_L.

(tangencies between the various budget lines and indifference curves) are labeled $H°$, H', H'' in the diagram. Figure 13.3 suggests that the *Price Expansion Path* (*PEP*) through these optimum positions, starting from the fixed endowment E, initially has negative slope but eventually may curve back and have positive slope. (In the region of negative slope, a higher wage induces the individual to work more hours; in the region of positive slope, a higher h_L leads the individual to work *less*.)

Chapter 4 (Section 4.4) showed how to separate the effects of a price change upon consumer choices into a *substitution effect* and an *income effect*. Similarly, a change in the hire-price will have both a substitution effect and an income effect upon a resource-supplier's decisions. If Albert is a lawyer choosing between work and leisure, an increase in his wage (his hourly billing rate) raises the price of leisure to him. Each round of golf, taking time from work, now costs him more. So the substitution effect leads him, other things equal, to choose less leisure as his wage rises.

But there also is an income effect. At the higher wage, the hours Albert devotes to work generate greater earnings. Since leisure is a normal superior good, his higher income leads him to want *more* leisure. So the income and substitution effects act in opposite directions. The higher billing rate motivates him to work more; the increased income motivates him to work less.

In dealing with consumer choices in Chapter 4, the income effect of a price change was usually a minor consideration as compared to the substitution effect. A consumer generally buys many different commodities, so a lower or higher price for any single good ordinarily has little effect upon his or her overall real income. But each worker is typically a highly specialized supplier of one single resource: his or her own labor. So

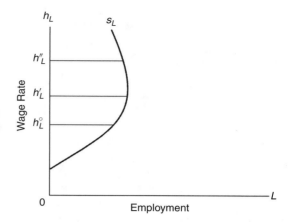

Figure 13.4. Backward-Bending Supply Curve of Labor

The individual supply curve of labor shown here has normal positive slope for wage rates up to h'_L but "bends backward" above that wage.

the worker's real income is strongly affected by changes in the wage rate. So the income effect of a wage change and the substitution effect are both important for the worker's resource-supply decision.

Turning to the Price Expansion Path in Figure 13.3, starting from point E the slope is initially negative. At very low wage rates, where the individual works only a few hours, the substitution effect is always more powerful than the income effect. The reason is that a change in the wage rate can scarcely enrich anyone who works only a few hours. The enrichment due to a wage increase is $L \times \Delta h_L$, where Δh_L is a small change in the wage. When L is also small, the income effect of the price change, $L \times \Delta h_L$, must be small. Only in the upper regions of the Price Expansion Path, where many hours are worked, is L sufficiently large to make the enrichment $L \times \Delta h_L$ large. Only then can the income effect overcome the substitution effect and make the Price Expansion Path have a negative slope. The picture in Figure 13.3 shows such a slope reversal for the Price Expansion Path.

A slope reversal, while possible, is not inevitable. The income effect might never become large enough to outweigh the substitution effect, in which case the Price Expansion Path would then never enter such a "backward-bending" region.

CONCLUSION

The income and substitution effects of a change in hire-price h_L run in opposite directions. At low wage rates the substitution effect must dominate: a person who works at all will initially work more hours as the wage h_L rises. At high wage rates, however, the income effect may dominate: as the wage rises still further, he or she may choose to work less.

The resource-owner's Price Expansion Path (PEP) of Figure 13.3 translates directly into his or her *resource-supply curve* (s_L). In Figure 13.4 the amount of labor L appears on the horizontal axis and the hire-price h_L on the vertical axis. The absolute slopes of the budget lines EK°, EK', and EK'' in Figure 13.3 become the hire-prices h_L°, h_L', and h_L'' in Figure 13.4. The "backward-bending" region of the Price Expansion Path in the earlier diagram leads to a corresponding "backward-bending" segment in the individual's supply curve. In Figure 13.4 the backward-bending segment – where a higher wage leads to fewer hours worked – begins at hire-price h_L'.

EXAMPLE 13.2 NURSING SERVICES: "BACKWARD-BENDING" SUPPLY?

Charles Link and Russell Settle examined the labor supply of married female professional nurses as reported in 1970 Census data.[a] They found that the labor supply curve bent backward, with the bend occurring (depending on race, age, and personal characteristics) at after-tax rates between $2.20 and $3.00 in 1970 dollars (corresponding to $8.61 to $11.75 in 2003 dollars). Furthermore, most of the nurses were in the backward-bending range.

Apart from her own wages, a powerful influence upon a married nurse's labor supply decisions is her husband's income. Among married white registered nurses, for example, a $1 increase in the husband's wage (if the husband worked 2,000 hours, that would mean a $2,000 increase in family income) was associated with 140 to 252 fewer nursing hours worked per year.

The connection with the husband's income may partially explain why the supply curve for female nursing bends backward. Many nurses are married to other health care professionals. Several general forces, for example, changes in Medicare and Medicaid benefits, tend to influence the demand for all health care personnel simultaneously. So any rise in female nurses' wage rate is likely to correlate with a corresponding increase in husbands' wages. Then the statistically observed backward-bending effect may not be a response to nurses' own wage rates but rather to the higher family incomes inclusive of the correlated change in husbands' wages.

Another important consideration is that a nurse-and-doctor married couple are likely to have large family income, putting them in a high tax bracket. So, if the nurse receives a higher pretax wage, the after-tax gain in terms of family income might be quite small.

COMMENT

A backward-bending supply curve for nursing services poses a serious difficulty for medical planners. When additional nursing services are demanded, market forces will dictate higher wages for nurses. But then the new supply-demand equilibrium will have less rather than more nursing hours provided! (In the long run, however, higher wages in nursing will attract newcomers into the profession. That is, the long-run supply curve is almost sure to be more elastic, and indeed positively sloped.)

---

[a] Charles Link and Russell Settle, "Wage Incentives and Married Professional Nurses: A Case of Backward-Bending Supply?" *Economic Inquiry*, v. 19 (January 1981).

An Application: The Incentive Effects of "Welfare" and Social Security

Programs to help the poor may reduce the incentive to work. Figure 13.5 illustrates a simplified "welfare" system in which a government agency guarantees a minimum income of, say, $6,000 per year. If income is below this, the agency will make up the difference. So for a low-wage worker, accepting market employment means that welfare benefits are lost, dollar for dollar, for earnings up to $6,000.

Suppose Beverly has no outside source of nonlabor income. In the absence of a welfare system, her optimum in the diagram would be the tangency point G along the budget line EK. At a wage of $28 per day she works 250 days, earning $7,000 per year; she has 115 days a year of "leisure." If she is guaranteed $6,000 in welfare benefits, her budget line becomes the kinked line MLK. Given the shape of her indifference curves,

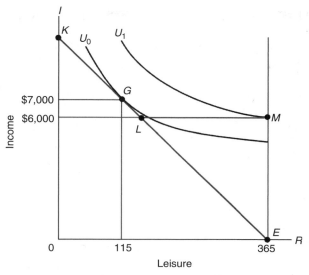

Figure 13.5. Employment versus "Welfare"

In the absence of a welfare system the individual's optimum is at G on indifference curve U_0; he or she earns $7,000 and works $365 - 115 = 250$ days per year. If the welfare guarantee is $6,000, on condition that the person's earned income is less than that, the effective budget line is the kinked line MLK. Along this budget line the optimum is the no-work position M on indifference curve U_1.

the optimum is now at M, where she does not work at all. (True, by not working she sacrifices $1,000 of income, but she values the increased leisure more than the lost income.)

By a parallel analysis, Social Security can reduce beneficiaries' incentive to work. Indeed, when Social Security was proposed in the depression years of the early 1930s, an argument made in its favor was that the elderly should be encouraged to retire, to "make room" for younger workers and thereby reduce unemployment. Current thinking, in contrast, has emphasized the loss of national income when still-productive workers are induced to retire.

EXAMPLE 13.3 RETIREMENT DECISIONS[a]

Until around 1950, most older men continued to participate in the labor force. The participation rate for men over 60 was 64% in 1880, and it remained about the same for decades thereafter.

In 1935 the Social Security Act came into effect and provided taxpayer-financed pensions, but only to *nonworking* retirees. Starting about then, the labor force participation rate of the elderly began falling sharply. It continued to decline thereafter, in part due to the steady liberalization of Social Security benefits. (Other factors, among them the growth in private pensions, may also have been involved.) By 1980 the labor force participation rate for men over 60 had fallen to 32%. This drop is even more striking when it is appreciated that health advances between 1880 and 1980 would otherwise have surely led to *increasing* labor force participation by the elderly. In addition, jobs have tended to become less physically demanding, which should also have led to greater participation by the elderly. So Social Security evidently had an extremely powerful effect in reducing the willingness of the elderly to remain employed.

The last column of the table (using a different data series that covers men over 65 rather than 60) shows that since 1980 participation rates have stabilized. The reason perhaps is that, owing to concerns about the financial viability of the Social Security system, benefit increases have tapered off in recent decades.

U.S. labor force participation rate (%)

Year	Men over 60*	Men over 65**
1880	64	
1900	67	
1920	65	
1940	55	
1960	46	
1980	32	19.0
1990		16.3
2000		17.5
2010 (projected)		19.5

*Source: Estimated visually from Lumsdaine and Wise (1990), Fig. 5a.
**Source: Bureau of Labor Statistics. Office of Occupational Statistics and Employment Projections, 2003, Table 3.

[a] Discussion based in part on Robin L. Lumsdaine and David A. Wise, "Aging and Labor Force Participation: A Review of Trends and Explanations," National Bureau of Economic Research Working Paper 3420 (August 1990).

Not only *time* spent at work, but also the intensity of *effort* may respond to financial considerations.

EXAMPLE 13.4 FOOTRACES AND EFFORT

Financial rewards affect employment not only quantitatively (how many hours to work?) but also qualitatively (how much effort to put in?). Michael T. Maloney and Robert E. McCormick collected evidence on the relation between reward and effort in a rather unusual income-earning activity: long-distance footraces.[a]

The authors studied invitational races offering monetary prizes in the southeastern United States during 1987–1991, for distances of 1 mile and upward. (Ten-kilometer distances were the most frequent.) They investigated whether higher prizes induced more expert runners to enter, and whether the *prize spread* – the difference between first and second place, between second and third, and so forth – affected effort.

Winners' average running times were presumably influenced by both a selection effect (who chooses to run?) and an effort effect (how hard do runners try for the prize?).

Performance turned out to be sensitive both to the size of the average prize and to the prize differentials. The elasticity of winning time relative to size of prize was about −0.017. This means that a doubling of the prize money (100% increase) was associated, on average, with a 1.7% reduction in the winning time. Both the selection effect and the effort effect appear to have been operative. Higher prizes appear to have attracted more proficient athletes, and motivated them to put in more intense effort as well. In 10-kilometer races, on average an increase in the prize from $1,000 to $2,000 reduced the average winning finishing time by around 35 seconds (from 34 minutes, 40 seconds).

For the prize differentials, the elasticity was about −0.039. (As these differentials rise, the top finalists take home a larger fraction of the prize money. A doubling of the average prize spread (in 10-kilometer races that would be an increase from a mean of $238 to $476) on average reduced the winning finishing time in 10-kilometer races by about 81 seconds.

So, the indications are, increased financial rewards did indeed induce greater effort from participants in these footraces.

[a] Michael T. Maloney and Robert E. McCormick, "The Response of Workers to Wages in Tournaments: Evidence from Foot Races," *Journal of Sports Economics*, v. 1 (March 2000).

13.2 PERSONNEL ECONOMICS: MANAGERIAL APPLICATIONS OF EMPLOYMENT THEORY

The Principal-Agent Problem

The effort that an employee ("the agent") devotes to the job can be only imperfectly monitored by the firm ("the principal"). A taxi driver, working out of sight of his supervisors, would be tempted to shirk if paid a straight hourly wage. Compensating him by a fraction of the amount shown on the meter, as is typically the case in current practice, reduces but does not eliminate the incentive to shirk. True, tips also reward diligence, and on the negative side there is the fear of being fired. Still, unless the driver receives the full marginal dollar paid by the rider, an incentive problem remains.

One theoretical solution is a two-part payment scheme. The driver gets all the revenue registered on the meter, plus tips, but must make a fixed payment each period to the firm. Then, since the driver keeps every extra dollar paid by the customer, he is properly motivated to exert himself to earn that extra dollar.

With such a payment arrangement, it is almost as if the driver rents the car and then becomes a firm himself. In Figure 13.6 effort e is scaled on the horizontal axis with dollars on the vertical axis. (Compare Figure 6.1 of Chapter 6.) Assume as shown in the diagram that Total Revenue is a straight-line function of effort. The driver also has a Total Cost curve, which here has a fixed and a variable element. The fixed element is his opportunity cost – the dollar amount he could earn in some other line of activity. Variable Cost is the dollar valuation he places upon the utility sacrifices associated with increased effort.

The difference between Total Revenue and Total Cost is greatest at the effort level e^* where the TR and TC curves are parallel (so that Marginal Revenue and Marginal Cost are equal). At that effort level the vertical difference is AB. Of the Total Revenue EA, the amount EG covers the driver's opportunity cost in alternative employment and the amount GB compensates him for the extra effort expended as he works more hours driving. The remainder, AB, would be profit for an ordinary firm, but here it is the maximum the driver would be willing to pay for the privilege of using the car.

A difficulty with this solution is that the Total Cost function is a psychological variable, and would vary from driver to driver. Taxicab firms would have to guess at the fixed

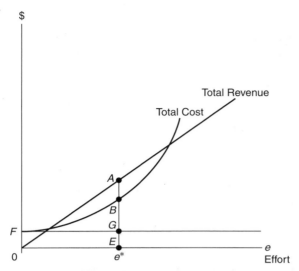

Figure 13.6. The Principal-Agent Problem

Effort e is scaled on the horizontal axis, and dollars on the vertical axis. The driver's Total Cost curve has a fixed element – the dollar amount he could earn in some other line of activity – and a variable element representing the dollar valuation he places upon the utility sacrifices associated with increased effort. His optimal effort is e^*, where the difference between Total Revenue and Total Cost is greatest. (The TR and TC curves are parallel, so Marginal Revenue and Marginal Cost are equal.) Of the Total Revenue EA, the amount EG covers the driver's opportunity cost in alternative employment and the amount GB compensates him for the extra effort expended as he works more hours driving. The remainder AB is the maximum the driver would be willing to pay for the privilege of using the car.

amount AB to be charged drivers for use of the car. On the other hand, the firms have to guess now at the best fraction to pay drivers of the amount on the meter, and in addition have to be concerned about monitoring drivers to deter shirking.

Paying by the Piece[5]

Historically, the two main modern forms of employee compensation have been payment by the hour and payment by the piece. Payment by the piece is, other things equal, superior from the point of view of motivating employees to produce. But, on the negative side, *quality* tends to suffer if only the *quantity* of output enters into the pay package. Also, it is sometimes argued, piece-rate systems tend to trigger excessively intense competition among employees that is bad for health and morale.

Figure 13.7 compares how time-wage and piece-wage systems affect a worker's decisions. As in the preceding diagram, effort e is scaled on the horizontal axis and income on the vertical axis. Figure 13.7 is an indifference-curve diagram rather than a Revenue/Cost diagram. By assumption effort is a bad, so the indifference curves here have *positive* slope. For simplicity, effort and output are supposed to be perfectly correlated.

---

[5] This discussion is based on Edward Lazear, "Performance Pay and Productivity," *American Economic Review*, v. 90 (December 2000).

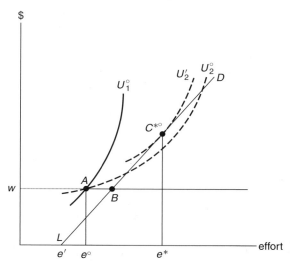

Figure 13.7. Payment by the Price

Effort e is scaled on the horizontal axis and income on the vertical axis. Since effort is a bad, the indifference curves have positive slope. Under a time-rate system subject to a required minimal effort/output level e°, the worker's opportunity constraint rises vertically from e° on the horizontal axis to point A and then becomes horizontal for higher levels of effort. Through point A, the solid indifference curve U_1° represents a worker with strong aversion to effort and the dashed curve U_2° a worker with lesser aversion to effort. Under such a *time-rate* system both types prefer point A, delivering only the minimum amount of effort. A possible *piece-rate* payment scheme is pictured by the line LBD. The worker is paid nothing at all until effort/output level e' is achieved, and then receives a positive constant marginal (per-piece) payment indicated by the slope of LBD. The worker with the greater aversion to effort prefers the time-rate scheme. The other worker prefers the piece-rate scheme, allowing her to attain point C^* on indifference curve U_2', higher on her preference scale than her U_2° curve through point A.

Under a time-rate system, suppose the firm offers the worker a wage w, subject to the proviso that she must deliver a certain minimal effort/output level e°. In the diagram her opportunity constraint rises vertically from e° on the horizontal axis to point A with coordinates e°, w – and then becomes a horizontal line for higher levels of effort. Two distinct possible indifference curves through point A are plotted, U_1° and U_2°. The solid curve U_1° represents a "type-1" worker, characterized by relatively strong aversion to effort. The dashed curve U_2° represents a "type-2" employee characterized by lesser aversion to effort. Although the indifference curves are not the same, under this *time-rate* system both types still prefer point A. That is, each delivers only the minimum amount of effort required to retain his or her job.

A possible *piece-rate* payment scheme is pictured by the line LBD. The worker is paid nothing at all until effort (output) level e' is achieved. Beyond e' she receives a positive constant marginal (per-piece) payment v indicated by the slope of LBD.

Imagine that the worker has the option of enrolling either under the time-rate scheme or the piece-rate scheme. The type-1 worker, with her greater aversion to effort, will remain with the time-rate scheme. Despite the new opportunity, the most preferred attainable point for her is still point A on indifference curve U_1°. But the type-2 employee finds the piece-rate opportunity attractive. She can attain point C^*, where LBD is tangent to her indifference curve U_2', higher on her preference scale than her U_2^0 curve through point A.

So a piece-rate system would leave a type-1 employee unaffected – at least in the short run – while allowing type-2 employees to do better than before. As for the firm, so long as the piece rate (allowing also for the associated costs of materials, utilities, etc.) is less than the firm's Marginal Revenue, it will enjoy higher profits to the extent that any employees choose the piece-rate scheme.

EXAMPLE 13.5 EMPLOYEE COMPENSATION AT SAFELITE

In 1994–1995 the Safelite Glass Corporation (a major producer of auto glass) shifted glass installers in its various factories from time rates to piece rates. During the transition period both methods of compensation were in use. The company provided Edward P. Lazear with data allowing him to compare performance under the two systems.[a]

Compensation at Safelite –1994–1995

	Hourly wage system (averages)	Piece rate system (averages)
Units per worker per day	2.70	3.24
Actual pay	$2,228	$2,283
Cost per unit	$44.83	$35.24

Source: Adapted from Lazear, Table 2.

The table indicates that piece rates led to a substantial increase in worker productivity – about 0.54 units, a 20% improvement. After certain adjustments, the author estimated that the gain was even larger, around 44%. Correspondingly, the firm's cost per unit dropped sharply. As indicated by the text and diagram above, the improvement had two main sources: (1) an *incentive effect* (some employees will choose to work harder) and (2) a *sorting effect* (the more productive workers were more likely to choose to be paid by the piece).

It is not clear, however, why actual average pay per worker went up so very little, from $2,228 to only $2,283 (or about 2.5%). The author suggested one possible explanation, that the system was introduced first for factories in low-wage areas, so that the low-wage and therefore less skilled workers were overrepresented in the piece wage data and underrepresented in the hourly wage data. Allowing for this factor, he estimated that those workers who changed over from time to piece rates received about a 7% increase in compensation on average.

What about the quality of product? Quality problems in the production of auto glass usually show up quickly in the form of broken windshields, and the company's monitoring system was able to control that source of fault. In fact, it appears that quality rose after the shift to piece rates.

COMMENT

In view of the advantages described in the text and illustrated by the Safelite experience, it is puzzling that piece rates remain quite uncommon in American industrial practice. It appears that a peak of 30% of U.S. workers received incentive pay in 1945, and the proportion has since been declining.[b] A likely explanation is that American manufacturing workers are less and less involved in the routine repetitive activities that lend themselves to measuring output by the piece.

[a] Edward P. Lazear, "Performance Pay and Productivity," *American Economic Review*, v. 90 (December 2000).

[b] John Pencavel, "Work Effort, On-the-Job Screening, and Alternative Methods of Remuneration," *Research in Labor Economics*, v. 33 (January 1978).

Signalling

Even if worker productivity is not immediately visible to employers, the preceding discussion showed that under a piece rate system workers might automatically sort themselves into high-pay high-productivity and low-pay low-productivity groups. This section discusses another way in which workers could be induced to sort themselves in accordance with productivity.

Suppose half the job candidates available for a certain position have high ability and half have low ability. Imagine that the wage has to be set in advance, before the firm knows how much the applicant will produce on the job. Employers, however, can observe whether the applicant has acquired an educational credential, such as a B.A. degree. The key idea here is that, even if education is not itself productive, high-ability workers are more likely than low-ability workers to acquire the credential.

The table here shows, for high-ability and low-ability workers, hypothetical figures for Marginal Revenue Product and for cost of education. Since the two types are equally numerous, the average of the Marginal Revenue Products is $(10 + 6)/2 = 8$. If the firm were to ignore the educational credential and hire a candidate at random, it could therefore afford to pay a wage of 8. This would be a "pooling equilibrium." (The firm will normally still be making a profit, since – owing to the Law of Diminishing Returns – all but the marginal worker in each category will be producing more than the tabulated *mrp* figure.)

	High ability	Low ability
Marginal revenue product	10	6
Cost of credential	1	5

Starting from a pooling equilibrium, suppose the firm were to offer a wage of 10 to applicants with a credential and 6 to applicants without one. Since a high-ability worker gains 2 at a cost of 1, he should rationally acquire the credential. Now there is a possible "separating equilibrium." The high-ability worker would obtain the credential and the low-ability worker would not. No one is motivated to deviate, so the separating equilibrium associated with this wage schedule is stable.

What would happen if, holding everything else the same, the cost of the credential to the high-quality worker were 3 rather than 1? The separating equilibrium, with the wage schedule just described, will still be stable. A high-quality worker who deviates can save the cost of 3, but as a result would be classed with the low-ability workers and suffer a wage reduction of 4 ($= 10 - 6$). But now the pooling equilibrium would also be stable! If the firm paid everyone 8, a high-ability worker who acquires the credential would gain only 2 (= 10 − 8) at a cost of 3. So, under certain circumstances, an economic situation may have more than a single stable equilibrium.

With many firms in the industry, however, pooling equilibria become unlikely. If there are any firms at all offering the separating wage schedule, high-ability workers will migrate toward those firms.

EXAMPLE 13.6 SIGNALS AND HANDICAPS

Just as high-ability workers may try to signal quality to employers by obtaining an educational credential, in the realm of biology higher-quality males try to signal their quality to females. The peacock's tail is a famous example.

Biologists explain that the process works because of "the handicap principle."[a] In the preceding text discussion, signalling worked even if the educational credential did not contribute to productivity. The handsome tail of the peacock is an even more extreme case, since it actually hampers the animal's "productivity," that is, his ability to obtain food and escape predators. But the crucial point is that such a handicap is *less* burdensome to a superior-quality animal with better health and stronger muscles. So, at least under certain conditions,[b] natural selection has operated to make the females prefer to mate with males bearing exceptionally handsome tails.

An amazing range of biological features serve as biological credentials of quality. Just as peahens prefer peacocks with beautiful tails, female deer look for males with huge antlers, female bower birds look for males who produce the largest and most attractively decorated nests, and female frogs prefer males with loud croaks as an indicator of muscular strength. In all these cases lower-quality males either are physically unable to emit the signal, or else can do only at excessive cost in comparison with the higher-quality males.

COMMENT

Looking at human females, is it possible they are particularly attracted to males who are better able to bear the burden of purchasing an expensive diamond engagement ring?[c]

---

[a] Amotz and Avishag Zahavi, *The Handicap Principle: A Missing Piece of Darwin's Puzzle*, Oxford University Press, 1997.

[b] Kjell Hausken and Jack Hirshleifer, "The Truthful Signalling Hypothesis: An Explicit General Equilibrium Model," *Journal of Theoretical Biology*, v. 228 (2004).

[c] Margaret F. Brinig, "Rings and Promises," *Journal of Law, Economics, and Organization*, v. 6 (1990). The author's thesis is that an engagement ring serves as a kind of hostage, which the fiancé stands to lose if he reneges on his commitment. This is not inconsistent with the handicap explanation, since only a more intensely desirous male (and hence, other things equal, a more desirable mate for the female) will want to grant such a surety.

13.3   FACTOR-MARKET EQUILIBRIUM

From Individual Supply to Market Supply

The market supply S_L shown in Figure 13.8 is the horizontal summation of the individual resource-supply curves s_L of Figure 13.4. One point of interest: even if many or indeed all of the *individual* supply curves bend backward as in Figure 13.4, the *market* supply curve in Figure 13.8 need not have this shape. Although many or most if the workers currently in any industry may prefer to work fewer hours as the wage rises, new workers

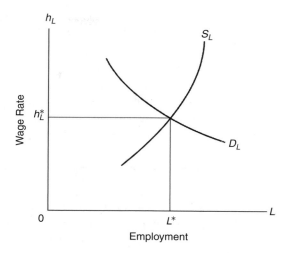

Figure 13.8. Equilibrium in the Labor Market

The intersection of the aggregate demand curve for labor D_L and the aggregate supply curve of labor S_L determines the equilibrium wage rate h_L^* and the level of market employment L^*.

will be attracted from other industries or from leisure. So the supply of a particular type of labor to a single industry or trade will only rarely bend backward. Imagine, for example, that the wages of supermarket cashiers rise. Cashiers currently employed may now choose to work fewer hours, but a flood of new applicants will likely be attracted away from other jobs and toward cashiering.

Demand and Supply Together

The intersection of the resource supply and resource demand curves determines market equilibrium – in this case, the amounts of resources exchanged and the associated hire-prices. The forces that influence and modify these quantities and prices can be separated into those that operate through supply and those that operate through demand.

The determinants on the *demand side* affect Marginal Revenue Product – where, recalling the definition, Marginal Revenue Product is defined as Marginal Product × Marginal Revenue ($mrp \equiv mp \times MR$).

1. *Technology.* The state of technical progress determines the Marginal Product functions for each separate resource and the degree of complementarity among resources.
2. *Demand for final products.* The intensity of consumers' desires for any particular good determines the demand curve for that good, and therefore affects the Marginal Revenue Products of the resources involved in producing that good.
3. *Supply of complementary or anticomplementary inputs.* Depending upon the degree of complementarity, the Marginal Product of any particular resource is affected by the availability of other inputs.

Among the influences on the *supply side* are:

1. *Preferences.* Attitudes toward work versus leisure, or working in one line of activity versus another, influence the resource-supply curves.
2. *Wealth.* As an important aspect of preferences, wealthier people generally prefer to retain more of their owned resources for reservation uses. So, other things equal, the greater the wealth of the owner, the less the supply offered on the market.

3. *Demography.* The size of the population and its age-sex composition will affect the supply of labor to the market, and possibly the supply of land and of other resources. (Recall the discussion of the Black Death in the previous chapter.)

4. *Social forces and legislation.* Historically, and even to some extent today, women have been excluded from many jobs. Child labor has also long been regulated. Similar restrictions, for example environmental regulations, often limit how and to what extent land and other nonhuman resources can be devoted to market employment.

EXAMPLE 13.7 SCIENTISTS

Companies vary in their willingness to grant their scientific staff freedom to engage in independent research. One would expect scientists to be willing to accept a lower wage from firms more tolerant of independent research. In a diagram like Figure 13.8, the supply curve S_L of scientific personnel would lie further to the right for more tolerant firms.

In 1998–1999 the economist Scott Stern surveyed biology Ph.D.'s who sought nonacademic positions in business firms, research institutes, or government laboratories.[a] The author found a strong inverse association between research freedom and the wage accepted. On average scientists accepted a wage penalty of 25% in order to take jobs with firms allowing their employees to publish results in the open scientific literature.

Recall, however, that the supply side is only half the picture. The demand side also needs to be considered. Independent research diverts time and effort and therefore (from the point of view of the company) reduces the employee's productivity. (This loss might be offset to the extent that independent research has synergistic or complementary effects of possible benefit to the firm.)

So, although the supply effect probably dominates, demand considerations may also be involved in explaining the quite large pay differentials between firms offering different degrees of research independence to their scientific staff.

---

[a] Scott Stern, "Do Scientists Pay to Be Scientists," National Bureau of Economic Research, Working Paper 7410 (October 1999).

An Application: Sources of Growing Wage Inequality

Wage rates earned by high-paid workers, in comparison with low-paid workers, have been increasing since around 1970.

EXAMPLE 13.8 RISING WAGE-RATE INEQUALITY

Making use of U.S. Census data, Chinhui Juhn, Kevin M. Murphy, and Brooks Pierce developed indexes showing wage trends for the period 1963 to 1989.[a] The table here compares real weekly wage rates of men at the 90th percentile, the 50th percentile (the median), and the 10th percentile of the wage distribution. Relative to the base year 1963 = 100 the three indices rose together to about 120 in 1969, but diverged sharply thereafter. As of 1989 the median remained about the same as in 1969. But the index for the 90th percentile index rose to about 140 by 1989, while the 10th percentile fell to about 95. So in terms of wage rates, between 1969 and 1989 high-wage workers gained while low-wage workers lost ground.

Changing wage inequality, 1963–1989 (1963 = 100)

Year	90th percentile	Median	10th percentile
1963	100	100	100
1969	120	120	120
1975	120	117	110
1981	126	119	102
1987	139	122	98
1989	140	120	94

Source: Estimated visually from selected data in Juhn, Murphy, and Pierce, Figure 1 (p. 415).

Wage-rate inequality differs from *income inequality*. Higher-wage workers also tend to earn more from nonlabor sources such as interest and rents. On the other hand, high-income individuals on average have larger families. Even more important is that higher-wage workers generally pay higher taxes and receive fewer government income supplements.

Another element in the picture is that higher-wage workers have been working more hours. A study by Dora Costa indicated that in the 1890s the lowest 10% of workers worked nearly 11 hours per day, while the top 10% worked just under 9 hours. But by 1991 the hours worked by the bottom 10% dropped sharply to only 7.5 hours, whereas for the top 10% the hours worked dropped only slightly to 8.5 hours.[b]

Still another consideration is that many families include both high-wage workers (father and mother may be corporate executives) and low-wage workers (their teen-age children may work part-time at McDonalds). Also, there is a life-cycle aspect to low versus high incomes. A young person typically starts at a low wage, but with age and experience gradually achieves higher pay. So high pay and low pay may to some extent average out over a working lifetime.

---

[a] Chinhui Juhn, Kevin M. Murphy, and Brooks Pierce, "Wage Inequality and the Rise in Returns to Skill," *Journal of Political Economy*, v. 101 (June 1993).

[b] Dora Costa, "The Unequal Work Day: A Long Term View," National Bureau of Economic Research Working Paper No. 6419 (February 1998).

Several explanations of growing wage inequality have been offered.

1. *International competition.* In recent decades, barriers to international trade have declined. Increasing trade, associated with greater international division of labor, has improved real incomes worldwide. (See the discussion of The Fundamental Theorem of Exchange in Chapter 7.) Still, some groups have been hurt. In particular, low-skilled low-wage workers in the United States must now compete with low-skilled but even lower-wage workers in countries like China and India.

On the other hand, American *high-skilled* workers now must similarly compete with high-skilled but less highly paid workers in countries such as Japan and Germany. So it is unclear whether freer trade, of itself, increases wage inequality in the United States.

2. *Technological change.* Computers and related developments have increased the demand for literacy, adaptability, and analytic ability. Low-skilled workers, with little to offer on the market except personal traits like patience or muscular strength, have gained little from this type of technological progress. (Except as consumers, of course.) On the other hand, the rising educational levels of American workers means that the *supply* of workers capable of handling computers and other modern technologies has also risen. Since both demand and supply of American high-skilled workers have increased relative to American low-skilled workers, again it is unclear whether the net effect is to increase U.S. wage inequality.

3. *Immigration.* Although individual exceptions are numerous, the bulk of recent immigrants (mainly from Latin America and Asia) have been low-skilled workers. Their entry into the U.S. labor force has reduced wages at the bottom of the distribution – and, owing to factor complementarity, has likely raised wages at the top. So immigration has certainly increased wage inequality within the United States. (At the same time, these population movements have tended to reduce the wage inequality *between* the United States and countries such as Mexico and India.)

4. *Weakened unionization.* Trade unions as factor-market cartels tend to raise wages. In recent decades unionization has declined sharply, reducing this source of pressure for higher wages. But unions primarily represent workers toward the middle of the wage distribution, or even higher. So the lesser degree of unionization cannot be the cause of low-wage workers losing ground.

Several more speculative ideas are also worth mentioning.

5. *Winner-take-all markets.*[6] The contention here is that, in many lines of activity, workers now more often compete for a few big prizes rather than for many smaller ones. In earlier periods smaller cities and towns supported opera houses, athletic teams, and a wide variety of local commercial and noncommercial enterprises that have now largely disappeared. Better transportation and better communications now allow consumers everywhere to be served by world-class firms and entertained by superstars. Hence opportunities have shrunk for persons with only moderate talents. (Notice that this argument is more consistent with a shift of income away from the *middle*, rather than away from the *bottom* of the talent distribution.)

6. *The paradox of increasing opportunity.* In a totally stratified world, with everyone locked at birth into the limited types of employment open to his or her social class, the distribution of true talent would be more or less the same from top to bottom. Then, even though workers at the bottom have no choice but to be porters or servants, the more skilled of them will become first-rate porters and first-rate servants. Consumers will, accordingly, be willing to pay them more. But in a world of freer opportunity, proficient workers will rapidly rise out of the bottom stratum. So increasing opportunity implies that the people left behind at the bottom will, over the years tend to have less and less in the way of marketable skills.[7]

---

[6] Robert H. Frank and Philip J. Cook, *The Winner-Take-All Society*, New York: The Free Press, 1995.

[7] Yet talent in the sense of *marketable* skills may not be the best measure of true merit. Many great artists, for example, were hardly appreciated in their own lifetimes. Vincent Van Gogh never sold a painting in his life.

13.4 MONOPOLIES AND CARTELS IN FACTOR SUPPLY

Monopsony on the *demand side* of the factor market was studied in the preceding chapter. Here the discussion turns to monopoly on the *supply side* of the input market.

Since every firm's product is unique in some ways, each firm has some monopoly power in the product market. Similarly for resources: each worker, each machine, each acre of land is in some way distinctive. But with so many close substitutes, individual resource-owners rarely have any significant monopoly power in the factor market. (Among the exceptions are the unique services of motion picture stars and athletic champions.)

A monopolist on the supply side of the factor market is in a situation much like the product-market monopolies studied in Chapter 8, so a detailed analysis will not be necessary here. But although *monopolies* on the supply side of the factor market are rare, resource-suppliers do commonly achieve monopoly power through *cartels*. By combining into a trade union, workers with no monopoly power individually may, by collectively restricting the supply of labor, raise their wages.

As explained in Chapter 8, cartels have a major weak point: "chiselling." If a union raises wages, individual members have an incentive to gain increased employment by accepting less than the standard pay. As noted in Chapter 8, cartels are sometimes favored or sustained by government action, and that is the case for labor unions in most modern nations. Under the National Labor Relations Act in the United States, an election is normally held to choose a collective bargaining agent. A union that wins a majority of the votes becomes the *exclusive* bargaining agent for all workers in the collective-bargaining unit, regardless of minority wishes. Once a collective-bargaining agent is officially certified, the firm is forbidden to bargain with individual workers. Chiselling is effectively illegal: no single worker can work additional hours by accepting a lower hourly wage, nor can any outsider get a job by offering to work for less.

A disadvantage of unions, from the workers' point of view, is that the wage gain is generally associated with reduced employment. (However, rather than discharge existing workers, firms usually find it more convenient to hire fewer *new* employees. This means that any declines in employment affect mostly those potential new workers who would otherwise be hired.) Another disadvantage is that unionized firms are likely to be less profitable, so in the long run they tend to lose business to nonunion firms.

EXAMPLE 13.9 UNIONIZATION IN THE PRIVATE AND PUBLIC SECTORS

In the past, trade unions mainly represented workers in the private sector. Unions have historically been prevalent in manufacturing, representing employees of large corporations such as General Motors together with small firms in competitive industries such as the needle trades. Unions have also been important in mining, construction, and in some sectors of retailing such as supermarkets. Government employment, in contrast, was not a major area of union strength.

But this picture is no longer accurate. As the table indicates, in 1983 union membership already accounted for only 17% of workers in the private sector, as opposed to 37% of employees in the public sector. By 2002 unionization in the private sector had fallen drastically to only 8%, but continued to rise (though only slightly) to 38% in the public sector.

Union representation in private versus public employment (millions of workers, and percent unionized)

	1983		2002	
	All employees	Unionized	All employees	Unionized
Private sector	71.2	11.9 (17%)	100.6	8.7 (8%)
Public sector	15.6	5.7 (37%)	19.4	7.3 (38%)

Source: B. T. Hirsch and D. T. Macpherson, *Union Membership and Earnings Data Book* (2003), as cited in David Blanchflower and Alex Bryson (September 2003), "What Effect Do Unions Have on Wages...," National Bureau of Economic Research Working Paper 9973, Table 2.

It might at first seem puzzling that unions are so disproportionately represented in the public sector. After all, almost all government agencies have personnel policies such as Civil Service that reduce the need for employees to turn to unions for collective protection against arbitrary actions of bosses and supervisors.

The most obvious explanation is that union members are voters, and union treasuries are major sources of funding for electoral campaigns. Acting as an employer a government decision-maker might be inclined to resist unionization, but as a politician he or she is likely to be beholden to union leaders. More important, probably, is the power of competition. Employers in the private sector are always under great pressure to hold down costs. So they are strongly motivated to resist unions pushing for higher wages and employee benefits. If General Motors signs an unusually generous union contract, it will probably have to raise prices on its autos and thus lose business to domestic competitors like Ford or to foreign competitors like Toyota. Government agencies are under much less competitive pressure. If the state of New Jersey pays exceptionally high wages to its administrative personnel, it may have to raise taxes. But only in the very long run is New Jersey likely to lose business and population to Pennsylvania or Maryland.

Professional associations have sometimes been accused of acting as cartels. The American Medical Association has pressed for higher standards in medical education, which have raised physician quality to the benefit of consumers. But these higher standards have also reduced the number of practicing physicians, reducing the availability of medical services as well as raising doctors' incomes.

Loosely organized resource-supply cartels such as professional associations usually shun collective bargaining. Instead, they aim to achieve their ends by restricting entry to the trade. Whereas workers who chisel on rates of pay may be difficult to detect, entry into a profession is usually highly visible and so easier to control. In the supply-demand equilibrium of Figure 13.8, entry control could shift the supply curve S_L so far to the left as to achieve a monopoly-like outcome. Some of the programs aimed to assist American farmers (see Example 2.7) have also achieved cartel-like effects by control of entry into agricultural production.

One notable exception to tight control over occupational entry is the legal profession. Whereas the medical and dental and accounting professions have always concerned themselves about excessive numbers of practitioners, law schools in the United States have greatly increased the supply of new lawyers without apparent objection from established lawyers. This exception is, however, understandable. An additional physician or dentist or accountant or barber takes away business from his or her fellows. In contrast, each additional attorney – by adding to the number of lawsuits, writs, presentments, depositions, hearings, trials, pleadings, demurrers, rejoinders, and appeals – probably makes more business for other practitioners of the trade.

13.5 THE "FUNCTIONAL" DISTRIBUTION OF INCOME

The Traditional Classification: Land, Labor, and Capital

Resources have traditionally been classified under the headings of labor, land, and capital. These were once thought to correspond to three so-called "functional" categories of factor incomes: labor receives wages, land receives rent, and capital receives interest.

This classification made some sociological sense in the emerging period of economic thought, especially in England during the late 18th and early 19th centuries. Land was mainly owned by the old aristocracy. Capital (by which was meant material assets other than land) was owned by the rising middle classes. Labor was provided by the workers.

Even if there is some historical merit to this classification, the claim that these three inputs are "functionally distinct" in economic terms is analytically invalid.

LAND VERSUS CAPITAL: *Land* is traditionally defined as the "natural and inexhaustible productive powers of the soil." *Capital*, in contrast with land, supposedly represents "produced means of production." But the powers of the soil – its fertility, topographical features, and geographical location – are often largely a human creation. It took human effort to discover the vast new lands of America or to drain marshes and clear wasteland in England. Even for developed land, maintaining its fertility may require continuing human exertion and sacrifice.

One might think that land and capital differ on the supply side. Land is supposedly fixed in quantity (the supply curve is vertical), whereas capital is a produced resource whose supply curve slopes upward. But the supply of land is not absolutely fixed. More land will be provided when the price is right. It can even be reclaimed from the ocean.[8] And existing land will be allowed to erode away if the reward for maintaining it is insufficient. Furthermore, even if the amount of physical land were fixed, as long as there are reservation uses its supply *to the market* will still respond to its price.

LABOR VERSUS CAPITAL: Nor is there any "functional" distinction between labor and capital. In modern society what a person has to sell is not raw labor power, but trained and educated capacity to apply effort. Just as an owned tool may be part of a worker's capital, so is training ("human capital"). The capacity of a human being to do useful labor is as much a produced means of production as any building or machine.

EXAMPLE 13.10 INCOME SOURCES OF THE WEALTHY IN BRITAIN

In the past 150 years a remarkable historical change has taken place in the sources of incomes received by wealthy people in Great Britain. The table here, based upon a study by Peter H. Lindert,[a] compares the upper 10% of the population in 1867

---

[8] The most famous example is the massive drainage of the Zuider Zee by the Dutch. Large areas of Boston and San Francisco are also built on reclaimed land.

with that in 1972–1973. In 1867 investment income – earnings from resources other than land or labor – was the largest component, labor earnings a distant second, and land rents were still substantial. In contrast, by the 1970s land rents had become negligible and the fraction accounted for by investment income had shrunk drastically. Labor earnings had become by far the most important source of income, even for the wealthy.

Although the change is most striking for the wealthy, a similar pattern was observed for the population at large. The author estimated that the overall nationwide share of national income attributable to human skills rose from around 15% in 1867 to 52% in the years 1972–1973.

Sources of income in Britain (top 10% of population)

	England and Wales 1867	United Kingdom 1972–3
Land rents	13%	1%
Investment income	69	15
Labor earnings	18	84
Total	100%	100%

Source: Adapted from Lindert, p. 1155.

COMMENT

The growth of "labor earnings" mainly reflects increased education and training (investment in human capital). And since buildings, machines, transportation and communication networks tend to *complement* labor, the vast accumulation of such nonhuman capital in the course of a century has also helped raise wage rates and labor incomes.

[a] Peter H. Lindert, "Unequal English Wealth Since 1670," *Journal of Political Economy*, v. 94 (December 1986).

Supply conditions for different types of resources diverge in important ways. Human capital has the disadvantage of dying along with its possessor. Longer expected life spans reduce this disadvantage, which is perhaps one reason why young people have been increasingly acquiring more education and training. On the plus side human capital also has the convenient feature of portability; it moves about with its owner. Portability helps contribute to flexibility in the geographical deployment of resources, and is therefore increasingly important in a dynamic economy. Portability is also a crucial consideration for resource-owners threatened by possible confiscation. So one would expect education to be highly valued (in comparison with land, for example) by minority groups vulnerable to expropriation, and by people in general during periods of political turmoil.

Capital, Rate of Return, and Interest

Capital is best thought of as a generic term for all *sources* of productive services. These sources must be distinguished from the *productive services* themselves. The human being is the source of labor services, but the labor service is the employee-hour (or other time unit). Similarly, land is a source of productive services, but land-service is measured in some unit like acre-years. And again, it is necessary to distinguish buildings and machines (sources) from the services of building and machines.

The *sources* of input services constitute an individual's or a nation's capital. Land is capital. Machines and buildings are capital. And the strength, skill, and training of the labor force are human capital.

Markets may exist both for the sources of productive services and for the services themselves. Markets for resources determine the asset price of a machine or building or an acre of land. Markets for productive services determine the hire-price for a year's use of a machine or building or an acre of land. Labor is a special case. In modern times human labor can be hired, but humans cannot be bought as assets.[9] In some periods, however, human slaves have been bought and sold. And on the other hand, some systems of law have forbidden sale of certain nonhuman resources, notably land (as in the British system of entail).

EXAMPLE 13.11 CAPITAL IN THE SLAVE-OWNING SOUTH – COMPENSATED EMANCIPATION?

Louis Rose studied the value of various categories of wealth in the 15 states where slaves were emancipated by President Lincoln's proclamation.[a] The table indicates that, at $3,685 millions of 1860 dollars, slaves accounted for about 24% of the aggregate wealth in the hands of white property-owners. Slave values varied with age and other characteristics, the average being around $933. Emancipation eliminated the value of this property to the slave-owners, but generated a corresponding economic gain to the slaves themselves in the form of the transferred ownership of their own persons.

Wealth data, 15 southern states, 1860 millions of dollars

Value of (nonfarm) real estate and personal property	$8,644
Value of land in farms	2,550
Value of implements and machinery in use	104
Value of livestock	515
Value of slaves emancipated	3,685
Total	15,498

Source: Adapted from Rose, pp. 43, 49.

In view of the enormous costs of the Civil War, economists have asked why the North and South did not agree on *compensated emancipation*? (President Lincoln initially favored gradual compensated emancipation, but his proposals aroused little support in either North or South.) One part of the answer is that each side expected to win in a quick (cheap) war. Northern leaders felt they need not pay for emancipation, whereas the South thought it could maintain slavery at little cost.

The costs of the Civil War turned out to be far higher than either side anticipated. In terms of 1860 dollars, Gerald Gunderson estimated the costs (counting government outlays, plus loss of trade and civilian output, but *excluding* any charge for lives lost!) as totaling $2.188 billion for the North and $2.017 billion for the South, for a total of $4.205 billion.[b] He calculated that compensated emancipation would have cost around $90 per capita as a one-time charge levied upon the entire population of the

---

[9] This is not absolutely true. Workers, subject to certain legal constraints, might be able to sign contracts binding them to work for an employer over a period of years. Such a contract might be a valuable asset and as such salable to other potential employers.

United States (including the slave-owners as well as the freed slaves themselves). This sum is large. In 1860 the national income was only around $100 per capita, so the sum required would have come to about 90% of one year's national income. But the cost of the war as estimated by Gunderson – and this figure is undoubtedly too low – was even larger, around $140 per capita or 140% of a year's national income.

To get a truer picture of the cost of the war, Claudia Dale Goldin estimated the loss of potential consumption by all persons alive in 1860 – thus allowing for wartime sacrifices and also their postwar consequences.[c] This came to around $10 billion, over twice Gunderson's total. (However, even the Goldin figure is surely still an underestimate, since it omits "intangible" considerations like pain and suffering.)

Returning to Gunderson's calculations, and looking at the regions separately, the cost of the war came to $96 per free Northerner and $380 per free Southerner. In addition, white Southerners lost what they saw as the value of their slave investments. (Recall that this was not a *net* regional loss, since the gain to the freedmen offset the loss to their former owners. But benefits to freedmen of course played no role in the calculations of the Southern leaders.) So, even limiting ourselves to such "cold-blooded" calculations, the War would appear to have been a miscalculation even for the North – and it was the grossest of blunders for the South. The North should have been willing to offer compensated emancipation, and Southern whites should have been delighted to accept it. (Chapter 17 will take up the question of why, despite the gains always achievable by avoiding it, conflict – in the form of war, crime, and politics – continues to occur.)

---

[a] Louis Rose, "Capital Losses of Southern Slaveholders Due to Emancipation," *Western Economic Journal*, v. 3 (Fall 1964).

[b] Gerald Gunderson, "The Origin of the American Civil War," *Journal of Economic History*, v. 34 (December 1974).

[c] Claudia Dale Goldin, "The Economics of Emancipation," *Journal of Economic History*, v. 33 (March 1973).

The word "capital" is commonly used in two quite different senses that often lead to confusion. The two meanings can be separated by distinguishing between *real capital* and *capital value*. Real capital (or capital goods) refers to the physical sources of productive services: land, buildings, labor power, and so on. *Capital value* is the market valuation of these sources. This distinction parallels the difference between the *physical* Marginal Product *mp* of an acre of land (bushels of wheat per year) and the *Value of the Marginal Product vmp* (dollar value of the bushels produced per year).

When both the resource and the service are traded in markets, the price of the source as an asset (its capital value) is economically related to the hire-price of using it over some period of time. This relationship leads to the concept called the *rate of return* (ROR). Suppose an acre of land has a price of $1,000 as an asset, and its physical Marginal Product is 50 bushels of wheat per year. If the price of wheat is $2 per bushel, the Value of the Marginal Product and therefore the hire-price is $100 per year. Then, other things equal, the rate of return earned from the investment in land is $100/$1,000, or 10% per year. More generally, the rate of return from holding any asset is:

$$\text{Rate of return} \equiv \frac{\text{Annual net earnings}}{\text{Capital value}} \qquad (13.5)$$

In the numerator on the right-hand side of this equation, annual net earnings is the "cash flow" generated by the asset, adjusted for *depreciation or appreciation.*

Let z_A be the cash flow, while P_A represents the capital value (asset price) of asset A and ΔP_A its anticipated change in value (appreciation or depreciation) during the year. If the asset is rented to another party, the cash flow will be its hire-price. Or, for an asset directly owned, z_A will be the value of its physical yield:

$$ROR_A \equiv \frac{Z_a + \Delta P_A}{P_A} \tag{13.5'}$$

PROPOSITION: In equilibrium, the rates of return earned on all assets will be equal.

For any two assets A and B, if ROR_A is greater than ROR_B, then resource-owners will want to buy A and sell B. So the price P_A will rise, while P_B will fall. The rate of return on A will then fall and the rate of return on B rise, until the two rates of return are brought into equality.

So an asset expected to *depreciate* in value during a given time period must command a correspondingly higher hire-price, whereas holding assets expected to *appreciate* may be attractive despite a small cash flow. A land speculator may be willing to pay a steep price for a city lot intended to remain vacant for a period of time, earning zero cash flow. He would do so, however, only if he expects the value of the site to appreciate enough to make the investment worthwhile.

EXERCISE 13.2

Suppose the going rate of return is 5%. Let there be three assets: A (acres of land), B (barrels of aging wine), and M (machines). The wine requires costly storage, but is expected to appreciate in value. Machines, in contrast, generate a big positive cash flow but depreciate in value. Land yields a more modest cash-flow (its hire-price), but is not expected to appreciate or depreciate. Using the data in the table, find the asset prices P_A, P_B, and P_M.

Asset	Annual cash flow (z)	Anticipated appreciation (ΔP)
A	50	0%
B	-30	8
M	100	-5

ANSWER: Anticipated land appreciation is $\Delta P_A = 0$, so equation (13.5') has the simple form $0.05 = 50/P_A$; the solution is $P_A = 1,000$. For wine, the anticipated appreciation is $\Delta P_B = 0.08 P_B$. The equation becomes $0.05 = (-30 + 0.08 P_B)/P_B$, so $P_B = 1,000$. For machines, appreciation is $\Delta P_M = -0.05 P_M$, so the equation is $0.05 = (100 - 0.05 P_M)/P_M$. Once again the solution is $P_M = 1,000$. So these three widely different assets have the same capital values. The divergences in their cash flows are offset by the anticipated appreciation or depreciation.

Though a full analysis will be deferred to Chapter 15 ("The Economics of Time"), it can be shown that in equilibrium the common rate of return on all assets also equals the *rate of interest* (r). Thus, for all assets A, B, ..., in equilibrium:

$$ROR_A = ROR_B = \cdots = r \tag{13.5''}$$

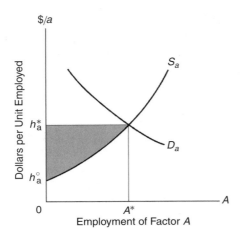

Figure 13.9. Economic Rent

Economic rent is the shaded area lying above the factor supply curve S_a and below the market equilibrium hire-price h_a^*.

So in equilibrium the interest rate equals the ratio between the net earnings of any asset and its capital value. (Or, inverting this relation, asset value can logically be determined by "capitalizing" net earnings – that is, dividing by the interest rate.) How the rate of interest is determined by the productivity of assets together with the time-preferences of consumers will be the central topic of Chapter 15.

CONCLUSION

Interest is not the return to a particular factor called capital. Rather, in equilibrium the interest rate equals the rate of return on the capital value of each and every asset or factor of production. The interest rate is then the ratio of annual *net* earnings (that is, allowing for depreciation or appreciation and for cash flow) from any resource, divided by its resource price.

13.6 ECONOMIC RENT

Economists give the term *economic rent* a special meaning. It must be distinguished from the usual concept of rent as the hire-price for annual use of an acre of land, a building, or a machine. Instead, economic rent is defined as the *excess return* to any input. That is, economic rent is the difference between the actual payment received (the hire-price) and the lowest payment the owner would have been willing to accept. Economic rent is therefore closely related to the concept of Producer Surplus introduced in Chapter 7.

In Figure 13.9 the economic rent received by the owners of resource A is the shaded area above the supply curve and below the hire-price h_a^*. (Note the similarity to the picture of Producer Surplus in Figure 7.7; the difference is that the horizontal axis here is scaled in units of input A rather than in units of output Q.) There is an "excess" return because the sellers receive h_a^* for each unit of A^* sold, whereas the supply curve shows that lower hire-prices would have been accepted for all but the very last unit.

The amount of economic rent (the size of the shaded area) is sensitive to the shape of the supply curve S_a. The less elastic the supply (the steeper the curve) in the neighborhood of the equilibrium, the greater the economic rent. In the limit, if S_a were vertical at $A = A^*$, the entire payment $h_a A^*$ would be economic rent.

Economic rent is a slippery category, since its magnitude depends upon the range of alternatives considered. It was noted earlier in the chapter that the more narrowly defined is a particular employment of a resource, the more elastic (flatter) is the supply curve of that activity. Even if the supply of labor in general is rather inelastic, the supply of labor to a narrow activity such as cashier services is likely to be quite elastic. (A higher wage for cashiers is likely to draw in employees currently working in substitute occupations such as typists or salespersons.) This means that the economic rent – the excess return of working as a cashier rather than shifting to the next best job – is small. But if the alternative to working as a cashier is no job at all, the supply curve is likely to be inelastic: economic rent will be large.

Confusions over economic rent have played a role in American politics. Henry George[10] based his famous "single tax" proposal on the idea that, since land is in fixed supply (its supply curve is supposedly vertical), all or almost all land rent could be taxed away without affecting the amount of land made available for productive use. (Supposedly, owners would submit to having even 99% of their land rents taxed away rather than leaving the property totally idle.) In short, Henry George thought that all land rent was *economic rent*.

For several reasons not all land rent is economic rent: (1) As previously noted, the physical amount of land is not literally fixed. Heavy taxes on land rent would not only discourage reclaiming new land from the ocean, but would rule out the investments needed to prevent erosion and degradation of existing land. (2) Even if the physical supply of land were fixed, its *market supply* is not. Landowners have reservation uses. If net after-tax rent receipts are too low, owners can retain their land tracts as residential estates or use them to engage in home farming. (3) A high tax on land would reduce the owner's incentives to seek the *best* use of his or her land, since all or almost all of the additional earnings would be lost in taxes.

SUMMARY   In input markets, the supply side consists of individual owners of resources whereas firms, as employers of resources, constitute the demand side.

The owner of any resource must decide between offering it on the market to obtain income, or else retaining it for personal reservation uses. To maximize utility, a price-taking resource-owner would equates his or her personal Marginal Rate of Substitution in Resource Supply to the hire-price of the resource. As endowed income rises, an Income Expansion Path (IEP) is traced out. Similarly, as hire-price h_a varies a Price Expansion Path (PEP) is traced out. Changes in the hire-price h_a will have both an income effect and a substitution effect upon the supply of input. These work in opposite directions, so that the supply curve of a resource may have a backward-bending range.

A *principal-agent problem* arises when the firm (the principal) cannot perfectly monitor an employee (the agent). One solution is a two-part pay scheme: the employee is paid his or her Marginal Revenue Product, but only after making a fixed lump-sum payment to the firm. Another possible solution is payment by the piece instead of by the hour.

When the productivity of a job applicant is not immediately visible to an employer, a high-ability person may *signal* ability, for example by obtaining an educational credential. The necessary condition is that the credential must be less costly for a high-ability

---

[10] Henry George, 1839–1897, American economist and reformer. In 1886 he ran for mayor of New York, coming in second in a field of three candidates.

worker than for a low-ability worker to acquire. In a *separating equilibrium*, the signalling is effective; higher-ability workers receive higher wages. But it is also possible that signalling does not work, leading to a *pooling equilibrium* in which all qualities of workers receive the same wage.

In a competitive factor market, the equilibrium hire-price and quantity for any input are found at the intersection of the market supply and demand curves. Demand for inputs tends to rise with technological progress, with higher consumer demand for final products, and with increased supply of cooperating inputs. Increased wealth increases the overall availability of a resource, but can also induce people to retain more for reservation uses, thereby reducing supply.

Monopolies on the supply side of a resource market are rare. More common are cartels whose members act as a collective monopolist. Owing to the "chiselling" problem, resource cartels like other cartels can rarely survive without government support. Labor unions are the most important type of resource cartel. Certain professional associations achieve much the same effect by limiting entry into the profession.

A traditional classification divides resources into the categories of land (resources provided by Nature), capital (resources provided by human sacrifice and saving), and labor (the human resource itself). But a more economically meaningful distinction is between *productive services* (such as an employee-hour of labor or an acre-year of land) and the *sources of these services*. For any resource A, the relation between the price or "capital value" of the source P_A and the hire-price h_a defines the rate of return ROR_A, after adjusting for possible appreciation or depreciation during the hiring period. So if P_A is the price of the asset, $ROR_A \equiv (h_a + \Delta P_A)/P_A$.

Economic rent is the excess of what a resource-owner receives in the market over the minimum required to draw the resource away from reservation uses. Economic rent is smaller the greater is the range of alternatives considered.

QUESTIONS

[†]The answers to daggered questions appear at the end of the book.

For Review

1. "Leisure" refers to reservation uses of labor. Name other resources likely to have significant nonmarket or reservation uses.

2. Explain, in terms of income and substitution effects, why the market supply curve of a resource service can bend backward.

[†]3. If leisure were an inferior good, would a backward-bending supply curve of labor be possible?

[†]4. Why must the substitution effect dominate the income effect at very low wage rates?

[†]5. Is the supply curve of a resource to a particular employment likely to be more or less elastic than the supply to all market uses? Why?

6. In what way does the market opportunity set of an input-monopolist differ from that of a competitive supplier of input services? How will the optimum of the resource-owner be affected?

[†]7. Physicians commonly work unusually long hours, and are often praised for their dedication to healing the sick and alleviating human suffering. Show why, even if physicians are not exceptionally tenderhearted, they would still be likely to work long hours.

8. Explain the traditional "functional" classification of inputs of production.
†9. How can land and labor power be thought of as capital?
†10. What is the relationship between the hire-price of an input and the purchase price of that input?
11. What causes the rate of return ROR on all assets to tend toward equality?
†12. What is economic rent? What is its relation to Producer Surplus?
†13. A firm that previously pays a time-rate introduces a piece-rate. How do you expect output to change? If given a choice, what kind of employees would you expect to choose the time-rate and the piece rate?
†14. Why hasn't the piece-rate replaced the time-rate as the dominant means of compensating manufacturing workers in the United States?

For Further Thought and Discussion

†1. What would be the effect on women's demand for "leisure" (the desire for reservation or nonmarket uses of time) of:
   a. a decline in the birth rate;
   b. improved household technology (as with the introduction of washing machines, vacuum cleaners, and so on);
   c. a fall in the price of prepared foods?

   In each case, what would be the effect on *men's* supply of labor?
†2. If changing circumstances have reduced women's preferences for reservation uses of their time (see question above), what effect would such a change have upon the supply curve of female labor? Upon the relative market wages of male and female workers?
3. What would be the effect upon the budget line and the resource-owner's optimum of a progressive income tax on labor earnings? of a time-and-a-half rule for overtime work?
4. Diagram a situation in which a resource-owner devotes all of his or her resource to reservation uses. Does this necessarily imply that income *I* must be a "bad" or a "neuter" commodity at the solution point? Diagram a situation in which the resource-owner's optimum is such that no reservation uses *R* are retained. Does this imply that *R* must be a "bad" or a "neuter" commodity at the solution point? Explain.
†5. In modern times, real wealth and real wage rates have steadily increased throughout the Western world. But average working hours in market employment have steadily fallen. Would the pure income effect (due to rising per capita wealth) tend to reduce market employment? Would the pure substitution effect (due to the relative price shift represented by the rising wage rate) tend to have this effect? Comment upon the relative importance of the two in light of the evidence.
†6. Historians generally believe that slave labor is less productive than free labor. Analyze this contention.
7. Consider proposals that wage rates should reflect "comparable worth" rather than supply and demand. Some states and other political jurisdictions have already accepted this principle for determining salaries of public employees. A flourishing business of comparable-worth consultants provides formulas to compute salaries in accordance with the knowledge and skill required, the complexity of the task, the physical demands of the job, and so forth. But these various formulas differ drastically from one another. Is there any way of objectively determining comparable worth apart from supply and demand? What consequences would you anticipate if a wage set in accordance with comparable worth diverged from that indicated by supply and demand?

8. According to the single-tax movement, a land tax would not affect the productive uses of land since the supply of land is fixed. Is this valid? Distinguish between a tax on *market uses* of land, versus a tax on *ownership* of land.

†9. Compare the consequences of a tax upon labor earnings (market uses of labor) versus a tax upon "labor capacity" (that is, a tax calculated upon the individual's *ability to earn*, whether he or she works or not).

†10. What *supply-side* considerations help explain the relatively high wages received by U.S. workers?

11. Over a century ago Karl Marx, in what is known as *the immiserization hypothesis*, predicted that workers' wages and incomes in the advanced industrial countries would tend to fall – thus bringing on a socialist revolution. This prediction has failed. Some defenders of Marx have argued that immiserization did not occur because in the meantime capitalism has adopted "socialistic" reforms. Among these might perhaps be classed minimum-wage laws, the 40-hour week, welfare relief for the unemployed, and laws encouraging trade unions and collective bargaining. What effects would you expect each of these reforms to have upon wage rates? upon workers' incomes?

†12. Wage rates are high in New York City, compared to the rest of the United States. But so is the cost of living. Would you conclude that typical New York workers really are, or are not, more productive than workers elsewhere?

†13. If "welfare" is introduced, a person might shift from working positive to zero hours. Is this due to the income effect or the substitution effect, or both?

†14. For the consumer, the income and substitution effects tend to reinforce one another. For the resource supplier, they seem to be opposed. Explain.

†15. When a firm borrows to take on a high level of debt, it faces a risk that if its future cash flows are poor, it will have trouble repaying the debt – "financial distress." Financial economists have documented that financial distress imposes costs on the firm – direct and indirect. Could a high level of debt be a signal for high firm quality?

†16. Suppose that the marginal cost of extracting oil is continuously increasing with the amount of oil extracted, that there is no technological progress over time, and that it is prohibitively costly to extract the last drop of oil from the ground. In the long run, will society "run out of oil"?

V EXCHANGE

14 | Exchange, Transaction Costs, and Money

The Fundamental Theorem of Exchange – that buyers and sellers both gain from trade – was introduced in Chapter 7. Many economic fallacies, for example, the most common arguments for protective tariffs, overlook the point that voluntary trade benefits both sides.

Still, some objections might be raised. Suppose a buyer paid good money for a beachfront lot that proves to be miles out to sea. The answer is that the parties here did not truly agree on an exchange. Owing to trickery, there was no "meeting of the minds." Another problem: a momentary want may misrepresent a person's true preferences. Esau sold his birthright to Jacob for a mess of pottage (*Genesis*, Chapter 25) and regretted the transaction afterward. Third and most serious, many of us would be better off not satisfying even our most intense desires. Think of a drug addict. Getting what you wish for is often the worst thing that could happen to you. Still, it can always be said that rational participants in voluntary exchange *believe* they will both gain.

Mutual gain from trade involves two distinct elements. The first is an improved (mutually preferred) *allocation of consumption goods*. Suppose Ida and John are endowed with equal quantities of tea and coffee, but Ida prefers tea and John prefers coffee. The potential gain from trade is obvious. Alternatively, suppose Ida and John both prefer bread with butter, but Ida is initially endowed with all the bread and John with all the butter. Again, both can benefit from trade.

The second source of mutual gain is *rearrangement of production*. If Ida is better at baking bread and John at churning butter, trade permits each to concentrate on his or her area of superiority.

CONCLUSION

Voluntary exchange is mutually beneficial because (1) Each person obtains a consumption basket he or she prefers to the original endowment. (2) People can specialize in production, thereby increasing the totals of goods available.

This chapter will probe more deeply into these gains from exchange. It will also deal with *transaction costs* that limit the benefits from trade, and with money as a way of minimizing transaction costs. Later on the discussion will follow up a topic introduced in Chapter 11 – asymmetrical information in exchange. An important trade mechanism, auctions, for which asymmetrical information plays a crucial role, will then be analyzed.

14.1   PURE EXCHANGE: THE EDGEWORTH BOX

The first benefit of trade is that, through exchange, people can obtain baskets of goods that better match everyone's desires.

In the mid-1800s, the United States exported wheat to Britain in exchange for manufactured goods. Using the notation X for manufactures and Y for wheat, typical citizens of the two countries are pictured in Figure 14.1. In Panel (a) Ida, the American, has an endowment at position E_i near the vertical axis. (She starts with a relatively large amount of wheat Y.) Panel (b) shows that John, the Briton, has an endowment at E_j, near the horizontal axis. (He starts with a relatively large amount of manufactures X.) The bold lines indicate the desired directions of exchange. If Ida moves down and to the right (giving up wheat for manufactures) while John moves up and to the left (giving up manufactures for wheat), each can attain a higher indifference curve.

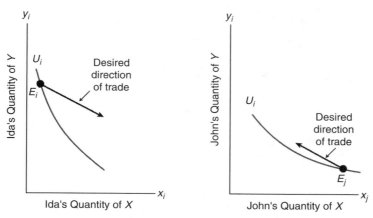

Figure 14.1. Desired Directions of Trade

In panel (a) Ida, a typical American, is endowed with a relatively large amount of wheat Y. In panel (b) John, a typical Briton, is endowed with a relatively large amount of manufactures X. Given normal diversified preferences as indicated by their respective indifference curves U_i and U_j, they can both benefit by trade.

The *Edgeworth box* of Figure 14.2 shows this information in a different way. Panel (b) of the previous diagram has been rotated 180° (so that John's origin is at the upper right corner of the box) and superimposed upon Panel (a) in such a way that the two endowment positions E_i and E_j coincide at point E. Ida's preference directions remain up and to the right, but John's are now down and to the left. (Turning the book upside down will confirm that John's indifference curves have the usual position and shape, when referred to his origin at the upper right corner.)

The size of the Edgeworth box is determined by the total quantities available. At point E Ida is endowed with $\overline{y}_i$ units of wheat and John with $\overline{y}_j$ units. The height of the box is thus $\overline{Y} \equiv \overline{y}_i + \overline{y}_j$. Similarly, the width of the box is determined by the total amount of manufactures available: $\overline{X} \equiv \overline{x}_i + \overline{x}_j$.

Exchange is pictured as follows. The two individuals are initially at the joint endowment position E. The indifference curves U_i'' for Ida and U_j'' for John through point E generate a lens-shaped "region of mutual advantage" (the shaded area). As Ida sells John wheat in exchange for manufactures, the position of the two parties (that is, the division of wheat and manufactures between them) moves southeast in the diagram. If they agree to the particular distribution of wheat and manufactures represented by point T within the shaded area, they will respectively attain higher indifference curves U_i''' and U_i'''. (Remember that John's origin is at the upper right corner, making his preference directions down and to the left.) So Ida and John should be willing to trade from the endowment position E to points such as T or F. They would not *both*, however, be willing to trade from E to points such as R, S, or V.

Suppose that Ida and John do agree on a redistribution of wheat and manufactures so as to arrive at point T. The indifference curves U_i''' for Ida and U_j''' for John through point T generate a smaller lens-shaped region of mutual advantage (the darker shaded area). This means that, starting from point T, the parties can still engage in *additional* mutually advantageous trading.

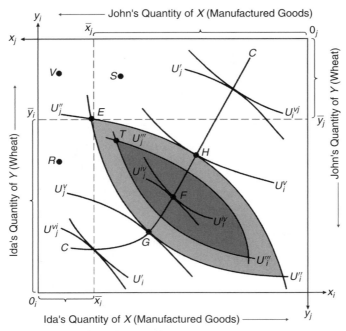

Figure 14.2. The Edgeworth Box

For Ida, amounts of X and Y are measured by distances to the right of and above her origin 0_i. For John the axes are inverted: amounts of X and Y are measured by distances to the left of and below his origin 0_j. Ida's preferences are represented by indifference curves U_i', U_i'',... with utility increasing upward and to the right; John's preferences are represented by indifference curves U_j', U_j'',... with utility increasing downward and to the left. The width of the box corresponds to the fixed social total $\overline{X} \equiv x_i + x_j$ and the height to the fixed social total $\overline{Y} \equiv y_i + y_j$. Any point in the diagram represents an allocation of these totals between Ida and John. The allocations that both prefer to the endowment position E are shown by the lightly shaded "region of mutual advantage"; the heavily shaded region is mutually preferred to point T.

In contrast, consider point F. At F the indifference curves U_i^{iv} for Ida and U_j^{iv} for John are mutually tangent. As is clear from the geometry, moving in any direction from point F must make either Ida or John (or both of them) worse off. In other words, at point F it is no longer possible to construct a region of mutual advantage.

Point F, however, is only one of many mutual tangencies. Connecting all the mutual tangencies traces out the *Contract Curve* (*CC*) shown in the diagram. Every point on the Contract Curve is a potential equilibrium. Were the traders to arrive at such a point, no additional voluntary (mutually advantageous) exchanges would be possible. The portion GH of the Contract Curve within the region of mutual advantage associated with point E shows all the potential equilibria achievable starting from E as endowment point.

What happens when trade is blocked? History provides some lessons.

EXAMPLE 14.1 JEFFERSON'S TRADE EMBARGO

From 1792 to 1815 Britain and France were almost continually at war. A British blockade often confiscated American cargos allegedly being shipped to France. Seamen on American vessels were also frequently taken by force (impressed) into the British Navy. To put a stop to impressment, and to pressure Britain into respecting American merchant shipping, President Thomas Jefferson proposed and the U.S. Congress voted a nearly complete embargo upon international commerce as of December 1807. The idea was that, to gain a renewal of American exports of cotton, wheat, tobacco, and so forth, the British would have to make important concesssions.

The economic effects of the embargo were studied by Douglas A. Irwin.[a] American exports fell from $150.4 million in 1807 to only $45.4 million in 1808 – a drop of about 70%. U.S. imports fell around 60%, from $144.7 million to $58.1 million. As would be expected, prices were also drastically affected. The domestic prices of American export commodities such as cotton, tobacco, flour, and rice all fell sharply. As for imported goods, a price index of 18 commodities normally entering the port of Boston rose from around 97 in January 1808 to 129 in January 1809. The author estimated that the embargo reduced the U.S. Gross National Product by around 8% during the period it was in effect.

So U.S. exporters and importers, and of course American ocean shipping as a business, were all hit hard. Meanwhile Britain, having comand of the seas, was able to access sources around the world for products previously imported from America and to ship and sell her own exports abroad. The embargo, having failed in its purpose after causing great damage to U.S. interests, was repealed by Congress in March 1809.

---

[a] Douglas A. Irwin, "The Welfare Cost of Autarky: Evidence from the Jeffersonian Trade Embargo, 1807–1809," mimeo (December 6, 2001).

Failing to learn the lesson of Jefferson's embargo, the southern Confederacy attempted a similar trade policy during the American Civil War.

EXAMPLE 14.2 ECONOMIC BLOCKADE AND THE AMERICAN CIVIL WAR[a]

Before the Civil War, the Northern and Southern states had engaged in mutually advantageous economic exchange. The Southern surplus of cotton was mainly sold to the North, with the proceeds used to buy Northern manufactured products. Less than 10% of the prewar (1860) total national value of manufactures had been produced in the South.[b]

The war-caused interruption of trade hit the Confederacy much harder than the Union. The Union blockade choked off Southern imports from the Northern states and also from Europe. For the North, cotton imports from India and Egypt and the West Indies replaced Southern fiber, though at higher cost.

Confederate trade policy was seriously misguided. The South's leaders failed to realize the vulnerability of their cotton-based economy to the interruption of trade. In 1861 and 1862 it was still possible to ship cotton abroad, the sea blockade having not yet become effective. The Confederate government discouraged this traffic. Believing that "Cotton is king," the Southern authorities withheld the large crops of those years in the hope that economic pressures would force the North to accept secession.

The Confederate government also banned overland smuggling through the lines, partly on moralistic grounds, partly again to withhold "King Cotton." This was illogical, since most of the cotton run by sea through the blockade to Cuba or Bermuda was transshipped to the North anyway. But more important, a strict ban on trade through the lines was, for the North, a logical complement to the sea blockade that was strangling the Southern economy. It was in the interest of the South to break the blockade by land and by sea.

Actually, much illegal trade did pass through the lines, despite attempts of officials on both sides to stop that traffic. Curiously, even today historians commonly take a moralistic attitude on this question. They fail to appreciate that the land blockade was a wise policy for the Union, but an unwise one for the Confederacy.

---

[a] Discussion based on J. Hirshleifer, *Economic Behaviour in Adversity* (Chicago, University of Chicago Press, 1987), Chapter 1.

[b] Albert D. Kirwan, ed., *The Confederacy* (New York: Meridian Books, 1959), p. 63.

The Edgeworth box can also be used to illustrate market equilibrium. Think now of Ida and John as representing many traders on each side of the market, all behaving as *price-takers* (having no monopoly or monopsony power).

In Figure 14.3 *KL* is a possible budget line for both Ida and John. (A single budget line suffices for the two of them, since they look at the line from different directions: Ida's budget line is read from her origin at the lower left corner of the box, and John's from the upper right corner.) Recall from Chapter 4 that the price ratio between any two goods corresponds to the absolute value of the budget-line slope. Accordingly, in Figure 14.3 the manufactures/wheat price ratio P_x/P_y is the absolute slope of the dashed line *KL*. At this price ratio Ida would want to consume the combination of wheat and manufactures shown by Q_i. In other words, *KL* is tangent to her best attainable indifference curve at point Q_i. John would similarly want to consume at Q_j, where *KL* is tangent to his best attainable indifference curve. But points Q_i and Q_j differ! This means that the quantity of manufactures that Ida wishes to buy differs from the quantity that John wants to sell. Nor do the wheat quantities match up. So the price ratio represented by the slope of *KL* cannot be an equilibrium.

Now consider the steeper budget line $K'L'$, representing a higher price of manufactures relative to wheat. Along $K'L'$, Ida wants to consume at her tangency point Q_i^*, while John wants to consume at his tangency point Q_j^*. These two points do coincide. The amount of wheat that Ida wants to sell at that price ratio exactly equals the amount John wants to buy. (And then, of course, the quantity of manufactures that John wants to sell equals the quantity that Ida wants to buy.) So the slope of $K'L'$ represents the equilibrium price ratio.

> **PROPOSITION:** In the Edgeworth box, the equilibrium allocation of the two commodities lies in the region of mutual advantage. At the equilibrium price ratio, the traders' indifference curves are tangent to one another and to the common budget line.

Expressed mathematically, at equilibrium the following equations must hold:

$$P_x x_i + P_y y_i = P_x \overline{x}_i + P_y \overline{y}_i \quad \text{and} \quad P_x x_j + P_y y_j = P_x \overline{x}_j + P_y \overline{y}_j \quad (14.1)$$

$$MRSC_i = P_x/P_y = MRSC_j \quad (14.2)$$

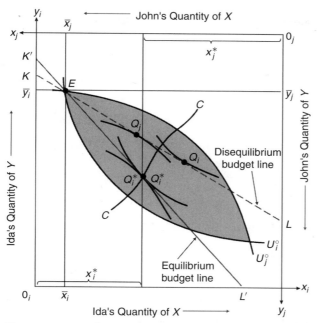

Figure 14.3. Budget Lines and Competitive Equilibrium

Any price ratio determines the slope of a budget line through the endowment position E. Ida's opportunity set lies below this line, and John's lies above it. The dashed budget line KL does not correspond to a competitive market equilibrium for these two traders, since along KL Ida's optimum Q_i lies at a different point from John's optimum Q_j. $K'L'$ does correspond to an equilibrium price ratio, because the optimum positions Q_i^* and Q_j^* coincide. The equilibrium must occur at a mutual tangency of the indifference curves.

Equations (14.1) say that Ida is on her budget line and that John is on his. In each case the market value of the chosen consumption basket (the left-hand side of the equation) equals the market value of the endowed basket (the right-hand side). Equations (14.2) indicate, as a second requirement of equilibrium, that for each person the absolute value of the slope of the indifference curve (the Marginal Rate of Substitution in Consumption *MRSC*) must equal the absolute value of the slope of the budget line (or, equivalently, the price ratio).

EXERCISE 14.1

Ida's Marginal Rate of Substitution in Consumption is $MRSC_i = y_i/x_i$. For John, $MRSC_j = y_j/x_j$. Ida's endowment is $\bar{x}_i = 10$, $\bar{y}_i = 100$, while John's endowment is $\bar{x}_j = 50$, $\bar{y}_j = 20$. Suppose wheat Y is the numeraire (so that $P_y \equiv 1$). Verify that the competitive equilibrium price for manufactures is $P_x^* = 2$.

ANSWER: Ida wants to consume at the point on her budget line where the slope (with the sign reversed) of her indifference curve ($MRSC_i$) equals the price ratio. For her, equations (14.1) and (14.2) become:

$$2x_i + y_i = 10P_x + 100(1) \quad \text{and} \quad y_i/x_i = 2$$

Setting $P_x = 2$ and solving, Ida's optimum is $x_i^* = 30$, $y_i^* = 60$.

For John the corresponding equations are:

$$2x_j + y_j = 50P_x + 20(1) \quad \text{and} \quad y_j/x_j = 2$$

Solving, John chooses an identical combination: $x_j^* = 30$, $y_j^* = 60$. So far so good, but it must still be verified that the total quantities demanded equal the total amounts available:

$$x_i + x_j = 60 = \overline{X} \equiv 10 + 50 \quad \text{and} \quad y_i + y_j = 120 \equiv \overline{Y} \equiv 100 + 20$$

Since the demands and supplies do match, $P_x^* = 2$ is indeed the equilibrium price.

14.2 SUPPLY AND DEMAND IN PURE EXCHANGE

The Edgeworth box illustrates the properties of an exchange equilibrium. To understand *how* equilibrium is reached, the analysis uses the familiar concepts of supply and demand.

The Price Expansion Path (*PEP*) in Panel (a) of Figure 14.4 resembles the Price Expansion Path of Chapter 4, except for one feature. In Chapter 4 the endowment point *E* was on the vertical (*Y*) axis. In other words, in Chapter 4 the individual initially had none of the other commodity (*X*). Here, in Figure 14.4, the endowment points are in the interior, meaning that each person starts out with positive amounts of both goods. This change has an important result. In Chapter 4 the person endowed only with good *Y* could never be a supplier of the other good *X*. But Ida's endowment point here lies close to but not quite at the vertical axis. (Mid-19th-century America produced lots of wheat, but also some manufactures.) So *usually* Ida will supply wheat and demand manufactures, but not necessarily *always*. At some sufficiently high price ratio P_x/P_y (some budget line so steep) she will want to stay with her endowment combination and neither buy nor sell anything at all. This is called her "autarky" price ratio.[1] And at price ratios higher than that (even steeper budget lines through E_i), she would sell wheat. That is, her optimum consumption basket would lie above and to the left of E_i. Similarly, Panel (b) shows that at most price ratios John will sell *X* and buy *Y*. But at a sufficiently low price ratio P_x/P_y his market behavior would reverse.

The data in the Price Expansion Path curves of Figure 14.4 can generate two different kinds of supply and demand curves. The first runs in terms of *full* quantities, the second in terms of *transaction* quantities.

1. At any price, a person's *full demand* (or *consumption demand*) is the amount of the commodity entering into his or her desired consumption basket.
2. A person's *transaction demand* (sometimes called *excess demand*) is the quantity he or she buys in the market as a function of price. It equals full demand less the endowed amount of the good.
3. A person's *full supply* of a good, in a world of pure exchange, is his or her endowed quantity.[2]

---

[1] "Autarky" means self-sufficiency. (Not to be confused with "autarchy," which means absolute rule by a monarch.)
[2] When production is allowed for in the following section, this definition of full supply will be revised.

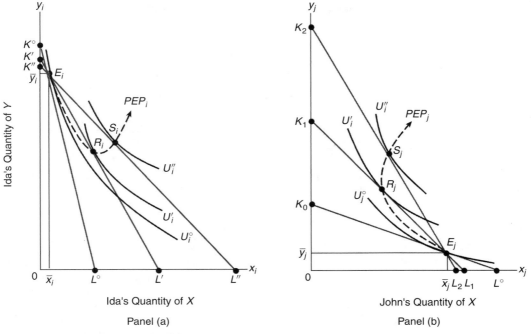

Ida's Quantity of X

Panel (a)

John's Quantity of X

Panel (b)

Figure 14.4. Price Expansion Paths

A change in the price ratio tilts the budget lines through the endowment positions E_i in Panel (a) and E_j in Panel (b). For price ratios leading to points on *PEP* to the right of E_i, Ida will be a net demander of X. At the autarky price ratio (budget line $K°L°$) Ida will stand pat and not trade; for still higher price ratios she will be a supplier of X (there is a range of PEP_i to the left of E_i, though not shown in the diagram). A corresponding analysis holds for John in Panel (b).

4. A person's *transaction supply* of X is the quantity offered for sale as price varies. It equals the endowed quantity less the amount retained for consumption.

Symbolically, for any commodity X and any individual i, suppose the endowed amount is $\bar{x}_i$ and the consumed amount is x_i. Then:

Full demand: x_i
Full supply: $\bar{x}_i$
Transaction demand: $x_i^t \equiv x_i - \bar{x}_i$
Transaction supply: $-x_i^t \equiv \bar{x}_i - x_i$

(Transaction supply is the negative of transaction demand.)

The "full" quantities are those demanded from or supplied *to the economy*. The "transaction" quantities are the amounts demanded from or supplied *to the market*. The difference is represented by the endowed amounts that individuals retain for their own consumption.

To appreciate the significance of the distinction between full quantities and transaction quantities, consider taxation. Some taxes are levied upon consumption or upon use of a good. Examples include annual auto license fees and property taxes. Here it is the *full* quantities that are taxed. In contrast, sales taxes are imposed only upon *transaction*

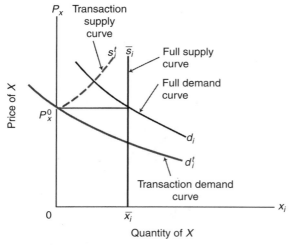

Figure 14.5. Individual Full and Transaction Supply and Demand Curves (Pure Exchange)

Ida's full demand curve d_i shows, at any price P_x, her desired consumption quantity. The full supply curve $\bar{s}_i$ represents her fixed endowment quantity. The transaction demand curve d_i^t shows, at any price P_x, the amount she demands from the market (horizontal difference between d_i and $\bar{s}_i$). In the range where transaction demand d_i^t is negative, it is usually more convenient to speak of a positive *transaction supply* curve, s_i^t. Transaction demand and transaction supply are exactly zero at the autarky price P_x^o.

quantities, what people buy or sell. A farmer who churns butter for his own family would escape a sales tax, but would remain subject to a consumption or use tax on butter.

When transaction taxes rise, it becomes more attractive to "do it yourself," that is, to self-supply one's wants rather than to deal in the market. A *tariff* is a transaction tax that applies to international trading. So tariffs encourage self-supply ("do it yourself") on the international level. Tariffs necessarily entail some loss of the mutual advantages of trade.

In Panel (a) of Figure 14.4, at any price ratio (absolute value of the slope of the budget line), Ida's full demand for manufactures is the x-coordinate of her consumption optimum along the budget line. The Price Expansion Path PEP_i traces out all such points. Her transaction demand x_i^t is this horizontal distance x_i less her endowed amount $\bar{x}_i$. Notice that though full demand x_i is never negative, her transaction demand x_i^t can be negative. (The price ratio P_x/P_y can be so steep that Ida sells manufactures.)

These patterns are reflected in the individual supply and demand curves shown in Figure 14.5. Here wheat Y is taken to be the numeraire ($P_y \equiv 1$), making the price ratio P_x/P_y equal to P_x. At each P_x the individual's *full demand* curve d_i shows the desired consumption quantity x_i. The *full supply* curve is the fixed endowed amount $\bar{x}_i$, while the *transaction demand* curve d_i^t shows the difference between the two. At Ida's autarky price P_x^o, her full demand equals her full supply – her transaction demand is zero. (For prices above the autarky price, the negative transaction demand curve d_i^t can also be shown as a positive transaction supply curve s_i^t – the dashed curve.)

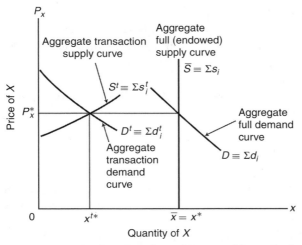

Figure 14.6. Market Supply and Demand (Pure Exchange)

The aggregate full supply curve $\overline{S}$ and full demand curve D are horizontal sums of the corresponding individual curves of the preceding diagram. The aggregate transaction supply and transaction demand curves S^t and D^t are similarly derived. The equilibrium price P_x^* is determined by the intersection of either pair of curves. In equilibrium the aggregate full quantity consumed is X^*; the aggregate transaction quantity is X^{t*}. (The difference is the aggregate quantity self-supplied by individuals for their own consumption.)

Corresponding definitions apply for the *aggregate* quantities, where in each case the symbol X corresponds to the sum of the individual amounts:

Full demand: $\qquad X$
Full supply: $\qquad \overline{X}$
Transaction demand: $\quad X^t \equiv X - \overline{X}$
Transaction supply: $\quad -X^t \equiv \overline{X} - X$

The individual supply-demand data are aggregated for the market as a whole in Figure 14.6. The vertical aggregate full supply curve labelled $\overline{S} \equiv \Sigma s_i$ represents the horizontal sum of the individual supply curves. Similar definitions apply for the aggregate full demand curve $D \equiv \Sigma d_i$, the aggregate transaction demand curve $D^t \equiv \Sigma d_i^t$, and the aggregate supply curve $S^t \equiv \Sigma s_i^t$.

Two additional points are worth noting. First, although the *individual* transaction demand and supply curves of Figure 14.5 intersected along the vertical axis, the *aggregate* transaction supply and demand curves will intersect in the interior – unless literally everyone in the market has exactly the same autarky price P_x^o. (Only in exceptional circumstances will the price that makes Ida want to consume her endowment basket of commodities be the same as the price that will make other individuals such as John, Kate, and Louis also want to consume at their endowments.) Second, the intersection of the *individual* full demand and full supply curves and, equivalently, the intersection of the corresponding transaction demand and supply curves, occurred at that person's autarky price P_x^o. But the intersection of the *aggregate* full demand and full supply curves (or equivalently, of the aggregate transaction demand and supply curves) occurs at the market equilibrium price P_x^*.

CONCLUSION

The point where the *aggregate full supply* curve intersects the *aggregate full demand* curve shows the economy-wide consumption of the good, which must equal the aggregate economywide supply. The point where the *aggregate transaction supply* curve intersects the *aggregate transaction demand* curve shows the amount of the good actually exchanged between buyers and sellers. The two pairs of curves intersect at the same equilibrium price.

EXERCISE 14.2

Use the data of Exercise 14.1 to find (a) the individual full supply and demand curves and the corresponding aggregate curves; (b) the corresponding transaction supply and demand curves. Verify that the market equilibrium price $P_x^* = 2$ is attained, calculating either in terms of full supply and demand or in terms of transaction supply and demand.

ANSWER: (a) From equations (14.1), Ida's budget equation can be written $P_x x_i + y_i = 10 P_x + 100$. Her Marginal Rate of Substitution in Consumption is y_i/x_i, so from (14.2) one can write $y_i/x_i = P_x$. Substituting in the budget equation and eliminating y_i generates her full demand for manufactures: $x_i = 5 + 50/P_x$. For John the conditions are $P_x x_j + y_j = 50 P_x + 20$ and $y_j/x_j = P_x$, leading to his full demand equation $x_j = 25 + 10/P_x$. Summing, the *aggregate* full demand equation is therefore $X \equiv x_i + x_j = 30 + 60/P_x$. The full supplies are $\bar{x}_i = 10$ and $\bar{x}_j = 50$, summing to $\bar{X} = 60$. Setting aggregate supply equal to aggregate demand, the solution is indeed $P_x^* = 2$. (b) In the neighborhood of equilibrium, Ida will sell and John will buy manufactures. Ida's transaction demand is $x_i - \bar{x}_i = -5 + 50/P_x$. Since she is the only buyer, this is also the aggregate transaction demand D^t. John's transaction supply is $\bar{x}_j - x_j = 10/P_x - 25$; since he is the only supplier, this is also the aggregate transaction supply S^t. Setting $D^t = S^t$, the solution once again is $P_x^* = 2$.

An Application: Market Experiments in Economics

Critics sometimes charge that economics cannot be a science because economics does not subject its theories to the test of experiment. That accusation has been invalid for at least 30 years.

Among other topics, economic experiments have examined the standard economic assumptions about individual behavior: rationality (as in the Example "Transitivity and Age" in Chapter 3) and self-interested preferences (as in the Example "Selfish Economics Students?" in Chapter 1). Experiments have also dealt with groups of individuals interacting through markets.

Imagine such an experiment conducted in the classroom.[3] Each subject would privately receive a message identifying him or her as a potential buyer or seller. If a

---

[3] Actually, the classroom is far from an ideal environment for a controlled scientific experiment. Students as experimental subjects may be influenced by personal friendships or enmities, or by desire to please or annoy the instructor. Also, it is difficult to provide financial incentives. While classroom experiments may be suggestive, more scientific weight attaches to laboratory experiments conducted under controlled conditions, as in the Example that follows.

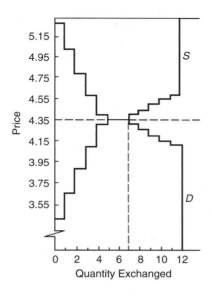

Figure 14.7. Equilibrium in a Market Experiment

Although the traders know only their individual willingness to pay (if a buyer) or cost (if a seller), the experimenter can aggregate this information into supply and demand curves so as to predict the result. The supply and demand curves have a "staircase" form here, because the commodity can be exchanged in whole units only. The equilibrium price is 4.35. If a small "commission" is paid for each executed transaction, the equilibrium quantity is 7.

buyer, the message might say:

> You are to be loaned 100 tokens, with which you can buy up to 3 units of a commodity at a price of 6 tokens each. The first unit you buy can be resold to the experimenter for 16 tokens, the second for 11 tokens, the third for 3 tokens. After you repay the 100 tokens loaned to you, the remainder will be your profit. At the end of the experiment this profit can be converted into dollars for you to take away.

So, for example, if the subject bought two units of the commodity for 6 tokens each, she could take home $(16 - 6) + (11 - 6) = 15$ dollars.

For a seller, the private information would similarly indicate the cost in tokens and the prices at which units could be sold to the experimenter. At the end of the experiment, the subject on the supply side of the market could take home the aggregate difference between sales revenue and cost.

Each subject sees only his or her own personal "willingness to pay" or "cost" information, so no participant can be aware of the theoretical equilibrium price. But, summing over all the data, the experimenter can construct market supply and demand curves so as to determine the outcome implied by economic theory. (One complication: since the commodity can be exchanged in whole units only, the supply and demand curves are not smooth but have a staircase form, as in Figure 14.7. The staircases might intersect not at a single point but rather over a unit step. To avoid ambiguity, a small additional bonus could be paid to the subjects for each completed transaction. This ensures that the right-hand edge of the step (the larger of the two quantities) will be the theoretical equilibrium amount traded.)

As for the details of the trading process, the subjects could seek trading partners by just milling about, or some more organized procedure might be used. The terms of completed transactions could be publicly announced (as on the ticker of the New York Stock Exchange) or possibly kept confidential between the parties. Market intermediaries such as brokers or dealers might or might not be involved in the experimental setup.

The crucial point is that, despite all these possible procedural variations, the experimental outcomes have almost always come close to the theoretical supply-demand equilibrium:

> Students were both surprised and amazed at the conclusion of the experiment when the entrusted student opened a sealed envelope containing the correctly predicted equilibrium price and quantity.[4]

EXAMPLE 14.3 A MARKET EXPERIMENT USING A COMPUTERIZED SUPPLY-DEMAND PROCESS

On the New York Stock Exchange (NYSE), traders can strike deals with one another around a trading post. Or they can leave bids or offers with a specialist at the post. The specialist, on the basis of his or her "book" of bids and offers, hand, publicly quotes standing prices to buy or to sell. All executed transactions are announced on the stock ticker.

Vernon L. Smith and Arlington W. Williams[a] conducted several experiments designed to examine different "rules of the game" for market exchanges. One of their experiments used a computerized version of the NYSE procedure. On the computer each subject could make a bid or offer, or could accept a deal offered by another trader. All finalized contracts appeared on everyone's computer screen. Subjects were also informed about the best not-yet-executed bids to buy or sell. To be displayed to the entire market, a trader's price proposal had to state better terms – for buyers a higher bid, for sellers a lower offer – than the best outstanding not-yet-executed quotation. This "bid-ask spread reduction rule" corresponds to one of the regulations of the New York Stock Exchange. Proposals not meeting this rule were placed in a queue. After execution of a contract, the best bid and the best offer in the queue were automatically moved up and became public information.

One of the experiments had just four buyers and four sellers. Recall that, on the usual interpretation, competitive supply-demand equilibrium requires many traders on each side. The question investigated was whether, even with only a few traders, the textbook prediction – that the competitive equilibrium outcome would be at the intersection of the supply curve and demand curve – would be achieved.

The table illustrates results with "inexperienced" subjects – that is, individuals who had not participated in any previous experiments. Each subject was given *private* information about his or her "resale price" (if a buyer) or "cost" if a seller, for each of three units of the commodity. There were eight trading periods. In each period an arbitrary constant was added to or subtracted from each subject's private information about resale value or cost. Otherwise, conditions remained the same throughout. Although the competitive equilibrium price accordingly varied, the numbers were so chosen that in every period the supply-demand intersection involved an exchange of exactly 7 units.

The table shows the highest-price and lowest-price contracts executed each period, measured in terms of divergence from the theoretical equilibrium price. After the first few periods, trading generally settled down in the near neighborhood

---

[4] David Gillette and Robert DelMas, "Psycho-economics: Studies in Decision Making," *Classroom Experiences*, v. 1 (Fall 1992), Department of Economics, Management, and Accounting, Marietta College, quoted in Vernon L. Smith, "Economics in the Laboratory," *Journal of Economic Perspectives*, v. 8 (Winter 1994).

of the supply-demand intersection – exactly 7 units, or in a few cases 6 units – were in fact traded.

Price and quantity in an experimental market

Period	High	Low	Quantity traded	Units exchanged at exact equilibrium price
1	+0.10	−0.20	6	1
2	+0.30	0	6	3
3	+0.15	−0.15	7	2
4	+0.05	−0.10	7	3
5	+0.05	−0.10	6	4
6	+0.05	0	7	5
7	+0.10	0	7	6
8	+0.05	0	7	5

Source: Estimated visually from Smith and Williams, Figure 2 (p. 318).

[a] Vernon L. Smith and Arlington W. Williams, "An Experimental Comparison of Alternative Rules for Competitive Market Exchange," in Richard Engelbrecht-Wiggans, Martin Shubik, and Robert M. Stark, eds., *Auctions, Bidding, and Contracting: Uses and Theory* (New York: New York University Press, 1993).

The trading processes devised for economic experiments have had real-world impact. U.S. Treasury procedures for marketing government bonds and for selling rights to the radio spectrum (to be described later in the chapter) have been influenced by the techniques and rules designed for and studied in economic experiments.

14.3 EXCHANGE AND PRODUCTION

In pure exchange, each person is assumed to possess an endowed basket of goods. But in reality goods must be *produced* from people's endowed resources.

An isolated Robinson Crusoe has *only* productive opportunities. In Figure 14.8 the shaded region shows Robinson's *productive opportunity set* – the possible baskets of goods X and Y that could be produced from his available resources. The upper-right boundary QQ of the production opportunity set is called the *Production Possibility Curve* (*PPC*). Symbolically:

$$Q(x, y) = 0 \quad \text{The Production Possibility Curve} \quad (14.3)$$

For example, $Q(x, y)$ could take the algebraic form $x^2 + y^2 - 16$ with x and y positive, which would be a quarter-circle in the diagram. Such a "concave" shape of the Production Possibility Curve would reflect diminishing returns. Suppose an individual or a nation tried to specialize in the production of good Y, that is, tried to move toward the vertical axis along QQ. As specialization is pushed further and further, each increment Δy will require a greater and greater sacrifice $-\Delta x$. Geometrically, the curve becomes flatter (the absolute slope $|\Delta y/\Delta x|$ decreases) moving to the left along the Production Possibility Curve.

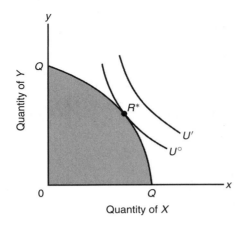

Figure 14.8. Productive and Consumptive Optimum: Robinson Crusoe

Crusoe's opportunity set (the shaded region) shows the combinations he can produce in isolation. It is bounded by a Production-Possibility Curve QQ subject to diminishing returns to specialization in producing either X or Y. Since an isolated Robinson Crusoe must produce what he consumes, the best attainable position is the tangency of QQ with indifference curve U° at point R^*.

Robinson's optimum balance between X and Y would be at R^* in the diagram, where the Production Possibility Curve QQ is tangent to his highest attainable indifference curve U°. Since Robinson cannot trade, he can consume only what he himself produces. So point R^* is both a *production optimum* and a *consumption optimum* for Robinson Crusoe.

At the R^* tangency, the slope of Robinson's indifference curve must equal the slope along his Production Possibility Curve:

$$MRSC = MRT \quad \text{Robinson Crusoe Optimum} \qquad (14.4)$$

$MRSC$ is the familiar Marginal Rate of Substitution in Consumption, the absolute slope along an indifference curve. The new symbol MRT stands for the *Marginal Rate of Transformation*, the absolute value of the slope $|\Delta y / \Delta x|$ along the Production Possibility Curve. It shows how much of good Y must be sacrificed to achieve a unit increase in X.

CONCLUSION

An isolated individual, who can produce but cannot trade, has a combined production/consumption optimum at the point along the boundary of the production opportunity set where his or her Marginal Rate of Substitution in Consumption equals the Marginal Rate of Transformation.

Only rarely will an individual be in the position of a Robinson Crusoe. But nations as a whole have sometimes cut themselves off from external trade (as in Example 14.1 above). As another instance, Japan closed itself to international commerce for over two centuries before Commodore Matthew C. Perry's visit in 1854.

EXAMPLE 14.4 ANIMAL ROBINSON CRUSOES

Trade is a human invention. Nonhuman animals also make economic decisions, but they do so under Robinson Crusoe conditions.

Let X and Y be two types of prey. Owing to diminishing returns, the predator's productive opportunity set typically is shaped like the shaded region in Figure 14.8. The more the predator concentrates on consuming prey species X, the scarcer and more difficult it becomes to capture X rather than Y (the Marginal Rate of Transformation becomes steeper towards the right). The predator also has preferences as represented by the indifference curves in the diagram. Each such curve represents a set of equally acceptable diets. The convexity of the indifference curves reflects

**Figure 14.9. Production Optimum
and Consumption Optimum**

If a market exists, the individual can exchange X for Y at the market price ratio P_x/P_y, as well as engage in production. The production optimum is at the tangency Q^*, on the highest attainable budget line MM. Along this budget line, the consumption optimum C^* is on indifference curve U' which represents a higer level of utility than the autarky optimum R^* on indifference curve $U°$.

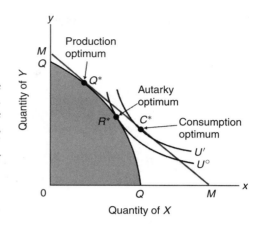

the fact that diversity in consumption helps provide the varied metabolic inputs required by living organisms. The optimal position for the animal is at the tangency point R^*, which will ordinarily represent an interior (mixed-diet) solution.[a]

Now consider what happens in periods of food shortage. The opportunity set of Figure 14.8 would shrink toward the origin. As a reasonable assumption about preferences, suppose that at low levels of nutrition only calorie intake counts. Then all prey sources would become close substitutes, valued simply in proportion to calorie content. So in accordance with the discussion in Chapter 4 (see Figure 4.7), at low levels of consumption the indifference curves would be nearly straight lines. Then, if one species has a higher caloric payoff than another, the predator would concentrate heavily upon that single species. In contrast, under conditions of abundance different prey species such as X and Y are no longer just interchangeable sources of calories. Instead, they satisfy a variety of nutritional needs. So at higher levels of abundance the indifference curves will have more normal curvature and predators will tend to choose a more balanced diet. They will be selected to hunt a number of species, rather than only one or a very few.

This analysis has taken only "demand side" effects into account. But there are "supply side" considerations as well. For example, it may be that the food shortage is due to reduced availability of only one of the two prey species. This shortfall would affect the shape of the predator's Produciton Possibility Curve of Figure 14.8 rather than the indifference curves. If a previously plentiful prey species has become more scarce, then under conditions of shortage a wider rather than a narrower range of prey will be sought.

[a] See Martin L. Cody, "Optimization in Ecology," *Science*, v. 183 (March 22, 1974).

[b] Such supply-side considerations are analyzed in Robert H. MacArthur and Eric R. Pianka, "On Optimal Use of a Patchy Environment," *The American Naturalist*, v. 100 (1966).

Now consider the more general and typical situation, a world of *both* production and exchange. (Imagine that Robinson Crusoe's island has been discovered, so he can now trade with the rest of the world.) In Figure 14.9 the Production Possibility Curve *PPC* remains as before. But now there are also opportunities to buy and sell, as indicated by the budget line *MM* with slope $\Delta y/\Delta x = -P_x/P_y$. (Budget lines, all with this slope and therefore parallel to one another, could be drawn through each and every point on the Production Possibility curve. But as is evident from the geometry, *MM* is the highest and best attainable budget line.)

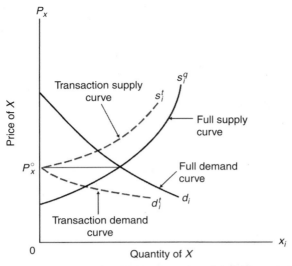

Figure 14.10. Individual Demand and Supply with Production

As P_x rises, Ida produces more X, so full supply curve s_i^q has positive slope. Her full demand curve d_i normally has negative slope. Transaction supply and demand for X are exactly zero at her autarky price P_x^o, the price at which the full demand curve and the full supply curve intersect. Above this price full supply exceeds full demand, so there will be positive transaction supply s_i^t – increasing as P_x rises. Below this price full demand exceeds full supply, so there will be positive transaction demand d_i^t – increasing as P_x falls.

The opportunity to trade allows a person *to separate production from consumption*. If Ida has the productive and trading opportunities shown in Figure 14.9, she does best by producing the basket Q^* and consuming the basket C^*. Think of this as a two-step procedure. First, Ida chooses a production optimum Q^* where her Production Possibility Curve QQ is tangent to the highest attainable budget line MM. (Note that, in comparison with the Robinson Crusoe solution R^*, Ida "specializes" in the production of good Y – wheat.) Second, by trading some of her extra wheat for good X, manufactures, she moves down and to the right along MM. Specifically, she will move to her consumption optimum C^*, where MM is tangent to her highest attainable indifference curve U'. As shown in the diagram, U' represents a higher preference level than the U^o associated with her no-trade solution R^*.

Ida's budget-line equation can be written:

$$P_x x_i + P_y y_i = P_x x_i^q + P_y y_i^q \tag{14.5}$$

This resembles equations (14.1), the budget equation in pure exchange. On the right-hand side, however, the *produced* quantities x_i^q, y_i^q appear in place of the *endowed* quantities $\bar{x}_i$, $\bar{y}_i$. (In pure exchange Ida started from her endowed combination E, but now the base-point for trading is her production optimum Q^*.)

Corresponding to equations (14.2), which applied for pure exchange, and to equation (14.4), which applied for Robinson Crusoe, in a world of both production and exchange there is a double slope-equality condition:

$$MRT = \frac{P_x}{P_y} \qquad \text{Tangency Condition – Production Optimum} \tag{14.6a}$$

$$MRSC = \frac{P_x}{P_y} \qquad \text{Tangency Condition – Consumption Optimum} \tag{14.6b}$$

The first condition represents the tangency at Q^*; the second condition represents the tangency at C^*.

These two equations together imply equation (14.4), $MRSC = MRT$, an equality that also held for Robinson Crusoe. So at their respective optimum positions, both for Robinson (a nontrader) and for Ida (a trader) the slope of the Production Possibility Curve equals the slope of an indifference curve. But for Robinson these equalities hold *at the same point* R^*. For Ida, in contrast, the Marginal Rate of Transformation *at her production optimum* Q^* equals the Marginal Rate of Substitution in Consumption *at her consumption optimum* C^*.

EXERCISE 14.3

Let x be the amount of manufactures and y the amount of wheat that Robinson Crusoe can produce. His Production Possibility curve is described by the equation $x^2/2 + y = 150$. By tabulating $\Delta y/\Delta x$ along this Production Possibility Curve (or by using calculus) it can be shown that the absolute slope along the Production Possibility Curve is $|\Delta y/\Delta x| \equiv MRT = x$. Suppose the slope of his indifference curve is $-MRSC = -y/x$. (a) Find Robinson's combined production-consumption optimum R^*. (b) Ida has exactly the same productive opportunities and preferences. She can, however, also trade in a market where, with wheat as numeraire (so that $P_y \equiv 1$), the price of manufactures is $P_x = 5$. Determine Ida's production optimum Q^* and consumption optimum C^*. (c) Verify that Robinson would like to change places with Ida.

ANSWER: (a) Setting $MRT = MRSC$ leads to $x = y/x$, so that $y = x^2$. Substituting in the equation for the Production Possibility Curve, Robinson's R^* solution is $x = 10$, $y = 100$. (b) Ida finds her production optimum Q^* by setting $|\Delta y/\Delta x| \equiv MRT = P_x/P_y = 5/1 = 5$. Solving, Q^* can be expressed in compact notation as $(x^q, y^q) = (5, 137.5)$. To find her consumption optimum, use the budget equation (14.5): $5x + y = (5)(5) + 137.5$. Also needed is the slope-equality equation (14.6b), which here becomes $y/x = 5$. Solving these two equations simultaneously, Ida's C^* solution is $(x^*, y^*) = (16.25, 81.25)$. (c) Ida prefers her C^* to her no-trade solution R^*. (She could always obtain the R^* combination by not trading, yet chooses to trade instead.) Since Robinson has the same preferences and productive opportunities, he would prefer Ida's C^* over his own R^*.

Figure 14.10 translates the information pictured in Figure 14.9 into individual supply and demand curves. Once again it will be useful to distinguish *full supply and demand* from *transaction supply and demand*:

Full demand: x_i
Full supply: x_i^q
Transaction demand: $x_i^t \equiv x_i - x_i^q$
Transaction supply: $-x_i^t \equiv x_i^q - x_i$

(As compared with the definitions of these variables in Section 14.2, the only difference here is that the *produced* magnitude x_i^q replaces the *endowed* magnitude $\bar{x}_i$.)

Figure 14.10 resembles Figure 14.5, with one important difference. In pure exchange Ida's full supply of manufactures was her fixed endowed quantity $\bar{x}_i$ – the vertical line $\bar{s}_i$ in Figure 14.5. But in a world of production and exchange, a person's full supply (that is,

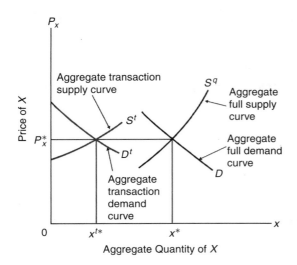

Figure 14.11. Market Supply and Demand, with Production

The aggregate full supply curve S^q and full demand curve D are horizontal sums of the corresponding individual curves of the preceding diagram. The aggregate transaction supply and transaction demand curves S^t and D^t are similarly derived. The equilibrium price P_x^* is determined by the intersection of either pair of curves. In equilibrium the aggregate full quantity produced and consumed is X^*; the aggregate transaction quantity is X^{t*}. (The difference is the aggregate quantity self-supplied by individuals for their own consumption.)

the amount produced) will vary with price. Taking wheat as numeraire (so that $P_y \equiv 1$), as price P_x rises the market line MM in Figure 14.9 would become steeper. The tangency point Q^* therefore shifts down and to the right along the Production Possibility Curve, and so the x-coordinate of Q^* increases. That is, as the price of manufactures rises relative to the price of wheat, Ida produces more manufactures (X) and less wheat (Y). So in Figure 14.10 her full supply curve s_i^q shows x^q as a rising function of P_x. Similarly, her full demand curve d_i represents the x-coordinate of her consumption optimum C^*.

What about *transaction* demand and supply? As in the preceding section, Ida's transaction demand x_i^t is her net demand from the market (the difference between full demand and full supply). And the transaction supply $-x_i^t$ is her net supply to the market (the difference between full supply and full demand). At Ida's *autarky price* P_x^o the net amounts demanded and supplied are zero: her Q^* and C^* solutions coincide. [*Note*: Robinson Crusoe was *necessarily* in an autarky situation. But for a person with trading opportunities, autarky will be preferred only at some single specific price ratio.]

Last, for the market as a whole, in Figure 14.11 the curves shown are the horizontal sums of the corresponding curves in the preceding diagram. The aggregate supply curve now has positive slope: more of X is produced as its price rises. But otherwise the picture is essentially the same as Figure 14.6 that dealt with pure exchange.

The analysis of pure exchange in Section 14.2 illustrated the first advantage of trade: existing stocks of commodities are redistributed to better match people's desires. The analysis of production and exchange here allows us to see the second advantage: *specialization in production* enlarges the total availabilities of goods.

In Figure 14.12 the two panels show Production Possibility Curves QQ for Ida as a typical American and for John as a typical Briton. (Recall that America is assumed relatively superior in producing wheat, and Britain in producing manufactures.) In the absence of trade, Ida and John can only achieve their respective "Robinson Crusoe" solutions R_i^* and R_j^*. Since they desire to consume both commodities, in isolation each would have to produce some of a good that the other could produce more efficiently. The

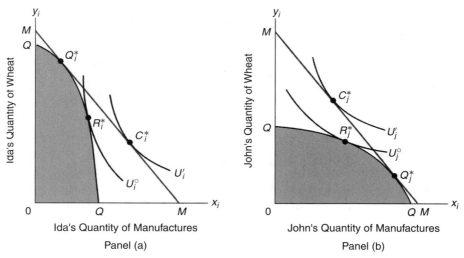

Figure 14.12. Productive Specialization

In the absence of exchange, Ida (a typical American) and John (a typical Briton) would produce and consume at R_i^* and R_j^*, respectively. Trade permits each to specialize in producing the commodity favored by his or her productive opportunities, trading off the excess so as to still achieve a diversified pattern of consumption.

opening of trade makes budget lines MM with slope $-P_x/P_y$ available to both parties. Ida's situation in Panel (a) is essentially the same as in Figure 14.9. Her production optimum is Q_i^*, where she specializes in producing wheat. But this specialization does not reduce diversity in consumption: she obtains manufactures by selling her excess wheat, enjoying the consumption optimum C_i^*. Correspondingly, John specializes in producing manufactures. The final positions, C_i^* for Ida and C_j^* for John, are superior to their no-trade optimum positions R_i^* and R_j^*.

These two great advantages of trade – improved (mutually preferred) distributions of consumption goods, and specialization in production that makes larger totals available – have led economists generally to favor free trade both within and among nations.

EXAMPLE 14.5 REGIONAL SPECIALIZATION IN THE UNITED STATES

The two main explanations for geographical specialization of production are *comparative advantage* and *increasing returns*.

Comparative advantage reflects different resource endowments in different regions and countries: bananas are more easily produced in Panama, and furs in Siberia. The increasing-returns explanation for regional specialization is illustrated by the fact that most musical wind instruments produced in America come from one small city: Elkhart, Indiana. For this line of production Elkhart has no evident resource superiority over other small Indiana cities like Kokomo or Muncie, not to mention similar cities in Ohio and Illinois. For more or less accidental reasons, one or a few instrument firms may have initially located in Elkhart. Others followed to take advantage of an existing pool of skilled employees and supporting services. So there may be advantages of locational concentration, even when it hardly matters just where the concentration occurs.

Technological advances have reduced transport costs for both products and resources over time. Reduced costs of *transporting products* tend to increase regional specialization. Production should become increasingly concentrated at the best productive locations, regardless of whether it is comparative advantage or increasing returns that makes those locations best. In contrast, reduced costs of *transporting resources* – increasing mobility of labor and capital goods – tends to decrease regional specialization. Earlier in American history, California concentrated on agriculture and New England on manufacturing. But over time human labor and other mobile resources were able to move toward California and away from New England, tending to make both regions less specialized than before.

Sukkoo Kim[a] analyzed the changing extent of geographical specialization for U.S. Census regions, using data back to 1860. The table shows regional localization indices averaged over 20 manufacturing industries, for selected years from 1860 to 1987. As can be seen, the index rose at first, but fell throughout the 20th century. U.S. manufacturing industry today is considerably less geographically specialized than in 1860. Since then, it appears, improved movement of resources (tending to reduce regional specialization) has more than offset the improved movement of products that favors regional specialization.

Localization of U.S. manufacturing industry, 1860–1987

Year	Localization index
1860	0.273
1914	0.311
1947	0.259
1987	0.197

Source: Extracted from Table III in Kim (p. 896).

[a] Sukkoo Kim, "Expansion of Markets and the Geographic Distribution of Economic Activities: The Trends in U.S. Regional Manufacturing Structure, 1860–1987," *Quarterly Journal of Economics*, v. 110 (November 1995).

14.4 IMPERFECT MARKETS: COSTS OF EXCHANGE

How Perfect Are Markets?

In a perfect market, all trading takes place at a single price known to all participants. In addition, there are no charges or fees for buying or selling. But markets can never be quite perfect.

1. *Imperfect communication*: In actual markets, some demanders may be unaware of the prices asked by some potential suppliers, and some suppliers may not know the prices that demanders are willing to offer.
2. *Nonunique prices*: An ideal perfect market immediately reaches the single market-clearing price. But actual trading takes place over time. In a city market, customers or suppliers arriving early may receive prices differing from those realized

later in the day. (One effect of *speculation* is to reduce such variations from equilibrium. When speculators have beliefs that are approximately correct, buying when they believe the price is accidentally too low, and selling when it is too high, they prevent prices from moving too far from their market-clearing values.)

3. *Costly transactions*: In perfect markets, it costs nothing to engage in trade. But imperfect communication, for example, can force buyers and sellers to deal through a broker – a middleman. Middleman services are useful, but they must be paid for. In addition, transaction taxes may also burden exchange.

How large are the costs of exchange? In 2001 about 13% of U.S. employment fell into the occupational category Wholesale and Retail Trade. And workers classified under Transportation and Communication, Finance, Insurance, and Real Estate may also have been providing middleman services. (By way of comparison, about 11% were employed in manufacturing and about 2% in agriculture.)

But in estimating the actual cost of the exchange process to the economy, it is essential to distinguish between (1) *market trading* and (2) the *physical transfer* of commodities. Any economy that integrates the activities of many individuals – whether an economy of saints, of ants, or of utility-maximizers under free markets – will still require physical transfers of goods from one person to another. Activities and costs bound up with physical transfers of goods are not necessarily due to market exchange.

Imagine an extreme command economy, where the central authority makes all economic decisions. Aiming at efficient specialization in production, the dictator might order farmers to grow crops and turn them over to railroads. The railroads would be ordered to ship the produced commodities to cities. Factories would be ordered to process them into consumable products and turn them over to retail outlets, and so forth.

Along this chain, activities such as handling, shipping, storing, and record-keeping will all inevitably absorb resources. The resources devoted to these activities are not exchange costs but rather *production costs*. "Adding" transportation to a good, to bring it closer to a consumer, is in principle the same as "adding" baking services to dough to make it into bread. So transportation workers are not middlemen in the sense used here. Similarly, many of the persons employed in wholesale and retail establishments work at warehousing or record-keeping, processes that would take place even in a command economy. So the costs due specifically to the process of *exchange* are smaller than might have first been thought.

The true costs of exchange are those that stem from the fact that markets involve voluntary transactions. Offers must be communicated from one individual to another. Contracts must be negotiated, and their execution verified. Buyers and sellers must both guard against fraud or other nonperformance.[5] All the expenses of an institution such as the New York Stock Exchange, for example, fall under one or more of these headings. (Without private ownership there would be no corporate shares and so no need for a stock exchange.)

---

[5] A command economy would also suffer from severe communication and enforcement problems. "Costs of command" are likely to far exceed the costs of market exchange.

EXAMPLE 14.6 COSTS OF TRADING – NYSE VERSUS NASDAQ

Organized marketplaces such as the New York Stock Exchange (NYSE) and the National Association of Securities Dealers Automated Quotations (NASDAQ) approach the ideal of a perfect market. The institution guarantees the quality of the merchandise and the payment arrangements. In dealing on the NYSE or NASDAQ the buyer need not be concerned whether the stock certificates acquired are counterfeit, and the seller need not fear that the buyer is paying with a bad check.

On the New York Stock Exchange, as described in Example 14.3 above, a specialist in each security maintains a continuous market in that stock. The specialist can, but need not, hold an inventory of the stock. Various rules prohibit the specialist from favoring his or her own orders over those of the customers.

The newer electronic trading system known as NASDAQ operates differently. It has no central trading location. Trading is executed by computer. It has no specialists; instead a group of around 500 firms act as dealers that maintain inventories of particular listed stocks. At any moment of time competing dealers quote their own bids to buy or offers to sell. So on NASDAQ traders buy from or sell to a dealer, whereas on the NYSE traders mostly buy from one another – the specialist serving as intermediary. The NASDAQ dealer is more like a shopkeeper, the NYSE specialist more like a broker. (These intermediaries are distinct from the customers' own brokers, who merely transmit orders to the NYSE or NASDAQ or other exchanges.)

A study by Roger D. Huang and Hans R. Stoll compared execution costs for comparable stocks in 1991 at the NYSE and NASDAQ.[a] Execution costs were measured as the bid-ask spread, that is, the average gap between the price that a buyer paid and a seller accepted. The study was limited to 175 matched pairs of stocks, one on each of the exchanges. As shown in the table, the effective average spreads on the NYSE were much lower than on NASDAQ, suggesting that the NYSE trading procedures were more efficient.

One possible partial explanation is that NASDAQ generally lists stocks of lesser-known companies, for which the market will be thinner. In thin markets buying will usually require paying a bigger premium, and selling will require accepting a greater discount. Although the authors matched what they regarded as "comparable" stocks on the two exchange, imperfect matching may explain some of the observed cost differential.

The authors' preferred explanation was that the market procedures of NASDAQ are inherently less competitive. The NYSE specialist, though appearing to have monopoly power, is subject to competition from floor traders who can buy and sell amongst themselves. In contrast, although no dealer on NASDAQ has a guaranteed monopoly, the dealers are spread over many securities. So only a few of them may be competing to execute orders for any single stock.

The data reported by the authors refer only to *trading costs*, exclusive of the commissions that retail customers might have paid to their own brokers. This makes a difference, because NYSE specialists take a commission on orders processed through them. NASDAQ trades, being "net," involve no commissions – apart from whatever the retail customer may pay his broker. The authors regard 5 cents each way (or 10 cents for the full spread) as a reasonable estimate of the extent that commissions increase the bid-ask spread on the NYSE. Even with this correction, a substantial gap in favor of the NYSE remains.

Bid-ask spreads – NYSE versus NASDAQ

Trade size	Effective spread	
	NYSE	NASDAQ
Small	15.4	39.8
Medium	17.0	31.2
Large	17.0	27.0

Source: Adapted from Huang and Stoll, Table 2.

[a] Roger D. Huang and Hans R. Stoll, "Dealer versus Auction Markets: A Paired Comparison of Execution Costs on NASDAQ and the NYSE," *Journal of Financial Economics*, v. 41 (1996).

In the discussion that follows, markets will generally be assumed perfect *except* for transaction costs. One can imagine that middlemen have totally eliminated other types of market imperfections (such as limited communication or "incorrect trades" at nonequilibrium prices). But of course these efficient middlemen must be paid. Costs of exchange have important consequences for the scope of trading, which in turn reflects the degree of specialization in production and consumption.

Costs of exchange usually increase with (1) the volume of goods traded and (2) the frequency of trades. If the charge per unit of the good traded is a constant, transaction costs would be *proportional to volume*. Alternatively, if each purchase regardless of size requires payment of a fixed fee, that would be a *lump-sum transaction charge*. Actual charges, such as the commission schedules published by stock brokers, may involve both proportional and lump-sum elements.

Proportional Transaction Costs

If you buy a house today and resell it tomorrow, you are unlikely to get back what you paid. The same holds true for cars, furniture, CDs, or almost any consumer product. This gap between buying price and selling price represents proportional transaction costs, such as a real-estate broker's fee. (But recall that brokers and other middlemen help overcome imperfections of markets. Reselling your house without employing a broker is always possible, but most people find brokers' services worth the money.)

Proportional transaction charges resemble the per-unit taxes on exchange discussed in Chapter 2. If a tax of $\$G$ per unit is levied upon purchases or sales of commodity X, as illustrated in Figure 14.13, then the gross price P_x^+ paid by buyers would necessarily be $\$G$ greater than the net price P_x^- received by sellers. The shaded area in the diagram represents the government's aggregate tax receipts $G \times X'$, where X' is the quantity exchanged.

To apply this picture to proportional transaction costs, think of the price gap $G \equiv P_x^+ - P_x^-$ as the *per-unit trading fee* charged by middlemen. A jobber may buy raincoats from a Dallas retailer for $10 each, in the knowledge that he can resell them in Mexico for $15 net of shipping cost – in effect, receiving a trading fee of $5 per unit.[6] The shaded area

[6] Do not infer that the jobber is necessarily underhanded or unethical. He may have incurred considerable costs in learning of the existence of customers in Mexico. Also, jobbing is normally a competitive industry that anyone can enter. So, in accordance with the Zero-Profit Theorem of Chapter 7, the jobber likely earns only a normal return on his time and trouble.

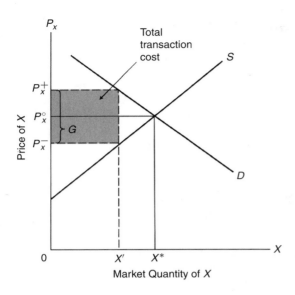

Figure 14.13. Proportional Transaction Costs

Here there is a proportional transaction charge, in the amount of G per unit of commodity X exchanged. In equilibrium, there must be a price gap of this amount between the price paid by demanders (P_x^+) and the price received by suppliers (P_x^-). The quantity exchanged is X', and the shaded area represents the aggregate transaction costs.

in the diagram now represents the aggregate amount received by middlemen for their services. Note that a proportional transaction charge, like a per-unit tax, means that the quantity exchanged X' is necessarily smaller than the "ideal" equilibrium amount X^*. (But if the goods could not be sold without the middleman's help, this "ideal" amount is only hypothetical.)

Figure 14.14 shows how proportional transaction costs could affect Ida, a typical trader with endowment E in a world of pure exchange. Were markets perfect, Ida could trade in either direction along her budget line KL with slope $-P_x/P_y$ (or $-P_x$, taking Y as the numeraire so that $P_y \equiv 1$). Allowing for a proportional trading charge, however, her trading opportunities are represented by the broken dashed line $K'EL'$. Starting from E, suppose Ida would like to buy more X (she wants to move down and to the right.). Since the gross price P_x^+ she now faces is higher than the hypothetical

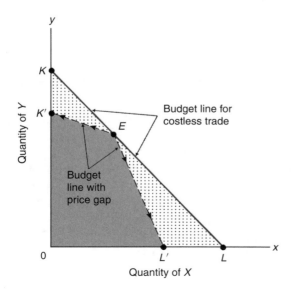

Figure 14.14. Individual Trading Opportunities: Proportional Transaction Costs

The budget line for costless exchange is KL. With a proportional transaction charge, starting from endowment E a buyer of X has to pay the high (gross) price reflected by the slope of EL'; similarly, a seller receives only the low (net) price reflected by the slope of EK'. The consumer's optimum might occur along EL', along EK', or else at the autarky position E.

perfect-markets price P_x, the dashed line-segment EL' is steeper than EL. In the reverse case, if Ida wanted to sell some of her endowed X (that is, to move up and to the left from E) she would receive only the lower net price P_x^- reflected in the flat slope of the line-segment EK'. So transaction costs shrink the opportunity set from the theoretical triangle OKL to the smaller quadrilateral $OK'EL'$.

Transaction costs could be so steep that an individual or nation would forego trade entirely and choose autarky.

EXERCISE 14.4

Abner has endowment $E = (\bar{x}, \bar{y}) = (60, 60)$. His Marginal Rate of Substitution in Consumption is $MRSC = 3y/x$. The market price is $P_x = 2.5$. (a) Verify that, were markets perfect, his consumption optimum would be $C^* = (x^*, y^*) = (63, 52.5)$. (He buys 3 units of X, paying 7.5 units of Y.) (b) Now suppose that a trading charge is imposed, so that Abner has to pay $P_x^+ = 3.5$ to buy a unit of X, but receives only $P_x^- = 1.5$ if he sells. Thus, $G \equiv (P_x^+ - P_x^-) = 2$. Does his consumption optimum change, and if so how?

ANSWER: (a) Abner's budget equation and slope-equality condition are needed to specify the tangency. His budget equation is $P_x x + P_y y = P_x \bar{x} + P_y \bar{y}$, or numerically here $2.5x + y = 2.5(60) + 60 = 210$. The slope-equality condition $MRSC = P_x/P_y$ is numerically $3y/x = 2.5$. Solving these simultaneously, the solution is indeed $(x^*, y^*) = (63, 52.5)$. (b) Since at the perfect-markets price $P_x = 2.5$ Abner bought rather than sold X, at the even lower *net price* $P_x^- = 1.5$ he will not now want to sell X. So the only question is whether he will buy X or stick with his endowment E. Let us examine the first possibility. Following the method of Part (a) but using the gross price $P_x^+ = 3.5$, it can be verified that the indicated solution for Abner would be $(x^*, y^*) = (57.9, 67.5)$ approximately. But $57.9 < 60$, so the assumption that he would buy X is contradicted. The conclusion, therefore, is that Abner will prefer to remain at his endowment position $(60,60)$.

On the basis of Figure 14.14, individual and market demand and supply curves allowing for proportional trading costs are illustrated in Figure 14.15. In Panel (a), P_x^o is the perfect-markets autarky price for Ida: the price at which she would stay with her endowment E even in the absence of transaction charges. From the preceding discussion, if the *gross* price P_x^+ is less than P_x^o she will still want to buy X – despite the transaction charge. In this price range, the demand curve $d(P_x^+)$ applies. By similar reasoning, if the *net* price P_x^- were higher than P_x^o, she would want to sell X. This information is summarized as her supply curve $s(P_x^-)$.

So Ida's market behavior as buyer or seller is depicted by the *inner pair* of curves in Panel (a). The outer curves are the supply curve in terms of the gross price $s(P_x^+)$ and the demand curve in terms of the net price $d(P_x^-)$. Each of these differs from its "partner" curve by the constant vertical distance G – the price gap. Last, since Ida will not want to buy if $P_x^+ > P_x^o$ and will not want to sell if $P_x^- < P_x^o$, she will stay with her endowment position only when *both* of these conditions hold. In the diagram, this means that the *gross price* P_x^+ must lie between M and P_x^o on the vertical axis, or equivalently that the *net price* P_x^- must lie between P_x^o and N.

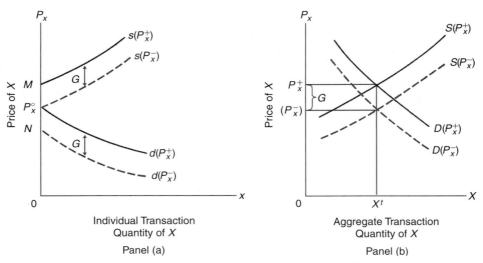

Figure 14.15. Supply and Demand: Proportional Transaction Costs

In Panel (a) the inner pair of curves show an individual's transaction supply as a function of the *net* selling price P_x^- (where this exceeds the autarky price P_x^o), and transaction demand as a function of the *gross* buying price P_x^+ (where this is less than the autarky price). The upper solid curve shows supply as related to the gross price; the lower dashed curve shows demand as related to the net price. Panel (b) pictures the marketwide aggregates of these four curves. The equilibrium transaction quantity X^t is found at the intersection of the two solid curves (which are defined in terms of the gross prices) or else the intersection of the two dashed curves (which are defined in terms of the net prices); the equilibrium gross and net prices are determined accordingly.

Summing over all the traders in the market, the corresponding pairs of aggregate market supply and demand curves are shown in Panel (b). It now becomes clear why it was convenient to draw all four curves in Panel (a). The intersection of $S(P_x^+)$ and $D(P_x^+)$, the two solid curves, determines the equilibrium *gross* (buying) price P_x^+. The intersection of the two dashed curves $S(P_x^-)$ and $D(P_x^-)$ intersect determines the *net* (selling) price P_x^-. The two intersections occur *at the same market quantity X^t*, but the gross and net equilibrium prices differ by the fixed gap G– the proportional transaction cost.

What would happen if middleman charges were to increase? In Panel (a) the *inner* pair of curves would not change, since they directly represent individual behavior in terms of the relevant (gross or net) prices. But as G rises the *outer* pair of curves would move further outward. Since the equilibrium solution determined in Panel (b) necessarily involves an intersection with one or the other of the outer curves, higher transaction costs would reduce the volume of transactions.

CONCLUSION

Proportional transaction costs create a gap between the buying price and the selling price. The larger the gap, the more likely individuals are to choose autarky solutions, and the smaller will be the aggregate volume of market trading.

For sufficiently large G, the curves may fail to intersect in the positive quadrant of the diagram. This means that the market is nonviable. Some markets do disappear as a country gets wealthier, among them markets for used containers and for old clothes.

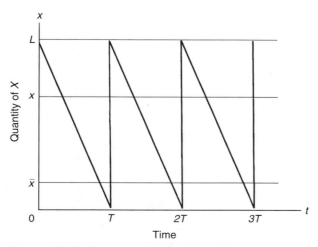

Figure 14.16. Inventory History for a Consumer

The individual has a self-supplied continuous endowment flow $\bar{x}$ and a continuous consumption flow x. The difference is made up by discrete market purchases at time intervals T. At each multiple of T, inventory falls to zero and a new stock quantity L is purchased.

It has become cheaper to discard used goods than to pay for the required middleman services.

Lump-Sum Transaction Costs

Proportional transaction costs can explain certain facts about the world, such as the gap between buying and selling prices. But another important fact remains to be explained: why do buyers or sellers ever hold *inventories*? Why keep milk in the refrigerator rather than go out and buy it whenever you are thirsty? The evident explanation is that it is infeasible to trade at each and every minute of the clock. A consumer has to hold inventories if his or her consumption moments imperfectly synchronize with convenient times for trips to the market. And a storekeeper must hold inventories while awaiting the irregular visits of customers.

When costs of exchange take the form of a fixed lump-sum fee per transaction, consumers have an incentive to trade less frequently (so as to make fewer trips to the market). On the other hand, the less frequent the trades, the larger are the inventories buyers and sellers must hold. The costs of holding inventories must therefore be balanced against the costs of frequent trading.

In a world of pure exchange, suppose the transaction cost is a fixed amount F for each trade. Think of it as an entry fee. For simplicity, suppose John consumes commodity X continuously at a level flow x over time. He also has a corresponding level endowment flow $\bar{x}$ over time. If $x > \bar{x}$ his inventories are regularly depleted over time. To replenish them, at regular time-intervals $T, 2T, 3T, \ldots$ he makes a purchase of size L. He can thereby maintain a constant consumption flow of $x = \bar{x} + (L/T)$. For example, if $\bar{x}$ is 10 units per day, if his order size is $L = 140$ units, and the time-interval T is 7 days, a consumption rate of $x = 10 + (140/7) = 30$ units per day can be maintained. Such an inventory history is shown in Figure 14.16.

(For John to be a net buyer of good X, he must of course be a net seller of some other commodity Y. A similar diagram, showing regular accumulation rather than diminution of inventory between trades, would picture his inventory history for commodity Y.)

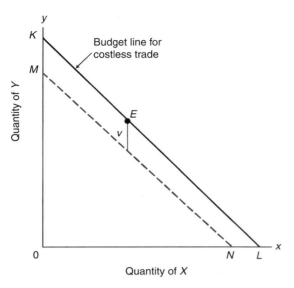

Figure 14.17. Individual Trading Opportunities: Lump-Sum Transaction Costs

The budget line for costless trade is KL as before. A lump-sum transaction charge does not create a gap between buying price and selling price. Thus, the effective budget line MN remains parallel to KL but is lower down, reflecting the reduced trading opportunities. The vertical distance between KL and MN reflects the transaction charge and the cost of holding inventories between purchase intervals. The consumer's optimum might occur anywhere along MN; in addition, however, the endowment point E on MN remains available as a possible autarky solution.

Intuitively, high lump-sum transaction costs, like high proportional transaction charges, would affect market supply and demand curves, and could lead an individual to avoid trading. This is correct, but the analysis is now somewhat different.

Proportional transaction costs, as pictured in Figure 14.14, break the perfect-markets budget line KL into a steeper buying-price segment and a flatter selling-price segment. Therefore only one basket on the original KL remains available, the endowment point E. Lump-sum transaction costs also break up the budget line, but in a different way. In Figure 14.17, once again the single point E on KL remains available. But if the individual chooses to trade at all, the relevant budget line MN is parallel to KL (since the market price P_x is unaffected) but lower down.

How far down? Two elements must be considered: the transaction charges themselves, and the costs of holding inventories. Over the buying interval T, the transaction charge per unit of time is F/T. Let h denote the per-unit inventory holding cost per unit of time. (Both of these are paid, let us assume, in units of the numeraire good Y.) Since on average the amount of inventory held is $L/2$, the vertical distance between KL and MN is given by:

$$V \equiv \frac{F}{T} + \frac{hTL}{2} \qquad (14.7)$$

A larger buying interval T spreads out the fixed charge F, reducing the first term on the right-hand side. But it means increasing the inventory holding costs reflected in the second term.

The implications for the individual's supply and demand curves are shown in Figure 14.18, which assumes a particular choice of T. Here there is no gap between the buying and selling price. And the autarky price P_x^o, where the individual would prefer not to trade even in the absence of transaction costs, remains as before. Within some range of prices above and below P_x^o no trading occurs. But as the market price increasingly diverges from P_x^o, it become attractive to incur the average trading fee F/T and associated inventory holding costs $hTL/2$.

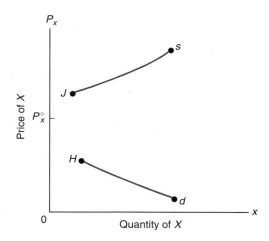

Figure 14.18. Individual Net Supply and Demand: Lump-Sum Transaction Cost

If there is a lump-sum cost per transaction, the individual will enter the market as a supplier or a demander only if the market price diverges from the autarky price P_x^o by at least a certain discrete amount. If the price divergence is just great enough, the individual will offer or demand a minimal discrete quantity – represented by the point J where the supply curve begins and the point H where the demand curve begins.

Figure 14.18 has the interesting feature that the supply and demand curves start at interior points J and H rather than at the vertical axis. The price P_x must be some distance above or below the autarky price P_x^o before it becomes economically worthwhile to enter the market at all. And when the price moves enough to make entering the market worthwhile, there will also be a minimum positive quantity traded.

As usual, these individual transaction supply and demand curves can be aggregated into market-wide supply and demand curves. For lump-sum transaction costs, as for proportional transaction costs, the market supply and demand curves may not intersect. If so, the market disappears.

CONCLUSION

Lump-sum transaction costs do not create a price gap. But they induce consumers to make trades only at discrete intervals, so that both buyers and sellers have to hold inventories. Heavy transaction charges and the resulting high inventory costs make individual autarky solutions more likely, reducing the aggregate volume of market trade. At the extreme, the market can become nonviable.

EXAMPLE 14.7 HOME OWNERSHIP AND UNEMPLOYMENT

In the period 1950–1960, a study by Andrew J. Oswald pointed out, most European nations had lower unemployment rates than the United States.[a] But by the 1990s European unemployment rates had become much higher than U.S. rates. Also, in the earlier period the U.S. fraction of owner-occupied housing was 80%, while European workers were mostly renters. By the 1990s, again, this difference was also largely reversed. In part as a result of subsidies and other incentives, by the 1990s owner-occupied rates in many European nations had risen to levels ranging from 28% in Switzerland to 80% in Spain, and in the 50–70% range for major countries such as the United Kingdom, France, and Italy.

The author argued that these trends were connected. It was rising home-ownership that led to rising rates of unemployment. This pattern tended to hold over time, across nations, and even within nations (for example, among the different cantons of Switzerland). For the various European nations, Oswald's analysis indicated, an increase of 10 percentage points in the home ownership fraction was associated with a fall of 4 percentage points in the proportion of men working.

The conjectured explanation involved transaction costs. A dynamic economy dictates that workers change jobs. But such adjustments often require a change of residence. A renter can, relatively easily, move his residence to accept a job offer in a different city or region. But the transaction costs of selling an existing house and possibly buying another – involving both proportional and lump-sum elements – are often burdensome. So, it appears, rather than incur these costs many European workers remain unemployed in the hope that a new job, not requiring a change of residence, will become available.

[a] Andrew J. Oswald, "The Housing Market and Europe's Unemployment: A Non-technical Paper" (May 1999, mimeo).

14.5   THE ROLE OF MONEY

Money is a device that reduces the costs of market trading. But recall that the costs of market trading in the proper sense – of bargaining and negotiating – must be distinguished from the much larger costs of physical movements and transfers of goods. These latter are really costs of production. So long as there is specialization and a division of labor, costs will be incurred in shipping goods, storing them while awaiting delivery, breaking bulk in repackaging, and so forth – whether or not the economy runs on the basis of market trading. Money can do nothing to reduce the costs of these physical processes.

Money facilitates trade in two main ways: as a *medium of exchange* and as a *temporary store of value*. These functions can be best visualized by comparing three hypothetical social regimes: (1) a pure command economy, with no trading but only dictated physical commodity turnovers, (2) a barter economy (with trading but without any monetary commodity), and (3) a money economy.

Money as Medium of Exchange

Suppose an economy has N individuals and N goods, and that everyone specializes in producing just one of the commodities. But each person would still like to consume all N goods. What is desired is *specialization in production* but *diversity in consumption* – the normal situation.

Imagine that the dictator in a pure command regime is perfectly efficient and benevolent. Such an economy has no costs of trading – no bidding, negotiating, or contracting. Even so, *transfer costs*, for example transportation expenses, may make some of the possible commodity movements uneconomic. Suppose oranges are produced in California and lobsters in Maine. Lobsters could be so expensive to ship that the dictator would correctly decide that overall efficiency required Californians to do without them. That is, Californians' "willingness to pay" does not cover the cost of producing and shipping lobsters. But oranges are less costly to ship, let us suppose, and so the dictator correctly commands that some California oranges be sent to Maine.

Now suppose a revolution displaces the dictator, substituting a regime of barter trade. In this regime, only two-party trade is feasible. (Multiparty barter trades are exceedingly costly to negotiate and enforce.)

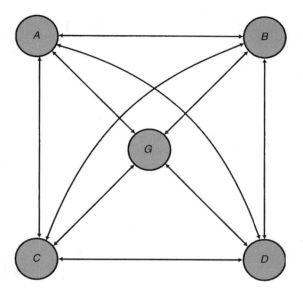

Figure 14.19. Trading Channels: Five Goods

With five commodities, under two-way barter there would have to be 10 channels of trade or markets. If commodity *G* were instead the sole medium of exchange, only four markets would be needed.

Since each of the N persons can trade with $N - 1$ others, the number of possible trading pairs is $N(N - 1)$. If $N = 3$, each individuals can deal with two others, making a total of six possible trades. But whereas the dictator could evaluate the economic efficiency of all of these $N(N - 1)$ possible trades, under bilateral barter only $N(N - 1)/2$ *two-way channels of exchange* are possible. If shipment of Maine lobsters to California is economically unfeasible owing to high transportation costs, then the California oranges cannot go to Maine either – since a lobsters-for-oranges deal cannot be arranged. Compared to an ideal command economy, therefore, a barter economy incurs the costs of negotiating trades; it also leads to inferior (inefficient) production and consumption arrangements.

The inefficiency of barter opens up a role for money as a medium of exchange. The commodity serving as money can be one of the original goods, or can be an artificial new commodity (like paper currency). In either case, the effect is to make multilateral trading possible through *indirect* exchanges.

Suppose, to begin with, that one of the initial commodities is chosen as the medium of exchange. In the prisoner-of-war situation of Chapter 4 cigarettes served this function, but assume here that the medium of exchange is gold. In a money economy other commodities are no longer traded for one another, but only for gold. This drastically reduces the number of different types of transactions, and thereby the costs of finding trading partners and of negotiating and enforcing trades.

Returning to a barter economy, if there were four ordinary consumption goods *A, B, C, D* plus gold *G*, Figure 14.19 pictures the $(5 \times 4)/2 = 10$ trading channels required. But if all other goods are traded only for gold, four channels will suffice. In general, with N commodities apart from gold, a money economy requires only $N - 1$ types of transactions.

This direct gain from reduced transaction costs is actually less important than the widened range of available transactions. Money makes possible triangular or still more complex exchanges without requiring anything beyond bilateral trades. Consider the lobster-orange example once again. In a monetary economy the Maine lobsters still cannot go to California: the transportation costs are too high, and money cannot change that fact. But the California oranges can now go to Maine! The Maine lobstermen can pay for oranges in gold, which they obtain by selling lobsters to other, non-California customers.

Last, most important of all, this widened range of transactions allows more specialization in production and division of labor. Relaxing the assumption that each trader or trading group produces only one of the N commodities, suppose instead that Californians produced a variety of products for domestic consumption – but at relatively high cost. The new possibility of shipping oranges to Maine, which was closed off under two-way barter, makes it possible for Californians to concentrate more heavily in their activity of comparative advantage: orange growing.

One element of cost is likely to be greater in a gold economy than in a barter economy: increased handling and shipping gold itself. Clearing arrangements have evolved to reduce these costs. Also, gold can be replaced by something less costly, for example, paper money. To further reduce handling and shipping costs, modern economies use a nonphysical, purely abstract medium of exchange – banking deposits.

Money as Temporary Store of Value

The second important role of money is as a temporary store of value (sometimes called an "abode of purchasing power"). Inventories of money help bridge time intervals between receipts and payments. By carrying an inventory of money, a baker can sell bread today while deferring purchases of meat until tomorrow.

Think again of the hypothetical pure command economy. Even there, inventories are required for production. But if a revolution overthrows the dictator in favor of a regime of bilateral barter exchange, additional *trading inventories* are required. Suppose three individuals 1, 2, and 3 are the specialized producers of commodities A, B, and C, respectively. Imagine that the desired pattern of trade is triangular: commodity A is to flow from person 1 to 2, commodity B from 2 to 3, and commodity C from 3 to 1. If multilateral trading is ruled out, we have the "double coincidence" problem of barter. Consider individual 2, who wants commodity A from individual 1. But individual 2 produces nothing that individual 1 wants. Although individual 2 can provide commodity B to individual 3, the latter produces nothing that individual 2 desires.

The solution is for some or all individuals to hold trading inventories of the third commodity, the one they neither produce nor consume. "Trade goods" are accepted in exchange for commodities produced, in order to have something available to exchange for commodities a person wants to consume.

Rather than hold inventories of many different types of trade goods, it is efficient for everyone to accept in exchange some single "store of value" commodity – money. The monetary commodity should be both cheap to produce and cheap to store, and preferably should not be eroded by consumption over time. (Loss of the monetary medium owing to consumption was a problem with cigarettes in the P.O.W. example of Chapter 4.) Again, there will be a natural tendency to move toward a purely abstract money commodity such as banking deposits, which are almost costless to produce and to store and are never actually consumed.

CONCLUSION

Money reduces the costs of market trading. (But not the costs of the physical transfers of goods required in any economic system with a division of labor.) When one commodity is the sole *medium of exchange*, fewer two-way transaction channels are required. And a medium of exchange makes possible triangular or even more complex trade patterns that would be impossible under barter. Where inventories of goods must be carried solely for trading purposes, costs of exchange are minimized if there is a consensus to use a single monetary commodity, which then also serves as everyone's temporary *store of value.*

14.6 AN APPLICATION: AUCTIONS

Several different exchange mechanisms have been discussed so far in the chapter. In broker markets a middleman brings buyers and sellers together, for a commission. In dealer markets the middleman instead holds an inventory of the good, hoping to make money on the difference between his or her buying price and selling price. This section of the chapter covers a third important mechanism – auctions.

The typical auction involves a single seller facing several potential buyers. The item offered may be unique, for example, an Old Master painting. Or it may be a quantity that can be divided among the bidders. When the U.S. Treasury auctions off a new issue of government bonds, buyers may submit bids for larger or smaller amounts of the bonds.

Since auctions involve a single seller, ordinarily one would expect the monopoly analysis of Chapter 8 to apply. But that analysis assumed the seller knows the buyers' demand curve. Auctions are a way of dealing with asymmetrical information (as discussed in Chapter 12). Specifically, the seller does not know the buyers' willingness to pay – their "reservation values." Nor do the buyers know one another's reservation values.

EXAMPLE 14.8 BIDDING FOR THE RADIO SPECTRUM[a]

The radio spectrum is a valuable resource. Rights to broadcast or to transmit radio messages are worth billions of dollars to television and radio stations, telephone companies, commercial paging services, and other users.

In the United States the Federal Communications Commission (FCC) assigns these rights. The traditional method began with hearings before an FCC administrative law judge. The judge's recommendation and the FCC's final decision were supposed to be based upon the benefits to the general public – a vague criterion. The process typically took years, was arguably subject to personal or ideological bias, tended to attract improper political influence, and generated a great deal of litigation.

In 1982 Congress allowed the FCC to use lotteries instead. Lotteries avoided some of the above difficulties, but were subject to other disadvantages. Since a valuable property was being given away free of charge, applicants were numerous. In 1984 the FCC received over half a million applications to enter a lottery for cellular licenses. Most of the successful lottery applicants, it turned out, never intended to use the spectrum themselves. They were just free-loaders, planning (if awarded a license) to resell them to an actual operating company.

For many years economists had pointed out a better way of assigning property rights in the radio spectrum – *auctions*. Although the FCC and industry insiders were skeptical, in 1993 Congress authorized the FCC to hold auctions. The first two auctions, in July and October 1994, dealt with tiny slivers of the radio spectrum reserved for personal communication services such as portable phones and pagers. Because the values of many of the licenses were interconnected (for example, bidders strongly preferred geographical contiguity), designers of the bidding process faced important analytic and practical problems. These were ingeniously resolved by the staff of the FCC and their consulting economists. The upshot: though little of the radio spectrum was involved – only 1.2 MHz – the winning bidders paid the government over a billion dollars.

This success was followed by a much more ambitious and complicated auction. Running from December 1994 to March 1995, licenses to 60 MHz of spectrum (bands wide enough to be usable for voice and data services) over the larger trading areas of the United States were sold. (Another auction was planned to cover the smaller trading areas.) An astonishing total of $7.7 billion was paid by the winning bidders. Thus the government gained "money out of thin air," for property rights that had previously been given away by administrative procedures or lotteries.

---

[a] Discussion based upon Peter C. Cramton, "Money out of Thin Air: The Nationwide Narrowband PCS Auction," University of Maryland, 25 September 1994, and R. Preston McAfee and John McMillan, "Analyzing the Airwaves Auction," *Journal of Economic Perspectives*, v. 10 (Winter 1996).

In terms of the bidding procedure, auctions fall into two main categories: sealed-bid versus public outcry.

The public outcry method is used in two types of auctions:

(1) *English (ascending-price) auction*. This is the familiar system of open public bids. The person making the highest offer wins the item being sold, and must pay the amount bid.
(2) *Dutch (descending-price) auction*. In the famous flower auctions at Aalsmeer in Holland, a clock visible to all participants is started at a high price. The price drops in steps until one of the potential buyers makes a bid by pushing a button. The winner pays the amount bid, as shown on the clock.

In the sealed-bid method, all offers are submitted in sealed envelopes to be opened simultaneously. The highest bid naturally wins. But there are two types of sealed-bid auctions, corresponding to the amount that the winning bidder pays.

(3) *Sealed-bid first-price auction*. The winner pays the amount bid.
(4) *Sealed-bid second-price auction*. Here the sale price, although paid by the winner, is only the amount offered by the runner-up – the second-highest bid.

(Among possible auction variations not considered here, the seller might charge an entry fee for the right to bid – or alternatively might offer bidders a small recompense in order to encourage participation. Also, sellers sometimes set a minimum "reserve price" which must be met if the sale is to be finalized.)

For analytical purposes, it will be understood that bids must be stated in unit steps – of a dollar or penny or whatever – no fractions are permitted.

It turns out that the English open-outcry auction is logically very similar to the sealed-bid second-price auction. And the Dutch auction resembles the sealed-bid first-price auction.

The English Auction

The English auction is the familiar open outcry proceeding. At any point everyone knows the current top bid and the history of previous bids. The auction stops when no one is willing to go beyond the current high bid; the item is then sold to the high bidder at that price.

In an English auction your best strategy is to bid one unit step higher than the current top bid offered by some other buyer, *provided* that bid was less than your reservation value. When all bidders follow this strategy, two results follow. (i) The person with the highest reservation value gets the good. (ii) The price paid is one unit step above the valuation of the person with the second-highest reservation value. So if the item is worth $200 to you but the top opposing bid is $100, you need offer only $101 (assuming that bids must be stated to the dollar) to win.

Sealed-Bid Second-Price Auction

In this form of auction the high bidder is the winner, but pays only the amount of the second-highest (runner-up) bid. Surprisingly perhaps, this leads to essentially the same result as the English open-outcry auction.

In a sealed-bid second-price auction a rational participant should always truthfully bid his or her reservation value. As participant, your bid determines only *whether* you win the auction; it does not affect the *price* you pay if you win. That price is determined by the second-highest bidder. So bidding below your reservation value reduces your chances of winning, without improving the price you pay if you win. It follows that you should not bid below your reservation value. And, of course, it never makes sense to bid above it.

If all bidders follow this strategy, once again the person with the highest reservation price gets the good, just as in the English auction. The price paid differs in only one small way. In the sealed-bid second-price auction the price paid is the runner-up valuation, that is, the bid submitted by the person with the second-highest reservation value. So if you bid your reservation value of $200 and the runner-up bid is $100, you need only pay $100.

These first two auctions are easy to analyze because the optimal strategies depend only upon the participant's own valuation of the item, and not at all upon what he or she believes other bidders might be thinking or doing. But for the other pair, the Dutch open-outcry auction and the sealed-bid first-price auction, rational calculation requires making conjectures about the reservation values and strategies of the other participants.

Sealed-Bid First-Price Auction

In a sealed-bid first-price auction, suppose there are only two bidders, 1 and 2. Furthermore, suppose each of them correctly believes the other's reservation value is equally likely to be any number from $0 to $1,000.

Now consider bidder 1. His valuation will be some V_1 between these limits. It can be shown that his bid b_1 should be exactly half that amount; that is, he should set

$b_1 = V_1/2$. And of course the same would apply for the other bidder: she should set $b_2 = V_2/2$. The reasoning goes as follows.

The bid b_1 will win for bidder 1 only if that amount exceeds b_2. For concreteness, imagine his bid is $b_1 = \$400$. Bidder 2, if she also adopts the above strategy, will bid less than $400 only if her valuation V_2 is less than $800. Since by assumption her V_2 is equally likely to be any number between $0 and $1,000, there is an 80% chance it will be less than $800 – in which case her bid will be under $400. So bidder 1's bid of $400 has an 80% chance of winning. And if he does win, his gain G_1 (corresponding to the Consumer Surplus concept of Chapter 7) will be $G_1 \equiv V_1 - b_1$. So on average his gain would be 0.8 ($800 − $400) = $320.

Expressing this algebraically, bidder 1's expected gain $E(G_1)$ is:

$$E(G_1) \equiv \frac{2b_1}{1,000}(V_1 - b_1) \tag{14.8}$$

The fraction on the right-hand side is the probability that bidder 1 makes the high bid. Since bidder 2 by assumption follows the indicated strategy (her bid b_2 is half her valuation V_2), her probability of bidding less than b_1 is the probability that her valuation V_2 is less than $2b_1$, to wit $2b_1/1,000$. The parenthesis on the right-hand side is bidder 1's gain if he does win the bidding. (The same equation will hold for bidder 2, after changing the subscripts.)

Now, on the assumption that bidder 2 follows the indicated strategy (so that b_2 is half her valuation V_2), what is the best bid for bidder 1? This can be solved as a straightforward calculus problem,[7] but the answer can be seen intuitively. If the player bids $0, he will of course never win. Thus $b_1 = 0$ implies $E(G_1) = 0$. At the other extreme, if the player bids his full value V_1 (so that $b_1 = V_1$), again there is no gain: $E(G_1) = 0$. By the symmetry of the formula, it is easy to see that the best b_1 is half-way between: $b_1 = V_1/2$.

To summarize the argument: if the other bidder's strategy is to bid half her valuation, it pays you to do the same. Since this applies to each player, bidding half your reservation value is an equilibrium – neither bidder has any motivation to change his or her strategy.

The Dutch Auction

For the best strategy under the Dutch (descending-price) auction, the reasoning (continuing with the simple special case of two bidders described above) is identical. Each participant should bid half of his or her reservation value. The participant should let the clock run down until it reaches half of his or her reservation value, and then stop the clock (if the opponent has not already done so). The chance of winning (the fraction on the right-hand side of equation (14.8)) and the amount gained in that event (the parenthesis following the fraction) are the same as for the sealed-bid first-price auction.

EXAMPLE 14.9 eBAY VERSUS AMAZON – SNIPING

On-line auctions are conducted by both eBay and Amazon. On eBay, auctions have a "hard close." Bids must be submitted before a prespecified terminal time. On

---

[7] *Mathematical Footnote:* As the first-order condition for a maximum, differentiating $E(G_1)$ with respect to b_1 and setting equal to zero leads immediately to $b_1 = V_1/2$.

Amazon, in contrast, bidding remains open until 10 minutes have passed without a new bid. Only in the absence of a new bid does the auction close. This difference has important implications for what has become known as "sniping" – last-minute bidding.

Both auction systems are of the English open-outcry type. Since bidders may find it inconvenient to continuously monitor the progress of the auction, both systems provide for "proxy bids." A proxy bid becomes activated when the bidding rises to one unit below it, at which point it becomes the current high bid.

Amazon and eBay both recommend that proxy bidders submit their full reservation prices, in which case they need not submit any later bids or even attend to the progress of the auction. Since these are second-price auctions, the winner does not have to pay his or her full reservation price but only an amount one unit higher than the runner-up. So the recommendations are in line with the analysis in the preceding text.

Nevertheless, it has been observed, bidders do attend to the course of the auction, and – despite the above reasoning – "sniping is common." As another disadvantage, owing to uncertainty as to whether a last-minute bid will arrive in time, engaging in sniping involves a risk of nonexecution. So it is not immediately evident why sniping takes place.

Alvin E. Roth and Axel Ockenfels asked whether there might be circumstances in which sniping is rational.[a] One possibility is that snipers may be taking advantage of the irrationality of other, possibly naive, participants. If opposing bidders (perhaps foolishly) sometimes do not submit their full reservation prices but instead move up one step at a time, a fast-reacting sniper can possibly win the bidding at a low price, less than the opponent would ultimately have been willing to pay. Furthermore, if there is informational asymmetry, it could make sense for a very well-informed or experienced participant to hold off until the very end, so as not to disclose his or her superior knowledge. Regardless of the reason, however, sniping should be less prevalent under the Amazon "soft close" system, where the bidding has no predetermined termination time.

The authors compared eBay versus Amazon bidding for two types of product – antiques and computers. For computers they found that, on eBay, 9% of all last bids were submitted in the final 5 minutes, as compared with only 1% for Amazon. For antiques on eBay, 16% were submitted in the last 5 minutes, and again only 1% for Amazon. Thus, as expected, the "hard close" on eBay led to more last-minute bidding. And, in addition, there was more last-minute bidding for antiques than for computers. Antiques being much less standardized than computers, the antiques market is more subject to informational asymmetry. So, very likely, well-informed bidders for antiques were holding off in order not to prematurely disclose their valuations to other market participants.

[a] Alvin E. Roth and Axel Ockenfels, "Last-Minute Bidding and the Rules for Ending Second-Price Auctions: Evidence from eBay and Amazon Auctions on the Internet," *American Economic Review* v. 92 (September 2002).

CONCLUSION

If the participants follow rational strategies, the English auction leads to the same result as the sealed-bid second-price auction, with the small modification that the price in the English auction is higher by the unit step specified in the bidding procedure. And the Dutch auction leads to the same result as the sealed-bid first-price auction. The best strategy in the English auction and the sealed-bid second-price auction depends only upon the player's own valuation of the item offered for sale. But for the Dutch auction and the sealed-bid first-price auction, beliefs about the other participants' valuations and strategies have to be specified to determine a person's optimal bidding strategy.

SUMMARY   One of the two major benefits of trade is that the achieved allocation of goods is mutually preferred to the initial endowments. For two goods X and Y, the Edgeworth box shows how traders can both gain by trading into the region of mutual advantage. At the competitive equilibrium, each individual's Marginal Rate of Substitution in Consumption $MRSC$ (the absolute slope $|\Delta y/\Delta x|$ along the indifference curve) equals the market price ratio P_x/P_y.

The second major benefit of trade is that each individual can specialize in accordance with his or her comparative advantage in production. The Marginal Rate of Transformation MRT is the absolute slope $|\Delta y/\Delta x|$ along the Production Possibility Curve. For an isolated Robinson Crusoe, the combined production-consumption optimum satisfies the condition $MRT = MRSC$. But in a world of production and exchange, the individual's optimal production point is determined by the condition $MRT = P_x/P_y$ and the optimal consumption point by the condition $MRSC = P_x/P_y$. The fact that the production optimum and the consumption optimum can differ corresponds to productive specialization, which makes available increased quantities of both goods.

For any good X, *full demand* (desired consumption) differs from *transaction demand* (the amount demanded in the market). Similarly, *full supply* differs from *transaction supply*. The magnitudes differ by the quantities that individuals retain for their own consumption. Market equilibrium can be expressed in terms of the intersection of the full supply and demand curves, or in terms of the intersection of the transaction supply and demand curves.

Perfect markets are characterized by (1) *perfect communication* (traders are aware of all buy/sell offers), (2) *instantaneous equilibrium* (all transactions are executed simultaneously at a single common price), and (3) *zero transaction costs*. Actual markets can only approximate these ideal conditions.

Any economic system with specialization and the division of labor incurs *transfer costs* – transportation, warehousing, retail distribution, and so on – associated with storing or moving goods among locations or among individuals. These transfer costs would persist even in a total command economy. An economy with voluntary exchange also incurs a second kind of cost, *trading costs*. Trading costs stem from the need to negotiate deals and write contracts among self-interested individuals. Yet, history has shown, trade brings about better results than a command economy could ever achieve.

"Middlemen" reduce costs of trading, but must themselves be compensated for their services. Costs of trading depend on the amounts traded and on the frequency of trading. *Proportional* transaction costs, which create a gap between buying price and selling price, reduce the equilibrium amounts traded in markets. *Lump-sum* costs, which are incurred each time a transaction takes place, diminish the optimum frequency of transactions.

Both types of transaction costs reduce specialization in production and make autarky more likely.

Money reduces the cost of trading in two main ways:

(1) As a *medium of exchange*, money reduces the number of different channels of two-way exchanges, in comparison with barter. This lowers the costs of collecting information, keeping records, and shipping goods to settle transactions. Even more important, triangular or even more complex patterns of trade become possible.

(2) As a *store of value*, money can replace the costlier trading inventories that would have to be carried under barter.

There are four main types of auctions, which logically fall into two paired categories.

(1) In the *English (ascending-price) auction* and the *sealed-bid second-price auction*, the item sold goes to the party with the highest reservation value. He or she only pays, however, the reservation value – that is, the maximum amount offered – of the runner-up. (Plus a unit step up for the English auction.) In these auctions each participant needs to know only his or her own reservation value.

(2) In the *Dutch (descending-price)* auction and the *sealed-bid first-price auction*, each person's rational strategy will depend also upon his or her conjectures as to the opponent's reservation value and strategy. In the simplest special case where the personal valuations are correctly conjectured to be uniformly distributed between zero and an upper bound, the equilibrium strategy is to bid exactly half one's own valuation.

QUESTIONS

†The answers to daggered questions appear at the end of the book.

For Review

1. Explain how the possibility of trade can lead to consumption benefits (improved allocations of given social totals of goods among the different individuals) and to production benefits (larger social totals of desired goods). How is the consumptive improvement illustrated in the Edgeworth box? Can the productive improvement be illustrated in the Edgeworth box?

†2. a. If two persons have identical preferences (indifference-curve maps), does it follow that they cannot trade to mutual advantage?
   b. What if they have identical preferences and identical endowments in a world of pure exchange?
   c. In a world of production, what if they have identical preferences and identical productive opportunities?

†3. We normally observe specialization in production but diversification in consumption.
   a. What shapes of the individuals' Production Possibility Curves and preference maps lead to this pattern of behavior?
   b. Could this specialization in production but diversification in consumption be achieved in the absence of trade?

4. What is meant by an individual's autarky price for a particular good? What happens at higher prices? At lower prices?

5. What condition must hold for each individual at a competitive equilibrium in a world of pure exchange? What additional condition characterizes the market as a whole?

†6. What are the production and consumption conditions that must hold for each individual in a world of production and exchange? What additional conditions characterize the market as a whole?

†7. If market equilibrium takes place at the intersection of the aggregate transaction demand and transaction supply curves, how can the intersection of the *full* demand and *full* supply curves also determine the equilibrium?

8. "For every individual, the s_i^t and d_i^t curves must intersect along the vertical axis, as in Figure 14.10. It is therefore impossible for the aggregate S^t and D^t curves to intersect in the interior, as in Figure 14.11." True or false? Explain.

9. What are perfect markets? What is perfect competition?

†10. a.   Can autarky occur in costless exchange?

b.   Why is autarky more likely the higher are transaction costs?

11. Some markets are illegal (markets for babies, narcotic drugs, government favors, and so on). Law enforcement that is not totally effective can be regarded as imposing a transaction cost upon participants. In terms of this chapter's analysis, what effects would you anticipate from increased law-enforcement effort against the narcotic traffic? Would the volume of transactions be affected? What about the gross price paid by buyers in comparison with the net price received by sellers?

12. Illustrate how sufficiently heavy proportional transaction costs might make a market nonviable. Do the same for lump-sum transaction costs.

†13. Since the existence of markets necessarily involves some burden of transaction costs, wouldn't a command economy dispensing with markets always be more efficient? Explain.

14. Distinguish between the costs of transferring goods from one individual to another and exchange costs. How would you classify transportation of goods between producer and consumer? What about the costs of negotiating a contract? Enforcing a contract?

†15. Other things equal, if the bid-ask spread for a stock increases, do you expect the amount of trading to increase or decrease?

For Further Thought and Discussion

1. From Omar Khayyam:

I often wonder what the Vintners buy
One half so precious as the Goods they sell.

Omar seems to be suggesting that vintners ought not to engage in exchange, since wine is more precious than anything else. Where is the fallacy in his reasoning?

†2. Compare the likely effects of taxes levied upon consumption, upon production, and upon exchange of a commodity.

†3. Suppose Robinson Crusoe is superior to Friday in producing both fish and bananas. For example, it may take Robinson 1 hour to catch a fish and 2 hours to pick a bunch of bananas, while it takes Friday 4 hours to do either. Show that they still can engage in mutually beneficial exchange. (In international trade this is called *the principle of comparative advantage.*)

†4. Imagine an initial Edgeworth-box competitive equilibrium, starting from an endowment position where individual i has all of commodity G (grain) and individual j has all of commodity Y (*numeraire*). Suppose i's endowment of grain doubles, everything else remaining unchanged. Can we be sure that i is better off at the new competitive

equilibrium? that *j* is better off? that at least one of them is better off? [*Hint:* Are wheat farmers necessarily better off if the crop is large? What about consumers of wheat?]

5. Give examples of markets that have existed historically, but do not now exist. Can you explain their disappearance?

6. According to the economist Kenneth E. Boulding, a tariff can be regarded as a "negative railroad." Whereas a railroad connects trading communities, a tariff separates them. Is the analogy valid?

†7. The text stated that, in a world of two commodities *X* and *Y*, trade would normally lead to greater quantities produced of both goods. Is this necessarily the case? Might there possibly be, say, greater production of *X* but reduced production of *Y*? Explain. [*Hint:* Consider the case where only trader *i* (Ida) has productive opportunities, while trader *j* (James) has a fixed endowment.]

†8. Flowers provide bees with nectar, while bees facilitate the pollination of flowers. Is this exchange?

9. Fresh fruits are cheaper at farm roadstands than in city markets. Does the price difference reflect transfer costs or trading costs, or are there elements of each?

10. Give examples of exchange costs that are reduced by the existence of money as a medium of exchange. Of money as a store of value.

†11. If rationing is introduced, money is no longer a fully effective medium of exchange. What types of additional exchange costs emerge in a world where ration coupons and cash are *both* required to effectuate a transaction?

†12. According to elementary textbooks, a commodity selected to serve as money should be portable, divisible, storable, generally recognizable, and homogeneous. In terms of the discussion in this chapter, why are these desirable qualities? Can you think of other desirable qualities? [*Hint:* Think of cigarettes serving as money in a prisoner-of-war camp.]

13. Consider again the Edgeworth Box in Figure 14.2. We saw that Ida and John should be willing to trade from the endowment position *E* to points such as *T* or *F*. However, they would not *both* be willing to trade from *E* to points like *R*, *S*, or *V*. Which of them (if any) would be willing to move from *E* to *R*? From *E* to *S*? From *E* to *V*?

†14. In Figure 14.11 what does the horizontal distance between the equilibrium aggregate and transaction quantities, X^* and X^{t*}, represent?

15. Prove that the price at which the *full* supply and demand curves intersect must be the same as the price at which the *transaction* supply and demand curves intersect (as pictured in both Figure 14.5 and 14.6).

16. Consider an experiment with the following instructions. "This information is confidential, for your eyes only. You are to be loaned 100 tokens, with which you can buy units of a commodity at a price of 6 tokens each. The first unit you buy can be resold to the experimenter for 16 tokens, the second for 11 tokens, the third for 3 tokens. After you repay the loaned 100 tokens, the remainder will be your "profit." At the end of the experiment your 'profit' can be converted into dollars for you to take away."

So, for example, if the subject correctly bought two units for 6 tokens each, he could take home $(16 - 6) + (11 - 6) = 15$ dollars.

Verify that, if the stated resale values are regarded as the subject's "marginal willingness to pay" for successive units, the $15 amount corresponds to his or her *Consumer Surplus.*

At the end of the experiment, the subject could take home a profit equal to the aggregate difference between sales proceeds and cost. Verify that this difference corresponds to *Producer Surplus.*

17. In Figure 14.14, show that, depending upon the location and shape of her indifference curves, Ida could prefer any of the following three possibilities: (1) a tangency along line-segment EL' (she sells some of her endowed Y for X); (2) a tangency along line-segment EK' (she sells some of her endowed X for Y); or (3) a nontangency solution at point E (she sticks with her endowment position, i.e., she chooses autarky).

18. For the individual pictured in Figure 14.17 show that for some patterns of preferences, transaction costs, and ruling price P_x, he could be either a buyer of X or a seller or else stand pat at his endowment position E.

†19. In Figure 14.18 the supply and demand curves start at interior points J and H rather than at the vertical axis. The price P_x must be sufficiently above or below the autarky price P_x^o before it becomes worthwhile to enter the market. Verify that when trade does become worthwhile, there will also be a minimum positive quantity traded.

VI ECONOMICS AND TIME

15 The Economics of Time

The text so far has covered two types of decisions: (1) how to spend income (what consumption goods to buy?) and (2) how to earn income (how hard to work, what amounts of resource services to offer on the market?). This chapter examines another economic choice: (3) how to provide for the present versus the future.

To balance between present and future consumption, people save and invest. A person who *saves* is refraining from current consumption. A person who *invests* is creating "capital" – either physical capital such as factories and machines or human capital (education and training).

An isolated Robinson Crusoe has to simultaneously save and invest. He saves by not eating up all of his current corn crop; he invests by planting the saved corn as seed. In a multiperson economy, however, those who save and those who invest may be different people. Savers might put money in the bank or buy corporate securities. The financial system transfers this purchasing power to finance other people's investments – building a house, enlarging a factory, or acquiring a college education.[1] Although any single person's saving might exceed the amount he or she invests, the economywide *totals* of saving and investment must be equal.

Why save or invest rather than consume today? Only so you, or someone you designate, can consume more in the future. A person builds a house to obtain future shelter; an orchardist plants a tree to harvest fruit in later years; a worker takes a course of training to win a higher-paying job.

Sections 15.1 through 15.3 cover the logic of individual decisions and equilibrium outcomes involving a balance between present and future. Section 15.4 discusses an important practical topic: the criteria used by business firms and by government agencies for evaluating investment projects. Section 15.5 shows how the artifact of *money* affects investment and interest. Section 15.6 looks into why interest rates vary across different financial instruments on the basis of risk or term. Section 15.7 examines the fundamental considerations that determine when levels of saving and investment in the overall economy are great or small, and when interest rates are high or low.

15.1   PRESENT VERSUS FUTURE

Assume for simplicity that there is only a single consumption good – corn (C). The objects of choice are C_0 (this year's corn), C_1 (corn 1 year from now), C_2 (corn 2 years from now), and so on. The corresponding prices are P_0, P_1, P_2, and so on. [*Note:* These are the prices *today*, for corn to be delivered at the specified dates.] Let current corn C_0 be the numeraire or basis of pricing, so that $P_0 \equiv 1$.

Choosing between this year's corn and next year's corn (between C_0 and C_1) follows the same economic logic as choosing between this year's wheat and this year's manufactures. Just as supply and demand determine today's price ratio P_w/P_m between wheat and manufactures, supply and demand determine today's price ratio P_1/P_0 between this year's corn and next year's corn.

Letting the lower-case symbols c_0 and c_1 designate specific quantities of the goods C_0 and C_1, and using Δc_0 and Δc_1 to signify small changes, the annual *rate of interest*

---

[1] In ordinary discussions, this distinction between saving and investment is sometimes neglected. A financial writer may recommend that readers "invest" in stocks or bonds or savings deposits. Strictly speaking, buying financial instruments represents saving, not investment.

Table 15.1 Interest-rate equivalents

Short-term interest rates	Long-term interest rates
$\dfrac{P_1}{P_0} = \dfrac{1}{1 + r_1}$	$\dfrac{P_1}{P_0} = \dfrac{1}{1 + R_1}$
$\dfrac{P_2}{P_1} = \dfrac{1}{1 + r_2}$	$\dfrac{P_2}{P_0} = \dfrac{1}{(1 + R_2)^2}$
$\cdots$	$\cdots$
$\dfrac{P_T}{P_{T-1}} = \dfrac{1}{1 + r_T}$	$\dfrac{P_T}{P_0} = \dfrac{1}{(1 + R_T)^T}$

is defined by the expression:

$$-\frac{\Delta c_1}{\Delta c_0} \equiv \frac{P_0}{P_1} \equiv 1 + r_1 \qquad (15.1)$$

The minus sign on the left-hand side indicates that a person can obtain an increment of current corn (Δc_0) only by giving up some future corn (Δc_1), and vice versa. Furthermore, since in market exchange the value offered and the value received are equal, $P_0 \Delta c_0$ must equal $-P_1 \Delta c_1$, or $-\Delta c_1/\Delta c_0 = P_0/P_1$. The second identity in equation (15.1) defines the interest rate r_1 as the premium on the value of current corn relative to future corn. So P_1, the value today of 1-year future corn, is "discounted" in comparison with P_0 by the factor $1 + r_1$.

DEFINITION: The annual real rate of interest r_1 is the *extra* amount of 1-year future corn that must be paid in the market to receive a unit of current corn.

EXERCISE 15.1

(a) If the interest rate is $r_1 = 10\%$, what is P_1 (the price today of a 1-year future claim to corn)? (b) What if $r_1 = 100\%$? (c) If future claims become almost valueless (P_1 approaches zero), what would happen to r_1?

ANSWER: (a) Using equation (15.1), if $r_1 = 10\%$ then $P_1 \equiv 1/(1 + r_1) = 1/1.1$, which is approximately 0.909. (b) If $r_1 = 100\%$ then $P_1 = \frac{1}{2} = 0.5$. (c) As P_1 approaches zero, r_1 goes to infinity.

Can interest rates be negative? From equation (15.1), negative interest rates mean that claims to future income are worth more than current claims (in today's market). Though unusual, this is not impossible. It might come about if people anticipate great scarcities in the future. But there is a limit: interest rates cannot be less than -100%. If $r < -1$, in equation (15.1) either P_0 or P_1 must be negative – contradicting the assumption that current corn and future corn are both *goods* rather than bads.

So far only two periods have been considered: "now" (date 0) and "1 year from now" (date 1). More generally, individuals will make choices about corn at various dates $C_0, C_1, C_2, \ldots, C_T$ in the light of prices $P_0, P_1, P_2, \ldots, P_T$ – where T is the terminal date or economic horizon. Two useful ways of generalizing equation (15.1) are illustrated in Table 15.1. First, consider the successive year-to-year price ratios $P_1/P_0, P_2/P_1, \ldots, P_T/P_{T-1}$. These can be used to define the 1-year *short-term* interest rates $r_1, r_2, \ldots, r_T$ shown in the first column of the table. Here $1 + r_1$ is the discount factor for transactions between date 0 and date 1, $1 + r_2$ is the discount factor between date 1 and date 2, and so on.

Alternatively, consider the ratios P_1/P_0, P_2/P_0, ..., P_T/P_0, where P_0 appears in all the denominators. In the second column of Table 15.1 these ratios are used to define the *long-term* interest rates R_1, R_2, ..., R_T associated with transactions between date 0 and any future date up to T. Notice that R_2 is a kind of average of r_1 and r_2. The worth today of a unit of corn 2 years off could be found either by using the long-term discounting formula for P_2/P_0 in the second column of the table, or else by successively using the short-term 1-year discounting formulas for P_2/P_1 and P_1/P_0.

EXERCISE 15.2

(a) Let $P_0 \equiv 1$, and suppose that $r_1 = 10\%$ and $r_2 = 20\%$. (a) What is the worth *at date 1* of a bushel of corn at date 2? (b) What is the worth *today* of a bushel of corn at date 2? (c) What is the implied long-term interest rate R_2?

ANSWER: (a) This worth is P_2/P_1. Using Table 15.1, when $r_2 = 20\%$ the ratio equals $1/1.2 = 0.833$. (b) $P_2/P_0 \equiv (P_2/P_1) \times (P_1/P_0)$, and the previous exercise showed that when $r_1 = 10\%$, $P_1/P_0 = 0.909$. So a bushel 2 years off is worth $0.833 \times 0.909 = 0.758$ today. (c) Using the second column of Table 15.1, set $0.758 = 1/(1 + R_2)^2$. The numerical solution is $R_2 = 15.9\%$, approximately.

The next two exercises illustrate the power of compound interest.

EXERCISE 15.3

(a) If $P_0 \equiv 1$ as usual, and supposing that all the short-term interest rates r_1, r_2, ... are equal to some common value $r = 10\%$, what is the value of a bushel of corn to be received in 5 years? 10 years? 20 years? (b) Same question, if $r = 20\%$?

ANSWER: [Questions like these can be answered by using financial functions in a spreadsheet, a financial calculator, or interest tables published in many financial and accounting texts]: (a) At 10%, a payment 5 years in the future is worth 0.683 today, a payment 10 years off is worth 0.386, and a payment 20 years off is worth 0.159. (b) At 20%, the corresponding numbers are 0.402, 0.162, and 0.026.

So as the length of the term increases, compound interest more and more drastically erodes the value today of a future payment. And the effect becomes disproportionately stronger at higher interest rates.

EXERCISE 15.4

Suppose you had to plan ahead whether to cut a tree for timber after 10 years or after 20 years. (a) If $r = 5\%$, how much greater must the timber value be at after 20 years to justify letting the tree grow that long? (b) If $r = 10\%$?

ANSWER: (a) Using interest tables, at 5% a unit payment 10 years off is worth 0.615 today, whereas a payment 20 years off is worth only 0.377. To justify not cutting until 20 years, the timber value at that date would have to be greater by at least the proportion $0.615/0.377 = 1.63$, approximately. (b) At $r = 10\%$ the timber value would have to be greater by the ratio $0.463/0.215 = 2.15$.

Figure 15.1. Consumption This Year versus Consumption Next Year

The choice between C_0 and C_1 involves the preference map (indifference curves U', U'', U'''), endowment E, and budget line KL. The intertemporal consumption optimum is C^*. The individual shown here chooses to lend the amount $\bar{c}_0 - c_0^*$ of current claims, receiving in repayment the amount $c_1^* - \bar{c}_1$ of future claims. $\overline{W}_0$ is the endowed wealth measured in units of current claims C_0.

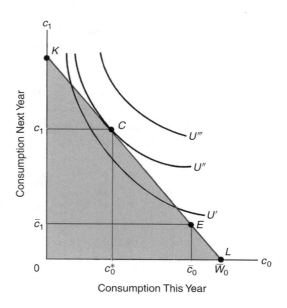

Consumption This Year

15.2 CONSUMPTION CHOICES OVER TIME: PURE EXCHANGE

In the intertemporal context, pure exchange means that no net investment is taking place. Building a house or planting a tree are ruled out, since they change the physical totals of present and future goods. And if no investment is taking place, aggregate saving must also equal zero. Some individuals might be saving, but their saving (lending) has to be balanced by "dis-saving" (borrowing) on the part of others.

Borrowing-Lending Equilibrium with Zero Net Investment

Figure 15.1, which pictures choices between consumption this year and consumption next year (between C_0 and C_1), closely resembles the "optimum of the consumer" diagrams in Chapter 4. Once again there are indifference curves U', U'', U''', ... and a budget line KL. But the endowment position $E \equiv (\bar{c}_0, \bar{c}_1)$ is in the interior. So the individual – call him Karl – has an initial entitlement that consists of positive amounts $\bar{c}_0$ of this year's corn and $\bar{c}_1$ of next year's corn.

Suppose Karl wants to consume more than his endowed $\bar{c}_0$ units of corn in the current period. Since productive investment is ruled out under the pure-exchange assumption, Karl can do so only by borrowing from someone else. Or if, instead, he prefers to consume more than $\bar{c}_1$ next year, he can do so only by lending to others at a positive rate of interest. In the diagram, *lending* means moving northwest along the budget line KL from E – giving up current corn in exchange for future corn.[2] Moving southeast along KL, increasing c_0 at the expense of c_1, is *borrowing*. As pictured in Figure 15.1, the utility-maximizing consumption basket is the tangency point $C^* \equiv (c_0^*, c_1^*)$. At Karl's optimum he lends $\bar{c}_0 - c_0^*$ units of current corn, expecting to be repaid $c_1^* - \bar{c}_1$ units of next year's corn.

What if, with the same preferences and budget line, the endowment position E had instead been located northwest of C^* along the budget line? Then moving from the

---

[2] "Lending" includes depositing funds in a savings account or buying financial instruments like stocks and bonds.

new E to the optimum C^* means that Karl would borrow $c_0^* - \bar{c}_0^*$ and repay $\bar{c}_1 - \bar{c}_1^*$. A person whose endowment is mainly in the form of future income is like the "heir with great expectations" in Charles Dickens's novel: he has little money today, but can borrow on the strength of his rich future prospects.[3]

In the "optimum of the consumer" diagrams of Chapter 4, the absolute slope of the budget line was $-\Delta y/\Delta x = P_x/P_y$, the price ratio between goods X and Y. Similarly here in Figure 15.1 the absolute slope of the budget line – the market rate at which individuals can trade current corn against future corn (can lend or borrow) – is $-\Delta c_1/\Delta c_0 = P_0/P_1$. From equation (15.1), this ratio also equals $1 + r_1$. So a higher interest rate means a steeper slope of the budget line.

In Chapter 4 the individual's *income I* constrained his or her choices, as shown by the budget equation $P_x x + P_y y = I$. That equation was valid because of an implicit assumption that all decisions concerned only a single time-period. In making choices over time, it is not a single period's income that limits consumption choices, but rather overall wealth.

A person endowed with rights to given quantities $\bar{c}_0$ and $\bar{c}_1$ of present and future corn has *endowed wealth* $\overline{W}_0$, which is defined as:

$$\overline{W}_0 \equiv P_0\bar{c}_0 + P_1\bar{c}_1 \tag{15.2}$$

(The subscript 0 is attached because wealth signifies a present market value, the worth *today* of income claims in both present and future.)

DEFINITION: Endowed wealth $\overline{W}_0$ is the present value of an individual's endowment $(\bar{c}_0, \bar{c}_1)$ of present and future claims.

Since $P_0 \equiv 1$ and $P_1 \equiv 1/(1 + r_1)$, the definition in equation (15.2) can also be written:

$$\overline{W}_0 \equiv \bar{c}_0 + \frac{\bar{c}_1}{1 + r_1} \tag{15.2'}$$

Endowed wealth is shown in Figure 15.1 as the horizontal intercept of the budget line KL.

It is endowed wealth, indicated in the diagram by the budget line, that constrains consumption choices in the present or the future. The equation of this intertemporal budget line can also be expressed in two ways:

$$P_0 c_0 + P_1 c_1 = \overline{W}_0 \tag{15.3}$$

$$c_0 + \frac{c_1}{1 + r_1} = \overline{W}_0 \tag{15.3'}$$

Equation (15.3) resembles (15.2), and (15.3') resembles (15.2'). But do not confuse them! Equations (15.2) and (15.2') *define* endowed wealth $\overline{W}_0$ (notice the identity sign $\equiv$) in terms of the given endowments $\bar{c}_0$ and $\bar{c}_1$ as known constants. But in equations (15.3) and (15.3'), c_0 and c_1 (without the overbars) are consumer choice variables and $\overline{W}_0$ is the constraint.

---

[3] Nineteenth-century British novels frequently refer to a financial instrument known as the "post-obit." Heirs to an entailed estate could borrow, with no interest or repayment of principal due until after succession to the estate. (Under British law the successor to an entailed estate could not be disinherited, and so remained a relatively good credit risk despite possibly having wasteful habits.)

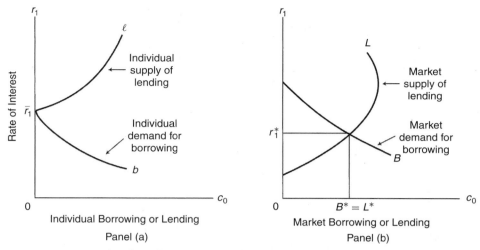

Figure 15.2. Supply of Lending, Demand for Borrowing

Panel (a) depicts an *individual's* supply of lending curve ℓ (the transaction supply of C_0) and demand for borrowing curve b (the transaction demand for C_0) as functions of the interest rate r_1. In Panel (b) the intersection of the *market* supply of lending curve L and the *market* demand for borrowing curve B determines the equilibrium interest rate r_1^* and the amount of borrowing and lending $B^* = L^*$.

Moving from the individual to the market level of analysis, supply and demand for current corn C_0 can be expressed as functions of the interest rate r_1. (The analysis parallels Section 14.2 of the preceding chapter). Karl's individual *supply of lending* is his *transaction supply of current corn*. If he is endowed with $\overline{c}_0$ units and chooses to consume only c_0 units, he will be lending the difference $\overline{c}_0 - c_0$. Similarly, his individual *demand for borrowing* is his *transaction demand for current corn*, the difference $c_0 - \overline{c}_0$. Whether he prefers to borrow or to lend will of course depend upon the interest rate. This is shown in Panel (a) of Figure 15.2 by the b curve (his individual demand for borrowing) and the ℓ curve (his individual supply of lending). At Karl's "autarky" interest rate $\overline{r}_1$ he will be satisfied to stay put, neither lending nor borrowing.

Panel (b) shows the aggregate B and L curves, which are the horizontal summations of the individual b and ℓ curves. The intersection of B and L determines the equilibrium amounts of borrowing and lending $B^* = L^*$ and the equilibrium rate of interest r_1^*.

An Application: Double Taxation of Saving?

Income is taxed when initially earned. But then any amount saved is taxed a second time when it generates earnings in future years. Does this mean that income taxes discourage saving?

Figure 15.3 shows an individual's (Karl's) indifference curves. The endowment position E is assumed to lie along the horizontal axis: $E \equiv (\overline{c}_0, 0)$. So Karl must save if he is to consume in the future. In the absence of taxes his budget line would be EK with absolute slope $1 + r_1$. The line EK intercepts the vertical axis at $\overline{c}_0(1 + r_1)$, which is his maximum attainable amount of future corn. His consumption optimum is C^*.

To verify whether income taxation is biased against saving, a baseline for comparison is needed. An appropriate baseline is a tax levied upon *consumption* rather than on income. (For the moment, assume that the market interest rate r_1 remains unchanged.)

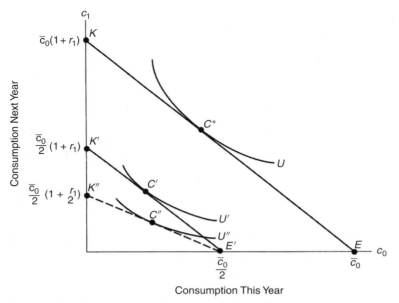

Figure 15.3. Consumption Tax versus Income Tax

A *consumption tax*, that bears equally heavily upon C_0 and C_1 shifts the budget line proportionately downward from EK to $E'K'$. The original consumption optimum C^* shifts to C' – present consumption, future consumption, and saving all fall about proportionately. An *income tax* bears upon all of current income (whether or not saved) as well as upon future consumption and income, so the budget line becomes $E'K''$. Comparing the income tax optimum C'' with the consumption tax optimum C', the amount of saving (horizontal distance between E' and C' or C'') may be about the same, but net provision for the future is less.

Consider a consumption tax at the rate of 50%. This means that current endowed amounts *intended* for consumption (that is, any amounts not saved) are reduced by one-half. (This can be viewed as a 100% tax on *actual* consumption expenditures: a person who buys a loaf of bread must pay an equivalent amount to the tax collector.)

For such a consumption tax the relevant budget line is $E'K'$, both intercepts of EK having been shifted halfway to the origin. If Karl had maximized his current consumption and saved nothing, his attainable c_0 would equal half his endowed c_0. And if he had chosen instead to forego current consumption entirely, saving as much as possible, after paying next year's consumption tax his maximum attainable c_1 would be half of $c_0(1 + r_1)$. Any intermediate choice lies upon the line $E'K'$ connecting these two intercepts. Since the budget lines EK and $E'K'$ are parallel, a *consumption* tax has no systematic bias between current and future consumption. The new optimum C' shifts more or less proportionately inward to the origin from the original C^*.

If instead a 50% *income* tax is imposed, however, the relevant budget line becomes $E'K''$. To see why, note that 50% of current income $\bar{c}_0$ has to be paid at date 0 *regardless* of the consumption/saving decision. (Whereas under a consumption tax, if Karl saves the maximum possible amount $\bar{c}_0/2$, he pays no tax for the current period.) And after paying $\bar{c}_0/2$ at date 0, Karl remains liable for a 50% tax at date 1 upon his income for that period. Specifically, his date 1 tax liability would be $\ell r_1/2$, where ℓ is the amount lent (saved). In the extreme case where he saves as much as possible ($\ell = \bar{c}_0/2$), the net after-tax amount remaining is the intercept of the budget line $E'K''$ on the vertical axis:

$\bar{c}_0/2 \times (1 + r_1/2)$. Along this budget line his consumption optimum might be a point like C'' in the diagram.

Returning to the original issue, as compared with a consumption tax is an income tax *biased against saving*? Is it *biased against future consumption*? It turns out these are two different questions! Geometrically, when C' (the optimum under the consumption tax) and C'' (the optimum under the income tax) are compared, the amounts saved (as defined by the horizontal distance from point E') are similar. But C'' lies below C', which means that future consumption is less.

The explanation reflects the income effect and substitution effect of the tax, regarded as a price change. A 50% income tax is a heavier burden than a 50% consumption tax; the opportunity set for $E'K''$ is smaller than for $E'K'$. The *income effect* therefore suggests that Karl should want to consume less of both C_0 and C_1.[4] But the income tax also makes C_1 more expensive relative to C_0 (the budget line is flatter), so the *substitution effect* encourages current consumption relative to future consumption. Since the income and substitution effects counterbalance one another with regard to current consumption, the amount of current saving might remain about the same. But when it comes to future consumption the income and substitution effects reinforce one another, so future consumption is definitely less.

CONCLUSION

Income taxes, compared with taxes on consumption, might or might not discourage saving but will reduce future consumption.

A more complete analysis would next trace out how the different tax systems might affect the market interest rate, which was assumed constant in the discussion above. Intuitively, since a consumption tax reduces current and future consumption more or less proportionately, it has no systematic effect on r_1. (The possible effect of an income tax upon interest rates is addressed in a question at the end of the chapter.)

EXAMPLE 15.1 SCHOLARSHIPS AND SAVINGS

Families often make big sacrifices to finance their children's college studies. To ease the burden, colleges offer various forms of financial aid. Such aid is usually "means-tested": the richer the family, the less the assistance provided. Although means testing is entirely reasonable, the effect is to penalize parental saving.

Using data from the 1986 Survey of Consumer Finances, Martin Feldstein[a] analyzed the "uniform methodology" employed until the late 1980s by the College Entrance Examination Board for adjusting financial aid on the basis of family assets and income. For parents of students receiving financial aid, in 1986 the formula reduced aid on a graduated schedule: the reduction was 22% of the first $7,300 of the family's "adjusted available income," rising in steps to a reduction of 47% for family income above $14,500. For a family with several college-bound children, the calculated aid reduction would be multiplied accordingly.

The more a family saves in precollege years, the greater will be its accumulated assets and the larger the income those assets generate. But higher family income means less financial aid. Consider a typical household with a head 45 years old, two precollege children, and annual income of $45,000. For such a family, Feldstein

---

[4] On the assumption that current consumption and future consumption are both normal superior goods.

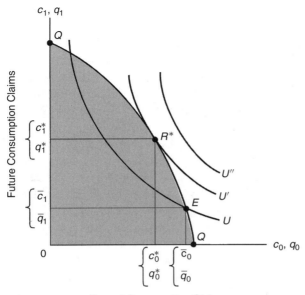

Figure 15.4. Robinson Crusoe Optimum Over Time

Robinson Crusoe has no intertemporal exchange (borrowing-lending) opportunities, but can engage in productive transformations between consumption this year and consumption next year. QQ is the Production-Possibility Curve through his endowment E. The Crusoe optimum is at R^*, where QQ is tangent to the highest attainable indifference curve. This is an autarky solution: the amounts produced (q_0^*, q_1^*) equal the amounts consumed (c_0^*, c_1^*).

estimated, the penalty on saving is so severe that the rational response would be for the family to reduce its saving by $23,124 (as of the date of the first child's entry to college). The reduction comes to about 50% of the amount of financial assets that the typical family would otherwise have accumulated. For the nation as a whole, the reduction amounted to about $66 billion!

COMMENT

The effect upon saving is so large because, whereas ordinary income taxes are payable whether or not the taxpayer is saving part of his or her income, means-tested financial aid penalizes *only* a family that sacrifices to provide for the future. Parents who consume all their current income, and save nothing for their children's college education, would escape the burden of this implicit tax.

[a] Martin Feldstein, "College Scholarship Rules and Private Saving," *American Economic Review*, v. 85 (June 1995).

15.3 PRODUCTION AND CONSUMPTION OVER TIME: SAVING AND INVESTMENT

In a pure exchange economy, the net total of savings must be zero: the aggregate savings of lenders must equal the aggregate "dis-savings" of borrowers. What happens when investment (productive) opportunities are available?

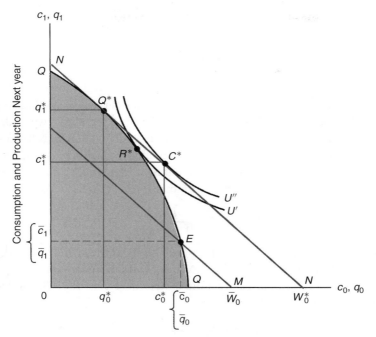

Figure 15.5. Intertemporal Production Optimum and Consumption Optimum, with Exchange

The individual here has intertemporal productive opportunities (the Production-Possibility Curve QQ) as well as exchange opportunities indicated by budget lines such as MM and NN of slope $-P_0/P_1 = -(1 + r)$. The production optimum Q^* involves investment in the amount $\overline{q}_0 - q_0^*$. The consumption optimum C^* indicates that the individual saves only $\overline{c}_0 - c_0^*$; the remainder of the investment is financed by borrowing in the market.

Figure 15.4 pictures an isolated Robinson Crusoe, who has *only* productive opportunities as indicated by the Production Possibility Curve QQ. (Note the similarity to Figure 14.8 of the previous chapter.) For Robinson, at any date t *corn consumed* (c_t) and *corn produced* (q_t) must be the same: he can consume only what he produces. His endowment E can therefore be written either as ($\overline{c}_0, \overline{c}_1$) or as ($\overline{q}_0, \overline{q}_1$). Robinson's optimum occurs at point $R^* = (c_0^*, c_1^*) = (q_0^*, q_1^*)$, where the Production-Possibility Curve is tangent to his highest attainable indifference curve.

Robinson's saving (corn not currently consumed) is the horizontal distance $\overline{c}_0 - c_1^*$. Since he cannot lend (there is no one to lend to), Robinson saves only to have seed corn for planting, that is, for productive investment. His scale of plantings (investment) exactly equals his sacrificed consumption of current corn (saving): $\overline{c}_0 - c_1^* = \overline{q}_0 - q_1^*$. (The same holds true for an isolated country. In the absence of foreign trade, a country's investment must come from its own saving.) Robinson's return on investment is the increment of future corn: $q_1^* - \overline{q}_0 = c_1^* - \overline{c}_1$.

Figure 15.5 depicts an individual, say Ida, with access to *both* productive opportunities and market opportunities. (Compare Figure 14.9 in the preceding chapter.) As before, the productive opportunities are represented by the Production Possibility Curve QQ. The market opportunities are shown by budget lines of slope $-P_0/P_1 \equiv -(1 + r)$

through attainable points on QQ. Each budget line is associated with a specific level of wealth:

$$W_0 \equiv q_0 + \frac{q_1}{1 + r_1} \qquad (15.4)$$

In Figure 15.5, for each budget line the level of wealth W_0 is the intercept along the horizontal axis. Two of these budget lines are of special interest. (1) MM through the endowment position E is like the budget line KL of Figure 15.1: it shows what Ida could achieve by lending or borrowing alone. The horizontal intercept of MM is the endowed wealth $\overline{W}_0$. (2) NN in Figure 15.5, the highest attainable budget line, is tangent to the Production-Possibility Curve QQ at point Q^*, that is, at Ida's *production optimum*. The horizontal intercept of NN is the maximum attainable level of wealth W_0^*.

$$W_0^* \equiv q_0^* + \frac{q_1^*}{1 + r_1} \qquad (15.5)$$

Having maximized wealth by choosing the production optimum, Ida can then engage in market exchange (borrow or lend) along NN so as to attain her *consumption optimum* at point C^*. (Note that C^* is on a higher indifference curve than R^*.) The budget-line equation corresponding to NN is:

$$c_0 + \frac{c_1}{1 + r_1} = W_0^{*5} \qquad (15.6)$$

In Figure 15.5 Ida *invests* (plants seed corn) in the amount indicated by the horizontal distance $\overline{q}_0 - q_0^*$. But her *saving* is only the horizontal distance $\overline{c}_0 - c_0^*$. She "finances" the remainder of her investment by borrowing some of the savings (consumption sacrifices) of other individuals – to be repaid out of her future investment yield $q_1^* - \overline{q}_1$.

From the picture in Figure 15.5 it would be possible to generate curves showing Ida's individual levels of saving s, investment i, lending ℓ, and borrowing b – all as functions of the rate of interest r_1. Omitting this step, Figure 15.6 moves directly to the market aggregate curves for S, I, L, and B representing the horizontal summations of the individual s, i, ℓ, and b curves.

The market equilibrium is shown in two ways: (1) The equilibrium interest rate balances S and I (the supply of saving equals the demand for investment). (2) The equilibrium interest rate balances L and B (the supply of lending equals the demand for borrowing). (Note the similarity to Figure 14.11 of the preceding chapter.) The difference between the equilibrium amount of saving and investment ($S^* = I^*$) as compared with the equilibrium amount of borrowing and lending ($L^* = B^*$) equals the investments that people "self-finance" through their own saving.

CONCLUSION

In a regime of pure exchange, a person can achieve a preferred intertemporal pattern of consumption only by borrowing or lending. At the equilibrium interest rate the overall market supply of lending equals the overall market demand for borrowing ($L^* = B^*$). But when intertemporal production (investing) is also possible, each individual chooses his or her optimal scale of investment and lending or borrowing. The

---

[5] The maximum attainable level of wealth W_0^* is *defined* in the identity (15.5), but in the conditional equation (15.6) appears as a *constraint* upon the possible consumption choices (c_0, c_1).

Figure 15.6. Intertemporal Equilibrium with Productive Investment

When productive investment takes place, the equilibrium interest rate r^* simultaneously balances (1) the aggregate supply of saving S with the aggregate demand for investment I and (2) the aggregate supply of lending L with the aggregate demand for borrowing B. The difference between the two magnitudes, at any interest rate r, is accounted for by the amount of investment self-financed out of investors' own savings.

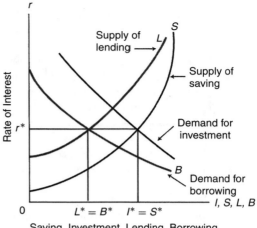

equilibrium interest rate balances the aggregate supply of saving with the aggregate demand for investment ($S^* = I^*$), and also equates the aggregate supply of lending with the aggregate demand for borrowing ($L^* = B^*$).

EXAMPLE 15.2 GROWTH VERSUS INVESTMENT: INTERNATIONAL COMPARISONS

Some nations save and invest more than others. One would expect nations to grow more rapidly the more they invest. The table suggests that this indeed occurs.

Growth, investment, and saving (1973–1984)

	Growth rate of of GDP (%)	Investment rate (%)	Saving rate (%)
Five highest growth rates			
Egypt	8.5	25	12
Yemen Arab Republic	8.1	21	−22
Cameroon	7.1	26	33
Syrian Arab Republic	7.0	24	12
Indonesia	6.8	21	20
Five lowest growth rates			
Zambia	0.4	14	15
El Salvador	−0.3	12	4
Ghana	−0.9	6	5
Zaire	−1.0	NA	NA
Uganda	−1.3	8	6

Source: Selected from The World Bank, *The World Development Report* (1986).

COMMENT

In interpreting these data, note how saving and investment differ. Heavy investment in a country can be taking place despite low saving if funds are flowing in from abroad. Yemen clearly falls into this category. It had a high investment rate along with a hugely negative saving rate! Conversely, a high saving rate by residents of a country may not be reflected in GDP growth if the savings are all invested abroad. Overall, however, there is bound to be some correlation between investment and savings, since it is generally easier and safer for people to invest at home rather than abroad. In this table, the countries with very low saving rates almost all suffered from great political disturbances. The countries with extraordinarily high investment rates were mainly beneficiaries of the oil boom, with investment funds coming in from external sources such as the international oil companies.

15.4   INVESTMENT DECISIONS AND PROJECT ANALYSIS

Apart from choosing how much to save or invest, decision-makers also need to select specific saving instruments and investment projects. Typically there will be many possible projects and instruments: big versus small, quick-yielding versus slow-yielding, risky versus safe. What is needed is an appropriate *criterion* for choosing among financial instruments and investment projects.

The Separation Theorem

A crucial implication of the previous analysis is:

> **THE SEPARATION THEOREM: A person's production optimum position Q^* is entirely independent of his or her personal preferences.**

In Figure 15.5, Ida's indifference curves did not matter for finding her production optimum. Although her intertemporal consumption optimum C^* involved her time-preferences, her Q^* depended only on the shape of the Production Possibility curve QQ and the slope of the market lines.

Important practical results follow if the Separation Theorem is applicable. Suppose owners of a firm were to delegate all production decisions to a manager. To faithfully carry out their wishes, the manager need know nothing about their time-preferences! All the owners have to care about is that the manager maximizes the firm's wealth, that is, achieves the production optimum Q^*. What if the time preferences of the firm's multiple owners diverge? Some owners may want to consume more in early years; others might be more willing to defer consumption. Either way, they can all agree that it's best to maximize everyone's wealth. So the Separation Theorem makes it possible for large numbers of owners to come together and form a corporation in which managers make production decisions on their behalf.

Strictly speaking, however, the Separation Theorem applies only if the markets for borrowing and lending are perfect and costless. Owing to *transaction costs* (as discussed in the preceding chapter), individuals and firms can typically borrow only at a higher interest rate than the rate at which they can lend. If so, the choice of Q^* on the Production Possibility curve would be influenced by time-preferences after all.

The Separation Theorem is therefore an ideal that never *perfectly* applies. But even if time-preferences do matter for production decisions, individuals sharing similar time-preferences can group together as owners of firms. This explains why utility stocks, which typically pay high current dividends, are usually owned by older people. In contrast, younger investors tend to prefer high-tech stocks paying little or no current dividends, but offering better growth prospects.

The Present-Value Rule

What is the appropriate *decision rule* for choosing among financial instruments or investment projects? Any project is characterized by a sequence of dated cash flows or payments $z_0, z_1, \ldots, z_T$ from the present up to some horizon T. Investment projects involve sacrifices earlier in time for benefits later on. They begin with an *outlay phase* (one or more initial periods where the z_t tend to be negative) followed by a *payoff phase* (periods with mainly positive z_t). For "disinvestment" projects, which pull income from the future toward the present, these phases would be reversed.

The fundamental criterion for selecting among projects is known as the *Present-Value Rule*. For the simplest case of two periods – date 0 (now) and date 1 (one year from now) – the Present Value V_0 of a project with dated cash flows z_0 and z_1 is defined as:

$$V_0 \equiv z_0 + \frac{z_1}{1 + r_1} \quad \text{Definition of Present Value, two periods} \quad (15.7)$$

There are different versions of the Present-Value Rule depending upon whether the projects considered are or are not independent of one another.

> **PRESENT-VALUE RULE #1 (Independent Projects):** Adopt any project with positive Present Value and reject any project with negative Present Value.

This follows from the fact that the Present Value V_0 of a project represents the *additional wealth* it generates for its owners, as can be seen by comparing equation (15.7) with the definition of wealth in equation (15.4). Any positive increment of wealth is desirable.

But what if two projects are interdependent, meaning that adopting one or them changes the payoffs of another? An extreme of negative interdependence occurs when projects are *mutually exclusive*. For example, a landowner may have to choose between putting a gas station or an office building on his lot. For this case:

> **PRESENT-VALUE RULE #2 (Mutually Exclusive Projects):** Adopt the project with largest Present Value V_0, provided V_0 is positive.

The general Present-Value Rule #3 allows for all forms of possible interdependence, positive or negative:

> **PRESENT-VALUE RULE #3:** Tabulate *all* the possible combinations of projects available, including doing nothing. Then choose the *set* of projects that maximizes overall Present Value.

Rule #3 has the same form as Rule #2, since the available projects can be grouped into mutually exclusive combinations. Suppose a firm has three possible projects, A, B, and C. Regardless of whether the individual projects are independent or not, they can be sorted into the eight mutually exclusive combinations A, B, C, AB, AC, BC, ABC, and no project at all. Whichever combination has highest V_0 is the firm's wealth-maximizing investment choice.

EXERCISE 15.5

(a) A project has anticipated cash flows $z_0 = -100$ and $z_1 = 125$. Is this an investment or a disinvestment project? (b) What is its Present Value V_0 when the interest rate r_1 is 10 %? At $r_1 = 20\%$?

ANSWER: (a) Since z_0 is negative and z_1 is positive, this is an *investment* project. It involves current sacrifice for future benefit. (b) If $r_1 = 10\%$, equation (15.7) shows that $V_0 = -100 + 125/(1+0.1) = 13.64$. If $r_1 = 20\%$, the Present Value is $V_0 = 4.167$.

Notice that Present Value V_0 falls as the discount rate r rises. This must hold for all two-date investment projects, as is evident from equation (15.7).

EXERCISE 15.6

The table here shows payment sequences for two projects M and N. The first two rows show the payments when either project is adopted separately, and the third row shows what happens when they are adopted in combination. (Owing to interdependence, the date-0 outlays and the date-1 payoffs shown for MN are *not* simple summations of the magnitudes for M and N.) If the interest rate were 20% and you could adopt only M or N, which (if any) should you choose? What if you could adopt both together?

Project	z_0	z_1
M	−100	125
N	−50	90
MN	−160	240

ANSWER: If only one of them can be adopted, M and N are mutually exclusive. At 20%, $V_0(M) = -100 + 125/1.2 = 4.17$ and $V_0(N) = -50 + 90/1.2 = 25$. Since N has the higher Present Value (and since this is positive), N should be adopted. If the combination MN is also an available option, the calculation becomes $V_0(MN) = -160 + 240/1.2 = 40$. So the combination is better than either project alone.

Generalizing equation (15.7) to any number of dates, the Present Value of a stream of payments from date 0 to a "horizon" date T can be expressed in terms either of the *long-term* interest rates or of the *short-term* interest rates that were defined in Table 15.1:

$$V_0 \equiv z_0 + \frac{z_1}{1+R_1} + \frac{z_2}{(1+R_2)^2} + \cdots + \frac{z_T}{(1+R_T)^T} \qquad (15.8)$$

$$V_0 \equiv z_0 + \frac{z_1}{1+r_1} + \frac{z_2}{(1+r_2)(1+r_1)} + \cdots + \frac{z_T}{(1+r_T)\cdots(1+r_2)(1+r_1)} \qquad (15.9)$$

For some purposes the first formulation is more convenient, for other purposes the second. The formulations are logically the same, since the long-term rate R_T is an average of the short-term rates $r_1, r_2, \ldots, r_T$ between now and date T.

If the current rate will maintain itself indefinitely into the future, the r_t all equal some common value r. Then equations (15.8) and (15.9) both reduce to:

$$V_0 \equiv z_0 + \frac{z_1}{1+r} + \frac{z_2}{(1+r)^2} + \cdots + \frac{z_T}{(1+r)^T} \qquad (15.10)$$

EXERCISE 15.7

(a) Suppose it costs $0.10 to plant a tree. Let the timber value of the tree (net of harvesting cost), if cut at any time t from the date of planting, be $g = \sqrt{t}$. A partial tabulation would be:

Year of cut (t):	1	4	9	16
Value of timber (g):	1	2	3	4

Considering only the possibilities tabulated (that is, do not interpolate within the table, or extend it beyond 16 years), what is the best time to cut the tree if the interest rate is constant over time at 5%? (b) Suppose that after a tree is harvested a new one can be planted in its place. Of the possibilities above, which period represents the best cutting cycle?

ANSWER: (a) Since the harvesting periods are mutually exclusive, Present-Value Rule #2 can be used.

Year of cut	Present value
1	$-0.10 + 1/1.05 = -0.01 + 0.95 = 0.85$
4	$-0.10 + 2/1.05^4 = -0.10 + 1.65 = 1.55$
9	$-0.10 + 3/1.05^9 = -0.10 + 1.93 = 1.83$
16	$-0.10 + 4/1.05^{16} = -0.10 + 1.83 = 1.73$

Evidently, it's best to cut after 9 years.
(b) For the 1-year cycle, the Present Value equation is:

$$V_0 = -0.1 + \frac{1-0.1}{1+r} + \frac{1-0.1}{(1+r)^2} + \cdots$$

where the annual net return of $1 - $0.1 = 0.90 repeats itself forever. The Present Value works out to $V_0 = 17.90. For the 4-year cycle:

$$V_0 \equiv -0.1 + \frac{2-0.1}{(1+r)^4} + \frac{2-0.1}{(1+r)^8} + \cdots$$

Here the net return is $1.90, repeating itself every 4 years forever. The Present Value is $V_0 = 8.54. By analogous calculations it can be shown that for the 9-year cycle $V_0 = 5.16 and that for the 16-year cycle $V_0 = 3.20. Thus, allowing for the possibility of replanting shortens the optimal cycling time from $t = 4$ to $t = 1$. The essential reason is that the tree's growth rate, in value terms, is greatest in earlier years and then tapers off.

For all investment or saving projects (that is, for projects that have mainly negative cash flows in earlier years and positive cash flows in later years), the Present Value is greater at lower rates of interest. This is easily understandable, since the interest rate is a measure of how much the future is discounted. Low interest rates mean that the positive cash flows of future years are discounted less; that is, they carry more weight in the overall calculation, thus enlarging Present Value. (Conversely, disinvestment projects are more attractive the higher the rate of interest.)

EXAMPLE 15.3 IS SOCIAL SECURITY A GOOD DEAL?

The U.S. Social Security system provides old-age pensions to millions of Americans. In contrast with private pension contracts, participation in Social Security is compulsory. Partly for this reason, there has been continuing debate over almost every aspect of the program.

One question has been whether, viewed as a saving program, Social Security is a "good deal" for participants. That is, viewed as an individual's saving project, is its Present Value positive? The question is difficult to answer, owing to the many changes that have been made and will surely continue to be made as to required contributions (what percentage of wages has to be paid in Social Security taxes), benefit levels (what pension amounts will be received), and eligibility rules (for example, at what age can a person retire and become a beneficiary).

Looking at the past, it is possible to examine the results for earlier participants. After its initiation in 1935 early enrollees in Social Security did very well. Early participants who had made contributions even for only a very few years received retirement benefits that were calculated much as if they had been under Social Security and contributing to the program all their working lives! (This factor added enormously to the initial political acceptability of the program.) Another initially favorable feature was the large ratio of working contributors to retirees. But these unusually advantageous circumstances were only temporary. By now almost all beneficiaries have been paying into the program all their working lives, as will be the case for new entrants from now on. And the aging of the U.S. population has reduced the fraction of contributors relative to beneficiaries.

Looking toward the future, whether Social Security is a good deal in terms of Present Value depends upon a host of more or less arguable assumptions about what will happen in future years. Although no single evaluation can be expected to resolve debate, a study by Liqun Lee and Andrew J. Rettenmeier offered several interesting results.[a]

The authors estimated future levels of taxes and benefits and estimated participants' projected earnings, retirement choices, and longevity. Some illustrative results are shown in the table, for Present Values calculated at a relatively low discount rate of 4%. (As the text indicates, a low discount rate increases the indicated Present Values of investment projects or saving programs.)

For single men the Present Values shown in the table are all negative! The results for single women, and for married men with nonworking wives, are only slightly more favorable: for these groups the Present Values are positive only for workers in the earliest birth years and with the lowest education levels.

The *relatively* more favorable results for those of earlier birth years reflects the initially low Social Security taxes. Rising longevity and the increasingly unfavorable ratio of pensioners to contributors have since caused tax rates to rise sharply. "Progressive" elements have been incorporated from the beginning, to assure a decent minimum standard of benefit even for low-earning workers. So low-income contributors have always done relatively better than high-income contributors. Nevertheless, the table indicates negative Present Values for all the groups tabulated.

COMMENT

Although these results may be questioned in detail, it appears that for most partici-pants Social Security is financially a bad deal. True, Social Security was not intended to be an actuarially sound pension program but has always involved a redistributive element. But even for the least well off participants, the Present Value of Social Se-curity as a savings program is at best only barely positive. Considerations of this kind have motivated proposals for reforms of Social Security that would bring it closer to an actuarially based pension program, while granting participants better control over the placement of their individual contributions.

Projected present values of social security investments – single men

Birth year	High School graduates	College graduates	Graduate school
1940	$-27,000	$-33,000	$-33,000
1950	-32,000	-45,000	-49,000
1960	-34,000	-53,000	-59,000
1970	-33,000	-58,000	-75,000
1980	-32,000	-63,000	-93,000

Source: Estimated visually from Lee and Rettenmeier, Figure 2.

[a] Liqun Lee and Andrew J. Rettenmeier, "Social Security and Education," National Center for Policy Analysis, Policy Report No. 240 (January 2001).

Women planning on an academic career suffer from several disadvantages. One of them is the likelihood of a career interruption due to family obligations, especially child-bearing and child-rearing. Such an interruption would make a woman's income payments stream in equation (15.10) likely to have fewer positive entries than a man's, on average and other things equal. The Present Value of her academic career being lower, a woman would rationally be less inclined to make the necessary investment in training (to build up her human capital) for a career.

A subtler factor strengthens this effect. Human capital tends to "decay" during career interruptions, since training may be forgotten or made obsolete by newer developments.

EXAMPLE 15.4 INTERRUPTED CAREERS AND THE DISCOUNTED VALUE OF KNOWLEDGE

John M. McDowell studied how the decay of knowledge in different fields influ-enced the training and specialization of male and female academics.[a] The decay rate of knowledge was estimated by the declining frequency of article citations by later authors. The annual average decay rate was 18.30% for leading journals in physics and 14.50% in chemistry, but only 3.85% for leading journals in history and 2.67% in English. (This means, for example, that a physics article cited 100 times in year t would on average be cited only $100 - 18.3 = 81.7$ times in year $t + 1$. For history, an article cited 100 times in year t would on average be cited only a little less in the next year: $100 - 3.85 = 96.15$ times.) These decay rates were then used to estimate, via a Present-Value calculation like equation (15.10), the "discounted present value of knowledge" in the various fields.

Present value of knowledge and costs of interrupted careers

	Discounted value (at age 35)	Loss of human capital due to career interruption (3-year)
Physics	4.53	42.30%
Chemistry	5.08	35.27%
History	8.03	10.91%
English	8.63	7.70%

Source: McDowell, Table 2, p. 757.

The high decay rates in physics and chemistry lead to correspondingly lower figures for the Present Values of knowledge in those fields. And so the decay rates also imply greater losses in those fields from career interruptions. Loss of a midcareer year is more costly, in terms of human capital, for a researcher in physics or chemistry than for a researcher in English or history.

Since women are far more likely than men to experience career interruptions, women undertaking academic careers would (other things equal) rationally tend to avoid physics and chemistry in favor of history and English, fields in which knowledge "decays" at a slower rate. In fact, women do tend to specialize more in these latter areas. On the other hand, with falling birth rates the handicap of family responsibilities for women has been declining. So, as expected, in recent years the proportion of women in fields such as physics and chemistry has been increasing.

[a] John M. McDowell, "Obsolescence of Knowledge and Career Publication Profiles," *American Economic Review*, v. 72 (September 1982).

Certain special assumptions simplify equation (15.10). Suppose the benefits of some asset or project begin at date 1 and continue on to infinity (the "economic horizon" is $T = \infty$), and that these positive future receipts $z_1, z_2, \ldots$ are all equal to some common z. Then, as the footnote shows, the Present Value of these benefits, denoted B_0, is given by:[6]

$$B_0 \equiv \frac{z}{r} \tag{15.11}$$

For example, if the interest rate is $r = 10\%$, the Present Value of $10 per year forever is $B_0 = \$10.00/0.10 = \$100$. Put another way, $100 in the bank at 10% interest would yield $z = \$10$ per year forever.

[6] *Mathematical Footnote:* Under the special assumptions above, equation (15.10) can be written:

$$B_0 = z \left| \frac{1}{1+r} + \frac{1}{(1+r)^2} + \cdots \right|$$

Let $1/(1+r)$ be denoted k. Then:

$$B_0 = z(1 + k + k^2 + \cdots) - z$$

Using the formula for the sum of an infinite series, the expression within parentheses equals $1/(1-k)$. And from the definition of k, simple algebra shows that $1 = k + r/(1+r)$. Making the indicated substitutions:

$$B_0 = z \left| \frac{1+r}{r} \right| - z = \frac{z}{r}$$

As for the current-period element z_0, think of it as the asset's acquisition cost c_0 or price P. The asset's overall Present Value is evidently the amount by which the Present Value of the *benefits alone*, denoted B_0, exceeds the acquisition cost:

$$V_0 \equiv B_0 - P \equiv \frac{z}{r} - c_0 \qquad (15.11')$$

In equilibrium the acquisition cost or market price of any asset must equal the present value of the benefits it generates. Thus:

$$P = \frac{z}{r} \quad \text{or} \quad r = \frac{z}{P} \, ^7 \qquad (15.11'')$$

This justifies the discussion in Chapter 13 that expressed the interest rate as the ratio between the hire-price h_A of a resource and the value or price P_A of the resource itself: $r = h_A / P_A$. Since h_A is the annual amount received if the asset is rented out, and the asset price P_A corresponds to P here, the hire-price h_A corresponds to the benefit z in equation (15.11'').

The Rate of Return (ROR) Rule

Another decision rule for evaluating projects makes use of the Rate of Return (ROR), sometimes called the Internal Rate of Return. The Present Value and Rate of Return rules often agree, but not always.

The Present-Value Rule, in its most general form, calls for adopting the overall set of investment (or disinvestment) projects that maximizes V_0. The underlying justification is that, since V_0 is an increment to owners' wealth, the best overall set of projects is the one that maximizes this increment. In the special case of independent projects (Present-Value Rule #1), each and every project with positive Present Value ($V_0 > 0$) should be adopted.

The Rate of Return for any project is defined by setting up an equation in Present Value form, but with the discount rate treated as an unknown. The discount rate that makes this Present Value equal to zero is the Rate of Return ROR, here symbolized as ρ. Thus, adapting equation (15.10):

$$0 \equiv z_0 + \frac{z_1}{1+\rho} + \frac{z_2}{(1+\rho)^2} + \cdots + \frac{z_T}{(1+\rho)^T} \quad \text{Definition of } \rho \qquad (15.12)$$

The associated *rule*, in the simplest case of independent projects, is to adopt any project whose ROR exceeds the market rate of interest: That is, adopt if $\rho > r$. The underlying thought is that the ROR represents a kind of "growth rate" of value over time. If funds invested in a project grow in value more rapidly than compounding at the market interest rate, it makes sense to adopt the project.

For independent projects in the two-period (date 0 and date 1) case, the Present-Value Rule and the *ROR* Rule agree: $V_0 > 0$ implies $\rho > r$.[8] And this is also true for the special case discussed above, where a project has a date-0 acquisition cost c_0 and yields annual benefits z forever.[9]

---

[7] In this equation an equals sign ($=$) rather than an identity sign ($\equiv$) appears. The expression here is not an identity, but a condition of equilibrium.

[8] *Mathematical Footnote*: For the two-date case, by assumption: $z_0 + \frac{z_1}{1+r} > 0$. And by definition, $z_0 + \frac{z_1}{1+\rho} \equiv 0$. So $\rho > r$.

[9] *Mathematical Footnote*: For the special case just described, $c_0 + \frac{z}{r} > 0$ and $c_0 + \frac{z}{\rho} > 0$. Once again, ρ must be greater than r.

The equivalence between these Present Value and Rate of Return rules holds for *any* sequence of payments $z_0, z_1, \ldots, z_T$ meeting the strict definition of an investment project. To wit, a single outlay phase (an initial sequence of negative or zero elements beginning with z_0) is followed by a single payoff phase (a sequence of positive or zero elements); in other words, the signs reverse only once. For example, the payments streams $(z_0, z_1, z_2) = (-5, 1, 5)$ or $(-1, -5, 8)$ meet this condition, whereas the stream $(z_0, z_1, z_2) = (-1, 5, -2)$ does not.[10]

CONCLUSION

For independent projects, if the payments stream has only a single reversal of signs (an investment phase followed by a payoff phase), then the Present-Value Rule ("Adopt if $V_0 > 0$") is equivalent to the Rate of Return Rule ("Adopt if $\rho > r$").

Discrepancies between the two rules arise in two classes of cases: (1) independent projects that violate the single-reversal condition, and (2) interdependent projects of all types.

(1) Consider the project defined by the twice-reversing payments stream $(z_0, z_1, z_2) = (-1, 5, -6)$. Calculating the Rate of Return ρ leads to *two* solutions: $\rho = 100\%$ and $\rho = 200\%$.[11] Or consider the payments stream $(z_0, z_1, z_2) = (-1, 3, -2.5)$. Here the algebraic formula for ρ yields *no* solution at all in real numbers. How then can ρ be compared with r?[12]

The difficulty is immediately explained in terms of the Present Value concept. Figure 15.7 shows, for a number of possible payment sequences (projects), how V_0 changes as the discount rate varies from $r = -100\%$ upward. Project *I*, whose payments sequence is $(-1, 0, 4)$, is an investment project in the strict sense, since its V_0 declines throughout as r rises. As follows from the definition of the Rate of Return concept, its ρ is represented by the point where the $V_0(I)$ curve cuts the horizontal axis. Project II, with sequence $(-1, 5, -6)$, has positive V_0 (and therefore warrants adopting) for all r *between* 100% and 200%; otherwise the Present Value is negative and the project should be rejected. The two algebraic solutions for ρ correspond to the two intersections of $V_0(II)$ with the horizontal axis. Last, Project III, with sequence $(-1, 3, -2.5)$, has negative V_0 for *all* r. In accordance with the Present Value Rule, it should never be adopted.[13]

---

[10] *Mathematical Footnote*: In the simplest situation, a *single* negative z_0 would be followed by a series of positive values up to z_T. Using the same method as in the preceding footnote, by assumption:

$$z_0 + \frac{z_1}{1+r} + \frac{z_2}{(1+r)^2} + \cdots + \frac{z_T}{(1+r)^T} > 0$$

That is, Present Value V_0 is positive. And by definition:

$$z_0 + \frac{z_1}{1+\rho} + \frac{z_2}{(1+\rho)^2} + \cdots + \frac{z_T}{(1+\rho)^T} = 0$$

Comparing these two equations shows that $\rho > r$.

(If the outlay phase extends for several dates before the payoff phase begins, the proof is somewhat more difficult and will not be provided here.)

[11] *Mathematical Footnote*: $0 = -z_0 + \frac{z_1}{1+\rho} + \frac{z_2}{(1+\rho)^2}$ is a quadratic equation. Such an equation may have two, one, or zero solutions among the real numbers.

[12] These two examples involve something stronger than reversal of signs in the benefit stream: in each case the *summed magnitude of the negative elements* exceeds the sum of the positive elements. It has been proved mathematically that only under this condition will the Rate of Return calculation lack a unique result. Such situations, however, may be realistic. A mining project might involve an initial outlay (z_0 is negative), followed by one or more years of positive z_1, z_2, z_3, etc. But once the mine is exhausted, very large costs (negative z_T) may be incurred closing it down at the terminal date T.

[13] This statement is true for interest rates r that are constant over time. The project $(-1, 3, -2.5)$ can have positive V_0 if r_1 and r_2 differ. Using equation (15.9), it may be verified that $V_0 > 0$ when $r_1 = 100\%$ and $r_2 = 200\%$.

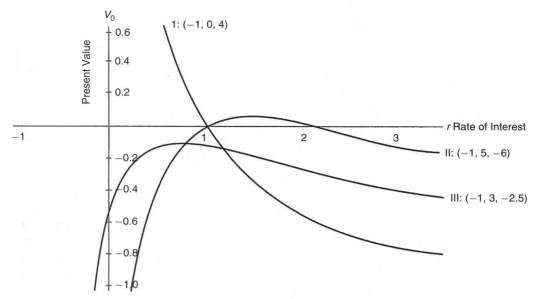

Figure 15.7. Present Values and Rates of Return for Three Projects

As the payments for project I show only a single alternation (from negative to positive), it is a simple investment project. Its Present Value is a declining function of the interest rate r. Projects II and III each involve more than sign alternation; their Present Values first rise and then fall as r increases. Project I has a unique Rate of Return $\rho = 100\%$ at the intersection of its V_0 curve with the horizontal axis. Project II has two such intersections, $\rho = 100\%$ and 200%; project III has none. Thus, evaluating projects by a comparison of ρ with r can be ambiguous or even impossible.

So, for independent projects, the Present Value Rule is clearly the more fundamental. Among other things, it tells us when the alternative ROR rule is or is not valid.

(2) An even more serious problem with the Rate of Return investment criterion arises in considering *interdependent* projects. In the extreme case of mutually exclusive projects, it is not even clear what the Rate of Return Rule would be. Should the investor adopt that single one of the set of mutually exclusive projects with the *highest* ρ? That could be a serious mistake. The project with highest ρ may be of such small scale as to provide little wealth gain; a larger-scale project with a lower ρ might generate a much greater wealth increment.

EXERCISE 15.8

(a) For the projects tabulated in Exercise 15.6, calculate the Rates of Return for M, N, and MN.
(b) If M and N are mutually exclusive options, which has higher ρ? Is that project the same as the one with higher Present Value V_0? (c) If MN is also available as a third mutually exclusive option, which of the three possibilities M, N, and MN has the highest ρ? Is that the same as the one with highest Present Value V_0?

ANSWER: (a) Substituting the tabulated payoffs for M, equation (15.12) becomes $0 \equiv -100 + \frac{125}{1+\rho}$. The solution is $\rho(M) = 25\%$. Similar computations lead to the results $\rho(N) = 80\%$, $\rho(MN) = 50\%$. (b) The value of ρ is higher for M than for N. And N also was shown in Exercise 15.6 to have higher Present Value. So here there is no

> disagreement. (c) When MN is also considered, in terms of ρ, project N remains the highest of the three. But N is not the best choice. Exercise 15.6 showed that MN has the highest Present Value V_0.

So the Rate of Return Rule ("Adopt if $\rho > r$") is an unreliable guide for investment decision. That does not mean the Rate of Return is mathematically incorrect as a *concept*, only that it must be used with caution in choosing among investment projects.

Nevertheless, both in business practice and in economic analysis Rates of Return are calculated and used for investment choices. Why? Sometimes doing so is simply a mistake. But there are a fluctuating number of other considerations.

Perhaps the most important concerns the division of labor. A company might find it convenient to employ *project specialists* who would filter through the investment options by calculating the Rate of Return associated with each. These project appraisers would not need to know the discount rate r, a fluctuating number that might better be estimated by *finance specialists* acquainted with the terms on which the company can obtain project funding. Top management can make the decision in the light of the information on ρ and r provided by the two sets of subordinates. Despite some risk of error, if most projects are independent and if their payoffs involve no serious sign reversals, the administrative convenience of such a division of labor may warrant using the Rate of Return Rule.

In economic analysis as well, once again it is often convenient to have a criterion like ρ that describes investment options without necessarily having to know the interest rate that applies for calculating Present Value. An economist might use ρ, for example, to compare the gains from acquiring a college education over different periods of time or among different countries – without attempting to take account of possible historical or geographical differences in interest rates. Still, Rate of Return comparisons alone would not allow us to say that college education was a better investment in 1980 than in 1990, or a better investment in country X than in country Y.

EXAMPLE 15.5 RATE OF RETURN TO EDUCATION – INTERNATIONAL COMPARISONS

In 2002 George Psacharopoulos and Harry Anthony Patrinos reported on a World Bank survey of rates of return on educational investments in many countries.[a] The "social" rates of return reported in the table here are generally lower than the "private" rates of return that would enter into individuals' calculations. The reason is that government subsidies to education tend to raise its perceived *private* profitability, but since these subsidies divert resources from elsewhere in the economy they are not included in the *social* calculation.

Social rates of return to education

Region	Primary	Secondary	Higher
Asia (non-OECD)	16.2	11.1	11.0
Latin America/Caribbean	17.4	12.9	12.3
OECD	8.5	9.4	8.5
Sub-Saharan Africa	25.4	18.4	11.3
World	18.9	13.1	10.8

Source: Selected from Psacharopoulos and Patrinos, Table 1.

The data refer to the most recent years available, mainly from 1994 on. The OECD countries are 30 generally richer nations including the United States, Canada, Japan, Australia, South Korea, and many European countries. Notice that the social rates of return are highest in the less developed countries, especially for primary education. The Rate of Return also tends to decline moving from primary to more advanced levels of education, which accords with the principle of diminishing returns.

COMMENT

Investment in education probably meets the single-alternation condition justifying use of the Rate of Return rule. That is, costs do tend to be followed by benefits without further sign reversals. On the other hand, ROR comparisons between (say) OECD and Latin America are highly dubious, since (as explained in the text) the same level of education might involve rather different *scales* of investment. So, although it may be wise policy in terms of worldwide well-being to transfer educational resources from OECD nations to Latin America (for example), that really cannot be demonstrated by a Rate of Return comparison.

[a] George Psacharopoulos and Harry Anthony Patrinos, "Returns to Investment in Education: A Further Update," World Bank Policy Research Working Paper 2881 (September 2002).

15.5 REAL INTEREST AND MONETARY INTEREST: ALLOWING FOR INFLATION

This chapter has so far dealt only with the *real* rate of interest. Microeconomics usually looks behind the "veil of money" to think in terms of real goods, in this case present corn versus future corn.

But in actual markets, people almost always deal in terms of *monetary* rates of interest. What is the relation between the real and monetary rates? Suppose a bank pays 8% interest. That means that if you deposit $100 you can withdraw $108 at the end of the year. But, if the cost of living rises, the $108 after a year will buy you less than $108 at the beginning of the year. Perhaps the end-of-year $108 will buy only as much as $103 would have bought at the beginning of the year. If so, although 8% is the *monetary* rate of interest, the *real* rate of interest is only about 3%.

The real rate of interest is the extra amount of future corn that must be offered in the market in exchange for a unit of current corn. Rewriting equation (15.1), the real interest rate between date 0 and date 1 is again:

$$1 + r_1 \equiv -\frac{\Delta c_1}{\Delta c_0} \tag{15.13}$$

Whereas the real rate of interest r_1 is the *premium on current corn relative to future corn*, the monetary interest rate r_1' is the *premium on current money over future money*. Thus r_1' is the extra amount of future money that must be offered in exchange for current money:

$$1 + r_1' \equiv -\frac{\Delta m_1}{\Delta m_0} \tag{15.14}$$

The relationship between r_1 and r'_1 involves the *price level*, the amount of money required at any date to buy real goods. There will be a current and a future price level, defined as:

$$P_0^m \equiv -\frac{\Delta m_0}{\Delta c_0} \quad \text{and} \quad P_1^m \equiv -\frac{\Delta m_1}{\Delta c_1} \tag{15.15}$$

Consider the identity:

$$\frac{\Delta m_1}{\Delta m_0} \equiv \frac{\Delta m_1}{\Delta c_1} \frac{\Delta c_1}{\Delta c_0} \frac{\Delta c_0}{\Delta m_0} \tag{15.16}$$

Substituting from the preceding equations:

$$1 + r'_1 \equiv \frac{P_1^m}{P_0^m}(1 + r_1)$$

Finally, define a_1, *the anticipated rate of price inflation* between date 0 and date 1, as:

$$1 + a_1 \equiv \frac{P_1^m}{P_0^m} \tag{15.17}$$

It follows immediately that:

$$1 + r'_1 \equiv (1 + a_1)(1 + r_1)$$

Or, simplifying:

$$r'_1 = r_1 + a_1 + a_1 r_1 \tag{15.18}$$

So, between dates 0 and 1, the monetary rate of interest equals the real rate of interest plus the anticipated rate of price inflation, plus their cross-product. When r_1 and a_1 remain in their usual ranges in the low percentage points, the cross-product term can, to a good approximation, be ignored. The shorter the period of compounding, the better the approximation. For continuously compounded interest the cross-product drops out entirely, so that:[14]

$$r'_1 = r_1 + a_1 \tag{15.19}$$

This equation is known as "the Fisher hypothesis."[15] An obvious implication is that when people expect inflation to be high, the money interest rate r'_1 will be high.

> **PROPOSITION:** To a good approximation, the money rate of interest equals the real rate of interest plus the anticipated rate of price inflation.

[14] *Mathematical Footnote*: If i is an annually compounded interest rate, a unit investment at date 0 will grow to $1 + i$ units at the end of one year. With quarterly compounding, the end-of-year terminal value will be $(1 + i/4)^4$. Generalizing, for any compounding frequency f per year, terminal value will be $(1 + i/f)^f$. Define $h \equiv f/i$, so that this becomes $[(1 + 1/h)^h]^i$. For continuous compounding, we let f approach infinity, which means that h also approaches infinity. But, as $h \to \infty$, the expression within brackets becomes e, the base of the natural logarithms. So at the end of a year, with continuous compounding the terminal value becomes e^i. In terms of continuously compounded rates for the monetary rate of interest r'_1, the real rate of interest r_1, and the anticipated rate of inflation a_1:

$$e^{r'_1} \equiv e^{r_1} e^{a_1}$$

Taking logarithms, it follows that $r'_1 = r_1 + a_1$.

[15] After the American economist Irving Fisher (1867–1947). Indeed, the entire analysis of intertemporal choice in this chapter derives from Fisher's classic formulation in *The Theory of Interest* (Macmillan, 1930).

EXAMPLE 15.6 REAL AND MONETARY RATES OF INTEREST IN THE UNITED KINGDOM

The British Treasury sells ordinary bonds paying fixed *monetary* rates of interest (r'). Also sold are inflation-adjusted bonds that offer, in effect, fixed *real* rates of interest (r).

Using the difference between the stated interest rates on the two types of bond as a measure of anticipated inflation (a) at that date, G. Thomas Woodward[a] examined 14 different bond maturities from 1982 to 2024. For each maturity, he used data from April 1982 to August 1990 in order to statistically estimate equations in the form

$$r' = H + Ka$$

If the Fisher hypothesis (equation 15.19) is valid, H should correspond to the *real* rate of interest over the period and K should equal 1. For technical statistical reasons, however, it was difficult to estimate H. So the only issue was how close the estimated K was to 1.

Generally, for the 14 different maturities the estimates of K were fairly close to 1. However, except for the near maturities, they tended to be on the high side – in the neighborhood of 1.1 or 1.2. The author considered whether this divergence might be due to income taxes. (If taxes must be paid on interest earnings, the effective difference between r' and r will be less than appears from the crude data.) After adjustment for taxes, most of the indicated K values were indeed close to *1*, except that some of the near maturities fell a bit below. As a possible explanation, monetary theory indicates that very short-maturity instruments substitute for money, and therefore are held in part for "liquidity" rather than for pure investment purposes. Overall, the author concluded, the Fisher hypothesis is well supported by the British evidence.

---

[a] G. Thomas Woodward, "Evidence of the Fisher Effect from UK Indexed Bonds," *Review of Economics and Statistics*, v. 74 (May 1992).

The analysis in this section has implications for ongoing debates in macroeconomics. According to one view, expansion of the money supply tends to *reduce* monetary interest rates. If the government unexpectedly pays some of its bills with newly printed money, people find themselves holding unexpectedly large current cash balances. Provided they do not anticipate having correspondingly larger future cash balances, they should be willing to trade larger amounts of current money for claims on future money. A higher $\Delta m_0 / \Delta m_1$, or equivalently a lower $\Delta m_1 / \Delta m_0$ (in absolute value, of course), means that the monetary interest rate r_1' in equation (15.15) must fall.

The opposed view is that expansion of the money supply tends to *raise* the monetary rate of interest. An increase in current money may lead people to believe that the government will make future money balances larger still. Given general anticipations of higher $\Delta m_1 / \Delta m_0$, the monetary interest rate r_1' will rise. In short, an expansion of the money supply lowers the monetary rate r_1' if it is believed to be a unique event, but continuing monetary expansion can generate inflationary expectations that raise r_1'.

It is important to appreciate that high monetary rates of interest do not necessarily imply high *real* yields to investors. In fact, taking inflation and taxes into account, the experience of investors over the past half-century has been unimpressive, as is indicated in Example 15.7 below.

15.6   THE MULTIPLICITY OF INTEREST RATES

Many different interest rates coexist in the market at any moment of time. One important distinction, between real and monetary rates, has just been discussed and explained. Varying interest rates are observed, however, even *within* each of these categories. Example 15.7 reveals great divergences in the historical yields of different types of financial instruments, among them Treasury bills, long-term bonds, and common stocks. Or consider dealings with your bank. A savings account might pay around 4% a year. But if you want to borrow, the same bank may demand a rate of 7% on a long-term mortgage, 12% on a commercial loan, or 15% to finance a consumer purchase.

In Chapter 11, Section 11.1 contrasted a job offer yielding risky income with one offering sure income. Risk was associated with income variability, that is, with different amounts of income received in different possible states of the world. The analysis showed that, owing to risk aversion, a given amount of sure income would be preferred to a prospect of risky income yielding the same amount on average (as a mathematical expectation).

Extending the Chapter 11 analysis, suppose there are possible states or events $s = 1, 2, \ldots, S$ that might affect the net benefit at date 1, each with associated probability π_s. (In accordance with the laws of probability, the π_s must sum to 1.) Denote the date-1 benefit in each possible state as z_{1s}. Then the mathematical expectation $\hat{z}_1$ is:

$$\hat{z}_1 \equiv \pi z_{11} + \pi_1 z_{12} + \cdots + \pi_s z_{1s} \tag{15.20}$$

For assessing variability a convenient measure is the *standard deviation σ*:

$$\sigma(z_1) \equiv [\pi_1(z_{11} - \hat{z}_1)^2 + \pi_2(z_{12} - \hat{z}_1)^2 + \cdots + \pi_s(z_{1s} - \hat{z}_1)^2]^{1/2} \tag{15.21}$$

Holding the standard deviation constant, a higher expectation $\hat{z}_1$ will always be desired. And, given risk aversion, for any level of expectation people will generally prefer a lower standard deviation $\sigma(z_1)$.

Does the market reflect preference for or aversion to variability risk? The empirical evidence is that risk aversion dominates in financial markets. Thus, as Example 15.7 shows, over the period 1926–2002 investors were willing to hold U.S. Treasury bills (low variability risk) even though they yielded a real return of only 0.8% a year, whereas to hold common stocks of small companies (high variability risk) they required a real yield of 13.5%.

EXAMPLE 15.7 NOMINAL AND REAL YIELDS, 1926–2002

Roger G. Ibbotson and associates examined the average annual long-term returns from various financial instruments between 1926 and 2002.[a] In the table the first column shows the arithmetic mean of the compounded annual *monetary* (nominal) returns received by holders of various types of securities over the 76-year period. The second column shows the inflation-adjusted or *real* average annual returns. The third column shows the standard deviation σ of the real returns, a statistical measure of risk. As can be seen, higher average returns are associated with greater riskiness.

Thus, government issues paid low real returns, whereas stocks of (relatively risky) small companies on average paid high rates of return.

Nominal and real rate yields per annum, 1926–2002

	Average nominal yield	Average real yield	Standard deviation of real yield
U.S. Treasury bills	3.8	0.8	4.0
Long-term government bonds	5.8	2.9	10.6
Long-term corporate bonds	6.2	3.2	9.9
Large company stocks	12.2	9.0	20.6
Small company stocks	16.9	13.5	32.6

Source: Adapted from Ibbotson Associates, Tables 6-7 and 6-8.

COMMENT

Allowing for income taxes, and in particular the interaction between taxes and inflation, makes the historical record for investors look much worse. Taxes and inflation interact to the disadvantage of investors because income taxes are levied upon *nominal* rather than real returns. Suppose someone buys a common stock for $100, receives $3 in dividends, and sells the stock for $110 at the end of the year. The nominal before-tax return is 13%. But suppose the rate of inflation is 10% and the person's marginal tax rate is 25%. He or she will pay $0.75 in tax on the dividends, and $2.50 on the capital gain, leaving $113.00 − $3.25 = $109.75 at the end of the year. But with 10% inflation, the purchasing power of this $109.75 is only $109.75/1.10 = $99.77, so the real yield has been negative. In fact, when inflation and taxes are both taken into account, U.S. investors have on average incurred negative real yields over much of the past half-century! One should not be surprised, therefore, that many observers find the fraction of income devoted to saving in the United States to be disturbingly low.

[a] Ibbotson Associates, *Stocks, Bonds, Bills and Inflation: SBBI 2003 Yearbook.*

In view of the evidence for risk aversion in financial markets, how is it that *gambling* – deliberately seeking risk – remains popular? Without necessarily providing a full answer, the following points should be noted: (1) Apart from "pathological" cases, people generally gamble in ways that put in jeopardy only a small fraction of their wealth, for example, by placing only small lottery bets. Such gambling can be regarded as a kind of consumption good, buying a thrill at low cost. The financial markets, in contrast, reflect the fact that investors avoid risk in making big decisions about their overall asset portfolios. (2) Even a risk-averse person will accept some gambles, provided the subjective expectation of return is sufficiently high. For a horse-racing expert, betting at the track may yield a high expectation of return.[16]

As a possibly related point, the next Example shows that investments in works of art – though quite risky – have *not* yielded investors high rates of return.

---

[16] And someone who receives a revelation from on high, as to which horse will win, may think he's onto a sure thing, not a gamble at all!

EXAMPLE 15.8 ART APPRECIATION

Works of art are, among other things, ways of holding savings. Since prices may be much higher or lower when the time comes to sell, investing in art is subject to variability risk. James E. Pesando examined the variability risk and the rate of return on investment in modern prints, using 1977–1992 data for repeat sales of the same prints at auction.[a] There were 27,961 repeat sales for the 28 artists covered. The table here shows that the average 1.51% real return on prints was lower than the return on 180-day Treasury bills – despite the fact that (as measured by the standard deviation of return) investing in prints is much riskier.

Real returns per year, 1977–1992

	Mean (%)	Standard deviation (%)
Prints	1.51	19.94
Stocks	8.14	22.47
U.S. government bonds	2.54	21.83
180-day Treasury bills	2.23	3.43

Source: Pesando, Table 2, p. 1080.

COMMENT

The probable explanation is that buyers obtain nonpecuniary benefits from owning works of art, in particular the pleasure of viewing and displaying their art collections. So works of art are more than mere financial instruments, and therefore command a lower financial return.

[a] James E. Pesando, "Art as an Investment: The Market for Modern Prints," *American Economic Review*, v. 83 (December 1993).

In contrast with Example 15.7, the Example here indicates that in this period U.S. government bonds (but not 180-day Treasury bills) had relatively high variability risk. The reported standard deviation for these bonds exceeds the σ for prints and even approaches the σ for common stocks. The main reason is that, owing mainly to changing anticipations of inflation, monetary interest rates fluctuated considerably during the period 1977–1992. As seen earlier in the chapter, Present Values of future payments are highly sensitive to changes in the rate of interest, and so the market values of longer-term government bonds fluctuated considerably from year to year.

Two other forces, related to riskiness, also help explain the multiplicity of observed interest rates:

1. *Transaction costs*: Interest rates often reflect an element of transaction cost. Consumption loans typically carry high interest rates because it is troublesome to investigate many small borrowers and to enforce penalties for default.
2. *Term*: There is a "term structure" of interest rates. Today's short-term rate r_1 may differ from the "forward" short-term rates r_2, r_3, etc. Or, as this is more usually expressed, the short-term rate r_1 may differ from the longer-term rates R_2, R_3, etc. as defined in Table 15.1.

Interest rates almost always rise as term increases. In January 2004, for example, U.S. Treasury issues maturing within 3–6 months typically were paying around 0.85%, while issues maturing in 20 years yielded 4.9%. In financial parlance, the "yield curve is rising."

Rising yield curves mainly reflect investors' desire for *flexibility*. Since placing funds in a short-term loan or investment leaves you in a relatively flexible position, you're willing to accept a low rate of return. In contrast, you will probably require a higher expected return in exchange for "locking in" to a long-term investment. (Because of resale opportunities, investors are not *literally* locked in to a long-term investment such as a 20-year corporate bond. However, in attempting to sell off the unmatured bond, you may find that whatever forces make you want to sell also make potential buyers reluctant to buy.)

An Application: The Discount Rate for Project Analysis

That investments vary in riskiness has important implications for project analysis (as discussed in Section 15.4 above). Dealing for simplicity with independent projects only, both the Present Value Rule ("Accept if $V_0 > 0$") and the Rate of Return Rule ("Accept if $\rho > r$") require selection of an appropriate interest or discount rate r. Which of the multiplicity of coexisting interest rates is the appropriate one?

It seems straightforward that *the discount rate employed in evaluating a project should correspond to its risk*. If the project under consideration is no riskier than a Treasury bond, it would be appropriate to discount its anticipated returns at the relatively low interest rate carried by such government obligations. If, as is more likely, a project has about the same riskiness as the firm's other ongoing activities, then the discount rate should be the rate of return that the financial markets require for providing funds to the company (its overall "cost of capital").[17]

One type of mistake is common in project analysis. Suppose a company such as General Motors is considering an independent project whose riskiness is typical of its activities overall. According to the discussion above, the expected project returns should be discounted at General Motors' overall "cost of capital," say 10%. Imagine that, at that rate, the project fails the Present Value Rule, that is, $V_0 < 0$. Now suppose a financial analyst says: "We don't really have to sell new stock or issue new bonds to finance this project. If we were instead to mortgage one of our downtown office buildings, with that collateral a bank would be happy to provide funds at a much lower rate, say 6%. Since at 6% the project has positive Present Value, let's go ahead with it."

The error here is like trying to pull yourself up by your own bootstraps. A low-interest loan might well be obtained by putting an office building up as collateral. But that collateral is no longer available to protect the holders of *other* General Motors

---

[17] In the modern finance literature, the riskiness of corporate securities is measured by "beta," a concept that reflects both the standard deviation σ of the security itself and its correlation with the overall market. Suppose company X's stock has high σ, so that its return is variable, but the return is negatively correlated with general stock price movements. Then for the representative investor, whose portfolio can be regarded as a cross-section of the entire stock market, stock X reduces risk – holding it offsets the riskiness of the market as a whole. Consequently, its stock price P_X should be relatively high and its expectation of return low. The returns on most stocks will of course be *positively* correlated with the market as a whole; the increased risk implies that their expected returns would have to be correspondingly high. See F. Black, M. C. Jensen, and M. Scholes, "The Capital-Asset Pricing Model: Some Empirical Tests," in M. C. Jensen, ed., *Studies in the Theory of Capital Markets* (New York: Praeger, 1972).

securities, which therefore become riskier and will thus tend to fall in value. Another way to look at this is to realize that the aggregate value of the firm's assets must equal the value of its stock and liabilities taken together.[18] If a project is adopted that fails the Present Value test under a discount rate corresponding to the additional risk the project imposes upon the firm's overall activities then the value of General Motors will fall.

EXERCISE 15.9

X Corporation has a simple capital structure, consisting solely of common stock. Its expected annual profit, assumed to continue indefinitely, is $100 a year, with standard deviation $50. The capital market views this pattern as warranting a discount rate of $r = 10\%$. So X's stock, calculated using equation (15.11″) in the form $P = \hat{z}/r$, is worth $100/0.10 = \$1,000$.

Management is considering a new project which would cost $200 and provide additional net profit of $20 a year, with standard deviation $10. Making the simplifying assumption of perfect correlation of the new project with old operations, after adoption the overall standard deviation of net profit would be $60. (a) Is the project worth adopting, if financed with a new issue of common stock? (b) What would happen if the project were financed instead by new mortgage debt, issued on a riskless basis at 6%?

ANSWER: (a) Since $\hat{z}/\sigma(z) = \$120/\$60$ is in the same ratio as the previous $100/$50, new common stockholders should be willing to provide the additional $200 of new funds at the same 10% cost of capital. The company overall is then worth $120/0.10 = \$1,200$, of which the new stock accounts for $200. The existing shareholders' stock is still worth $1,000. Since $V_0 = 0$, the project is just on the borderline of warranting adoption. (b) The company overall is still worth $1,200. Since by assumption the riskless bonds are worth $200 at 6%, the old shares are still worth $1,000. It is true that for the existing shareholders the expected annual net profit $\hat{z}$ rises by 8% (from $100 to $100 + $20 = $12 = \$108$), but these shareholders now face a 20% increase in variability $\sigma(z)$, from $50 to $60. So the expected profit $\hat{z}$ is discounted at a higher rate. In fact, the new discount rate will be 10.8%, since $108/0.108 = \$1,000$.

The principle that the discount rate should reflect the riskiness that the project contributes to overall operations has important implications for government investments. Like General Motors, but even more so, the U.S. government could acquire funds for a risky activity while still borrowing on a riskless ("full faith and credit") basis. But if the rate of return on a government project does not sufficiently reflect its riskiness, adopting it will reduce the overall wealth of the citizenry.[19]

15.7 THE FUNDAMENTALS OF INVESTMENT, SAVING, AND INTEREST

At certain times and in some geographical areas investment and saving have historically been high, and low at other times and places. Similarly for interest rates: in some periods and at some places they have been high, at others low.

---

[18] This proposition is known as the Modigliani–Miller Theorem. See F. Modigliani and M. H. Miller, "The Cost of Capital, Corporation Finance and the Theory of Investment," *American Economic Review*, v. 48 (June 1958).
[19] J. Hirshleifer, "Investment Decision Criteria: Private Decisions" and "Investment Decision Criteria: Public Decisions" in *The New Palgrave Dictionary of Money & Finance* (London: The Macmillan Press, 1992).

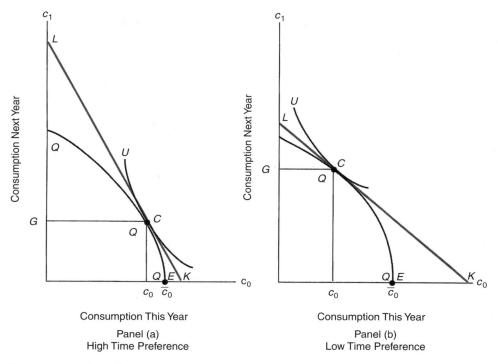

Figure 15.8. The Effects of Time Preference on Investment and Interest: Representative-Individual Model

In a representative-individual model the equilibrium is determined by the tangency of the Production-Possibility Curve QQ with the highest attainable indifference curve. (Although a budget line KL exists, because everyone is alike no trading takes place.) In Panel (a) time preference is high (the indifference curves are steep); thus, the equilibrium interest rate is also high and little investment takes place. In Panel (b) time preference is low (the indifference curves are flat); the equilibrium interest rate is therefore low and a great deal of investment takes place.

What explains these differences? Saving, investment, and interest rates all relate to comparisons between present and future, so time is the crucial consideration. The three fundamental determinants are *time-preference*, *time-endowment*, and *time-productivity*.

1. *Time-preference*: The more impatient people are, the more they prefer current consumption. Think in terms of a "representative individual" (RI). The two panels of Figure 15.8 illustrate the implications of steep indifference curves (high time-preference) and flat indifference curves (low time-preference). In each case, the representative individual's preference map is juxtaposed against a typical Production Possibility Curve QQ. For simplicity the endowment point E is assumed to lie on the horizontal axis.

In a representative-individual model, the equilibrium is at the tangency of QQ with the highest attainable indifference curve. The *RI*'s budget line necessarily goes through this tangency, since the *RI*, having no one to trade with, cannot diverge from the endowment position. Recall from equation (15.1) that the absolute slope of the budget line equals $1 + r_1$. So the slope of this tangent budget line determines the interest rate.[20]

---

[20] Figure 15.8 resembles the Robinson Crusoe diagram of Figure 15.4. But whereas in Figure 15.4 the tangency R^* was an *optimum* position for Robinson, here the corresponding point $Q^* = C^*$ is the *equilibrium* of an economy with identical individuals. The crucial difference is that in a Crusoe situation there is no budget

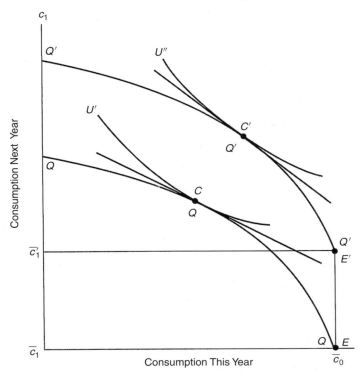

Figure 15.9. The Effects of Time Endowment on Investment and Interest: Representative-Individual Model

Here the endowment shifts vertically from E to E', owing to an increase in the future-dated element from $\bar{c}_1 = 0$ to c_1'. Assuming the technological possibilities for transforming current income into future income remain unchanged, the Production-Possibility Curve QQ also shifts vertically upward to the position $Q'Q'$. The effect is to raise the interest rate (as shown by the slopes of the budget lines that can be drawn through Q and Q') and decrease the scale of investment.

For the high time-preference picture in Panel (a), it is evident that the scale of saving and investment $\bar{c}_0 - c_0^*$ will be low and the interest rate r_1 (steepness of the equilibrium budget line) high. The reverse holds for the low time-preference picture in Panel (b).

Low time-preference is associated with personal characteristics such as farsightedness, strong family ties, willingness to defer enjoyment, and the like. The later years of the Roman Empire were characterized by a decline in such "puritanical" attitudes. With this shift toward high time-preference, interest rates accordingly rose.

Time-preference is linked to biological factors. The inevitability of death is the overwhelming ground for positive time-preference – wanting to consume here and now. The main countervailing factor is that one's descendants provide a vicarious way of surviving past one's own life. In recent times these considerations have operated in opposite directions. Rising life spans have put off death, and hence have encouraged saving. But smaller family sizes have discouraged it.

2. *Time-endowment*: The effects of differing time-endowments are pictured in Figure 15.9. First suppose the representative endowment E is again on the horizontal axis. The solution $Q^* = C^*$ is as before at the tangency of the Production-Possibility Curve

line. But in a representative individual picture, a budget line can be drawn through the tangency point. Anyone can trade but, with everyone alike, at the equilibrium price ratio no trade takes place.

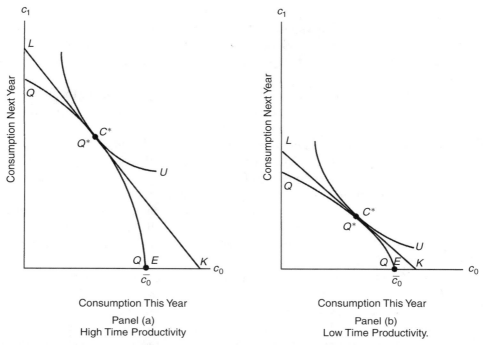

Figure 15.10. The Effects of Time Productivity on Investment and Interest: Representative-Individual Model

In Panel (a) time productivity is high (the Production-Possibility Curve QQ is steep), so the equilibrium interest rate is also high. In Panel (b) time productivity is low (the QQ curve is relatively flat); the equilibrium interest rate is therefore low. At the equilibrium $Q^* = C^*$ in Panel (b), although the consumption provided for the future is certainly less than in Panel (a), we cannot definitely say whether the scale of investment is also less.

QQ with the highest attainable indifference curve. The absolute slope of the equilibrium budget line through $Q^* = C^*$ once again determines the interest rate r_1. The amount of investment is shown by the horizontal distance between E and Q^*.

A change in time-endowment toward the future is pictured in the diagram by an upward shift of the RI's endowment point to the position E'. If *time-productivity* remains the same, the technological possibilities for transforming current income into future income are unchanged. Geometrically, the new Production-Possibility Curve $Q'Q'$ through E' will be vertically parallel to QQ. The new optimum is $Q'^* = C'^*$. From the geometry, the new equilibrium interest rate r_1' is higher than r_1 (the RI's new equilibrium budget line has steeper slope). And the scale of investment (the horizontal distance between E' and Q'^*) will be less.

Alternatively, consider a community hit with disaster. A catastrophe usually damages goods relatively close to consumption more drastically than it injures the basic productive powers of the economy. A drought or a hurricane may destroy crops while leaving long-term productive fundamentals – fertility of the soil, mineral resources, and human skills – unimpaired. Since present incomes are affected more seriously than anticipated future incomes, the endowment point will shift not up as in Figure 15.9, but instead to the left. The scale of investment will tend to fall, while the interest rate will tend to rise.

3. *Time-productivity:* In the two panels of Figure 15.10, higher and lower time-productivity of investment are represented by steeper and flatter Production-Possibility

Curves *QQ*. With high time-productivity, interest rates will tend to be high; with low time-productivity, interest rates will be low. This difference has been observed in comparisons between newer and more productive versus older and more mature communities. For example, interest rates historically have been higher in America than in Britain, and higher in California than in New England.

If time-productivity rises, there will be increased provision for the future. But as this increased provision can be provided with less current sacrifice, the effect on the scale of investment can go either way.

Two other factors supplement the fundamentals described above.

4. *Degree of isolation*: The interest rate in a locality that is financially linked with other regions cannot diverge too far from the normal rates in the outside world. If a divergence were to appear, investments and loans would flow from the low-interest area to the high-interest area. The differences historically observed between interest rates in Britain and America, or between New England and California, have therefore been much smaller than they would have been had the communities been more fully isolated from one another.

5. *Risk*: Riskiness is correlated with futurity. Today already exists, tomorrow is somewhat uncertain, and the farther future is increasingly shrouded in mist. For people who are risk-averse, a future endowment that is more uncertain (has higher perceived variability risk) is like a future endowment that is effectively smaller. So increased riskiness of the future acts like an impoverishment of the future, which can strengthen the "precautionary" motivation to save (saving for a rainy day).

SUMMARY   A person *saves* by consuming less than his or her income. He or she *invests* by physically transforming potential current income into future income – for example, planting seed corn. If personal investment exceeds personal saving, the individual must borrow from other savers. In the reverse case, the difference is lent out to other investors.

Individuals' choices as to present consumption versus future consumption determine the price ratios between current and future real goods. The price ratio P_0/P_1 can also be written as $1 + r_1$, which defines the real rate of interest r_1 between real consumption at date 0 (the present) and at date 1 (1 year from now).

In a world of intertemporal pure exchange, investment opportunities are absent. Each individual's wealth – the market value of his or her endowment – is fixed. He or she borrows or lends to achieve an optimum time-pattern of consumption.

When investment opportunities do exist, the individual maximizes wealth by choosing a *production optimum* together with a utility-maximizing *consumption optimum*. The intersection of the aggregate supply curve of saving and the aggregate demand curve for investment equates the aggregate amount of saving and investment and determines the equilibrium rate of interest. At this interest rate, aggregate borrowing also equals aggregate lending.

This analysis generalizes to any number of dates, so as to determine the time sequences of consumption, saving and investment, and lending and borrowing – together with the "term structure" of short-term and long-term interest rates.

If markets for intertemporal claims ("capital markets") are perfect, the Separation Theorem holds: production decisions can be aimed solely at maximizing wealth, independently of time-preferences. And a manager who maximizes the wealth of the firm will be making the correct production decisions for all the owners individually, regardless of their possibly differing time-preferences.

A project or set of projects that increases wealth has positive Present Value. With cash flow z_i in period i, and a constant interest rate r, Present Value V_0 is defined as:

$$V_0 \equiv z_0 + \frac{z_1}{1+r} + \cdots + \frac{z_T}{(1+r)^T}$$

The Present Value Rule for project selection directs the decision-maker to select the overall set of projects that maximizes wealth.

The Rate of Return (ROR) concept is defined as the value of ρ that satisfies the equation:

$$0 \equiv z_0 + \frac{z_1}{1+\rho} + \cdots + \frac{z_T}{(1+\rho)^T}$$

The ROR Rule for project selection says to adopt all projects for which $\rho > r$, and among mutually exclusive projects to choose the one of greatest ρ. This rule often arrives at the same project choices as the Present Value Rule, but under certain conditions – notably, where projects differ substantially in scale – can lead to significant error.

Each firm has a "cost of capital" that represents the financial markets' evaluation of the riskiness of its anticipated annual payoffs z. If the riskiness of a new project is typical of the existing activities of the business, the appropriate discount rate would be the same as the firm's overall cost of capital.

The *real* interest rate r_1 is the premium on current real goods over future real goods. The money interest rate r_1' is the premium on current money over future money. The relation between the real interest rate and the money interest rate depends on the anticipated rate of price-level inflation a_1:

$$r_1' = r_1 + a_1$$

The fundamental determinants of the real interest rate and the scale of investment in a community include *time-preferences* (more urgent desires for current goods tend to reduce investment and raise interest rates), *time-endowments* (anticipations of higher future income raise interest rates and reduce investment), and *time-productivity* (better productive opportunities raise both investment and interest rates). Owing to risk aversion, high riskiness attaching to future anticipated income has much the same effect as a quantitative reduction in that future income.

QUESTIONS

†The answers to daggered questions appear at the end of the book.

For Review

1. Explain the analogy between the intertemporal optimum of the consumer (choice between current consumption C_0 and future consumption C_1) and the optimum of the consumer at a moment of time (choice between consumption of commodity X and commodity Y).

†2. Which is correct, and explain:
   a. The annual rate of interest is the ratio P_0/P_1, the price of a current consumption claim divided by the price of a consumption claim dated one year in the future.

   b.   The annual rate of interest is the *premium* on the value of current relative to 1-year future claims, as given by the expression $(P_0/P_1) - 1$.

3. What is wealth? How does it relate to current and future incomes?

†4. In intertemporal market equilibrium under pure exchange, aggregate borrowing B equals aggregate lending L. What can be said about the equilibrium of saving S and investment I? Is the amount $I = S$ necessarily smaller or larger than the amount $B = L$?

†5. Turning to equilibrium in a production economy, aggregate saving must equal aggregate investment. What can be said about borrowing and lending?

6. What is the Separation Theorem? What is its importance? What would tend to happen if it were not applicable?

†7. a.   What is the Present Value Rule?
   b.   Will this rule always lead decisionmakers to correct choices of projects when the Separation Theorem holds?
   c.   What if the Separation Theorem does not hold?

8. Explain the relation between the rate of interest r as defined in the equation $r \equiv (P_0/P_1) - 1$ and as defined in the equation $r \equiv z/V_0$.

9. What is the *money* rate of interest, and how is it related to the *real* rate of interest?

†10. In Example 15.3 on the benefits of Social Security, if the discount rate used were 5% instead of 4%, do you think the discounted value of social security for single men would remain negative?

†11. How can a country invest more than it saves?

For Further Thought and Discussion

1. In a two-period preference diagram, illustrate the following endowments. Indicate whether the person is likely to be a borrower or a lender.
   a.   A young woman with an elderly, wealthy, loving uncle in Australia.
   b.   A farmer whose crop has been destroyed by a hurricane.
   c.   A sugar-beet farmer who has just learned that this year's sugar-cane crop has been destroyed by a hurricane.
   d.   A 35-year-old star baseball player.

†2. "Saving need not equal investment for any single individual, but the two must be equal for the market as a whole." Is this necessarily true in equilibrium? Would it be true in a disequilibrium situation, as might result from a floor or ceiling upon interest rates?

†3. Resources in a newly settled country are likely to have great potential but are as yet undeveloped.
   a.   Would you expect the real interest rate to be high or low?
   b.   Comparing situations in which the new country is or is not in close contact with the rest of the world, in which situation will the interest rate be higher?
   c.   In which will more investment take place? Explain.

†4. One country is "stagnant" (i.e., has little investment and economic growth) because productive opportunities yielding a good return on investment are lacking. Another "stagnant" country has excellent investment opportunities, but has little investment because the citizens' time-preferences are very high. Which country would tend to have a high, and which a low, real interest rate? Explain.

5. Money interest rates throughout the world have generally been higher since World War II than in the prewar period. Indicate which of the following might provide part of the explanation and analyze:

a. Higher rates of time-preference (changes in tastes).

b. Higher rates of time-productivity (changes in investment opportunities).

c. Lower ratios of current to anticipated future incomes (increased relative scarcity of current endowments).

d. Higher rates of inflation (changes in anticipations as to monetary policies of governments).

†6. a. Are negative rates of interest impossible?

b. Is there a limit upon how negative the interest rate can be?

7. "Annual income twenty pounds, annual expenditure nineteen pounds, result happiness. Annual income twenty pounds, annual expenditure twenty-one pounds, result misery" – Mr. Micawber in Charles Dickens' *David Copperfield*. Is this sound economics? Analyze.

†8. An issue of *Consumer Reports* magazine asked whether a homebuyer might advantageously finance purchase of appliances by an addition to his or her home mortgage. The alternatives considered were (1) buy appliances through a retail store for $675, financed by a two-year contract at 15% interest; and (2) buy the same appliances for $450 through the homebuilder, financed by a mortgage add-on 27-year contract at 7.75% interest. The article contended that the first option was superior. The justification offered was that, for the two-year 15% contract, the total of interest-plus-principal payments would add up to only $785 – whereas, for the 27-year mortgage add-on contract at 7.75%, the total payments would eventually sum to $1,075. Analyze.

†9. During World War II it was necessary to decide how much of military expenditures was to be financed by taxation and how much by government borrowing. Some economists argued that financing the war by borrowing would "shift the burden to future generations." Is this correct? How would you go about determining how much of the cost of a war is borne by the current generation versus future generations?

10. How would a tax on income affect saving and investment in a world of pure exchange? In a world of production and exchange?

†11. Why might the stock of a small company on average earn a higher rate of return than the yield on a government bond?

VII POLITICAL ECONOMY

16 Welfare Economics: The Market and the State

The book to this point has dealt mainly with economics as a *positive* science. It analyzed how the market economy works, whether or not the outcomes are regarded as desirable. But economists also study *normative* issues – public policy. Are price controls wise? Should immigration be limited? Are low taxes with small government better than high taxes with big government? Are regulations to protect the environment a good idea?

What economists call welfare economics, the subject of this chapter, asks how public policies should be evaluated. Such an evaluation will of course depend upon the goals of policy, especially the need to balance between *efficiency* and *equity*, discussed in the first section of the chapter. The second section reviews the Theorem of the Invisible Hand, a proposition suggesting that the market economy may achieve efficiency. The section that follows covers "market failures" – ways in which the Invisible Hand might go wrong. Two related areas of possible failure, *the commons* and *the problem of public goods*, are treated next. It turns out that these failures stem from unsuitable or incomplete assignment of property rights. The next main section therefore deals with attempts to acquire property rights over resources or to defend against others' efforts to gain such control.

16.1   GOALS OF ECONOMIC POLICY

Two of the many possible goals of policy are efficiency and equity. Think of efficiency as representing the *size of the economic pie* (bigger is better), and equity as representing the *distribution of slices* (fairer is better).

Efficiency versus Equity

To begin with, suppose a person's well-being depends only upon his or her own income, measured in terms of a generalized consumption good (corn). As a two-person community, for John and Kathy the shaded area in Figure 16.1 shows the social opportunity set – all the achievable income combinations I_j, I_k.

The curve II' bounding the social opportunity set is the *Social Opportunity Frontier*. As drawn, the curve is concave to the origin, so that total social income $\overline{I}$ is larger toward the middle rather than at the corners. So if a change in social arrangements allows Kathy to get more, John need not lose the entire amount that Kathy gains.

Consider first the *efficiency* goal of public policy. As a first definition, it might be thought that efficient social policy should maximize the sum of incomes, $\overline{I} \equiv I_j + I_k$. In Figure 16.1 the level of summed income is held constant along an "iso-income" line such as MM'. Along each such line one more bushel of corn for John means one less bushel for Kathy, so the slope of MM' equals -1. The maximum level of summed income is achieved at point I^* where the Social Opportunity Frontier II' is tangent to a line of slope -1, in this case line MM'.

Economists, however, define efficiency more broadly. Not just I^* but *all* the points on the Social Opportunity Frontier are efficient outcomes. The reason: at any point on that curve, it is impossible to make *both* John and Kathy better off – or to make one of them better off without making the other worse off. So, at any income combination represented by a point on II', it would be impossible to achieve unanimous consent to move to any other point on the curve, or for that matter to any other point within the social opportunity set. Thus all points on the Social Opportunity Frontier are said to be *Pareto-efficient* (or *Pareto-optimal*).[1]

----

[1] Vilfredo Pareto (1848–1923), Italian economist and sociologist.

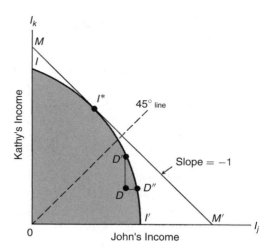

Figure 16.1. Social Allocations of Income

The shaded region is the social opportunity set, showing the attainable combinations of income for John (I_j) and Kathy (I_k); its boundary is the Social Opportunity Frontier II'. Total social income is maximized at I^*, where II' is tangent to line MM' of slope -1.

DEFINITION: (1) An allocation A of goods in an economy is "Pareto-preferred" to some other allocation B if, under A, everyone is at least as well off as under B and at least one person is better off. (2) An allocation is "Pareto-efficient" (or "Pareto-optimal") if no available alternative is Pareto-preferred to it.

Consider the allocation D in the interior of the shaded social opportunity set of Figure 16.1. Comparing D with D', Kathy is better off at D' and John is no worse off, so D' is Pareto-preferred to D. At D'' John is better off than at D, while Kathy is no worse off. So D'' is also Pareto-preferred to D. In fact, any point within the roughly triangular area $D'DD''$, other than D itself, is Pareto-preferred to D.

Generalizing this reasoning, for any point like D *in the interior* of the social opportunity set, some points on the Social Opportunity Frontier II' are Pareto-preferred to it. So no point in the interior of the social opportunity set can be Pareto-efficient. But comparing any two allocations like D' and D'' along II' itself, any gain to one party comes with a loss to the other – so no point on II' is Pareto-preferred to any other. Thus the Social Opportunity Frontier is the set of Pareto-efficient allocations.

Dealing with a single real-income commodity (corn) is a simplification. In the analysis that follows, the efficiency concept will be extended to multiple commodities. It is also possible, though with techniques more advanced than those covered in this book, to allow for the *effort and risk* required to generate income, and for the *reservation uses of resources* (leisure) that must be sacrificed.

Some other complications pose problems that have not been and perhaps can never be resolved. For example, if John benevolently values Kathy's consumption, as measured by his willingness to sacrifice some of his own consumption to increase hers, then is Kathy's income also John's income? And if instead John regards Kathy as an enemy, can a reduction of Kathy's income be regarded as an increase in John's? Setting aside these problems, the discussion here assume that John's satisfaction depends solely upon his own income I_j and Kathy's satisfaction solely upon her own income I_k.

Turning to distributive equity or fairness, several possible criteria have been advocated. Among these are (1) *Equality*: everyone should have the same income; (2) *Market achievement*: incomes should represent economic performance, as measured by success in the market; (3) *Ownership*: no one should be deprived of legally acquired property except as punishment for crime.

There are problems with each of these criteria. Equality may at first seem appealing. But does a lazy person deserve to live as opulently as a hard worker? Or consider *achievement*. High income may result not from good work but from good luck, among other things from being fortunate to have inherited wealth or talent. As for *ownership*, the current distribution of property may again be largely the result of luck, or may even reflect successful criminal activity in the past.

Debates about equity are endless. For that reason, economists commonly concentrate upon the efficiency effects of alternative public policies.

Utilitarianism

Underlying welfare economics is a philosophical view known as utilitarianism.[2] Utilitarians contend that (1) All social policies, rules, and institutions are to be judged solely by their *consequences*. And (2) the only relevant consequences are *individual gratifications* ("pleasures and pains").

The first assertion represents a kind of social pragmatism. For utilitarians, social practices and institutions (for example, voting, the market, capital punishment, the family, the nation) are means or instruments. They should not be adopted or rejected, opposed or supported, because they agree with or disagree with the Bible, or with natural law, or with ethical principles. Instead, the only criterion is: Does this arrangement lead to desirable social outcomes? Where others might say "The ends do not justify the means," the utilitarian replies, "What can justifies the means but the ends attained?"

The second assertion represents a kind of radical individualism. Policies may or may not serve God's purposes, may or may not advance science and learning, may or may not promote the nation's survival. All of this is irrelevant for the utilitarian philosopher, who asks only whether the results satisfy individual desires. President John F. Kennedy once declared "Ask not what your country can do for you, ask what you can do for your country." A utilitarian would reply, "Why be a citizen of a country except for what it can do for you?"

Opponents of utilitarianism might argue, for example, that social policy should be directed at giving individuals not what they want but at what they ought to have. As our sacred texts tell us, and as history demonstrates, getting what you want may be catastrophic for you. Furthermore, what people want is by no means a fully autonomous choice but is itself largely the consequence of external pressures and social conditioning.

Although these reservations have merit, economics is not ethics. *Economics is the science of the instrumental.* Economic analysis takes people's goals, whether selfish or altruistic, as given. Positive economics analyzes how people go about achieving their self-evaluated goals, and normative economics asks what social policies can either facilitate or interfere with their doing so.

Efficiency as the Sum of Consumer Surplus and Producer Surplus

So far the discussion has run in terms of a single "real income" commodity. When there are many commodities, the analog of maximizing real income I is maximizing the sum of Consumer Surplus and Producer Surplus ($CS + PS$) across all goods.

---

[2] Like the term "utility" introduced in Chapter 3, the word "utilitarianism" was popularized by the British philosopher Jeremy Bentham (1748–1832).

Figure 16.2. Pareto-Preferred and Pareto-Optimal Allocations

Given an initial allocation of income E, the points in the shaded lens-shaped area are all *Pareto-preferred* to E. The Contract Curve *CC* represents the set of *Pareto-optimal* allocations. Only points within the range *DD'* along the Contract Curve are both Pareto-optimal and Pareto-preferred to E. At *M*, the midpoint of the diagram, the individuals consume identical amounts of both goods. In general, however, *M* will be neither Pareto-optimal nor Pareto-preferred to *E*: the dotted area is the set of points Pareto-preferred to *M*.

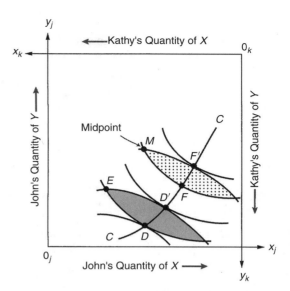

Consumer Surplus and Producer Surplus were covered in Chapter 7 – see especially Figure 7.7. Section 7.4 examined the "efficiency loss" associated with barriers to trade such as taxes, production quotas, and price controls. To review the key idea, for any output quantity *Q* in Figure 7.7, the area under the demand curve represents consumers' *aggregate willingness to pay* for that amount of product. The area under the supply curve represents the *aggregate opportunity cost*, the value of the alternative goods and services (including leisure) foregone. The difference between the two areas – the shaded area – therefore represents the aggregate net benefit of producing the specified amount of this product rather than devoting the required resources to leisure or to producing other goods. Efficiency increases with the sum of Consumer Surplus and Producer Surplus, regardless of the division between them. (The actual division between Producer Surplus and Consumer Surplus is a *distributive* rather than an efficiency issue.)

Efficient Allocations in the Edgeworth Box

In Figure 16.2 (compare Figure 14.2) suppose point *E* is the endowment position – the initial allocation of goods *X* and *Y* between John and Kathy. Then the shaded area in the diagram, the lens-shaped "region of mutual advantage," is the set of allocations of *X* and *Y* that are *Pareto-preferred* to *E*. (For each person, any point within the shaded area lies on a higher indifference curve in comparison with point *E*.)

Now consider the Contract Curve *CC'*, the curve drawn through all the mutual tangencies of John and Kathy's indifference curves. For any point like *F* on *CC'*, no region of mutual advantage exists. So the consumers would never unanimously agree to move away from *F* to any other allocation. The Contract Curve therefore corresponds to the set of *Pareto-efficient* (or *Pareto-optimal*) allocations.

Notice that many allocations that are Pareto-preferred to *E* are not themselves Pareto-optimal (that is, they lie off the Contract Curve). Correspondingly, some Pareto-optimal points along the Contract Curve are not Pareto-preferred to *E*. The only allocations that are *both* Pareto-optimal and Pareto-preferred to *E* are points lying along the Contract Curve within the region of mutual advantage, that is, in the range *DD'* along *CC'*. (Recall that, as shown in Figure 14.3, the competitive equilibrium meets both of these conditions. So the competitive equilibrium is Pareto-efficient, and it is also Pareto-preferred in comparison with the endowment position E.)

At the mid-point, M, John and Kathy have equal amounts of both goods. Notice that, since tastes differ, neither party may find such equality appealing. In fact, as shown in the diagram, if M lies off the Contract Curve CC' then the individuals would be happy to trade away from it to some "unequal" point lying in the region of mutual advantage relative to point M. The dotted area in Figure 16.2 show the points that John and Kathy both prefer to M.

"Equity" Reconsidered

Despite the difficulty of defining equity or fairness, people have strong feelings about them. And those feelings have economic consequences.

EXAMPLE 16.1 EFFICIENCY VERSUS EQUITY IN "ULTIMATUM GAME" EXPERIMENTS

In an experimental situation known as the Ultimatum Game, individuals are paired off and asked to divide a sum of money, say $50.

One member of each pair is randomly chosen to be the Proposer. His task is to suggest a division of the amount at stake. For example, he might offer to retain $30, leaving $20 for the other player. The other party, the Responder, can accept the proposal. If she does, the money is then divided accordingly. Or she can reject, in which case neither party receives anything.

Suppose the Proposer were to suggest retaining $49 for himself, leaving only $1 for the Responder. If cash is a good for both parties, the efficiency criterion would dictate that Responder accept the offer. Even if the deal seems grossly inequitable, both would be better off as opposed to the alternative of receiving nothing at all.

Alvin E. Roth and colleagues conducted parallel Ultimate Game experiments in four countries: Israel, Yugoslavia, Japan, and the United States.[a] The amount at stake was usually $10, or its equivalent in other currencies. (In some sessions the amount was set at $30, but the different scales of payoff did not importantly affect the results.) Proposer and Responder were physically separated, so no player ever knew the identity of his or her partner. Each subject played 10 rounds, changing partners every round.

The table here summarizes results of U.S. experiments in which the amount at stake was $30 – translated into 1,000 tokens available for distribution between the parties. There were 10 pairs of subjects. At the end of play, a participant's accumulated tokens, worth $0.03 each, could be turned in for cash. Since each player participated in ten rounds, he or she could earn as much as $300.

Although it might seem plausible that Proposers could successfully offer highly inequitable splits – for example, keeping all but one token for themselves – in the experiment all 10 Proposers offered their partners substantial fractions of the 1,000 tokens. The first round saw no offer less than 450 tokens (and that lowest offer of 450 was rejected). Half of the Proposers offered an exact split of 500 tokens each. The mean offer overall was 497.5, and 80% of the offers were accepted. Why were Proposers so generous? The two main possible explanations are: (1) The Proposers were themselves unselfishly concerned about fairness. Or (2) the Proposers were *selfish but prudent*, fearing that an inadequate offer would be rejected.

By the 10th round, it turned out that Proposers were keeping somewhat more for themselves. The mean offer fell to 402.5. Nevertheless, the acceptance rate rose to 90%. This suggests that on the basis of experience Proposers were, on the whole, correctly judging how much they could retain for themselves without running an excessive risk of rejection.

The main conclusion of the experiment (and many other studies have confirmed this) is that Responders are willing to sacrifice some income rather than be treated inequitably. And Proposers, knowing this, avoid making offers believed to have too large a chance of being rejected.

Furthermore, the experiments conducted in different countries led to very similar results. So willingness to sacrifice income to avoid being treated inequitably is a widely held, if not universal, attitude.

The ultimatum game – experimental results

Tokens offered (of 1000)	First round		Tenth round	
	# of Proposers (1st round)	# accepted (1st round)	# of Proposers (10th round)	# accepted (10th round)
300	0	–	1	1
350	0	–	0	–
375	0	–	0	–
400	0	–	0	–
425	0	–	2	1
450	1	0	1	1
475	2	2	1	1
500	5	4	4	4
525	1	1	1	1
550	1	1	0	–
	Mean offer: 497.5	Acceptance rate: 80%	Mean offer: 402.5	Acceptance rate: 90%

Source: Adapted visually from Roth et al., Figure 3 (p. 1083).

[a] Alvin E. Roth, Vesna Prasnikar, Masahiro Okuno-Fujiwara, and Shmuel Zamier, "Bargaining and Market Behavior in Jerusalem, Ljubljana, Pittsburgh, and Tokyo: An Experimental Study," *American Economic Review*, v. 81 (December 1991).

One possible meaning of fairness is that an allocation of goods should be *envy-free*. A distribution of goods between John and Kathy is said to be envy-free if neither would prefer to change places with the other.

EXERCISE 16.1

John's endowment is $(\overline{x}_j, \overline{y}_j) = (50, 10)$ and Kathy's is $(\overline{x}_k, \overline{y}_k) = (20, 30)$. John's utility function is $U_j = x_j^2 y_j$ and Kathy's is $U_k = x_k y_k^2$. Is the endowed allocation envy-free?

ANSWER: John's utility from his endowed basket is $U_j = 50^2 \times 10 = 25{,}000$; his utility from Kathy's basket would be $20^2 \times 30 = 12{,}000$. So he does not want to change places. Similarly, Kathy's utility from her own basket is $U_k = 18{,}000$, whereas John's basket would give her utility of only 5,000. Since neither would want to change places, this endowment allocation is envy-free.

An Application: How to Divide a Cake

When divorcing couples split up marital property, they face a problem of fair division. Similar issues arise when nations negotiate over disputed territory, or when a gang of bank robbers divides up the loot. For concreteness, think of dividing a cake. The cake need not be uniform: part might be chocolate, part vanilla. Or some portions may have lots of raisins, others very few. So what is "fair" will depend in part upon the tastes of the parties.

If there are only two claimants, a well-known principle (attributed to King Solomon) applies. One person, chosen by toss of a coin, cuts the cake; the other has the first choice. For Abigail, the cutter, the problem is what principle to follow in making the division. As for the chooser, Bill, his principle is obvious: after Abigail has made the cut, he takes whichever piece he prefers.

If the cake is sliced in an arbitrary way, the result might be neither efficient nor equitable. For example, if one party loves raisins and the other hates them, the cake might conceivably be cut in such a way that a different division could make them both better off. And of course it might be cut in such a way that at least one claimant envies the other's slice. The question is whether Abigail, following her own self-interest, will rationally cut the cake in a way that is both efficient and envy-free.

Abigail's rational strategy will depend upon what she knows about Bill's preferences. Only the two extreme cases will be considered here: (1) Abigail has *perfect knowledge* of Bill's preferences. (2) Abigail is *completely ignorant* of Bill's preferences.

PERFECT KNOWLEDGE   Suppose the cake is exactly half chocolate, half vanilla. Imagine that Abigail knows that Bill loves chocolate, whereas she herself is indifferent. Then it makes sense for her to split the cake into two portions: a smaller chocolate slice for Bill and a bigger one containing the remainder of the chocolate, plus all the vanilla, for herself. The question is, how unequal should she make the slices?

Call b the fraction of the entire cake (consisting of some but not all of the chocolate portion) she carves off for Bill. And suppose she knows that Bill's relative preference for chocolate over vanilla is always in the constant ratio r. Then Abigail will want to make Bill almost (but not quite) indifferent between his assigned chocolate portion and the remainder of the cake – the portion she intends to retain.

Bill will be indifferent if:

$$rb = \frac{1}{2} + r\left(\frac{1}{2} - b\right) \tag{16.1}$$

The left-hand side of this equation is Bill's evaluation of the chocolate portion: his fraction b of the entire cake multiplied by r, his relative preference for chocolate. The right-hand side is Bill's evaluation of the other portion. It consists of the vanilla half of the cake, entering with a weight of 1, plus the remaining chocolate fraction of the cake weighted by r.

Solving the equation, the result is:

$$b = \frac{1+r}{4r} \tag{16.2}$$

So if, for example, Abigail knows that $r = 2$ (Bill requires twice as much vanilla before being willing to give up a piece of chocolate), she should give Bill 3/8 of the cake, in the form of 3/4 of the chocolate portion. To which she would have to add a crumb, to make Bill definitely prefer his slice rather than remaining indifferent.

COMPLETE IGNORANCE   Suppose, in contrast, that Abigail is completely ignorant as to Bill's preferences. As between any two portions into which she might carve the cake, she has no idea which Bill would prefer. She herself prefers more cake to less, but she does not even know whether that's true for Bill. Then, assuming she is risk-averse, her rational strategy is to cut in such a way as to make *herself* indifferent between the two portions.

If she is neutral as between chocolate and vanilla, she should simply cut the cake in half – and it does not matter which way she does so. If instead she were, say, to split the cake into 2/3 versus 1/3 portions, hoping that Bill will choose the smaller of the two, she is exposing herself to risk. Being risk-averse, she prefers having the mathematical expectation of income (here, "income" is cake) for sure rather than face such a risk. Specifically, half the cake for sure is better for her than equal chances of 2/3 versus 1/3.

But suppose she likes chocolate better than vanilla, in the ratio r. Then, owing again to risk aversion, she will want to make herself indifferent between the two portions into which she cuts the cake, thereby achieving a sure level of utility regardless of what Bill chooses. The equations above are now applicable for Abigail, after the symbol "b" that represented Bill's share is changed to the symbol "a" for Abigail's share. So if for her $r = 2$, the solution is $a = 3/8$. That means she will cut off 3/4 of the chocolate half, being indifferent now as to whether Bill chooses that portion or the other.

This solution is envy-free. Since Bill has his choice, by definition he does not envy Abigail – who gets the portion he has rejected. And Abigail, being indifferent, does not envy Bill whichever portion he chooses. Furthermore, the solution is efficient, since no modification would make both parties feel better off.

In a more general situation, the two parties might be dividing up not a single cake, but a collection of different goods. Or more than two parties may be involved in the negotiation. For these extensions, finding solutions that are both efficient and equitable has turned out to pose difficult mathematical and analytical problems. They have been studied most thoroughly by the political scientist Steven Brams and his colleagues.[3] Only one of the many possible situations will be covered here.

Suppose Abigail and Bill are a divorcing couple. There are three goods involved: the house, the car, and the bank account. Step 1 of what Brams calls the "Adjusted Winner" procedure initially assigns each party 100 points to distribute over the three goods. Imagine that Abigail assigns 70 points to the house, 5 to the auto, and 25 to the bank account. Bill assigns 55 points to the house, 15 to the auto, and 30 to the bank account. In Step 2, whoever assigns a higher number to any item tentatively "wins" it. In this case, Abigail gets the house and Bill gets the bank account and the car. But this solution is not envy-free: Bill, with only 45 points, would prefer to change places with Abigail and get the house (since it's worth 55 points to him). Brams' Step 3 is an adjustment that equalizes the final points achieved. In this case Abigail would give up part of the house, possibly by a space-sharing or time-sharing arrangement. (Or by selling the house and dividing the proceeds.) In the final solution they both end up with equal numbers of points, an outcome that is both efficient and envy-free.

The Adjusted Winner procedure, which has been only very partially described here, is not a "purely academic" matter. It has proved to be of practical importance. And in fact New York University, Steven Brams's institution, has obtained a patent on this system for solving the fair division problem.

---

[3] Steven J. Brams and Alan D. Taylor, *Fair Division: From Cake-Cutting to Dispute Resolution* (Cambridge, UK: Cambridge University Press, 1998).

THE THEOREM OF THE INVISIBLE HAND: THE ROLE OF PRICES

Adam Smith asserted that "the invisible hand" of self-interest leads individuals to engage in activities that promote the best interests of all. This principle is sometimes called The Fundamental Theorem of Economics.

> **THE THEOREM OF THE INVISIBLE HAND:** Under perfect competition, utility-maximizing behavior by individuals, and profit-maximizing behavior by firms, leads to a Pareto-efficient outcome.

This section analyzes three distinguishable aspects of Pareto efficiency: *efficient consumption*, *efficient production*, and *efficient balance between production and consumption*. Market prices guide individuals toward all three of these ends.

Efficient Consumption

Efficient consumption is achieved when, on the margin, no one is willing to give up more of Y for X than is any other individual. If this condition fails to hold between any two persons, they could both gain by trade. Suppose that John, from his endowed allocation of goods, is willing to give up six apples for one more quart of milk. And suppose Kathy is willing to give up one endowed quart of milk for three apples. Then they could both benefit by trade: Kathy should sell milk to John at a price anywhere between three and six apples per quart.

Writing this more formally, making use of the concept of Marginal Rate of Substitution in Consumption (Chapter 4), the condition for efficiency in consumption between John and Kathy is:

$$MRSC^j = MRSC^k \tag{16.3}$$

Recall the more intuitive concept of Marginal Value that was introduced in Section 4.1 of Chapter 4. (Marginal Value is the person's marginal "willingness to pay" for X in terms of the numeraire good Y.) In this more intuitive terminology, the above condition can be written:

$$MV^j_x = MV^k_x \tag{16.3'}$$

That is, efficiency in consumption is achieved when, for each and every good X, everyone's Marginal Value (marginal willingness to pay) is the same.[4]

Efficient Production

For given quantities of goods X and Y to be produced efficiently across firms, no producer should be able to transform a unit of Y into X at a different rate from another producer.[5] So the Marginal Rates of Transformation MRT between goods X and Y should be equal for all producers. Suppose firm f could produce one shirt with the material and labor it uses for one dress, while firm g could make two shirts with the resources used to produce a dress. It would be better to switch some shirt production to firm g and some dress production to firm f. Firm f could produce one less shirt, allowing it to produce

---

[4] As a technical qualification, these formulas hold, strictly speaking, only for individuals consuming positive quantities of each good.

[5] "Transformation" does not mean that a unit of good Y is literally converted into a unit of good X. Rather, resources are reallocated to generate more of X and less of Y.

one more dress. Output of dresses would be unchanged, but output of shirts would increase. The efficiency condition can be written:

$$MRT^f = MRT^g \tag{16.4}$$

Again using more intuitive terminology, the amount of the numeraire Y foregone in producing one more unit of X is simply the *Marginal Cost* of X. So:

$$MC_x^f = MC_x^g \tag{16.4'}$$

That is, for production of X to be efficient among firms, each firm should produce X at the same Marginal Cost.

Efficient Balance between Production and Consumption

The rate at which any producer f can reallocate resources to transform Y into X should equal the rate at which any consumer j is willing to give up Y for X in his consumption basket:

$$MRT^f = MRSC^j \tag{16.5}$$

Were this condition violated, consumers could be made better off. Suppose that some firm could produce one dress with the resources used to produce one shirt, but that a consumer was willing to give up two shirts for one dress. Then if the firm produced one less shirt, the consumer could have one more dress, even though she would be willing to give up two shirts. The extra shirt she gets to enjoy makes her better off.

In the more intuitive terminology, for any good X the Marginal Cost of any producer should equal the Marginal Value to any consumer:

$$MC_x^f = MV_x^j \tag{16.5'}$$

One might imagine that achieving these ideal conditions of efficiency would require a benevolent dictator, operating with the help of a dedicated and efficient bureaucracy. Whether or not that would be practical, the crucial point is that – according to the Theorem of the Invisible Hand – the same result is achieved, without any central planning at all, through *the signals that market prices provide*!

As usual, let commodity Y be the numeraire, so that $P_y \equiv 1$. In a market system, different producers like firms f and g do not *directly* aim at equating their Marginal Rates of Transformation as in equation (16.4). Instead, from the analysis in Chapter 6, under competitive conditions each firm sets its Marginal Cost MC_x equal to the market price P_x. And similarly, consumers j and k do not *directly* aim at equating their Marginal Rates of Substitution in Consumption as in equation (16.3). Rather, as was seen in Chapter 4, each person sets his or her Marginal Value MV_x (marginal "willingness to pay") equal to the same price P_x. Thus market prices bring about efficiency by "mediating" all production and consumption decisions throughout the economy. Using the two forms of notation, this can be portrayed pictorially:

$$
\begin{matrix}
MRT^f & & MRT^g & & MC^f & & MC^g \\
= & = & & & = & = & \\
& P_x/P_y & & \text{or} & & P_x & \\
= & = & & & = & = & \\
MRS_C^j & & MRS_C^k & & MV^j & & MV^k
\end{matrix}
\tag{16.6}
$$

CONCLUSION

In market equilibrium under competitive conditions, prices lead self-interested individuals to meet the conditions of efficient production, efficient consumption, and efficient balance of production and consumption.

16.3   "MARKET FAILURES"

Alas, in an imperfect world the Theorem of the Invisible Hand is too good to be true. Things can and do go wrong.

Monopoly

Non-price-taking behavior (whether due to monopoly, cartels, oligopoly or to any of the market-structure situations analyzed in Chapters 8 through 10) violates the efficiency conditions of the preceding section.

For monopoly, Chapter 8 showed that the profit-maximizing monopolist would set Marginal Cost = Marginal Revenue. But since Marginal Revenue is less than Price, this is inconsistent with setting Marginal Cost = Price, as called for by the efficiency conditions of equation (16.6). Compared to an efficient outcome, a monopolist produces too little. Similarly, a monopolistic resource-supplier would offer too little of the resource on the input market.

Figure 8.5 showed the efficiency loss due to smaller monopoly output as the sum of the reductions in Consumer Surplus and Producer Surplus. The monopolist, while sacrificing some Producer Surplus owing to reduced output, still comes out ahead – thanks to the shaded "transfer" from Consumer Surplus to Producer Surplus on the remaining amount produced. In the terminology of this chapter, the transfer is a *redistribution*: the gain to the monopolist from a higher price on the smaller quantity produced is balanced by the loss to consumers. (Whether such a redistribution can be considered desirable is a matter of equity, but the efficiency loss persists.)

CONCLUSION

Under monopoly there is "too little" market exchange. Consequently, there will also be "too little" productive specialization and "too little" market employment of inputs.

Externalities

Externalities arise when individuals or firms are involuntarily affected, either favorably or unfavorably, by the decisions of another party – where the decision-maker causing the externality is not penalized for the damage he imposes upon others or rewarded for any benefits conferred. Examples include business firms that pollute water supplies, thoughtless drivers who make life more difficult for other motorists, and homeowners whose pets disturb the neighbors.

It is essential to distinguish between *direct* and *pecuniary* externalities. The examples just mentioned were "direct" externalities, and the analysis will concentrate on these. "Pecuniary" externalities arise when actions affect other parties *only through market prices*. Suppose women enter some industry previously closed to them. The female entrants may be close substitutes for the male workers already in the industry, who are

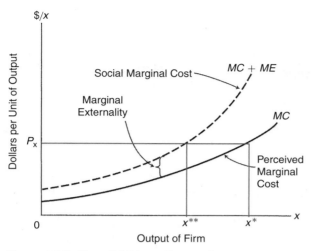

Figure 16.3. Harmful Direct Externality

The competitive firm produces output x^* where perceived Marginal Cost MC equals price P_x. The true social Marginal Cost, however, is the vertical summation $MC + ME$ (dashed curve), where ME is the Marginal Externality. Thus, the efficient output is $x^{**} < x^*$.

therefore likely to see their wages fall. But this externality is only pecuniary. From the technological point of view, the male workers remain just as productive as they were before. What has happened is that their skills have become less scarce, so they are paid less.

The crucial point is that *pecuniary externalities cancel out!* The loss to the male workers (lower wage received) is balanced by an identical gain to the firms employing them. (A benefit that, remembering the Zero-profit Theorem of Chapter 7, ultimately filters down to consumers through lower prices for the product.) Pecuniary externalities are redistributive: they concern not the size of the pie, but who gets what slice. The questions they raise fall under the heading of equity rather than of efficiency.

Returning to *direct* externalities, consider pollution. Aerial emissions can cause smog; chemical pollution may make water undrinkable; heat pollution may kill fish in a stream. Congestion is also a kind of pollution. Each additional visitor at an Internet site in peak periods slows the downloads for other users; each additional broadcasting station crowds the airways, impairing the reception of other stations' signals; each additional barrel of oil extracted raises the cost of pumping at neighboring oil wells.

But a direct externality may also be beneficial. An upstream user's activities could improve the quality of water downstream. Similarly, as discussed in Chapter 7, a farmer in a marshy area who drains his land may lower water levels and make neighboring lands more productive.

Figure 16.3 pictures a harmful direct externality. A competitive (price-taking) firm maximizes profit by setting its Marginal Cost MC equal to the market price P_x; the associated output is x^*. The damage to others is the Marginal Externality ME. The true Social Marginal Cost for society as a whole is $SMC \equiv MC + ME$. Taking the externality into account, setting $SMC = P$ implies a smaller ideal output x^{**}. Correspondingly, for a beneficial externality the SMC curve would lie below MC, and the ideal firm output would exceed x^*.

CONCLUSION

Direct externalities, beneficial or harmful, lead the Invisible Hand astray. Efficiency requires that a decision-maker generating a harmful direct externality should produce less than the private profit-maximizing level of output. Or, if the externality is beneficial, output should be expanded beyond the profit-maximizing amount. (*Pecuniary* externalities, though they may raise issues of fairness, are irrelevant to efficiency.)

Several policies have been adopted or proposed to reduce the inefficiencies stemming from direct externalities.

1. *Taxes and subsidies*: A tax on harmful externalities would induce firms to reduce the damage imposed on others. An ideal corrective tax would be equal to the Marginal Externality in Figure 16.5. Then the private Marginal Cost plus the tax penalty would sum to the Social Marginal Cost of production. Correspondingly, for a beneficial externality, a corrective subsidy would induce an increase in the externality-generating activity.

EXAMPLE 16.2 THE MARGINAL EXCESS BURDEN OF TAXATION IN THE UNITED KINGDOM

Transaction taxes impose a "wedge" between buying prices and selling prices. This means that the efficiency condition $MC_x = MV_x$ will be violated. Recall the discussion of *gross price* versus *net (after-tax) price* in Chapter 2. Buyers will set MV_x, the Marginal Value of a unit of X, equal to the gross price P_x^+; sellers will set Marginal Cost equal to the net price P_x^-.

In a 2001 study, Ian W. H. Parry estimated the "marginal excess burden" (*MEB*) in the United Kingdom of taxes on employment (including income taxation and payroll taxes such as Social Security), taxes on gasoline, and taxes on "sin goods" – cigarettes and alcohol.[a]

For employment taxes, the table indicates a marginal excess burden of 0.26 for transfer spending. This means that when £1 of income is diverted by taxation to a recipient group, the cost to the rest of society is £1.26. Transfers financed by taxes on employment, for example, reduce national income because they weaken the incentive to work. The marginal excess burden for employment taxes is therefore sensitive to the supply elasticity of labor. (The marginal excess burden of 0.26 shown in the table reflects a middling estimate of this elasticity.)

"Sin taxes" and gasoline taxes, on the other hand, to the extent that they merely compensate for direct externalities, are not distortions. Smoking is associated with air pollution, and is a fire hazard. Alcohol is associated with crime and auto accidents. Driving is associated with air pollution and congestion. For these taxes, the estimates of Marginal Excess Burden in the table measure the consequences of imposing tax levels *in excess of* the estimated external damages.

It turns out that for cigarette taxation the Marginal Excess Burden is large, larger than the Marginal Excess Burden for employment taxation, whereas for alcohol the Marginal Excess Burden is relatively small. The main reason is that cigarettes are taxed more heavily in proportion to market price. Taxes accounted for around 65% of the retail price of cigarettes, but only about 27% of the price of alcoholic drinks. Gasoline is taxed at much higher rates in the United Kingdom than in the United

States, indeed at more than the estimated external damage effects. Consequently, as shown in the table, the associated Marginal Excess Burden is high.

Marginal excess burden (MEB) of specified taxes in the United Kingdom

Tax upon	MEB (pence, per £ of tax revenue)
Employment	26
Cigarettes	75
Alcohol	24
Gasoline	79

Source: Adapted from Parry, Tables 2–5.

[a] Ian W. H. Parry, "Comparing the Marginal Excess Burden of Labor, Petrol, Cigarette, and Alcohol Taxes: An Application to the United Kingdom." Resources for the Future, Inc., Discussion Paper 00-33REV (2001).

EXAMPLE 16.3 MORE ON "SIN TAXES"

Exceptionally high taxes are often imposed upon cigarettes and liquor ("sin taxes"). One reason is that smoking and drinking generate adverse externalities – costs imposed upon others. The question arises, how big are these costs?

With the aim of determining whether smokers and drinkers "pay their way" in terms of the burden imposed upon others, Willard G. Manning et al. assessed the magnitude of these externalities.[a] Since future effects (such as increased mortality risks) had to be allowed for, calculation of present values was required (as discussed in Chapter 15). The results here show the result of such calculations in 1986 dollars, using a 5% discount rate.

External costs of smoking and drinking (1986 dollars)

	Cost per pack of cigarettes	Cost per excess ounce of alcohol*
Medical care	$0.26	$0.10
Sick leave	0.01	0.05
Group life insurance	0.05	0.02
Nursing home	−0.03	0.00
Retirement pension	−0.24	0.03
Fires	0.02	–
Foregone taxes on earnings	0.09	0.06
Motor vehicle accidents	–	0.93
Totals	$0.15	$1.19

* "Excess" ounces are amounts over two reported drinks per day.
Source: Adapted from Manning et al., Tables 2 and 4.

Some of these numbers are negative, meaning that the effects upon other parties were on balance favorable. By dying earlier, for example, smokers reduce the burden imposed upon retirement pension systems!

In calculating the cigarette externality, there is a question how to deal with "passive" smoking. The authors estimated that harmful effect at $0.14 per pack. But because the primary sufferers are members of the smokers' own families, the authors did not count this as an *externality*. The costs of fires due to smoking, estimated at $0.09 per pack, were omitted for the same reason.

As shown in the table, for cigarettes the external cost per pack was estimated at $0.15, or $0.38 upon adding the within-family effects of passive smoking and fires. In comparison, the average tax on cigarettes was $0.37 per pack. For alcohol, the tabulated cost per excess ounce ($1.19) was multiplied by 0.4 to obtain $0.48 as the cost per ounce – which compares with an average tax of only $0.23 per ounce. So (as is consistent with the preceding Example) cigarettes appear to be fully taxed or even "over-taxed" relative to the externality imposed on others. On the other hand, alcohol is under-taxed.

COMMENT

This study disregarded the distinction in the text above between direct and pecuniary externalities. Recall that, on efficiency grounds, only *direct* externalities warrant a corrective marginal tax. For cigarettes, passive smoking and fire losses (apart from those suffered by the smoker) do represent direct externalities. For alcohol, similarly, the tabulated external motor vehicle accident cost represents a direct externality. But *all* the other categories shown in the table are pecuniary rather than direct externalities! The effects upon retirement pensions, for example, are only financial transfers, as are the medical costs paid by employers or other parties.

So, from the efficiency point of view alone, to correct for harmful externalities the cigarette tax should be only $0.02 per pack (external fire cost), or $0.25 if both passive smoking ($0.14) and the intrafamily effects of fires ($0.09) are added. For alcohol, the tax should reflect only the motor-vehicle accident cost ($0.93 × 0.4 = $0.37). Despite these revisions, however, the conclusion remains that cigarettes are over-taxed and alcohol is under-taxed.

Of course, it might reasonably be regarded as "fair" to penalize smokers if other parties such as employers or taxpayers bear their medical costs. But once again, that is a *distributive* issue. The efficient discouragement of externalities should penalize only direct, not pecuniary effects.

---

[a] Willard G. Manning, Emmett B. Keeler, Joseph P. Newhouse, Elizabeth M. Sloss, and Jeffrey Wasserman, "The Taxes of Sin: Do Smokers and Drinkers Pay Their Way?" *Journal of the American Medical Association*, v. 261 (March 17, 1989).

2. *Unitization:* Suppose upstream uses affect the quality of downstream river water. Then, regardless of whether the externality is harmful or beneficial, merging or "unitizing" the upstream and downstream users under the control of a single decision-maker would *internalize* the externality.

3. *Property reassignment and licenses:* The way in which property rights are assigned, and even more important their *tradability*, lies at the heart of the externality problem. Suppose a downstream user is initially entitled to pure water. Then the upstream user could buy the downstream user's consent to emit some pollutants. If on the other hand the upstream party was initially entitled to pollute, the downstream user could compensate him for reducing pollution.

EXAMPLE 16.4 SMOG

Under the 1990 Clean Air Act, the Environmental Protection Agency (EPA) can issue tradable licenses allowing emissions of five principal air pollutants. The commodity exchanged is called an emission reduction credit. The basic idea was that a firm setting up an industrial process or other source of emissions would have to buy an emission reduction credit from some other party; the seller would, accordingly, have to reduce its level of emissions. Since only *changes* in emissions required a license, the "status quo" provided the initial basis for the assignment of rights. Trading in these rights was permitted, but subject to bureaucratic approval.

Vivien Foster and Robert W. Hahn studied the working of this market in the Los Angeles area.[a] It turned out that most of the transactions took place entirely *within* firms. In such trades a firm gained the right to increase emissions in one plant or activity by cutting back elsewhere. Thus the main effect was to allow firms greater internal flexibility to meet an unchanged total of emissions. Nevertheless, there was a large estimated cost saving, between $0.5 and $12 billion. Despite the limitations, over 10,000 tons of pollutant rights per year were traded in 1985–1992, with total spending of about $2 billion on emission reduction credits.

The main limit to the volume of trading was that the regulatory agency (the South Coast Air Quality Management District) reserved the right to approve all transactions. In fact, it approved less than 20% of the proposed trades. About half the remainder were rejected entirely; the other half were approved only after revisions. Firms incurred substantial fees and suffered long delays. Apart from bureaucratic inefficiencies, it appears there were technical difficulties in certifying the claimed emissions reductions (the "commodity" being sold) and in determining the benchmark against which reductions are measured.

COMMENT

If interfirm trading of credits were also permitted, much larger efficiency gains could have been achieved. The effect of the program is to restrict emissions of atmospheric pollutants to those activities that can "pay their way" in terms of reducing emissions elsewhere.

---

[a] Vivien Foster and Robert W. Hahn, "Designing More Efficient Markets: Lessons from Los Angeles Smog Control," *Journal of Law and Economics*, v. 38 (April 1995).

The Coase Theorem

When it comes to achieving efficiency, more vital than the initial assignment of property rights is ensuring that the allotted rights are exchangeable in markets. This point is summarized in the Coase Theorem:[6]

> **THE COASE THEOREM:** If property rights are well-defined, and if the parties involved can reach and enforce agreements at zero transaction costs, then the final outcome will be efficient regardless of the initial assignments of property rights.

The thrust of the Coase Theorem is that the Invisible Hand can be effective even in the presence of externalities. Market forces can sometimes bring these "external" effects into the calculations of the parties involved. Suppose a firm has the legal right to pollute,

[6] R. H. Coase, "The Problem of Social Cost," *Journal of Law and Economics*, v. 3 (October 1960).

for example, by using river water in a way that impairs its quality for a downstream user. The injured downstream firm can still contract with the upstream firm to pollute less. Alternatively, perhaps the downstream firm has a legal right to clean water. Then the upstream firm could offer compensation in return for permission to pollute. (When the externality is beneficial, the argument applies in reverse.) In each case the offer will be accepted only if both parties gain thereby, so that overall efficiency is enhanced. So it is not necessary for the upstream and downstream firms to be "unitized" – negotiations among the firms can do the job. As long as the legal rights are marketable and well-defined, the Invisible Hand leads to an efficient outcome.

So far so good. But consider monopoly once again. Monopoly entails inefficient underproduction of the monopolized good. According to the Coase Theorem, a monopolist firm and its customers should agree upon a more efficient arrangement. For example, the consumers could offer an additional lump-sum payment in return for the monopolist producing more output. So the inefficiency due to monopoly should disappear, along with externalities!

But this will not work – the Coase Theorem will fail – if the required negotiations are infeasible or too costly. In the pollution example, many affected parties might have to agree upon terms to offer the polluter. Or consider common-pool resources such as oil fields. According to the Coase Theorem, unitization or some other efficient reorganization should result from voluntary agreement among the producers. In practice, however, special legislation has proved necessary to compel compliance by holdouts. Nor is the difficulty of reaching a negotiated solution always due to large numbers. With small numbers a different kind of problem appears: *strategic behavior*, as was discussed in Chapter 10. So for either large numbers or small numbers of bargainers, the mere possibility of a mutually advantageous agreement does not guarantee that such an agreement will ever be reached.

EXAMPLE 16.5 THE COASE THEOREM AND SHOPPING MALLS

Shopping malls generally need an "anchor" as attractor – usually a department store. By bringing in traffic, and possibly in other ways, the anchor store confers beneficial *externalities* upon all the independent and satellite shops within the mall.

Conceivably, all the smaller stores might get together and negotiate to invite an anchor store, offering terms that would compensate the larger store for the externalities it would confer. But such negotiations would be difficult. The solution is to have a separate firm operate the mall, in the process charging rentals that would reflect the externality.

B. Peter Pashigian and Eric D. Gould surveyed several regional and superregional malls in the United States.[a] As shown in the table, mall owners allow for the externality by offering lower rentals to department stores as anchors. Calculating in terms of the percent ratio of rent per square foot to sales per square foot, independent department stores in regional malls paid 1.3%, whereas other store types typically paid about 8%. And, as the figures indicate, this was not because the anchor stores had higher sales than the other store types – quite the contrary, their sales per square foot were lower. For the superregional malls, the contrast was even stronger. The authors explain that anchor stores in superregional malls usually are enterprises with exceptionally high reputations, which attract more shoppers than anchor stores in regional chains.

Sales and rentals in shopping malls

	Super-regional malls		Regional malls	
	Median sales/sq.ft	Median rent/$sales	Median sales/sq.ft	Median rent/$sales
Independent department stores	$178	1.5%	$134	1.3%
Clothing and accessories	237	7.9	205	7.5
Gift/specialty	250	8.8	200	8.5
Jewelry	555	7.6	499	7.3

Source: Adapted from Pashigian and Gould, Table 2.

[a] B. Peter Pashigian and Eric D. Gould, "Internalizing Externalities: The Pricing of Space in Shopping Malls," *Journal of Law and Economics*, v. 41 (April 1988).

16.4 THE COMMONS: THE CONSEQUENCES OF UNRESTRICTED ACCESS

Imagine a common pool of underground water, where no single user has any right to exclude others from using the resource. Then each user, pumping from his own well, lowers the water table for everyone else, thus raising their costs of extraction. The consequence of such unrestricted access is called "the tragedy of the commons." In terms of Figure 16.3, a harmful direct externality is involved. Unrestricted access leads to congestion which is costly for everyone. Public parks and roads and highways, and telephone service and Internet connections, are also common pools – they are subject to congestion if there is unrestricted access.

Consider cable modems. Each neighborhood is served by a cable of fixed capacity, which here serves as the common pool. As users attempt to download more data they place increasing pressure upon the common pool. Congestion occurs – the data move more slowly.

Suppose that, in accordance with the principle of diminishing returns, the marginal benefit to each user declines with the amount downloaded. This could occur because the user is likely to first download the most desired files. Imagine that the number of consumers is fixed, and that they have identical preferences. Each consumer's choice variable is how many megabytes of data to download.

Figure 16.4 shows the situation of a typical consumer, Lee. The marginal benefit to Lee, were he the sole user of the service, is shown by curve d_1d_1. Now suppose there are other users, each downloading 3 megabytes per day. Under these conditions Lee's marginal benefit is shown by the curve d_3d_3. (The d_3d_3 curve is lower than the d_1d_1 curve because congestion reduces Lee's satisfaction from any given number of downloads.) And, if each other user downloads 5 megabytes per day, making congestion worse, the marginal benefit to Lee is shown by the still lower curve d_5d_5.

To find the overall demand curve *DD* for the service, only the mutually consistent points are relevant, that is, points where Lee's consumption is the same as everyone else's. First, the demand curve goes through point *A* at the intersection with the vertical

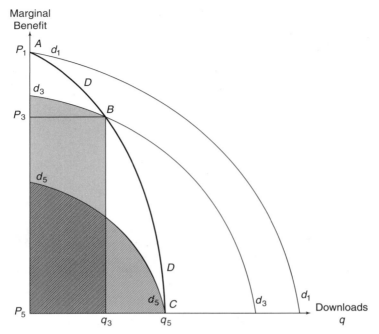

Figure 16.4. Congestion of the Commons

Curve d_1d_1 shows the marginal benefit to typical consumer as sole user. The d_3d_3 curve shows the reduced marginal benefit if there are other users downloading 3 megabytes per day, and similarly for the d_5d_5 curve. The overall demand curve DD goes through all the mutually consistent points, where this consumer downloads the same as everyone else. At the choke price P_1 everyone is frozen out of the market. The zero price P_5 represents unrestricted access, the total benefit being the hatched area under the curve d_5d_5. At price P_3 each consumer would download only 3 megabytes a day. The total benefit would then be the shaded area under the curve d_3d_3, over the range from $q = 0$ to $q = q_3$. This is larger than the shaded area under the curve d_5d_5 over the range from $q = 0$ to $q = q_5$, showing that consumers value uncrowded service.

axis. This is the choke price P_1 for Lee and (since everyone is identical) for all users – a price so high as to freeze all of them out of the market. The lower price P_3 is associated with the consistent point B along d_3d_3, where Lee and everyone else each downloads $q_3 = 3$ megabytes daily. The third consistent point shown is C on curve d_5d_5, where each user downloads $q_5 = 5$ megabytes. Connecting all the consistent consumption points such as A and B and C generates the demand curve DD.

Since point C lies along the horizontal axis, it represents what would occur at the price $P_5 = 0$, that is, if access were unrestricted. Here the market is saturated, with everyone's marginal benefit zero. But the Consumer Surplus remains positive, as shown by the shaded area under the curve d_5d_5.

Benefits would be higher if each consumer could be induced to download only 3 megabytes a day. Such a desirable restriction upon access could be achieved by imposing a price P_3 per megabyte. The total benefit would then be the shaded area under the curve d_3d_3 over the range from $q = 0$ to $q = q_3$, which as drawn is larger than the shaded area under the curve d_5d_5 over the range from $q = 0$ to $q = q_5$. The reason is that an uncrowded service is worth more to consumers. True, Consumer Surplus is now less by the amount of the required consumer payments P_3q_3, but that revenue rebounds to the benefit of the suppliers. Still, were the curves drawn differently, the area under the curve d_5d_5 might be larger. Although it may be desirable to restrict access, the restriction could be too severe.

To determine what amount of restriction is best requires knowing the cost of providing the cable service. Suppose there is a constant per-unit cost represented by the height P_3 along the vertical axis. Were it impossible to restrict access, users would ignore this cost and would arrive at the equilibrium point C. Allowing for the true cost represented by the rectangle P_3q_3 would make it clear that the restrictive solution at point A is more efficient than the unrestricted solution at point C. At quantity q_5 the cost area would be represented by a rectangle P_3q_5 (not drawn in the diagram) that would be greater than the entire Consumer Surplus under curve d_5d_5. The most efficient restriction would be the point along the demand curve DD that maximizes the next Consumer Surplus, after deducting the cost of providing the service.

EXAMPLE 16.6 THE FISHERY AS A COMMONS – SUCCESSFUL RESTRICTION OF ACCESS

The halibut fishery off British Columbia has been subject to drastic overexploitation, as described by R. Quentin Grafton and Dale Squires.[a] For many years the International Pacific Halibut Commission, a U.S.–Canadian agency, restricted fishing in order to maintain the halibut stock. Up to 1990, the Halibut Commission attempted to achieve this goal mainly by shortening the fishing season.

As the table shows, from 65 days in 1980 the fishing season was regularly reduced, ending with a 1990 season of just 6 days per year! Such a short fishing season is extraordinarily inefficient. There was a "rush to fish." Fishing firms were led to multiply the number and increase the size of vessels employed, in order to grab as many fish as possible in the narrow window of time available. In addition, consumers found fresh fish available only for a short period of the year, so the crop generated less revenue for the industry.

In 1990 a new system of quotas was introduced. Quotas were assigned to all the 435 vessels then engaged in the fishery, and some transfers of quotas between vessels were permitted. The favorable consequences are visible in the table. Although the total catch declined for a year or two after 1990, the expansion of the season from 6 to 245 days allowed the introduction of more efficient fishing practices. There have also been safety improvements and reduced wastage. The increased year-round availability of fresh halibut better satisfied consumer desires, and so received higher prices on average. Transferability of quotas allowed the retirement of some of the less efficient vessels and permitted a reduction of personnel. As a sign of the health of the industry and growing confidence in the system, the market price of tradable fishing quotas has been increasing.

The British Columbia Halibut Fishery

Year	Season length (days)	Number of vessels	Catch (millions of lbs.)
1980	65	333	5.7
1995	22	334	9.6
1990	6	435	8.6
1991	214	433	7.2

1992	240	431	7.6
1993	245	351	10.6
1994	245	313	9.9
1995	245	294	9.5
1996	245	281	9.5

Source: Adapted from Grafton and Squires, Table 1.

[a] R. Quentin Grafton and Dale Squires, "Private Property and Economic Efficiency: A Study of a Common-Pool Resource," *Journal of Law and Economics*, v. 43 (October 2000).

16.5 PUBLIC GOODS

Lighthouses alert ships to danger. But if one ship benefits from the light signal, that in no way prevents other ships from also benefitting. Similarly for television broadcasts: one viewer's watching a program does not reduce its availability to other viewers. This property characterizes what are called *public goods*.

> **DEFINITION:** A commodity is a public good if its consumption by any one person does not reduce the amount available to others. Putting it another way, providing a public good to *anyone* makes it possible, without additional cost, to provide it to *everyone*.[7]

Do not confuse public goods with the commons goods (such as highways or fisheries) analyzed in the preceding section. The "tragedy of the commons" is due to unrestricted access. Ocean fisheries may have open access, but fish are not public goods: a mackerel eaten by one person is no longer available for anyone else. Cars may have unrestricted access to a highway, but the space taken by one vehicle is not available to any other car. The defining characteristic of a public good is *concurrent consumption*: one person's use does not interfere with another's.

Some goods combine the two features: anyone suitably equipped can receive a radio broadcast (unrestricted access), and no listener interferes with any other (concurrent consumption). But when a broadcast is "scrambled" to restrict access, as is done in pay TV, it remains a public good – since all those with access receive the broadcast concurrently.

There are also goods in the intermediate range of the spectrum between wholly private and wholly public. A stage performance is a public good to members of a given audience, but the capacity of the theater limits the number who can be concurrently served. Such partial public goods are termed "club goods."

Efficient Production and Consumption of Public Goods

Think of Robinson Crusoe and Friday on their island. Apart from an ordinary private good, say bananas (B), let wood (W) be a public good burned to heat their joint living quarters. (A log on the fire that keeps Robinson warm also does the same for Friday.)

---

[7] Public goods are sometimes called "collective goods." This is poor terminology. Humans are not part of a superorganism, and hence do not consume goods collectively.

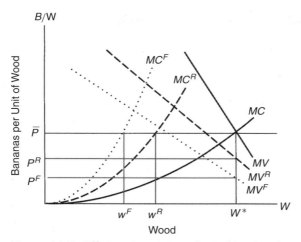

Figure 16.5. Efficient Provision of a Public Good

Wood W is a public good for Robinson Crusoe and Friday. The social Marginal Cost MC of providing the public good is the *horizontal* sum of the individual MC curves; the social Marginal Value MV is the *vertical* sum of the individual MV curves. The efficient output of the public good is W^*. Since each individual should produce to the point where his MC is equal to the marginal social value $\overline{P}$ of the public good, Crusoe should supply w^R and Friday w^F. If the value $\overline{P}$ is divided into amounts P^R and P^F to be paid by Crusoe and Friday, respectively, each would demand the entire amount of the public good produced.

As before, the efficiency conditions can be written in two forms:

$$MRT^R = MRT^F = MRSC^R + MRSC^F \qquad (16.7)$$

$$MC^R = MC^F = MV^R + MV^F \qquad (16.7')$$

Here MC^R is Robinson's Marginal Cost (of producing wood in terms of bananas sacrificed), and MRT^R is the same concept in Marginal Rate of Transformation terminology. Notice that, in contrast with equations (16.5) and (16.5'), here each right-hand-side is a *sum* – reflecting the crucial point that units produced by any supplier become available to each and every consumer.

> **PROPOSITION:** For a public good, one that can be concurrently consumed, the efficiency conditions require that the different producers' Marginal Costs equal one another and also equal *the sum* of the consumers' separate Marginal Values.

Figure 16.5 shows how these conditions may be met. Robinson's rising Marginal Cost curve MC^R and falling Marginal Value curve MV^R for the public good are shown as solid. Friday's corresponding MC^F and MV^F curves as dashed. The overall or community-wide Marginal Cost curve, labelled MC, is the *horizontal sum* of MC^R and MC^F. However, the overall Marginal Value curve, labelled MV, is the *vertical sum* of MV^R and MV^F.[8] The intersection of MC and MV determines the efficient total W^* of wood supplied and consumed. Of this quantity, to meet the efficiency conditions Robinson

---

[8] For simplicity in constructing the diagram, no "income effect" has been allowed for. Normally, MV^R, Robinson's marginal willingness to pay for additional wood, should be a little larger the more wood that Friday has provided, since Friday's doing so enriches Robinson (and vice versa). The next section will take the income effect into account.

should supply w^R and Friday w^F. If so, the Marginal Costs of the two suppliers are equal $(MC^R = MC^F)$ and the supply quantities w^R and w^F sum to W^*. As for the demand quantities, the crucial point is that *both* Robinson and Friday consume the entire $W^* -$ the sum of the amounts produced.

EXERCISE 16.2

Robinson's demand for the public good is given by $MV^R = 80 - 2W$; Friday's demand is given by $MV^F = 30 - W$. The Marginal Cost functions are $MC^R = 2 + 4w^R$ and $MC^F = 2 + 6w^F$. Find the efficient output W^* for the public good, and the separate production quantities w^R and w^F.

ANSWER: Adding the demand curves *vertically*, the aggregate Marginal Value curve is $MV = 110 - 3W$. The Marginal Cost curves MC^R and MC^F must be summed *horizontally*. Skipping over the algebraic details, but using the fact that $w^R + w^F \equiv W$, the aggregate Marginal Cost curve is $MC = (12W + 10)/5$. Setting $MV = MC$, the efficient quantity is $W^* = 20$. To find the separate amounts produced, note first that at this W^* the vertically summed Marginal Value is $MV = 50$. Setting the Marginal Costs MC^R and MC^F each equal to 50 leads to the separate outputs $w^R = 12$, $w^F = 8$.

Is there a set of prices that would induce the individual decision-makers to arrive at the Pareto-efficient outcome described by these efficiency conditions?

First, at the optimum aggregate output W^* the social marginal value (the height of the MV curve) is $\overline{P}$. If, as *producers* of the public good, Robinson and Friday could receive the price $\overline{P}$ then the familiar profit-maximization rules $MC^R = \overline{P}$ and $MC^F = \overline{P}$ would lead them to produce the correct quantities w^R and w^F. On the other hand, if as *consumers* they were each charged the price $\overline{P}$, their demand quantities (determined by setting $MV^R = \overline{P}$ and $MV^F = \overline{P}$) would be too small. Since achieving efficiency requires that they each consume the entire amount W^*, Robinson as consumer should be charged only his demand price (the height of his MV^R curve at W^*), denoted by P^R. Similarly, Friday's price P^F should be his demand price at W^*. It is the *sum* of these efficient consumer prices that ought to equal the price $\overline{P}$ paid to producers.

In summary, the set of prices $(\overline{P}, P^R, P^F)$ that would give correct "Invisible Hand" signals to the separate individuals is:

$$\begin{cases} MC^R = MC^F = \overline{P} \\ MV^R = P^R \quad \text{and} \quad MV^F = P^F \\ \overline{P} = P^R + P^F \end{cases} \qquad (16.8)$$

But could these prices emerge from a market process? The answer is no. For the price system to work, sellers must be able to exclude nonpayers. If so, a monopolist supplier would want to restrict output and therefore would violate the condition Marginal Cost = Price. Nor could the result be achieved under competitive conditions. Since the efficient prices P^R and P^F charged demanders will generally differ, *price discrimination* would be required. But competitive suppliers cannot engage in price discrimination.

CONCLUSION

The efficiency conditions for provision of public goods require that each supplier's Marginal Cost equal the sum of all the demanders' Marginal Values. If nonpayers can be excluded, a system of prices exists that would elicit the efficient total supply and would charge enough to demanders to clear the market. But this system of prices cannot be achieved under competition or under monopoly.

EXERCISE 16.3

(a) Using the same data as in the preceding Exercise, find the set of prices that would lead to the efficient production and consumption quantities. (b) Suppose that Robinson and Friday as producers are competitive price-takers, ruling out price discrimination. What would be the outcome?

ANSWER: (a) From the preceding Exercise, at the efficient solution $MC^R = MC^F = MV = 50$. Therefore the price paid to each supplier would be $\overline{P} = 50$. But to induce consumers to buy the full quantity $W^* = 20$, each consumer must be charged only his separate Marginal Value for this amount of W. Finding the Marginal Values at $W = 20$ from the preceding exercise, the answers are $MV^R = 40 = P^R$ and $MV^F = 10 = P^F$. (b) If as a consumer Robinson can be charged no more than Friday, the *effective* vertical sum of the demand curves in the relevant range is twice the height of Friday's alone, or $MV = 60 - 2W$. Setting $MC = MV = \overline{P}$ as before leads to $W^* = 13.18$, $\overline{P} = 33.64$, $P^R = P^F = 16.82$. At these prices Friday would want to consume exactly the 13.18 units of W produced. Robinson would want to consume even more, but could not do so. In the absence of price discrimination, the quantity of the public good produced is less than the efficient quantity.

Voluntary Provision of Nonexcludable Public Goods – Free-Riding

A self-interested individual might want to provide some of a public good simply for his or her own use. A family might be willing to pay for better neighborhood street lighting, just for their own safety, even if they care nothing about the benefits to other residents. Two important results apply for the private provision of public goods.

> **PROPOSITION 1:** Wealthy people will provide disproportionately more of the public good.

> **PROPOSITION 2:** As community size increases, provision of the public good grows in absolute terms, but less than proportionately to population size.

The key problem hampering the voluntary private provision of public goods is *free-riding*. Although each consumer has some incentive to provide the good, everyone prefers that others pick up the tab.

In Figure 16.6 the quantity b_R scaled along the horizontal axis indicates Robinson's amounts of the private good (bananas). Along the vertical axis, w_R^q indicates his production of the public good (wood) and W_R^c is his consumption of the public good. (As before, Robinson will be consuming both what he produces and what Friday produces.) Suppose Robinson's initial endowment position is E^o; he starts with b_R^o bananas but no

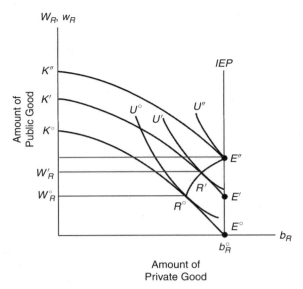

Figure 16.6. Choice between a Private and a Public Good

In Friday's absence, Robinson Crusoe's endowment is E°, where he has zero of the public good W and b_r° of the private good B. His Production Possibility Curve is $E^\circ K^\circ$, and his productive-consumptive optimum is R°. If Friday provides any W, Crusoe's endowment position shifts upward by the same amount. As a function of Friday's provision, Crusoe's optimum positions trace out an Income Expansion Path *IEP*. If B and W are both normal goods for him, Crusoe's *IEP* curve will have positive slope, becoming vertical when the limiting quantity b_r° is reached.

wood. The Production Possibility Curve $E^\circ K^\circ$ shows his opportunities for productive transformations between wood and bananas.

Were Robinson alone on the island, his optimum would be at R° where he produces w_R° units of wood and consumes the same quantity. Now imagine that Friday comes along, providing an additional amount of wood equal to the vertical distance between E° and E'. Robinson's endowment now shifts upward from E° to E'. His Production Possibility Curve also shifts upward to become $E'K'$. The new optimum is R'. If bananas and wood are normal superior goods, Robinson will end up consuming more of both in comparison with what he consumed in isolation. Thanks to Friday's arrival, Robinson will be consuming more of the public good but producing less! That is, he will be sacrificing fewer bananas.

As Friday hypothetically produces more and more of the public good, Robinson's optimum solutions trace out an Income Expansion Path *IEP* (compare Figure 4.9) that includes points R°, R', and E'' in the diagram. Eventually, when the amount of wood that Friday produces equals the distance $E'' - E^\circ$, Robinson's Income Expansion Path hits the barrier formed by the vertical line through b_R°. Beyond this point, Friday is providing so much of the public good that Robinson need produce none at all himself. He becomes a complete "free rider."

Patterned upon the Reaction Curves used in the analysis of duopoly in Chapter 10 (see Figure 10.1), Reaction Curves for Robinson and Friday can be constructed. Using the information summarized by the Income Expansion Path, in Figure 16.7 the Reaction Curve RC_R shows how much w_R^q Robinson will produce in response to any

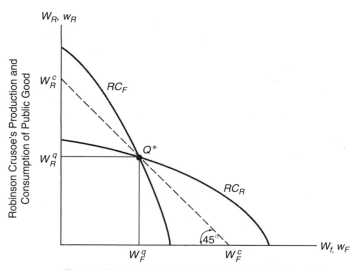

Figure 16.7. Cournot Solution for Supply of a Public Good

Robinson Crusoe's Reaction Curve RC_R shows the quantity of the public good W that he will produce in response to any given amount provided by Friday. Similarly, RC_F is Friday's Reaction Curve. The intersection Q^* shows Crusoe's and Friday's production quantities for the public good, w_R^q and w_F^q. The consumption quantities are the same for each, being the sum $W_R^c = W_F^c = w_R^q + w_F^q$ shown geometrically as the equal intercepts along the axes of the line through Q^* with slope -1.

quantity w_F^q of the public good that Friday produces. Friday's Reaction Curve, RC_F, is defined correspondingly. (Compare the duopolists' Reaction Curves in Figure 10.1.) Note that RC_R is flatter than the dashed line of slope -1. This indicates that as Friday produces an additional unit of wood, Robinson reduces his own production – but by less than one unit. Friday's Reaction Curve RC_F, by similar reasoning, is steeper than the line of slope -1.

The Nash equilibrium (see the discussion in Chapter 10) is at the point Q^*, where the two Reaction Curves intersect. Each person is satisfied with his own production decision, given the other's choice. The location of Q^* determines the *production quantities* of the public good. What about the *consumption quantities*? Since each person consumes the total wood produced, each consumes the sum $w_R^q + w_F^q$. These consumption quantities, W_R^c and W_F^c, are shown geometrically by the intercepts at the axes of the dashed line (of slope -1) drawn through Q^*.

Returning to Proposition 1 above, suppose Robinson becomes wealthier – meaning that he starts with a bigger endowment of the private good (bananas) in Figure 16.6. If the previous endowment position (with Friday producing some of the public good) were E', the new endowment position would shift to the right. The Production Possibility Curve $E'K'$ would also shift to the right. Robinson would now want to produce more wood just for his own use (R' would shift up and to the right). So, in Figure 16.8, his Reaction Curve RC_R would shift upward. This means that the intersection point Q^* shifts up and to the left: Robinson produces more of the public good, and Friday produces less. Thus, wealthy individuals have to provide *disproportionately* more of the public good, because free riding becomes increasingly possible and attractive for the poorer members of the community.

EXERCISE 16.4

Suppose Robinson's Income Expansion Path, as shown in Figure 16.6, is given by the equation $W_R^c = 2b_R$ (up to the point where the vertical barrier at b_R^o is reached). The equation for his Production Possibility Curve is $W_R^c + b_R = b_R^o + w_F^q$. (This equation would correspond to a straight-line Production Possibility Curve in Figure 16.6.) Friday's Income Expansion Path and Production Possibility Curve are defined similarly. Robinson's endowment, however, is larger: $b_R = 1,800$ and $b_F = 900$. Find: (a) the Reaction Curves, (b) the amounts of the public good produced, and (c) the consumption solutions.

ANSWER: (a) Substituting from Robinson's Income Expansion Path equation, the equation for his Production Possibility Curve is $W_R^c + W_R^c/2 = 1,800 + w_F^q$, or $W_R^c = 1,200 + 2w_F^q/3$. But $W_R^c \equiv w_R^q + w_F^q$, and so $w_R^q = 1,200 - w_F^q/3$. This is the equation for Robinson's Reaction Curve in terms of quantities *produced*. (Robinson reduces his production of W by one-third of a unit for each additional unit provided by Friday.) Similarly, Friday's Reaction Curve is $w_F^q = 600 - w_R^q/3$. (b) Solving the two Reaction Curve equations, the Nash equilibrium is $w_R^q = 1,125$ and $w_F^q = 225$. Since their wealth ratio in terms of endowed bananas was $1,800/900 = 2$, Robinson is providing a *disproportionately* larger amount of the public good, as claimed in Proposition 1. (c) Both Robinson and Friday consume 1,350 of W and 675 of B. (So, despite Robinson's larger endowment, he provides so much more of the public good as to end up no better off than Friday!)

Turning now to Proposition 2, suppose a third person – call her Saturday – joins Robinson and Friday. Now think of Robinson's Reaction Curve RC_R in Figure 16.7 as his response to the *combined* production of Friday and Saturday (reinterpreting the horizontal axis accordingly). Since Friday will reduce his production by less than 1:1 in response to any additional units of the public good that Saturday provides, Friday and Saturday's combined production is greater than what Friday would have produced alone. Consequently, the combined Friday-plus-Saturday Reaction Curve lies further to the right than the Reaction Curve RC_F pictured in the diagram; the intersection point Q^* must therefore move down and to the right. More generally, as new members enter a community, each of the original citizens produces less of the public good. Even so, since the cutback is less than one-for-one, *total* provision of the public good increases with community size,

In equation (16.7′), as the number of people in the community grows, the sum on the right increases. Consequently, to achieve efficiency each person should now produce more of the public good. But, as just seen, each individual producer will then want to *reduce* production. Hence the shortfall rises, at an increasing rate, as community size grows.

EXERCISE 16.5

Starting with the community of Exercise 16.4, let the new arrival, Saturday, have the same preferences and endowment as Friday. Compare with the previous result.

ANSWER: Let i index the individuals R, F, and S. As before, each of the Income Expansion Paths has the form $W_i^c = 2b_i$. The Production Possibility Curves now become:

$$\text{(Robinson)} \quad W_R^c + b_R = 1{,}800 + w_F^q + w_S^q$$

$$\text{(Friday)} \quad W_F^c + b_F = 900 + w_R^q + w_S^q$$

$$\text{(Saturday)} \quad W_S^c + b_S = 900 + w_F^q + w_R^q$$

Substituting from the respective Income Expansion Path equations:

$$W_R^c = 1{,}200 + 2\left(w_F^q + w_S^q\right)/3$$

$$W_F^c = 600 + 2\left(w_R^q + w_S^q\right)/3$$

$$W_S^c = 600 + 2\left(w_F^q + w_R^q\right)/3$$

Since all the consumed quantities on the left-hand side of these equations must equal each other and also must equal the *sum* of the three produced quantities:

$$w_R^q = 1{,}200 - \left(w_F^q + w_S^q\right)/3$$

$$w_F^q = 600 - \left(w_R^q + w_S^q\right)/3$$

$$w_S^q = 600 - \left(w_F^q + w_R^q\right)/3$$

Solving simultaneously gives the produced amounts of the public good:

$$w_R^q = 1{,}080, \quad w_F^q = 180, \quad w_S^q = 180$$

The total of W produced is 1,440. Since both Robinson and Friday have cut back in response to Saturday's production, this is only a little larger than the previous two-person total of 1,350 units. Each of the three individuals now consumes 1,440 of W and 720 of B.

The deficient motivation for privately supplying public goods, at least in large communities, may justify their provision by government instead. It is sometimes asserted that production of public goods determines the proper scope of government. Arguably, "private goods" ought to be privately supplied and "public goods" ought to be publicly supplied. Nevertheless, private firms do supply public goods. Television broadcasting is the obvious example, but even lighthouse services have at times been privately provided. And on the other hand government agencies, while supplying public goods such as national defense, also produce a vast range of private goods such as electric power (Tennessee Valley Authority), irrigation water (the U.S. Bureau of Reclamation), insurance (Social Security), education (public schools), and postal services (the U.S. Postal Service).

An Extension: Weakest-Link versus Best-Shot Models of Public Goods[9]

So far the amount of the public good available to each member of the community was assumed to be the *sum* of the amounts provided by the separate individuals. (When Robinson and Friday both provide wood, the total availability is the sum of the two

[9] This discussion is based upon Jack Hirshleifer, "From Weakest-Link to Best-Shot: The Voluntary Provision of Public Goods," *Public Choice*, v. 41 (1983), pp. 371–386.

Table 16.1 Standard public good case (Prisoners' Dilemma)

		Column player	
		Contribute	Do not contribute
Row player	Contribute	1, 1	−1, 2
	Do not contribute	2, −1	0, 0

contributions.) But this is only one of many possibilities. The amount available of a public good may in some instances be determined by the *minimum* amount individually provided (the "weakest link" case). Or it may depend only on the *maximum* of the individual amounts supplied (the "best shot" case).

Suppose the public good is a chain bridge, where each member of the community is responsible for one link of the chain. The weakest link determines the strength of the bridge as a whole. Or imagine a flat island subject to flooding, where each landholder is responsible for the section of the dike bordering his or her land. Since dike failure will flood the entire island, this also is a weakest-link public good; the lowest portion of the dike determines the amount of flood protection.[10] An example of the opposite case, a best-shot situation, is medical research. For example, several different antipolio vaccines were developed, but only the best of them ended up being used.

These different models of public goods can be analyzed in terms of the game-theory payoff matrices introduced in Chapter 10.

Start with standard public goods, where everyone benefits from the *sum* of the individual contributions. In Table 16.1 each individual can choose to Contribute or to Not Contribute. Suppose Arthur and Betty can each contribute at a cost $c = 3$ each. If only one contributes, each of them gets the benefit $b = 2$; if both contribute, the benefit to each is $b = 4$. The upper-right cell shows the payoffs when Row (Arthur) contributes and Column (Betty) does not. The first number in that cell, Arthur's payoff -1, is the sum of -3 and $+2$. The second number, Betty's payoff, is 2 (since she incurs no cost). Comparison with Table 10.3 in Chapter 10 shows that Table 16.1 is a *Prisoners' Dilemma.*

As described in Section 10.1, the Nash equilibrium under simultaneous play[11] is such that each person's decision is a best response to the other player's choice. In Table 16.1 the equilibrium is at the lower-right cell where both choose Not Contribute, with payoffs (0,0). This is inefficient. If both parties instead chose Contribute, they would arrive at the upper-left cell with payoffs (1,1). The problem is that if either Contributes, then the other's best response is Not Contribute. So the upper-left cell is not an equilibrium.

Now consider the weakest-link case shown in Table 16.2. Here each person gets a benefit of $b = 2$ only if *both* contribute, at a cost of $c = 1$ each. The *efficient* outcome remains the upper-left cell, with payoffs (1,1). This is a Nash equilibrium. Notice, however, that the lower-right cell, with payoffs (0,0), is also a Nash equilibrium. There is a also a third Nash equilibrium, involving the "mixed strategies" that were defined in

---

[10] Benjamin Franklin appears to have had in mind the weakest-link model when, at the signing of the Declaration of Independence in 1776, he said: "We must all hang together, or assuredly we shall all hang separately."

[11] Chapter 10 also covered solution concepts for situations in which the players move *in sequence* rather than simultaneously. In this chapter the simultaneous-move protocol is assumed.

Table 16.2 Weakest-link public good

		Column player	
		Contribute	Do not contribute
Row player	Contribute	1, 1	−1, 0
	Do not contribute	0, −1	0, 0

Section 10.1. At this mixed-strategy Nash solution each player chooses Contribute with probability 50% and Not Contribute with probability 50%, leading again to a payoff of zero to each.[12]

Which of these three weakest-link Nash equilibria will apply? The sensible thing is for each player to choose Contribute. Notice that all the Nash solutions are symmetrical; that is, the players' choices match one another. If so, it makes more sense to match at (Contribute, Contribute) rather than at any of the Pareto-inferior strategy-pairs. Nevertheless, all that can rigorously be said is that – in contrast with the standard public goods or "summation" case – when public goods take the weakest-link form an efficient solution *could* be attained.

Now consider a best-shot public good (Table 16.3). Here suppose the cost of contributing remains $c = 1$, but each player receives the benefit $b = 2$ whenever *either* contributes. The table has two asymmetric Nash equilibria in pure strategies: either Row contributes and Column does not with payoffs (2,1), or vice versa with payoffs (1,2). Furthermore, these are both Pareto-optimal outcomes (an efficient amount of the public good is provided). Once again there is a symmetrical "mixed strategy" solution, with each player choosing Contribute and Not contribute with 50% probability. The payoffs for the symmetrical mixed-strategy solution are (1,1). In view of the payoffs (2,1) and (1,2) of the asymmetrical solutions, the Nash equilibrium with payoffs (1,1) is inefficient. Still, each of the possible equilibria gets closer to efficiency, in comparison with the standard "summation" case.

CONCLUSION

For public goods whose availability to consumers depends, as is usually assumed, upon the *sum* of the amounts individually provided, the Nash equilibrium under simultaneous play is always inefficient. When the amount available depends upon the minimum contribution (weakest-link) or the maximum contribution (best-shot), the Nash equilibrium comes closer to or actually achieves Pareto efficiency.

As a final thought, recall that the Coase Theorem is always at work to overcome "market failures." Counteracting the tendency to underprovide public goods, members of a community may be able to negotiate with one another to their mutual advantage – signing contracts that essentially say "I will increase my contribution if you do."

---

[12] Suppose Betty plays her two (column) strategies with 50% probability each. Arthur's payoff if he chooses the Contribute row will then be the average of +1 and −1, or 0. And if Arthur chooses the "Not contribute" row, it will be the average of 0 and 0, or 0 once again. A similar calculation holds for Betty's choices if Arthur chooses a 50:50 mixture. This pair of mixed strategies is an equilibrium since, given the other's choice, neither player gains from changing.

Table 16.3 Best-shot public good

		Column player	
		Contribute	Do not contribute
Row player	Contribute	1, 1	1, 2
	Do not contribute	2, 1	0, 0

EXAMPLE 16.7 ALLIANCES: WEAKEST-LINK OR BEST-SHOT?

John A. C. Conybeare, James C. Murdoch, and Todd Sandler asked whether some important historic military alliances represented summation, weakest-link, or best-shot situations.[a] For a weakest-link alliance, success (fighting power) would be determined by the *smallest* of the national military contributions; for a best-shot alliance, by the *largest*.

In the period before the first World War, the Triple Alliance (Germany, Austria, Italy) faced the Triple Entente (Britain, France, Russia). And after World War II the NATO alliance led by the United States faced the Warsaw Pact led by the Soviet Union. For each alliance, the authors tentatively identified the likely weakest-link and best-shot nations. In the Warsaw Pact, for example, the Soviet Union was the obvious "best shot" (biggest contributor).

For an alliance of the weakest-link type, the authors postulated that the nations would have arrived at the largest *symmetrical* solution (corresponding to the Contribute, Contribute outcome in the upper-left cell of Table 16.2). For a best-shot alliance, an *asymmetrical* solution (one of the off-diagonal cells of Table 16.3) was assumed – the "best shot" making a positive contribution, the others not.

Of course, a nation rarely if ever spends literally zero on defense. Defense effort, although motivated in part by alliance considerations, almost always also serves private national purposes such as maintaining internal order. So for each member of an alliance, defense spending is partly a private good, partly a public good.

Taking up the best-shot model first, for each alliance the authors identified the likely best-shot nation. Suppose that, owing perhaps to a rise in national income, the best shot increases its defense budget. Now consider the response of its allies. In a strict best-shot model these other allies would have been contributing zero to begin with, and would now continue to contribute zero. But since their own defense efforts are only partly public goods, they will have a motive to respond. Such an ally would increase its defense budget if the "private good" aspect of its defense effort were a *complement* (as defined in Chapter 4, Section 4.2) to the public good provided by the best-shot nation. Or, if it were instead a *substitute* (*anticomplement*), the ally would react by reducing its defense budget.

So the prediction is that, in a best-shot alliance, other allies' defense expenditures would respond in some way – positively in the case of complements, negatively if anticomplements – to increases in the defense budget of the best shot. (And they would not react at all to increases in the defense efforts of other, non-best-shot, members of the alliance.) By similar reasoning, in a weakest-link alliance the other allies' defense expenditures would respond in a nonzero way only to increases in the defense budget of the nation identified as the weakest link.

For the pre-World War I alliances, military manpower data for the period 1880–1914 indicated that the Triple Alliance satisfied the predictions for a best-shot situation. The implication is that the best-shot nation, Germany, provided all or almost all of the "public" aspect of alliance military expenditures. Although Austria and Italy also had large defense budgets, these mostly served those nations' separate private national purposes. The opposed Triple Entente, in contrast, fit the weakest-link predictions – Britain being the weakest-link nation. More generally, the authors suggested, *offensive* coalitions such as the Triple Alliance are usually best-shot situations, while *defensive* alliances like the Triple Entente tend to be weakest-link.

COMMENT

The alliance model here assumes that each nation decides independently on its level of military effort. But members of an alliance can surely negotiate with one another. They can sign treaties effectively saying "I will contribute more effort if you do the same." As the Coase Theorem tells us, such negotiation would allow a closer approximation to Pareto efficiency. In fact, intra-alliance negotiations figured importantly in the history of all the alliances studied here.

[a] John A. C. Conybeare, James C. Murdoch, and Todd Sandler, "Alternative Collective-Goods Models of Military Alliances: Theory and Empirics," *Economic Inquiry*, v. 32 (October 1994).

16.6 APPROPRIATIVE ACTIVITY AND RENT-SEEKING

According to the Coase Theorem, "market failures" such as externalities can, ideally, be overcome by market trading of property rights. But for this to be possible, property rights must be well-defined to begin with. What happens when they are not?

Property rights are poorly defined if (1) not all resources are appropriated (some resources do not belong legally to anyone), or if (2) rights to use some resources, although defined in a formal legal sense, are only imperfectly enforced. When property rights are imperfectly enforced, stealing can be profitable. It may even be possible to take others' property without doing anything illegal, for example by filing groundless lawsuits, by legislation transferring control of resources, or by adverse possession of land. And on the other side, the present owners of property may undertake defensive measures: patrolling to prevent theft or invasion, hiring expensive lawyers to fight lawsuits, lobbying against new legislation, and so forth. All such proceedings, both offensive or defensive, come under the heading of *appropriative activity* – efforts to impose or else to prevent involuntary changes in the ownership of property.

The "rush to fish," as the consequence of a limited fishing season, is another type of costly appropriative activity, as is the "rush to pump" when neighboring oil wells draw upon a common underlying petroleum source. A famous historical instance was the Oklahoma land rush of 1889, a race to stake out former Indian territories. "Rushing" is attempting to gain control of currently *unappropriated* resources. Settling new territories, fishing and hunting, and pumping oil are all productive actions in and of themselves. The inefficiency arises from the extra costs incurred when everyone races to act before others do.

It is essential to understand that the efficiency loss due to appropriative activity is not a consequence of the *existence* of property rights under law. It arises because their assignment or their enforcement is imperfect. A totally lawless society would not avoid appropriative activity. On the contrary, under anarchy the struggle to acquire and defend one's control over resources would become every person's main occupation.

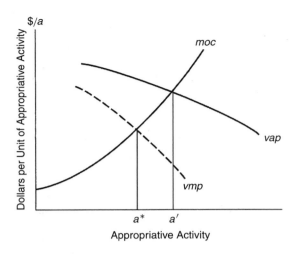

Figure 16.8. Appropriative Activity and Preclusive Competition

The efficient level of appropriative activity for any individual is a^*, where Marginal Opportunity Cost *moc* equals Value of the Marginal Product *vmp*. However, if the resource is unowned (such as fish in the ocean), the individual will want to set *moc* equal to the Value of the Average Product *vap* at activity level $a' > a^*$. Thus, preclusive competition leads to excessive appropriative effort.

The race to acquire unappropriated resources is called *preclusive competition.* Figure 16.8 illustrates both the efficient level of effort in the attempt to acquire such resources and the extent of inefficient "rushing" that can be anticipated. Think of a community of fishermen. The appropriative (fishing) effort of a typical individual is scaled on the horizontal axis. The efficient level of fishing is a^*. Here the typical individual's rising curve of *Marginal Opportunity Cost* (*moc*) – representing the value of the best other uses of resources devoted to appropriative effort – intersects the falling *Value of the Marginal Product* (*vmp*) curve. But the privately optimal level of effort is at a'; here the *moc* curve intersects the *Value of the Average Product* (*vap*) curve.

The key idea is that, though an additional hour of effort by any fisherman will land more fish, some of those same fish would have been caught by other fishermen. The true Marginal Product is what remains after subtracting this externality. Assuming for simplicity that all the fishermen are identical, each gets as much as any other when they fish the same number of hours. Hence each enjoys the *Average Product*, the total fish catch divided by the total of hours spent.

EXERCISE 16.7

An isolated village contains a cultivated banana grove. Bananas (B) are the only consumption good. There are $L = 12$ villagers, of whom L_g work in the banana grove. The production function for bananas in the grove is $B_g = 12L_g - L_g^2$. The remaining villagers L_w work in the surrounding wilderness; the production function for bananas there is $B_w = 2L_w$. For simplicity, assume none of the workers desires leisure and that no other resources or products need be considered. (a) How would you divide the 12 laborers between grove and wilderness to maximize banana output? (b) Compare the results if the grove were instead "unappropriated" property, so that any villager could enter and pick what she pleases. (c) What property rights could be assigned to achieve efficiency without a centralized dictatorship? [*Note*: Since bananas are the only good, there is no need to distinguish between physical Marginal Product and Value of the Marginal Product, or between physical Average Product and Value of the Average Product.]

ANSWER: Starting with the production function in the grove, the *Marginal Product* function can be found (by calculus or by plotting) to be $vmp_g = 12 - 2L_g$.

Figure 16.9. Possible Additional Monopoly Efficiency Loss Due to Rent Seeking

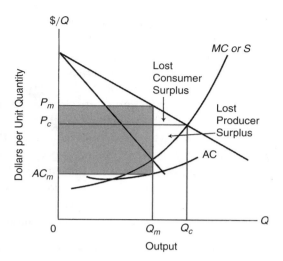

Figure 8.5 showed the lost Consumer Surplus and Producer Surplus owing to the fact that the monopoly output Q_m was smaller than the output Q_c for a competitive industry. *Additional* efficiency loss may result from rent-seeking competition for the monopoly privilege. The maximum a firm could bid in such a competition is the monopoly profit – the difference $P_m - AC_m$ multiplied by the monopoly's profit-maximizing output Q_m. (Whether this area is an efficiency loss or simply a distributive transfer depends upon the extent to which the rent-seeking competition involves real wastage of resources.)

The Marginal Opportunity Cost (*moc*) here is the constant return to labor in the wilderness: $moc = 2$. The efficient outcome requires that $moc = vmp_g$, or that $2 = 12 - 2L_g$. The result is the efficient assignment: $L_g = 5$, $L_w = 7$. The banana outputs are $B_g = 35$ and $B_w = 14$, summing to a total of 49. (b) If the grove is unowned, the villagers will instead equate the *Average Products* in the grove and in the wilderness. (Or else workers would shift from where the average is lower to where it is higher.) Setting $B_g/L_g = B_w/L_w$ implies $L_g = 10$ and $L_w = 2$. The Total Product of 24 is the same as if the grove did not exist at all! (c) One possibility is to grant each villager 1/12 of the grove as individual property. Then each person would work 5/12 of the time in the grove and 7/12 of the time in the wilderness.

Suppose individuals or firms compete to acquire property rights in the form of legal privileges, such as licenses or franchises. This type of appropriative activity is called *rent-seeking*. Figure 16.9 here adapts the familiar monopoly analysis pictured in Figure 8.5, which showed the efficiency loss under monopoly as the sum of the foregone Consumer Surplus and Producer Surplus. The loss occurred because the monopoly output Q_m is smaller than the competitive output Q_c. The new idea underlying Figure 16.9 is that rent-seeking is responsible for an *additional* efficiency loss.

Specifically, think of potential monopolists competing for the monopoly privilege. Suppose each candidate would be willing to spend any amount up to the monopoly profit it would otherwise achieve. In Figure 16.9 the size of this maximum bid is shown by the shaded area: this is the difference between the monopolist's price P_m and its level of Average Cost AC_m at the monopoly output Q_m, multiplied by Q_m.

The (dotted) efficiency loss identified in Figure 8.5 (the lost Consumer Surplus and Producer Surplus) still remains. Whether rent-seeking imposes any *additional* efficiency loss depends upon how the appropriative competition takes place.

Suppose a local community chooses to grant a monopoly TV cable franchise. It might sell the right at a public auction (see Example 14.8). Then the winning bidder's payment is not an efficiency loss but only a transfer to the community treasury. (True, organizing and participating in auctions involves some paperwork and perhaps may require some hard thinking by bidders, but the inefficient waste of resources is likely to be small.) Alternatively, franchise rights may be obtained by a bribery auction. If so, the proceeds go not to the community but to the politicians or bureaucrats in a position to demand the bribe. Again, this is mainly a transfer, so (ethics aside) the efficiency loss will be small.

Some forms of rent-seeking competition involve greater costs. Suppose the franchise is awarded at the discretion of individuals who, though too honest to accept bribes, can be influenced in other ways: for example, by expensive lobbyists, by costly litigation, by commercial and political pressures, or by broadcasters' promises to carry certain favored programs in place of others more desired by consumers. Last, the privilege may be acquired by competitive violence. In Prohibition-era Chicago, the Capone gang used warfare to achieve near-monopoly control of bootlegging.[13] These forms of appropriative competition involve substantial social costs.

The upshot is that rent-seeking competitions for monopoly positions can magnify the waste of resources, over and above the losses of Consumer Surplus and Producer Surplus associated with smaller monopoly output.

EXAMPLE 16.8 RENT-SEEKING IN STATE CAPITALS

Rent-seeking, attempting to acquire rights or privileges from government, is difficult to measure. There is no physically visible output. And inputs such as bribes, threats, promises, or favors may take hidden or intangible forms.

In an ingenious approach, Russell S. Sobel and Thomas A. Garrett reasoned that much rent-seeking necessarily takes place at the seats of government, specifically state capitals in the United States.[a] They compared the prevalence of enterprises that might be associated with rent-seeking activity in the counties containing the 50 state capitals with their prevalence in 50 noncapital counties – matched in terms of demography, levels of income, and so forth.

The authors distinguished *direct* rent-seeking activities (campaign contributions and in-kind gifts) from *indirect* rent-seeking efforts (demonstrations, advertising, and policy-oriented research). In what may be excessively harsh language, the first category of rent-seeking corresponds roughly to bribery, the second to propaganda.

The table shows a selection of the results. The "industries" are 33 of the 4-digit Standard Industrial Classification categories of enterprises as listed in the U.S. Census Bureau, *1995 County Business Patterns*, selected by the authors as likely to be associated with rent-seeking activities. The data column shows the number of establishments in each industry, per capita, as a ratio; the numerator is the median of the 50 capital counties and the denominator is the median of the matched non-state-capital counties. A ratio exceeding 1 shows that the industry in question is "overrepresented" in state capitals. (The authors also estimated the total volume of rent-seeking in other ways that cannot be covered here.) All the activities shown in the table are overrepresented in capital counties.

Quite apart from rent-seeking, normal processes of government administration – without regard to rent-seeking – necessarily lead to disproportionate representation of certain types of business and social enterprises. Governments must maintain police forces, for example, and so industries supplying police equipment are likely to cluster near the seats of government. For this reason, as estimates of the scale of rent-seeking the comparisons shown in the table err to some extent on the high side. On the other hand, since some rent-seeking also take place outside of capital

---

[13] See Kenneth Allsop, *The Bootleggers: The Story of Chicago's Prohibition Era*, 2nd ed. (New Rochelle, NY: Arlington House, 1968).

counties, there is also an error in the opposite direction. Whether the two errors cancel out remains doubtful.

COMMENT

The concentration of associations of various types in state capitals surely reflects their rent-seeking activities. It may be surprising that legal services are not more heavily overrepresented. That probably reflects the fact that these activities are needed and utilized in all types of communities, whether state capitals or not.

Establishments in capital versus matched comparison counties

SIC #	Industry	Ratio of capital/noncapital establishments
	Direct rent-seeking industries (selected)	
8100	Legal services	1.52
8600	Membership organizations	1.59
8610	Business associations	3.31
8620	Professional organizations	4.57
8630	Labor organizations	1.83
8640	Civil and social associations	1.50
8650	Political organizations	11.16
	Indirect rent-seeking industries (selected)	
2710	Newspapers	1.31
2720	Periodicals	1.32
4830	Radio and television broadcasting	1.27
7310	Advertising	1.31
8733	Noncommercial research organizations	1.92

Source: Adapted from Sobel and Garrett, Table 1b.

[a] Russell S. Sobel and Thomas A. Garrett, "On the Measurement of Rent-Seeking and Its Social Opportunity Cost," *Public Choice*, v. 112 (2002).

SUMMARY   The analysis of economic policy has concentrated on two policy goals: *efficiency* (the size of the pie) and *equity* (the distribution of slices). Efficiency is increased by any Pareto-preferred change, that is, any change that increases the utility of some person or persons without reducing the utility of anyone else. An outcome is Pareto-efficient (or Pareto-optimal, or just efficient for short) when no other outcomes are Pareto-preferred to it. (Nevertheless, an efficient outcome need not be Pareto-preferred to every outcome that is inefficient.)

The Social Opportunity Frontier shows the maximum achievable income for any person, given the income of the others. All points on the Social Opportunity Frontier are efficient. For two commodities, the Contract Curve within the Edgeworth box corresponds to the Social Opportunity Frontier. A practical measure of efficiency is the sum of Consumer Surplus and Producer Surplus.

The Theorem of the Invisible Hand states that, under ideal conditions, a laissez-faire economy uses resources efficiently. Guided by market prices, in equilibrium individuals and firms will choose *efficient patterns of consumption* (for each commodity, all consumers will have equal Marginal Values), *efficient patterns of production* (for each commodity, all firms will have equal Marginal Costs), and *efficient balances between consumption and production* (for each commodity, Marginal Cost will equal Marginal Value).

The Invisible Hand may fail owing to monopolies (monopolized goods are underproduced) or to direct externalities (goods imposing costs upon others are overproduced; goods generating benefits to others are underproduced). The Coase Theorem, however, indicates that when property rights are well defined, and when agreements are easily negotiated and enforced, voluntary agreements tend to overcome these inefficiencies.

Common-pool problems are another source of market failure. In a "commons" such as an ocean fishery or an underground oil pool, property rights are not well defined. The consequence is a wasteful "rush to fish" or "rush to pump."

Public goods represent a special kind of externality, where providing the good to anyone makes it possible, without additional cost, to provide it for everyone. Although it is possible to define an efficient set of prices that would lead producers to generate and consumers to demand efficient quantities of a public good, these prices could not be arrived at by market processes. However, some amounts of public goods will rationally be voluntarily provided, with the wealthy supplying a disproportionately large fraction. If reliance is upon voluntary provision alone, the gap between the efficient amount and the quantity supplied becomes more severe the larger the community.

When the amount of the public good available for consumption is determined not by the *sum* of the individual contributions, as usually assumed, but instead by the *smallest* (weakest-link) or by the *largest* (best-shot) individual contribution, the aggregate provision comes closer to the Pareto-efficient level.

Where property rights are imperfect, appropriative activity and rent-seeking – struggles to achieve control of resources – constitute another important source of efficiency loss.

QUESTIONS

†The answers to daggered questions appear at the end of the book.

For Review

1. Explain and justify the normally "concave" shape of the Social-Opportunity Frontier in Figure 16.1.
2. In the Edgeworth Box (Figure 16.2), explain the difference between *Pareto-preferred* and *Pareto-optimal* allocations.
†3. a. What meaning, if any, can be given to the concept of a "social optimum"?
    b. How valid is efficiency or Pareto optimality as a criterion of social optimality?
4. Why is it true that in equilibrium all consumers have the same Marginal Rates of Substitution in Consumption, even though they differ in tastes and incomes?
5. What is the Theorem of the Invisible Hand?
6. What are the conditions of efficiency and are they reached in a free-market economy? Can the conditions be achieved, in principle, without use of the market?
7. Why does disequilibrium of markets lead to inefficiency?
†8. a. Explain why a monopolist in the product market is said to hire "too little" of the factors it uses for production.

b. Does it follow that too large a proportion of the community's resources are employed by competitive firms?

9. What are public goods? What are externalities? Is a public good a special case of an externality?

10. How would inability to exclude nonpayers affect the private supply of public goods? The private supply of private goods?

†11. a. Under what circumstances does the "free rider" problem emerge?
 b. It has been asserted that all government is fundamentally a response to the free-rider problem. How valid is this claim?

†12. a. What is the efficiency condition for optimal provision of a public good?
 b. In the case of public goods why do we sum individual demand curves vertically, whereas for private goods we sum horizontally?

†13. Mosquito control at the local level is an example of a pure public good. Suppose that in an economy consisting of two identical persons, each has the following Marginal Value function for mosquito control: $MV^i = MV^j = 100 - y$, where y is the quantity of mosquito control. Let the Marginal Cost of mosquito control be $10. What is the socially optimal level of control?

†14. a. What limits the possibility of private supply of public goods?
 b. Will public provision mean that a more nearly optimal amount will be supplied?

15. What is Coase's Theorem? Explain the relevance of each of the following conditions for the applicability of the theorem:
 a. Well-defined property rights.
 b. Low costs of negotiating and enforcing agreements.

16. What is "appropriative activity"? What is "rent-seeking"? What are the implications of such activities for economic efficiency?

†17. What is the possible advantage of imposing "sin taxes" on alcohol or cigarettes, or a tax on gasoline, as compared with other products? Distinguish between direct and pecuniary externalities.

†18. Why do countries negotiate international treaties to limit the amount of fishing?

†19. Why are "anchor" department stores in shopping malls charged lower rents than other stores?

For Further Thought and Discussion

†1. Analyze the following fragment of a conversation based upon Robert Browning's poem, "My Last Duchess":

But my dear Dr. H., your own textbook proves that in terms of economic efficiency I was amply justified in taking the life of my last duchess. For, being of not inconsiderable means, I was willing to pay more for her death than she could have pay to prevent it.

In terms of economic efficiency, was the Duke justified in murdering his wife?

†2. "An efficient allocation of resources maximizes the dollar value of national income." True or false? Explain.

3. Give an example of an externality that is mutually beneficial. Of one that is mutually harmful. Can there be a case in which in one direction the effect is beneficial but in the other direction harmful?

†4. What real-world considerations may forestall the working of Coase's Theorem by making property rights ambiguous or uncertain? By raising the costs of negotiating and enforcing contracts?

†5. "An ideal market would achieve a Pareto-efficient outcome, but only one that is Pareto-preferred to the endowment situation; an ideal dictatorship would not be so limited." True or false? Explain.

†6. Steps have been taken in the United States to ban the commercial market in human blood. (One argument is that commercially provided blood is more likely to be infected with hepatitis than volunteered blood.) Can this ban be justified on efficiency grounds, or any other grounds?

†7. One "market intervention" is the law against polygamy. Historically, many societies have permitted polygyny (multiple wives) and some even polyandry (multiple husbands). It has been contended that the laws banning one husband from having multiple wives work to the disadvantage of women, just as a law forbidding more than one car per customer would hurt suppliers of cars.

   a.   Is this analogy sound?
   b.   Who are the main losers and main gainers from monogamy laws?
   c.   Can the monogamy laws be defended in terms of efficiency?
   d.   Can the same laws be defended in terms of equality?

†8. Through the millennia, humans have hunted many species to extinction. How is this related to the problem of the commons?

†9. Consider a toll charged in order to recover the past cost of building a road. It could be argued that to be efficient, the toll should instead be set close to zero – because a higher toll will deter some individuals from driving, whereas the incremental cost of another driver is close to zero once the road has been built. Do you agree?

†10. Michael Heller describes how during the late 1990s, valuable retail floor space in Russia was left vacant for long periods, while at the same time flimsy metal kiosks sprang up on the street and did thriving business. His proposed explanation is "the tragedy of the anticommons": that too many government authorities and individuals were able to block usage of retail floor space by regulation or property infringement claims. The tragedy of the anticommons leads to under- rather than over-usage of scarce resources. Heller and Rebecca Eisenberg have argued also that patents on gene-related technologies not specifically limited to a single specific commercial application are creating a tragedy of the anticommons for biomedical research. In other words, granting more intellectual property rights may decrease the development of new medications and treatments. Why might the tragedy of the anticommons be a special problem for fields involving research?

17 Government, Politics, and Conflict

Chapter 16 dealt with "market failures," ways in which the Invisible Hand might go wrong when it came to achieving economic efficiency. When market incentives fail, it is natural to turn to government for remedies. Section 17.1 considers the other side of the coin: *government failures*. Are government actions likely to realize citizens' desired ends, any more than private actions? Section 17.2 looks at the likely outcomes of democratic politics and majority voting. Finally, although the text so far has dealt almost exclusively with how people make a living through mutually advantageous market transactions, a crucially important alternative way of acquiring resources is taken up in Section 17.3: the method of conflict, confiscation, and war.

17.1   THE OTHER SIDE OF THE COIN: GOVERNMENT FAILURES

Economists once thought of economic policy as a shotgun with two barrels. The first barrel favored free trade and laissez faire, owing to the efficiency advantages of a market economy guided by the Invisible Hand. The second barrel favored state intervention and regulation in order to correct imperfections and failures of the market economy. (For example, antitrust action to counter monopolies, and taxes or subsidies to correct for externalities.)

Neither barrel of the shotgun hits the target. Suppose the Invisible Hand worked perfectly. Even so, the efficient allocations of goods and resources achieved by the market economy might violate other goals of public policy, such as distributive equity or preservation of community values. On the other hand, in considering flaws of the market system we must guard against "the Nirvana fallacy" – the presumption that an ideal vision of government intervention will be reflected in actual practice.

Underlying the analysis in this chapter is the assumption that political decisions are guided by the same motivations as decisions in the marketplace. Although people are not wholly selfish, their political decisions are unlikely to be any more altruistic than their market decisions.

There is one crucial difference between market decisions and political decisions. Market transactions are *voluntary*. One person consents to sell, and the other consents to buy. But politics largely concerns *involuntary* transactions. A government agency may provide a public road, even though some taxpayers may derive no benefit and still have to pay for it. A citizen opposed to what government does cannot just abstain or go away. To a far greater degree than private individuals or firms, the state can *coerce* compliance.

Corruption as Government Failure

The widespread prevalence of government failures is suggested by the daily news of corrupt, high-handed, or inefficient government actions. Does that matter? For one thing, corruption is likely to depress economic growth.

EXAMPLE 17.1 CORRUPTION AND GROWTH – INTERNATIONAL COMPARISON

Vito Tanzi and Hamid Davoodi examined the relation between perceived levels of corruption and real GDP growth for 97 countries in 1997.[a] Using a scaled corruption measure provided by a private organization called Transparency International, the authors' regression analysis suggested that at the lowest level of corruption (score 0) the annual growth rate of national GDP was on average around 3%, whereas at the most severe level of corruption (score 10) the average growth rate was likely to be only 0%.

There is a direction-of-causation problem here. Rather than corruption reducing growth, it might be that high growth leads to less corruption. Such reverse causation could be plausible for the connection between corruption and the *level* rather than the growth of wealth. For one thing, wealthier countries can afford to pay government officials higher salaries, making them less dependent upon bribes. But even if *high-income* countries are more successful in controlling corruption, there seems to be no clear reason why a *high rate of income growth* should reduce corruption. So the conclusion that corruption hurts economic growth does not seem vulnerable to the reverse-causation objection.

[a] Vito Tanzi and Hamid Davoodi, "Corruption, Growth, and Public Finances," in Arvind K. Jain, ed., *The Political Economy of Corruption* (London and New York: Taylor and Francis, 2001).

Political Competition and Its Limits

Even when officials are high-handed or corrupt, governments are never wholly free of control by citizens. In the polity as in the market economy, the main mechanism of control is *competition*. Political parties are in some ways like business firms. Just as firms offer goods to consumers at a price, political parties offer packages of government policies at a "price" in the form of taxes and other burdens. To win elections and gain prestige and pay and power, parties and politicians try to at least give the appearance of meeting citizens' desires.

Perfect competition in the economy corresponds to perfect democracy in the polity.[1] In the market economy, perfect competition among firms drives profits to zero in long-run equilibrium (see Chapter 7). So suppliers are powerless to do anything other than what consumers want. Any firm that fails to satisfy consumers will be driven out of business. In the ideal polity, perfect competition among politicians similarly drives "political profit" to zero. Since failure to satisfy the citizens would mean losing office, parties or elected officials would ideally have no power to do anything but what citizens wanted. Thus, Adam Smith's Invisible Hand – the force that induces individuals, in their own self-interest, to satisfy the needs of others – applies, up to a point, in politics. To some extent at least, political parties do seem to respond to the interests of voters.

EXAMPLE 17.2 WHAT HAPPENED WHEN WOMEN GOT THE VOTE?

The scale of government, as a proportion of GNP, grew drastically in the 20th century. Since almost all of that growth took place after World War I, it is natural to examine social and political changes that occurred around that period. John R. Lott, Jr. and Lawrence W. Kenny[a] drew attention to a possibly unexpected explanation – women's suffrage. (Although some states had extended the vote to women earlier, the 19th Amendment, making woman suffrage universal, was not ratified until 1920.) The connection is that women, now voting in increasing numbers, were more favorable than men to increased government spending.

The table shows, averaging over states of the Union, per capita state government expenditures by year, before and after that state granted women the vote. (Year 0 is

[1] Gary S. Becker, "Competition and Democracy," *Journal of Law and Economics*, v. 1 (October 1958).

the year that women began voting in that state.) As can be seen, before extension of the suffrage (the "minus" years) the trend of per capita state expenditure was just about horizontal. Then, in the "plus" years, the trend took a sharp upward turn.

Average state expenditures, per capita (1996 dollars)

Years (before and after woman suffrage)	Expenditures
−10	$102
−8	105
−6	115
−4	120
−2	110
0	100
+2	115
+4	130
+6	140
+8	170
+10	205

Source: Estimated visually from Lott and Kenny, Figure 2.

Many other factors possibly influencing government spending were also at work during this period. After a statistical analysis allowing for other possible causes, the authors estimated that around 16% of the observed growth of government was attributable specifically to woman suffrage.

Why might women on average favor larger-scale government activity more than men do? One reason is that, since time immemorial, the prime source of physical protection and economic support for women has been marriage. But in the 20th century divorce became easier. No longer able to rely confidently upon men's marriage commitment, women have turned to government as a second line of defense. As a related point, women – and especially women raising children without husbands – are on average poorer than men, so they benefit disproportionately from government redistribution of income from the rich to the poor.

[a] John R. Lott, Jr. and Lawrence W. Kenny, "Did Women's Suffrage Change the Size and Scope of Government?" *Journal of Political Economy*, v. 107 (1999).

But, viewed as instruments whereby citizen-consumers can achieve their desires, political mechanisms suffer from serious shortcomings.

Just as ideal democracy in the polity corresponds to perfect competition in the market, *political dictatorship* corresponds to *monopoly*. But dictatorship is a far more drastic matter than market monopoly. Customers can usually avoid doing business with a market monopolist, but citizens cannot easily escape an oppressive government. Furthermore, the market monopolist only wants our money; the dictator may want our very lives.

Although the contest for political power is more competitive in democracies than in dictatorships, political competition involves strong economies of scale. As a result, democratic nations often have only two (or a very few) effective political parties. So even where democratic political competition exists, the situation is closer to *oligopoly* (Chapter 10) than to perfect competition.

Furthermore, citizens usually vote not for policies, but for delegates in the legislative or executive branches of government. These delegates supposedly represent the citizens in making policy choices. But elections are infrequent. Whereas consumers make and reconsider market choices every day, citizens can choose or recall their political representatives only at election intervals measured in years. And some of the most important political decision-makers, such as U.S. Supreme Court justices, are only indirectly "elected" and once chosen are beyond effective recall.

The limited options available further weaken citizens' control of delegates. Many issues are bundled in elections. A voter may prefer the position of one candidate on one question, of a competing candidate on a second issue, and so forth. But the delegate elected will represent (or misrepresent) the voter in all decisions to be made during his or her term of office. So, even in a democracy, delegates may have considerable leeway to further their own interests. Corruption, as described in the preceding Example, is one evident consequence.

Curiously, government officials may sometimes respond too readily to voter interests!

EXAMPLE 17.3 TORT AWARDS – IN-STATE VERSUS OUT-OF-STATE

Eric Helland and Alexander Tabarrok studied tort awards in more than 7,000 personal injury lawsuits tried in state courts during the period 1990–1995.[a] For judges elected in partisan voting (that is, with party labels appearing on the ballot), awards against out-of-state defendants were around 2.36 times the size of awards against in-state defendants. The situation was somewhat improved when judges were elected in nonpartisan balloting. Presumably, judicial candidates in nonpartisan elections cater less to voter prejudice and self-interest. But even then a large bias against out-of-state defendants remained.

Average tort awards – In-state versus out-of-state defendants

	Out-of-state defendant	In-state defendant	Out-of-state/ in-state
Partisan elections	$652,720	$276,320	2.36
Nonpartisan elections	384,540	207,570	1.85

Source: Adapted from Holland and Tabarrok, Table 1.

[a] Eric Helland and Alexander Tabarrok, "Exporting Tort Awards," *Regulation*, v. 23 (2000).

Excessive awards to in-state plaintiffs are not a failure of political delegation or representation. The judges here are not violating "the will of the people." Instead, they are pandering to improper, narrowly self-interested desires of a democratic majority. The problem is not corrupt politicians, but a corrupt citizenry.

Politics and Special Interests

"Special interests" (for example, firms in a particular industry) often obtain political favors such as tariffs or subsidies at the expense of the general consuming public.

Government favors to a particular industry are, for the firms in that industry, a public good. Tariff protection benefits all the domestic firms in an industry. The analysis in Chapter 16 showed that, when it comes to providing a public good, small groups can better overcome the free-rider problem. When the number of firms in an industry is small, they may not find it too difficult to get together and lobby for privileges and entitlements.

Special interests are also more strongly *motivated* to form pressure groups. Firms in the affected industry are likely to gain far more from the tariff than any comparably sized group in the population stands to lose – even though, overall, the public may suffer a much greater loss. As a generalization, since production tends to be more specialized than consumption, it has been argued that government interventions tend to favor producers over consumers.

EXAMPLE 17.4 GOVERNMENT AID TO AGRICULTURE – PRODUCTIVE OR REDISTRIBUTIVE?

Gordon C. Rausser compared the extent to which U.S. agricultural programs contributed to *productive efficiency*, as opposed to the aim of *redistributing wealth* toward special-interest beneficiaries.[a]

Agricultural programs might improve efficiency in several ways. Compiling better statistics reduces transaction costs and makes markets more perfect (see Chapter 13). Also, governmental research can contribute to developing new products, to finding new uses for old crops, to controlling pests, and so on. (Research tends to be a public good, so private industry will likely underinvest in it.) Third, regulation might correct for externalities, as discussed in Chapter 16. For example, withdrawing acres from production might conceivably help protect the environment.

On the other hand, policies that raise prices by cartel-like restrictions on agricultural output, or that provide income supplements to farmers or to other agricultural interests, do not contribute to efficiency. Their purpose is mainly redistributive.

In the table, commodities are ranked in order of "Producer Subsidy Equivalents" (PSEs), defined as the percentage of total farmer receipts represented by payments from the public sector. (Only the author's four highest-ranking and four lowest-ranking commodities are shown here.) The other columns show the percentages of each commodity's Producer Subsidy Equivalent that the author interpreted as productive versus redistributive; these two columns sum to 100%. Thus for sugar, 77.4% of farmers' receipts are accounted for by public sector assistance; of that assistance, only 7.9% was classified as productive, the remaining 92.1% being redistributive.

The table indicates that the four programs with a large subsidy fraction were overwhelmingly redistributive, whereas the four low-subsidy programs mainly provided productive assistance to the industry.

The high-subsidy programs were typically characterized by inelastic demand. A productive government intervention, such as Federally funded research leading to a less costly irrigation technique, is likely to elicit an increase in market supply. But if demand is highly inelastic, larger output implies a sharply lower price. So suppliers of an inelastic-demand commodity are likely to be uninterested in government activities aimed at improving productivity. Instead, they will want to concentrate their lobbying upon programs aimed at redistributing income in their favor.

U.S. Agricultural programs – productive versus redistributive

	Producer subsidy equivalents (1982–1986 averages)		
	Total	% productive	% redistributive
4 Highest			
Sugar	77.4	7.9%	92.1%
Milk	53.9	7.8	92.2
Rice	45.0	6.4	93.6
Wheat	36.5	13.5	86.5
4 Lowest			
Beef	8.7	55.5	44.5
Soybeans	8.5	74.3	25.7
Poultry	8.3	65.0	35.0
Pork	8.5	82.5	17.6

Source: Adapted from Rausser, Table 3.

[a] Gordon C. Rausser, "Predatory versus Productive Government: The case of U.S. Agricultural Policies," *Journal of Economic Perspectives*, v. 6 (Summer 1992).

On the other hand, there is a countervailing force. Although a small specialized group finds it easier to organize and bring its weight to bear, it remains a group small in number. Landlords can organize against rent controls more effectively than tenants can organize for them, but a politician must recognize that there are many more tenant votes than landlord votes.[2]

17.2 VOTING AS AN INSTRUMENT OF CONTROL

In a democracy, citizens choose their delegates by voting. But the effectiveness of a single vote is so tiny that the ordinary citizen might seem to have little reason to go to the polls. The election of a preferred candidate might be worth a lot to the voter, yet a single ballot is highly unlikely to determine the outcome. Even the phenomenally close presidential election of 2000 was decided in Florida by several hundred votes, not by a single vote. Or if the citizen merely wants to demonstrate support for a candidate, one vote more or less would scarcely be noticed. And even if the voter has no selfish aims at all but intends to cast a purely public-spirited ballot, that single vote will no more measurably advance the public interest than it would serve the voter's own selfish interest.

As a separate point, in the marketplace you usually get what you pay for. But in the political arena, elected candidates frequently violate their campaign promises. These considerations together lead to what has been called "rational ignorance." Because it is difficult for a voter to find a candidate who supports the whole bundle of his or her preferred policies, and because it is difficult to ensure that elected officials abide by their promises, and because even an informed vote is unlikely to matter, the rational voter will devote little effort to determining what are the best policies or who is the best candidate. Voting is cheap, but voting *intelligently* is costly.

[2] Agitation in favor of rent controls is encouraged by the fact that housing as a consumer good accounts for a very large part of a family's budget. This concentrated financial interest makes it more worthwhile for tenants to bear the cost of forming a pressure group to push for rent control.

EXAMPLE 17.5 DETERMINANTS OF VOTER TURNOUT

A rational citizen's choice of whether to vote will depend upon the costs and benefits. In this light Ron Shachar and Barry Nalebuff examined state-by-state voting turnout for the 11 Presidential elections from 1948 to 1988.[a] Among their results were the following:

1. *The larger the state population, the smaller the percent turnout.* This seems consistent with rational behavior, since the larger the population the smaller is the probability of a single voter determining the election. Statistically, an increase of 1,000,000 in the eligible voting population of a state was associated with a decline of 1.5 percentage points in the fraction voting.
2. *The more one-sided the election, the smaller the turnout.* Again this is rational, since in a one-sided election there would be even less chance of a single ballot affecting the outcome. The evidence indicated that a predicted 60:40 split within a state led to about 1% lower participation than with a predicted 55:45 split.
3. *Coincidence of Presidential with gubernatorial elections increased turnout.* It is more rational to vote if the election is more important. Having a gubernatorial race also on the ballot makes an election more important. Statistically, a coinciding gubernatorial election raised participation by about 2.4%.
4. *Rain on election day reduces turnout.* Since a rational voter takes account of the cost of voting, it is not surprising that each inch of rain on election day reduced the voting proportion by 3.5 percentage points.
5. *Higher levels of education increased turnout.* Educated voters can, presumably, more easily overcome the "rational ignorance" problem and cast an informed ballot. An increase of 10% in the proportion of the citizenry with four or more years of high school increased turnout by 2.2%.

COMMENT

Although these results illustrate that *differences* in the participation rate seem consistent with the canons of rationality, the problem remains: why vote at all? The underlying explanation, the authors argue, is the activity of political leaders. Leaders are strongly motivated to induce their supporters to vote, and go to considerable cost to achieve that end – for example, by organizing get-out-the-vote campaigns on election day. But probably the major explanation is psychological. Most voters derive a sense of civic pride upon casting a ballot, a reward that outweighs the cost of going to the polls.

[a] Ron Shachar and Barry Nalebuff, "Follow the Leader: Theory and Evidence on Political Participation," *American Economic Review*, v. 89 (June 1999).

Majority and Minority – "Log-Rolling"

Candidates in democratic elections have to win a majority, so they are likely to neglect minority interests. The market, in contrast, takes appropriate account of both majority and minority preferences. If 75% of consumers prefer chocolate and 25% prefer vanilla, the market will normally provide the two flavors in just about those proportions.

Though often considered an evil, political "log-rolling" is an important safeguard for minorities. Suppose minority legislators from farm states care deeply about drought relief. To attract the votes of other congressmen on this issue, they may promise to support mass transit or neighborhood renewal, programs of interest to urban legislators. In this way the *intensity* of minority preferences may help counterbalance the mere numbers of the majority.

EXAMPLE 17.6 LOG-ROLLING IN THE U.S. CONGRESS

Agricultural interests often have difficulty gaining Congressional approval for farm subsidy programs. And urban legislators did not always succeed in obtaining higher welfare payments for poorer city residents.

John Ferejohn described how, in the 1960s, a coalition of rural and urban legislators secured both these ends, making use of food stamp programs.[a] Food stamps, distributed mostly to urban lower-income people, offer reduced prices for foods using "surplus" agricultural products – so they potentially benefited both these groups. (At the expense of the general taxpayers, of course.) Rural interests had previously failed to support food stamp programs, preferring more direct subsidies. And urban interests usually opposed farm programs because they meant higher food prices and higher taxes. The political problem was how to make a log-rolling deal stick between two groups with such divergent interests.

As a typical example, in 1964 the House Agricultural Committee disapproved a food stamp bill: 5 Democrats, plus all 14 Republicans, were allied in the negative. The Democratic leadership responded by persuading another committee, the Rules Committee, to hold up approval of an entirely different bill, one that would have helped tobacco growers. Two of the Democratic dissenters on the Agricultural Committee, who favored tobacco producers, were thereby induced to swing over and favor the food stamp program.

Had the two programs, food stamps and farm subsidies, been considered and voted on separately they would likely both have been defeated. Proponents of each of the programs could get their own desired measure passed only by striking a deal to work together. Eventually the proponents arranged to have the programs packaged from the very beginning, in a consolidated "omnibus" bill. This tactic proved effective and survived a determined effort by the Reagan administration to separate the two programs.

---

[a] John Ferejohn, "Logrolling in an Institutional Context: A Case Study of Food Stamp Legislation," in Gerald C. Wright, Leroy Rieselbach, and Lawrence Dodd, eds., *Congress and Policy Change* (New York: Agathon Press, 1986).

Log-rolling brings market considerations into politics. Legislators' votes on some issues are "bought," to be "paid for" by votes on other issues. Log-rolling is an instance of the mutual advantage of trade for the participants (though not necessarily to the advantage of the citizenry in general).

The Cycling Paradox

Imagine that Abner, Betty, and Carlos are choosing among three proposals, *X*, *Y*, and *Z*. Suppose their voting preferences over the three options, ranked from highest to lowest, are as follows:

Preferences subject to cycling

Abner	Betty	Carlos
X	Y	Z
Y	Z	X
Z	X	Y

For example, Abner prefers X over Y, and Y over Z. Notice that a majority (Abner and Carlos) prefer X over Y, a majority (Abner and Better) prefer Y over Z, but a majority (Betty and Carlos) prefer Z over X! This is the paradox. In the terminology of Chapter 3, majority-rule choices can be *intransitive.*

In contrast, the paradox does not hold for the following alternative set of preferences:

Preferences not subject to cycling

Abner	Betty	Carlos
X	Y	Z
Y	X	X
Z	Z	Y

Here X has a majority over Y, Y has a majority over Z, but Z does not have a majority over X.

Where cycling is possible, as with the first set of preferences, the voting sequence (the "agenda") can determine the final outcome. Suppose Abner can determine the order of voting. He could call first for a vote between Y and Z, the winner to be matched against X. Policy Y would win the first vote. But in the second vote, his favored policy X would win over Y. Given the same power over the agenda, Betty or Carlos could also assure outcomes in their own favor. For the second set of preferences, on the other hand, control over the agenda would not work. Z can never win, and a choice between X and Y will always end up in favor of X. These preferences are "agenda-proof."

The Median-Voter Theorem

If an issue is to be decided in dichotomous (yes/no) voting, for example, when the U.S. Senate is asked to confirm a Presidential appointment, under reasonable assumptions the outcome will coincide with the preferences of the median voter (senator). To see why, imagine lining up the senators in order of their support for the candidate. The senator in the middle (the median senator) must necessarily be among the majority. If there is a strong preponderance on one side, by definition the median senator will be in that group. Or, at the extreme, if the other senators are equally split, then the middle senator's own choice makes the majority.[3]

Or, suppose the issue to be decided is quantitative, for example, the size of the government budget. In Figure 17.1, voters a through e are located at positions along a horizontal axis representing their ideal choices for the level of government spending (say, as a percentage of GNP). Suppose also that in moving away from the ideal point

---

[3] Justice Sandra Day O'Connor has been called "the most powerful woman in American history" because she is so often the swing (median) voter on issues before the U.S. Supreme Court.

% of GNP Devoted to Government Budget

Figure 17.1. The Median-Voter Theorem: Single Choice Dimension

Voters *a* through *e* choose by majority rule, from proposals *V* through *Z* for the size of the government budget. The segment $\overline{ae}$ is Pareto-optimal. Regardless of the agenda, the ultimate winner will be either *X* or *Y* (the proposals lying on either size of the median voter's preferred position *c*), depending on which of the two the median voter prefers.

each voter always prefers an option closer to his or her ideal over one that is farther away in the same direction. (Note that twice the distance need not be either half as good or three-quarters as good. The assumption here involves only *ranking* of preferences in a given direction.[4]) Furthermore, distances in *different* directions cannot be compared at all.

Here the interval from *a* to *e* along the horizontal axis is the set of Pareto-optimal (or Pareto-efficient) choices. Starting from any point outside the segment, all voters would favor moving to *some* point or points within that range. And starting from any point inside the segment, unanimous agreement could not be attained for moving to any point outside. It is not necessarily true, however, that *every* point within the segment $\overline{ae}$ is unanimously preferred over every point outside the segment. (A *Pareto-optimal* allocation is not necessarily *Pareto-preferred* to any arbitrary starting position – see Chapter 16.)

Suppose points *V*, *W*, *X*, *Y*, *Z* represent the alternative proposals being considered (percentages of GNP to be devoted to government). For there to be a unique equilibrium that is "agenda-proof" (independent of the voting sequence), some single option must win a majority vote against each one of the others. Will there necessarily be such a winner in Figure 17.1? A majority of voters (*b*, *c*, *d*, and *e*) prefer *X* over *V* or *W*. Similarly, *Y* wins against *Z* by attracting voters *a*, *b*, and *c*. So, regardless of the order of successive votes between pairs of alternatives, the final winner must be either *X* or *Y* – the options lying on either side of *c*, the ideal choice of the median voter. Whether *X* or *Y* becomes the winner will therefore depend solely on which of the two the median voter *c* prefers.[5]

Suppose that instead of only the specific alternatives *V* through *Z*, each numerical budget from 0 to 100% were possible. Then the outcome must be *exactly* at *c*, the ideal position of the median voter.

> **THE MEDIAN-VOTER THEOREM:** In majority-rule voting on a single issue, if each voter always prefers proposals that are nearer over those farther from his or her ideal positions in any given direction, a unique agenda-proof equilibrium exists. (There will be no cycling.) Furthermore, the outcome must be in the Pareto-efficient region.
>
> With separated discrete options, the outcome will be whichever the median voter prefers of the two proposals to either side of his or her ideal outcome. If the options are continuous, the result will be exactly at the ideal position of the median voter.

---

[4] Distance here is an "ordinal" (rather than "cardinal") utility measure, in the sense of Chapter 3, Section 3.2.

[5] This cannot be determined from the diagram. Although, as drawn, point *Y* is closer than point *X* to *c*, the median voter's ideal position, *X* and *Y* lie in opposite directions. Distances in different directions are not comparable in utility terms.

The cycling problem did not arise in this discussion because preferences were assumed to be *single-peaked*. That is, each voter was expected to prefer an option nearer his or her position over an outcome in the same direction but farther away. It would violate single-peakedness if, for example, a voter for whom the ideal budget size was 90% of GNP nevertheless preferred 10% over 50%. (Such a preference ordering might seem rather strange, yet in some circumstances violations of single-peakedness can be logical.)[6]

EXAMPLE 17.7 THE MEDIAN VOTER AND PARTY POLITICS

In modern politics voters must choose among political parties. Since parties represent a range of different views, supporting one or another party generally requires the individual voter to compromise his or her own preferences. The question then arises, will the median-voter theorem be satisfied? That is, will the winning party include the median voter?

John D. Huber and G. Bingham Powell, Jr. studied how well the median-voter theorem was satisfied under alternative political systems in several democratic nations.[a] In what they termed the Majority Control system, the majority group, either a single party or a coalition, has essentially complete control. In what they called the Proportional Influence system, each political party had some influence on government actions, more or less in proportion to its support in the electorate. The authors recognized also an intermediate Mixed system. The 12 democratic countries studied were classified as follows:

Majority Control: Australia, Great Britain, New Zealand
Mixed: France, Germany, Ireland, Spain, Sweden
Proportional Influence: Belgium, Denmark, Italy, the Netherlands

One might at first expect the median-voter theorem to be most closely reflected under the Proportional Influence system, since government decisions will then take into account the relative support that each party receives from the voters. This is not quite obvious. Although the Majority Control system gives most of the power to one party or coalition, representing perhaps only one side of the political spectrum, electoral competition leads the different parties to "move to the middle." So the winning group is likely to contain the median voter.

Measuring along a left-right scale, the authors assigned a position to the median voter and to the government. They then estimated the percentage of voters falling between these two positions. The size of the gap can be regarded as measuring the divergence of government policy from the preferences of the median voter.

Their analysis indicated that the median-voter theorem was most closely approximated by the Proportional Influence system. Under the Majority Control system 28% of the population fell in this gap; under the Proportional Influence system only 20% did. As expected, the Mixed system lay in between, with 23% of the population in the gap.

---

[a] John D. Huber and G. Bingham Powell, Jr., "Congruence between Citizens and Policymakers in Two Visions of Liberal Democracy," *World Politics*, v. 46 (April 1994).

Figure 17.2 shows the ideal points for three voters (*a*, *b*, and *c*) facing not one but two issues – for example, the size of the government budget and the number of

---

[6] One example: in a war it can make sense either to fight to the limit or else to surrender entirely, rather than fight only half-heartedly.

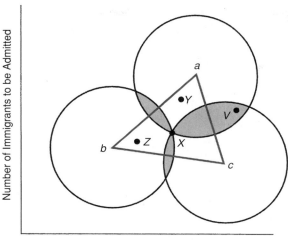

Size of Budget

Figure 17.2. Two Choice Dimensions

The three voters have ideal points at *a*, *b*, and *c*. The triangular region *abc* is the Pareto-optimal set, the boundaries of which are the mutual-tangency points of the circular indifference curves. For a typical point *X* within *abc*, there are three petal-shaped areas. Each of these areas is a set of proposals that can command a 2:1 majority over *X*. So cycling is inevitable if all possible positions are in contention. Furthermore, the petal-shaped regions include points such as *V* that are outside the Pareto-optimal set. However, if *X*, *Y*, and *Z* are the only alternatives offered the voters, *X* is a noncycling equilibrium.

immigrants to be admitted.[7] For convenience, assume that the indifference curves are *circular* around the ideal points. (Since utility then depends only upon distance, this means that preferences in different directions can be compared.)[8] The Pareto-optimal set is the triangular area connecting the three voters' ideal points *a*, *b*, *c*. The *ab* boundary of the triangle goes through the mutual tangencies of the indifference curves of individuals *a* and *b*, and similarly for the other boundaries of the triangle.

The indifference curves through any point such as *X* necessarily intersect to determine three shaded petal-shaped areas. These areas represent policy options that command a 2:1 majority over *X*. (The petal at the upper left, for example, is the set of policies that voters *a* and *b* both prefer to *X*.) So policy *X* will lose in majority voting whenever a policy point located in any of the petals is offered as an alternative. Since such a petal diagram can be constructed *for any point whatsoever*, cycling is inevitable when all points in the diagram are available policy options. If, however, only a number of discrete alternatives are to be voted on, cycling need not occur. For example, if only the specific options X, Y, Z were offered, then X would defeat each of the others regardless of the agenda.

As drawn, X lies within the efficient triangle abc. This shows that a non-Pareto-optimal point such as V could win a majority over a Pareto-efficient point like X – something that could not happen under single-issue majority voting.

---

[7] The discussion that follows is based upon Gordon Tullock, *Toward a Mathematics of Politics* (Ann Arbor: University of Michigan Press, 1967), Chapters 2–3.

[8] *Cardinal* utility is still not involved, however. In comparing two options, whichever lies at a greater distance from the ideal point (regardless of direction) is less preferred – but the *magnitude* of the preference (utility) difference is not quantified.

PROPOSITION: When the agenda under majority voting allows a continuous range of options over two quantitative issues, cycling is inevitable even with single-peaked preferences. In contrast, if the agenda consists of only a *discrete* set of options, cycling need not always occur. In either case, a policy outside the Pareto-optimal region may command a majority against efficient policies within the region.

17.3   CONFLICT AND COOPERATION

Markets – despite "failures" due to monopoly, externalities, and so forth – accomplish a remarkable task. They bring about cooperation even when each individual acts selfishly. And the previous discussion showed that, in the polity as well, majority-rule voting may also permit self-interested individuals to achieve a degree of cooperation.

Apart from markets and politics, people engage in an enormous variety of other social interactions, ranging from warfare to parental love. In all these domains the fundamental elements of economic analysis – scarcity, costs, opportunities, and preferences (goals) – continue to apply. As a crucial generalization, there are two main methods of achieving one's goals in the face of scarcity, two main ways of "making a living": (1) the way of productive cooperation guided by market exchange, and (2) the way of conflict. Following the first path, a person can engage in production for self-use, or in a social context in order to exchange the product with other parties. The second method of making a living – the way of conflict – is simply to grab or confiscate what you need or want. The way of conflict is omnipresent in the animal world. Lions prey on antelope, birds eat insects, and bacteria parasitize higher life forms. On the human level the way of conflict is illustrated by war among nations and violent crime within societies. And even a number of nonviolent human activities – litigation, strikes and lockouts, and redistributive politics – are conflictual activities, struggles to grab or defend resources. In the business world, rather than try to produce at lower cost, a firm might sabotage its rivals' deliveries or bribe its executives.

The key point is that in exchange the participating individuals achieve a mutual benefit. But a party pursuing the way of conflict is seeking a one-sided advantage. In consequence at least one contender, and possibly both, must lose out. For the way of production and exchange, competition promotes economic efficiency. But competition by means of conflict is disastrous.

Sources of Cooperation and Conflict

Among the considerations that determine whether individuals or groups will rationally lean toward cooperation or conflict are:[9]

1. *Preferences: sympathy versus antipathy* – Are the parties benevolent or malevolent toward one another, or simply neutral? The inclinations on either side need not be reciprocated by the other. (A mother may love her children even if they don't love her.)

---

[9] The analysis here is based in part upon Donald Wittman, "How a War Ends," *Journal of Conflict Resolution*, v. 23 (December 1979), David Friedman, "Many, Few, One: Social Harmony and the Shrunken Choice Set," *American Economic Review*, v. 70 (March 1980), and Jack Hirshleifer, "Conflict and Settlement," *The New Palgrave: A Dictionary of Economics*, v. 1 (London: Macmillan, 1987).

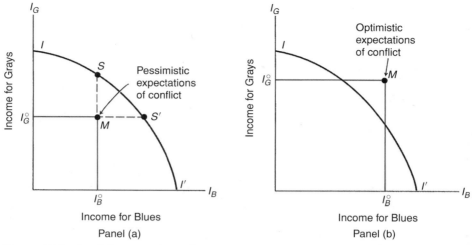

Figure 17.3. Confidence and Conflict

In Panel (a) the Blues anticipate that, in the event of conflict, they will achieve the equivalent of an income of I_B^o. The Grays similarly anticipate I_G^o. There is a region of mutual advantage MSS' achievable by a compromise agreement; the efficient solutions lie along the range SS'. In Panel (b) there is no possibility of a compromise solution.

2. *Opportunities: harmonious versus opposed interests* – Sometimes I help myself best by helping you, sometimes by hurting you. ("I got nothing 'gainst you, Wyatt Earp, but this town ain't big enough for the two of us.")

3. *Beliefs: pessimism versus optimism* – Either side can be optimistic or pessimistic about the consequences of friendly or of unfriendly behavior. Usually, greater uncertainty attaches to the outcome of hostile interactions. (War is, notoriously, the domain of uncertainty.)

In Panel (a) of Figure 17.3 the curve II' (like the similar curve in Figure 16.1) is the Social Opportunity Frontier *SOF*, the upper bound upon the income combinations attainable by two decision-makers. Think of the two sides either as individuals or as groups – the Blues and the Grays. And "income" may stand for territory, power, or ability to buy goods.

The diagram illustrates the role of pessimism versus optimism in the decision between conflict and settlement. (For simplicity, it is assumed here that uncertainty attaches *only* to the outcome of conflict.)

Specifically, suppose the Blues believe that a conflict would leave them with an income of I_B^o. The corresponding outcome anticipated by the Grays is I_G^o. Point M in the diagram pictures these beliefs. Starting from point M, the roughly triangular area MSS' represents a "region of mutual advantage" – where (both parties believe) they can gain by peaceful compromise. An efficient solution would lie somewhere in the range SS' along the *SOF* curve.

In Panel (b) each side is more optimistic than in Panel (a) about winning the battle in the event of conflict. Here point M lies outside the opportunity set, so there is no region of mutual advantage. *Each* expects to do better by fighting than by settling, so a clash is inevitable. (But since such beliefs are mutually inconsistent, one or the other party – or both – must be overestimating its chances.)

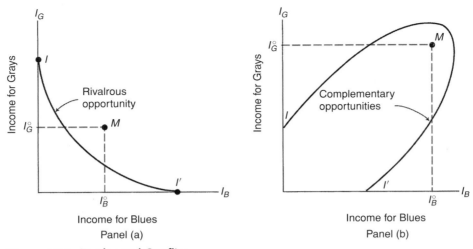

Figure 17.4. Rivalry and Conflict

In Panel (a) the two parties' peaceful opportunities are highly rivalrous. A compromise settlement is unlikely even if M is near the origin (even if conflict is perceived as not very profitable). In Panel (b) the peaceful opportunities are highly complementary. A compromise is easier to achieve even if the perceptions of the returns from conflict are relatively high (even if M is far from the origin).

After having experienced the test of battle, each side will likely learn the hard truth about its limited strength. This may not immediately lead to a peaceful settlement, however. The loser in battle will become more amenable to compromise, but the winner may become more intransigent.

One influence working toward eventual settlement is exhaustion of resources. As both sides become poorer, the additional wastage due to fighting becomes increasingly painful, while the possible spoils of victory get smaller.

Figure 17.3 highlighted *differences of beliefs* (pessimism or optimism) as a source of conflict. Figure 17.4 illustrates the role of *opportunities*. Panel (a) represents strong rivalry: the shape of the Social Opportunity Frontier II' shows that the interests of the two parties are sharply opposed. (One side must end up rich, the other poor – the only question being which is which.) Here even relatively pessimistic anticipations I_B^o and I_G^o about the outcome of a conflict may not lead to a compromise settlement, since point M lies outside the opportunity set. Panel (b) represents the opposite situation, where the two parties' interests are strongly complementary; each can get rich by helping the other. Accordingly, even if each contender were optimistic about winning the conflict, both would still likely prefer a compromise.

Last, Figure 17.5 illustrates the role of sympathetic or antipathetic preferences. In Panel (a) the two parties are mutually malevolent. For the Blues, Gray income I_G is a *bad* (as indicated by the positively sloping indifference curve U_B^o). Similarly the utility of the Grays declines with the income of the Blues. Antipathy reduces the size of MSS', the region of mutual advantage, and thus makes peaceful settlement less probable. In Panel (b) on the other hand, the parties are mutually sympathetic, enlarging the MSS' region and making peaceful settlement more likely.

Summarizing, a rational choice between conflict and settlement depends upon the costs and benefits of peace versus war, and in particular upon the parties' preferences, opportunities, and beliefs.

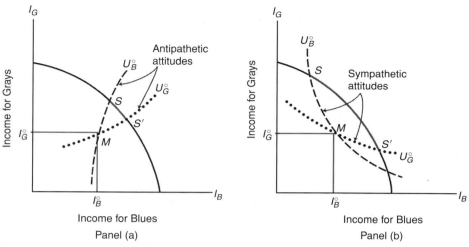

Figure 17.5. Antipathy and Conflict

In Panel (a) the parties are mutually antipathetic, which diminishes the region of mutual advantage MMS' and makes conflict more likely. In Panel (b) the parties are mutually sympathetic, making MMS' large and conflict therefore less likely.

EXAMPLE 17.8 THE RATIONALITY OF GOING TO WAR

The political scientists Bruce Bueno de Mesquita and David Lalman studied the initiation of wars among major powers in the 19th and 20th centuries.[a] They asked whether nations tended to initiate conflict rationally, that is, only when – in the opinion of the decision-makers on each side – doing so seemed advantageous. Their analysis was based upon the premise that each nation could be regarded as having a single utility function, which its leader maximized in making decisions about initiating conflict.

One of their studies, using data from 109 disputes among the major powers, examined the decision to make war in the light of decision-makers' beliefs about the probabilities of success. (The probability beliefs were calculated via a complex computation involving, among other things, the military capabilities of each nation and the likelihood of obtaining support from other nations.)

In the table, "expect success" means that the nation's leaders (in the opinion of the authors) assigned a better than 50% chance of winning the war and "does not expect success" means a less than 50% chance. Of the 109 disputes between major powers, only 16 ended in war. Among those 16, in 5 (31%) cases both sides expected success and in 11 (69%) at least one side did not. For the disputes that did not lead to war, in contrast, in only 16% of the cases did both sides expect success. So, it appears, more pessimistic expectations about the chances of victory did indeed make national leaders more reluctant to wage war.

War occurrence as related to estimated probabilities of success

	War	No war	Totals
Both sides expect success	5 (31%)	15 (16%)	83 (76%)
At least one side does not expect success	11 (69%)	78 (84%)	26 (24%)
Totals	16 (100%)	93 (100%)	109 (100%)

Source: Derived from text of Bueno de Mesquita and Lalman, p. 206.

Why should wars ever occur at all in cases where at least one side expects defeat? Why doesn't the prospective loser make concessions that would satisfy the aims of the other side? The reason is that beliefs about the likelihood of success are not the only factors involved in choosing between conflict and settlement. As explained in the preceding text, among the other factors are antipathy between the parties, the intensity of their rivalry over resources, and how bad their positions are likely to be if they give way without resorting to war.

COMMENT

It may be hard to determine which side "initiates" a conflict. In the American Civil War, the Confederates fired the first shots at Fort Sumter. But, it could be argued, it was the Union's refusal to let the Southern states secede that made war inevitable.

[a] Bruce Bueno de Mesquita and David Lalman, *War and Reason* (New Haven, CT, Yale University Press, 1992).

EXAMPLE 17.9 RAID OR TRADE?

In popular literature and films, the historical transfer of Indian lands to white ownership is usually pictured as an entirely conflictual interaction. The whites simply took what they wanted by force of arms. Terry L. Anderson and Fred S. McChesney showed that the situation was more complex.[a] A major method of peaceful transfer of Indian lands was by treaty. Under these treaties, overall around $400,000,000 – a huge sum in those days – was paid out to the Indians as individuals or tribes.

In the early years, land was so plentiful that (for the most part) the Indians did not attempt to defend territory. As indicated in the table, only about 41 Indian-white battles were listed in the period up to 1829. But after about 1850 the number of battles per decade rose sharply to a peak of 786 in 1860–1869 (the Civil War decade), tapering off thereafter.

To explain the changing balance between fighting and negotiated settlement, Anderson and McChesney pointed to several factors. One evident change was the increasing military power of the white invaders, owing partly to improved weapons (such as breech-loading and repeating rifles) and partly to growing numbers.

While the military imbalance might be expected to influence the *terms* of settlements arrived at, it need not have affected the *likelihood* of arriving at a settlement. It appears, however, that the Indians were slow to recognize these changes; undue "optimism" about their military chances (as discussed in the preceding text) made them reluctant to offer concessions.

The factor most emphasized by Anderson and McChesney was the difficulty of negotiating and enforcing agreements. In the early period, the Indians east of the Mississippi were largely agriculturalists with well-defined individual and tribal territories. In contrast, the tribes encountered west of the Mississippi mostly ranged nomadically over huge areas of land having no clear ownership. This difference made negotiated purchase much more difficult. Also, the greater distances made it harder for the authorities on both sides to maintain discipline over their own members. As a result, groups of whites were able to invade Indian lands despite the opposition of the Federal authorities. And on the other side, individual tribal warriors were only imperfectly subject to control even when their chiefs recognized the need for restraint.

Indian-white battles by decade

	Number of battles
Before 1830	41
1830–1839	63
1840–1849	53
1850–1859	190
1860–1869	786
1870–1879	530
1880–1889	131
After 1889	13

Source: Adapted from Anderson and McChesney, Table 1 (p. 58).

A specific treaty negotiation was described by the legal scholar Felix S. Cohen.[b] In 1794 the United States agreed to compensate the Iroquois nation, for a cession of territory, $4,500 annually forever. That sum has been faithfully paid to this date. Referring back to the analysis of compound interest in Chapter 15, compound interest tables indicate that a payment of $4,500 annually, calculating at a moderate interest rate of 4% for the period of 210 years between 1794 and 2004, would cumulate to the remarkable total of over $82.7 billion dollars! On the other hand, the annual benefits derived from the lands ceded by the Iroquois would also compound in value over the same period. So it cannot immediately be determined whether the Iroquois were overpaid or underpaid. But it is clear that they received significant compensation for the sacrifice of their lands.

[a] Terry L. Anderson and Fred S. McChesney, "Raid or Trade? An Economic Model of Indian-White Relations," *Journal of Law and Economics*, v. 37 (April 1994).

[b] Felix S. Cohen, "Original Indian Title," Minnesota Law Review, v. 32 (1947–1948).

The text has distinguished between two main paths of economic activity, two ways of "making a living": (1) productive cooperation as guided by markets, or (2) conflict. When individuals or groups cooperate, they increase the size of the pie available to society. When they engage in conflict, the consequence is inefficient fighting over the slices.

EXAMPLE 17.10 A LITIGATION EXPLOSION?

The United States, allegedly, is suffering from a litigation explosion. Newspaper reports about outlandish grounds for suit and huge legal judgements do suggest that, in recent decades, litigation has greatly increased. On the other hand, some spokesmen for the legal profession have dismissed the supposed growth in litigation as more hype than reality.

One way of examining the issue is to look at changes in the number of lawyers over recent decades compared with changes in the numbers in comparable professions such as accountants, engineers, and physicians. True, not all lawyers are engaged in lawsuits, and some members of these other professions are involved in litigation. Nevertheless, the relative numbers are a strong indication.

The table here makes use of U.S. Census data starting in 1970. It appears that the number of lawyers has indeed grown faster than the other professions listed, at least up to 1990. The lawyer/engineer ratio, for example, more than doubled from $274/1{,}208 = 0.23$ in 1970 to $780/1{,}673 = 0.47$ in 1990. As of 2002 the ratio was about the same, at $695/1{,}478 = 0.47$. Similarly, despite the rapid growth of medicine in the United States, the ratio of lawyers to physicians rose a remarkable 40% – from $274/290 = 0.94$ in 1970 to $780/584 = 1.34$ in 1990. However, the ratio has declined somewhat to $695/583 = 1.19$ in 2002.

Numbers in various professions (thousands)

	1970	1980	1990	2002
Accountants	704	993	1,554	976*
Engineers	1,208	1,382	1,673	1,478
Physicians	290	431	584	583
Lawyers	274	522	780	695

* This figure is for the year 2000, the latest available.

Sources: Before 2000, Sander and Williams,[a] p. 433, and personal communication from Richard H. Sander. For 2000/2002, U.S. Bureau of Labor Statistics, *Occupational Outlook Handbook*, 2002–2003 and 2004–2005 Editions.

COMMENT

It does not necessarily follow that the amount of litigation and the number of lawyers are now "too high." Perhaps in earlier years they were "too low." Although legal conflict is economically inefficient, it may serve other purposes. In particular, recall that while *efficiency* is one social criterion, *equity* is another. If increased litigation has improved equity, which is a debatable matter, the tradeoff may have been socially beneficial.

[a] Richard J. Sander and E. Douglas Williams, "Why Are There So Many Lawyers? Perspectives on a Turbulent Market," *Law and Social Inquiry*, 1989.

CONCLUSION

Individuals, groups, and nations may sometimes find it rational to pursue the way of conflict rather than the way of cooperation through production and exchange. The distribution and use of resources in and between societies will therefore depend upon the incentives for conflict versus settlement.

Engaging in conflict is evidently inconsistent with the Coase Theorem (Section 16.3 of the preceding chapter). That theorem says that all possible mutually advantageous agreements will be realized. War being costly, settlements and compromises are always available that would be better for both sides. The text pointed out earlier that the Coase Theorem appeared to "prove too much" in suggesting that monopoly would not permanently exist, that individuals would voluntarily contract with one another to internalize all externalities, and so on. For that reason, textbook statements of the Coase Theorem usually list several necessary qualifications, among them well-defined property rights and the absence of transaction costs. Still, even if markets were perfect, considerations such as antipathy, rivalry, and overconfidence can make conflictual activity appear to be (or even actually be) profitable to at least one side. So economically inefficient activities such as war, crime, and redistributive politics are bound to persist.

Table 17.1 Payoff matrices for four games (larger numbers indicate higher utility)

	Land or sea			Prisoners' dilemma	
	Land	Sea		Disarm	Arm
Land	2, 1	1, 2	Disarm	3, 3	1, 4
Sea	1, 2	2, 1	Arm	4, 1	*2, 2
	Chicken			Battle of the sexes	
	Soft	Tough		Patton	Montgomery
Soft	3, 3	*2, 4	Patton	*3, 2	1, 1
Tough	*4, 2	1, 1	Montgomery	1, 1	*2, 3

* = Nash solution in pure strategies (see text).

Conflict and Game Theory

The theory of games, introduced in Chapter 10, helps explain how cooperative and conflictual motives are intertwined. Summarizing the main points of the analysis in Section 10.1:

1. It is essential to distinguish the *pattern of payoffs* from the *protocol of play*.
2. Alternative patterns of payoffs, which can be thought as different environments in which the players might interact, are illustrated by matrices like those pictured in Section 10.1 and in this chapter.
3. The protocol of play can be thought of as the "rules of the game." For example, do the players move simultaneously or in sequence? If they move in sequence, who moves first? When does the game end?
4. For sequential play, the "perfect equilibrium" solution concept assumes that each player aims to maximize his own payoff, on the assumption that every other player will also be maximizing her own payoff.
5. For simultaneous play, a *dominant* strategy will always be chosen. If there is no dominant strategy, the *Nash equilibrium* is expected to hold: each player's choice is a best response to the strategies of other players. A Nash solution may not be unique, or may not even exist in terms of pure strategies. But if *mixed strategies* are allowed, at least one Nash solution exists.

The matrices in Table 17.1 illustrate four possible payoff environments. They are arranged in order of decreasing opposition of interests. Land or Sea is the most rivalrous environment. At the other extreme, in Battle of the Sexes the players' interests are the most compatible.[10]

The first matrix, Land or Sea, corresponds to a duel for survival: a "this town ain't big enough for the two of us" situation. Whenever one side is better off, the other is worse off. Since the parties' interests are totally opposed to one another, this is the most rivalrous of the four cases.[11]

For the second matrix, Prisoners' Dilemma, the opposition of interests is somewhat moderated. Chapter 10 mentioned several applications, among them "chiselling" in

[10] Battle of the Sexes still contains an element of opposed interests. The Right or Left matrix described in Section 10.1 was characterized by *completely* harmonious interests. (The payoffs for both players were equal throughout.)
[11] The elements of each cell, if interpreted as cardinal magnitudes, sum to a constant (equal to 3 here). Constant-sum environments are totally rivalrous.

cartels. Or think of an arms race, where the strategy options are Arm or Disarm. The Pareto-efficient solution is Disarm/Disarm, and this would presumably be attained if international treaties were perfectly enforceable. But since they are not, under standard game-theory assumptions Arm/Arm will be the equilibrium reached.

In the third matrix, Chicken,[12] the alternative strategies are Tough and Soft. Chicken-type payoffs are illustrated by union-management bargaining under threat of strike or lockout, or settlement negotiations before a court trial. Here a side that plays Tough hopes to force the opponent to give way and choose Soft. But if they both play Tough, the outcome is the worst possible for each (1,1 payoffs). Chicken involves less intense rivalry than Prisoners' Dilemma, owing to the mutual interest in avoiding the worst possible payoffs.

The last matrix in the table – Battle of the Sexes[13] – represents the mildest rivalry of the four. In Battle of the Sexes the two parties want to coordinate their strategies, thereby achieving one of the mutually preferred diagonal cells. The problem is *which* of the two alternative patterns of coordination will be arrived at. That is, who will reap the larger share of the mutual gain? Think of struggles within an alliance. In the early fall of 1944, after breaking out of the Normandy perimeter, American forces under General Patton were nearing the German border from eastern France. Meanwhile, British troops under Field Marshal Montgomery were approaching Germany through Belgium and Holland. Owing to supply limitations, the Allied high command agreed there had to be a single line of attack. Both allies would gain by defeating the Germans. But the Americans wanted to win by supplying Patton; the British preferred to do so by supplying Montgomery. The attack by Montgomery was chosen. (Probably the wrong decision, as it led to the Allied disaster at Arnhem.)

The game-theoretic issues include: What is the outcome likely to be? Will an efficient (conflict-minimizing) result be achieved? Which party is likely to gain the advantage? The answers to these questions do not depend upon the pattern of payoffs alone. It is also necessary to specify the protocol or rules of the game. Only the simplest rules will be considered here: *sequential moves* versus *simultaneous moves* in a single round of play.

For the four different payoff patterns of Table 17.1, features of the equilibria are summarized in Table 17.2.

The upper part of Table 17.2 describes outcomes under the sequential-play protocol (using the "perfect equilibrium" solution concept). Some of the highlights are:

1. *Pareto-efficient* outcomes – situations where it is no longer possible to improve any player's payoff without injuring another party – are achieved in all but one of the matrices shown. The exception is Prisoners' Dilemma. (Notice that, in Land or Sea, all four cells are Pareto-efficient!)
2. When rivalry is greatest (Land or Sea) the advantage lies with the second mover, who can observe the opponent move before choosing. But the advantage tends to shift in favor of the first mover as rivalry declines (Compare Chicken and Battle of the Sexes).

---

[12] The traditional story has two teenagers racing their jalopies toward one another on a one-lane road. Whoever turns aside first is the chicken.

[13] This story involves a married couple planning an evening out. Although they want to be together, the wife prefers the opera while the husband prefers a boxing match.

Table 17.2 Equilibria for four different payoff matrices

	Land or sea	Prisoners' dilemma	Chicken	Battle of the sexes
Degree of rivalry	Great	Large	Moderate	Small
Sequential-move game (row moves first)				
Outcome (payoff)	1, 2	2, 2	4, 2	3, 2
(cells)	upper right or lower left	lower right	lower left	upper left
Efficient?	yes	no	yes	yes
Advantage to	second mover	neither	first mover	first mover
Simultaneous-move game (symmetrical solutions with possible mixed strategies)				
Outcome (payoff)	1.5, 1.5	2, 2	2.5, 2.5	1.67, 1.67
Probability mix	0.5, 0.5	0, 1	0.5, 0.5	0.67, 0.33
Efficient?	yes	no	no	no
Advantage to	neither	neither	neither	neither

With the exception of the Prisoners' Dilemma, all the equilibria tabulated in the lower half of Table 17.2 involve mixed strategies.

Consider a specific example: Chicken. Recall that, in the Nash solution, each player makes a best response to the other player's choice. Column having chosen his strategy, if Row's best response is a strategy mixture it must be that she is *indifferent* between the elements of her mixture – in this case, between Tough or Soft. (Were she not indifferent, she would always choose the better of the two as an unmixed or "pure" strategy.) It remains to show how to determine the mixing probabilities.

Denote Row's equilibrium probability for playing Soft as p_R and Column's as p_C; the probabilities for playing Tough are $1 - p_R$ for Row and $1 - p_C$ for Column. Following the procedure outlined in Section 10.1 of Chapter 10, the calculation goes as follows. Row's average payoff if she chooses her upper strategy (Soft) is $3p_C + 2(1 - p_C)$. If she chooses Tough her average payoff is $4p_C + 1(1 - p_C)$. Setting these equal (since at equilibrium she must be indifferent), the solution is $p_C = 0.5$. Since $1 - p_C = 0.5$ as well, the mixture of playing Soft with probability 0.5 and playing Tough with probability 0.5 (indicated by the pair (0.5,0.5)) is the equilibrium strategy for Column. And, because the payoff matrix is symmetric, (0.5,0.5) is also the equilibrium mixture for Row.[14]

As can be seen in Table 17.2, the equilibrium mixture for the assumed payoffs in the Land or Sea matrix is also (0.5,0.5) for each side. For Prisoners' Dilemma the probability mix is shown as (0,1) – meaning that each player chooses the second strategy (Arm) with 100% probability. (So that outcome is a pure-strategy equilibrium.) Last, in Battle of the Sexes each player chooses, with probability 2/3, the strategy more favorable to himself or herself.

At a mixed-strategy equilibrium, the player is indifferent over his or her pure-strategy choices. But this means that, if the equilibrium involves mixed strategies on both sides, either player can deviate without losing thereby. In this sense, all mixed-strategy equilibria are "weak." A Nash equilibrium in pure strategies, in contrast, could be either "strong" (meaning that whichever side deviates suffers a reduced payoff) or "weak."

---

[14] Mixed-strategy equilibria will not always be 50:50, but will depend upon the numerical entries in the assumed payoff matrix.

Returning to Table 17.2, some highlights of the results for *simultaneous-move* games (in the lower part of the Table) are:

1. Since only symmetrical solutions are shown, in Table 17.2 neither party ever gains any advantage over the other.
2. *Efficient* outcomes were achieved for the sequential-move game in the case of both Chicken and Battle of the Sexes. But under the simultaneous-move protocol the outcome may be inefficient. In Chicken, a player who wants to avoid exploitation must play Tough with positive probability. But then there is a chance that the two will both play Tough, leading to the inefficient outcome (1,1). Similarly, under Battle of the Sexes with mixed strategies, again there is some positive chance that the players end up at one or the other of the two inefficient outcomes with payoffs (1,1).

The theory of games is not limited to the elementary interactions so far examined. To list just a few of the many possible complications and extensions: (i) Only two-person games have been considered, but in many important situations three or even more players interact simultaneously. (ii) A single round of play was assumed above. More generally, the parties may expect to engage in repeated interactions. They might play the same game over many times, or else shift from one payoff matrix or protocol to another in some specified way. (iii) In addition to the simple strategies considered here, one or more of the players could choose a *conditional* strategy – for example, a strategy involving threats or promises. The following section ("An Application: Should You Pay Ransom?") considers some of these additional issues.

All the matrices considered so far had *symmetric* payoffs between the two players. The exercise that follows illustrates an environment with *asymmetric* payoffs.

EXERCISE 17.2

A thief can choose between two strategies: Steal (*S*) or Refrain (*R*). Similarly, a property owner can choose between Defend (*D*) and Not-Defend (*ND*). Suppose the payoff *rankings* (higher numbers preferred) for Owner and Thief are:

Owner's rankings:	*Thief's rankings:*
4 for Not-Defend, Refrain	4 for Not-Defend, Steal
3 for Defend, Refrain	3 for Defend, Refrain
2 for Defend, Steal	2 for Not-Defend, Refrain
1 for Not-Defend, Steal	1 for Defend, Steal

(a) Write down the 2×2 payoff matrix, letting Owner be the row player and Thief the column player. (b) Suppose Owner's choosing "Defend" means building a high fence, whose presence or absence will be fully visible in advance to potential thieves. If so, do the players move simultaneously or instead sequentially? And if they move sequentially, who moves first? What is the solution? (c) Suppose instead that choosing "Defend" means installing a secret burglar alarm, where Thief will be unable to determine whether the alarm was installed. Same question as above.

ANSWER: (a) The payoff matrix is

		Thief	
		S	R
Owner	D	2, 1	3, 3
	ND	1, 4	4, 2

(b) The players here move sequentially, with Owner moving first. The "perfect equilibrium" is the strategy-pair (D,R) with payoffs (3,3). (The owner builds a fence, in which case the thief does not attempt to steal.) (c) Here the players move simultaneously. (Though Owner decides on investing in a burglar alarm before Thief makes his choice, Thief does not *know* which action she has chosen. So from an informational point of view they move simultaneously.) No Nash equilibrium in pure strategies exists, so the solution involves mixed strategies. Using the method described in the text, recall that the chosen probabilities must leave the opponent indifferent. Thief's payoff from S is $p_O + 4(1 - p_O)$ and from R is $3p_O + 2(1 - p_O)$. Setting these equal, the solution is $p_O = 0.5$. A similar calculation shows that $p_T = 0.5$ leaves Owner indifferent. So each player mixes with 50:50 probabilities.

An Application: Should You Pay Ransom?

A criminal has kidnapped your child. He threatens to kill her unless a ransom is paid. Does it make sense to pay? (The analysis here involves two elements not previously considered: *conditional strategies* and the possibility of *repeated games*.)

Your strategies as parent are Pay and Don't Pay. The kidnapper's are to Kill or Release the victim. You as parent move first, and the kidnapper moves last.

Naturally you would prefer to pay the ransom if that would assure your child's release. But the kidnapper might kill your child anyway in order to leave no witness alive.

Suppose your preference ranking (larger numbers indicating more desired outcomes) is:

"I don't pay, he releases"	4
"I pay, he releases"	3
"I don't pay, he kills"	2
"I pay, he kills"	1

You are not sure about the kidnapper's rankings, but suppose they are:

"Ransom paid, child released"	4
"Ransom paid, child killed"	3
"Ransom not paid, child released"	2
"Ransom not paid, child killed"	1

These rankings are shown in Matrix 1 of Table 17.3. This kidnapper is in a sense "nice"! That is, regardless of what you do, he prefers to release the child. (Perhaps he fears that, if caught, he will suffer a more severe penalty for a kidnap-murder than for a kidnap alone.)

Table 17.3 Should you pay ransom?

Matrix 1 ("Nice" kidnapper)			Matrix 2 ("Nasty" kidnapper)			Matrix 3 ("Nice" kidnapper if paid)		
	Kill	Release		Kill	Release		Kill	Release
Pay	1,3	3,4	Pay	1,4	3,3	Pay	1,3	3,4
Don't Pay	2,1	4,2	Don't Pay	2,2	4,1	Don't Pay	2,1	4,2

With the preferences shown in Matrix 1 of Table 17.3, since you move first, at this point you should choose Don't Pay. (If the kidnapper's preferences are known to you and if you believe he is rational.) The kidnapper will then choose Release. So the equilibrium payoffs are 4 for you and 2 for the kidnapper. This outcome is Pareto-efficient: there is no way of improving the payoff for either side without making the opponent worse off.

Alternatively, the kidnapper might be "nasty," meaning that whatever you do he prefers to Kill. (He is more concerned about the risk of leaving a witness alive to identify him than about the risk of more severe punishment should he be caught.) Then the payoffs would be as shown in Matrix 2 of Table 17.3.

Assume again that you know the kidnapper's preferences and believe he will act rationally. Your optimal choice remains Don't Pay! (Your child will be murdered regardless of what you do, so you might as well keep your money.) The equilibrium payoffs are (2, 2). This outcome is *not* Pareto-efficient: both sides would benefit by changing from (Don't Pay, Kill) to (Pay, Release) if an agreement to do so could be reached and enforced. But of course, that's the difficulty.

If a "nice" kidnapper would Release regardless of your action, and a "nasty" kidnapper would Kill regardless of your action, it would seem that – even if you don't know whether he is "nice" or "nasty" – the best choice remains not to pay.

So is paying a ransom *always* irrational? Not necessarily! Consider the possible payoff rankings for the kidnapper shown in Matrix 3 of Table 17.3. Here the kidnapper is "nice" only if you Pay, but turns "nasty" if you choose Don't Pay.

Here are two ways a kidnapper might attempt to convince the parent that his preferences are really as shown in Matrix 3.

(1) *Argument 1*: "I am really a 'nice' person. But being nice is a superior good for me; in fact, only when I have lots of money can I afford to be nice. If you pay the ransom, I'll be rich enough to do so."

(2) *Argument 2*: "I'm neither 'nice' or 'nasty'; I'm just in this business to make money. To remain in the kidnapping business I must convince parents that I will carry out my threats and promises. In other words, my actions will be dictated by the ranking shown in Matrix 3 – else my reputation would be wrecked. So you can count on me to choose Release if you choose pay, but Kill otherwise."

In the first scenario, the kidnapper is claiming that meeting his demands would "appease" him. Consider this analogy. In the Munich crisis that preceded World War II, Adolph Hitler claimed that, if appeased at the expense of Czechoslovakia, he would make no more territorial demands. (But given his way at Munich, Hitler did not abide by his promise. Almost immediately afterward he made demands on Polish territory, at which point the British and the French abandoned their efforts to appease him.)

In the second scenario, the kidnapper says he has a *reputation* to protect. If parents hear that he releases victims without receiving a ransom, they would not pay. The same holds if people learn that he kills victims even if parents do pay. So, he argues, you can have confidence that he will release the child if you pay, but otherwise will kill her.

Is this convincing? Imagine you know the kidnapper is always "nice" or always "nasty," so that argument (1) can be set aside. Suppose for the moment that the kidnapper plans to commit exactly one more crime after this one, and that this is known to all concerned. Then the parent should reason as follows: "The kidnapper, once he commits his next and final crime, will go out of business. So, for the parent of the next victim, the reputation argument cannot apply. Then the parent of the next victim will rationally refuse to pay ransom. But since that will happen regardless of whether or not I pay ransom now, the effect of my action upon the kidnapper's reputation is irrelevant. Thus, I too should refuse to pay."

Furthermore, this chain of reasoning is valid no matter how many future crimes the kidnapper plans to commit, so long as it is some definite number! On the final crime, the parent should not pay ransom. Thus, the kidnapper's reputation will be irrelevant for the parent of the next-to-last victim, and therefore for the next-to-next-to-last, and so on all the way back to the present crime.[15] So, only if you think the kidnapper is validly making argument (1) – that being nice is a superior good for him – should you as parent pay ransom.

It is possible of course that the kidnapper is not rational, or that you as parent do not believe he will be choosing rationally. If so, your choice, whether or not to pay ransom should depend upon your beliefs as to how and in what way the kidnapper's decision processes work.

SUMMARY   Individuals, it is reasonable to assume, are about equally selfish or un-selfish in their market behavior and in their political behavior. The main differences are that (1) in the market sphere transactions are voluntary, whereas the political sphere is characterized by coercive interactions; (2) in the market sphere, generally speaking, "you get what you pay for," but in the polity the connection between individual choices (votes) and actual outcomes is very loose.

In an ideally democratic state, competition for political leadership resembles competition in the marketplace. Competition for office forces political parties to satisfy citizens' wishes. But political competition is highly imperfect: citizens vote infrequently, there are only a few political parties among which to choose, many issues are bundled in the position of each candidate, and a voter has little motivation to incur the informational costs necessary to cast an intelligent ballot.

Majority rule gives inadequate weight to minority desires. On the other hand, "log-rolling" allows intense minority preferences on some issues to be exchanged for votes on other issues. In principle, log-rolling or even direct buying of votes can lead to Pareto-efficient outcomes.

---

[15] The reasoning would not apply if the kidnapper were planning an infinite rather than a finite number of crimes, for then there would be no last crime. But since the kidnapper is mortal, we need not worry about a nonending sequence of crimes. Alternatively, it can be shown mathematically that the kidnapper's threat is credible if at moment of time there is some sufficiently large *probability* of the sequence continuing – that is, of the kidnapper going on to commit another crime. But this also could not always be true for a mortal criminal.

Majority rule can lead to *cycling*: proposal *X* may be favored by a majority over *Y*, *Y* over *Z*, and *Z* in turn over *X*. Where conditions rule out cycling, there is a strong tendency for the option favored by the *median voter* to win out in majority voting.

Cooperation through exchange is not the only way of making a living. It is often possible to get ahead by pursuing the way of conflict – grabbing or confiscating the resources you want. Conflict situations include warfare, industrial disputes, litigation, crime, and redistributive politics. Whereas the way of cooperation through exchange achieves mutual benefit, when the way of conflict is adopted at least one side must lose – and possibly both. Elements involved in the choice of conflict as opposed to cooperative settlement include antipathetic preferences, rivalry for resources, overconfidence in one's ability to deliver and bear punishment, and nonenforceability of agreements. The Coase Theorem (that all mutually advantageous bargains will always be achieved), apart from its other limitations, is not applicable in circumstances leading one or more contenders to rationally choose the way of conflict. So we cannot expect the abolition of war, crime, and redistributive politics.

QUESTIONS
†The answers to daggered questions appear at the end of the book.

For Review

†1. In market competition among firms, economic profit tends to be eliminated (the "zero-profit theorem" of Chapter 7). Does something analogous tend to occur in political competition between parties? Why or why not?

†2. What are some of the major obstacles preventing the expression of the "will of the people" through the political system? How are these analogous to, and how different from, the difficulties of the market system?

3. How may the delegation of decision-making power to political representatives lead to decisions diverging from the desires of constituents? Considering the corporation as a kind of political system, what protections and escape hatches do stockholders have that may not be available to members of the polity?

4. How do the goals and opportunities of bureaucrats differ from those of elected officials? How do they differ from those of managers of private firms?

†5. a. Is a unanimous consent rule, in which dissident votes must be purchased, an ideal political system – apart from transaction costs?
   b. Does the process of "log-rolling" approximate this result?
   c. What are some objections to log-rolling?

6. What conditions are necessary for the validity of the Median-Voter Theorem? What types of elections are likely to meet these conditions?

7. Show how emotional antipathy, rivalry for resources, and overconfidence all tend to promote conflict.

8. In a situation where there would be a mutual gain from agreement, show how agreement might not be achieved when outside enforcement is absent.

†9. What are "self-enforcing agreements"? Give an example.

10. Show how different types of conflict can be represented in game-theory terms. Which are more and which are less likely to lead to cooperative solutions?

11. Why do "single-peaked" preferences rule out majority-vote cycling if there is only a single dimension of choice? What happens if there is more than one dimension?

†12. Why might elected state judges tend to find against out-of-state defendants more often than against in-state defendants?

†13. Why might elasticity of demand for a commodity affect whether government agricultural programs will tend to be designed to improve productivity, versus restricting output?

For Further Thought and Discussion

†1. We could regard the first section of the chapter as an "economic" approach to politics, considering government as a (more or less imperfect) provider of goods that citizens desire. Explain this approach to the political process. Are there other approaches?

†2. Would the fidelity of the political system to citizen desires be improved by any or all of the following: more frequent elections, more numerous legislatures, elected rather than appointed judges, the spoils system rather than the merit system in the civil service? Comment.

†3. If votes could be bought for money, would both the rich and the poor be better off, in accordance with the mutual advantage of trade? What is the objection to buying votes for money?

4. Under what political mechanisms or situations do majorities tend to exploit minorities? Under what mechanisms or situations is it the other way around?

†5. Which is more likely to gain legislative approval: a bill that redistributes cash income from the rich to the poor, or one that establishes a bureaucracy to provide services to the poor? Explain.

†6. Suppose there were a sudden unexpected increase in demand for a product now provided through the government sector. Would you expect any systematic differences in the price-quantity response as compared with a product provided through the private sector?

7. Under a system that might be called "open corruption," government officials (including judges) could sell their decisions to the highest bidder. How bad would this be?

†8. In rent-seeking competition there tends to be a higher intensity of struggle when the two sides have relatively equal valuations for the prize. Can you explain why?

9. Draw figures analogous to those in Figures 17.3, 17.4, and 17.5 where beliefs, opportunities, or preferences are not symmetrical. For example, suppose the Blues are sympathetic to the Grays but the Grays are hostile to the Blues.

†10. Under what conditions, if any, can the argument for appeasement make sense?

11. Can you give an intuitive explanation for why, when the degree of rivalry is greatest, the advantage lies with the second-mover, whereas when rivalry is least the advantage lies with the first-mover)?

12. According to the 19th century New York political operator William "Boss" Tweed, leader of the corrupt Tammany Hall political machine, "I don't care who does the electing as long as I get to do the nominating." Are nominators more powerful than voters? Is it better to be able to control the agenda for voting between alternative legislative bills, or to be able to vote on these bills?

Answers to Selected Questions

CHAPTER 1

For Review

1. a. Economic theories or models provide testable propositions about the real world. These models must stand or fall on the accuracy of their predictions. It is the use of evidence that makes theories scientific.

   b. Here are some economic predictions: Vegetables will be cheaper in season than out of season. People will seldom be observed throwing money away. Advertisers will claim that their products are better than competitors' products. To take a more extended example: Sharply higher gasoline prices will reduce auto travel generally, and also reduce average highway speeds (with a consequent drop in motor accidents). They will also encourage sales of smaller cars. In the longer run a trend to more compact cities will be observed. (Of course, all such predictions must be understood in an "other things equal" sense.)

   c. Economics does not explain why tastes or social attitudes change. We do not understand the determinants of ideological movements such as fascism, Marxism, or Christianity, or the full causes of important social trends such as growth of government. And even important issues of a more narrowly defined "economic" nature, for example the causes of business fluctuations, remain unresolved.

2. a. Rational behavior may be defined either in terms of method (the choice is made by calculating the costs and benefits of alternative actions) or in terms of results (the action chosen turns out to be well-suited for achieving one's goals). These two definitions do not fully agree.

   b. In terms of method, before placing a bet at roulette a gambler might calculate the odds and observe the behavior of the wheel. It would be irrational to bet on the basis of a dream or heavenly vision. In terms of results, on average casino gambling is unprofitable, so it's probably irrational to bet at all.

   c. Aggregated over many individuals, a limited degree of individual rationality will show up as a tendency toward rational behavior for the group as a whole. Even if the rational element is small, it operates in a consistent and predictable direction.

4. An obvious example is parental love. And billions of dollars are contributed annually to charities of all kinds.

7. a.   In a market economy, self-interested individuals will find it advantageous to provide goods and services to other people, via the process of exchange. What others are willing to pay enables the sellers to earn higher income and so better satisfy their own desires.

   b, c, d. No. If his or her own income is not increased by serving others, a self-interested individual will not do so voluntarily.

8. In the product market, firms sell goods and services to consumers, obtaining dollars in return. In the factor market, consumers in their capacity as resource owners trade factor services (e.g., labor time) to firms for dollars. The dollars that a consumer pays for goods and services must match the amounts received for providing factor services – that is, the consumer's income. Similarly, the dollars that firms pay for factor services must match overall with the revenues received for goods and services produced.

For Further Thought and Discussion

2. a.   That depends upon the direction of causation. Other things equal, the death penalty should be expected to reduce the murder rate. However, sometimes the causation runs the other way. If it was the high frequency of murder that led to the imposition of the death penalty, the jurisdiction with capital punishment might still have a high murder rate – even though the death penalty reduces the frequency.

   b.   Again, this depends upon the direction of causation. Other things equal, increasing the tax exemption should result in an increase in the birth rate. But if it was a perceived deficiency of births that led a nation to grant such an exemption, even if the birth rate rose somewhat it might still be lower than birth rates elsewhere.

3. If insurance companies refused to pay for the treatment of mental illness, and if the government did not finance treatment under Medicare, doctors would be less motivated to diagnose patients' psychological problems as "disease." This would surely lower the reported incidence of mental illness. Making medical treatment more costly would also induce potential patients to confront their problems rather than accept the dependent status of being "sick." These predicted effects do not depend upon whether Dr. Szasz's theory about mental illness is in fact correct.

6. The principle of the Invisible Hand applies to *market* interactions, which are both voluntary and mutual. Since the kinds of interactions mentioned in this question (crime, etc.) are not voluntary market exchanges, self-serving behavior may not benefit others.

7. Drivers who wore seat belts would feel safer than before, and might therefore take a little less care to avoid accidents. However, they would probably still remain safer overall. On the other hand, if drivers take less care, pedestrian deaths are likely to increase.

8. Dr. Johnson probably had in mind getting money by trade, as opposed to making a living by gambling or fighting. In short, he was thinking in terms of the Invisible Hand. Charles Baudelaire was probably upset by his publisher's refusal to give him a bigger advance on his royalties.

10. While "experts" proposing to keep disaster predictions secret may believe that people are irrational, that is not necessarily the case. The thought might be that some decisions that are individually rational – for example, jumping into your car to leave town – might lead to total paralysis of traffic. Whether earthquake predictions would indeed lead to individually irrational behavior or to socially dysfunctional consequences, or both, are

questions of social psychology. Economic analysis is not sufficient to justify or oppose a ban on predictions.

CHAPTER 2

For Review

1. a. Optimization. b. Equilibrium. c. Equilibrium. d. Optimization. e. Equilibrium. f. Optimization.

3. The price of a good X is the amount of another good (usually money) that must be given up in order to acquire a unit of X. Consequently, price is a ratio of amounts, or a ratio of quantities (money/X).

6. Yes. Shifting the supply curve up by $\$T$ leads to a solution at the intersection of the *gross* supply curve with the original demand curve. Shifting the demand curve down by $\$T$ leads to a solution at the intersection of the *net* demand curve with the original supply curve. As the only difference between the gross and net supply or demand curves is a vertical displacement of $\$T$, the intersections take place at the same quantity. The intersection of the gross supply curve with the demand curve determines the gross price. The intersection of the net demand curve with the supply curve determines the net price. But, of course, it is not necessary to carry out both constructions; either suffices since the gross price and net price are related by $P^+ \equiv P^- + T$.

8. a. Both. b. Raise the price paid by consumers. c., d. Reduce the price received by sellers.

10. a. A meaningful price ceiling is below the market equilibrium price; a meaningful price floor is above the equilibrium price.

 b. Because trade is voluntary, the quantity traded is the smaller of what sellers are willing to offer and what consumers are willing to buy. Price ceilings decrease the quantity that sellers wish to offer. Price floors decrease the quantity that consumers wish to buy. Both decrease the quantity traded.

 c. If a price floor above the equilibrium level is supported, sellers can make some sales for which there are no demanders (apart from the supporting agency). Transactions then depend solely on the existence of supply at that price. If the floor price is above the equilibrium price, the quantity sold will increase. The supporting agency, however, will accumulate inventories.

13. a. The marginal cost to the club is 30 cents per can. But for an additional can a member pays only his pro-rata share of the marginal cost to the club: $0.30/40 or 3/4 of a cent.

14. a. May be true or false. b. True. c. False. d. May be true or false. e. True. f. May be true or false.

15. As in Exercise 2.6, consumption under the tax is 36. For the 20% interdiction, solving the equations $P = 300 - Q^-$, $P = (60 + 2Q^+)/(1 - 0.2)$ and $Q^- = Q^+(1 - 0.2)$ gives consumption $Q^- = 54.55$ (and $P = 245.45$).

For Further Thought and Discussion

1. a. Wherever the Roman armies marched, the demand for foodstuffs increased because military demands were added to the normal civilian demands. With an unchanged supply curve, greater demand inevitably meant higher price.

 b. Diocletian's edict set a price ceiling below the (new) equilibrium price. As a result, there must have been unsatisfied buyers. It is likely that Diocletian's armies made up a large portion of these unsatisfied buyers. The soldiers possibly paid black market prices, went hungry, or most likely simply confiscated the food they wanted. [See

Jacob Burckhardt, *The Age of Constantine the Great* (New York: Pantheon, 1949), Chapter 2.]

2. a. The tax may be regarded as either shifting the supply curve up, or shifting the demand curve down. The tax would have a small effect upon quantity exchanged in the market, a small effect on the gross price paid by buyers, but a large effect upon the net price paid to sellers.

 b. The steep supply curve means that suppliers are willing to offer even a slightly larger quantity only at a much higher price. Since the tax reduces quantity sold by lowering the net demand, the net price received by sellers falls sharply. The gross price paid by consumers rises, but only slightly, since the market quantity declines just slightly.

4. a. Since it would be more costly to operate automobiles, the demand curve for cars would shift to the left, leading to a fall in their price.

 b. The price of big, heavy cars ("gas-guzzlers") would fall more.

5. a. As changes in economic conditions affect demand or supply (or both), the new supply-demand equilibrium is arrived at simply by shifting the affected curve or curves. No attention is paid to the process of moving from the old supply-demand intersection to the new.

 b. In the real world, these conditions are never precisely met. But in a market where traders are well informed, the model may closely approximate reality.

7. Fewer flights will be available, but the remaining flights will provide a higher quality of service. There will be less crowding and fewer delays. Ticket prices may or may not rise, since the fees paid by the airlines are counterbalanced by efficiency gains in scheduling flights. And of course, the airport will have additional income that can be used for a variety of purposes.

8. When quantity rises from $Q = 3$ to $Q = 6$, Total Revenue rises from 60 to 72. This provides an estimate of $(72 - 60)/3 = 4$ for the Marginal Revenue at the mid-point $Q = 4\ 1/2$. The decrease from $Q = 3$ to $Q = 0$ similarly provides an estimate of $(60 - 0)/3 = 20$ for the Marginal Revenue at $Q = 11/2$. Interpolating leads to the approximation $MR = (4 + 20)/2 = 12$ at $Q = 3$.

10. Since the "marginal" is below the "average" in this region, the "average" cannot be rising between $Q = 30$ and $Q = 35$.

12. Quantity must increase, but price can either increase or decrease. This is evident graphically. Intuitively, the increase in demand increases price and quantity (for a given supply curve), and the increase in supply increases quantity further, but at a lower price.

15. a. Demand and therefore price went up for exceptional talents, and down for average talents.

 b. Demand for the highest talent individuals fell. Demand for mass-produced music and drama featuring less talented artists also declined. Thus, the quality of recorded performances should have gone down. This quality reduction should reduce the attractiveness of recorded performances as opposed to live performances. So unrestrained copying could have led to somewhat greater demand for live performances, and therefore to higher demand for musicians of somewhat lesser talent. On the other hand, the cheap availability of pirated recordings would reduce the demand by other consumers for live music. Balancing these effects, overall this development might have raised demand for musicians with lesser talent, though this seems unlikely.

CHAPTER 3

For Review

1. a. Violates the Axiom of Comparison.
    b. Expresses indifference, but does not violate the laws.
    c. Indicates inconsistency, and thus also violates the Axiom of Comparison.
4. Utility simply indicates preference ranking. If Sally prefers bundle A to bundle B, economists say she gets higher utility from B.
6. Since ordinal utility indicates only direction of preference, only the sign and not the magnitude of Marginal Utility can be determined.
8. a. Ordinal. b. Cardinal. c. Interpersonal comparability.
9. Indifference curves show only level contours of utility. It remains necessary to indicate the directions of movement from lower to higher contours.

For Further Thought and Discussion

1. Even if it were possible to maximize the per capita amount of good (the "greatest good") in utility terms, adding more people ("the greatest number") would necessarily conflict with that goal. For example, would 200 units of "good" spread over 10 people (20 units per person) be better than 160 units spread over 20 people (only 8 per person, but there are more people sharing)?
2. Placement in a horse race, a tennis ladder, or a job seniority list. In materials science a measure commonly used for hardness is based on the relation "scratches." Diamond is harder than glass, and glass is harder than chalk, but this measure does not indicate how much harder.
4. Any shape that is symmetrical across the 45° line. This would indicate, for example, that I am indifferent between the combination "His Income is $2,000 while My Income is $1,000" and the combination "My Income is $2,000 while His Income is $1,000."
5. The preference map would take the form of rays out of the origin. Along any single ray, representing a fixed ratio of "My Income" to "His Income," the individual would be equally happy. For such an individual the preference directions would be such that "My Income" is a good, while "His Income" is a bad.
7. Utility theory describes the choices that an individual makes when faced with alternatives. If the student chooses the fresh fruit, the economist describes this behavior as a higher utility from choosing fresh fruit than from choosing the Napoleon. At a deeper level, people may feel conflicted about the different kinds of pleasures different goods provide, which raises the question of whether the student's behavior is rational. For example, people sometime succumb to temptation, and regret it afterward. Economists have developed extensions of utility theory to deal with imperfectly rational behavior, included problems of self-control.

CHAPTER 4

For Review

3. a. The budget line is the northeast boundary of an individual's market opportunity set. It shows the achievable consumption bundles if the individual spends all his income.
    b. The equation of the budget line is $I = P_x x + P_y y$.

    c. The slope of the budget line depends upon the relative prices of the goods X and Y. This slope is $-P_x/P_y$.

4. The optimum of the consumer is found geometrically as the point on the budget line touching the highest achievable indifference curve. If both goods are consumed, this is an interior solution. If only one good is consumed (if the budget line touches the highest indifference curve at one axis), this is a corner solution.

6. a. The Consumption Balance Equation is $MU_x/P_x = MU_y/P_y$. The Substitution Balance Equation is $MRS_C = P_x/P_y$ (or slope of indifference curve = slope of budget line). The Consumption Balance Equation can be reduced to the Substitution Balance Equation, but not vice versa. This is because the Consumption Balance Equation requires cardinal utility whereas the Substitution Balance Equation requires only ordinal utility. (Cardinal utility implies ordinal utility, but not vice versa.)

    b. Both equations apply to interior solutions. At a corner solution an *inequality* will ordinarily hold, dictating spending all of income upon one of the commodities.

11. a. If the Income Expansion Path has a positive slope, the Engel Curve for each good will have a positive slope.

    b. If X is an inferior good, the Engel Curve will have a negative slope.

14. If the Law of Demand holds, the Price Expansion Path never curls back (to the left).

18. As long as commodity X is a good (rather than a neuter or a bad), those receiving vouchers for X will consume at least the voucher equivalent. For those previously consuming less than this, the voucher will always increase consumption. For this reason, vouchers are particularly effective (relative to subsidies) in increasing consumption among persons who would otherwise have consumed little or none of a good.

For Further Thought and Discussion

1. a. An experiment could reveal the maximum amount of Y an individual might be willing to pay for a small increment of X. This would be an approximation of the MRS_C.

    b. No known experiment could reveal Marginal Utility.

3. a. In the Giffen range, the Price Expansion Path moves toward higher y but lower x. Since utility increases along the *PEP*, y must be increasing fast enough to more than compensate for the decrease in x. But in Figure 4.14 the amount of Y it is possible to acquire is bounded by the horizontal line through the starting point K. So this process can continue only over a limited range of the *PEP*, which must eventually turn up and to the right.

    b. This is impossible. Utility is increasing everywhere along the *PEP*, and the same starting point cannot have both lower and higher utility.

4. a. An increase in P_x would tend to shift the Income Expansion Path up and to the left.

    b. An increase in income would tend to displace the *PEP* up and to the right (assuming X and Y are both normal superior goods).

6. Here are two possibilities: (1) "Being a good woman" is a good for Becky, but one she can't afford until her income reaches five thousand a year. (2) Becky regards "being a good woman" as unpleasant (a bad, like hard labor). But for a fee (like wages for hard labor) of five thousand a year she would be a good woman.

7. The pair of close substitutes is more likely to have a member that is an inferior good. The reason is that complements tend to be consumed together, whereas substitutes do not. Therefore, increased income is likely to result in increased consumption of both bread and butter (complements). But comparing butter and margarine (substitutes), with increased income an individual is likely to consume less margarine, since he can now better afford the preferred (but more expensive) substitute – butter.

8. Since usually only a small fraction of income is spent on any single good X, the income effect (enrichment or impoverishment) due to a change in P_x will be relatively small.

10. The market price should rise, because increased quantities will be demanded. The effect will be to partially cancel the impact of the subsidy or voucher.

12. a. Coach travel is an inferior good here, since the purchased quantity falls as income rises. Specifically, if income were to rise above \$100, more first class travel and less coach travel would be purchased.

   b. If the traveler's budget is so small that he can complete the trip only by traveling entirely in coach, then he will do so. If the traveler's budget permits the trip to be completed by traveling entirely in first class, then only first-class travel will be purchased.

13. a. Yes.

   b. If the slope of the budget line is exactly the same as the slope of the indifference curve for the two perfect substitutes, then the individual does not care whether he consumes only one of the goods, or only the other good, or any mixture of the two.

19. No, the two Income Expansion Paths curves cannot intersect. Assuming $P_y = 1$ throughout, every point on the original *IEP* curve represents an indifference-curve tangency with a budget line of slope $-P_x$. Every point on the new *IEP'* curve represents a tangency with a budget line of slope $-P'_x$. If the two *IEP* curves crossed, their point of intersection would have to be where an indifference curve is tangent to two budget lines of different slopes, which is impossible.

20. The individual either will not change his demand at all, or will swing from buying 100% of one good to buying 100% of the other good. (We rule out the special case in which the price ratio is precisely the same as the slope of the straight-line indifference curves, in which case the quantity demanded is indeterminate.)

CHAPTER 5

For Review

2. Such Engel Curves (all straight lines through the origin, but with different slopes) depict the same proportionate response of changes in consumption to changes in income. For such curves, greater steepness does not show greater income elasticity but rather that x/I is higher – that is, that the commodity is absolutely more important in the consumer's budget.

5. a. *Elastic demand* means that the absolute value of the price elasticity of demand exceeds one. *Inelastic demand* means that the absolute value of the price elasticity of demand is less than one.

   b. For a linear demand curve, the elasticity at any point is the ratio of two slopes: the slope of a ray from the origin to the point on the curve, divided by the constant slope along the curve.

c.   For a nonlinear demand curve, the slope along the curve is interpreted as the slope of the tangent to the curve at that point. Thus the elasticity at any point along a nonlinear demand curve is the same as the elasticity along the straight line tangent at that point to the demand curve.

6. a. Negative infinity. b. Zero. c. -1.
9. Price elasticity is -1. Income elasticity is $+1$.
10. Permitting the sale of coupons would benefit both the wealthy and the poor. The poor could sell coupons for dollars, shift their income constraint outward, and attain a more preferred position. The wealthy could buy coupons for dollars, shift their ration constraint upward, and also attain a more preferred position.

For Further Thought and Discussion

2. a.   Since $PG = 100$, expenditure is constant at any price. Elasticity is therefore always 1. Since expenditure is constant, the share of the budget ("importance") is also the same at every price.

    b.   (Calculus is needed to answer this question.) The inverse slope of the demand curve can be shown to be $dG/dP = -200/P^3$. Multiply by P/G to obtain elasticity: $\eta = -200/(P^2 G)$. Since $P^2 G = 100$ (the demand equation), this reduces to $-200/100 = -2$. So the elasticity of demand is -2 at all prices. Since each 1% fall in price increases quantity by 2%, the budget share rises as price falls.

    c.   Using the same method as in (b), the slope is $-50/P^{1.5}$, and elasticity is $\eta = -50/(P^{0.5} G)$. This reduces to $-50/100 = -1/2$. Here a 1% fall in price increases quantity by only 0.5%, so "importance" falls as price falls.

    d.   "Importance" in the budget may change in either direction as price changes, even when elasticity is constant. In general, there is no necessary relation between importance and elasticity of demand.

3. a.   At low incomes consumers are likely to be interested only in nutrition. High-quality and low-quality beef are good substitutes as far as nutrition is concerned. At high incomes other characteristics such as flavor become increasingly important to consumers. Here, low-quality beef is not a good substitute for high-quality beef. Higher indifference curves would therefore have greater curvature.

    b.   Because high-quality beef is a luxury (it has a stronger positive income effect than low-quality beef), the price elasticity of demand for high-quality beef should be high relative to the price elasticity for low-quality beef.

5. The secretary's arithmetic is correct, but it does not follow that there's something wrong with the economics. The professor need not in fact be willing to pay more in total for two tickets than for three (which would indeed be irrational). The point is that if the price is only $10, he *does not have to* pay more for three tickets than he would have paid for two at a price of $20 each. Looking at this another way, the $10 is the worth of a third ticket to the professor, not the worth of each of three tickets. (If the objection were valid, it would never make sense for a consumer to have an inelastic demand for a good.)

6. This is indeed possible, though opinions may differ about how likely it is. Consumers seeking snob appeal gain utility from exclusiveness. At a high price, they pay more for the commodity but gain exclusivity. But if the exclusiveness were provided in some other way (as by the medieval Statute of Dress that made it illegal for the lower orders to wear upper-class clothes), presumably the Law of Demand would hold.

7. This is very much like the previous question, but here the consumer believes the high-price good is of higher quality. There is of course nothing paradoxical about someone

preferring high quality at a high price over low quality at a low price. Again, if the quality were guaranteed in some other way than by high price (perhaps by a consumer organization's rating of the product), presumably the Law of Demand would hold – a high-quality product at a low price would be chosen over the same high-quality product at a high price. Chapter 9 discusses this issue in greater depth.

11. a. The usual justification is that rationed commodities tend to be those that are "essential" to life or health. If ration allowances were exchangeable, rich people might end up with more than "their fair share" of these essential commodities. Note that this assumes that the poorer people who sell their allowances are foolish in giving up some "essentials" for nonessentials – or else possibly that poorer people have to be forced to remain in good working condition for the sake of the war effort, though they themselves might prefer otherwise!

   b. The adverse consequences include the loss of the gains from trade, plus the diversion of resources into black-market activities and the policing efforts required to minimize such activities.

CHAPTER 6

For Review

2. In a partnership, each partner is fully liable for all the liabilities of the enterprise. So having many partners is risky. The same holds when it become necessary to delegate management decisions. Since corporations are characterized by limited liability, larger organizations with professional management become more feasible.

3. a. Economic profit is the difference between the firm's Total Revenue and its Total (economic) Costs.

   b. Since owners receive profits, maximization of profit (owner wealth) is an appropriate goal for owners. Managers, if they are not also owners, have no claim on profits and so are only indirectly interested in maximizing profit. More directly, managers might be interested in power, growth, stability, and a favorable corporate image as well as in larger salaries and more pleasant working conditions.

   c. Owners try to develop mechanisms to impose their profit-maximizing goal upon managers. Lawsuits, proxy fights, and hostile takeover can punish managers who are not pursuing owners' goals. Similarly, profit-sharing and stock-option plans reward managers for pursuing owners' goals. These mechanisms are imperfect, though, so the likely result is that the firm will pursue some mixture of owner and manager goals.

6. a. Recall that Total Cost is Fixed Cost F plus Variable Cost VC. Since $AVC = 10 + 2.5q$, $VC = (AVC) \times q = 10q + 2.5q^2$, and Total Cost is $F + VC = 250 + 10q + 2.5q^2$.

   b. The firm maximizes profits at that output where $P = MC$, or numerically $50 = 10 + 5q$; the solution is $q = 8$.

   c. Profits are Total Revenue R minus Total Cost C. Here $R = Pq = 50(8) = 400$. Substituting in the cost equation $C = 250 + 10q + 2.5q^2$, we obtain $C = 490$. The firm is therefore losing $90. Nevertheless, since the price $P = 50$ is greater than $AVC = 10 + 2.5(8) = 30$, in the short run the firm should continue producing.

7. a. Yes. At the vertical axis, AC is greater than or equal to MC. (If there are fixed Costs, AC is infinite.) As MC falls from its initial level along the vertical axis, it makes AC fall as well.

b.   No. By proposition 2.2a, when *AC* is falling, *MC* lies below *AC*; but *MC* can be less than *AC* and still not be itself falling.

9. A firm will make short-run adjustments to changes in economic conditions if such changes are viewed as temporary. A firm will make long-run adjustments to changes in economic conditions if such changes are viewed as permanent.

10. This is a fallacy. In the long run the firm will increase its floor space (incur a fixed cost) only if doing so is cost-efficient. Otherwise it would hold floor space constant in the long run, not just the short run.

For Further Thought and Discussion

2. a.   Yes, assuming borrowers are rational and have voluntarily accepted the terms of the "contract."

   b.   Yes.

   c.   Not necessarily. Perhaps borrowers should be protected from their own mistakes. As a more important reason, almost every government reserves for itself a monopoly of lawful violence within its borders. (On this, see Chapter 17.)

3. Taking on additional traffic at a price lower than Average Cost would be financially advantageous if the price exceeded Marginal Cost. But even if Average Variable Cost is only one-third of Average Cost, Marginal Cost might not be low enough to warrant taking on the new traffic. (Indeed, Marginal Cost could then be larger than Average Cost.)

4. a.   If changing conditions are viewed as temporary, some inputs may be held fixed in the face of a contraction of output; this avoids the transaction costs incurred in selling the inputs and then buying them back when conditions return to normal – or, for an expansion of output, avoids the costs of buying inputs and later selling them back. A similar result holds when the firm's operations involve specialized resources. Resources specialized to the firm can only be sold at a low price to others, yet must be purchased at a high price. Then these resources may be held fixed during temporary changes in output.

   b.   The inputs that are held fixed are those that are highly specialized to the firm, or for which transaction costs are high.

7. The short-run Marginal Cost is the additional cost of temporarily increasing output. Whether these costs are paid immediately (overtime wages, increased usage of power, etc.) or at a later time (deferred maintenance), they are all costs. The factory manager is confusing short-run costs with costs that must be paid immediately. They are not the same.

8. The Short-run Marginal Cost curve must be rising.

9. a.   The Marginal Cost of providing service, when trains are running empty, is low. Another passenger can be transported at little *additional* cost. When trains are running full, the Marginal Cost is much higher. More trains must be run, or further unpleasant crowding must be imposed on passengers. Since Marginal Cost is very low in off hours, the transit line should encourage off-hour business, not discourage it. (The management consultant is confusing Marginal Cost with Average Cost.)

   b.   Commutation tickets will increase ridership at rush hours, but it is during these times that the trains are already full. If the cost of running additional trains or of imposing crowding on customers is high, then the transit line is likely to be worse off by selling commutation tickets. Discount tickets for *off-hour* riders, on the other hand, would likely increase revenues without much of an increase in cost. This type of discount would be a good idea. As a counterargument, however, more rush-hour train riders will likely mean less crowding of streets and highways. Weighing these two considerations, conceivably reduced-fare commutation tickets might be justified.

CHAPTER 7

For Review

1. Yes. Steepness and elasticity of supply, at a given point, must be inversely related.
2. While the issue of whether or not doubling all inputs would always double output is arguable, it is not economically relevant. In the real world, it is never possible to double *all* relevant inputs.
4. Where there are no "external" effects, the industry supply curve will be less steep than the firm supply curve but will have the same elasticity. (The quantitative response of output to price will be larger, but the *proportionate* response will be the same.)
6. a. In long-run equilibrium, the marginal firm is on the borderline between staying in the industry and leaving. The value of its opportunities elsewhere practically equals what it can earn in this industry. Consequently, the economic profit of the marginal firm will be (only negligibly above) zero.
   b. Inframarginal firms have access to some special resources particularly suited to producing in this industry. Other firms will bid for the right to use these special resources. When the inframarginal firm charges itself the opportunity cost – what it could get by offering the special resources to these other bidders – it is also left with zero economic profit.
10. External pecuniary effects are normally diseconomies, so the answer to the first question is no. External technological effects can be economies, so the answer to the second question is yes. In this situation, the industry supply curve slopes downward.

For Further Thought and Discussion

2. True. A competitive firm will produce positive output only if Marginal Cost exceeds Average Variable Cost (in the short run) or Average Cost (in the long run). So *AVC* in the former case, or *AC* in the latter case, must be rising.
4. a. Pecuniary. b. Technological. c. Pecuniary. d. Technological. (In all four cases, the effect is external to the individual firm but internal to the industry.)
5. No. All firms may be earning zero economic profit, and yet some may be able to survive even if product price falls. These will be the "inframarginal" firms (see last question in "For Review" section above).
7. a. If all coupons were used initially, allowing resale would only redistribute coupons. Only if some coupons were initially unused would sale of coupons tend to raise the price of petroleum and elicit more supply.
   b. Salability would cause a redistribution of coupons to those consumers having the highest demand prices for gasoline – at least as high as the sum of the product price and the price paid for a coupon.
   c. Without the sale of coupons, some buyers may receive little or no Consumer Surplus from their purchases of gasoline, while others who would receive great Consumer Surplus may be unable to make purchases. Salability will allow those previously

unable to make purchases to bid away the coupons from those currently receiving little Consumer Surplus from gasoline.

8. No. As a consequence of the reduced demand, the market price would fall below the ceiling price. Assuming some consumers with ration tickets were willing to pay as much as the choke price for supply, the new market equilibrium price would be below the ceiling price but above the choke price for supply – and so trade would take place. On the other hand, if the coupons were salable they would be resold to those who value them the most. Then there would be trading at the ceiling price.

10. No. The output from existing wells is based, even in the short run, on a calculation of the price received for oil versus the cost of pumping. The higher the price, the more it pays to pump. In the longer run, the higher the price, the more profitable it will be to extend the life of an existing well by heating, flooding, redrilling, etc.

12. a.   By reversing the analysis pictured in Figure 7.10, it can be seen that Consumer Surplus will increase (rather than decrease) because of the lower price to consumers, and Producer Surplus will increase (rather than decrease) because of the higher price to sellers.

   b.   No. A tax leads to inefficiency due to reduced exchange; a subsidy leads to inefficiency due to excessive exchange. (Since the price received by sellers exceeds the price paid by consumers, there will be units produced and sold whose value to consumers does not cover the Marginal Cost of production.) It may seem puzzling that Consumer Surplus and Producer Surplus both increase in this market and yet there is inefficiency. The explanation is that the subsidy here reduces Consumer Surplus and Producer Surplus *elsewhere* in the economy. Other industries must be taxed to finance the subsidy.

CHAPTER 8

For Review

1. Less: $48 is the price, but the additional unit reduces the revenues derived from the other 999 units.

2. To maximize profit, a monopolist will set $MR = MC$. Since Marginal Cost is always positive, the monopolist will always produce where Marginal Revenue is positive. $MR > 0$ implies elastic demand, that is $\eta < -1$.

3. It should be willing to pay more. True, if the firm continued to produce 1,000 panes, then its savings would be $10(1,000) = $10,000 – and on that basis it should pay no more than $10,000. However, since the machine is rented at a lump-sum rate, the *Marginal* Cost is now lower. At this lower MC the firm will want to produce more than 10,000 panes, so that (before paying for the machine) its profits increase by more than $10,000. Thus, the firm should be willing to pay more than $10,000.

5. In comparison with pure competition, monopoly results in a smaller rate of output. Because less is produced and traded, some of the gains from specialization and trade are lost; the sum of Consumer Surplus and Producer Surplus is smaller.

7. Owners of monopolies may be no more interested in nonprofit goals than owners of competitive firms, but reduced competitive pressure allows them to indulge such goals. As another matter, they may be less successful in imposing the goal of profit maximization upon managers, since owners of monopolies cannot measure their managers' performances by comparing them to competitors. Also, antitrust policy may act as a threat. (Profits that are too conspicuously large may attract antitrust prosecution.) Finally, many monopolies are regulated and so prevented from maximizing profits. For

any of these reasons, monopolies may not pursue profits as vigorously as do competitive firms.

9. In deriving the supply curve of the competitive industry, we assume that each separate firm sets output where Marginal Cost equals price. The height of the point on the supply curve therefore shows the Marginal Cost of each firm for that level of industry output. Consequently, that point on the supply curve also shows what the Marginal Cost would be if that industry were monopolized.

For Further Thought and Discussion

1. a. No, because theater admissions cannot normally be resold to others.
   b. No. It is probably true that the young, having less money, are less willing to pay for a movie ticket. That does not necessarily mean, however, that the young have a more elastic demand for movies.

2. Yes, there is a contradiction. A profit-maximizing monopolist always operates in the range of elastic demand (see For Review Question 2). But if demand is elastic, higher prices will have a big effect on quantity demanded.

4. a. At the simple monopoly optimum ($MR = MC$), price exceeds Marginal Cost. A perfectly discriminating monopolist, on the other hand, will expand output until price equals Marginal Cost. A perfectly discriminating monopolist therefore generally produces more than a simple monopolist. But if the income effect is very strong, this conclusion may not hold. The discriminating monopolist extracts more income from consumers at each level of output, which reduces demand for additional units.
   b. A market-segmentation monopolist will charge a price higher than the simple monopoly price to some market segments, and so sell less in those segments. But the monopolist will also charge a price lower than the simple monopoly price to the other segments and so sell more there. A market segmentation monopolist, then, may or may not produce and sell more than a simple monopolist.
   c. Whereas a multipart pricing monopolist will charge a price higher than the simple monopoly price for small purchases, the price will be less than the simple monopoly price for purchases beyond a certain size. Some customers will buy less because they purchase too little to receive the lower marginal price. Other customers will purchase enough to receive the lower marginal price and so will buy more (in the absence of a strong income effect) than if faced with a single monopoly price. The multipart pricing monopolist, therefore, also may or may not produce more than a simple monopolist.

5. Price discrimination can only be effective if resale of the commodity is difficult. Resale of services is more difficult than resale of manufactured goods.

6. a. Yes. The markets are divided between customers who are willing and customers who are not willing to take the trouble of collecting and using coupons. There should be little or no "leakage," since those not using coupons (and so paying higher prices) are unwilling to take the time and trouble needed to shift to the lower-price market.
   b. Yes, consumers with more elastic demands will find it more worthwhile to go to the trouble of using coupons.

10. Yes, the claims are contradictory. A profit-maximizing monopoly or cartel will not want to price its product in the region of inelastic demand (since inelastic demand implies that Marginal Revenue is negative).

13. Yes, a seller with market power will tend to charge a higher price for an inelastically demanded product. If library demand for hardbacks is inelastic, this is potentially consistent with a high price for hardbacks.

14. Yes. If theft is monopolized, the marginal yield of thieving to the "industry" as a whole is less than that perceived by the individual competitive thief. (One thief may steal on Tuesday what another thief wanted to steal on Wednesday.) Also, any increase in thievery tends to raise the intensity of defensive actions by potential victims, thereby reducing the returns to thieves in the aggregate. A monopolized theft industry would take all this into account and therefore engage in fewer (but on the average more remunerative) crimes.

CHAPTER 9

For Review

4. The monopolist is interested in producing services Z desired by consumers, where the service amount is $z = ql$ (quantity times "quality" – the latter being the service provided by each unit of physical product). Normally, there will be increasing Marginal Cost of expanding Z either by increasing quantity or by increasing quality. So, a monopolist who wants to produce a smaller service output will normally cut back on both quantity and quality.

5. a. No.
   b. If consumers were fully informed, it would not pay to suppress an invention that raised quality at given cost. (The only possible exception would be if the invention somehow destroyed the monopoly.)
   c. Consumers would not necessarily be better off. It is conceivable that adoption of a cost-reducing invention would lead the monopolist to produce a smaller amount of service than before at a higher price. And a similar result may come about for a quality-increasing invention.

7. Mass customization is the trend toward increased product variety available for the mass market in many kinds of products. By failing to account for the value of variety, standard national income measures such as GNP understate the real increases in consumer well-being that have taken place in recent decades.

8. No, advertising can increase competition by making consumers aware of competing sellers, forcing sellers to reduce prices.

For Further Thought and Discussion

1. Hospitals usually engage in oligopolistic or monopolistic competition. Even though these do not represent perfect competition, the analysis in this chapter suggests that a shift from such partial competition to actual monopoly is unlikely to increase efficiency. The assertions about "excessive" use of expensive equipment might however make sense in view of special features of the hospital market, notably the subsidies to medical care provided by governmental or private agencies. The greater the competition, the greater the likely response to a subsidy, the response here being both in terms of quantity and quality of service provided. But the fault, if any, is not excessive competition but rather the amount or type of subsidy offered users of medical services. If hospitals are installing too many expensive CAT scanners, the subsidy to users of such equipment should be reduced.

2. No, monopolistic competition emerges when consumers' tastes for different varieties provide each supplier with a degree of monopoly power over a "clientele" for its product.

If instead a single generally recognized quality attribute is desired by all consumers, they will purchase from whichever firm offers this attribute at the lowest price. If there are many firms, each can survive only by offering the same price as the others, *per unit of quality*. As price-taking suppliers of the service, firms are engaging in pure competition.

4. The demand curve would become $P = 200 - 8Q$. That is, it would start twice as high but fall four times as fast! Intuitively, the vertical intercept – the consumers' choke price – would be twice as high, since a purchaser would be willing to pay twice as much for the very first peach if it were known to be good. Now consider the horizontal intercept. Originally, consumers' marginal willingness to pay fell to zero at $Q = 50$. But 50 unknown-quality peaches translate to 25 good peaches. If the demand price for 25 good peaches is zero, the equation of the demand curve for good peaches must be as shown above.

5. The discussion of "Suppression of Inventions" showed that an invention lowering Total and Average Cost at every level of output might conceivably raise Marginal Cost in some ranges of output. If so, even for a competitive industry, a cost-reducing invention might reduce the quantity offered at some prices. (This could happen only over a limited range, and even so seems unlikely.) Since a quality-improving invention is logically equivalent to a cost-reducing invention (in terms of the cost of producing the attribute desired by consumers), a corresponding analysis applies: the invention might conceivably (though this seems improbable) reduce consumer welfare.

6. Think of oranges as providing various amounts of a desired attribute: flavor. High-quality oranges contain more attribute than low-quality oranges. But it costs no more to ship a high-quality than a low-quality orange. Thus shipping costs per unit of quality attribute will be less if high-quality oranges are shipped. Consequently, oranges shipped to distant locations tend to be of higher quality.

7. This is similar to the situation with oranges. The tax makes it *relatively* cheaper than before to supply high-quality (high-mileage) gasoline. Some firms that previously found it profitable to produce a lower grade of gasoline are likely now to shift over to a better grade.

9. Since there is some tradeoff between quantity and quality, restricting the number of acres planted motivated American farmers to specialize in high-yield but low-quality varieties. The reformed program had the opposite effect. Since the restriction was only upon the number of pounds produced, farmers profited by making each pound of tobacco a more valuable product. So American farmers shifted over to high-quality strains of tobacco. See J. A. Seagraves, "The Life Cycle of the Flue-Cured Tobacco Program," Department of Economics and Business, North Carolina State University, Working Paper No. 34 (March 1983).

13. For the first few years, the decline in price may overestimate the decline in quality of the average car, because owners may try to dispose of "lemons" while keeping cars that are running well.

CHAPTER 10

For Review

2. The Prisoners' Dilemma is a social interaction in which each participant is motivated to adopt a shortsightedly selfish strategy, with the result that all parties lose. The source of the difficulty is that an individual who cooperates cannot induce or compel the

others to do the same, so the unselfish player ends up worse off than the others. There is an unexploited mutual gain from exchange, due to inability to make binding agreements.

3. Monopolistic competition is a market structure in which each firm's product is differentiated from the others, but the number of firms rules out strategic behavior. In contrast, the essence of oligopoly is that the behavior of any one firm will noticeably affect the behavior of others.

4. In the Nash solution of game theory, each party does the best it can given the strategies of the others. The Cournot solution for oligopoly similarly assumes that each firm chooses the profit-maximizing quantity, given the choices made by the others.

8. a and b. One method of enforcing a collusive agreement is for "loyal" firms to match any price cut by a defecting firm, but to refrain from matching any price increase. This leads to each potential defector viewing its demand curve as kinked at the agreed level of prices.

9. Basically the offense should tend to benefit equally from a running play and a passing play, because if one were better than the other for the offense than the quarterback should increase the probability of calling that kind of play.

For Further Thought and Discussion

2. When duopolist firms "learn" about one another's behavior, many new possibilities open up. Conceivably, they may learn to behave more cooperatively, limiting output so as to approach a joint monopoly solution. On the other hand, as one firm learns that the other is inclined to restrict output, the first is tempted to "free-ride" and produce more. So the final result is unclear.

3. Even though the monopolist might find it more profitable to share the market with any single new entrant, doing so for one entrant may induce others also to enter. So the monopolist would want to build a reputation for always being a ruthless price-cutter against new entrants.

4. Yes. The kink would have a more extreme form under homogeneous oligopoly. A firm that raised its price, while other firms kept their prices constant, would lose all its business – so above the kink the demand curve would be flat (perfectly elastic). A firm that lowered price would find that other firms followed, so its demand below the kink would be no more elastic than the overall industry demand.

6. a. Table 10.9 shows that the symmetrical Collusive solution is not generally better than the Threat solution for both parties. If the threat can be made effective without having to be enforced very often, the "predatory price-cutter" can do better than under collusion.

   b. Predatory price-cutting is more likely to emerge where one firm is much more powerful or aggressive than the other, making its threat more credible.

9. a. In Table 10.1, under the sequential protocol the perfect equilibrium is not unique (though the payoffs are identical in either equilibrium). The first mover (whether Attacker or Defender) is always at a disadvantage, since the interests of Attacker and Defender are completely opposed. In Table 10.2 the perfect equilibrium is also not unique, but because the players' interests are completely aligned, there is no advantage or disadvantage to moving first.

   b. Perfect equilibrium outcomes are "efficient" in Table 10.1, because starting from any cell, a move to another cell cannot make one player better off without making the other player worse off. In Table 10.2, the perfect equilibrium Left, Left is inefficient, since both players would be better off with Right, Right (the other perfect equilibrium).

10. Outline of Answer: Find the algebraic solution for q_1 and q_2 in terms of P_1 and P_2. Then take the derivative, $\partial R_1/\partial P_1 = q_1 + P_1 \partial q_1/\partial P_1$. This leads to an equation for the RC_1 curve: $P_1 = 25 + 1/4 P_2$. Similar steps generate a similar RC_2 curve $P_2 = 25 + 1/4 P_1$. Solving the two equations gives $P_1 = P_2 = 33\ 1/3$, as in Figure 10.4. Similar calculations yield reaction curves for any value of s. As s become 0, the reaction curves approach the vertical and horizontal dashed lines at $P_1 = 50$ and $P_2 = 50$. As s approaches 1, the reaction curves approach the solution for identical products. RC_1 and RC_2 become diverging rays out of the origin, and the solution approaches $P_1 = P_2 = 0$.

CHAPTER 11

For Review

2. Otherwise the sickest individuals would buy a lot of insurance. To avoid losing money, insurance companies would have to set a very high price for insurance, which would discourage healthy people from buying insurance.

4. a.   High risk increases the risk premium and reduces the certainty equivalent.
   b.   High risk aversion also increases the risk premium and reduces the certainty equivalent.
   c.   High expected value increases the certainty equivalent. It may also reduce the risk premium, if being richer makes the individual less averse to the variability of the gamble.

5. No.

6. Insurance.

7. If the gamble is not fair, the individual may have to sacrifice some expected value in order to reduce risk.

8. The ability to decide whether to buy at the specified price after gaining information about subsequent movements in the stock's market price is valuable. If the stock price goes up, the call allows the holder to buy the stock at a cheap price and resell at a higher price at a profit. So the value of the option reflects the value of information about the future stock price movement.

11. A low-quality producer can mimic a high-quality producer by charging the same high price. If it is costly for consumers to learn about quality on their own, some consumers may choose not to investigate. If no consumers obtained information, then nothing would stop low-quality producers from charging a high price. However, there can be a mixed-strategy equilibrium in which each consumer acquires information with positive probability.

12. Advertising encourages consumers to try the product. Buyers of a high-quality brand will tend to have better experiences with the product than purchasers of a low-quality product. So buyers are more likely to recommend the high-quality product to their friends, and to buy it themselves in the future.

13. The gap can indicate that other potential employers evaluated the applicant and decided not to hire him. If the evaluator believes these previous evaluators possessed useful information, she may evaluate the candidate less favorably.

For Further Thought and Discussion

7. There is some cancellation of risks, but the cancellation is imperfect. Taking on extra gambles also creates the possibility of more extreme outcomes. So it is not irrational to avoid risk.

8. When A does badly B might not, and when B does badly A might not. So the variability of your wealth tends to be lower when divided between two asset classes.

9. When the company does poorly, there is a risk that the employee will be paid less or laid off when her stock in the company is also doing poorly. To diversify her risk, the employee should hold shares in unrelated companies, perhaps through a mutual fund.

10. Ordinarily the owner might be selling the television set because it didn't work very well. But if the owner needs to sell for other reasons, this adverse selection problem is reduced. So you should be willing to offer more.

12. Barbara is in a cascade. Even if her signal favors action b, she knows that Aaron's choice of a reflects his more accurate signal. So a cascade starts with the second individual.

13. The competitors may advertise and help expand the total size of the market for a new product. They may also may do research that generates public information that is useful for improving the product, which can also expand the size of the market. When there are competing standards vying for the market, other producers who use the same standard can help that standard capture the market.

CHAPTER 12

For Review

2. a. For a monopolist in the product market, Marginal Revenue is always less than product price. Consequently, for such a monopolist mrp_a lies below vmp_a. For a competitive form in the product market, on the other hand, Marginal Revenue equals product price so that mrp_a is identical to vmp_a.

   b. Whether the firm is a monopolist or a competitor in the product market, the mrp_a curve is the firm's demand curve for factor A (within the relevant range where mrp_a is a declining function of output).

4. a. All firms will be choosing output such that $mrp_a \equiv MR(mp_a) = h_a$, in the range where mrp_a is declining. For a competitive (price-taking) firm in the product market, price P is constant so that $MR \equiv P$. Such a firm will always produce in the region of diminishing marginal returns (where mp_a is declining). For a monopolist in the product market, MR is also declining, so $mrp_a \equiv MR(mpa)$ might be declining even though mp_a is constant or rising. So a monopolist might not employ so much of an input as to be in the region of diminishing mp_a. In either case, since it *may* be rational, the answer is yes.

   b. Yes, once again it may be rational, and a price-taking firm will *always* operate in this region. Although the equation $mrp_a = h_a$ can be satisfied in the region of diminishing marginal returns but rising average returns (where mp_a lies above ap_a), it can be verified that this implies $h_a > P(q/a)$, or $h_a a > Pq$. Since spending on input A alone would then exceed Total Revenue, this is irrational. So a competitive firm would always employ enough input to be in the region of diminishing average returns, and a monopolist firm might.

   c. Diminishing total returns means that mp_a is negative. It would never pay for a firm to employ so much of input A.

5. The conditions $mrp_a = h_a$ and $mrp_b = h_b$ imply that $mp_a/h_a = mp_b/h_b$. This equation states that an extra dollar spent on either input A or input B will increase output by the same amount. Consequently, input proportions are optimal. Multiplying both numerators by MR we obtain $mrp_a/h_a = mrp_b/h_b$. At the optimal factor employments both ratios must equal 1 and in addition $MC = h_a/mp_a = h_b/mp_b$. Thus we have $MR/MC = 1$; that is, the firm's scale of output is also optimal.

8. No, because firms can enter or leave the industry. The entry-exit effect tends to make the industry demand for a factor more elastic than the individual firm demands.

10. As use of an input increases, its marginal product eventually declines. By equation (12.5) with constant hire price (competitive factor market), the conclusion follows.

11. Increasing when the exponents sum to greater than one, constant when the exponents sum to 1, and decreasing when the exponents sum to less than one.

For Further Thought and Discussion

1. a. See Examples 12.1 through 12.3.
   b. This is a question of fact. The Laws of Diminishing Returns appear to be founded upon general physical aspects of the world. Note, however, that when economists say that marginal and average returns *eventually* diminish an initial range of increasing returns is not excluded. In some situations, notably "natural monopoly," it may be that the point of diminishing returns is never reached.

2. Even if two inputs are anticomplementary, each might have positive Marginal Product. It can than be rational to hire positive amounts of both inputs.

5. Since this chapter examines only the *demand* for labor, it does not cover all the supply considerations that might also have a bearing upon whether wages are high or low. Looking only at the demand side, demand for labor has been high in the United States mainly as a result of the presence of large amounts of complementary factors. In the early years these took the form of rich natural resources (fertile land, mineral wealth, navigable rivers). In more recent times, accumulations of complementary manufactured resources (machines, roads) have contributed to the demand for labor. Other possible sources of high demand for labor in the United States include rapid technological progress (see next question) and strong competition in product markets (so that *mrp* diverges very little from *vmp* in determining the firms' desired employment of labor).

6. Technological progress by definition tends to raise the Average Product of labor. It will tend to raise wage rates as well if the Marginal Product of labor also increases. While the effects on Average Product and Marginal Product are usually parallel, there are exceptions. A "labor-saving" invention may raise the productivity of the first few workers employed so much that the Marginal Product for larger numbers falls. There is another line of causation, however, associated with the general enrichment that technological progress brings about. Higher wealth increases the demand for products involving labor of all types. So wages will tend to rise as a result of revenue considerations as well as productivity considerations.

10. If there are productive efficiencies to having an employee work more than 35 hours per week (such as increased expertise), then marginal product as a function of the number of hours of labor input employed decreases. For a price-taking firm, this reduces the value of marginal product (*vmp*) at different possible levels of labor input a. So by the Factor Employment Condition (12.9) the total number of hours of labor demanded decreases. If this decrease is modest, firms may hire more workers

(since each worker is working fewer hours). Otherwise, firms are likely to hire fewer workers.

11. No, because other resources are needed to grow and distribute the lilies (e.g., time, land, water, fertilizer, transportation services, labor).

CHAPTER 13

For Review

3. No. The supply curve can bend backward only if the income effect opposes the substitution effect. If leisure were an inferior good, the enrichment due to a wage increase would lead to reduced choice of leisure (more supply of labor), thus reinforcing the substitution effect of the wage increase.

4. At very low wage rates, only a few hours are worked. A wage increase, multiplied by only a small number of hours, will have only a small enrichment effect compared with the substitution effect.

5. The supply curve to a particular employment is likely to be much more elastic. Different employments of labor are probably, from the worker's point of view, close substitutes. Then a relatively small change in the wage differential between two employments will induce a relatively large shift in labor supply from the less attractive to the more attractive employment.

7. At a high wage, a physician will tend to choose less leisure. Indeed, if the investment in medical training leaves the individual only as well off as before (on the same indifference curve), that person will surely work more, as shown in Figure 13.3. In that case only the substitution effect of the wage increase is effective; the income effect is exactly canceled by the income loss due to the cost of training. But if the physician ends up on a higher indifference curve as a result of the investment, there will be an income effect which would somewhat offset the substitution effect.

9. Each is a source of productive services, and thus is a portion of society's real capital.

10. This relationship is $h_a = rP_A$. In equilibrium, the hire-price of the factor equals the interest yield on the capital value or purchase price of the factor.

12. Economic rent is that portion of payment to a factor in excess of the amount required to call it into employment. Economic rent is a measure of the resource-owner's (seller's) net gain from trade in the factor market. It is analogous to Producer Surplus, which is a measure of the seller's net gain from trade in the product market.

13. The time-rate gives employees the incentive to provide the minimum effort needed to avoid being fired. The piece-rate provides an incentive for greater effort, if the employee is not too effort-averse. So output is likely to rise. Employees who are more effort-averse tend to prefer the time-rate, and employees who are less effort-averse prefer the piece-rate.

14. American manufacturing workers over time have become involved more with tasks that require thought and discretion rather than routine repetitive activities that lend themselves to measuring output by the piece.

For Further Thought and Discussion

1. a. A decline in the birth rate would reduce women's demand for "leisure" – that is, for nonmarket uses of their time. Note that "leisure" does not imply idleness.
   b. Here again, reduced time required for housework will reduce demand for "leisure" time.
   c. The same, once again. Same as b above.

2. Such a change in taste would lead to an outward shift in the market supply curve of female labor. More labor would be offered at each wage rate. And if males and females make up at least partially distinguishable types of labor, the outward shift in the supply of female labor would lead to a decrease in the equilibrium wage rate for female workers relative to male workers.

5. As long as leisure is a normal good, rising per capita wealth in the form of nonlabor income will lead to an increase in leisure and so to a decrease in the number of hours worked. As for rising real wages, there are both an income effect and a substitution effect to consider. The substitution effect always implies a decrease in leisure and an increase in hours worked, but the income effect works in the opposite direction. Since hours worked have been steadily falling as real wages have risen, the substitution effect of rising real wages appears to have been overwhelmed by the sum of the two income effects: that due to rising per capita wealth (property income), and the income effect of rising real wages.

6. Given the choice, a slave who obtained no reward for his labor would probably prefer all leisure (working less than a free person would), while the master would prefer to give the slave no leisure at all. So a master with strong control might be able to make his slave more productive than a free worker. However, it is costly to control a slave, so the master's control would not be absolute. The productivity of slave versus free labor is thus a question of circumstances. Where monitoring and negative incentives (punishments) are not too costly, slave labor may turn out to be very productive. But on the whole, the rewards (positive incentives) that free persons can achieve by working have been more effective, especially where motivation and intelligent effort are needed for doing a good job.

9. A tax on earnings generates a substitution effect (work less) and an income effect (normally work more, on the assumption that leisure is a normal good). The tax therefore has an ambiguous effect. A tax on labor capacity would generate only an income effect, and therefore (if leisure is a normal good) would increase the supply of labor.

10. In early years, the supply of American labor was small in comparison with the supply of cooperating factors such as land and natural resources. In more recent times, the large amount of accumulated capital has played a similar role. It is also possible that the abundance of recreational opportunities and larger homes have increased preference for leisure and thereby tended to raise market wage rates. Trade unions, which are a kind of labor cartel, may also play a role.

12. Yes, in equilibrium if workers in New York receive higher wages they are presumably more productive (have higher Marginal Product mp). This is probably mainly due, however, to the large amounts of cooperative inputs (streets, buildings, machinery) in such a large urban complex. What prevents workers elsewhere from all moving to New York is the high cost of living: crowding makes the New York prices of housing and other living amenities very high.

13. Welfare can be regarded as a decrease in the "price of leisure," but only over a certain range. If the person remains at her old optimum, there is no change of price, and hence neither an income effect nor a substitution effect. If the person responds to the price change by shifting to working zero hours, the substitution effect is certainly involved. Since the individual is also better off (in utility terms) there is also a wealth effect. The wealth effect reinforces the substitution effect in making the individual want to choose more leisure.

14. As the previous question suggests, for income versus leisure (two goods) the two effects are reinforcing. They oppose one another only when we speak of income versus work (a bad).

15. This situation fits that of the handicap principle: a firm with poor prospects faces a higher risk of trouble when it takes on high debt than a firm with excellent prospects. So taking on high debt can be a favorable signal. There is in fact evidence that firms shifting to higher levels of debt become more highly valued by investors (as reflected by increased stock prices).

16. No. The amount of extracted oil supplied to the market will increase with the oil price. As more oil is extracted, the marginal cost of extraction rises, so the price of oil will rise over time. This will lead to gradual reduction in oil consumption, until eventually the high price of oil makes other energy sources (such as solar power, nuclear power, hydroelectric power, and so forth) become relatively attractive.

CHAPTER 14

For Review

2. a. No. Mutually beneficial trade can occur as long as their *MRSC*s differ at their endowed positions (or at their Crusoe optimum positions, if production is possible).

   b. If individuals have identical preferences and endowments in a world of pure exchange, everyone's *MRSC* will be the same and no mutually beneficial trade can occur.

   c. Similarly, if they have identical preferences and identical productive opportunities, everyone's *MRSC* at the Crusoe optimum will be the same and no mutually beneficial trade can occur.

3. a. Asymmetrical Production-Possibility Curves lead to specialization in production: some people are better at producing bread, others at producing butter. (Another possible reason for specialization would be increasing returns.) There tends to be diversification in consumption because indifference curves are convex to (bowed toward) the origin.

   b. No. In the absence of trade an individual's degree of specialization in production and in consumption would have to be identical.

6. In a world of production and exchange (assuming interior solutions), at the production optimum each individual produces at a point along his Production-Possibility Curve such that *MRT* equals the ratio of market prices. Similarly, at the consumption optimum, each individual's *MRSC* equals the ratio of market prices. Additionally, for each good, the sum over all individuals of the produced quantities must equal the sum of the consumed quantities.

7. The intersection of the transaction demand and supply curves determines the point at which the quantity desired in exchange equals the quantity offered for exchange. The intersection of the *full* demand and supply curves determines the point at which the total quantity desired for consumption equals the total quantity available for consumption. Since the two pairs of curves differ only by the nontraded amounts of the good (endowed and self-consumed quantities in pure exchange, or produced and self-consumed quantities in a world of production), the price that brings desired transaction quantities into equilibrium must also bring desired full quantities into equilibrium.

10. a. Yes, but only in a very special case. Autarky will occur under costless exchange if for every individual the ratio of market prices exactly equals the *MRSC* and *MRT* at his or her Crusoe solution.

    b. Transaction costs create a gap between the gross and net price ratios. Any time an individual's *MRSC* and *MRT* at the Crusoe solution fall inside this gap, the individual will choose an autarky solution. The higher the transaction costs, the greater this gap and the more likely the autarky solution.

13. A command economy could avoid *transaction* costs by dispensing with markets, but the associated *enforcement* costs may be larger than the transaction costs saved. While market economies must use resources to integrate individual decisions, command economies must use resources to enforce central decisions. Even more important, probably, the commanders would need an enormous amount of information to make the economy function rationally – information automatically provided by price signals in market economies. And most important of all, the command economy will aim at "efficiency" in carrying out the desires of the commanders, which may be quite different from the desires of consumers.

15. Decrease. The (positive) gap between the price at which individuals can buy the stock and the price at which they can sell the stock is a measure of transaction cost.

For Further Thought and Discussion

2. A tax on consumption reduces the incentive to acquire the taxed good in any way, either by production or by exchange. There will be less consumption and consequently less production. A tax on production has similar effects. A tax on *exchange*, in contrast, will reduce production for the market but increase production for self-supply. On balance, consumption of the good will also be less since some of the cost-reducing advantages of specialization will be lost.

3. For Robinson, a bunch of bananas has an opportunity cost of two fish, whereas for Friday a bunch of bananas costs only one fish. Robinson has an absolute advantage in both activities, but Friday has a comparative advantage in picking bananas. Robinson could, for example, pick one less bunch of bananas and use the time to catch two fish. He could then sell one fish to Friday for one bunch of bananas and have the other fish left over to eat. In total, the community thus gains one fish from this specialization in production.

4. Clearly, at least one of the two parties must be better off, since there is more of G and no less of Y available. But i (the seller of good G) might end up worse off. If the demand for grain is inelastic, i will get less revenue in Y-units in the process of selling more G. More surprisingly, j (the buyer of G) might be the one ending up worse off – if Y is an inferior good for i.

7. If James has a fixed endowment, he cannot revise his production plans after the opening of trade with Ida. But Ida will almost always revise her production plans to produce more X and less Y, or vice versa. Either way there will be less total production of one of the two commodities. Thus, we cannot say that trade necessarily leads to larger production of *both* goods.

8. A Martian observer, unfamiliar with the mental limitations of flowers and bees, might indeed fail to appreciate the difference as compared with human exchange. Perhaps we're kidding ourselves, but we like to think that our exchanges are the result of choice. Presumably, bees are governed entirely by blind instinct, while the flowers are even further from having any choice as to whether or not to offer their nectar to bees.

11. If both ration coupons and cash are required for trade, traders must maintain inventories of coupons as well as cash. In addition, traders must transport, authenticate, and physically transfer ration coupons as well as cash. If coupons can be bought and sold, there is also the cost of the coupon market. If coupons cannot be bought and sold, there are the costs of enforcing (and the costs of evading) restrictions on the sale of coupons.

12. All these qualities reduce the cost of using money as medium of exchange or as store of value. A somewhat less obvious but very important quality, illustrated by the prisoner-of-war example, is that the monetary commodity should *not* also be a consumption good. And, of course, it should be cheap to produce.

14. The equilibrium aggregate quantity of X self-produced by consumers of X.

19. If the price were only slightly below the autarky price, then in the absence of transactions costs the individual would want to buy only a very small quantity. However, a lump-sum transaction cost places the individual on a lower budget line. When the individual shifts down from the autarky point and moves on the lower budget line he gets a small increment of consumption of X but suffers a large reduction in Y consumption. So on balance the individual is worse off.

CHAPTER 15

For Review

2. b is correct. The ratio P_0/P_1 is the rate at which current consumption claims can be traded for one-year future consumption claims. If a current consumption claim is foregone, the market will pay back that claim plus interest next year. So $P_0/P_1 \equiv 1 + r$. Consequently, $r \equiv (P_0/P_1) - 1$. The annual rate of interest is the premium on the relative value of current over one-year future consumption claims.

4. Investment must always equal zero in a world of pure exchange. So, at equilibrium, $I = S = 0$, yet $B = L$ will generally be positive.

5. In an economy with intertemporal production, once again $I = S$ and $B = L$. Here $I = S$ is positive, but this magnitude may be greater or smaller than the magnitude of $B = L$.

7. a.   The Present-Value Rule directs decision-makers to adopt any incremental project for which the Present Value is positive, and to reject projects for which Present Value is negative. And if projects are mutually exclusive, the one with highest Present Value should be adopted.

   b.   As long as the Separation Theorem holds, achieving the productive optimum is equivalent to wealth maximization. Since the Present-Value Rule is a wealth-maximizing rule, all those involved in a decision – even if their intertemporal preferences differ – will be satisfied if the Present-Value Rule is followed.

   c.   If the Separation Theorem does not hold, people's optimal project choices will depend upon their intertemporal preferences. So the Present-Value Rule will not necessarily lead to the best possible outcome for all.

10. Yes. Raising the discount rate would reduce the present value of the benefits by more than the costs, because the costs are paid earlier in the worker's career and the benefits are received later.

11. It can borrow from abroad and use the resources to invest.

For Further Thought and Discussion

2. At equilibrium it must be true that – even though saving need not equal investment for any individual – both actual and desired saving equal actual and desired investment in aggregate. (If this were not the case, the interest rate would adjust to bring about the equality.) If a ceiling were placed upon the interest rate, it will still be true that *actual* aggregate saving equals *actual* investment, but *desired* investment at the low legal

r would probably exceed actual investment and saving. A corresponding analysis would apply in the case of a floor. (Recall that, with floors or ceilings, it is always the *smaller* of demand and supply that governs the actual amounts traded.)

3. a. Since time-productivity will be relatively great in such a newly settled country, the real interest rate will tend to be high.

   b. The real interest rate will be higher if the country is isolated.

   c. Close contact with the rest of the world will lead to an inflow of resources that will increase total investment and decrease the real rate of interest in the new country.

4. If little investment is taking place because of low time-productivity, real interest rates will be low. If little investment is taking place because of high time-preference, interest rates will be high.

6. a. Negative rates of interest are possible. As Equation (15.1) indicates, all that is required is that future claims exchange at a premium against current claims ($P_0 < P_1$). Negative interest rates are rarely observed, however. In most situations attractive intertemporal productive opportunities increase the investment demand for current funds, while time-preference (impatience) raises the consumption demand for current funds. The combination assures that current funds will almost always exchange at a premium against the future funds.

   b. Yes. In Equation (15.1), since P_0/P_1 cannot be less than zero, r cannot fall below -1. In terms of percentages, the interest rate cannot be less than -100%.

8. The present worth of a stream of payments is not found by summing the simple total of the interest-plus-principal installments over the years. This mistakenly assumes that a future payment is worth as much as one today. In fact, at 7.75% a dollar payment deferred 27 years is worth today only about 13 cents. At 7.75% interest, the payments required by the 2-year contract ($392.50 1 year from now, and an equal amount 2 years from now) have present worth of $702.34. But the 27 annual payments (of $39.81 each) of the other contract have a present worth of only $445.21! So the consumer advice provided was seriously wrong. (Note that the quoted "price" of the appliances is irrelevant for these calculations; only the actual payments matter.)

9. Financing a war by borrowing does not "shift the burden to future generations" any more than financing a war by taxation. Borrowing and taxing are only intermediate processes. The extent to which the burden is shifted to future generations depends upon the degree to which financing the war reduces consumption or reduces investment. If consumption is reduced, the burden falls on the current generation. If investment is reduced, more of the burden falls upon future generations. So what matters is the extent to which citizens cut back on consumption or on investment when they either lend money or pay taxes to government.

11. The stock is likely to be riskier. Investors may insist on a higher average rate of return to compensate them for this risk.

CHAPTER 16

For Review

3. a. Given a social criterion, the "social optimum" is the allocation that best achieves the criterion. There seems to be little agreement as to any such social criterion, and so the term "social optimum" lacks objective meaning. For example, some people regard unregulated abortion as social progress; others see it as social calamity.

b. Efficiency seems a valid goal, but there are many reasons that it should not be the only element in a social criterion. First, considerations of equity may indicate some sacrifice of efficiency. Second, efficiency takes the satisfaction of individual wants as the sole measure of well-being. Some have argued that individuals are poor judges of what will actually benefit them, or that wants are not autonomous but really socially determined, or that supra-individualistic policy goals (liberty, justice, community) are also important.

8. a. The monopolist violates the efficiency condition $vmp_a = h_a$. Instead, the monopolist's profit-maximizing optimum satisfies the condition $mrp_a = h_a$. Since the mrp_a curve is lower than the vmp_a curve, the monopolist hires "too little" of the factors employed.

b. Yes, since monopolist firms employ "too little," resources are forced into competitive industries where they are less productive on the margin. So too large a proportion of society's resources are employed by competitive firms. (Also, some of the inputs not employed by monopolized industries are retained instead for nonmarket uses, which therefore also absorb too large a proportion of resources.)

11. a. A free-rider problem in the provision of goods will tend to arise whenever it is difficult to exclude nonpayers from the benefits of group action – as when public goods are provided even to those who do not contribute to defray the costs.

b. Not very valid. While much government activity concerns the provision of public goods – defense, law, and redistribution can all be viewed as having public-good characteristics – governments are also heavily involved with the provision of private goods. And "exploitative" governments may not be interested in serving the citizens at all.

12. a. This efficiency condition is $MC = \Sigma MV^i$, that is, the Marginal Cost of providing the public good must equal the sum of all the consumers' Marginal Values for the public good.

b. For a public good, since every consumer can receive the same unit, the vertical sum of the individual demand curves (individual Marginal Values) is the marginal social value. For a private good, only one consumer receives each unit. So the marginal social valuation of the private good is simply the marginal valuation of the consumer receiving that unit. However, this vertical sum of the individual demand curves is *not* the market demand curve for the public good; all it shows is the marginal social valuation of the public good.

13. These functions represent each person's marginal valuation schedule for mosquito control. Summing them, we obtain $MV = 200 - 2y$. Equating this to Marginal Cost $MC = 10$ leads to the solution $y^* = 95$.

14. a. The private supply of public goods is limited, first, by the difficulty and cost of exclusion. Nonpayers would have to be excluded for private provision to be feasible, and this may be impossible or quite costly. Where exclusion costs are sufficiently low, a private firm may provide a public good but is unlikely provide an efficient quantity. For efficient provision, firms would have to charge different prices to different individuals. Such price discrimination might be illegal or too costly.

b. Public provision may result in a quantity closer to the optimum, but of course not necessarily. Where exclusion is impossible or very costly, private provision is unlikely, and so public provision may be inevitable.

17. Consumption of these products can impose direct externalities. Cigarette smoking can lead to fire losses, and alcohol consumption can cause car accidents. Driving increases traffic congestion. By raising the cost of these activities, a tax can reduce the direct external costs imposed on others and thereby improve economic efficiency. Pecuniary externalities, in contrast, lead to distributive effects but not inefficiencies.

18. Fish in the ocean are a common resource. The negative externality between the fishing activities of different nations leads to overfishing. Limiting fishing protects the resource and increases economic efficiency.

19. Anchor stores are attractive enough to draw customers to the mall, thereby attracting customers to other stores. This is a positive externality. The mall pays for this benefit by discounting the rent to the anchor.

For Further Thought and Discussion

1. The Duke did not read the text carefully enough. If the Duchess were initially endowed with a property right to her own life, as we normally presume in a nonslave society, a Pareto-preferred movement toward an efficient solution would have to be *mutually* beneficial. It seems unlikely that the Duke could have paid enough to have the Duchess agree to her own death. If the Duke initially possessed the right to take the Duchess's life, on the other hand, his argument would be valid on efficiency grounds: it would be up to the Duchess to buy back from him the right to her life. Finally, as we have seen, the efficiency and equity criteria do not always agree, and – going beyond utilitarian considerations – ethical values need to be considered. In terms of equity or morality, he was certainly not "justified."

2. False. First, conventional national income measures fail to allow for a whole variety of sources of utility and disutility: for example, homemakers' services are not counted, nor is the value of leisure, nor (on the negative side) degradation of the environment. But the statement would not be true even if there were a perfect national income measure. Monopolization of a good, for example, might raise the market value of national income while reducing efficiency.

4. Property rights will be ill-defined when laws or court rulings are ambiguous and where legal precedents are conflicting or in a state of flux. Also, if it is costly to learn about one's rights, subjective uncertainty may persist even if the underlying legal theory is settled. The costs of negotiating and enforcing contracts tends to be high when multilateral contracting is required, or when individuals behave strategically in order to capture more of the gains from an agreement. Some potential trades are hampered by the difficulty of describing the good or service in advance, or of measuring delivery performance thereafter. For example, contracts for labor service cannot generally guarantee in advance how devotedly the worker will perform, and this may even be hard to measure afterward. In the used-car business, buyers find it difficult to determine quality prior to purchase, and writing a level of agreed quality into the contract is almost impossible.

5. True, since market reallocations of resources must be mutually beneficial. A dictator, in contrast, might achieve a Pareto-efficient outcome that was not Pareto-preferred to the original situation.

6. A ban on trade in blood is inefficient. The hepatitis problem is not a sufficient reason for a ban, since buyers are at liberty to use whatever method they deem appropriate in screening commercial donors. (As might have been anticipated, the prohibition of blood sales has caused dangerous blood "shortages.")

7. a.   Yes, the analogy is sound. Laws banning polygyny reduce the demand for wife-services. Since only women can provide those services, the laws work to the disadvantage of women in general (for exceptions, see b).

   b.   Women in general lose from monogamy laws, especially those who would prefer being a secondary wife of a desirable husband rather than remain unmarried or be an only wife of a less desirable spouse. Those men who would have been willing and able to acquire multiple wives also lose. The *gainers* from monogamy laws include women who are exceptionally desirable wives, assuming they prefer to be the sole wife. (If polygyny were legal, any such woman could still contract with her husband to be the sole wife but might have to pay a high price for that privilege.) But the biggest gainers from the monogamy law are undoubtedly those men who would otherwise have been unable to marry.

   c.   Monogamy laws cannot be defended in terms of efficiency.

   d.   Monogamy laws tend to increase equality among men, since males who are less attractive husbands have better chances of acquiring wives. They probably increase inequality among women, however, since they improve the ability of more-desirable wives to monopolize the best husbands.

8. Individuals have access to a common resource (food animals). Harvesting the resource reduces the pool available for others. This externality problem leads to over-hunting.

9. The efficient toll is not necessarily the amount needed to recover the cost of building the road. However, a toll close to zero is not efficient, because each additional car on the road increases congestion which is costly to other users.

10. Heller and Eisenberg argue that many research discoveries are like fragments that need to be assembled to create useful product. The developer of a product does not know how many and which fragments are needed before doing further costly research and development. The need to negotiate licenses with the patent-holders of numerous different fragments creates tremendous bargaining challenges for the developer of a new product.

CHAPTER 17

For Review

1. Yes, although a political party in office might capture a "profit" by looting the taxpayers, or more subtly by carrying out ideological programs in opposition to voters' desires, its ability to do so is limited by competition from other parties. Ideally, new parties would enter the politics "industry" until no profit opportunity remained. The surviving parties would have to follow what the voters desire. However, political competition is less effective than market competition (see next question), and so political profit may not be driven to zero.

2. The imperfections of the democratic political system in serving citizen desires are analogous to, but more severe than, the imperfections of the market. First, in the political system citizens almost never make choices directly on substantive issues; decisions are made by imperfectly controllable delegates. Second, citizens have only a very narrow range of choice even of delegates. They must select from a limited number of candidates (i.e., political competition is highly imperfect) at widely separated election intervals, whereas in the market individuals select almost continuously from a vast menu of choices. Third, democratic majority rule is likely to override minority desires. Fourth, the cost of acquiring information is much higher for political choices.

5. a.   Unanimous consent, involving the purchase of dissident votes, would permit only political changes that improved the welfare of each and every voter. In terms of Pareto-efficiency, this would be an ideal political system.

   b.   Log-rolling allows voters to trade votes on one issue for votes on another issue, and so often leads to a Pareto-preferred outcome – a series of decisions which together leave everyone better off.

   c.   The objections to log-rolling are due primarily to the fact that delegates, not citizens, actually vote on policies. Having made such a deal the delegate is better off, but not necessarily the citizens.

9. An agreement is self-enforcing when neither party can gain by defecting. For example, a physician and patient might have invested significant effort in getting to know one another. In order to maintain the relationship, the patient may pay the bills and the physician may provide good service, even in the absence of legal enforcement.

12. Elected judges may cater to in-state voters.

13. A productive government intervention such as research into how to reduce costs, is likely to elicit an increase in supply. If demand is highly inelastic, higher output implies a sharply lower price, and therefore lower revenues. So suppliers of an inelastic-demand commodity are likely to concentrate their lobbying in favor of programs that reduce output, thereby raising revenue.

For Further Thought and Discussion

1. The "economic approach" views politics as a kind of exchange process. Citizens shop for the type of government that provides them the highest utility. Political parties compete to become the government and so to capture the "profit" of being in power. Utility maximization, exchange, and competition are all involved. Later sections of the chapter analyze an alternative approach that views politics as a *conflict process* in which some individuals and groups attempt to exploit others.

2. More frequent elections, more numerous legislatures, and elected judges would allow citizens to more closely control government officials. However, the more frequent are elections and the more numerous the legislatures, the less important is any single vote and so the less informed will voters typically be. So it is not clear whether these proposals would improve the fidelity of the political system to citizen's desires. Replacing the merit system in civil service by the spoils system would give citizens more control over bu-reaucrats. The spoils system would therefore make the governmental mechanism more accountable to citizen desires, but might reduce the quality of personnel in government.

3. Voluntary trade is mutually beneficial. So if the poor trade votes to the rich for money, both gain. Objections to this practice are probably based on objections to the fact that the rich have more money to begin with.

5. There are important government programs that redistribute cash incomes. Social Secu-rity mainly falls into this category, being a redistribution from the working age-group to the retired age-group. But politicians generally prefer to establish service programs to "help" the poor by health care, job training, education, etc. Legislators gain by giving jobs to political supporters and bureaucrats get larger agencies.

6. To the extent that government is a provider of desired goods and services to citizens, the effects of changes in demand or costs should be similar to the effects changes in demand or costs of a privately provided good. The strength of the effects, however, will differ. A bureaucratic agency charged with providing goods may be interested in enlarging its budget and clientele, so would prefer keeping prices low to users. If so, an increase

in demand will lead to a larger increase in output and a smaller increase in price than under private provision.

8. Consider the extremes. If the prize is almost worthless to Arthur, he will put in little effort fighting for it. Knowing this, his opponent Betty, even though she values the prize more highly, will not need to put in a very big effort either.

10. If the opponent's malevolence is reduced by your transferring income or power to him, appeasement might make sense. The name holds if he is benevolent but opposes you owing merely to discordant interests, and if it is the case that receiving income from you increases his benevolence. (In each case, the result depends upon the numerical parameters.) The text describes a kidnapper who is nasty (will kill the victim) when poor, but when assuaged by a ransom payment turns "nice" (will release the victim) – keeping the cash, of course.

Name Index

Subject Index